SECRETUM SECRETORUM

VOLUME I · TEXT

EARLY ENGLISH TEXT SOCIETY

No. 276

1977

SECRETUM SECRETORUM

NINE ENGLISH VERSIONS

EDITED BY

M. A. MANZALAOUI

VOLUME I · TEXT

Published for
THE EARLY ENGLISH TEXT SOCIETY
by the
OXFORD UNIVERSITY PRESS
1977

Oxford University Press, Walton Street, Oxford OX2 6DP

OXFORD LONDON GLASGOW
NEW YORK TORONTO MELBOURNE WELLINGTON
IBADAN NAIROBI DAR ES SALAAM LUSAKA CAPE TOWN
KUALA LUMPUR SINGAPORE JAKARTA HONG KONG TOKYO
DELHI BOMBAY CALCUTTA MADRAS KARACHI

ISBN 0 19 722278 1

© *Early English Text Society, 1977*

*Printed in Great Britain
at the University Press, Oxford
by Vivian Ridler
Printer to the University*

ACKNOWLEDGEMENTS

THIS edition has been worked upon sporadically over a good many years. It is therefore a vain hope to try to single out every one of the many acts of assistance and generosity on the part of university and library administrators, friends and assistants, scholars and colleagues (the two latter terms are not, I should add, intended as excluding each other). Professor J. A. W. Bennett watched over the thesis out of which the notion of this edition grew, and I am happy to say that he is now following its fortunes as a member of the Council of the Society which is publishing it. The late Richard Walzer taught me almost everything I know about Arabic Aristotelianism. To both those scholars my academic and personal debts are greater than can be conveyed in the summary form of these acknowledgements. Among other scholars consulted have been Dr. S. Pinès, the late Samuel Stern, the late Martin Plessner, the late C. W. Coopland, Mr. B. Levine, and Dr. R. Hunt. The late E. Weil lent me the manuscript of the version of my text by Johannes de Caritate when it was in his hands; Mr. Robert B. Honeyman, its present owner, has since corresponded with me concerning it. Among the libraries whose staffs I must thank are the Bodleian, the Cambridge University Library, the British Library, the Wellcome Medical Historical Library, the Bibliothèque Nationale, the Bibliothèque de l'Arsenal; the Laurenziana, the Riccardiana, the Marucelliana, and the Biblioteca Nazionale of Florence, the Österreichische Bibliothek in Vienna, the Bayerische Staatsbibliothek in Munich, the Folger Shakespeare Library, the Library of Magdalen College, Oxford, the Central Library and the Library of the Faculty of Arts of the University of Alexandria, and the main Library of the University of British Columbia. I am also grateful to all the libraries, and in the case of the Johannes de Caritate manuscript the successive owners, who have given permission to reproduce plates from their manuscripts.

For study leaves, sabbaticals, and acts of generosity which have made the undertaking possible, I wish to thank the Universities of Alexandria and of British Columbia, the President and Fellows of Clare Hall, Cambridge, the President and Fellows of Magdalen

College, Oxford, the British Council, the Warden and Fellows of St. Antony's College, Oxford, and, particularly, the Canada Council for the Arts and Sciences. In addition to the award of several vacation grants and a Leave Grant, the Canada Council must be thanked for the funds which provided me, at one point of the work, with the assistance of Mr. Paul Whittal, to whom I am grateful for his revision of my typescript, and for some suggestions which have either saved me from making unnecessary or wrong-headed emendations, or have resulted in positive emendations which are embodied in the final text; it is to him that are due, for example, the emendation on 326/13 and the retention of the original reading without emending on 273b/15–16. Of the officers of the Early English Text Society, Mr. Neil Ker and Dr. Ian Doyle have made corrections and suggestions which have considerably improved this work. It has been my privilege to work with three successive Editorial Secretaries of the Society, Miss Patricia Kean, Mr. R. W. Burchfield, and Dr. Pamela Gradon—to the last of these a special expression of thanks is due for her meticulous overseeing and for a patient courtesy with which dilatory editors, I am sure, do not deserve to be treated.

In the final proof reading I had the assistance of Mr. Neil Mason, whose meticulous attention has saved the text from much that was faulty, and to whose judgement I have been very glad to defer on a number of occasions, e.g. in the punctuating of the two sentences which form p. 34, ll. 4–14, and in the wording of 204/29 and 210/31. For opinions on text no. V, the Shirleian *Decretum Aristotelis*, I am indebted to the members of my Palaeography class (English 501b) at the University of British Columbia in 1975–6, namely Miss Karen Levinson, Mr. Ian Carruthers, and, once again, Mr. Neil Mason; to Miss Levinson, for example, I owe the form of syntax and of punctuation adopted on 212/6–8 and 220/28, and to Mr. Carruthers, the form of emendation finally adopted on 207/1.

My thanks are due to Dr. Richard Holdaway of the Department of French at the University of British Columbia, who kindly gave me valuable advice on the French text of no. VIA, which he read in the proof stage. I have emended my text in several places in the light of his proposals, but he is not responsible for any errors that still remain.　　　　M. A. M.

CONTENTS

PLATES

INTRODUCTION

THE ARABIC TEXT

THE Latin pseudo-Aristotelian *Secretum secretorum* (or, as in some copies, *Secreta secretorum*) is found in about five hundred manuscripts, dating from the twelfth century onwards. It is a translation of the Arabic *Kitāb sirr al-asrār* (*The Book of the Secret of Secrets*).[1] *Sirr al-asrār* is in fact the sub-title in the Arabic: the main title can be translated as *The Book of the Science of Government, on the Good Ordering of Statecraft*.[2]

The Arabic text has been edited by Professor Abdel Rahman Badawi, in vol. i (the only volume to appear) of *al-Uṣūl al-Yūnāniyya lil-Naẓariyyāt al-Siyāsiyya fil-'Islām* (*Greek Origins of Political Theories in Islam*), Cairo, 1954. A modern English translation of the Arabic, by Ismail Ali, had already appeared in Steele's edition of the Latin *Secretum*, which forms Fascicule V (1920) of *Opera hactenus inedita Rogeri Baconi*, Oxford, 1909–40.

The Arabic work is extant in some fifty manuscripts; the earliest, a fragment, dates from A.D. 941/330 A.H.[3] The Proem to the *Sirr* describes it as the work of the well-known ninth-century translator Yaḥyā ibn-al-Biṭrīq (John son of the Patrician *or* of Patrick), working for the Caliph al-Ma'mūn in the great days of the movement of translation from Greek into Arabic.

The present editor is responsible for a full study of the known facts, and of the main problems, concerning the contents of the *Sirr* and its formation by a process of accretion, with some account

---

[1] The strict transliteration, showing accidence fully and accurately, is *Kitābu sirri l-asrār* (*The Book of the Secret of Secrets*). If the noun *Kitāb*, which is in the construct state, is omitted, the noun *Sirr* ceases to be in the genitive case, and the strict transliteration is then *Sirru l-asrār*. In common with much current orientalist practice, I here use 'broad' transliteration and give the definite article the fixed form *al-* irrespective of the elision with the case-ending of the preceding noun.

[2] *Kitāb 'ilm al-siyāsa fī tadbir al-riyāsa* (here again I give only a 'broad' transcription; a 'narrow' one would be *Kitābu 'ilmi s-siyāsati fī tadbiri r-riyāsaʰ*).

[3] B.L. MS. Or. 12070. This contains the Physiognomy only, but gives it in what is almost certainly a revised and shortened form, the form it takes in the later, or Long, recension of the *Sirr*: for the recensions of the Arabic see below, pp. x–xi.

of the Hellenic, Hellenistic, and later analogues of portions of the text. This is the article 'Kitāb Sirr al-asrār: Facts and Problems' (henceforward *FP*), *Oriens*, xxiii–xxiv, 1974 (for 1970–1), 148–257. Relevant information and opinions are given in the Preliminary Matter and Commentary in volume ii of the present edition. A summary review of the main facts is given below; the supporting evidence should be consulted in *FP*, since it is too bulky and diffuse to be reproduced here.

The *Sirr* purports to be an epistle from Aristotle to Alexander, dispatched to the latter during the course of his conquest of Persia, because Aristotle was too old to accompany him in person. It would seem to have been accepted by most medieval readers as a genuine Aristotelian text.

The first few pages of the First Discourse of the *Sirr*, corresponding to pp. 32 ff. of version III, the 'Ashmole' translation, as given below, correspond word for word to another Arabic pseudo-Aristotelian text, to which the later pages of the Discourse also bear a general resemblance. The text is the so-called *General Epistle* (*al-risālah al-'āmmiyyah*), part of a collection of pseudo-Aristotelian letters. The extant manuscripts of this are not earlier in date than the fourteenth century, but recent studies[1] suggest that this general Epistle belongs to the Umayyad court of the late eighth century. The first three Discourses of the *Sirr*, corresponding to 'Ashmole', pp. 32–46, 69–70, can be seen to owe a distant but recognizable debt to the *Nicomachean Ethics*.

There are two main recensions of the *Sirr*. One is in ten books; in his edition of the Latin, referred to above, Robert Steele named this the Eastern form, because he believed that manuscripts of this recension were associated with the eastern Arab world. In the present work it is named, more neutrally, the Long Form (*LF*). The other—Steele's 'Western Form'—is here referred to as the Short Form (*SF*): this itself is found in two variant forms, an eight-book one (*SF8*) and a seven-book one (*SF7*). The textual evidence suggests that almost certainly the Short Form, in its eight-book version, is the older form.

A text which had probably at first been exclusively a Mirror for Princes was, it would seem, turned into an encyclopedic manual by

---

[1] M. Grignaschi, 'Les Rasā'il 'Aristātalīsa 'ilā-l-Iskandar de Sālim Abū-l-'Ala' et l'activité culturelle à l'époque omayyade', *Bulletin d'Études Orientales de Damas*, xix (1965–6), 7–83.

the addition of a layer of scientific and occult material. In *SF* there is a solid block of this matter at the end of the work, divided up into several sections, each of which is given the Arabic name *bāb*.[1] This is not the term used for the major divisions on advice for princes, each of which is called a *maqālah*.[2] Unlike the *maqālah*s, the *bāb*s are not numbered. In *LF*, the *bāb*s have had their positions in the text reallocated. The bulk of the *bāb*s corresponds to pp. 48–69 and 89–113 of the 'Ashmole' version as printed below (except that the Physiognomy in 'Ashmole' is enlarged from other sources).

It is probably to a later reviser than the inserter of the *bāb*s that we owe the exchange of brief letters in the Proem, between Alexander and Aristotle ('Ashmole', pp. 28–9). This is not in the earlier and shorter of the two Latin translations, and was possibly missing from its Arabic original. It interrupts the matter, and even the Arabic syntax, of the Proem rather clumsily. It is found quoted as a separate entity by two tenth-century Arabic anthologists.

The revision of the Physiognomy *bāb*, earlier than A.D. 940, has already been referred to above. The next, and final, revision of the Arabic text is more important. In this, the reviser augmented the theoretical introduction at the head of each section (cf., e.g., 'Ashmole', pp. 69–71), and made lengthy additions of the same kind (cf. 'Ashmole', pp. 71–5). Almost all his more abstract additions, and some of those on more palpable topics, are to be found word for word in the Encyclopedia of the Ikhwān al-ṣafā, the Sincere Brethren, a name usually given in the faulty translation 'Brethren of Purity'. This group wrote in the third quarter of the tenth century, compiling and circulating their *Epistles*, a *summa* of medieval knowledge incorporating a heterogeneous metaphysic and an ecumenical attitude based largely upon Plotinian teachings, yet at the same time serving as political propaganda for the Fatimid dynasty.

Where the English translations are sufficiently literal, it is useful to be able to indicate, when possible, which sections of the *Sirr* correspond to the sections of these texts. By giving alphabetical sigils to the sections, the form of any Arabic, Latin, or western

---

[1] The plural is *abwāb*: the primary meaning of *bāb* is 'door' or 'gate'; hence Steele's use of the term *Gate*.

[2] Plural *maqālāt*: *maqālah* literally means a *discourse*, and is the term employed today for a newspaper *article*.

vernacular manuscript can be identified and described fairly closely in 'shorthand' terms by listing the sigils of the sections it contains. Steele's Latin edition makes use of a system of section-by-section sigils: unfortunately, Steele's system places all sections on the same footing and does not indicate the subordination of sub-sections to main divisions, and the historical stratification of the portions of the *Secretum*. A system making use of sigils in different series in subordination to one another (capital, minuscule, and Greek letters) enables the reader both to hold in mind the sub-ordination of sections within larger classifications, and the historical stratification of the sections of the *Secretum*. This is the method adopted in *FP*, and also used in the present edition. Notes relevant to the *Secretum* tradition as a whole, rather than to any individual English version, are given in the commentaries upon versions I and III: the use of the sigils in the *Commentary* in volume ii enables the reader who is studying another of the versions to consult the notes at the relevant point in its treatment of those two versions.

In order to make possible comparison with Steele's text and commentary, and with the Ismail Ali translation, as well as with the commentary in *FP*, the following table will be of help:

Contents	Steele's section-letter	New sigil
[Proem of Philippus Tripolitanus and dedication to Guy de Vere, Bishop of Tripoli]	a	S
[Philippus' list of contents]		z′
Dedication to the Caliph al-Ma'mūn by Yaḥyā ibn al-Biṭrīq	b	t
Recommendation of Aristotle		u
Alexander's letter to Aristotle		v
Aristotle's reply to Alexander		w
Proem of Yaḥyā	c	x
Aristotle's prefatory letter	d	y
Yaḥyā's List of Contents	e	z
Discourse I: Kinds of King	f	A
Discourse II: Conduct of a King		B
General instruction	g	a
Apologia for astronomy	h	b
[Proem of Johannes Hispaniensis, with dedication to Queen Tharasia, as sometimes inserted into full translation]		S′
Hygiene		c
Theoretical proem		α

Contents

[1] Steele (p. 108) omits this sigil by error.
[2] In the text (p. 164) Steele, as is consistent with his classification, gives this section a miniscule v as sigil; in his Introduction (p. lxiii) he inconsistently gives the sigil as a capital V.

Contents	Steele's section-letter	New sigil
Discourse IX: Wars		I
General advice	K	a
Astrology of victory	L	b
Onomantic calculation of victory from the names of the commanders	M	c
Discourse X: The Occult Sciences		J
Theory	N	a
Powers of the planets	O	b
Talismans, recipes, etc.	,,	c
The Philosopher's Stone	O/P	d
The Emerald Table of Hermes Trismegistus	O/P	e
Lapidary	P/R¹	f
Herbal	,,	g

THE LATIN VERSIONS

There are two Latin translations of the *Sirr*. The earlier is by Johannes Hispaniensis, and belongs to the middle of the twelfth century. Steele uses the form Hispalensis for this translator's name: the complicated question of the identity of the translator makes it more prudent to use the form found in the manuscripts of the *Secretum*, and not to suggest necessary identification of this Johannes (certainly responsible for a number of scientific texts) with Johannes Hispalensis, or John of Seville, a known translator of Arabic philosophical and quasi-philosophical works.[2] There are some 150 manuscripts of this version extant.[3] It consists of the

[1] By an oversight, Steele refers to the Lapidary and Herbal as P in his Introduction (p. lii), but as R in the body of the text (p. 118), where the sigil P is not allocated to any section. In the Ismail Ali text, P is used for my Jde, and R for my Jfg.

[2] See, e.g., Á. González Palencia, *El Arzobispo Don Raimundo de Toledo*, Barcelona, 1942; M. Alonso Alonso, 'Notas sobre los traductores toledanos Domingo Gundisalvo y Juan Hispano', *Al-Andalus*, viii (1943), 162 ff.; idem, 'Traducciones del árabe al latín por Juan Hispano (Ibn Dawûd)', *Al-Andalus*, xvii (1952), 129–51; M. T. D'Alverny, 'Notes sur les traductions médiévales des œuvres philosophiques d'Avicenne', *Archives d'histoire doctrinale et littéraire du moyen âge*, xix (1953), 337–58; L. Thorndyke, 'John of Seville', *Speculum*, xxxiv (1959), 20–38. For a summary of the controversy, and for his own views, see Richard Lemay, *Abu Ma'shar and Latin Aristotelianism in the Twelfth Century*, Beirut: American University of Beirut, 1962, pp. 9–16.

[3] Over sixty are listed in R. Förster, 'Handschriften und Ausgaben des pseudo-aristotelischen Secretum secretorum', *Centralblatt für Bibliothekswesen*, vi (1889). I hope to list the additional manuscripts in my study of the Latin version, mentioned below.

Latin translator's dedication and proem, and a translation of the major part of the Arabic proem, and of the earlier parts of the section on Hygiene, as found in *SF*. It thus takes the form: S'tuxyBcaa'ββ'γζ.

The Hispaniensis version has twice been edited: H. Suchier, *Denkmäler provenzalischer Literatur*, 2 vols., Halle, 1883, appendix, pp. 473–80; and J. Brinkmann, *Die apokryphen Gesundheitsregeln des Aristoteles für Alexander den Grossen in der Übersetzung des Johann von Toledo*, Leipzig, 1914.

There are two English versions of Hispaniensis: no. I below, *The Booke of Goode Governance and Guyding of þe Body*, and the Elizabethan version by Jankin Gwynne (who refers to the *Secretum* as *Tyrocaesar*—a distortion of *Sirr al-asrār*) which is printed as Appendix A (text no. X).

The full Latin translation belongs, in all probability, to the first half of the thirteenth century; it was known around the middle of the century to Roger Bacon, St. Albertus Magnus, Guibert de Tournai, Michael Scot, and the writer of the commentary on Boethius entitled *De consolatione et disciplina scolarium*.[1] A number of manuscripts belong to the thirteenth century. The translator was Philippus Tripolitanus, working for Guy de Vere of Valence, Bishop of Tripoli. Apart from the work of Stephanus of Pisa, this appears to be the only work translated from Arabic into Latin in Crusader lands,[2] the vast bulk of such translations having been carried out in Spain and in Sicily. The translation by Philippus has embedded in it part of Hispaniensis' translation of the Hygiene book, and partially repeats certain sections in new wording—hence the duplications indicated in the table of contents given above.

The Latin has twice been edited in modern times. The principal edition is that by Robert Steele. In his East German edition of the late thirteenth-century Middle High German version by the nun Hiltgart of Hürnheim, Reinhold Möller (1963) produced a fresh edition of the Latin, printed in parallel with the German, upon opposite pages.[3] Steele's Introduction, pp. vii–lxiii, remains the

[1] Steele, Introduction, pp. xviii f.
[2] Aldo Mieli, *La Science arabe et son rôle dans l'évolution scientifique mondiale* (Leiden, 1938), p. 225 n. 2. Adelard of Bath also visited the Levant and the Holy Land, even if his written works seem to belong to a later stage in his career (Mieli, pp. 224–5).
[3] Hiltgart von Hürnheim, ed. Reinhold Möller, *Mittelhochdeutsche Prosaübersetzung des 'Secretum secretorum'*, Berlin, 1963.

fullest study of the Latin, and many of the assertions made here are derived from Steele.

The manuscripts of Philippus, including abbreviations and adaptations of his work, known to Förster (see p. xiv, n. 3) are listed by him as some 200 in number: now some 350 extant manuscripts are known. The manuscripts have recently been studied and classified with considerable thoroughness by Dr. Friedrich Wurms, *Studien zu den deutschen und den lateinischen Prosafassungen des pseudo-aristotelischen 'Secretum secretorum'*, Hamburg dissertation, 1970 (privately printed, Clausthal-Zellerfeld: Bonecke). With these manuscripts and with the details of the contents and history of the Latin text, I hope to deal further elsewhere: some of these matters are here summarized, sometimes without full connecting links, and sometimes without any detailing of the supporting evidence.

Philippus starts his translation with a proem containing an encomium upon his episcopal patron, thus adding to, and paralleling, the encomia upon Alexander by the pseudo-Aristotle, and upon the Caliph by the Arabic 'translator'. The Physiognomy is usually found at the end of the text, and the Occult section in its place immediately after Hygiene. A common form of the Philippus text is: Sz΄tuvwxyABabcαα΄ββ΄γζ΄δεζηθιζ΄΄κλλ΄μμ΄νJ[a]bcdefgCabD abcdEFGHabIabBdαβγ. The recension of manuscripts of this general type has been named by Steele the 'Vulgate' *Secretum*.

The adaptations through which Philippus' versions passed are complex. They are examined in two unpublished dissertations: Willy Hermenau, 'Französische Bearbeitungen des Secretum Secretorum und ihr Verhältnis zu der lateinischen Übersetzung des Philippus Tripolitanus', Göttingen, 1922 (section I: 'Das lateinische Secretum Secretorum'), and Jacques Monfrin, *Le 'Secret des secrets': recherches sur les traductions françaises suivies du texte de Jofroi de Waterford et Servais Copale*, École des Chartes, Paris, 1947, part I (a summary is printed in the École des Chartes publication, *Positions des thèses soutenues par les élèves de la promotion de 1947 pour obtenir le diplôme d'archiviste paléographe*, pp. 94–9).

Wurms's systematic classification of the manuscripts largely, but not wholly, supersedes J. P. Gilson's work on Latin manuscripts of the *Secretum* in the British Library, as found in Steele, pp. xxv–xxviii. It is necessary here only to detail those forms and derivatives of Philippus which affect the translations in this volume, but some account is also taken in the exposition which follows of matters germane to the easily accessible literal translations printed by Steele in his *Three Prose Versions of the Secreta Secretorum* (E.E.T.S., E.S. 74, 1898)—henceforth *3PV*—as well as to the fifteenth-century Scottish version by Sir Gilbert of the Haye (ed. J. H. Stevenson, *Gilbert of the Haye's Prose Manuscript*, S.T.S., 2 vols., 1900–14; vol. i).

A. Roger Bacon produced a glossed version, divided into four books in the place of Philippus' ten. He complains (Steele, p. 39) that certain 'stulti' have expurgated the work: it is true that the Onomancy (section M) does not appear in the Latin, and is likely to be the portion which gave offence, since it consists of a form of divination. There is some indication that the section was translated by Philippus as part of his text: this is afforded by the nature of text no. II below, the version in MS. Sloane 213, which consists of the Physiognomy as in the *Secretum*, together with a version of the Onomancy of the *Sirr*. Text no. II thus appears to by-pass the Vulgate recension of the *Secretum*. It should be noted, however, that the transcribing of the Physiognomy section of the Vulgate separately from the remainder of the text is a well-established habit, attested by many Latin manuscripts, e.g. British Library Sloane 1313 and Egerton 874, Bodley Douce 45 and Lat. class. d. 17, and MS. Arras 741. Manuscripts in this tradition belong to Wurms's class I.3.

B. Among noteworthy departures from the original, many manuscripts of the Vulgate form of Tripolitanus omit the recipes for the final six electuaries in the medical section (i.e. section Bcμ', corresponding to the content of Version IV, pp. 82–8 below). Manuscripts of this type are from Steele's class E (Steele, p. xxvi) and include St. John's College, Oxford, 178 (thirteenth century) and Florence Riccardiana 108 (fifteenth century), as well as the texts listed by Steele.

Wurms's classification specifies those manuscripts which are known to include the later electuaries; they form his classes I.2.a and I.2.c.

C. Certain manuscripts include not only, as in the Vulgate version, the text of Hispaniensis' medical injunctions, which Tripolitanus made use of for his translation (Bc$\zeta'\zeta''$), but the title and dedication of Hispaniensis as well, i.e. section S' (e.g. Rawlinson C.274, f. 33: cf. Steele, p. xxvii).

D. The Vulgate *Secretum* and its derivation transfer the Physiognomy section, or make it the concluding portion of the work. Wurms's employment of this criterion to distinguish manuscripts of his class I.1 is misleading, since the same feature occurs in manuscripts of other classes, as, indeed, is clear from the descriptions he gives of his classes I.7.a and II.2.a.

E. Some manuscripts expand the Physiognomy, more particularly the section on Eyes, by combining with the Physiognomy of the *Sirr* two other texts, both of which can be found in vol. ii of Richard Förster, *Scriptores physiognomonici graeci et latini* (2 vols., Leipzig, 1893). The two texts are the *Anonymi de physiognomia liber* (Förster, pp. 3–145), and the relevant section of a medical treatise by Abū Bakr al-Rāzī, in the version by Gerard of Cremona, *Ababecri Rasis ad regem Mansorem de medicina* (Förster, pp. 163–79: cf. Wurms, class I.5).

F. One important feature is not noted by Steele. It is, however, taken into account by Hermenau (p. 7') and gives rise to what he terms the 'fehlerhaft' recension of the Vulgate. In the theoretical proem to the First Book (Section A), in the account of the constituents of successful rule, one manuscript tradition inverts the order of two consecutive portions of the exposition: the contents of Steele 42/8–24 are inserted immediately after Steele 41/3. Manuscripts of this type are B.L. Royal L2.E.xv, Berlin Hamilton 630, and Gdánsk Marianus F.180. Of this type, too, is the text of the Vulgate printed by Greyff at Reutlingen, and attributed to the year 1483 (Hein. 1779, British Library I.A. 10756). Presumably, in a prototype manuscript, the passage here in question was on a small-sized leaf which was turned over back to front: both the passage and the section which it wrongly precedes begin with the word *Causa*. This is Wurms's class I.4, but Wurms does not place in this category all the manuscripts known to belong to it.

G. Since there is considerable evidence of composite origin, it is extremely difficult, if not futile, to disentangle recensions in a thorough manner. Both the inverting of the expository matter in Ba and the expansion of the Physiognomy are found in Royal 12 E.xv and Rawlinson C.274. Both the embedding of the Hispaniensis proem and the expansion of the Physiognomy are found in B.L. MSS. Sloane 3554 and Harley 399. Peculiar to Royal 12 E.xv, however, is that Roger Bacon's glosses are included in it, although the text and its divisions do not correspond to those of

Bacon's recension as found in the manuscripts upon which Steele bases his edition.

H. There are a number of abbreviated, truncated, or fragmentary versions, including some with commentaries (see Förster, p. 13), and some of the items in Wurms's class III, where, however, some copies of the Hispaniensis translation appear to be included.

One abbreviated recension, popular in the fifteenth century, and perhaps originating in that period, is of particular interest, because it provided the basis for most of the printed versions of the fifteenth and sixteenth centuries, and for many of the French and English versions. This abbreviated *Tripolitanus* (henceforward *AbTrip*) omits much of the theoretical material, turning the text back to something not unlike the form of the *Sirr* before the final Arabic revision. Omitted in such manuscripts are the dedication by Tripolitanus (S), all the Hygiene section subsequent to Baths (Bcλ'–γ), all the occult material (J), most of the theoretical proem to the section on Ministers (D) and all the Army section (HI).

The theoretical proem to Justice (Ca) and that to Ministers appear in an abbreviated form, conflated. For this section, the symbol C/Da will be employed. The sections of the book are divided into paragraphs with headlines of their own, which do not always correspond to the sub-divisions in the Vulgate. This fact leads, at a superficial glance, to some confusion: caution is particularly required in dealing with the Hygiene section.

Manuscripts of this type are Bibliothèque Nationale 3029 and 7031. This recension is Steele's class F (p. xxvi) and Wurms's class II. A usual form consists of a shortened version of section S, followed by: tuvwxyABabcaa'ββ'γζ'δεηθιζ''CaDbcEFGHaBdβγ.

I. Since the *Secretum* is an encyclopedic work, its contents are sufficiently varied to have interested readers in many different modes, and in very varied fields of intellectual activity. A rough gauge of this variety is constituted by the other texts with which copies of the *Secretum* are transcribed or bound up. The *Secretum* is found in volumes of the genuine works of Aristotle (e.g. Florence, Riccardiana 113), and with other Mirrors for Princes (B.L. Royal 12 D.xv); it is found, either in partial or in complete form, connected with alchemical texts (Florence, Riccardiana Palatino 951). Some of the manuscripts mentioned under A above (see p. xvii) as containing the Physiognomy section, associate it with other

Physiognomies: B.L. MS. Egerton 847 includes it with two other
Physiognomies; Bodley MS. Douce 45 contains the Physiognomy
of the *Secretum* followed (f. 63) by a single page of al-Rāzī's text.
Presumably through association with it in the manuscript tradition,
a text will also be found incorporated into the body of the *Secretum*.
This conflation sometimes does not take place in the Latin, but in
a vernacular version. The *Liber diaetarum universalium* of Isaac
Judaeus is associated in manuscript with the Hispaniensis version
in MS. All Souls College 74 (thirteenth century) and B.L. Sloane
282; it is embedded in the full Tripolitanus text, in the French
version by Jofroi de Waterford and Servais Copale (Monfrin,
Positions de thèses, p. 98); thence it appears as an integral part of
James Yonge's translation (printed in *3PV*). The Tripolitanus
text is associated in manuscript and early printed versions with
Johannes Wallensis' treatise, the *Breviloquium de quattuor virtutibus
cardinalibus*[1]: e.g. in MSS. Corpus Christi, Oxford, 39 and B.L.
Burney 360, both of the fifteenth century. Both texts are already
found together in MS. Toulouse 736, a fourteenth-century manuscript in which the treatise on the cardinal virtues is itself attributed to Aristotle. The Cologne edition of *c.* 1472 (B.L. I.A.
3209 and Magdalen College, Oxford; Steele, p. xxx, no. 1) which
is apparently the *editio princeps*, associates the *Secretum* with the
Breviloquium and with a second treatise by Wallensis. Again, the
French of Waterford and Copale, and the English version by
James Yonge, embed it in the text.

J. Manuscript association which is thematically more tenuous
can sometimes be suspected of being the explanation of a later
conjoining of topics or conflation of texts. It is worth noting here,
particularly in view of one feature of Forrest's version of the
Secretum as discussed later, that there is a manuscript association
between the *Secretum* and treatises on the coronation of kings.
Our text is added in a later hand to the opening pages (ff. 2–12)
of the fifteenth-century B.L. MS. Additional 32097, which has as
its third item (originally the second) a text entitled *Processus factus
ad coronacionem regis Ricardi secundi* (ff. 13–20); the text *De corona-
tione regis*, which deals specifically with the coronation of Edward
IV, is found on ff. 25–8 of Bodley Douce 95 (fifteenth century)

---

[1] This treatise is also known as *Liber de instructione principum per quatuor
partes secundum quatuor virtutes cardinales* and *De virtutibus antiquorum principum et philosophorum*.

immediately preceding a text of the *Secretum*; in the fifteenth-century B.L. MS. Royal 12 D.iii, the *Secretum* is found (item 1, ff. 1–37) with the *Modus coronandi regem* (item 8), a copy of the text also found in B.L. Harley 2901 and (less closely agreeing as a text) Bodley Rawlinson C.425.

K. The ten-book division of the *Secretum* is altered into a four-part division in Bacon's recension, where Part I consists of all that precedes the Hygiene section (From S to Bb), Part II consists of the Hygiene (Bc), Part III, of all that follows this but precedes the Physiognomy in the Latin arrangement (J, C–I), and Part IV, of the *Physiognomy* (Bd). Bodley MS. Rawlinson C.274 is a good example of composite origin. It includes the Hispaniensis proem and the expanded Physiognomy, but (fols. 14 f.) has the opening theoretical passage in its correct order; it has embedded in it as part of the text some of Bacon's glosses; as an example of this, on f. 72 will be found Bacon's note on the scriptural authority for the classification of the ages of man, as in Steele, p. 131 n. 8 ('Nota quod distinccio jam facta etatum . . .' etc.). The manuscript is divided into ten books, as in the Vulgate, yet at the end of the list of Contents (f. 10) it announces a four-book division, as in Bacon. The description of the hypothetical third and fourth books in this intended division, however, is less unambiguous than in Steele's edition of Bacon (p. 28), for it is not clear that the fourth book is identical with the Physiognomy: where the Bacon recension has

Quarta est de mirabili eleccione amicorum et bajulorum regis per naturales proprietates corporum; *et hec sciencia* vocatur Phisonomia.

Rawlinson C.274 reads

Quarta de mirabili electione amicorum & baiulorum regis per naturales proprietates corporum. et liber sciencia uocatur phisonomia.

This leaves it possible for a reader (and a later redactor) to conceive of the bulk of the fourth book in this hypothetical division as consisting of the sections on ministers, envoys, etc. (with the Physiognomy as an appendage to it), and to assume that the title of the third book (*de mirabilibus utilitatibus nature & artis & morum*) refers, not to those sections, but to the latter portions of the medical section.

L. As Steele (pp. xxiii–iv) points out, in 1501 the Humanist Alexander Achillini published in Bologna a text which all subsequent sixteenth- and seventeenth-century editions followed, in

which he inserted passages on alchemy and talismans, and on
lapidary knowledge, deriving from the Short Form of the *Sirr al-
Asrār*. It is fairly certain that Achillini's insertions must derive
from Yehūdā al-Ḥarīzī's Hebrew translation, *Sōd ha-Sodōt*, carried out in Spain around the year 1200. It should further be noted
that Achillini's treatment of the Latin of Tripolitanus is elsewhere
curiously paraphrastic, whether or not this be due to a conflationary
rewriting that makes use of a knowledge of the wording of the
Hebrew text.

THE FRENCH VERSIONS

The different forms and translations in French are discussed
by Monfrin and by Hermenau. Apart from the translation of the
full Vulgate, the different French forms of *Ab Trip* (henceforward *Fr Ab*) must be noted. Three French forms of the *Ab Trip*
text can be distinguished. Two of them correspond to Hermenau's recensions B and C (Hermenau, pp. 44 ff.) and to the two
final classes of Jacques Monfrin's 'Traductions par choix' (*Positions
des thèses*, chapter ii, p. 96): they will henceforward be referred to
here as *Ab Trip B* and *Ab Trip C*. (Monfrin's first class of 'Traductions par choix', which we may classify as *Fr Ab A*, appears to be
a further derivative of *Ab Trip*.)[1]

---

[1] This form is closer to *Fr Ab B* than to *Fr Ab C*, and has no known English
derivatives. It is represented by B.L. MS. Additional 18179. The eulogy upon
Aristotle is lacking in its introductory material; it ends its Hygiene section with
Baths, and proceeds directly to Justice. Presumably through a misreading of the
word 'Tripoli' in its archetype, the Latin translator's name is given as 'Philippe
de *Thu*': his patron's name is given as 'Guy de Valence'. With both *Fr Ab B*
and *Fr Ab C* it shares the erroneous interpretation of the phrase concerning
wisdom written out upon parchment. The translation, however, is in wording
peculiar to it:

> Et pour ce, beau filz, que tu m'as aultres fois requis, par aultres tes lettres,
> que tu desiroyes asauoir le mouuement et le cours des estoilles auec l'art
> de alsimé et l'art de constraindre nature et d'autres pluiseurs choses que
> a-paines les pouroit comprendre esperit mortel . . . (Add. 18179, f. 6)

Among the features it shares with *Fr Ab B* as against *Fr Ab C* are the following:

B (3): the kingdom destroyed by excessive spending is not named:

> . . . qu'il en aduint jadis en vng pays ou quel quant la grandeur des despens
> surmonta les reuenues [*ms.* reuenuees] les seigneurs estendirent leurs mains
> au bien du commun . . . (Add. 18179, f. 9ᵛ)

B (4): The kingdoms destroyed through oath-breaking are those of the
albanoyens and *siciers* (Add. 18179, f. 22ᵛ).

B (5): The Magus is called a 'sarrasin' (Add. 18179, f. 56ᵛ).

B (6): Yaḥyā is named *Jehan fiz Patrice*.

B (7): The Physiognomy is omitted.

FrAbB, as in B.L. MS. Additional 18179 and St. John's College, Oxford, 102, is characterized by the following features:

B (1) As with all forms of *AbTrip* and *FrAb*, the theoretical proem to Justice is considerably cut down, and there is a mistranslation of Tripolitanus' phrase:

Preterea quod interrogasti et scire desideras est archanum tale quod humana pectora vix poterunt tollerare; quomodo ergo possunt in mortalibus pellibus depingi? (Steele, p. 40).

To take the wording of St. John's 102, this becomes

Et ce, beau filz, que tu m'as requis & que tu desires, a sauoir le mouuement & l'eure des estoilles, l'art d'A[lk]emie & l'art de contraindre natur & des aultres plusieurs choses, certes ce sont choses que a paine les pourroit comprendre humain entendement. Et comment doncque les pourroit comprendre aesprit mortel?

B (2) The omissions and errors peculiar to *FrAbC*, as noted below, do not occur. Thus this recension does contain the passage on the qualities of ministers (in Db) and the anecdote concerning the Jew (Dd).

B (3) The kingdom destroyed by excessive spending, as in Steele 44/19 (in A) is not named.

B (4) The two kingdoms destroyed as a result of oathbreaking, as in Steele 57/20–1 (in Ba), have names of the rough forms *aboniers* and *sorcies* (St. John's 102, f. 45^v).

B (5) In the anecdote of the Jew and the Magus, the Magus has become a Saracen.

B (6) The translator, whose name is not transformed in the manner of *FrAbC* (see below) is named Iehan filz Patrice (St. John's 102, f. 35).

B (7) The Physiognomy is omitted.

B (8) After the comparison of man to the animals (Dc as in Steele 143), comes an interpolated passage in which man's body is compared to the heavenly bodies and to natural phenomena.

The abbreviated form to which I refer as *FrAbC* is represented by the texts in MSS. Cambridge Ff.1.33, B.L. Royal 16 F.x and Harley 219 and the version printed by Vérard, Paris, 1497. It has the following features:

C (1) It shares with *FrAbB* the cutting down of the theoretical proem to Justice (Ca), and the mistranslation of the phrase concerning the parchment upon which books are written (as quoted in item no. 1 above). That it is a separate version of the original Latin *Ab Trip* can, however, be seen by comparing with the text as given above, the equivalent passage in Cambridge Ff.1.33, i.e. version VIA in the present volume:

> Et saichez que ce que tu m'as demandé et que tu desires tant santir sont tieulx secrés que humaine pensee a grant poine les pourroit aprandre ne soubtenir: comment donc peut il ou cuer d'omme mortel estre deprimés ne entendu ce qui n'apartient assauoir ne soit licite ne conuenable a traitier? (270b/13 to 272b/14 below)

C (2) Aristotle is called 'filz de Mahommet' of Macedonia.

C (3) The finder and Arabic translator of the original text has become 'Philipe . . . filz de Paris' (VIA, 12/3).

C (4) In the anecdote concerning him, 'Philemon' has become 'Phisonomias' (Ff.1.33, f. 32).

C (5) The kingdom destroyed by excessive spending is England (VIA, 20/16).

C (6) The kingdoms destroyed as a result of oathbreaking are those of the *Imbres* and (*As*)*syriens*.

C (7) Instead of coming to the *oracle of* the Sun, built by Asclepius (Steele 39), the translator comes to 'la cougnoissance du soleil laquelle fit Exculapidos' (VIA, 12/10–11).

C (8) Following an error in the Latin recension which forms their basis, manuscripts of this recension state that the belief of some of Aristotle's followers is that he ascended to Heaven as a *dove* of fire (*columba ignis), rather than in a column of fire (*in columna ignis*): thus, *en fourme d'une columbe de feu* (VIA, 9/24).

C (9) The passage on the qualities of ministers, the anecdote of the Jew and the Magus, etc., are omitted; the Physiognomy is retained.

ENGLISH VERSIONS

The present corpus consists of (1) one medieval translation of Hispaniensis and, in an appendix, a second one dating from the reign of Elizabeth I; (2) two translations of the full Latin form; (3) one fragmentary translation consisting of the Physiognomy and the Onomancy; (4) four medieval and early Tudor versions (two complete, two incomplete) of the French abbreviated texts, together with the relevant portion of the text of the French manuscript

almost certainly used by the translator of one of them: in con-
junction with these, but in an appendix to the volume, can be read
an early eighteenth-century translation of the Latin abbreviated
version; (5) an early Tudor adaptation in rhyme royal. There
are, thus, eight 'early English' translations (one from a printed
text), one verse rehandling, and, in addition, one French and
two 'early modern' English versions, reproduced as important
ancillaries.

I

The Booke of Goode Governance & Guyding of the Body: the
Middle English version of Johannes Hispaniensis' translation

The only known Middle English version of the Hispaniensis text
is contained in Bodleian MS. Rawlinson C.83.

The manuscript is a slim one of eight folios, on parchment, with
parchment binding; 21.5 × 15 cm.; twenty lines, with wide margins. The hand is fifteenth-century; rubricated, with red strokes
used to fill in the spaces between the pairs of black horizontal
lines drawn at the end of each chapter; red ink is also used to fill
in those letters which have rounded shapes—a characteristic also
of MS. Lyell 36, described on p. xxviii below. After the incipit,
the text proper (f. 2, l. 7) begins with an initial O containing a
sketch in ink, about 3.5 × 4 cm. This shows Aristotle, kneeling,
presenting the work to Alexander, enthroned; the two figures have
their names (*Alexander, Aristotiles*) written within scrolls. The
background shows the walls of a city or castle, and, beyond this,
a field in which, above some hillocks, the heads, spears, and banner
of a marching army can be seen, as well as what appears to be a
horse, drawn full face.

The manuscript bears the scribe's name, Wilhelmus, on the
front fly-leaf, followed by a monogram, apparently representing
the letters M I, upon a black shield. At the end (f. 8ᵛ) is the inscription *W.M ~ > G scripsit*; in this the W no doubt represents
the scribe's Christian name William: the remainder could, one
presumes, stand for a surname such as *Manning*.

In the margins the remarks 'nota' and 'nota bene' occur once or
twice. Against precept Four (f. 3ᵛ) is written 'incense Juniper'
apparently as a gloss to the word 'Gale'; against precept Fourteen
(f. 6) 'nota bene per dolorem capitis'. The manuscript has been

rendered partially illegible by scattered drops of liquid. An attempt has been made, for this edition, to read the stained portions under ultra-violet light.

II

Certeyne Rewles of Phisnomy and *A Calculacion to knowe by, of two Men feghtyng to-gidere, wheper sale be ouercomen*

The physiognomical section and the onomantic one are found translated together in B.L. MS. Sloane 213.

The text is on ff. 118^v–21; 19·5×27 cm. The portion of the manuscript formed by ff. 47–131, i.e. items 7–15, is a single unit and is in a characteristically fourteenth-century hand; it should perhaps be assigned to the years around 1400.[1] The bulk of the manuscript is in a later hand belonging to the fifteenth century. Ff. 161; in columns; twenty-four items, in Latin, French, and English. Many of the items are medical: they also include herbal, lapidary, astrological, and geometrical matter, and a treatise (item 19) on accountancy ('tabil marchaunte for all manere acountes'). Item 16 is a treatise, mainly astrological, in eight chapters; the matter with which we are concerned forms chapters 7 and 8. The other chapters run as follows:

1. (f. 111) howe al the yere es rewlede by the firste day of Januere.
2. (f. 111^v) what menes ilke thondere in the yere.
3. (f. 112^v) of evele and forbodden dayes.
4. (f. 113) what kynde was ilke day of the moon.
5. (f. 115) howe the seven planetes are frendes and enemyes.
6. (f. 117) descripcion of the four elementes and of the four complexiones.

Item 17, also in English, is a geometrical treatise.

Headings, numerals, and opening words of certain sentences are in red. An inscription dated 1560, on f. 5, runs 'Ex Bib*liotheca* Petr*i* de Cardonnet'.

---

[1] See the description of the language in volume ii. The old Sloane catalogue assigns some items in this section of the manuscript, including the *Phisnomy*, to the fourteenth century, but the *Index* to the Sloane collection more convincingly assigns to the fifteenth century ff. 51^v–63^v (Arnaldus de Villa Nova): s.v. *Villa Nova* in the Index.

III

The Secrete of Secretes: as in Bodleian MSS. Ashmole 396 and
Lyell 36

A full translation is contained in two fifteenth-century Bodleian
manuscripts, Ashmole 396 and the recent acquisition Lyell 36. I
refer to this anonymous translation as 'Ashmole', from the better
of the two manuscripts.

Ashmole 396 is a mid fifteenth-century parchment manuscript:
ff. 203, 27.5×20 cm. There are painted capitals (blue on red)
throughout, with illuminated initials in the first of the texts, i.e. the
Secretum, which takes up ff. 1–47. Headings in red ink. In binding,
a London indenture of 1608 has been used as end-paper. There are
a total of thirteen items in the manuscript, all English, dealing with
medicine, arithmetic, and astrology. The second item begins on
f. 48: it is an English version of the *Algorismus*, a treatise on arithmetic by Johannes de Sacro Bosco. This text has been printed,
from this manuscript, by Robert Steele, in *The Earliest Arithmetics
in English* (E.E.T.S., ES 118, 1922). Another item is a translation
of an astronomical treatise by the fourteenth-century John
Ashinden.

Catch-phrases are written within scrolls, at the ends of the
gatherings:

8ᵛ: to humble obedience
16ᵛ: for taking of hote
24ᵛ: in his love
32ᵛ: be-fore by ordre
40ᵛ: shynnyng and lightly.

Throughout the *Secretum*, with very great frequency (more so
than in the other texts in the manuscript) a seventeenth-century
hand has underlined passages, and written in marginal comments
to them. If this is the hand of Elias Ashmole, as Dr. Doyle has
suggested to me, the question arises whether he intended to print
the text. Marginal pointers have been inserted, to indicate passages of particular interest, in the form of a hand with a pointing
index finger (f. 6), or, more regularly, of a mark resembling a
Greek θ, with the horizontal stroke extended outside the oval.
These are so extremely frequent, averaging several to a page
throughout, that they cannot be indicated here. In the outer margin

have also been added chapter numbers in arabic numerals, while marginalia and other signs of study indicate a knowledgeable reader.

Lyell 36: 19.5 × 13.5 cm.; 202 ff., with about 26 lines to the page; late fifteenth century; paper and parchment usually alternating. Limp parchment wrapper, with remains of thong. Described in Albinia de la Mare, *Catalogue of the Collection of Medieval Manuscripts bequeathed to the Bodleian Library Oxford by James P. R. Lyell*, Oxford, 1971: an earlier description is in R. W. Hunt, 'The Lyell Bequest', *Bodleian Library Record*, iii (1950), 63 ff. A collection of tracts, astrological, gynaecological, etc., Latin and English. On f. 51 a new hand, careless, and difficult to read, begins; this is not at the start of a new quire, and is continuous with the early part, sharing with it the alternation of paper and parchment. Red ink is used for pointing, in vertical strokes, and for paragraph marks, at the head and in the body of chapters, as well as for the cartouches in which some of the headings are enclosed. The opening words of chapters are sometimes underlined in red. Red ink is used to fill in the small space between the double horizontal lines drawn in black at the conclusion of paragraphs; the individual letters of words are occasionally filled in with red ink: both these features are also found in Rawlinson C.83, described on pp. xxv–xxvi above. On f. 51 of the manuscript begins a tract of which the first words are 'Luna prima omnibus rebus'; this is followed by some 'Prognostica' attributed to Pythagoras. The *Secrete* is on ff. 85–127. After it comes (f. 128) a gynaecological treatise in English, beginning 'Ye schal understond that women have las hete'. Finally comes a text 'Cautele algorismi' (f. 154). In the text of the *Secrete* are some catchwords, written within rectangular cartouches, and very erratically employed. They are found as follows: on f. 90^v, which is apparently *not* the end of a gathering; on ff. 112^v, not followed by a repetition of the words upon the first recto of the gathering which follows; on f. 117^v, where the following recto is not the first of a new gathering and does not carry the catchword repeated.

The manuscript is defective: the opening of the text of the *Secretum* is lacking (for the misplacings in the text itself, see volume ii). The manuscript is, indeed, a wretched one, extremely unpleasant to use in every way: giving a disorderly text unintelligently transcribed in an ugly and careless hand, using ink which has now faded, and leaving only narrow margins. The book is in a bad state of preservation, its binding flimsy and crumpled. A letter addressed by Charles Singer to the bookseller Davis dated 19 June 1940, and formerly inserted in the manuscript, tentatively identifies the obstetric text with that in 'British Museum Sloane 2463 from folio 194 verso onwards', to which Miss De la Mare adds MSS. Sloane 5 and Royal 18 A.vi. All three of these manuscripts belong to the fifteenth century.

Another modern list of the contents, written in French, and earlier in date than this letter, is also inserted within the manuscript. It asserts that some leaves are missing after f. 112: but the text, if one includes the catchwords on f. 112ᵛ (which are not reproduced on f. 113), is continuous, and corresponds with Ashmole 396, f. 30ᵛ.

'Ashmole' contains the inversion of the passage in the theoretical proem to the first Book, discussed above (p. xviii); it also has the Hispaniensis proem embedded in it, and its Physiognomy is expanded in the manner of the Latin recension discussed under item E on p. xviii above.

IV

Johannes de Caritate, Þe Priuyté of Priuyteis

Another full version of the *Secretum* is found in a late fifteenth-century manuscript now the property of Mr. Robert B. Honeyman, Jr., of Rancho los Cerritos, San Juan Capistrano, California. My attention was drawn to this by Professor J. A. W. Bennett in 1950, when it was described (as item 237) in Catalogue no. 15 (Old Science and Medicine) of the late Ernst Weil of London, in the following terms:

Manuscript on Vellum . . . 6⅜ × 8½ in. [16.2 × 22 cm.] 118 leaves in a bastard hand, single lines, 21–23 to a page. Ample margins, prickings visible. With a large number of initials in burnished gold or azure. Contemporary panelled binding of brown calf, over wooden boards. The central panel is formed by intersecting rectangular frames filled with roll tools. . . .[1] Back with raised bands (very slightly damaged); clasps missing.

The hand is characterized by peculiarly broad, stubby down-strokes.

---

[1] Dr. Weil's reading of the letters in the tooling, here omitted, is inaccurate. See the description of the binding in the Preliminary Matter in volume ii.

Among the decorations are 'a fine initial A in burnished gold enclosing a thistle painted in varying shades of blue' (f. 40^v), and some 'elaborate pen work in red and purple frequently extending to the full length of the border'.[1]

Weil states that the quires consisted originally of eight leaves each, except the last but one, which he describes—with the addition of an interrogation mark—as 'a gathering of ten'. A few leaves are missing, as Dr. Weil points out, 'probably on account of fine initials, the offprints of some [of which] are showing'. It is possible that these missing illuminations contained illustrations as well as initials. I have taken the missing folios into consideration in numbering the leaves of the manuscript: they are ff. 1, 8, 34, 61, and 73: all contained the opening passages of sections of the text, i.e. the proem and each of the four books into which the body of the work has been divided. Fols. 33^v and 72 are blank, the recto of each containing the *explicit* to the Book which precedes. The missing folios enumerated above are the ones relevant to the textual study, and do not include fly-leaves. The full collation of the quires, however, is (to follow Weil, with one modification): 2 fly-leaves, 1^6 (first and last leaves missing),[2] 2^8–4^8, 5^7 (second leaf missing), 6^8–7^8, 8^7 (fifth leaf missing), 9^8, 10^7 (first leaf missing), 11^8–13^8, 14^3 (last five leaves missing), 15^8, 16^7.[3]

The *Priuyté* occupies ff. *1–107. There follows on ff. 109^v–122: 'The chef werke or operacion of alle clergé þat may be wrought by man', an alchemical text, in the same hand.

The text of the *Priuyté*, though written in a clear hand, seems to have been transcribed hastily. The word 'capitil' is frequently missing in the headings to the chapters, leaving an ordinal numerical adjective with no noun following it. The chapter numbers in the body of the text do not correspond with the numbering

---

[1] Dr. Weil's surmise that the style of these suggests 'a date well before the middle of the century' is in patent contradiction with the reference in the manuscript (see p. 114), which he himself quotes, to the reign of Henry VI as belonging to the past. Far from this reference proving that 'this manuscript . . . must have been written between 1422 and 1461', it proves only that the translation was carried out between 1422 and 1461 (or in 1471) and that the manuscript itself belongs to a later period than the original translation.

[2] Dr. Weil considers the first two leaves to be missing.

[3] To say with Dr. Weil that the last quire is a gathering of ten, with three leaves missing, seems to me an inadequate explanation of the manner in which the quire (in fact eight leaves with one missing) seems to consist partly of single leaves, to which no corresponding halves of bifolia were attached.

in the list of contents. The scribe has been through the manuscript, revising it, correcting words, adding letters above the line and phrases in the margin, and cancelling words and letters by erasure and expunction.

The *explicit* to Book I (ff. 33) reads:

> Parisiensis / Explicit prim*us* liber de Secretis secreto*rum*, sec*undum* translac*io*nem Joha*nn*is de Caritate.

This name is not, *pace* Dr. Weil, that of the Latin translator, the Latin text followed being a recension of Tripolitanus. An inscription on the front end-paper reads 'Johannes de Charitate D*o*ctor Parisiensis huius libri novissimus translator': but this is in a post-medieval hand, so that there is no justification for assuming that this attribution of a Paris doctorate to the translator is based upon anything other than an attempt to account for the presence (and syntactical function) of the word 'Parisiensis' in the *explicit*. It seems safe to assume that Johannes de Caritate was an Englishman: perhaps a John Charity, de Charité, Charté, Love or Lovelich, or perhaps a foundling named John, who was given the cognomen 'de Caritate'. The translation is dedicated to Sir Miles Stapleton of Norfolk. This will be further discussed in volume ii: it may be noted, in passing, that a letter possibly written by Margaret Paston, in 1466, in connection with the funeral of the writer's husband, mentions a 'Dom. John *Loveday*' who received 14*s*. 2*d*. for cloth for a riding cope.[1]

It is true that 'Parisiensis' could, conceivably, be the name of a person whom Johannes de Caritate had reason to consider in some way responsible for the *Latin* text of the *Secretum*: it could, arguably, be derived from the reference in one group of the *FrAb* texts to Philippus Tripolitanus as 'Philip of Paris', although this passage does not occur in the full Latin versions.

It is best, however, to assume that the wording of the *explicit* means that this portion of the manuscript was either produced by a scribe with the cognomen 'Parisiensis' or written out in Paris (or copied from one made there), and that it represents a translation by an Englishman of the name of Johannes de Caritate.[2]

---

[1] Blomefield, *Essay towards a Topographical History of the County of Norfolk* (11 vols., 1805), vi. 485.

[2] Dr. Weil posits a 'Jean de Charité' and adds 'he may come from the Cistercian abbey Charité in Franche-Comté or from Charité in Champagne'.

Back end-paper ii (verso) has some pen trials, and the inscription Johan*nes* Har. . . . This is the name of John Harcourt found on the margin of f. 61, and elsewhere upon the end-papers when examined[1] under ultra-violet light. The importance of these inscriptions is discussed in the Commentary: there also, the dedication of the translation to Stapleton, the possible locating of the provenance of this text at Paris, and the owning of it by John Harcourt and its seventeenth-century owner Richard Elde, are linked together in a surmise which must, of course, remain mere guesswork.

The Johannes de Caritate version is given a four-book division. The sections are as follows: I: all that precedes Hygiene (S to Ba); II: Hygiene, (Bb–cι) as far as Wines; III: the remainder of Hygiene (Bcζ''–ν); IV: the remainder of the text, from the Herbal and Lapidary onwards, concluding with the Physiognomy (C–J, Bd). Thus, Bacon's fourfold division is not followed, but the classification is close to that which can be seen by a reader, translator, or redactor, as the intention of the ambiguously worded version of Bacon's division, which MS. Rawlinson C.274 contains (see pp. xxv–xxvi above). It is possible that the Latin original used by Johannes was one in which the fourfold division suggested by that rubric was actually employed in the text. It is further noticeable that Johannes' Book II ends at the point where the Hygiene of the *Ab Trip* recensions ends, suggesting a possible contamination with that tradition, through some acquaintance with it.

A summary-form indication of the manner in which Johannes de Caritate divides up the sections of Philippus' text which he apportions among his four books is the following—it is a skeleton which is necessarily incomplete because of the portions missing from the manuscript at the start of each book, and somewhat misleading owing to the fact that Johannes substitutes his own equivalents for Philippus' preliminary passages, rather than reproducing them:

Book I: [Sz']vwABa

Book II: Bbca$a'\beta\beta'\gamma\zeta'\delta\zeta\eta\theta\iota$

Book III: Bc$\zeta''\kappa\lambda\mu\mu'\nu$

Book IV: J[ab] cdefgCabDabcdEFGHaIabBd$a\beta\gamma$

---

[1] This examination was carried out for me by Miss Désirée Hirst.

V

Decretum Aristotelis: þe secrete of secretes, and tresore incomperable
as in Bodleian MS. Ashmole 59, in the hand of John Shirley

Bodleian MS. Ashmole 59, in the hand of John Shirley, has been
studied by several scholars. For description and studies see the
catalogue of Ashmole manuscripts, and E. P. Hammond, articles in
Modern Language Notes, xix (1904), 35, in *Anglia*, xxvii (1904),
36, and xxx (1907), 320; *English Verse between Chaucer and Surrey*
(Durham, N.C., 1927), pp. 79 (n. 1), 192; *Chaucer: a Bibliographical
Manual* (New York, 1933), pp. 515 ff.; O. Gärtner, *John Shirley:
Sein Leben und Wirken* (Halle, 1904), pp. 22–25; F. N. Robinson,
Harvard Studies, v (1896), 185; A. Brusendorff, *The Chaucer
Tradition* (Oxford and Copenhagen, 1925), esp. pp. 207 ff. I have
received help from Dr. A. I. Doyle, whose work on Shirley has
now partly appeared in print.[1]

Ashmole 59 contains sixty-eight items. The section we are concerned with, i.e. that which is in Shirley's hand, consists of two
parchment and 130 paper leaves, about thirty-three lines to the
page, 27.5 × 19.5 cm. The manuscript contains Chaucer's *Com-
pleynt to Pité*, works by Gower and Lydgate, prophetic texts,
and gnomic writings in prose. For Shirley's 'device' on the title-
page, see Hammond, *English Verse*, pp. 192–3; for his verses
used as a bookplate, the same, together with the authorities referred to there, and H. S. Bennett, *Chaucer and the Fifteenth
Century*, pp. 116–18. Fols. 130ᵛ–134ᵛ have additions by other hands.

The *Decretum Aristotelis* (this title, in the explicit, is almost
certainly a slip for *Secretum* but it is retained here for its distinctiveness) is the opening item, on ff. 1–12ᵛ. A fragmentary version, it
occupies a quire to itself, although Miss Hammond (*Anglia*, xxx)
considers all of the 134 leaves to form a single production.
Brusendorff notes that the *Decretum* text is on a separate quire,
and further indicates the separate nature of the *third* portion of the
134 leaves (ff. 100–34). Miss Hammond herself (*MLN*, xix) notes
that the table of contents in the manuscript does not belong to
it. The text of the *Decretum* ends in the midst of the matter of the
Hygiene book, with the explicit (f. 12ᵛ) 'Et sic explicit Decretum
Aristo[te]lis'. This is followed by an incipit 'And begynneþe
þabstracte brevyaire compyled of divers balades &c.'. In place of

---

[1] *Medium Ævum*, xxx (1962), 93–101.

the catchword which is usual on the versos of this manuscript, f. 12ᵛ (the end of cap. xv in this translation) carries the figure 'xiij'. Although, as the manuscript stands, f. 13 is of course the following leaf, the numeral 'xiij'—a quire-number, but written as though it were a catchword—has been crossed through, and the numeral 'I' substituted, and so on for the following gatherings. Ashmole 59 must earlier have been intended as a portion of a larger volume: Dr. Doyle has pointed out to me that similar changes affect the Shirley manuscripts in Trinity College and Sion College.

It is difficult to assess how far the three self-contained sections of the 134 leaves (that is ff. 1–12, ff. 13–99, ff. 100–34) must be regarded as separate products of separate dates. The identical nature of the paper could be explained by the hypothesis that a scriptorium of the size of Shirley's may have made use, over an extended period, of a large quantity of identical writing material, purchased wholesale.

Miss Hammond (*Anglia*, xxvii) notes the general carelessness and haste of the 134 leaves, and dates them between the death of Humphrey of Gloucester (1447) and the death, at a ripe old age, of Shirley (1456). But this evidence, together with a passage dating after Lydgate's death (in 1449 or later) only fixes the date of ff. 13–100.

That ff. 1–12 and ff. 100–34 are closely connected in time and authorship is shown by a curious feature which they have in common, and which has hitherto escaped notice. This is the use in both texts of acrostics consisting of the letters of the alphabet in their correct order, used as opening letters of consecutive chapters.

Ff. 100–30 contain the *Chronicles of þe three kinges of Coloyne*. In this, chapters i to ix have the arbitrary initials TTWIWABFP. From chapter x (f. 107) to chapter xxxiii, the initials run as follows: ABCDEFGHIKLMNOPQRSTUXY 3 followed by a cruciform ampersand, the abbreviation sign for *con-* and the the letter sign ≡, apparently to be read as 'tytell'.[1] This last is dragged in forcibly (f. 123ᵛ) by an orthographical interruption of the quasi-scriptural story. The true beginning of the chapter, on f. 124, is formed by the words:

Whane all þat was necessarie and oportune was desposed and or-deynde by þees thre kinges . . .

[1] The name *tytell* has been used for the horizontal abbreviation stroke: see Samuel A. Tannenbaum, *The Handwriting of the Renaissance* (1931), p. 120.

But these words are preceded by a passage which runs as follows:

[f. 123ᵛ] ☰yttell tytle: Tytell is taken for a figur in diu*ers* langages and principally taken in scriptures and langages of Latyne for þe more savoury sowne of þe wordes, and þer-fore it is sette [f. 124] in þabsee for þe more redy writing of all maner of langages, and þe prola*cion*[1] of hem.

The next four initials, again (ff. 125–8) form the series ABCD, but the subsequent, and final, one (f. 128ᵛ) is P.

Curiously enough, another version of *The Chronicles of þe three kinges*, in B.L. MS. Royal 18 A.x, edited by C. Horstmann as E.E.T.S. o.s. 85 (1886), also contains an acrostic: by a manipulation of the opening phrases of the paragraphs initials are produced which spell out the names of two women who were presumably the owners or patronesses of that manuscript.[2] This need not detain us: what is of concern here is that the *Decretum* in Ashmole 59 contains an exact parallel to this feature of the Shirleian copy of *The Chronicles of þe three kinges*. The opening of the text transforms Yaḥyā's name into 'Marmaduke þe sonne of Patryke'— possible reasons for this curious alteration are discussed in volume II: I have used this feature to distinguish this translation by giving it the cognomen 'Marmaduke'. The initials of the opening words of each chapter (excluding the opening section) run in alphabetical order. Chapter i starts with an A. There follows a section starting with B, given a title but no chapter number. A section opening with C is numbered 'Capitulum ij'—this has been emended to iii in the present edition. It is clear that a section which did not form a separate chapter in the prototype has been made such for the sake of the acrostic, but that the original numbering has slipped past uncorrected. Chapter iv bears its correct number;

---

[1] prolacion: pronunciation.
[2] The names given are Margareta Moningtown and Mawde de Stranlea. Dr. Doyle writes 'Both names [are] associable with the S. Wales Border (Herefordshire etc.) at the beginning of the fifteenth century . . . Shirley seems to have had connexions (and origins?) in the same region, but there is nothing to relate Roy. 18 A.x and its contents to him.' Horstmann refers to the *Mappula Angliae* in B.L. MS. Harley 4011 for an acrostic which gives Osbert Bokenham's name.

The text of the *Chronicles* printed by Horstmann is of a different grouping from that in Ashmole 59. The versions closely related to Ashmole 59 are in: Douce 301, Cambridge Ee.4.2 and Kk.1.3, Cotton Titus A.xxv, Cambridge Patrick Papers 43, and a Bedford manuscript, now B.L. Add. 36983. Horstmann does not print any variants from Ashmole 59.

from there to chapter xi each chapter is regularly entitled 'capitulum'; the series gives the letters D E F G H I. Chapters x and xi have titles, but no numbers (they have been added to them in the text below): these chapters begin, respectively, with K and L. Chapter xii is numbered, and starts with M. Chapter xiii, unnumbered, gives N; chapters xiv–xv, numbered, give O and P. With this chapter, before the awkward letter Q is reached, the text breaks off. The jockeying with initial words is only jarring in the case of P, for the sake of which the general discussion of hygiene has been made to open with the words (222/26 ff. below)

People were assembled and come to-geder of þe moste naturale and renomed philosophre[s] þane beeing on lyve, for to determyne for a principal conclusion medicinable.

It is perhaps a dubious compliment to pay the deviser of the acrostic to say that not only was it unnoticed by previous investigators, but the present writer, the first modern transcriber of the text, remained quite unaware of it until he had reached the letter P on the penultimate page.

The presence of both acrostics in one manuscript suggests that they were a whim of Shirley's or of a close associate of his. Dr. Doyle writes to me of one friend of Shirley's: 'John Cok, brother of St. Bartholomew's hospital, dabbled a little in ciphers', but he knows of no connexion between him and this manuscript.

The Marmaduke version is so fragmentary and so obviously remanipulated by the translator that it is difficult to fix its source with any certainty. The text reproduces no portions of the *Secretum* that are not in the *Ab Trip* recensions. On most of the points which distinguish *Fr AbB* from *Fr AbC*, Marmaduke omits or modifies the passage in such a way as to afford no evidence. On one point it is in agreement with *Fr AbB*: the name of Guy de Valence is mentioned on f. 1. The probability is therefore that it belongs to the *Fr AbB* tradition, as does the version by Gilbert of the Haye.[1]

---

[1] The affiliation of the Haye version to that recension cannot be doubted, since it shares the features summed up above under the numbering (1), (3), (5), (7–8); the two kingdoms in question under point no. (4) are named by Haye the realms of the *Albanois* and *Sacienis* (p. 105); the translator (p. 74) is called Fair Pateris, which is likely (see point no. (6) on p. xxiii above) to be based on a misreading of *Iean [filz] Patrice* as *Beau Patrice*. In MS. St. John's 102 *Fr AbB* is associated with the *Livre de Chevalrie*, which is the fourth item in the manuscript. In Gilbert of the Haye's manuscript, the author's translations of the two texts are found together: curiously enough, J. H. Stephenson, editing both in

VI

John Shirley, *The Governance of Kynges and of Prynces*, as in
British Library MS. Add. 5467

Shirley's own translation is in B.L. MS. Add. 5467, ff. 211–224ᵛ.
This is a small paper manuscript of the second half of the fifteenth
century; 22.5 × 15.8 cm, ff. 225; usually twenty-six to thirty-two
lines to the page, but sometimes as few as nineteen.[1] The incipit
on f. 211 and the rubric on f. 213ᵛ are in a larger court hand, but
by the same scribe as the bulk of the text, which is in a more cur-
sive and angular script. Neither of the two hands of the volume
is Shirley's. Each opening of our text contains the running title:
[v] The governance of Kynges/[r] And of prynces. The lines of
the text are short, and a wide outer margin contains the numbers
of the chapters, and their titles: these form long narrow rubrics
of two or three words to a line.

Other texts in this manuscript include:

(1) Shirley's translation of *Le Livre de bonnes meurs*, translated, we
are informed on f. 97, 'in his grete and last age the yere of oure
lord a thousand foure hundreth Fourty', that is, when Shirley
was about seventy-four years old. Ends on f. 211.

(2) *The Cronycle of the Dethe of James Stewarde*, that is, of the
reign and murder of James I of Scotland, translated by Shirley,
as the colophon informs us 'oute of Latyne into oure moders
Englisshe tong'. This has been printed three times: in vol. i
of Pinkerton's *Antient Scotish Poems* (1756), in Glasgow in 1818,
and, for the Maitland Club, in 1837. Ff. 72ᵛ–82ᵛ.

The translation of the *Secretum* is entitled *The Governance of
Kynges and of Prynces, cleped The Secrete of Secretes*, and is written
with catchwords to its rectos. On the final page, f. 225ᵛ as it stands,
the text breaks off abruptly, after five lines of chapter xvi, but with
a catchword, indicating that the text had been continued further,
and perhaps completed.[2] The table of contents (ff. 211–13ᵛ) lists

one volume, fails to note anywhere the fact that a French version of the *Secretum*
(let alone one of the type here named *FrAbB*) is in the St. John's manuscript,
which he mentions in connection with the *Buke of Knychthede*.

[1] For a description of the manuscript and a full survey of its contents, see
Gärtner, op. cit., pp. 25–57.

[2] As mentioned in volume ii, the headings to chapter xlvii and further
chapters are included in the list of contents, thus indicating that the translation
had probably been continued.

fifty-eight chapters. The extant text reckons the preliminary material (f. 211 and verso), which precedes the table of contents, as a chapter, thereby turning the eulogy of Aristotle (chapter i in the table of contents) into chapter ii. There follow chapters iii to xv *in toto*, and the five lines of chapter xvi.

The table of contents omits all reference to the discourse on Justice. The position at which the heading should occur—since the *Governance* follows the arrangement of the *Ab Trip* recension—is at the very bottom of f. 213: omission in such a position may well be an oversight.

VIA

Le Secret des secrés: Cambridge University Library MS. Ff.1.33

Shirley's translation is very close textually to a French version of the *Secretum* found in Cambridge MS. Ff.1.33. This manuscript carries the name of John Shirley repeatedly in its margins, with the characteristic injunction 'No*ta* p*er* Shirley'.

Fol. 1ᵛ, apparently originally the front pastedown, contains Shirley's emblem. The Cambridge University Library Catalogue does not specifically state that Shirley owned the manuscript, but the fact is obvious.

The manuscript further contains a text of the *Livre de bonnes meurs*, Shirley's version of which, as we have seen, precedes the *Governance* in Add. 5467. The fourth item in the manuscript is the *Livre de eschez*, the translation by Jehan de Vignay of the *Ludus Scacchorum* of Jacobus de Cessolis: this explains[1] Shirley's attribution of the *Bonnes meurs* to him in his English translation. Assuming that Shirley's scriptorium produced version VI at a later date than his version V, i.e. not earlier than 1449, it should be noted that Shirley translated the *Bonnes meurs* some ten years before the *Secretum*, for, as noted above, he gives 1440 as the date of his version of the *Bonnes meurs*.

Internal evidence supports the supposition that the French *Secretum* in Cambridge Ff.1.33 is the original which Shirley used for his *Governance* (see further details in volume ii).

[1] See H. J. R. Murray, *A History of Chess*, Oxford, 1913, repr. 1962, pp. 545–6. I am indebted to the reader of the Oxford Press for this reference. Hoccleve's version of the *Secretum*, the *Regement for Princes*, includes matter from Jacobus de Cessolis' book.

The relevant section of this text has therefore been included in this corpus, printed opposite the text of the *Governance*. This enables the reader to have a glimpse of the original upon which Shirley worked, an opportunity of studying the workshop of a fifteenth-century book-producer.

MS. Ff.1.33 is a fine-looking octavo volume: 24×17 cm., 33 lines, foliated in two portions, ff. 106+76. It dates only some quarter of a century earlier than the English version: The scribe's colophon (pt. ii, f. 76) reads 'Et fut copié et escript à Bourges en Berry ou moys de may l'an de grace mil quatre cent et vingt.' The *Secret des secrés* takes up pp. 1–62.

In addition to the items mentioned, the manuscript contains *Le livre du gouvernement de santé que Ypocras fist et l'envoya a l'emperiere Sesar.*

VII

The Secrete of Secretes, as in University College Oxford MS. 85

MS. Univ. 85, deposited in the Bodleian Library, is a large and fine folio-sized manuscript on vellum, 34×25 cm., ff. 90, with wide margins, and twenty-eight lines to each page. The hand is neat and the decoration noteworthy; each of the items has a large miniature at its beginning, occupying all but a few lines at the bottom of the page. The texts are all in English and all translations; they are, following the numbered pages of this volume (since University College manuscripts are paginated rather than foliated):

p. 1: The *Quadrilogue* of Alain Chartier.
p. 70: *The Secrete of Secretes.*
p. 136: *Consideracions right necessarye to the good governance of a prince* [from Vegetius, Aegidius Colonna, and others].

The Chartier text has now been edited by Dr. Margaret S. Blayney in *Fifteenth-Century English Translations of Alain Chartier's 'Le Traité de l'Esperance' and 'Le Quadrilogue Invectif'*, E.E.T.S., 270, 1974.

There are decorations running down the left-hand margins at the beginnings of sections. Initials are regularly illuminated.

The hand of this manuscript has been identified with that of B.L. MS. Harley 4775 by Mr. Neil Ker and by Professor Auvo Kurvinen; to the latter I am grateful for bringing to my notice most of the following facts. The Harleian manuscript, like Univ. 85, is a large folio in vellum of the second half of the fifteenth century. It contains a translation, earlier than Caxton's, of Jacobus de Voragine's *Legenda aurea*. The translation is attributed to 1438 on the strength of the colophon in Bodleian MS. Douce 372: this manuscript was copied between 1438 and 1460, the latter being the date of its second colophon. The Harleian and Douce manuscripts agree so closely in wording and spelling as to make Miss Kurvinen consider them copies of one prototype manuscript, probably executed at about the same time: the Midland dialectal features are mild, and the extent of standardization suggests a London scriptorium. Miss Kurvinen's opinion upon the scribe, based mainly on a study of Harley 4775, is that 'he was a professional scribe who copied extremely faithfully, so that his text is likely to retain even some of the dialectal forms of his exempla' (private letter, 16 June 1955).

VIII

Robert Copland's printed version, *The Secrete of Secretes*, 1528; reprint by Kitson, 1572

Copland's printed version of 1528 (STC 770) is preserved in a unique copy in the Cambridge University Library. This is now reproduced as no. 220 in the facsimile series *The English Experience* (Amsterdam, 1970). There is no title-page.

The final leaf, f. J4, carries Copland's device, preceded by the colophon:

Thus endeth the secrete of secretes of Arystotle wi*th* the governayle of prynces and euery maner of estate with rules of helthe for body and soule very prouffytable for euery man, and also veray good to teche chyldren to lerne to rede Englysshe. Newly translated & enprynted by Robert Copland at Londo*n* in the flete-strete at the sygne of the Rose garla*n*de the yere of our lorde. M.CCCCC.xxviij. the .vij. day of August þe .xx yere of the reygne of our mooste dradde soverayne and naturall kynge Henry the .viij. defender of the fayth.

Copland's first dated book bears the imprint 1515, the second belongs to 1521. The *Secret* is one of three bearing the date 1528.[1]

---

[1] For Copland see W. Herbert, *Typographical Antiquities* iii (1816), 111–26; H. R. Plomer, 'Robert Copland', *Transactions of the Bibliographical Society*, iii (1895–6), 211–25; E. Gordon Duff *et al.*, *Handlists of English Printers, 1501–1556*, Pt. ii; Copland is in the section on the years 1515–33, by H. R. Plomer.

Kitson's reprint of Copland's translation (STC 770a) is also extant in a unique copy, in the Folger Shakespeare Library.

The title-page runs as follows:

THE SECRETE OF SE-/CRETES, CONTAINING THE / most excellent and learned instruction / *of Aristotle the prince of Philosophers:* / which he sent to the Emperour, King A-/lexander: very necessarye and profitable / for all maner of estates and degrees, / VVith some instructions in the / ende of this booke, touching / the iudgment of Phi-/ sognomie.

> Lordes and maisters, wise and honourable,
> Of this said booke make all a loking glas:
> For ye shal finde it good and profitable,
> With wisedome to bring your nedes to passe:
> Make your entent, as the aut[oures] was,
> Which grounded it on right hie grauit[ie],
> Counselling you to lyue in equytie.[1]

A full study of Kitson's text is in T. P. Harrison, 'The Folger *Secret of Secrets*, 1572', *Joseph Quincy Adams Memorial Studies*, ed. J. G. McManaway, G. J. Dawson, and E. E. Willoughby (Washington, 1948), pp. 601–20.[2]

Robert Copland died about 1547, and was succeeded, at the same address, the Rose-garland in Fleet Street, by William Copland, whose imprint appears until 1553. Kitson's impression is identical with Copland's apart from changes in punctuation and spelling: it comes, of course, from a separate press. Some of the initial letters of Copland's edition (they consist of woodcuts with grotesques within the letters), are used again, though the pages are certainly reset in a different chase, if not entirely set up anew, and the spelling has been 'modernized', in a reprint of ff. D4 to G3 of Copland's text, that is, the portion of the *Secretum* which deals with Hygiene.[3] This was printed by Wyer in 1535 (STC 6837) under a title which is derived from that of the first of the chapters of this portion, 'Of the dyfference of astronomy'. His incipit runs:

Here begyn/neth the dyfference of a-/stronomy, with the gouer-/nayle to kepe mans body / in helth, all the foure / seasons of the/yeare.

---

[1] Bracketed portions are indistinct in the extant copy.

[2] My thanks are due to Mr. Giles Dawson for having brought Professor Harrison's article to my attention.

[3] Some upper-case letters of a different fount have been substituted.

Wyer's volume consists of five gatherings, A–D⁴, F⁵; f. E5 bears the imprint:

Imprynted by / me Robert Wyer Dwellynge at the Syne / of Seynt John Euan-/gelyst, in Seynt Martyns Parysshe besyde / Charynge / Crose.

The copy in the British Library (C.40a 21) is, I believe, unique. It should be regarded as a reprint of this portion of Copland, and variants from it have been included in the textual footnotes below.

The Folger copy of Kitson's text bears the name of a seventeenth-century owner, R. Stephenson (sig. A2). Until the volume was acquired by the Folger Library, the reprint had been listed as a ghost, known only through having been mentioned as unobtainable in 1702, in the preface to the Walwyn version (see pp. xliv ff. below).

IX

William Forrest, *The Pleasaunt Poesye of Princelie Practise*, in British Library MS. Royal 17 D.iii, dated 1548

B.L. MS. Royal 17 D.iii, is fully described in the catalogue of the Royal manuscripts. It is a holograph manuscript of Sir William Forrest's *Pleasaunt Poesye of Princelie Practise*, a rhyme royal version of the *Secretum*. Ff. 77, 25.5×18.4 cm; about three and a half stanzas of rhyme royal to the page. Chapter headings are in alternate black and red words.

After the unfinished text there are several blank but lined folios. Forrest's hand can be seen in his other holograph manuscripts: B.L. Add. 34791 (a metrical version of the Psalms); B.L. Royal 17 A.xxi (a later form of the same work, written out in 1551); MS. University College, Oxford 88 (Part I of his *History of Joseph the Chaiste*, together with some other works); B.L. Royal 18 C.xiii (Part II of *Joseph*, written out in 1569, but composed in 1545: see *Bodleian Quarterly Record*, iii (1950), 22 f.); Bodl. MS. Wood empt. 2 (his *History of Griseld the Second*).

W. D. Macray's edition of this last-mentioned work (1875) contains a full account of Forrest's life and works.

Forrest's poem was written in 1548 for presentation to the Duke of Somerset, and through him to Edward VI: the date is on f. 8. In this manuscript the poem is unfinished; although the manuscript is in the royal collection, one presumes that Somerset's fall, in that year, came before Forrest could present it formally to him. Also originally dedicated to Somerset is Forrest's collection of Metrical Psalms, contained, as noted above, in a manuscript dated 1551. A full-page drawing (f. 7ᵛ) shows Forrest presenting the volume to Edward VI.

Of Forrest's interpolations one is, notably, an allegorized description of the coronation of an English king. This may be a spontaneous insertion, appropriate for the young Edward VI and for the months in which the poem must have been composed. In view, however, of the manuscript association of the *Secretum*, discussed above (pp. xx–xxi) with treatises on coronation ceremonial, it is at least a possibility that Forrest had at his disposal a Latin manuscript which included both a text of the *Secretum* and a description of the ceremonial.

Portions of the *Pleasaunt Poesye* have already appeared in print in S. J. Herrtage, *England in the Reign of King Henry the Eighth*, E.E.T.S., E.S. 32 (1878): these portions correspond to ll. 2570–3262 in the present edition.

APPENDIX A: X

Jenkin Gwynne, *Tyrocaesar* (1569), in Wellcome Medical Historical Library MS. 71

MS. 71 in the Wellcome Medical Historical Library, Euston Road, London, is described in S. A. J. Moorat, *Catalogue of Western Manuscripts on Medicine and Science in the Wellcome Historical Library*, vol. i, 1962. The manuscript consists of forty leaves, 27 × 21 cm; the contents are carefully written out on paper specially prepared with neat red ruling—about twenty lines of text to a page—with boldly defined margins, of which the outer one is particularly wide and is used for the author's own annotations. The manuscript is almost certainly the author's holograph, written out in the manner of Elizabethan texts prepared for the printers. Two hands, secretary and italic, are used—the latter being employed for emphasis.

The manuscript is dated 1569 (f. 4), and is dedicated to Sir Walter Mildmay, who was Chancellor of the Exchequer[1] and is

---

[1] Moorat (loc. cit.) writes that Mildmay was not Chancellor until 1574. But the *DNB* article on Mildmay gives the earlier date 1566 for the start of his occupancy of the post, while 1559 is given as the date by S. E. Lehmberg, *Sir Walter Mildmay and Tudor Government* (Austin, Texas, 1964), p. 48.

best known as the founder of Emmanuel College, Cambridge. Gwynne was a clerk of the Exchequer. The manuscript presumably passed from Mildmay's son Anthony to Francis Fane, first Earl of Westmoreland, who married Walter Mildmay's granddaughter Mary: for a slip pasted into the inside of the binding reads 'The Earl of Westmoreland 1856'—the reference being to John Fane, the eleventh earl, d. 1859.

Ff. 3–4^v contain a dedicatory letter, in which Gwynne speaks of repaying a debt of gratitude to Mildmay by translating the Latin text of Hispaniensis (or Joannes Hispanus, as he writes) for his patron. Many manuscripts of Hispaniensis, in the proem, transliterate the title *Sirr al-asrār* in some such form as *cyrotesrar*. In Gwynne's text this becomes *Tyrocaesar*.

The text of Hispaniensis is on ff. 5–8^v.

Ff. 8^v–16 contain a reproduction, with many gaps, of ll. 1240 to 2016 of the fifteenth-century rhyme royal version of the *Secretum* by John Lydgate and Benedict Burgh, the *Book of the Governaunce of Kynges and of Prynces*, edited by Robert Steele under the title *Secrees of Old Philisoffris* as E.E.T.S., E.s. 66 (1894). This section of the poem corresponds with the portion of the *Sirr* translated by Hispaniensis. Gwynne identifies the lines only as 'a pece of the said epistill Englisshed by some auncient learnede man, whose name I colde not fynde' (f. 8^v).

Fols. 16–22 contain Gwynne's own reflections upon the themes of the Hispaniensis text.

After the *Finis* which stands at the end of this section the remainder of the text, which is not here reproduced, consists of a series of alleged prophecies of events in the years and centuries to follow (ff. 22–40).

Gwynne states that he finds them 'not ympertinent to the matter' of man's health. A brief account of this section, and of the manuscript as a whole, is found in the present editor's article, 'Tyrocaesar: a manual for Sir Walter Mildmay', *Manuscripta*, xix (1975), 27–35.

APPENDIX B: XI

Aristotles's Secret of Secrets Contracted; The Walwyn version of 1702

In 1702 there appeared a new English translation of *AbTrip*. Only in a very restricted sense, by virtue of some of the remarks in the preface, can this be said to usher in the modern scholarly study of the *Secretum*, which was to start with Douce's annotations in some of the copies he owned (i.e. Bodleian MSS. Douce 95 and 128). The 1702 translation continues, in much the same spirit, the manner of the late medieval and early modern English translators. This being so, and because this translation is known only through the unique copy in the British Library, the text is here printed as an appendix to this corpus.

A description is as follows:

ARISTOTLES's / Secret of Secrets / Contracted; / Being the Sum of his Advice / TO / *Alexander* the Great, / About / The Preservation of Health / and Government. / Formerly Translated out of the / Original *Greek* into *Latin*, and di-/vers other Languages; and being / very scarse, is now faithfully ren-/dred into *English*, / For the Good of Mankind. / [line] / *LONDON*, / Printed for *H.Walwyn*, at the three Legs in / the *Poultry*, 1702.

i Title-page; iii–viii, The Bookseller to the Reader; 1–87, text. A⁴, B–D¹², GHI⁸.

The translator of the 'Walwyn' version informs us that he knew of an older English version, but that he translated from an abbreviated Latin printing, presumably one of those based upon *Ab Trip* (see Steele, pp. xxx f.), and from the edition of 1520. The latter is the Du Pré text (Paris, 16mo), which follows the Achillini text. Walwyn's version must therefore be considered an abbreviated conflation of *Ab Trip* and Achillini. As the critical apparatus below, and the Commentary to follow, will indicate, the obscurities in the Walwyn version often derive from a misreading or mistranslation either of a standard form of the Latin, or specifically of the Achillini wording.

INTER-RELATIONSHIP OF THE ENGLISH VERSIONS

The relationship of these English versions to their originals, to one another, and to the other known literal English versions, can be indicated in tabular form. In the table below, the three translations in *3PV*, and Sir Gilbert of the Haye's version, have been included. Short titles are used for them, as follows:

Reg.: *The Book of the Governaunce of Kyngis and of Pryncis, callid the Secrete of Secretes*; in B.L. MS. Royal 18 A.vii. Printed as item 1 in *3PV*.

Yonge: James Yonge, *The Gouernaunce of Prynces* (1422), as in Bodley
MS. Rawlinson B.490 (and, fragmentarily, Trinity College, Dublin
E.2.31). Item 3 in *3PV*.

Haye: Sir Gilbert of the Haye, *The Buke of the Governaunce of Princis*.

Of the above, Lambeth is a version of the Vulgate, Reg. of
FrAbC, and Haye, as discussed above, of *FrAbB*. Yonge's
version, itself containing interpolations relevant to the Lord Lieu-
tenant of Ireland, to whom it is addressed, is a translation of the
Waterford–Copale version, which has embedded in it the *Dietary*
of Isaac Judaeus and the *Breviloquium* of Johannes Wallensis.

It is difficult to devise a stemmatic arrangement of the three
unknown texts of *FrAbC* used respectively by Copland, and by the
translators of Reg. and Univ., and to relate them to Cambridge
Ff.1.33. The readings show no steady affiliations. Ff.1.33, Univ.,
and Copland all refer to the translator as 'Philip of Paris'; Reg.
omits this particular passage. The kingdom destroyed through
prodigality (in section A) is England in Ff.1.33 and in Univ.; the
passage is omitted in Reg. and Copland. The peoples destroyed
through oath-breaking (in section Ba) are *Imbres* and *Assyriens*
in Ff.1.33, *Ymbres* and *Syriens* in Univ.; in Reg. the *Assiryenes*
alone are mentioned; Copland omits them. In likening a king to
natural phenomena, Univ. and Copland omit the wind, giving
only the comparisons to rain and the changing seasons. In the
table below, therefore, no more detailed affiliation is attempted
than common derivation from French texts of the same recension
as Ff.1.33.

Since it is not clear that any portion of the Walwyn version de-
rives from a section of the Achillini text which is indebted to
Ḥarīzī's Hebrew translation, reference to Ḥarīzī and to his source,
the Short Form of the Arabic *Sirr*, is omitted in this table.

EDITORIAL POLICY: GENERAL REMARKS

The editor has attempted to produce a corpus of all known early
English versions of the *Secretum* which have not already been
edited. This embraces the fifteenth-century versions, and early-
sixteenth-century versions both from manuscript and from printed
sources. For the sake of completeness, variants from the 1572 re-
printing of Copland's text and from Wyer's fragment have been
included in the footnotes, and the Elizabethan manuscript version

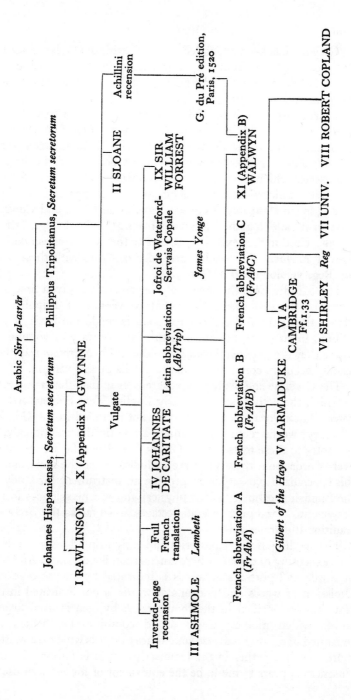

Arabic *Sirr al-asrār*

Johannes Hispaniensis, *Secretum secretorum*   Philippus Tripolitanus, *Secretum secretorum*

I RAWLINSON   X (Appendix A) GWYNNE   II SLOANE   Achillini recension

Vulgate   G. du Pré edition, Paris, 1520

Full French translation   IV JOHANNES DE CARITATE   Latin abbreviation (*AbTrip*)   Jofroi de Waterford-Servais Copale   IX SIR WILLIAM FORREST

Lambeth   *James Yonge*

Inverted-page recension   French abbreviation B (*FrAbB*)   French abbreviation C (*FrAbC*)   XI (Appendix B) WALWYN

III ASHMOLE

French abbreviation A (*FrAbA*)   *Gilbert of the Haye* V MARMADUKE   VI A CAMBRIDGE Ff.I.33

VI SHIRLEY   *Reg* VII UNIV.   VIII ROBERT COPLAND

by Gwynne has been appended, together with the Walwyn version
of 1702, which, far from constituting an early modern antiquarian
effort, is by its nature a continuation of the medieval and Renaissance manner of treating the text.

In order to make it possible to study the parallel treatment of
FrAbC by three English translators, the texts of the Univ. translation, and of the translations by Shirley and Copland, are printed
side by side, together with the relevant portion of the French
manuscript which the editor believes Shirley to have been following. When Shirley's text breaks off, the French text of Cambridge
Ff.1.33 is cut short in this corpus, leaving the Univ. and Copland
texts in parallel together. Readings from MS. Cambridge Ff.1.33
are also cited in the textual apparatus to the other English derivatives of *FrAbC*. The reader may also compare with these texts
the Reg. version of *FrAbC* in *3PV*.

The Middle English version of Hispaniensis is given first, followed by the earliest, and fragmentary, version of Tripolitanus.
Placed third, the full Ashmole version is made the basis of this
edition, in so far as the notes in the Commentary in volume II,
where they are of general concern to the whole *Secretum* tradition,
usually occur in comment upon the details of this version.

The Gwynne and Walwyn texts are later in date than the period
to which the activities of the Early English Text Society are de-
voted. Their vocabulary is therefore not included in the General
Glossary; words requiring comment are noticed, exceptionally, in
the notes to these texts. In the Glossary of Scientific Terms, however, words from these texts are included, since the main aim of
this specialized glossary is to provide an instrument for study of
the English vocabulary of the physical and arcane sciences in the
pre-scientific and proto-scienti ficstages, in so far as the *Secretum*
tradition illustrates this.

The spelling of the manuscript and early printed texts stands as
it is, excepting of course, where emendation is necessary. Addition
of words and portions of words is indicated by square brackets.
Omission of words and portions of words is not indicated in the
text, but is specified in the footnotes. A hyphen is used to join
words which modern usage would combine, but which are
separated in the original: also sometimes in words which are written
more closely together in the manuscripts than is normal, for this
closeness appears to me to be the equivalent of the modern use of

a hyphen. Punctuation is modernized: peculiarities of punctuation are pointed out in the separate discussions of the different texts, in the Preliminary Matter in volume ii, where further secondary information concerning the manuscripts will be found, to supplement the descriptions given in this Introduction.

Capital *I* is given as *J* where it represents the consonant. The double *ff* is reduced to a single *f* where it is clear that it represents nothing more than the scribe's grapheme for capital *F*, or, as in the case of the Johannes de Caritate manuscript, that it stands for a single *f* in all graphic contexts. The *þ* has been retained. In order to emphasize the continuity of the medieval tradition both in the printed books and in holograph manuscript works of the sixteenth century, the *y* of Copland and of Forrest has been represented by a *þ* where the dental fricative is intended. In the texts based upon printed books, i.e. those of Copland and of the 'Walwyn' version, the punctuation of the original edition is retained.

Most light downstrokes and other graphic signs added to final letters have been ignored, excepting where they patently represent a plural *-es/is*. Abbreviations have been silently expanded wherever a graphic sign has been interpreted as meaningful and not otiose. Expansion has sometimes been a matter of fairly arbitrary or subjective choice, since more than one possible reading has seemed equally persuasive; such doubtful cases are usually singled out in the footnotes. The abbreviations for the terminations *-es*, *-en*, *-eth* have been expanded as *-is*, *-in*, *-ith* where neighbouring scribal practice favours this. This has at times meant a change of policy within the course of a single text.

The editor's treatment of the signs which are sometimes contraction marks for *-n* and *-m* perhaps requires special mention. These signs are a straight horizontal stroke and, less often, a semicircular horizontal curve with a dot beneath. These have sometimes been expanded, but, where they seemed to have no function, however boldly they are written, they have been treated as otiose. In many instances the straight horizontal stroke has seemed to the editor to indicate that the minims it surmounts represent a nasal and not a vowel, i.e. while it is not strictly otiose, its function in such cases appears to be confirmatory and not supplemental. This would make the function of this stroke the converse of its function in modern German script. In such cases, the sign has not been represented here in any way. Decisions, however, have been more than usually difficult, and many readers, comparing the texts with their originals, may well disagree with the editor over specific instances.

The arbitrariness of decisions over expansions is particularly clear in the case of the mid-sixteenth-century holograph text of William Forrest, which combines italic hand with spelling of a particularly otiose type and an extremely generous use of contraction signs which an editor, in the interests of common sense as well as of compactness, is impelled, as far as possible, to treat as otiose. Forrest's is an example of a humanist manuscript text presenting a state of affairs halfway between that of a fifteenth-century text and that of an early printed book. His punctuation is of a more modern type than that of the other main texts, and as far as convenient it has been preserved. The elements which he uses (colon, semicolon, brackets) have been freely made use of in the editorial adjustments of the punctuation of his text. Forrest often joins words which are written separately today. Since his text is interesting as an example of authorial presentation, where I have separated such words the fact is, exceptionally, indicated in the footnotes.

Emendations are, where this is thought best, supported in the footnotes by citation of the Latin reading closest to the English translator's supposed original. Erroneous translations and readings requiring further explanation are, of course, treated in the Commentary in volume II: those which it is supposed might most cause the reader to hesitate are singled out in the footnotes in volume I by the cross-reference '*See n(ote)*'.

TEXTS

In the critical apparatus, the following sigil is used:

B   Roger Bacon, ed. Robert Steele, *Opera hactenus inedita*, fasc. v: *Secretum Secretorum*, Oxford, 1920.

In this apparatus, when a reading is given from a base text on its own, no sigil is used. When such a reading is followed in the same footnote by readings from other texts, the base text and all other texts are indicated by sigils which are listed on the introductory pages to the individual texts.

I

REGIMEN SANITATIS:
THE BOOKE OF GOODE GOVERNANCE
AND GUYDING OF þE BODY

A fifteenth-century version of Johannes Hispaniensis
in Bodleian MS. *Rawlinson C. 83*

Regimen Sanitatis | [f. 1ᵛ]

This booke, made for the rule and gouernaunce of mannis [f. 2]
body to kepe him in helth and goode disposicion of body,
was sent fro þe grete philosophir Aristotill to the nobill
prince King Alexander, of the which here begynnith the 5
prologe.

O nobil king, if thou wilt diligently rede and vnderstonde this
litil booke and tretice, and rule thi selfe aftir the doctrine, rulis
and preceptis in this booke or tretice writtin, thou shalt kepe thy
selfe in helth and goode disposicion of body, and haue continuaunce 10
of long life. Yitt notwithstanding the doctrine of this booke, thy
life may be shortid by othir chauncis, as of warre or othir perellis.
To preserue the frome deth happyng by such meanis, this booke
helpith not, but | onely to preserue the from deth which commith [f. 2ᵛ]
by sekenes. **Here endith the prologe, and begynnith the** 15
booke of gouernaunce for the helth of mannis body, the
which conteynith xv doctrines or preceptis, of þe which
here begynnith the first doctrine.
WHen thou rysist fro slepe in þe morning, first stretch thy
lymmis, þi leggys, thine armis, thy shuldris, thy necke, thyne hed. 20
This availith to sett thy lymmis in dwe ordre. Aftir þat, kembe
thine hed, for þat openith þe poris of þe hed, that fumositeis which
ascendith fro þe stomake in tyme of slepe by opening of þe poris

---

5 which] *followed by* begynnith *written in red ink* (*which is used for the whole
title*) *then crossed through in black ink*   12 as] *inserted above line*

may departe fro the. This doone, if it be somir season, wesshe thi
hondis, bifore þu goist oute fro thi chambir, with colde watir, for
þe coldenes of þe watir shettith þi naturell poris, and lettith þi
4 naturell hete to passe from the, which wold passe if þi poris were
[f. 3] not closid. And when þu commist fro thy chambre, walke | tem-
peratly a competent season bifore thou put thy self to any oþir
occupacion.

The secund doctrine or precept:

SE that thi clothis be precious and riȝt feire to the eye, for beauté
10 and preciousenes of þe clothis liȝtenith and gladdith the spiritte of
man, which gladnes of spiritte is cause of a continuaunce in helth
like as heuynes of spiritte and sorow inducith sikenes. Hit causith
also a man to be more quick in all his deedis, and þe bettir to
execute all that perteynith to his office.

15 **The thridde doctrine or precept:**

Dayly in the morning rubbe and clense þi mouth, and rubbe þi
teith with the leuis or barke of a soote tre and bitter withall, as
with the barke or leuis of the bay tre. þis manir of doing clensith
19 thy tieth and mouth, and resoluith flewme, by the meane wherof
[f. 3ᵛ] thou mayist more clerely | speke withoute cowghing or speting.
Also it excitith þine appetite to mete.

The fourth doctrine or precepte:

In þe m⟨orni⟩ng vse sum fumigacions. Let brenne such þingis
a⟨s c⟩ausith a soote fume, as incense, juniper, gale or levis of þe
25 baytre. And se þat þu receiue þe fume with þi nose, for þis
openith þe clausuris of þi brayne and disposith well þi hede, it
strengthith þi lymmis, þi shuldris and þi armis, it makith a⟨ll⟩
þi face and thy countenaunce gladly, and prolongith þe from age,
and lettith þe horenes of þe hede, and it conforteth ⟨all⟩ thy five
30 bodely wittis.

The v doctrine or precepte:

Aftir all þis anointe þi selfe with precious oynementis and sweete,
for sweete sauour is mete to the spiritte: it gladdith, refresshith and
confortith þe ⟨spirit⟩te like as holsum mete confortith þe body.
35 Which conforting of þe spiritte causith þe hert to be glad and

---

1 the] *preceded by a long vertical stroke, crossed through*   12 heuynes]
*damp has made this, and many other portions of the ms., illegible in normal light,
this state being at its worst on ff. 3ᵛ–5. Most such portions become legible, wholly
or partly, under ultra-violet radiation. Where certain enough of having deciphered
the letters, I make no indication; otherwise words, or portions of words, are placed
in angular brackets*

makith þe bloode pl⟨aye⟩full to renne in to þe veynis for the delectacion of þe hert.

The sixte doctrine or precept folowith : |

In þe morning bifore þu ⟨go⟩st furth, vse certeine electuaryis aftir [f. 4]
þe councell of men experte in phisike. Also þu shal ⟨ta⟩ke of þe 5
roote of rubarbe iij peny-⟨we3t⟩ diuerce tymes in þe morning
bifore þi going oute ⟨a⟩mong þe peple. For þis medicin profitith
gretely to purge and remoue flewme from þe mouth of þe stomake.
Hit dryith awey e⟨uyl⟩ humours of þe body, it expellith and
remouith fumo⟨site⟩is and wyndis within the body, it makith þi 10
mouth to be well sauourid, and all þi persone. Entre thi councell
and provide what ⟨is nee⟩din⟨ge⟩ for þi comon w⟨eal⟩.

The vijth precepte or doctrine.

IF ⟨it⟩ cum to þe a grete appetite to et⟨e th⟩ough it be b⟨i⟩f⟨or⟩e
þine oure acc⟨u⟩s⟨to⟩mid, yit ⟨thou m⟩ay go to thi dyner ⟨con⟩- 15
uenient ⟨acc⟩ording to þin⟨ ap⟩petite when i⟨t c⟩ummith, if it
be gret. For ellis shall þi naturall hete labour vpon corrupt ⟨hu⟩-
mours. This wise to folow þine ap⟨peti⟩te when it cummith if it be
grete avail⟨ith⟩ many ⟨w⟩ysis. ⟨It⟩ st⟨re⟩nthith thi body and 19
li3tenit⟨h⟩ it. It kindelith þe hete of þi stomak and | remouith [f. 4ᵛ]
flewme. Which if thou wilt not ete when þi grete appetite cummith,
it dullith þi stomak and destruith þin appetite ay⟨en⟩s anoþir tyme.

The viijth doctrine.

When þu art sett att þi mete, se þi metis be holsum, and in plenté of
diuerse kyndes of metis, and ete of þem þat þin appetite moste 25
meuith þe to, but ete sumwhat lasse þen inowgh, and rise sumwhat
with an appetite.

The ixth doctrine :

Ete þi liquid metis as potagis or sewis in þe bigyn⟨in⟩g of þi
refeccion. If þu first ete þi substancial me⟨tis⟩, and aftir þi liquid 30
metis, it sha⟨ll c⟩ause a confusion in þi stomak. And if þu shall
[eit] a⟨t⟩ one refeccion diuers potagis, sum rinning potagis and sum
stonding, ete first þi rinning potage, and aftir þi substanciall
m⟨ete⟩ in þe midd⟨ist⟩, and last þi stonding potage, as ge⟨l⟩yis
and such oþir last of all. Also se þi grete mete be et⟨in⟩ first and 35
receiuid in the botom of þi stomake, for þer is gretir hete þen in þe
over parte of þi stomak, and þ⟨er⟩for lett li3t metis of digestion be
lattir ete, for lesse hete is for | such metis sufficient. [f. 5]

---

18 appetite] *ms. wormeaten*   32 [eit] cum   34 mete] *ms. wormeaten*
(*verso of line 18 above*, appetite)

The xth. doctrine or precept.

Also se þi brede be made of pure flour clene departid fro þe branne and sumwhat levenid. But yitte in all þi diete for-gete not to leue with an appetite, for who so wille ete til he hath fulfillid his ap-
5 petite hath more þen ynouȝh, and so shall his mete ly in þe botom of his stomak not digestid.

The xjth doctrine or precepte:

Se þu be no grete drinker: þough þi drink be neuir so pleasant, numbir þi drinkyngis. Se þey be not verray many in one diete, be-
10 twene þi drinkingis se þer be a competent space, and se þi draȝt be not ouir grete, but mesurable. And aftir þi mete biware þu drinke no watir, be it neuir so pleasaunt vnto þe, for drinking of watir aftir þi mete coldith þi stomak and quenchith þi naturall hete. But if þi desire be so grete aftir þi mete to drink watir, for
15 grete hete of þe season, drink but litil, and se þe watir be well tastid and verry colde.

þe xijth doctrine.

[f. 5ᵛ] When þu art a-rise fro mete, walke a litil vpon soft gresse. | And if þu wilt slepe aftir þi dyner, lett þi slepe be litil and short,
20 and begyn þi slepe vpon þi riȝt side a litil season, and þen turne on þi left side and so make an ende of þi slepe. And be ware þu slepe not bifore mete, for such slepe shall make þi body ouir leene, and dry þi moisture naturall. But moderate slepe aftir mete shall re-fressh þe, and kepe þe in goode disposicion of body.

25 þe xiijth doctrine.

When þu hast ete þi mete, be ware þu ete not eftsonis, vn-til þi mete bifore receiuid be perfitely digestid. And when þat is, þu shalt knowe by .ij. tokenis. One is when þine appetite cummith to þe ayene after þi mete which þu hast receyuid. Anoþir tokin: if þi
30 spettel be sotel, and liȝtly will destende in to þi mouth. Iff þu take mete withoute appetite, þi naturall hete is feblid. And if þu haue a newe appetite, þi naturall hete is accendid.

The xiiijth. doctrine.

When þine appetite cummith, sone aftir, fall to þi mete, for if þu
35 absteine þe long fro þi mete aftir þine appetite is cum, þi stomake
[f. 6] shalbe fillid with corrupt humouris which | he drawith to him of þe refuce and superfluité of þe mete bifore digestid, and of such corrupt humours receyuid in þe stomac by abstinence of mete aftir

---

33–4 *outer margin* nota bene per | dolore capitis

þine appetite is cum, thine hed and þi brayne shall gretely be troublid by aking and oþir diseasis.

The xvth doctrine tretith of þe iiij seasons of þe yere:
THou must diligently take hede of iiij ceasons of þe yere which þis wise be namid: **Ver, Estas, Autumpnus, Hyemps.** First 5
Ver begynnith in March and continuith til þe hote somir begyn.
Estas begynnith in þe monnith of June and durith to þe middis of August. Then begynnith **Autumpnus,** callid Hervest, and durith to þe middis of Nouembir. And þen begynnith **Hyemps** callid wintir, and durith til þe begynning of Ver. The disposicions of þies 10
iiij ceasons of þe yere ben þies: **Ver** is temperate, hote and moiste, like vnto þe eyer. þen begynnith mannis bloode to encrese. Diett according for þat season be boylid capons and chicons. Also amongis herbis, letuce be holsum. Amongis liquouris þat | noris- [f. 6ᵛ]
shith, gotis milke is riȝt norisshing. Among grete flessh, yong 15
kidde and fatte. Also as for bloodeletting þat ceason callid Ver is most according. þis season also is conuenient for laxis, and baynis drye and moiste, also to take aromatik pocions made with spices. And if ony þing hath happenid in þe yer bifor, by wey of medicine or oþir, þis season may all be restorid and refourmid by þe menis 20
bifore rehercid. Then folowith a season callid **Estas** or summir, and is commonly excessifly hote and drie. And in þis season en- crecith rede coler, and is like to fire which is excedingly hote and drye. In þis season þu hast nede to absteyne the fro replecion of mete and drink, and in manir vse abstinence more þan in Ver, 25
and in especiall to absteine fro metis and drinkis þat be hote in wirking, and to vse metis þat be colde and moiste, and in sawcis to vse vinagre and sorel savce, and in fruitis to vse such þat be sum- what egre, as orangis and pomegranatis, to vse moiste baynis mesurably, and vttirly to eschiwe dry baynis for þat season, also 30
þen to be ware of letting of bloode, but if grete nede re-|quire, [f. 7]
walking and exercise moderately according, in þe morning and late towardis niȝt. Aftir þis folowith **Autumpnus** or harvest, which is sumwhat cold in þe regarde of þe summer, and also dry, and is like to þe erth, which is colde and drie. And in þis season 35
arisith and encrecith melancoly, callid in Latin Colera nigra. In þis season þu must absteine þe fro suche metis and frutis þat gendrith melancoly, as fro olde towgh bef and moton, fro olde gotis flessh,

---

13 capons and chicons] *both* -ons *terminations with presumably otiose contraction signs: intended forms possibly* capouns *and* chicouns

and in þis season þu mayist vse baynis and also laxis to purge
melancoly. Aftir þis folowith **Hyems**, callid wintir, which tyme is
colde and moiste like to watir. It begynnith toward thende of
Nouembre and continuith to Ver. In þis tyme of wintir conuenient
5 it is to ete hote metis and dry, as dove birdis, bakemetis well spicid,
rostid gete, swanis, wilde foule, drink goode rede wyne and miȝty.
Also þe potagis se þat þei be hote in wirking and well spicid. Absteine fro laxis and letting of bloode, but if grete nede require. In
9 þis ceason þu mayist vse oynementis and anoint þi body, and aftir
[f. 7ᵛ] rubbe it ayenst þe fire and dry it ayene. In þis | season vse no grete
abstinence from mete, for þen mannis digestion is strong and miȝty.

NOw, miȝty prince Alexander, kepe well this litill booke for þe
gyding of þi body as a jvell precious, for by þis þu shalt kepe
þi naturall moistur, and so folowith þi naturall hete, for so long
15 abydith naturall hete as doith naturall moistur, in so much as
naturall hete is radicate and kept in naturall moistur as in his
naturall fundament and ground. Thies ij, þat is to say, naturall
hete and naturall moisture, well kepte, continuith bodyly helth
and life. And age shall not gretely grow vpon þe. For man waxith
20 olde for one of ij causis. One cause is for wasting of naturall
moysture, and grete drynes, wherof growith febilnes of body.
A-nothir cause, which is accidentall, as by sekenes, wher vnto
man fallith for lak of goode guyding of his body, as in þis booke
is shewid. Thies be þo þingis þat makith mannis body well flesshid
25 and not lene, but raþir moiste: to ete and drink moderatly metis
[f. 8] and drinkis þat be sumwhat sweete. | Att s⟨u⟩m seasons to drink
warme gotis milke is holsum, and it preseruith well naturall hete
and moistur. Hit is also conuenient onis in a monith to provoke a
vomitt; it clensith þe stomak fro corrupt and rottin humours. When
30 few humours be in þe stomak þen is þe body in goode confort, and
is in goode disposicion to digest mete receyuid, and hath goode
moistur. And þe bettir for helth and digestion if þe man haue ioy
and gladnes, and with þat goode fortune, as glory, worship, fame
and worship of þe peple, victory of his ennemyis. Also if he may
35 beholde beauteuous parsonis, and delectabil bookis, and here
pleasaunt songis, and be in cumpany of such as a man louith, and
to were goode clothis, and to be anoyntid with swete oynementis.
And ayenwarde þies be þe þingis which chiefly disposith ill and
feblith þe body: to ete litil and drink much, to laboure ouir much,

26 sum] *ms. wormeaten*

and stond oft in þe sonne, to walke ouir much, to slepe bifore
mete, to slepe vpon hard strawe, to wassh in watir vnholsum, to ete
salt mete and dry, as bacon or beefe, in especiall | such as hath [f. 8ᵛ]
hongyd long in þe smoke, to d⟨ri⟩nke very old wynes, in speciall ny
the lyis, to be lette oft bloode, to haue þe cumpany of women oft, 5
ofte to be in drede and to haue grete sorow. þies be such þing þat
bringith a man soone to grete sikenes and febilnes of body and soone
to his ende. **Here endith the booke of goode gouernance and
guyding of þe body, writtin by Aristotill to þe full nobill
prince King Alexander, to kepe him in helth and to pre-** 10
serue him in long life.

.W. MA ～ ⟩G. scripsit

4 drinke] *ms. wormeaten (verso of 8/26 above,* sum)

II

CERTEYNE REWLES OF PHISNOMY

AND

A CALCULACION TO KNOW BY OF TUO MEN FEGHTYNGE TOGIDERE, WHEÞER SALE BE OUERCOMEN

From British Library MS. Sloane 213, ff. 118ᵛ–121ʳ

[f. 118ᵛᵃ] **Here sues certeyne rewles of phisnomy, to knowe by onely thoght when men lokes on any man, of what condicions he es.**

ALixander þe grete conquerour in alle his conquest and werres was
5 reuled by Aristotel þe worthiest philosopher þat euer was, whilk
Aristotel, when he myght no lenger walk for age, wrote many
bokes to þat same kyng Alixander, wher-by he suld gouerne hym,
amonge whilk bokes he wrote one of fisnomy, þat Alixander myght
knowe by onely sight þe condicyons of men when he sawe þem.
10 Of whilk phisnomy here sues summe of þe rewles. And Aristotel
sais howe þat in tyme of Ypocras þer was a philosopher hight
Philomon, þat was chefe mayster and hyest doctur of þis science.
[f. 118ᵛᵇ] And also he sais þe disciples of | Ypocras paynted þe fourme and
schappe of Ypocras in parchemyne, and bare it to Philomon, and
15 saide þus to him, 'Byholde þis figur, and deme and schewe to vs
þe qualités of þe complexion of it.' And when he had inly sene it
he saide þus, 'þis man es lucherus, deceitus, auarus and lufyng
liccherie.' And for he saide so þei wolde haue slayne hym, and þei
saide to him þus, 'A, you fole, þis es þe figur of þe worthyest and
20 best man in al þis werlde!' **Philomon** þerfor peced þem and
amendid his wordes and saide, 'þis es þe figure of þe wyse Ypocras,
wher-to asked ȝe þis of me to assay my science. Nowe I haue
schewed ȝowe þer-of what I fele as be my sciens.' Forþi when þei
come to Ypocras þei tolde him what þei had done and howe Philo-
25 mon saide to þem. And þan saide Ypocras, 'Trewly Philomon saide
sothe, and he lafte noght of þe leste letter of þe treuthe. Neuer-

þeles, sithen I biheld and knewe me schapli to þese thynges filthy
and reprouable, I ordeyned my soule kyng aboue my body, and
so I withdrewe my body fro þise thynges and I ouercome it in
wiȝholdyng of my foule luste.' þerfore sais Aristotel þus to Alixander: þis es þe praysyng and wisdome of þe werkes of Ypocras, for   5
phisik es noght elles bot abstynens, and conquest of foule couetus
lustes. Þerfore Aristotil to Alixander ordeyned certeyne reules of
Philomones sciens whilk schortly and compendiusly, þat es to say
profitabely, sues here. Lyuyd culoure, þat es like lede, and flaue
culour, þat es to say ȝalo as falowe leues, es token of littelyd defyeng. 10
Fle þerfore ilk lyuyd and flaue man, for he es bowyng and buxome
to vices and to liccherie. If þou se any man haunte to loke on þe,
and when þou lokes vp-on him he es sumdele agaste þer-of and
blenches, namely if þou be wrothe, he sighes and teres schewes in   14
his eighne, | þat man lufes and dredes þe; and if þe contrary hap-   [f. 119ra]
pen, þan þat man has envy to þe and despises þe. Be war and right
wele warre fro ilk man euele schapen and litteled, yf þer be in any
lymme [lessnyng], right als þou suld be warre fro þi dedly enemy.
þat man es euenest and best tempred whilk acordes in meneté, þat
es to say noþer to longe ne to schorte, noþer to thyk ne to thynne,   20
noþer to brode ne to narowe, noþer to mykel ne to litel, noþer to
white ne to blak ne to rede, bot faire broune rody, with blak eyghne,
blak heres and roundenes of visage, euenes of stature, with holnes
of body, whose wordes are selden bot when nede askes, mediocrité
of voyce, þat es to say noþer to smalle ne to grete, mediocrité also   25
of heuede whose culour es lufly white rody broune. Haue þat man
with þe and truyst to him for he es trewe. **Many heres and softe**
signyfies buxomnes and coldnes of braynes. Many heres vpon
aiþer schuldre signyfies foly. Many heres in þe brest and in þe
wombe, signyfies horribilté and syngulerté of kynde and littelynge   30
of sone conceyuyng, and luf of wronges. Forsothe ruf culour, þat
es to say like to fyne golde, es token of foly and of mekil wrath, and
of gylus waytynges. Blak here sygnyfies euenes and luf of rightwisnes. Medioker culour bitwene ruf and blak es lufly rody broune,
and þat signyfies luf of pece. **Forsothe þat es an envious man**   35
þat has grete eyghne and also he es vnschameful, slowe, sleuthfull
and vnbuxome, namely if his grete eyghne be lyuyd. He þat has
eyghne of heuenli culour or blak, namely blak broune, if þei be
medioker, þat es nouþer to mykel ne to litel, he es persable sone and
light of vnderstondyng, curius and trewe. He þat has extencion,   40

þat es to say strechynge oute o brode his eyghne, and extencion
[f. 119rb] of sembelande, es wicked and gylusly | waytynge. Who þat has
eyghne like an asse, he es a fole and of harde kynde and dulle.
Whose eyghne meues swiftely and his sight es scharpe, he es gylus,
5 vnfaithfull and theuysch. Whose eighne are rede, he es hardy
willy, stronge and myghty. þat man es werst of alle and moste
reprouable and moste to be fledde, whose eyghne haue alle
aboute spottes, white, rede or blak. **Browes of many heares**
signyfy vnconabilté of spekyng. þat es an envious man whose
10 browes are straght to þe temples. þat man es light of vnderstondyng, whose browes are grete and thynne and medioker in length
and schortnes. **Nose when it es sotyl and smalle,** he þat owes
it es wrathfull and angry. Who þat has a longe nose straght to þe
mouthe he es gentill, worthy and hardy. Whose nose es like an ape,
15 he es hasty. Schorte nose toknes a schrewe, and if þe noseholes be
wyde also, þat es a synger and liccherous. Whose nose holes has
grete openyng, he es hard and wrathfull; and when þe nose es brode
in þe mydell and goyng to heght, þat man es wordefull and lufyng to
lye and lyenge. þat man es euenest and best, whose nose es medioker
20 in length, and medioker in brede at þe ende, and þe holes are
noght to mykel. **Þe face þat es playne** with outen rounde hilles,
signyfies a stryuefull man, truandous, wrongewyse and vnclene.
And who þat has a medioker face in iowes and temples, sumdele tornyng to fatnes, he es sothfast trewe, lufyng, vndirstan-
25 dyng, seruysh and wyse-witty and wele made. He þat has a
wyde mouthe es batus and hardy. Grete lippes ar tokene of a
folische man. And who þat es fleschy and right fat on face,
he es litel wyse, vnbyhofull and lyeng. And who þat has a smalle
[f. 119va] face and sumdele lene, he es sotille of vnderstondyng | and cir-
30 cumspect, þat es to say vmbseyn, in his werkes. And who þat has
a litel face sumdele colored as safferon, he es dronkelewe, deceytous,
right vicious and werst. And who þat has a longe face, he es
wrongefull. **Who þat has grete swellyng temples and full
iowes,** he es right angry and wrathfull. Who þat has right mekil
35 eares he es foltisch, saue he es of gode mynde and noght forgetefull.
Who þat has right litel eares he es foltisch, theuysch and liccherous.
Eares in þe mene bitokenes vertues. Who þat has a grete voyce and
wele souned, he es batus and eloquent, þat es to say pertly spekynge.

15–16 Schorte . . . liccherous] *misplaced between* folische man. *and* And who
(*l. 27 below*)

To smalle voyce tokenes foly and wommanhede. Whose voyce es
medioker he es wise, puruyous, sothfast and rightwyse. Who þat
spekes swiftly, namely if þe voyce be smalle, he es hasty, vncurtas,
foltische, vnbihofull and besely lyeng. If þe voyce be to grete, he
es angry, wrathfull, ouerthrowyng godenes, and euel of kynde. 5
And he þat has a swete voyce es envyous and suspicious. Also a
faire voyce signyfies foly, vnwisdome, mekil wille and oftesithes
liccherie. Who þat meues ofte, namely with þe hondes, when he
spekes, he es vnclene, eloquente and deceytus. Who þat es
abstynent from meuyng of his handes, nameli when he has grete 10
cause to be stered, he es perfite of vndirstondyng, wele disposed,
hole and gode of councele. **Who þat has a longe smalle nek,**
he es foltisch and sonoure, þat es to say wele sounede. Who þat
has a right schort nek, he es ful queynte, sotel, gylous and fraudus.
Who þat has a grete nek, he es foltis, glotenous and grete eter. 15
Who þat has a grete wombe, he es indiscrete, foltisch, proude, and
lufyng liccheri. Mediokerte of wombe and straitnes of breste,
signyfies heght of vnderstondyng and of gode councele. Brede of
breste and gretenes of schuldres and of | rigge signyfies worthynes, [f. 119ᵛᵇ]
gentilnes, hardynes, heuenes of vnderstondyng and of wisdome. 20
Sotilté and smalnes of þe rigge signyfies a discordus man. Mediokerte of breste and euenes of rigge es approued þe best signe of all.
Grete fyngres and schorte, signyfies foly and vnwisdome. **Grete
fleschy fete** signyfies foly and luf of wrongwisnes. Litel fete and
lene are sumdele vertuus, þaugh oftesithe þei signyfie pride. 25
Medioker fete are best. Sotilté and smalnes of legges signyfies
ignoraunce and vnconny[n]gnes. Gretenes of legges, signyfy
hardynes and strength. Brode toos signyfy strength of þe body.
Mekil flesch in þe knees signyfie febilnes, vertue and vnderstondyng. Whose passes ar wyde, longe and late he sale spede and 30
be welthy in alle his wayes, werkes and dedes. Whose passes ar
schorte, he es hasty, wodisch inpacient, suspicius, vnmyghty in his
werkes and of euel wille. **Þat man es best of mynde and wele
made in kynde** who has medioker moyste nesch flesch, noght
to longe ne to schorte, white sumdele rody, þat is to say white rody 35
broune, meke and lufly sembelande, | playne and medioker blak [f. 120ʳᵃ]
heares, þat es to say noght to thik ne to thynne, and auburn rounde

---

22 *After* all *18 ll. left blank, possibly for an illustration*   27 vncon-
nyngnes] vnconnygnes *with* g *as corr. over (or badly ligatured with) the* n *here
preceding it*

blak eighne, medioker heuede and nek, aþer wele disposed to
oþer, sumdele brode schuldres, noght to fleschly in þe knees and
oþer ioyntes, clere voyce with mediokerte þer-of. Skilfull longe
handes with longe sutile fyngres, litel laghyng and sone done, bot
5 lest scornyng or none at alle, for mekil laghyng namely loude, longe
and ofte, with litel cause, schewes a wicked man and a fole. And
scornyng, lispyng, stameryng, and gamen at harme schewes a right
wicked and deceytus man. Also it es gode when þe sembelance of
man es medeled sumdele with honest schorte myrth, gladnes and
10 ioy. **Neuerþeles, sais Aristotil** to Alixander, I gif þe reules by
departyng of mans body, and temper þou þem in þin inwitt by
gode discrecion of vnderstondyng. And set noght þi sentence ne
dome in one of þese signes allone, bot gader þe wittenes to-gider of
ilk one. And where þe tokenes gifes þe dyuerse and ouerthwert
15 domes, go þou euer to þe better and more prouable party. And þus
þer þou knowes þi self or any oþer schaply and bowable to any
vice by way of þi compleccion, do þi self and councele oþer to do
as Ypocras did, and make þi soule to reule þi body by gode resone
and discrecion, withstandyng by vertue þo vyces to whilke þou art
20 conable borne of compleccion, and þan þou sale be praysed and
holden wyse bifore God mekil more þan if þe makyng of þi compleccion wer gyuen al to vertue. For he þat es made moste brothil
and stondes strengest, sal moste be thanked of God. Here-to acordes
25 seynt Poule, sayeng on þis maner, 'No man sale be crouned, bot
als he has lawfully and stalworthly stryuene.'

[f. 120rb] **Here sues a calculacion to | knowe by of tuo men feghtyng
to-gidere, wheþer sale be ouercomen.**

TAke tuo names of men whilk are gyuen þem in þeir birthe, if þou
wille wite of þem tuo feghtyng to-gider or stryuyng wheþer sale
30 ouercome, or of tuo folkes weddede wheþer sale lenger life, or of
tuo folk goyng any viage wheþer sale come ageyne, or of a seke man
wheþer he sale dye or life. Counte þe name of ilkone of þem by
þe letteres of þe Abc þat sues in þe ende of þis chapiter, and by þe
noumber þat es on ilk letter þer-of. And when þou has so done de-
35 parte al þe hole by nene, saue of þem þat are weddid, by seuene
loke þou departe. And by þe ouerplus of þo nene or of þo seuene,
þou salt se by one of þise eghte reules, who sale ouercome, who
sale raþer dye, who sale raþer come ageyne. And if you wille wite
of any seke wheþer he sale dye or life of þat sekenes, take þan þe

26] *Title run on in ms.*

name of þat seke and of þe lune and of þe day in whilk he toke his
sekenes, and acounte as we taght bifore: and if þe seke mans name
ouercomes he sale life, and if þe lune ouercome, with-outen doute
he sale dye. By þis experiment Alixander þe grettest conqueroure
þat euer was ouercome many batayles. Wherfore þe first reule es 5
þis: **One and one**: þe lesse sale ouercome. One and tuo: he þat
has tuo sale ouercome. One and thre: he þat has one sale ouercome.
One and foure: he þat has foure sale ouercome. One and fyue: he
þat has one sale ouercome. One and sex: he þat has sex sale
ouercome. One and seuene: he þat has one sale ouercome. One 10
and eighte: he þat has eghte sale ouercome. One and nyne: he þat
has one sale ouercome. **Tuo and tuo**: þe strenger sale | ouercome. [f. 120ᵛᵃ]
Tuo and thre: he þat has thre sale ouercome. Tuo and foure: who
has tuo sale ouercome. Tuo and fyue: who has fyue sale ouercome.
Two and sex: who has tuo sale ouercome. Tuo and seuen: who 15
has seuen sale ouercome. Tuo and eghte: who has tuo sale ouercome. Tuo and nyne: who has nyne sale ouercome. **Thre and
thre**: þe lesse sale ouercome. Thre and foure: who has foure sale
ouercome. Thre and fyue: who has thre sale ouercome. Thre and
sex: who has sex sal ouercome. Thre and seuen: who has thre 20
sale ouercome. Thre and eght: who has eght sale ouercome. Thre
and nyne: who has thre sale ouercome. **Foure and foure**: þe
strenger sale ouercome. Foure and fyue: who has fyue sale ouercome. Foure and sex: who has foure sale ouercome. Foure and
seuen: who has seuene sale ouercome. Foure and eghte: who has 25
foure sale ouercome. Foure and nyne: who has nyne sale ouercome.
Fyue and fyue: þe les sale ouercome. Fyue and sex: who has
sex sale ouercome. Fyue and seuen: who has fyue sale ouercome.
Fyue and eght: who has eght sale ouercome. Fyue and nyne: who
has fyue sale ouercome. **Sex and sex**: þe strenger sale ouercome. 30
Sex and seuene: who has seuen sale ouercome. Sex and eght:
who has sex sale ouercome. Sex and nyne: who has nyne sale
ouercome. **Seuen and seuen**: þe les sal ouercome. Seuen and
eght: who has eght sale ouercome. Seuen and nyne: who has seuen
sale ouercome. **Eght and eght**: þe strenger sale ouercome. Eght 35
and nyne: who has nyne sale ouercome. **Nyne and nyne**: þe lesse
sale ouercome. Nowe after þe reules go we se þe Abece of þis
crafte, wher-by, as we bifore hight, þise countes sale be caste.
A:3. B:3. C:22. D:14. E:25. F:3. G:7. H:6. J:15. K:15. L:22.
M:23. N:15. O:8. P:13. Q:21. R:13. S:11. T:8. V:5. X:6. 40

[f. 120vb] Y:3. Z:4. Also here sues | anoþer Abece, wher-by if þou acounte
wel þou may also wite of a man and his wife wheþer sale soner dye.
Take þe names of þem bothe, and acounte þe letteres of þo names
by þe noumbre of þis suyng Abece, and when þou has done, if
5 al þe hole noumbre be euene, with-outen doute þe man sale dye,
and if it be odde, þan es it þe womman. A:1. B:4. C:4. D:4. E:4.
F:4. G:2. H:2. J:2. K:2. L:3. M:2. N:2. O:1. P:1. Q:3.
R:3. S:1. T:2. V:2. X:3. Z:4. Also here sues anoþer Abece
where-by þou may knowe of what planet ilk man es.

	.1.	.2.	.3.
10	A. E. J. S.	B. K. Q. R.	G. L.

	.4.	.5.	.6.	.7.
	D. M. T.	N.	C. O. V.	Z.

	.8.	.9.
15	F.P.	X.

Departe þis by nene vnto an hondreth, and if one or 8 be ouer,
þan þe sonne es his planet. If 2 or 9 be ouer, þan Venus es his
planet. If 3, þan he es of Mercurie. If 4, þan he es of þe mone.
If 5, þan he es of Saturne. If 6, þan he es of Jupiter. If 7, þan he
20 es of Mars.

.1.	.1.	.6.	.3.
Adam	Andreu	Aldene	Anfos

.9.	.9.	.9.
Benaster	Bec	Daueide

25 Also here sues anoþer Abece to knowe by of what signe in þe
Zodiak ilk man es, þat es to say, vnder whilk signe he es borne,
and to whilk signe he es moste like. Also her by you may knowe
his fortune and þe moneth in whilk he sale dye. Also her-by you
may knowe þe fortune and infortune of many thynges, tounes,
30 cites and castelles. A:2. B:21. C:20. D:41. E:5. F:24. G:3.
H:20. J:10. K:13. L:42. M:12. N:22. O:13. P:21. Q:20.

---

8 X:3] *foll. by* Y *crossed out in red ink, with the space after it left blank*
16 Departe...and] *run on opposite final items of table*   22 Aldene] Aldon:
see n.   24 Benaster] Benastru: *see n.*   Daueide] Dauide: *see n.*   25 Also...
anoþer] *the text from* Also *to the* an *of* anoþer *is run on opposite final items of table*

R:27. S:22. T:41. V:13. X:20. Y:10. Z:7. Wherfor, if þou wilt
knowe by þis Abece any man, als it es saide bifore, take | his name [f. 121ʳᵃ]
and his moderes name, and also if [þ]ou wilt knowe of any toune by
þis Abece, as it es saide bifore, þan take þat tounes name and þe
name of þe cite Jerusalem, for þat es moder of alle tounes, and þan 5
acounte þe letteres of þo names by þe noumber of his Abece. And
when þou hast alle done, departe it by eght and twenty. And if
one or tuo leue ouer, þan þat þou sekes longes to þe Weþer. And
if thre, foure or fyue leue ouer, þan þat þou sekes longes to þe
Bole. And if sex or seuene, þan longes it to þe Gemyns. And if 10
eght or nyne, þan longes it to þe Canker. And if ten, elleuene or
tuelfe, þan longes it to þe Lyon. And if thrittene or fourtene, þan
longes it to þe Virgyn. And if fiften or sexten, þan longes it to
þe Liber. And if seuentene, eghtene or nyntene, þan longes it to þe
Scorpion. And if twenti, or one and twenti, þan longes it to þe 15
Sagittari. And if tuo and twenti, or thre and twenti, þan longes it to
þe Capricorn. And if four and twenti, fyue and twenti, or sex and
twenti, þan longes it to þe Aquari. And if seuen and twenti, or
eght and twenty, þan longes it to þe Fisches.

3 þou] you

III

THE 'ASHMOLE' VERSION
THE SECRETE OF SECRETES

Fifteenth-century version (written perhaps soon after 1445) of the augmented Latin recension represented by Bodleian MS. Rawlinson C.274 and B.L. MS. Royal 12 E.xv. Contained in late fifteenth-century Bodleian MSS. Ashmole 396 and Lyell 36.

Critical text based on Ashmole 396, with emendations from Lyell 36, and with selected parallel readings in the footnotes from manuscript and printed sources indicated, and from B.

A = Ashmole 396

L = Lyell 36

R = Rawlinson C.274

S = vol. ii of Richard Förster, *Scriptores physiognomonici graeci et latini*, 2 vols., Leipzig, 1893, extracts therefrom being from the following texts:

(1) *Anonymi de physiognomonia liber* (pp. 3–145)
(2) *Abubecri Rasis ad regem Mansorem de re medicina liber II translatus ex arabico in latinum a Gerardo Cremonensi* (pp. 163–79)
(3) The physiognomical portion of the *Sirr* itself (pp. 183–222)

[f. 1] **TO his most excellent lord, and in worshippyng of Cristen religion hardiest, Guy of Valence, the gracious Bisshop of Tripolis, Philipp of his clerkes the lest, hymself and his seruice he offreth to his trew devocion.**

And by asmoch as the mone is brighter than other sterres and
5 thurgh the good radiacion of the sonne more shynynger, in so moche the clernesse of [y]our engyne and science passeth all others in littratures that ben in this side of the Mediterrayn See, as wele

---

1 *All of version in Lyell 36 missing, until matter of p. 35 below*   4 his] this
(*poss. intended reading*)

barbares as Latines. For ther is none of hole mynde that may more
swetly saver in science than he. With largesse of graces by Hym of
Whom all godes proceden and alle yiftes ben destribuyt, it semeth
that vnto the fulnesse of science and of grace he hath give. For
sothly in these ben founde the vniuersall graces of the faders be- 5
fore, that is to sey, Noe-is shamfastnesse, Abraham-is trouth,
Isaac-is confidence, Jacob-is longa[n]y[m]yté, Moyses-is suf-
fraunce, Josue-is stablenesse, Job-is pacience, Ely-is deuocion,
Elisé-is profession, Dauid-is benignité, Salomon-is wisedam,
Danyel-is chastité, Isaye-is faire speche, perseuerance and fourme 10
with other seyntes vertues, dwellen fully in Thy Holynesse, more-
ouer in liberall sciences best lettred, in Holy Chirch lawe most
perfite, and in dyvyne and mortall lawes best taught. Therfor
it is worth that youre mekenesse have this present boke in the
which of all science some profite is conteyned, for whan Y was 15
with yow at Antioch, and this precious margarite ther found, it
plesed youre lordship that I shold translate it out of Arabik into
Latyne. And forsoth Y was he that coveyted youre comaundement
to obeye, and to youre wille, for the obedience that I owe to youre
sage wolle serve, this boke, that Latynes lakked, and is so rare 20
that it is hadde but with full fewe Arabies, I have translated, and
that with full grete labour, and light speche, fro Arabik speche
into Latyne vnto youre magnitude and honoure, chesyng out
omwhile a letter of a letter, omwhile sense of sense, that is to sey,
wysedome of wisedome, sithen that Arabies have oo maner of 25
speche, and Latyne men another. The which boke | the most [f. 1ᵛ]
perfite philosophier Aristotiles made, at the request and desire of
kyng Alisaundre his disciple, that desired of hym to write what
shold happe or betyde hym, and that he wolde shewe hym the   .
secretes of certeyn actes and konnynges, that is to sey, the maner 30
of comparacion and pousté of sterres by astronomye, and the art
of alkymye by nature, and the art of constreynyng and naturell
worchyng in [in]cantacions and aerymancie, piromancy, ydro-
mancy, and geomancie. The which fully he myght not at fulle declare, for croked age and bodely vanyté. And how be it that he 35
purposed tho science and the secretes of theym in full privé wise,
natheles to the wille and askyng of so grete a lord neyther he
shuld ne durst not gayn seye. Willyng forsoth in parcell openly

---

7 longanymyté] longamynyte   9 profession] ss *apparently*
corrected from cc

satisfye and declare, and in parcell speke couertly, he made this
boke spekyng by apparaunces, examples and signes, techyng
outward, by littrature, philosophik and phisik doctrine, pertenyng
vnto lordes for kepyng of the helth of their bodies, and vnto
5 ineffabill profite in knowlechyng of the hevenly bodies. Inward,
fully to purpose, he shewith by apparence secretely to his prynce
Alexaundre the pryncipall purpose instantly of that that he asketh
of hym, dyvydyng this boke in x distinctions or bookes, of the
which euery of hem conteyneth chapiters and terminat parcels or
10 articles, that vndre certeyn titles the purpose of thasker may be
found, and specially for the profite of the reders. Therfor, the
begynnyng of this boke and of all the x bokes, and the titules of all
the chapiters therof [Y shewe]. To your most prudence, most meke
fader, of the new Y translate this werk to your glory and honoure,
15 to thentent that my mynde and memorye may the stedfastlyer
abide and endure in service at the deuocion of your mynde,
bisechyng full mekely that yf ought in this werk may be found
profitable or acceptable to youre plesaunce, that the thanke therof
be referred to Hym that taught it me, of Whom all grace cometh,
20 and to Aristotell that made it. And yf ought vtterly be found or
inconveniently, that vnto my vnknowyng I pray yow may be
deputed, rather than to malice. Nathelesse youre assured speche
and certaynté in interpretacion and spekyng in propreté that so
[f. 2] lightly haboundeth | I beseche to full-fille it there I want, and
25 correct there as Y lak, thurgh godly mekenesse the which you
longe kepe sauf and sownde vnto trewe men-is glory and honoure.
And after full longe tyme space, graunt He vs to eterne blisse by
mercy graciously to come.

Here begynneth the chapiters of the [booke]

30

| Of the prologe of John that transulated this booke | [Chapter-heading in actual text] Of a prohemy of a worthy doctoure of the comenda-cion of Aristotle | [Page in text] 27 |

13 Y shewe] collegi et descripsi B 27   29 of the booke] of the comendacion of the prohemy of the doctour in comendacion of Aristotle. (*The words* of
the comendacion *rendered otiose by the words* of the prohemy ... comendacion
*while entire phrase is presumably the title of the first chapter, rendered redundant
as part of the list of contents by the chapter heading of ll. 32 f.*: of the prologe
... booke.)   33 transulated] *intended form perh.* translated

22–3 o .. dyversitees] *written as separate chapter-heading*

Oppynyons of philosophers 61
Of knowyng of metes 62

Of knowyng of metes
Of knowyng of waters⎫ [Not
                     ⎬ in
Of knowyng of wynes ⎭ text]

[For next item in text, see below, l. 29]

5

Of that wher thurgh the body waxeth fatte
Of that that maketh it lene and voydeth it

Of thynges that fatten the body and maken it lene 59

Of takyng of medycynes and houres therto competent 63 10

Of yevyng of medecynes and of the hours therto appropred 64 15

Of disposicion of vaynes
Of makyng of hony for medycynes
Of the first medycyne
Of the seconde 20
Of the thirde
Of the fourthe
Of the fyveth
Of the sixt
Of the seventh 25
Of the eyght
Of the most last and fynall medycyne

[Not in text]

Of blode-lettyng and of houres accordyng therto

Of blode-lettyng by fleobotomye, and of houres therto competent 63 30

The [6] Boke of the nature of certeyn herbes and stones, and of Aristotles secretes 64 35

[For next item in text see below, p. 26, l. 11]

Of knowlechyng of the qualities of men

Here begynneth the 10 Boke, of Phisonomye, to

32 6 Boke] 5 Boke

38 mene] *medial* e *badly formed*

[Book 1]

Of a prohemy of a worthy doctoure of the comendacion of Aristotle

God almyghty kepe oure kynge to the glorye of trew Cristen men
in bileve, and conferme his kyngdom in kepyng of Goddes lawe 25
and yeve hym enduryng to the honoure and lavde of all good men.
I, servyng as a seruant, have executed the charge that was yeve
me, and Y have put me in peyne to inquere after the morall boke
of gouernaill of prynces, that is cleped 'The Secrete of Secretes',
the whiche boke made the prince of philosophiers, Aristotle the 30
sonne of Nichomach to his | disciple the grete Emperoure [f. 3ᵛ]
Alexaundre, the sone of Philipp, Kyng of Grekis, the which
Alexandre, as it is seid, had two hornes. The which boke he made
in his age, whan he wax febill in bodyly strengthes, and myght
not bere dayly labours, neyther a-bide and suffre the juparties 35

22–3 Of¹ . . . Aristotle] *written as though constituting two items in continuation
of the preceding list of contents, each with illuminated initial, the second starting with*
Of the comendacion

and perilles of waies, neyther kyngly besynesse dayly exercisse.
And Alexandre hym as his maister he chose and gretely loved for
bicause he was a man of grete, profounde, hole and holsome
counseile, and of litterature, of full grete and penetratif intellect,
5 wakyng in lawfull studies, in kynde thewes and spirituell sciences
and contemplatif charitees, he was discrete, humble, and a lover
of justice, a seyer of trouth. And therfor many of the philosophiers
trowed that he was of the nombre of prophetes. And it was founde
in an olde boke of Greges that almyghty God sent to hym his
10 aungell seying that, 'Rather Y wolle name the an aungell than
a man'. Truly he had many tokens, and many myracles and
straunge he dud, that wold be to longe to telle them all by ordure.
Wherfor of his deth there ben dyuers oppynyons. For some secte
that is called Peripatatik seith that he assended vnto the emperiall
15 heven in a piller of fire. For he caused that Alexandre lyved so
longe, thurgh obseruance of his counseill, and kepyng of his
comaundement, and therby he wanne citees and gate the tryvmphe
and victorie of many regions, and of all the world there as he came
he allone helde and had the monarchie. His fame ranne thurgh
20 all the clymates of the world. Many peples and dyuers nacions
be-came subgettis to his comaundement and empire, bothe
Arabiens and Persiens. There was none that durst resiste or gaynsey
hym in worde or dede. For sothe many moralis made and wrote
Aristotle, for the grete love of hert, and to have accomplisshed his
25 secrete purposes. One of his epistles is that he wrote to Alexandre
vpon a-nother he wrote to hym, whan he had wonne Perse and
putte theire lordes in captiuité, and wrote to Aristotle thus:

O worthy doctour and of justice gouernoure, I signifie to the
that thurgh prudence I have founde in the lande of Perse a certeyn
30 peple that have reson and penetrable intellect, that studyen how
they may lordship purchace, and to gete the reame. Wherfor we
[f. 4] purpose to | do in all thynge with thaym as thou wilt decree vs by
thy wrytyng signatif.

Vnto whom Aristotle aunswered thus:

35 Yf thow maist chaunge the ayer of that contree into water, and
also the disposicion of the citees, thow shalt have thy wille and
purpose with them. And yf thow may not, lordship there vpon

2 Alexandre] Alex*andre unusual use of abbreviation, occurring at end of line*
9 Greges] gg*es*   13 secte] secretes

hem with goodnesse and graciously hire them with benignité, and make theym trust the. And I hope that thurgh Goddes helpe they all shall be to thy plesance and likyng subgettis, and obeye thy comaundementis, and that by the love that they shall have to the. And so pesibly shalt thou lordship them with tryvmphe and 5 victory.

Alexandre this epistle resceyved, and diligently the counseils therof dud and folowed, so that the Persiens were aboue all other nacions most obedient to his empire.

John the sone of Patrik, þe most perfite interpretatour and 10 truest, that translated this boke, seide that he left neyther place ne temple in the whiche philosophiers weren woned to leve theire secrete labours and worchynges, the whiche þat he sought not, so ferre that he visited euery konnyng man that was noysed or knowe, that medled with wrytyng of philosophers in ferre contrees 15 about. So that at the last he come to the oratorye of the sone, and there reuerence giwe to the stappes of the foote, by devocion there he founde a man solitary that ay had studyed in philosophie and was perfitest, vnto whom he humbled hym, in as moche as possible was to a seruant, diligently and deuoutly besought that he wold 20 shewe hym the secretes of that oratory, the which frely graunted hym his desires. After his longe labour and tarying there, and his entent accomplised, with joye he retourned home, yeldyng many-fold thankes to God his Maker, and than, at the peticion of this honourable prynce, he laboured, studied, and translated this boke, 25 first fro Grewe to Caldee speche, and fro þat into Arrabike.

All the first, therfor, as Y have found in that boke, I have translated the Boke of the most p[er]fite Aristotle, in the which boke | he aunswered vnto the peticions of Kyng [f. 4ᵛ] **Alexandre vndre þis fourme:** 30

O sonne, gloriosest Emperour rightfullest, God conferme the in the way of knowlechyng, and in the pathe of trouthe, and represse thy bestiall appetites, and strength He thy reame, and illumyne He thy engyne to His service and honoure. An epistle reuerently, as it was sittyng, I have resceyved, and fully vndrestonde how ye 35 desire my persone to be with yow, and mervaile why Y am absent fro yow, and reprove me for Y have litell care for youre grete werkes. Therfor Y purpose to hast me in makyng of a rule and

28 perfite] profite   36 mervaile] a *badly formed, over a corr.*

canon to Youre Highnesse, that shall be as a balance forto weye
with all thy werkes, in shewyng of my good wille to you as a rule
most sure to all thynge that thow wilt, and that that Y shold shewe
the yf Y were ther with the present, mervailyng why thou blamest
5 me for myne absence, for ye know wele, or shold knowe, that I
abiured never for no contempt to come to youre most leef glory,
but croked age and feblenesse of body have biseged me, and made
me vnlusty and vnable forto goo or ride. Wherfor askest thow and
desirest to know, suche secretes that with vnnethes manes brest
10 may conseyve or vndrestande thy high desires and peticions,
therfor, how myght it be depeynted or wryten in a dede skynne?
That thow askest, and that it sitteth the to aske and knowe, and
it is lefull to me to entrete and trete of, I owe and am bound to
aunswere, as thow art bounde of duté and discrecion to aske me
15 no more but that that [I deliuer the] in the secretes of this boke.
Yf thou hede it wele, rede it wele, and vndrestande it wele, thou
shalt fully fynde it. And I wene ther shall be none obstakell betwix the and it, or it and [the]. For God hath yeve the so grete an
vnderstandyng, a swyftnesse of engyne, and knowlechyng of lit-
20 terature and science, and specially by my precedent doctryne that
Y gaf you be-fore this, that by thy-self thow shalt reprove and
fyguratyfly vndrestande all that thou desirest, and teche it forthe
to whom thow wilt. For the desire of thy fervent wille shall open
[f. 5]   to the | the way to the accomplysshyng of thy purpose to brynge
[f. 5 ll. 16ff.] it to the ende desired, oure Lorde grauntyng. | The cause and the
26 substaunce, why by fegures I telle the my secrete, spekyng with
the by examples, signes and apperaunces, [is] for [that] I drede
gretly that this boke shall come to vntrewe men-is handes, and
to the power of proude men, and so shuld come to them þe last
30 good and Goddes pryveté, vnto the whiche the high God demed
them vn-able to have it and vnworthy, I fully a trespasser of
dyvyne grace and a maker open and a bewrier of hevenly secretes
and prevités. Therfor, vndre attestacion of dyvyne jugement Y
detect and open this sacrament, in the wise as it was tolde me.
35 Wete thow wele therfor, that who so openeth and [un]buryeth
hid thynges and privetees, hym full sone after many infortunes

---

11 depeynted] *second* e *badly formed*   15 I deliuer the] tradidi B 40   18 the] it
25 The cause] *preceded by passage written in red as chapter heading:* [b]y sparying
taxes and talages of thy subgitz and by rew[t]he, *and by a number of lines*
(f. 5, ll. 3–16), *here reassigned to normal position in text of Secretum* (31/25 to
32/3): *see n.*   27 is for that] for

foloweth. Wherfor thou maist not be sure fro contyngencijs and
badnesse a-comyng, if thow do so, wherfro oure Lord the kepe
fro all suche, and fro all werk vn-honest fro hens forth. And
before all other thynges I reduce to thy mynde that hoolefull
techyng, that at all tymes I was accustumed to expone to the, and 5
to enfourme thy noble saule therwith. And that shall be to the thy
solas and heleful myrroure. It sitteth euery kyng of necessité to
have | sustynaunce to maynteyne with his reame, and strength of [f. 5ᵛ]
men to defende it with, and to comfort it. For he most gouerne
rightfully, and have lordship vpon his subgettis, and thay sub- 10
gettes vnyformely obey to his lordship. For oftymes thurgh in-
obedience of subgettes, the pousté of lordship is febled, and
subgettes wolle wayte to be maisters. And I shall shewe yow the
cause why and wherfor subgettes ben enduced to obeye lordes.
The cause is double, one is outward, and that other is ynward. 15
And it is not longe sithe that Y declared to the the cause outward,
that is to sey, to spende wysely thy good amonge theym, and
exercise thow largesse amonge theym, rewardyng euery accordyng to his demerites and seruice. And with this a kyng most
have a-nother cautell of the which here-after I purpose to make 20
mension, in the chapiter of richesse &c, and of aides &c, to induce
them all to his entente. And this is in the first degree. And this
maner of aide hath two causes, inward and outward. [Out]ward
is that a kyng exercise justice aboute taxe talages and pensions
vpon his subgettes and trew men | [b]y sparyng thaides, taxes and [f. 5, ll. 3 ff.]
talages of [his] subgitz, and by rew[t]he. The cause inward is the 26
secrete of philosophers and of rightfull men, whom the holy God
hath before other chosen and His holy sentence commended. And
Y comende it to the for a secrete, with others that thou shall fynde
in this boke vndre dyuerse tytles, in the whiche outward the grete 30
philosophie, as it entendeth, thow shalt fynde, and doctryne. Inward forsothe, the cause fynall is conteyned: there is thy fynall
and pryncipall purpose. Whan therfor thow perceyvest the techyng
of decrees and þe demonstracion of discrete men tha[n] perfitly
and fully shalt thou brynge aboute thy desire. Wherfor the most 35

18 one] with A retribuendo singulis B 42   23 Outward] Inward A: see
n.   25–6 by sparyng . . . rewthe] written as rubric to section, followed by
substance of 31/26 (The cause inward . . .) to 32/3 (. . . fynde theryn), all being
placed on f. 5, ll. 3–16, preceding substance of text as given above, 30/25 to 31/25
Misplacement probably already in Latin original: see n.   25 by] y   26 his] thy
rewthe] rewhe   31 philosophie] foll. by finall: see n.   34 than] that

wysest and gloriosest God, illumyne He thy reson, and so clere
He thyne intellect that thow maist perceyve the sacrament of this
[*f. 5ᵛ, l. 21*] science, that thou fynde theryn [that that thou desyrest,] | desyryng
rychesse there as it is, and ay callyng to His helpe, That departeth
5 His rychesse habondantly into the soules of wise men, and to
studyantis geveth grace and comfort. For at Hym is no thynge
harde, with out Whom it is full harde to have possession.

Of kynges and theire maners aboute larges and avaryce

There ben 4 maners of kynges, a kynge that is large to hym-
10 self and to his subgettes, a kynge nygard to hym-self and to his
subgettes, a kynge nygard to hym-self, and large to his subgettes,
and a kyng large to hym-self and nygard to his subgettes. The
Italyens holden oppynyon that it is no vice to a kynge to be
nygardus to hym-self, and large to his subgettes. The Indiens
15 seyen, that he is good that is avareus to his subgettis. The Persiens gayn-seyen the Indiens, for they holde the kyng nought
worth, but yf he be large to hym-self and to his subgettes. But
[f. 6] amonge all, after my sentence, he is worst | and of merite to be
reproved, he that is large to hym-self, and nygard to his subgettes,
20 for sone his reigne is like to be destroyed. Ther-for it is full necessarye subtily forto enquire of these vertues and vices, and forto
shewe what thynge is largesse or scantnesse, and where the errour
of largesse is, and what myschief foloweth the withdrawyng
therof. Forsothe it is openly knowen that qualitees ben reprou-
25 able, and specially whan they discorden and breken in the myddell.
Also we knowen that the obseruance of largesse is full harde, and
his contrarie full light. For to exercise avarice and prodigalité is no
maistrye; forto contynue in largesse is and wolle be harde. Therfor
yf thow wilt gete largesse, considre thy power, pousté and myght,
30 and the tyme of necessitee, and the desertes and merites of men.
Therfore shalt thow give thy goodes after thy power, and that
with mesure vnto nedy and to worthy men. Who-so euer yeveth
his goodes to ydiotes, he trespasseth ayenst the rule of largesse.
For yf he yeveth his godes to hym that nedeth it not, therfor geteth
35 he neyther lavde nor thanke. And yf he yeve it to indigne and vnworthy folkes it is lost. And who inordinatly yeveth away his
goodes and richesse, he shall sone come to the bitter strone of

---

3 theryn . . . desirest] theryn, *ending misplaced passage, f. 5, l. 16*   desyryng]
text returns to f. 5ᵛ, l. 21

pouertee. And he is like to hym that wolde of his victorye make
a supersedeas to his enemye. Who-so euer yeveth of his good in
tyme of necessité to indigent and nedy men, such a kynge is large
to hym-self, and to his subgettes, [and] his reame shall be wele
prepared, stuffed and arraied, his comaundementes shall be 5
obeyed, observed, and kept. Of antecien tyme suche kynges had
lavde in the peple, and were cleped vertuous, large and moderat.
But who-so shewith out his goodes immoderatly or inordinatly to
vnworthy, and not to nedy folkes, suche kynge is reputed for a was-
tour of the comvne wele, and for a destroyer of the reame, for his 10
prudence and providence is ferre fro his kyngdome. Forsothe the
name of avarice accordeth not to a kynge, for it is disconvenient to
his reame magesté. And yf any kyng have eyther of these 2 vices, that
is to sey, avarice or prodigalité, he oweth thurgh thryfty counseill
and full grete diligence, to purveye to gete | vndre hym a discrete, [f. 6ᵛ
trew, chosen man, vnto whom he shall commytte þe disposicion 16
of the comone wele, and to gouerne wele the richesse of the reame.
   Alexandre, stedfastly I sey to the, that euery kyngdome that
contynueth yiftes and expenses aboue the ferme and extent therof
more þan it may bere, the kyng therof is distroyed, and he dis- 20
troyeth. I sey to the ayene, and wille not sesse to sey it, vnto the
mekenesse that thow hast of God, that declinacion fro prodigalité
and avarice, and acquisicion of largesse ben kynges glorye, and the
enduryng of reames, and this namely whan he absteyneth hym,
and withdraweth his hondes fro the goodes and the possessions 25
of his subgettes. For it is found writen by auctorité, that high and
verray goodnesse, clareté of intellect, and full perfeccion of lawe
is verryfied in a kynge, whan he absteyneth hym fro his subgettes
money and possessions. For the cause of distruccion of reames is
superfluyté of expenses aboue the revenves and rentes of citees. 30
And so failyng the kynges expenses, he streccheth his handes in
the goodes and rentes of his subgettes. And they cryen vnto the
most highest and gloriosest God. And He suffreth immyssions
of bad aungels to scorge thaym, so that the peple riseth ayenst her
gouernoures, and ny by putteth out thaire names out of the erthe, 35
as it happed late in Inde, and had not the glorious God holpen, that
contrey had be fully destroyed. Vnderstondeth wele that richesse
causeth enduryng of the soule animall, and is part therof, and
without richesse it may not endure. Therfore shvnne superfluous

4 and] of

habundant expenses, and lette temperaunce rewle largesse, for
euer folissh and superfluous yiftes is to be shoned of the substaunce
of largesse. And it is vertuous to leve it, and not to be-wayle it,
for that is the privyté of secretes. And reduce not to mynde suche
5 foule largesse in yiftes, but thynke on that it is of the kynde of
goodnesse, and of the substaunce of vertues to rewarde them
that have deserued it, to be mercyfull and to for-geve omwhile
inyvries, to honoure hem that shold be honoured and to yeve
9 reuerence to them that ben worth, to helpe þe symple and the
[f. 7] nedy, and further them that lakketh, and aunswere | innocentes yf
they salue the, represse thy tonge, amende wronges, flee foly and
ignorance. I have taught the all wayes as Y dud before, and into
thy brest Y wolle sowe bothe trust and lernyng, that it may be in
all thy wayes and werkes charité superfluant and science sufficiant
15 to thy gouernaile for terme of all thy lyf. And trewly I sey to the
now wisedam of philosophie abrevyat, and yf Y had seid to the
never no more, if thow had folowed that, it had be sufficiant to
gyde the, in all thy werkes in this world and in that other.

Therfor wete wele, that intellect, or vnderstondyng, is the hede
20 of gouernaile, the helthe of the soule, the conseruacion of vertue,
the spie of vyces. There-in forsoth we may spye that thynge that
we shold shonne and flee. Be it wele chesen, that, þat shold be
chosen, for there is in [it] the rote and begynnyng of vertue and
of all lavdable and honourable goodes. And the first instrument of
25 intellect is desire of good fame. For who so euer desireth it effec-
tually, he is like to be famous and gracious. And who it desireth
feyntly or feynyngly, thurgh sclaundre and defame he is like to be
confounded. Fame therfor is that thynge that pryncipally and fully
is delited to be had by hym-self, for no man joyeth ne hath appetite
30 to come to kynge or reame, that lakketh good fame. Therfore
the begynnyng of wisedome and vndrestandyng is for to have good
fame, wherethurgh all kyngdomes and lordshippes ben gat and
kept. For yf they be goten other-wise or kept, it is thurgh envie,
and envie engendreth lesynges, the whiche is the mater and moder
35 of all reprovable vices. Envye also engendreth detraccion. Detraccion engendreth hate. Haate engendreth wronge; wronge, defences
and pretinacy ther-in. Pretynacy engendreth wrathe; wrathe, de-
spisyng and defences; defences, repugnant enemytés. Enemytees
gendreth bataille; bataille, deth and destruccion of citees, and that
40 is contrarie to nature, for thurgh resistence and repugnacie is

destroyed nature. Studye therfor, and love and desire goode fame.
For reson thurgh good fame chesith trouthe, and trouthe is the
rote and mater of all laudable werkes and goodnesse, and is the
contrarie to lesynges, and it engendreth justice. Justice engendreth
trust and confidence; | and confidence, largesse; and largesse, 5
famuliarité and service; famuliarité, frendship; frendship, coun- [f. 7ᵛ]
seill and helpe. For these causes the world was, and lawes to men
establisshed. And this accordeth with reson. And thus it is open,
that who desireth gouernaile for good fame, it is goode and durable.

O Alexaundre, declyne fro bestiall desires and likynges, for 10
they ben correptible. And carnell appetites enclynen the inwitte of
man to corruptible foule lust, and lykyng of the bestiall soule, ne
discrecion had before. And therof the body is corrupted, also
thurgh many-fold harmes that foloweth the carnall appetites.
Vndrestonde therfor that flesshly lust and lykyng engendreth 15
carnell love, carnell love engendreth avarice, avarice engendreth
richesse, richesse shamelesnesse, shamelesnesse presumpsion,
presumpcion vntrouth, vntrouth theft, theft shame and reproff,
that ledeth hym to prison and captiuité, and to execucion of the
lawe-is rigour, and to destruccion of famuliarité, and to rvyne of 20
all. And that is contrarye to nature.

Of Prudence

First and pryncipally it sitteth to a kynge as touchyng hym-self,
that his laudable wisedome be knowen in the peple, and so the 25
fame of his name rynne abrode, and that he with his men be homely
seyn amonge them, and reyson them. And that shall cause hym to
have honoure and lavde of them, and to be dreded whan they
wolle se hym in wisedome, eloquent, and prudently doyng.
Sorowfull Y am that by certeyn signes me may knowe whether 30
wisedom or dulnesse ben strongest in a kynge. For what kyng
vndresetteth his reame to the law of God, he is worthy to reigne
and honourably forto lordship. And forsoth who suffreth his lawes
to be in seruage, and not executyng it by justice, ther-yn he is

---

3 and goodnesse] and *ins. above*   12 corruptible] L (f. 85) *begins here,*
with corruptabull   23 hym-self] hys selfe L   25 rynne] renyth L
27–8 they woll se] þat þay se L   29 me] ȝe L (*impersonal* me *regularly
represented in* L *by* ȝe *or other personal pronoun; this variant will not normally
be indicated hereafter*)   31 to reigne] for to regne L   32 who] who so L
lawes] lawys L   33 ther-yn] And ther yn A þer in L

a transgressour of trouth, and a dispiser of his law. And who so
dispiseth his lawe of men shall be dispised, for he is condempned
in the lawe. Ayene I sey that wise dyvyne philosophiers seyn, that
at the begynnyng it sitteth that reame magisté be attempred with
5 lawfull institutis, and not by fayned apparences, but in dede
[f. 8] doynges, and that | they know hym forto drede the most highest
God, and forto be subgette to dyvyne power, &c. For whan they
se hym to drede and worship God, they all wille love and drede
bothe. But yf he shewe hym outward to be religious, and his
10 werkes to be bad inward, of God he is reprovable, and of men de-
spisable. For it wolle be to harde to kepe privé bad werkes, but
the peple wolle sone know them. And so thurgh synne his empire
shall be dymynued, and the diademe of his glorye, and lak his
honoure. What more to sey or to do, sithen ther is no price ne no
15 tresour to by tham therwith ayene? Moreouer it sitteth to a kyng
to worship konnyng men of lawe, to reuerence religious, to reise vp
wise men, and to speke with them, and to meve doutfull questions,
honestly to aske and discretly to aunswere, hys wyser and his
nobler gretly to honoure, euery man after his degré and state.
20 Also it is sittyng to a kyng to know thynges a-comyng, and to
mynde vpon tham, and by prudencye to put defences ayenst
chaunces a-comyng, or the more paciently suffre them yf other
prouision or helpe may not be had.

Of kynges providence

25 It sitteth to a kynge to have pité, and to can refrayne the wrath
and the movyng of the soule, that he may escape all sodeyne con-
tencions, and no thynge to do with-out avisement, and resonably to
know his errour, and wisely to revoke it. For it is a full high wisedome in a kyng to gouerne hym-self, and whan he wolle se ony
30 good or profitable thynge that oweth to be do, he to do it, and that
with discrecion, not to hasty neyther to slowe, þat he be not reputed to hasty neyther to slowe in the peple, as impetuous other
remiss. It sitteth to his dignité honorably to be clothed, and euer in
faire garnementis and robes passyng oþer in fairenesse. And he
35 shold were dere, riche and straunge ornamentes. Sittyng also it is

---

1 dispiser] r *indistinct* A dyspysar L   3 that . . . seyn] Hyt ys wyse
diuine Philosophers saying L   6 forto drede] to drede L   10 bad]
made L   14 ne] noth*er* L   22 the] else L   26 movyng] mornyng L
escape] scape L   sodeyne] man*er* L   31 be] may L   32 in] to L

for a kyng to have a pr[e]rogatif in his arraie above all others,
wherby his dignité is worshiped and made faire, his pousté or
myght not hurt, and due reuerence to hym at all tyme yeve. It
sitteth a kyng to be wele faukened, out-spekyng clere voice havyng,
the which is moche worth and profitable, and specialy in tyme of 5
bataille. |

Of kynges contynence   [f. 8ᵛ]

O Alexandre, full faire and honourable it is a kynge to absteyne
hym fro moche speche, but yf nede asketh it. For it is trewe that
the eeres of men ben all-wey thristyng to hir kynges to speke fre. 10
Thurgh his speche lightly they ben satisfyed, for gladly they wolde
hire hym.

Of kynges consuetude

It sitteth a kynge to absteyne hym and not moche vse the feliship
of his subgettes and specially of vile persones, for to moche famu- 15
lierité bryngeth contempt. And therfor full faire is the condicion
of Indiens in disposicion of their kyngdome and in ordinacion of
kynges, for they have establisshed that thaire kynge ones a-yere
shall appere and be seyn amonge his peple, in kyngly apparaill and
with host armed, sitting nobly vpon a courser arraied in his fairest 20
array of armes. And they maketh the comone peple [stand] a
goode way of, and the states of nobles and barons to be about hym.
Than vsen they to expe[di]te and spede high causes and besynesse
and many [workes], and than declaren they actes and gestes of
tyme passed, and what peyn and charge the kyng hath had for the 25
comone weel, and how trewly and lovyngly he hath demened hym
to and for thaym. And that day to yeve grete yiftes, and to pardon
surfetes, and to lose prisoners, and releve pouer folkes, and to tell
what werkes he hath made and wille do. And whan the sermon is
done, the kynge shall sitte, and of his most principall consellers, 30
one shall stonde vp that is right wise and wele favkoned and declare his honour and comende hym, yevyng lavde and thankes to
the glorious God, that ordeyned so good a prynce vpon so laudable
peple and so obeisant as they Indiens be. And after laudes geven
to God, and the kynges comendacion made, he shall turne to the 35

1 prerogatif] prorogatif *with abbreviation sign for* ro A prerogatyf L   in . .
arraie] be for oþer in hus aray L   2 worshiped] d *corr. from* s   9 hym]
hym sylf L   14 a] to a L   vse] to vse L   23 expedite] explete AL
24 workes] et preteritos rerum eventus declarare B 49   28 lose] lawse L
35 made] y-made L

peple, and preyse theire good maners, joying for their beyng there
[f. 9] present, inducying theym out-ward by resons | to humble obedience,
love and reuerence of the kyng. That endit, the peple shall studie
how they may yeve to the kyng most lavde, havse his name and
5 good werkes, and comende his wisedame, pray to God for his lyf
and welfare, and that thurgh citees and townes, and teche and
induce thair childre, fro infancie, to love, worship and drede the
kyng. And this is the principalist wise, wher-thurgh in that contré
the good name and fame of the kynge is enhanced, b[o]t[h] prively
10 and openly. At that tyme he vsed also forto punyssh wikked men,
as robers, men-sleers and way-kepers, and correct others. That
tyme he vsed also to reles part of his tributis, and dispense with
marchantis of theire customes, and other rentes in parcell relesse,
and tham truly kepe and defende. And this [is] a speciall cause why
15 that Inde is so full of peple and richesse, for theder rynne all merchauntes fro euery side of the world. There be they wele reconied,
and there wynnen they, bothe riche and poore, bothe denizines
and foreyns. Therof groweth the kynges tributes and rentes so
grete, for there is none that dare offende by wronge a merchaunt.
20 They maketh them to bere theire good name and fame thurgh all
the world, for there shall euery man have his duté. And that
stuffeth and kepeth their citees, multiplieth their rentes, and
accreseth therby the kynges honoure and glory, wherfor quaken the
enemyes and dare not stere. So lyveth the kyng suerly and pesibly,
25 and hath the desires of his wille.

Of finall intencion of a kynge

O Alexandre, coveyte not þat thynge that is corruptible and
transitorye, and that thou most sone leve. Aske after incorruptible
richesse, the euer-lastyng lyf, the eterne kyngdome and durable
30 glorye. Dresse therfor thy thoughtes all-wayes in goodnesse, take
on the to be manly and glorious, eschewe the waies of leons and
bestes in their vnclennesse, be not incredible and inflexible to
spare them that thow hast had victorye of. Thynke on thynges a-
comyng, and be ware of sodayn chaunces, for thow wotest not
35 what to-morow wolle brynge yn. Folowe not thy desires in etyng,
drynkyng, wyvyng and in dayly slepe. |

---

1 there] in L   8 principalist wise] principall vse L   that] this L
9 both] but AL   11 men-sleers] mansleers L   32 incredible and
inflexible] vncredible an vnflexibile L   36 slepe] slepe. slepe. slepe. L

Of kynges disport and solas   [f. 9ᵛ]

To the magisté imperiall it sitteth trew [to haue] priuat men
with whom he shall delite with dyuers maners of instrumentes, and
kyndes of orgaynes, at what tyme he woll be hevy or vnlusty.
Man-is soule naturelly in such thynges delyteth, his wittes resteth, 5
his besynesse and other curiosité vanyssheth. All his body therby is
strengthed. If thy nature therfore wolle delite in such thynges, at
the most vse it a 3 or 4 dayes for recreacion, as ye thynke that it is
to do. But most honest and best it is to do it secretly and seld.
And whan thou art in that pleasaunce absteyne the fro drynke, and 10
suffre others to spare it not, and lette hem drynke atavnt, and out-
drynke other. And fayne the hurt of the wyne, and than shalt thow
here and see many secretes. But vse this not oft: but twyes or
thryes in a yere. Thow shalt have all-so about the of thy meynyall
seruantes and speciall that sholl brynge to the trew report of what is 15
seid and done in thy reame. Whan thow art amonge thy barons,
honoure wise men, and them that thow seest owith to be honoured.
Mayntene euery man after his degré is. Pray one to come to the
to-day, and another to-morow, and brynge them in as their degree
asketh, and so honour them. Loke that ther be none of thyne 20
astates or nobles, high ne pouere, but þat thow make hym know
thy largesse, by the clemence of thy magisté open to all men, and
the noblesse of thy liberall witte.

Of kynges discrecion

It sitteth a kynge, more-ouer, to have discrecion, contynence and 25
sapience, and to be ware of grennyng and of lavghteryng. For oft
laughteryng putteth a-way reuerence, and engendreth age. Also
wete wele, that a kyng is more owe to honoure men in his court,
and in his consistory and lawe places, than elles-where, for there
hath honoure his interest. Yf any do wronge, he is to be pvnysshed 30
after the qualité of his persone, that others may be ferded [þer-]
with, and lerne to leve wronge. For ther is a punysshment appropred to the nobles and estates, another to the juges, merchantes
and rich men, and another to the comoners and subgettis. Good

---

2 to haue] and AL   6 other] eny L   8 that it is] hit for L
14 a yere] þe ere L   15 speciall] specially L   18 after . . . is] is om. L
20 honour them] honoreth þam as þer degre askyth L   26 of] ins. above
31 that] and L   31–2 þer-with] þer supplied from L   33 merchantes] and
marchawyndes L   34 comoners] second o badly formed, apparently over corr. e

it is þerfore to kepe rigour and contynence, that betwix the kyng
[f. 10] and his subgettes | may be distynccions of persones. For is writen
in Esculapius-is boke, that he is a lavdable and able-to-be-
beloved kyng, that is like to an egle lordshippyng a-monge hi[r]
5 briddes and other fovles, for she is not like to none other brid
that is subgette to her. Therfor, in thy court or presence yf any
be that doth, or presumeth to do, ony offence, wronge or iniury,
it is to be considred with what sprite he doth it with, other by pley
and casuelly, or in contempt and derogacion of thy magesté and
10 dignité royall. Yf it happ by the first maner, lightly it oweth to be
corrected, and yf by the seconde maner, suffre hym deye.

Of kynges reverence

O Alexandre, the obedience of lordship is attended in 4 maners,
that is to sey, in religion, love, curialité and reuerence. O Alexandre,
15 convert to the the good wille of thy subgettes, putte away jnyvries
and wronges fro tham, and yeve neuer to men occasion to speke
ill by the. For lightly the peple wille be moved, for to do and to
sey ill. Therfor have contynence with the, and yeve no cause to sey
bad by the, and so shalt thow eschewe her evell doyng. Wonder-
20 stande wele that ripe discrecion, wele handled, is glory of magesté,
of dignité, of lordly reuerence, and exaltacion of the reame. For
soth it is the hiest prudence, that thy reuerence remayne more in
the hertis of thy subgettes than thy love.

Of kynges worthynesse and symylytude

25 It is rad that a kyng in his reame is as rayne in the erthe, the
which of Goddes grace is called the blissyng of the heven, the lyf
of the erthe, of lyvyng thynges the helpe and kepyng. For thurgh
rayne the erthe is arrayed, it helpeþ in journeys the merchantes, to
bylders it fauoureth and yeveth solace. Nathelesse, of rayne cometh
30 thundres in the aier, layte falleth, waters swelleth, the sees tem-
pesteth, and many harmes oft cometh wher-thurgh many lyvyng
thynges ben perisshed. For all that, forsoth, men ben bounde to
worship the grete God in His magisté, the badde accidentes notwithstondyng, consideryng the tokens of grace, and the yiftes of

3–4 able-to-be-beloved] abull to be say to be louyd L   4 hir] his A þis
L   5 she] sche L   6 her] hyr L   17 by] of L   18 to sey] to
ins. above A to om. L   19–20 Wonderstande] Vnderstondyng L   25 as]
as a L   34 tokens] werkes L

mercy. For thurgh rayne all vegetuble thyng is quicned and
buddeth, and to all thynge wexyng, or growyng, that is lyvyng | is [f. 10ᵛ]
shad God-is blissyng. And therfor oft men have yeve lavde to God,
and for-yete harmes past that happed to them. And example of
the kynge is accordant to example of wyndes, that the most highest 5
God sendeth out, and streccheth them fro the tresoure of His
mercy, and by them ben clowdes enduced, that bryngeth forth
cornes, and frute of trees ben ripe, and resumeth spirit and strength
of the whiche the thynge desired is had, the waies opened in the
see, and many other goodes foloweth. And of wyndes also dyuers 10
impedimentis and perilles happeth both in see and land. Outward
doloures it enduceth to the entrayles of the hertes. With w[av]es
it discouereth and spratlith the richesse of men. Therby ben in the
aier corrupcions engendred, mortall venymes ben norisshed and
many-fold vnprofites foloweth. Nathelesse the lower creatures be- 15
secheth the clemencie of God the Maker to take fro them tho
badnesse. That notwithstandyng, He susteyneth wyndes to kepe
and reduce their cours, as he ordeyned them, that euery thyng
þurgh His wisedome by even weight and certeyn ordure ordeyned
and stabled, that it shold serve His seruaunt. And this come of His 20
inmense mercy and in-effabill goodness. This forsothe is the same
parable in wynter and somer, the coldes and the hetes whereof
by His high prouidence inevitably [He] hath stablished to generacion, propagacion and durabilité of thynges naturell. Nathelesse
many-fold inconvenientes and mortell perill hath come of colde 25
in the wynter and of hete in the somer. In like wise happeth in a
kyng, for full many vnprofites cometh fro hym to his subgettes
that displeseth them and maketh them speke greuously. For all
that, in tham is many and grete profites that shall shew wele.

Of kynges subuencion 30

O Alexandre, be ware of pouerté, honger, and of wrecched
necessité, and of debilité of sike folkes, and fede them. Helpe the
nedy in their indigence, of thy clemencie. Chese the an eloquent
man knowyng all or many speches, and a lover | of justice, that [f. 11]

---

4 happed to them] appeth þam L   6 streccheth] strengyth L   12 With
waves] With wyfes A þat wyfys L   17–18 kepe and reduce] kepe L   19 ordure
ordeyned] order orden L   20 seruant] seruantes L   this come] þis
come L   22 coldes] clowdes L   22–3 wherof by] wher by L
26 in the (2ce)] of L   31 pouerté, honger] of hunger and pouerte L
33 clemencie] Clemens L   34 or] oþer L

he may fulfille thy while and absence, and love and gouerne them.
In that standeth the obseruance of the law, the gladnesse of men,
and God-is plesyng. O Alexandre, make store and tresour of
many-fold greynes and seedes, profitable for men-is fode, ar the
5 yere of hunger come, so that whan it cometh, thy providence may
helpe all thy peple. For in tyme of necessité thow sholdest helpe
thy citezenis and open vp thy celers and garners, and see that it
be publisshed in the citees of all thy reame the plenté of thy stuffe,
store and tresour. This wool be hold a grete cautile, a gretter
10 providence, an helpe of the reame, helth of the peple, and a
kepyng of the citees. Than shall thy preceptes be obeyed, thy
dedes have prosperité and þi good fame reysed. Than shall they
all know that thy eyen sawe ferre of and fro, and than wolle they
preise thy clemencie, and drede for to offende thy magisté.

15   ## Of kynges mercy and myserecorde

O Alexandre, full oft have Y taught the, and now teche, that
thow kepe mercy, and my techyng. For yf thow do so, thow shalt
bryng about thy purpose, and thy kingdom shall be permanent:
that is for to sey, spare to shede the blode of mankynde. That is
20 convenient allone to God for to do, for he knoweth the secrete[s]
and the hid thynges of men-is hertis. Therfor take neuer vpon
the Goddes office, for it is not yeve to the to know Goddes
pryvetés, in asmoch as thou maist therfor shede not man-is blode
For the grete doctour Hermogenes wrote thus, 'Whan a creature
25 sleeth a creature like to hym, all the vertues of the heven cryen to
God-is magesté seying, "Lord, Lord, Thy seruaunt wolle be like
to The!" And yf he sle wrongfully, the highest Maker of all wolle
aunswere, "Suffre ye hym, for who sleeth shall be slayne! To Me
the vengeaunce is, and Y shall rewarde". And so oftymes the
30 vertues of heven shall represent in thair lavde the deth of hym
slayn, tille vengeance be take vpon the sleer of hym, the which
shall be one of the perseuerantes in eterne peynes.' |

[f. 11ᵛ]   ## Of kynges memorye and mynde

O Alexandre, of all peynes have mynde and notice. Many-folde

1 while] wyll qwyl L   2 the law] þi law L   4 fode] fodys L   5 whan]
when þat L   cometh] come L   7 citezenis] citezenys L   12–13 they all] all
they L   13 sawe] see L   14 clemencie] clemence L   for to] to L (*this
regular variant not recorded hereafter*)   17 For] *om.* L   19 to shede] *om.* L
20 secretes] secrete A secretes L: *see n.*   21 take neuer] neuyr take L

kynde of badnesse by experiment hast thow lerned. Reduce to
mynde the dedes of thy parentes and of thy elders be-fore the, and
discusse diligently their annales, out of the which thou shalt draw
out many good examples that thow may exercice. Dispise not the
lest of thy subgettis, for how be it that he be lytell and vile, for 5
sone by euer he may ascende to richesse and honoure, and than he
wolle be worthyer and myghtier to noye and to be noyed.

Of kynges feithe to be kept

Most meke Emperour, be ware that thow breke not thy feith giwe,
neyther thy bonde confermed, for that is appropred to vntrew 10
folkes and to ill lyvers, to yonglynes and to stottes. Kepe truly thy
promysse, for a bad ende wolle folow all vntrowth, and how be
it that of broken promysse some profite may happe, nathelesse
the spice therof is bad, it is an example reprovable and of the
kynde of badnesse. For vndrestonde wele that thurgh feith is 15
had congregacion of men, inhabitacion of citees, of peple comv-
nicacion, and of kynges dominacion. Thurgh feith castels ben
kept, citees defended, and kynges lordshippen. If feith were had
away, than wold all men turne [agayn] to their first estate, to be as
brute bestes. Most truest kyng, shone therfor forto breke thy 20
promysse and feith, and kepe thyn othes and thy bondes yf they
bere charge, witnessyng Hermogene that thow wotest not but þat
the two sprites or aungels, that kepeth the, one on thy right, and
that other on thy left side, that knowen all the privetees of thy
werkes that thow decreest to be done, woll declare them to the 25
Maker of all. Of and in trouth this o thynge alone shold and is
y-now to withdrawe the and all others from all inhonest werkes.
Who is he that compelleth the so oft to swere? It oweth not to be
do, but of full grete nede. Forsothe a kyng yf if he were gretly
prayed or desired to, he shold not swere. Thow wotest wele þat it 30
is not convenient to the dignyté and magisté of a kynge for to swere,
and whan he doth it he doth derogacion to his honour. | It is [f. 12]
accustumed to subgettes and seruantes for to swere. And yf thow
aske what was the distruccion of the Vngariens, of the Scithes, and
of the Barbares, and of the Assiriens, me may aunswere the, for 35

2 be-fore the] by-for thys L   5 and] or L   12 a bad . . . vntrowth]
all vntrowth wolle folow the contrarye therof a bad ende A (*and*, *substant*. L):
see n.   13 profite] thyng L   15 For] and L   18 had] kept L
19 agayn] *supplied from* a-gayn L   estate] state L   24 that . . thy] a noþer
att þe L   35 Assiriens] sisiares L

that their kynges vseden othes to fraude and decepcion of the peple,
and brake the feith and bondes that was made bitwene theire
negburhes in the next citees to hem for the helth and welfare of all
mankynde. They, as wikked and vntrew, abused theire othes to
5 their negburghes subuersion, and therfor the equité of the most
rightfullest God myght suffre them no lenger. O best taught sone
Alexandre, Y wille that thow wete that in ordinacion of the empire
and gouernaill, there ben certayn speciall techynges full morall
perteynyng to the, touchyng thy meynyall feleship and comone
10 peple-is gouernaunce, but here is no place therfor. Nathelesse, in
a certeyn place of this boke, I shall sette it for thy helthfull
techyng shortly and profitably, in obseruance wherof, God
grauntyng, thou shalt have long prosperité. Grucche never for
thyng past, for that is apropred to feble men and to women. Shewe
15 thy manhode, kepe curialité, exercise goodnesse. In this is proteccion of the reame, and distruccion of enemyes.

Of promocion of studies and of scoles

O Emperour full worthy, ordeyne scolehouses and stablissh
studies in th[e] citees of thy reame, and suffre them, and comaunde
20 thy men that they teche their children to studie in sciences of
litterature and of chyvalrye, and in liberall and noble konnynges,
and ther prudence shall helpe tham in that that is necessarie and
behouffull for tham. And yeve prerogatifes to good studiers and
lerners that profiten, so that ther-by other scolers may take an
25 example and a mater to wacche and lerne. Graciously hire their
peticions and epistles, and receyve them and hede tham, yevyng
lavde to lavdable folkes, and rewardyng that that deserueth it.
In this, and by it, shalt thow stere litter[a]ted to enhaunce their
worshippes, and to make thy gestes by wrytynges perpetuell. This
30 is a full comendable maner, this prudence is laudable; in this is
honoured the empire, all thy reame is made faire, the court of the
emperour is lighted, the kinges anuall gestes the better ben re-
[f. 12ᵛ] comended | to mynde. Who reised the kyngdome of Greke[s], who

2 betwene] be-twyx L   4 and] and as L   7 wete] schuldyst wete L
14 feble . . . women] a febleman and to woman L   17 *This chapter, and
matter that follows, preceded in L by the section on Justice, corresponding to pp.
69–71, which have been displaced and are inserted at this point in that ms.*
18 worthy, ordeyne] wel ordayn L   19 the] thy A þe L   20 sciences]
science L   23 studiers] *corrected from* studies A   25 example] Ensampull
L   27 folkes] folke L   28 litterated] li*tt*er*et*ed A letterated L
28–9 enhaunce their worshippes] Enehawynce to wurschyppe L   31 thy] þis L

bare their gestes to be perpetued aboute in the world? Suerly
that made the diligence of studiantes, the provesse of wisemen
that most effectuelly loveden sciences. Sothely a mayden in an
husbondman-is hous thurgh grete studie knew the cours of the
yere and of all the planettes, the festes and solempnytés of monthes 5
a-comyng, the planettes places, the cause of shortnesse of the day
and of nyghtes, and the revolucion of Pliades and of Boetes, the
cercle and the shortnesse of particuler daies, and the signes of the
sterres, the jugementes of thynges a-comyng, and infinite other
thynges that perteyneth to the art of the bodies above.   10

Of kepying of body

O Alexandre, at no tyme trust the werkes and seruices of women.
Comytte the not to them. And yf nede artith it, comytte the to her
that thow supposest is trewest to the, and loveth the best, for doute
it not, that all that tyme thy lyf standeth in her handes. O Alexandre, 15
be wele ware of mortell venyme, for it is not late syn men vseden
to empoison. It is knowen what multitude of kynges and of other
lordes have hasted the dayes of her deth thurgh pocions of venyme.
O good Alexandre, trust never to o phisicien or lech, for one is
myghty y-now to anoye the, [and] lightly dare he presume to do   20
wikkednesse and brynge it about. And yf it may be, have about
the at the lest x of tham. And are thow take ony medecyne, make
them accorde into one, and do by the counseill of the more partie.
And for to gedre the medcynes in tyme and seson due, thow
sholdest have one þat is trewe and konnyng in knowyng of the   25
kyndes of spices and thair qualitees after phisiciens counseill, and
compone them vndre certayn weight and mesure as it is accordant.
O Alexandre, mynde wele on that, that the Quene of Inde sent to
[yow] for frendship presentes and many full faire yiftes, and,
a-monge other, one of the full most faire mayden, that fro her   30
infancie was norisshed vp with venyme of | serpentes. And had [f. 13]
not I at that hovre loked the wyselyer for [cavtel] her þurgh, and
by art magik, and saw her shamles boldnesse, and how vncessyngly
she beheld euery man in the face, wherby Y perceyved that thurgh

2 that] he that L   14 supposest] suppose L   16 not] *om.* L
20 the, and] the The A þe L et de facili audet B59   21 and brynge] to
bryng L   24 in] be L   seson due] dew seson L   25 sholdest] schalt L
28 that, that] þat L   29 many . . yiftes] mony fold *gyftes* L   30 faire
mayden] fayryst mayd L   32-3 I . . . saw] þat and lokyd the wyse for hyr
thowȝth and be hur magike and see L

her infected lookes, or thurgh etyng with her, she wold have slayn
men, as by experiment thow proved wele afterward. And yf Y
had [not] certenly i-shewed the that, thy deth shold have come to
the thurgh the ardure that thow sholdest have in flesshly delyng
5   with her. O Alexandre, kepe therfor thy full noble soule that is full
high and angelyke, that is comended to the, not for to be dis-
honested, but forto be glorified, and not to be of the condicion of
vnclene spirites, but of the nombre of clene and wise.

Of houres to be chosen by astronomye

10   O Kyng most meke, yf it may be, rise not neyther sitte not, ete
not, neyther drynke not, neyther in maner no thynge do, with-out
the counseill of a perfite astronomyer. And vnderstond certaynly
that the gracious God made never thyng voide and ydell in nature,
but all thyng He made with a cause probable, and by the most
15   certayn reson. And by inquysicion of that resonable way, kn[e]w
our most perfite doctour Plato the nature of parties, and of thynges
componed of contrarie qualitees and colours, in thair generacions,
by comparison to thynges componed. And therby he gate knowlech
of sterres, comates, of Ideis, and other thynges fourmed. Yeve no
20   feith, good Prynce, to the seiyng of fooles and ill-willed folkes, that
seyne that the science of planetes is so hard that no man may
canne it or atteyne it. They woten not what they seith, for at the
power of vndrestandyng is no thyng hard, and euery thyng is
konable and lerneable by wey of reson. Also ther ben others not
25   small fooles, that seyn that God all thyng before sawe, and be-fore
from the begynnyng ordeyned, wherfor they seith, that there is no
profite in the precognicion therof. Sithen they shall be of nede,
therfor, what avayleth the science of sterres? Also tho badly erren.
29   I sey, how be it that it is necessarye that some thynges come,
[f. 13ᵛ] neuertheles | yf me knewe it ar it come, me myght the lightlyer
suffre it, or the prudentlier decline fro it, and so in maner eschewe
it and escape it. For in that, that in forsight Y know whan and what
shall come, thurgh good provision Y resceyve them and discretly

---

2 as . . . proved] and by experiment þer providet L   6 high] heȝth L
13 in nature] in natures A (and, substant. L); in naturis B 60   14 with a
cause] om. L   15 knew] know (cf. l. 30 and footnote) A vowel indistinct L:
see n.   18 knowlech] knowyng L   21–2 no . . . or] þer may no body
cunne to hit & L   24 wey] the way L   30 knewe] medial e apparently
corr. from o (cf. l. 15 and footnote) A knew (vowel indistinct) L   31 fro it]
hit fro L (this variant due to postposition will not be recorded hereafter)

suffre them passe with-out molestyng or grete grevaunce. **Example
in grace** : Whan m[e]n knowen that they shall have a cold wynter,
they arrayeth their howses hote, purveieth them of clothes, and
geteth them coles and wode, and stuffeth them with many other
thynges, wher-thurgh whan the wynter cometh, the colde of hit 5
hurteth hem not. And in hote somer tyme, thurgh colde metes and
drynkes, and colde herbes and spices, they escapeth the malice of
the hete of hit. In like wise, when they see byfore the yere of
honger and of indigence, thurgh conseruacion of cornes by foresight, and of other thynges lightly and with eesy grevaunce, they 10
shaken of that tyme. It is also full gretly helpyng to know thynges
a-comyng, for me may the better shone tham, and to the Sender
therof, that is to sey, to the most high Kyng, me may praye that
He of His high myght wolle put a-way all such badnesse from tham,
and other wise ordeyne it. For He predestineth neuer so þat shold 15
in any thyng be derogacion to His power. Forsothe, men may pray
to God-is clemencie with orisons, praiers and deuocions, by fastyng,
sacrafice, almesse, and by many-fold other goodes, for oure giltes
askyng pardone, and for our surfetes punycion or penaunce. And
than it is full lyke that God almyghty wolle putte away that that 20
they dreden or feeren. Therfor turne we ayene to the begone
sermon, and vnderstonde wele that astronomye is dyvyded in 3
parties, that is to sey, in ordinacion of hevenes and speres, and in
disposicion of the planetes, in division of the signes, and in longa-
cion of the planetes fro þe sone, and in their movynges. That part 25
of astronomye is cleped the science. The second part is of the
qualité and of the maner to know the movyng of the firmament
vpon the rysyng of the signes and treteth of thynges in beyng, or
they happe or come vndre the firmament of the moone. And this 29
part is cleped astrologie or | science of jugementes. And the more [f. 14]
worthy part of astronomye is the science of the thirde, that is to sey,
of the planettes, speres and signes. And vnderstonde wele that there
ben of fix sterres in the firmament [M and] 22, and 7 planettes,
of the which Y shall yeve playn informacion in oo part of this
booke. 35

1–2 Example in grace] *here and passim: see n.* 2 me] man A me*n* L
4 coles and wode] wodde & col L 11 gretly] grete L 12 shone]
escheue L 15 wise] wayes L ordeyne] ordynat L predestineth]
predestinate L 26 cleped] called L 30 part] *written* pt *with* -er
contraction 31 science] L sciences A: *see n.*

The Prologe of the Seconde Booke

For sothe now Y wille teche the medycynes and other privitees
that shall be sufficient y-now to the conservacion of thy helthe,
so that thow shalt nede none other leche, the which conservacion
5 of sanyté and of helthe is better and precioser than any medecyne,
and they ben full necessarie to the, and to the gouernaill of the
worlde.

Of conservancie of helthe

And vnderstonde wele that ther is no way to do no thyng by, ney-
10 ther to gete no thynge by, but only by myght and potencie. And
potencie is not had but by helthe. And ther is no helth, but there
as egalnesse is of complexions. And that may not be had with-out
attempraunce of humours and conservancie of sanité, and in
getyng of many other thynges. And revelacion þerof was made to
15 holy philosophers, the servantes of God, and to rightfull and to
prophetis such as were chosen and lighted with the spirite of
dyvyne sapience, and endowed them with yiftes of science. Of
them the other philosophres that have be sithe toke thair begynnyng, bothe Indiens, Persiens, Grekes, and Latynes, and wrote
20 vpon thair principles, of artis and sciences the secretes, for in their
writyng is no thynge founed, no thynge reproved, but of full wise
men approved. Who-so-euer is cause of perdicion of hym-self,
thurgh moch spekyng, he may be cause of perdicion of others. For
we chese that that we love, and asken that that we intenden. For
25 soth, wete þow shalt that the most highest God and gloriosest,
amonge all oþer philosophres most He illumyned the Grekes, and
inflamed them with knowyng and getyng of sciences and of the
privetees of naturell thynges. Of these elleswhere Y made feith
[f. 14ᵛ] to the, wherfor here-after Y entende | to procede and purpose to
30 determyne in this booke, our Lord therto grauntyng. Accorded
for sothe ben all wise and naturel philosophres, that a man is
componed of opposed elementes, and of 4 contrarye humours,
that at all tymes nedith norisshyng and drynkes, the which yf he
lak, the man is corrupted in his substaunce. And yf he vse that to

2 now ... the] syn Y wull teche þe now the L   8 conservancie] *Con-*
seruacion L   10 potencie] pote*n*cyon L   12 of] of h*is* L   13 attem-
praunce] a temporans L   conservancie] *conser*uaunce L   sanité] sante L
19 Indiens] iudiciens (*or* indiciens?) L   21 founed] fownd L   27 know-
yng] connyng L   sciences] science L   28 elleswhere] wele far L
30 determyne] dete*r*me L   34 the man] he L

oft or to scarce, he rynneth debilité of siknesse, and other inconvenientes many. And yf he vse it temperatly, he shall fynde
helpe of lyf, bodely strength, and of all his substance helth. Fully
therfore they ben accorded, that who trespasseth the due maner
hereof, full or fastyng, slepyng or wakyng, in movyng or rest, in 5
dissolucion or extencion of the wombe, or in blode-lettyng, he shall
not escape stronge sikenesse, and wexyng infirmytees, of the which
all and euery Y purpose to determyne vndre short congruyté,
yevyng a full certayne doctryne vpon the kyndes of siknesse, and
vpon thaire remedies. Also they all accorden that who can be ware 10
of to moch and of to lytell, conservyng an evenesse and temperance in dyetyng, he shall have helth and longe lyf. For Y
founde [nevere] there philosophres that discorded fro this, that
is to sey, how that all delites and plesances of this world,
honoures and flesshly lustes, naturely desireth to endure, wherfor 15
who coueyteth forto lyve, studye he to gete to thynges þat ben
apropred to enduryng, and tho that kepeth lyf, and renovnce he
the lustes of his propre wille and flesshly desires, and be ware all
way of superfluous and crapulous surfetes in etyng [and] drynkyng.
For Y herde sey that Ypocras kept a diete and surfete therby in 20
maner of feblenesse of his body, and a disciple of hys spake thus
to hym, 'O worthy doctour, yf thow woldest ete wele, thow
sholdest not suffre so moche feblenesse of thy body.' Ypocras
aunswered thus, 'Sone, Y ete for to lyve, but Y lyve not for to ete.
Foode is had forto endure with, not enduryng for foode.' 25
    'Truly,' seid he, 'I have know full many that while they lyved
they dem[y]n[u]ed þ[ai]r foode, and absteyned tham fro comestions and of other flesshly appetites, sparyng glotonye, lyvyng
temperatly by dyetyng, wher-|thurgh they were of the most [f. 15]
holest of body, of good operacion, of longe lyf, of assured ap- 30
petite, and of good movyng.' And this [is] openly proved in the
Arrabiens and in tham that oft walked in wildernesse and desertis.

1 debilité] the debylyte L   4 trespasseth] trespas L   8 determyne]
determe L   9 the] all L   10 who] so who L   13 founde nevere
there . . . discorded fro] fond . . . a-cordyth fro L   16 who] who so L
17–18 he the lustes] his lystes L   19 etyng and drynkyng] etynges and
drynkynges L   23 sholdest] schuld L   24 ete] eyte þus but for L
26 I have know] Y knev L   that while] qwen L   27 demynued] demunyed
A nine minims between de and ed, presumably for deminuied L   þair] þoor
A þer L   30 holest] helyng L   31 this is] possibly this on its own is
intended construction   proved] prouyth L   32 walked] walkyth L
2550C74   E

Therfor it is an open argument that abstinence fro comestions, fro constipacions and superfluyté, is the hyghest helthe.

In how many maners is helthe conserved

O Alexandre, in medecynes is conteyned the most certeyn and
5 most veray techyng, that the conseruance of helth standeth principally in 2 thynges. First that a man vse convenient metes accordyng to his age, to the seson and tyme of the yere, and to the custume of his nature, that is to sey, that he vse such metes and drynkes with the which he hath be brought forth before, the which
10 confermed his nature, þat is to say, that accordeth with his complexion. Secondly, that he be purged of all superfluous and corruptif humours. And vnderstande wele that the bodies of men, that ben receptacles of mete and drynke, ben thynned and resolued, as wele the bodies resceyvyng as the foode that is resceyved.
15 At the first they ben resolued by the hete naturell that drieth vp the moisture of the bodies, and is norisshed and fedde with the same humydité. Resolued they ben also by the hete of the sone and of wynde, that drieth vp all the moistur of bodies and of floodes. For whan the body is hote and vaporable, than is good to
20 vse grete metes, for that that is dissolued, and passeth fro the body, wolle be of grete quantité and of grose substance, for the grete hetes and vapoures of the body. And whan the bodies ben thynne and drye, than sotell and moist metes ben good. For that that is dissolued fro the body shall be of smale quantité, for his
25 streite issues. Certeyn therfor be it a techyng to conseruacion of helthe, that a man vse metes conuenient to his complexion. **Example of grace**: if any be of hote nature, vse he temperatly hote metes, and if he be of cold nature, vse he temperatly colde metes. The same sey Y of a moist and drye bodye. Therfor yf hete
30 be augmented and in-flame with to grete a swellyng, that is, than, other for hote metis and strong, other for hete outward lordship-
[f. 15ᵛ] pyng and | myghtyest, than opposed and contrarye metes helpen, that is to sey, coolde. For grosse metes and stronge ben good to a stronge and an hote stomak, for it fareth as a stronge fire, that

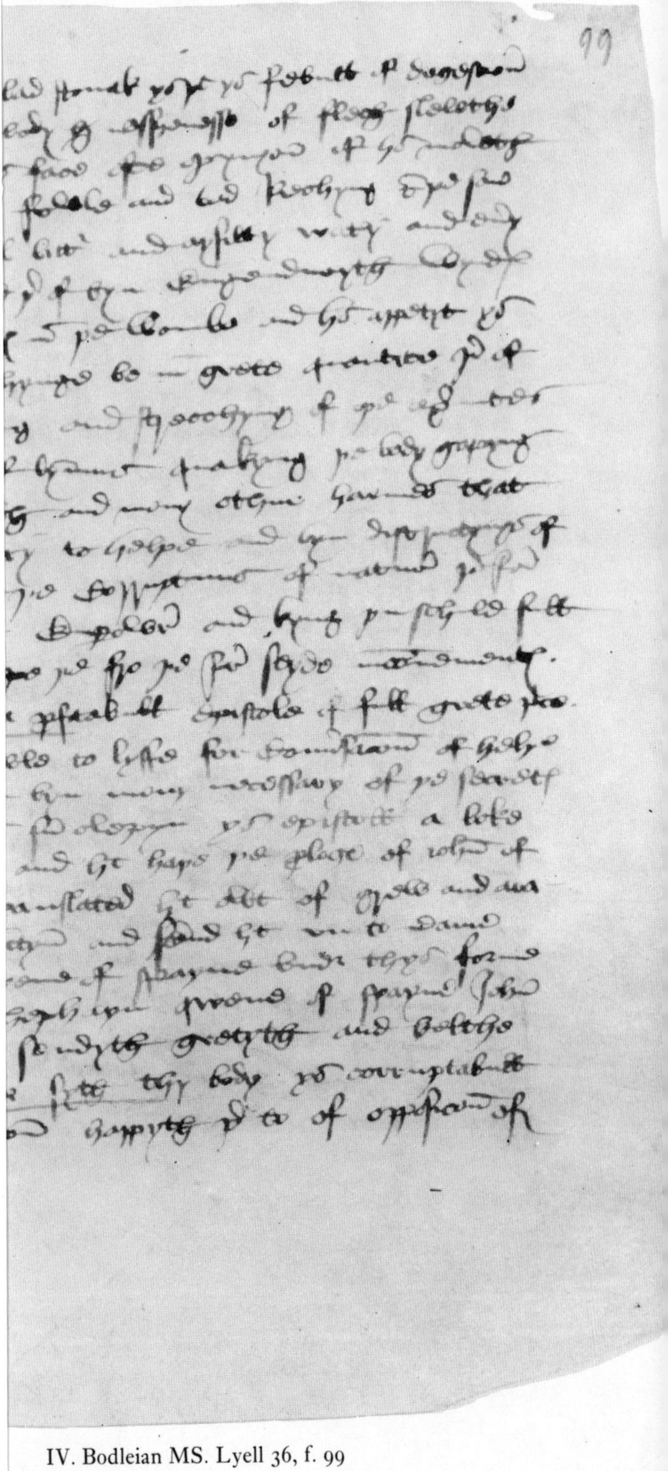

IV. Bodleian MS. Lyell 36, f. 99

hath myght to brenne grete wode. But whan the stomak is cold
and feble, than vse he sotell and light metes, for that stomak is
likened to a fire that brenneth but reedis, lockers and sotell wode.
The tokens of a good stomak ben lightnesse of the body, clernesse
of vnderstandyng, mevyng, and good appetite. The signes of a 5
bad stomak is: that [it] is feble of digestion by hevynesse of body,
nesshnesse of flessh, sleuthe, swellyng of face, oft openyng of his
mouth, gref of eyen, foule and bad rechyng and the savour to be
sowre, dol, bitter, aiselly, watery other stynkyng, and therof ben
engendred wyndes and swellynges in the wombe, and his appetite 10
is lost. Yf the thynge be in grete quantité, therof cometh spetyng
and strecchyng of the extremytees, reflexions of lymes, quakyng of
the body, gapyng of the mouthe, and many other harmes that ben
contrary to helth, and ben destructifes of the body and corruptifes
of nature. Therfor, most clement Emperour and Kyng, thow 15
sholdest full diligently kepe the fro the forseid inconveniences.

[Book 3]

Here foloweth a full profitable epistle of full grete price,
yevyng a rule to lyve, for conservacion of helthe, in the
which ben many necessaries of the secretes of medicyne. 20
Some clepen this epistle a booke by hym-self, and it hath
the prologe of John of Spayn that translated it out of Grewe
and Arrabik into Latyn and sende it to Dame Thephayne,
Quene of Spayn, vndre þis fourme: To Dame Thephayne,
Quene of Spayn, John of Spayne sendeth gretyng, or 25
helthe, &c.

O Alexandre, sith the body is corruptible, and corrupcion happeth therto of opposicion of complexion and of humours that ben
ther-yn, it is sittyng to me by this present werk to write vnto the
some maner of profites, and at all necessary, and of secretis of the 30
art of medicyne. With the which be gretly contented, sithen it is
vnhonest that a leche shold know all the infirmytés of kynges. If
diligently thow be-hold this exampler, and after the order of this
full precious booke, while thow lyvest shalt nede | no leche, but yf   [f. 16]
plage of pestilence other woundes in fyghtyng or bataill happe tham, 35

2 he] *om.* L   4 clernesse] and clerenesse L   6 it] *supplied from* yt L
7 of face] of h*is* face L   9 bitter] bitt*er* and L   other] and eu*er*y L
16 inconveniences] inco*m*uenient*es* L   20 necessaries] necessary L   medicyne]
medycynys L   23 to] vn-to L   25 gretyng or] gretyth or L   27 the] thy L
35 other] and other A (*and, substant.,* L)   or] and L   tham] þan L

omwhile all may not [be] shoned. Therfore, Alexandre, it behoveth the, whan thow risest fro slepe, walke esely and strecche
thy lymes and kembe thyn hede, for of strecchyng of thy lymmes
is thy body strengthed, and the combyng of thy hede draweth
5 out and putteth a-way all the vapours that while thow slepest
assendeth to thyn hede. In somer wassh with colde water, and in
wynter with hote, for tho thynges constreyneth and holden the
vapourantes hetes of þe hede or body, and therof wolle grow desire
of appetites to ete wele. Than clothe the with the best and softest
10 clothes and array the with the best garnementis, for naturelly thy
lyf is gladed therwith, and thy vertue and myght with fairenesse
and shynyng of clothes is delyted and comforted. Than shalt thow
froyte thy tethe and gomes with leves wele sauoured and hote and
drye [of] nature, other with leves of grene trees of bitter nature or
15 sovre. That helpeth and profiteth moch. They clenen the tethe and
the mouthe. It melteth fleme, it clenseth the tonge and clereth the
speche. More-ouer, it stereth appetites and wille to eete. Than
resceyve the fvme of appropred fumygacions to the seson of the
yere. Tha[t] profiteth moche, that openeth the closes of the brayn,
20 and yeveth wexyng to the armes, maketh the nek fatte. It clarefieth
þe visage and the sight, it strengtheth the 5 wittes, it shonneth and
tarieth hoorenesse. After that, vse the best vngementis in wirchyng
and sauour, accordyng to the seson of the yere, for with good odoure
is the soule plesed and refeid, for that is his foode, and the soule
25 comforted, the body is strengthed, the bloode rynneth and conforteth all the vaynes thurgh the plesaunce of the soule. Afterward
take a pocion of a lectuary made of aloes citryn and of rvbarb of 4
peny-weight, for that moche profiteth: it draweth flewme fro the
mouthe of the stomak, it moveth coller, it putteth a-way ventosité,
30 and yeldeth the movthe wele savoured. Afterward sitte with nobles
and estates, and speke with wise men, after the custume of kynges
and of prynces. And do that, that sitteth the forto do [first] whan
wille of etyng cometh to the, about the hovre that thow hast vsed
[f. 16ᵛ] afore. | Than meve thy body with esy labour as in goyng or
35 rydyng, other by some oþer exercise, for therof wolle growe moch
profite to the body and mervelously helpeth it. It veseth a-way and

---

3 of strecchyng] of þe strachyng L   15–16 the tethe and the mouthe]
þi tethe and þi mowth L   19 That] than A þen L   24 refeid] refeyt L
27 citryn] cicatud L   28 peny-weight] peny worth L   32 first] supplied
from furst L

breketh all ventositees, it streng[e]th the body and lighteth it, it
kyndli[t]h hete in the stomak, it constreyneth the joyntes of the
body, and breketh the superflue humours, and maketh flevme descende to the stomak, that is a-boylyng with mete by hote and drye.
Afterward se that many metes come before the, and of such as 5
thow likest and kanst chese, ete thow accordyng to thyn appetite,
with brede lightly reised, wele and perfitly lavayned and new and
wele bake, and wele fro bran sarsed, meenly with salt savoured,
settyng before that that shold be sette afore. **Example of grace:**
yf thow take dissoluyng potages, it dissolueth, and retentif potages 10
constreynen; but yf the resoluer be take be-fore, the constreyner,
take after, is slippered and make light degestion and goode eges-
tion. And yf thow vse the restreynyng first, the dissolver, for
because of his soft workyng, sheweth ill after, and in maner con-
fovndeth both. And yf thow vse in oone mete many nesshe and 15
sleper potages that wolle sone be digested, necessarye it is that he
take first the potage retentif, that the hete of the bothom of the
stomake may there leve his car[n]osité, for the hete that is there is
caused of the nyghnesse of the lyver, that maketh decoccion there.
This done, me most be ware of to moche etyng, be the mete never 20
so good, and withdraw the hand, while he hath appetit and desire
to ete. For of superfluyté of mete is the stomak stopped, the body
greved, the inwitte hurt, and the mete vndigested abideth in the
bothom noyovs, and vndified. Also restrayne the, and be ware
of drynkyng of water vpon thy mete, lest thow accustume it, for it 25
coldeth the stomak, and restrayneth the fire, and quencheth the
hete of digestion, confoundeth the mete, and gendreth impediment, specially if moch be dronke, for ther is no thynge worse than
it to the helthe of mannes body. And yf it may [not] come otherwise but nede arteth the to drynke water, as for hethe of the tyme, 30
oþer | for takyng of hote metes, other for hete of body other of [f. 17
stomak, lette it be cold, and lytell in quantité.

Of the maner and wise of slepyng

Whan thow risest from thy mete, in a sete, other in a covche, vpon
soft strawed clothes and sotell straw, rest the, and slepe temperatly, 35

2 kyndlith hete] kyndlich heteth A (*and, substant.*, L): *see n.*   10 retentif]
retentatyf L   12 make] *so also* L   15 sleper] slyder L   17 first]
ins. above A   18 carnosité] caroiosite A coriosite (*with* ri *altered from* n) L
for] therfor A (*and, substant.*, L)   20 me] ʒe L   21 he hath] ʒe have L
28 specially] and specyallych L

first on thy right side, and after on the left, and theron full-fille
thy slepe, for the lift side is colder, and nedeth þerfor more
calefaccion. But yf thow fele eny greuance in thy stomak or wombe,
than take a necessarye medecyne. Put on thy wombe an hevy, hote
5 shert, and gripe or hull in thyn armes a fair hote maiden. And yf
thow reche sourely, wete wele that thy stomak is coldred. To
remedy that, drynke hote water with some eygre sirope, and it
wolle purge vp the emprisoned mete corrupted and vndigested,
that causeth grete distruccion of the body. Movyng and exercise
10 before mete stirreth to the stomak naturell hete. But after mete it
noyeth, for than descendith esely the mete vndecoct to the lower
part of the stomak, and therof is gendred inclusion of wyndes,
and many-fold of other badnesse and vnprofites. Vnderstande also
wele, that slepyng before mete maketh a body thynne, and dryeth
15 vp his moysture and consumeth it. But after mete mervelously it
refressheth the body, filleth it, strengtheth it, and norissheth it,
for while the man slepeth the body resteth, and than the naturell
hete that ronne[th] thurgh all the body, is drawen inward to the
stomak and to his bothom. Than is the stomak strengthed in de-
20 coccion of the mete, than the resonable vertue asketh his rest.
And þerfor some philosophres seid, that eve suppers more profiteth
the body þan noone metes, for the noone mele resceyveth the hete
of the day whan all wittes worcheth, and the inwitte is wexed,
so that what me hireth than, it is roted neyþer resoned, and that for
25 man-is many-fold thoughtes, and many other vnprofitable inconveniences that cometh aboute hym thurgh hete and movyng.
[f. 17ᵛ] And at merydie, the naturell hete is shad by all the outward | part
of the body, wherby the stomak is febled to digest the mete. And
sothly in the eve souper happeth the contrarye, for the body may
30 have tranquyllité of his labour, and than may rest body and soule.
And also the nyght naturelly is cold, that dreveth the naturell hete
to the inward part, or to the lowest, of the stomak.

Of kepyng of vsage or of custume

Also it is not [to be unwyst], that who that vseth to ete twyes a

---

1 the left] þi lyfte syde L   14 body] manys body L   15 after mete]
written as one word, and separated by vertical stroke   18 ronneth] Ronne A
Rennyth L   20 the mete] h*i*s mete L   24–6 so that . . . inconveniences]
and so that my herith ys rotyd noþer resoned and þat for mony-fold-ys ma*n*nys
thouȝth and mony old vnprofitabull *conuenientes* L: *see n.*   32 to¹] in to L
34 to be unwyst] ignorare tu non debes B 75: *see n.*   twyes] ij tymys L

day, if he wold kepe o certayn houre and o certayne mele, sothly he
shall suffre therby ano[y]. And so shall he that now eteth but ones
a day, and before he was vsed to ete twies, for his stomak may not,
ne wille not, diffie and digest his mete, and it norissheth hym not.
For who-so-euer all-wayes before obserued a certayn houre in   5
etyng and drynkyng, and he sodeynly chaungeth that houre to
a-nother, he shall mow sone perceyve that it profiteth not his
nature but hurteth it. For custume is a-nother nature. Therfor yf
any necessitee that hath no lawe compelleth the to chaunge thyn
vsage, thy dyet in etyng, do it discretly and wisely, that the   10
chaunge be by lytell and lytell, o tyme after a-nother, and so with
the helpe of God it shall be wele. And be wele ware er thow ete eft
sones, that thy stomak be clene and voide fro the first mete, and
that shalt thow know by thy appetite and hungery desires, and by
thynnesse of thy spetell that sotelly wille rynne in thy mouthe.   15
For who so euer taketh mete habondantly without nede of his body,
that is with-out wille and appetite, the last eten mete shall fynde
the naturell hete as a gellé, for the plenté of coold humours that
vndefieth the mete. So is the stomak wexed that the last take mete
fyndeth no hete, for to moche intendyng or beynge ther-to-gedre.   20
For many thynges intended, the witte is the lasse to euery of them.
But who-so-euer eteth with good wille, desire and appetit, than þe
mete fyndeth hete in the stomak, as fire kendeled and redy to boyle
and digest it. And whan euer [in] thy stomak good appetite |
cometh to the, forth-with yf thow maist, ete and aunswere it. For   [f. 18]
els ille humours wolle descende in to it, and draw downe to them   26
all the superfluyté of the body, that shall trouble the brayn with
fulle badde vapours, and afterward, whan hete cometh, the mete
in the stomak shall be but tepide hote and vndigest, and not profiteth the body, but rather noyeth it and sleeth it.   30

The 4 Boke that treteth of the 4 tymes of þe yere
Of veer, somer, hervest and wynter

Oure intencion in this booke is shortly for to determyne of and
vp-on the 4 tymes of the yere, vpon the qualité and propreté

1 o certayn] a certeyn L   o certayne] a certeyn L   2 anoy] anoþer
AL   4 ne wille . . . digest] well degeste and defye L   9 lawe] lay L
15 sotelly] sofly L   18 a gellé] gely L   20 ther-to-gedre] therto
gedre   22 desire and] seiser or L   26 ille] euyl L   them] hyt L
29–30 profiteth] profit L   30 sleeth] stryyth L

of euery tyme of them, and of thair variance. For sothe, Alexandre, thow sholdest suerly kepe tho 4 tymes of the yere that ben thus distingued.

Of veere

5   Ueer begynneth whan the sonne entreth the signe of Aries, and dureth 93 daies, 23 houres and 15 minutes of an houre, that is to sey, it begynneth the 11 day of March and endith the 13 day of Juyn. At his begynnyng, day and nyght ben even of oo length. In regions, the tyme waxyng swete, the aier waxeth clere, softly
10 blowen the wyndes, snowes dissoluen, ryvers rynnen. Amonge montaynes walleth welles, moysture is exhaunced to the tree toppe, braunches budden, sedes rysen, cornes wexen, medowes wexen grene. Faire and fressh ben flovres, clad with newe leves ben trees, the soile is arraied with herbes and grasses. Engendren bestes,
15 pastures ben arraied and resumen a newe strength, briddes syngen, the nyghtyngale sovneth and resonett. The erth all fully re-sceyve[th] his garnementis and fairenesse, and is as a faire spouse and a full specious damysell arraied with broches, and clad with many-fold coloures that she may appere to me in the day of hir
20 mariage. **Veer** also is a tyme that is hote and moist, and that
[f. 18ᵛ] temperatly, and is lyke to the aier. And | in it is the blode meved, and is shad thurgh all the parties of the body, and ther-in profiteth all thyng that is lyke and even of complexions, that is to sey, temperat. And so most thy diete be in that tyme. Italiens tha[n]
25 vsen to ete chekons, corlewes, egges (not passyng v at a mele), wilde betis that Arabiens clepen scariol, and then vse they to drynke gotis mylke. No seson of the yere is better than he, neyther profitabler to lettyng of blode. It is not bad to vse women ther-yn, so it be not ayenst the lawe, and to meve þe body, and to lose the
30 wombe, to entre and to vse bathes and swetis, to drynke spices for digestion. And than purgacions shold be take. What-euer errour happe in þe medicynes, whether be it by digestion or dimi-nvacion, other of to moche digestion other of inanycion, this seson with his humydité and habilité in party restoreth.

---

2 sholdest] schalt L   8 oo] oon L   11 toppe] toppͦ A toppe (*perhaps for* toppe*s*) L   16–17 resceyveth] resceyved A rescauyth L   17 garne-mentis] garment*es* L   19 me] þe L   23 complexions] complexions A complexion L   24 than] that A (*and, substant.,* L)   32 happe] happͦ (*cf.* happe 60/27) A happe L   þe] *ins. above*

Of somer

Somer begynneth whan the sonne entreth the signe of the
Crabbe, and dureth 93 dayes, 9 houres, 20 minutes of an houre,
that is to sey [it begynneth] the [xiii] day of June and durith tille
the 14 day of Septembre. In this tyme ben the dayes at the lengest, 5
and nyghtes in all regions discresen, hetes cresen, wyndes swollen,
tranquyllité in the [s]ee, clernes in the aier, cornes dryen and
rypen, serpentes comen forth, venymes ben shad, bodily vertues
ben strengthed, and þe world is as a spouse full in the body and age,
with hetes swellyng. Somer tyme is hote and drye, wher-in collir 10
stirreth. Me most in that seson be ware and absteyne fro all thynge
that is hote and drye in complexion, for they wolle stirr collir.
Fro to hote metes and drynkes, and fro crapulous etyng, me most
absteyne, lest the naturell hete queynt therby. Ete that tyme all
thyng that is colde and moist of complexion, as veel, with vynegre, 15
or eysell, cucurbitis and pulletis ensayned, potage also made vp on
barly floure, and frutis of egre savour, as soure apples, pome
garnatis. | And vse scarcely veneryen actis, fro all bledyng be ware, [f. 19]
and specialy in pryncipall veynes, but yf nede art it, and scarcely
also entre bathes. Therfor ete in that tyme, as be-fore is rehersed, 20
cold and moiste metes, so that with coldnesse the violence of hete,
and with moisture the malice of drynesse, may be repressed. In
like wise thurgh all the sesons of the yere me most with contrari[e]s
cure contraries.

Of hervest 25

Hervest begynneth whan the sone entreth the signe of Libra
and conteyneth 89 [dayes], 6 houres. This is fro the 14 day of
Septembre vnto the 12 day of Decembre. In this tyme dayes and
nyghtes ben lyke longe, in the seconde tourne. And here-in the
nyght accreseth, the aier wexeth cold, the northern wyndes 30
blowen, the tymes chaungen, the flodes decresen, welles dymyn-
ven, greves wydreth, frutis enden, the face of therth lakketh fairenesse, voules asken hote regions, bestes thaire dennes, serpentes
crepen in thair holes, and theder gadre foode for the wynter. The
world is like a woman of full age lakkyng clothes, [l]evyng yougth 35

4 xiii] ix AL   5 14] xij L   6 hetes] and hett*es* L   wyndes] and wynd*es*
L   7 see] yere A ʒee L   14 queynt] qwenche L   23 contraries]
contrarious A contraryes L   27 conteyneth] continuyth L   14] ix L
28 vnto] in to L   29 lyke] elyke L   31 welles] þe well*es* L
35 levyng] yevyng A ʒevuyng L   yought] yowthys *followed by canc.* la L

and hastyng to age. The hervest is colde and drye, wheryn ryseth
malencoly. Me most therfor in þat seson vse hote and moiste metes
as chekons, lambe, wyne olde and sotell, and swete grapes. Be ware
of all thyng that gendreth malancolie, movyng of the body, and
5 vsyng of veneryne actes, more than in somer. Vse þan baynes. And
purgacions, yf nede be, in this tyme may be had and take. In this
seson, yf me nede, me may take vomytes, and that meenly, about
noone or whan þe day is hotest, for in such houres ben engendred
and gadereth all superfluytees in man. Purgacion of the wombe or
10 of the body shall be take that tyme, and perismon and agnaricon
and all other thynges that draweth blak collir and repressen the
humours of melancoly.

Of the wynter

[f. 19ᵛ] The wynter begynneth whan the sone entreth the signe of | Capry-
15 corne and conteyneth 88 dayes, 15 houres, 14 minutes, that is
to sey, from the 12 day of Decembre, tille the 11 day of Marche. In
this tyme the nyght is longest and the dayes shortest, colde hath
myght, wyndes ben sharp, the leves of trees [all] fallen [down],
all grene thynge dyen and waxen hard as stones, the most part of
20 bestiall kepe tham in caves of montayns, for the most cold and
moisture þat is than, the aier is derk, the tyme blak, the bestes
quaken, for the seson febleth the vertues of thaire bodies. And than
is the worlde as an olde woman, greued and decreped in age, lakkyng
clothes, neygh to deth. The wynter is colde and moist, wher-in
25 flevme is augmented, wher-in me most chaunge oure dietyng. Than
turne to hote metes of hote matir and nature, as coluer peions,
moton, and rosted metes, and all fat soupyng and hote metes, as
figis, nottis and fyne rede wyne and hote letuaries. Absteyne thein
fro lousyng of the body and lettyng of blode, but yf it nede the
30 more. Vse not to moche mete, noþer venereyn actes, lest that digestion be febled. Than me most chaunge thaire. In chafyng of þe
body, in enoyntyng therof, and frotyng, [vse] oynementis hote.
And vse temperat bathes. It noyeth not moche in that seson to vse
women, movyng of body, grete drynkyng, moch etyng, for because
35 of cold outward the naturell hete draweth inward and causeth

---

3 lambe] lombes L   10 perismon] perisiom L   13 the] om. L
15 conteyneth] continuth L   17 dayes] day L   18 all fallen down]
supplied from all fallyn dowyn L   21 þat] ins. above A   the aier . . . black]
þe ayr ys blacke and dricke L   26 matir and nature] natur and hote mater L
28 thein] þe L   34 for because] for cawse L

good digestion. In veer and somer, the wombe is colde, and the
povres open, and the hete is shad thurgh all the body, and
the stomake hath litell þerof, and so digestion is letted and the
humours moved. Vnderstande þis wele, and God kepe the, and
farewell. O Alexandre, kepe wele þis precious prefixed diet and 5
hede euery part therof. Conserve naturell hete, for as longe as
temperat hete is in a man, and moisture not passyng the myddell,
than therof cometh naturell hete, and than helth in lyf is like to
abide, and so sanyté may be longe kept. For in 2 maners age
cometh. In that one by due law and cours of nature, in wexyng 10
colde, and the body wastyng and drying, and so destroying the
creature. A-nother maner accidentall, as of sikenesse and of other
causes, and bad cures and hedynges. |

Of thynges that fatten the body and maken it lene   [f. 20]

These fatten and moysten the body: sureté, fulsomnes of swete 15
metes and of dyuerse drynkes that ben swete, as mylke and meth,
hote drenkes other sharp, and slepyng after mete vpon soft beddes
and the place wele savoured, accordyng to the tyme, in colde places
and moist, and seeld entré into swete bathes of fressh water and
litell tariyng ther-in, that the body take moysture of the bathe and 20
not the bathe of the body, for thurgh tarying there the body wold
be febled. All redolent herbes that accordeth with the helthe of
the body loke that they be in it, as, in the wynter, wermode that
is of hote nature; roses also and violettes, and all colde herbes, in
the somer. A vomyte also wassheth the body and purgeth the 25
stomak of all bad humours and putrified. And whan fewe humours
be in the stomak the hete is comforted forto digest and forto dewe
the body and yeve it humydité and fatnesse. And moche the more
and profitabler yf he be mery and glad, and yf he myght have
resonable glory and honoure, and of his enemyes victorye, hope 30
and trust in the peple, in pleyes and sightes to delyte, to se faire
faces and vesages, and beholde delitable bokes, and to here swete
songes and delitable, to laugh amonge tham that loven hym, to be
clad in the best clothyng of colour and teyntour, and to be wele
an-oynted with the best accordyng oynementis to the tyme. Of 35

3 letted] lyttyd L   12 as] ys as L   18 wele] the place wele A (and,
substant., L); supra stramenta mollia et odorifera in locis ac temporibus con-
venientibus B 82   23 the body] manys body L   33 delitable] delicius L
hym] þe L   34 clothyng ... teyntour] cloþyng colours and tinctores L

the contrarye these dryen, feblen and maken leene the body:
to ete and drynk lytell, labour oft, and to moche stonde in the sone,
with-out mesure walke, slepe before mete vpon hard beddes, to be
vexed in mynd, to entre bathes there as sulphure water is, and sitte
5 longe ther-yn, vse ete drye, salt, and resty mete, and to drynke full
olde wyne oft, to take and make many seeges, oft to lette blode and
to lak mesure ther-in, to be to besy in venerien actis, to be vexed
with bad thoughtes, to have drede oft and sorow. All these and
many other dryen and feblen the body.

10   A rewle of Ypocras

If any man constipat or replete entreth bayn, or bath, the dolour |
[f. 20ᵛ] of ydropesye, other of the intestines and bowels, he may be sure of.
Also who deliteth with a woman the belly full, he shall be paraletik
yf he vse it moch. Neither is good than to rynne ne to ride moche.
15 Who to-geder oft eteth fyssh and drynketh mylke with-all, lepre or
perell in his eye it disposeth. Wyne and mylke in like wise worchen.
This litell werk vnto Kyng Alexandre, the prynce of leches wrote,
that he, thurgh the tenoure therof and the maners obserued, shold
nede none other leche.

20 **Here foloweth the 5 Boke of the 4 pryncipall lymmes, and
first of the passions and sikenesse of the hede and his
remedies**

The body is dyvyded in 4 parties. The first part is the hede. Whan
any superfluyté is gendred ther-in, thow maist know it by these
25 signes: that is to sey, by dazovnesse of eyen, hevynes of browes,
repercussion of the tymples, the sownyng of the eeres and stoppyng
of the nastrels. Who-so-euer feele this happe to hym, take and
boyle efros in pelletes in swete wyne, with the rootes of pullege,
and wast half, and of the residue euery mornyng put a sponefull
30 in thi mouth, tille thow fele that it profiteth the. And vse with thy
mete mvstard sede of a peny weight, wele poudred, with confitis
thurgh xij oignementes: that he vse to slepe with. If he leve that

2 stonde] to stand L   5 ete] to ete L   6 to take] and to take L
13 who] who so L   14 moche] to much L   16 in his eye] in yen L
28 effros in pelletes] i. pelletes *in outer margin in scribe's hand, with no indication of precise insertion-point* A eufrace and pellatory L effresim pullei R f. 43
esdentum B 84: *see n.*   with the rootes of pullege] *om.* L & radicibus pullegei
R f. 43 cum radicibus pullegii B 84: *see n.*   32 thurgh] wi*th* L   that he
vse to] to make hym to vse L cum pulvere confecto ex xii unguentis, et hoc
in dormitacione sua utatur B 84

and for-yitte it, it is to be doughted of perieleus siknesse, that is
to sey, corrupcion of his sight, dolour of his brayn, and many other
infirmitees, fro the whiche at all tymes God kepe the.

Of syknesse of the brest and his remedies

The brest is the 2 part. If ther-in be gendred superfluytees, these 5
signes foloweth: the tonge is hevy, the movth bitter, in the stomak
moch sowrenesse, and he felith the cough. Me most therfor lisse
etyng and drynkyng, vse vomytes, and ther-after take sugre
roset, with a stik of aloes, and shave it, and after that take the
quantité of a notte of the grete electuarye that is made with ligne 10
aloes, vt supra.

And yf thow do not so thow may lightly cacche the passions
of thy side and reynes and rynne into an excesse and into other
siknesses.

Of sikenesse of the genytaill and thair medecyne | 15

The coddes ben [þe oþer] parties. And yf any superfluyté be [f. 21]
gadered in tham, or impediment, to lak appetit is the signe therof.
Who feleth hym greved ther-in, he most take 2 herbes, drochachen
and arianes, and boyle herbe and rote in white wyne, and euery
mornyng vse it, tempered with water and hony, and absteyne fro 20
moche etyng and drynkyng.

And yf he leve behynde this medecyne, he may be aferde of
dolour of coddis, of the longis, and of the stone.

Oppynyons of philosophers

It is writte in olde storyes that a myghty kyng brought to-gedre 25
the best leches of Indiens, Grekis, and Medis, and Persiens, and
enyoyned them to make hym a medecyne that, it vsed, me shall
nede none other medecyne. Holsomly, seid the Greke, that who
wold take euery mornyng hote water, other rose water 2 sponefull
seuerelly, it wille cause helth and that he shall nede none other 30
medecyne. And the Persien seid that it profiteth moche to take,
fastyng, of the greynes of myle. I for sothe sey that who slepeth
so moch that he fyndeth no ponderosité in his body, and specially

3 at all tymes] al þe tyme L   5 2] second L   11 vt supra] *badly*
drawn horizontal stroke partly under, partly through, these words, perh. cancelling
them   16 þe oþer parties] L parties 2 A   17 gadered] genduryd L
18 drochachen] drochiachen L   28 Holsomly] *see n.*

wombe, he nedeth not to be a-ferd. And who eteth euery mornyng
7 dragmes of radissh, bake, wele sweted, he nede not fere no sikenesse of flewme neyther govt, his mynde therby wolle be amended,
his intellect lighted. And who in tyme convenient vseth it accord-
5 yng to his complexion, he shall be sure and have no cause to drede
feuere quartayn. And who vseth to ete nvttes with fyges and with
a fewe braunches of rewe, venyme that day shall not anoye hym.
O high Kyng, studye in all wise to kepe and hold thy naturell hete.
For as longe as temperat hete is in the man, and moisture naturell,
10 the hete is tempered and strengthed, for helthe restoreth in tham
twayn. And vndrestande wele in this place that destruccion and
corrupcion of the body cometh of 2 causes, that one is naturell,
that other innaturell. Naturell cometh of repugnancie and contra-
14 diccion of 4 contrarie qualitees, as thus drynesse lordshippeth the
[f. 21ᵛ] body. Corruption for-sothe | cometh a-yenst kynde, of some actuell
or accidentall cause, as of bataill, or spornyng with a stone, other
of other chaunces, by siknesse oþer ill counseill.

Of knowyng of metes

Of metes some ben sotell, some grosse, and some meen. Sotell
20 engendreth clere blode and good, and they ben white, chekons of
hennes wele norisshed and fatte, and egges. For-sothe, grosse
metes ben good to hote men, and labourers, and for diners to them
that slepen after noone. Meene metes engendren none inflam-
macion, neither superfluyté, as lambe, kyd, wether castrot, and all
25 flessh that ben hote and moist. Nathelesse it semeth that moisture
faileth in these fleshis whan they ben rosted and wexen hard, and
so hote and drye. Therfor yf any such flessh be rosted, ete it hote
and sone, and specially whan any spices is rosted with them, for
than it is best. Metes that engendren malencoly ben bugles, befes,
30 kyne, and suche other grosse flessh. Nathelesse bestes of that nature,
wele fed and yonge, brought forth in watery and moist shadowed
pasture, ben best, swettest, and holsomest. The same may me sey
of fisshes. And vndrestand wele that fisshes of smale substaunce,
of sotell skynne, and light to be chaved, the which ben brought
35 forth in salt water rynnyng, ben lightest and best. Nathelesse the

3 wolle be amended] will be well a-mendyth L   7 shall not anoye]
non schall ny L   8 wise] wayes L   13 repugnancie] repugnans L
14 as thus] *see n.*   16 or sporning with] off spurnyng of L   29-30 bugles,
befes, kyne] bugill bestes & kyne L   30 nature] L natures A   32 best]
bestes L   33 of fisshes] in fyschys L   35 best] bestes L

fisshes that ben engendred in the see and brought out of it, ben holsomest. Me most beware of tho fisshes that ben of grete substance, and of hard skynne, for such fisshes comonly ben venemous. And at this tyme of fisshes this is sufficiant, for in the boke that Y made the of potages and medecynes, thow shalt fynd this 5 mater sufficiantly determyned.

Of blode-lettyng by fleobotomye, and of houres therto competent

Yf thow wolt lette blode, se that the moone be assendyng and past the coniunccion and the sones orbe, and se that she be not in the 10 Crabbe, Fisshes, neither Yonglynes. And more be ware þat the moone applie to the sone of none aspect, and specially 4le or opposicion. And be ware that the mone make no coniunccion bad in watry signes, and se that Mercury be not in thascendent, neyther in the 7 hous. The same sey Y of Saturne. And vndrestond 15 that the last half of the mones mo[n]the is better to lette blode in than is the first. And | lette the moone be in Libra or Scorpion, [f. 22] with-out aspect or raies of the noyous planetes, other of bad sterres fix, for and she be in the second half reproued or infortuned, than is she werst of all. But in kuttyng or garsyng of the 20 flessh, lette the mone be accresyng to his light without loke of ony noyous sterre, and not opposid to Mercury, but joyned with Venus, other biholdyng Venus and Mercury of frendlinesse. Whan the moone happeth in thascendent, than hath she domynacion there, and so she hath in euery of the 12 houses, aduerbialy, now good, 25 now bad, now strong, now feble. But euer be ware of hir in thascendent.

Of takyng of medycynes, and houres therto competent

Whan thow wolt take ony medecyne laxatif, sette the mone in the Scorpion, Libra, other in Pisces. But be ware that she neygh not to 30 Saturne, for than congeleth she the humours and the medecyne in the body. And the ferther she be fro Saturne, the better it is. But drede not her beyng with Mercury. Therfor thynk that þe begynnyng of thi werk, and the surenesse of thy body, after the

---

9 lette] be lett L   past] passe L   12 4le] for quartile cf. 89/14
14 in thascendent] ascendyng L   16 monthe] movthe A (and, substant., L)
20 kuttyng or garsyng] kittyng or carvyng, garcyng L   32 she] that sche
L   34 thy] y written over e A þe L

good constellacion of the moone, and her absence fro noyous
sterres and after her prosperité in her ascense.

Of yevyng of medecynes and of houres therto appropred

Ar thow yeve medecyne, se in what signe the sone is. And yf it be
5 in a colerik signe, me most make sharper the medcyne. And yf in
a melancolik signe, moche more. And yf in a flevmatik signe, moch
lasse. After the qualité and reson of the signe whan it is hurt and
constreyned, the nature of the wombe is to be lax. More-ouer,
thow most se in like wise yf the mone be in a colerik, flevmatik,
10 other malancolik signe. And yf the bothe luminaries be-hold and
resceyve other in colerik signes, the medecyne than yeve shall
some men litell anoye, and yf they in malencolik signes do so,
moche lasse, for it is but seld vsed. But yf they bothe be in flevmatik signes, the medecyne take lightly worcheth, and specialy
15 yf the moone be accresyng.

The [6] booke, of the nature of certayn herbes and stones, and of Aristotles secretes. |

[f. 22ᵛ] [O]f the qualité, propreté and vertue of some herbes, and of thair
profites by short trete in this chapiter &c, I wolle determyne, but
20 in oure other booke fully of thaire propreté and of the strengthes
of herbes, and natures of plantis, we have declared. And therfor
what we sey now of plantes and stones, as touchyng þis werk it is
now. But now, Alexandre, thow shalt wele vndrestand that as in
plantes ben dyvers natures and strengthes, so in stones beth many
25 kyndes and vertues. The price of thair fairenesse and the profites
ben inestimable, and specially they be convenient to the magesté
roiall of a prince, for they maken faire the diademes of kynges, þei
comforten the sight of the eyen, they plesen the soule. It arraieth
the dignité. And [by] thair vertues full gracious, siknesse ben ex-
30 pelled fro men-is bodies, and with-out them litell worth is medecyne, and specialy where me wold have grevous siknesse put a-way.
Full grete and mervelous vertue is bothe in plantes and in stones,

---

5 sharper] scharpe L   5–6 in a melancolik] it be in malencoly L
6 yf in a flevmatik] yff hit be in fleumatycke L   7 qualité] over erasure A
9 a colerik] in colerike signe L   10 other malancolik signe] or malencolye L
12 malencolik signes] malencolye signe L   16 L omits all from here to the
section Of Justice, as given below pp. 69–71, and places that section before the section
Of promocion of studies and of scoles, as on p. 44 above. At this point, L proceeds
with the Eighth Book as on p. 71 below   The 6] The 5   18 Of] Yf A

but fro mankynd they ben hid. But we in oure boke of stones and
plantes have þeir propretees and vertues more fully exponed. **In
primis,** therfor, O Alexandre, I wolle yeve the amonge the
secretes the grettest þat þurgh Goddes myght shall helpe the
to bryng about thy purpose, and to kepe secré the priveté. Therfor 5
take the stone animal, vegetable, and mynerall, the which is no
stone, neither hath the nature of a stone. And this stone is like
in maner to stones of montaynes, of mynes, and of plantes animal,
and it is founde in euery place, in euery tyme, in euery man, and
it is conuertible to all colours, and ther-in ben contened all 10
elementes, and it is cleped the litell world. And Y wolle name hym
by his propre name, as þe comone peple calleth it, that is to sey,
the terme of an egge, that is to sey, the philosophers egge. Dyvyde
hym therfor in 4 parties, for euery part hath o nature, and than
compone hym egally and proporcionly, so that ther be no dyvysion 15
ther-in neyther repugnance, and thow shalt have thy purpose,
God grauntyng it the. This maner is profitable, but Y wolle
dyvyde hym | to the in speciall operacions. Dyvyde it in 4, and 2 [f. 23]
maners may be do wele, and with-out corrupcion. Therfor, whan
thow hast water of the aier, and aier of fire, and fire of erthe, than 20
shalt thou have fully this craft. Dispose therfor thy aiery substaunce by discrecion, and dispose the substance, by cause, by
moisture, and hete, till þei accorde and joyne, and discorde nether
deceuere not. And than joyne to them 2 vertues operatifes, water
and fire, and than is thy werk accomplisshed. For and thow medled 25
it with water soole, it will make it white, and yf thow medle it
with fire, it wolle be rede, God grauntyng. Oure fader Hermogenes,
that is cleped treble in philosophie, he spoke best ther-in, seiyng:
Trouth hath hym so, and it is no doute, that the lover to the heigher,
and the heigher to the lower aunsweren. The worcher forsoth of 30
all myracles is the one and sool God, of and fro Whom cometh
all meruelous operacions. So all thynges were created of o soole
substance, and of o soole disposicion, the fader wherof is the
sone, and the moone moder, that brought hym forth by blast or
aier in the wombe, the erthe taken fro it, to whom is seid the increat 35
fader, tresour of myracles, and yever of vertues. Of fire is made
erthe. Depart the erthe fro the fire, for the sotiller is worthier than
the more grosse, and the thynne thyng than the thik. This most
be do wisely and discretly. It ascendith fro the erth into þe heven,

29 lover] o *corr. from* e

and falleth fro heven to the erthe, and therof sleith the higher and
the lower vertue. And [þus] it lordship[pes] in þe lower and in the
heigher, and thow shalt lordship aboue and beneth, which forsoth
is the light of lightes, and therfor fro the wolle fle all derknesse.
5 The higher vertue ouer-cometh all, for sothe all thynne thyng doth
in dense thynges. After the disposicion of the more world rynneth
this worchyng. And for this prophetisyng of the trynyté of God
Hermogenes i[s] called **Triplex,** trebill in philosophie, as Aristotle
9 seith. Of the mervailes of this world is that stone, that fighteth
[f. 23ᵛ] with waters and wyndes. Thow shalt se | hym rise vp on the water,
whan the waters rynnen with wyndes. And it is born in the
Mediterrayn See. His propreté is this: yf thow take this stone and
put hym in a-nother stone, and bere hym with the, this is impossible: that any host shall endure ayenst the, other resist ayenst the,
15 but fle hedyngly before the. Ther ben 2 stones of mervelous vertue,
that ben found in derk places, of the which one is white, that other
is rede, and ben found in spotillissh waters. Thair operacions ben
these: the white begynneth to appere vpone the water in the fallyng
of the sone, and abideth vpon the water till mydnyght, and than
20 begynneth to discende downward, and at the sone rysyng she is
at the bothome. The rede stone worcheth contrarye, for whan the
sone ariseth she begynneth to appere, and so to mydday, and than
begynneth to descende tille the sone-fallyng. The propretees of tho
2 stones also ben these: yf thou woldest honge of the rede stone
25 a weight of a car[a]t vpon one of the hors of thyne host, the hors of
thyn host shall not cesse neying tille þu put the stone a-way. The
operacion of the white stone is the contrarie, for the horse that bere
it shall never nye tille thow remove it a-way. Therfor they be good
to stere thretyng, and to werkes of hostes. The propretees of tho
30 stones also ben these: yf two stryve to-gedre, put the white stone
in one of thair mouthes, and yf he be in the right he shall anon
speke, and yf he be not, he shall wex dombe as long as it is in his
mouth. The rede stone worcheth to the contrarye. And Y wille
determyne to the the propretees and vertues of stones in enchaunte-
35 mentis, and of some [plantes], in the next tretys. Thow hast fully
of the precedentes knowen, whan Y treted to the [of] nature[s] and
secretis of kynde, of thair degrees, of disposicion of plantes, and of
disposicion of mynerall after the essense and beyng therof, and

2 þus] yf   8 is] it   18 vpone] *over erasure*   25 carat] pondus
denarii B 118; *blank left for word* R f. 63   36 of natures] and naturell

whan it resceyveth his propre fourme after his nature and begynnyng, fro the natures above, that is myghtyest and lordshippyng
there-in. And in plantis water is myghtyest in nature, and in
mynerall the erthe, and in | stones. Plantes resceyveth their nature   [f. 24]
of water by extension, as water resceyveth it by movyng and im-   5
pulsion of wyndes in his place. And as water is of dyuers figures,
so dyuers figures ben in plantes, for all figures ben ther-in. And
sithen water is most myghtyest in plantes, and it sheweth not but
by diffusion, and Mercury is worker of dissolucion of waters, and
in his heven vncessably worcheth it, than he must gouerne it as   10
euery planet gouerneth that thyng þat is accordyng and conuenient
to his nature. **Example of grace**: Saturne gouerneth the erth,
Mercury the water, Jupiter the aier, the sone the fire. These
inconvenientes be not found in the planetes but in the operacions
that they have, contynuell and perpetuell, by the vniuersell vertue   15
aboue, that is above all the vertues of these operacions, but here is
no place to shewe the highnesse therof. Natheles here Y make
mension, for it is full necessary and profitable for the tretis suyng,
in the which we shall declare of other thynges, and of indyvyduis of
certeyn vegetable plantis. Therfor the knowlechyng of the pro-   20
pretees of these thynges bilongeth to philosophers. Forsoth the
operacion of naturell thynges pertenyth leeches. And Y wolle
that thy prudence be not hid, that all thyng lakkyng light of þe
nombre vegetable is gouerned of Satourne and yeve to hym, and
all thynge that flovreth and is lumynous is yoven to be gouerned   25
of Mercury, and all thyng vegetable that floureth and bereth no
frute is yove to Mars and by hym gouerned. After-ward compone
and joyne these dyvysions, and sey all vegetable beryng forth frut
[not florisshyng], as palme, is yove to Saturne, and to the sone,
and all florisshyng not beryng fruyt, is ruled by Mercury and Mars.   30
Also some vegetables ben by bowes, some by seedes, and some
ben with-out seedes or plantacion. Therfor is shewed openly that
euery spice of vegitable hath his propre disposicion, that is com-
plexioned, and foloweth the vertue, of one of the planetis, other of
more, after he hath take it, and helpeth euery propreté the vertue   35
of the planet þat he is propred to | by vertue naturall that disposeth   [f. 24ᵛ]

19 indyvyduis] *stroke of second* i *over first minim of* u   28–9 vegetable
beryng forth frut not florisshyng] florisshyng vegetable not beryng forth frut A:
perhaps for not-florisshyng vegetable beryng forth frut   29 not] *run through
with horizontal stroke, apparently an erroneous canc.: see n.*

his spices vnto hete, sauour, odour and figure. And the naturell
soule gedreth all the propretees and vertues naturell, for they
rynnen therfro and foloweth it, and yeveth enduryng to them,
for as long tyme as their nature have signified and diffined. For
5 there is none act with-out movyng, and no operacion with-out
terme. And so shalt thow fynde some spices anoying, and some
helpyng, and some engendren gladnesse, and some love, some
hate. Some geven reuerence and honour to the berer, some abieccion and contempt. Some causeth fals dremes, some trew visions.
10 Some gendreth man-hode and strength, some sleuth and feblenesse. Some heleth the bodies and kepeth þem fro venyme
mortell, some corrupteth the body, and inducith in tham deth.
And I shall make to the mencion of all these spices, with open
argumentis and probacions therof. Sothly that spice of vegetable
15 that engendreth reuerence and honour, it is a tre havyng leves
wrapped to-gedre. The fourme of the leves and fruyt is rounde,
the tre of hym-self is moist and most swete of odour. Who-so-euer
taketh of that tree in his name and bereth it with hym, the vertue
of hym yeveth hym reuerence and honour. And ther is a-nother tre
20 that ryseth as longe as a mannes arme, havyng longe leves and
moist, havyng ther-in white leves. Who-so-euer bereth a substance
therof, he shall be honoured and exalted. And ther is a-nother tre
that hath full grete leves, and his palmites ben streight vpon the
erth, and the odour is good. And who-so-euer bereth therof he
25 shall be glad, light, worthy and myghty. With hym it is not good
for to stryve or fight, for his aduersary shall be slayn, and in his
operacion [he] shall have victorie. And of spices of trees is a certayn spice that hath cropp, and is planted, havyng oblong leves,
and the leves falleth fro the tree as she bere fruyt, and she hath
30 3 rede oblong floures of swete savour and odour. Who eteth tho
floures, he shall have joye and laughter, and who plukketh it vp
with leves and crop, and shaketh a-way the flour thynkyng of any
[f. 25] femynyn persone, that wolle stere her to kendle | in his love. Ther
is a-noþer tre cleped androsmon, and it groweth in þe land of Zyn,
35 and it is pleted to-gedre, havyng dry leves, and full lytell and
passyng smal sedes rounde, and withyn white. Yf þu take 7 cornes
of þat sede in the name of ony persone and bray þem in his name,
Venus arisyng, so that her ray[i]es touche them, yeve it hym to
drynk or ete, and þi drede shall abide stille in his hert, and euer

38 rayies] raynes (*or* rayiies?): *see n.*

he shall obeye the, duryng all þi lyf. And of spices and plantes
ther is oone þat gendreth langour, whos crop is planted, whos
bowes strecchen out as long as a man-is arme. þe floures ben white,
havyng leves and beryng no fruyt. Of þe propreté it is of Mars and
of Mercury, the nature of it of fire and of thaier. þe berer þerof 5
shall never be with ou[t] langour while it is on hym. And þer
is anoþer of the kynde of plantes, and it is sanatif, the sede þerof
sowe, the rotes square, the leves rounde, the floures of celestyn
colour. And the sede ben rede, and the odour swete and of good
tast. Who drynkeþ therof or smelleth, þe odour of it heleth hym 10
of þe pose, oþer of melancoly of thoughty mynde, of swellyng of
feere, of frenesy, and of many other siknesse. There is a-nother
plant cleped farrolidon and gendreth [hate and contempt].

Ther is anoþer plant cleped matynison and it is worthy to gete
love and reuerence therby. O Alexandre, I have fulfilled that I 15
promysed to the to trete vpon, and openly I have soiled it. Therfor
alwayes be manly and vertuous, and þe glorious God gouerne,
dresse and kepe the, Whos goodnesse euery creature perceyveth.

The 7 Boke, of Justice, and of the goodnesse that foloweth and cometh therof, &c. 20

Justice is a laudable comendacion of the propreté of the Highest,
Symplest, and Gloriosest, wherfor the reame shall be his whom
God hath chosen to and stablisshed hym vpon His seruauntes, to
whom is comytted the besynesse and þe gouernaill of his subgettes,
the which therfor shall espy, kepe and defende the possessions, 25
richesse, and the blood of his subgettes, and all their | werkes, as [f. 25ᵛ]
he were thair God. In this he is likened to God, that he shold
folow Hym in all his werkes. God forsothe is wise and konnyng,
and His precony and names ben glorious. In Hym is the magnitude
of lordship. He is most of all and aboue comendacion. Therfor 30
wisedom is contrarie to Iniustice, and his contrarye is Justice.
Thurgh meene of Justice, the hevens were created, and stablisshed
above the erthe. In Justice also were the holy prophetes sent.
Justice forsoth is the fourme of intellect, the which the glorious
God created, and brought forth His creature to hym. And by 35

13 hate and contempt] A *breaks off with* gendreth *in middle of line, and starts new paragraph* 19 *In* L, *this and following section displaced* (fols. 92 ff.), *occurring earlier, following section* Of kynges feithe (*as on pp. 43 f. above*), *and before section* Of promocion of studies (*as on p. 44 above*) 21 a laudable] a hie lawdabull L 23 vpon] þer-to L 29 names ben] name ys L

Justice the erthe was edified, and ordeyned were kynges, and obeying
and tamyng of subgettes, and by Justice is made meke terrible
thynges, and thynges remote approchen neygh. Soules therby ben
losed and delyuered fro all vices, and ayenst their kyng fro all
5 corrupcion. And therfor the Indiens seid, justice of the gouernour
and kyng is profitabler to the subgettes than plenté of tyme. And
also they seid þat the domynacion of a rightfull man is better than
the even rayn. It was founde in a stone writen and graven in Caldee
speche, that a kyng and Intellect ben brethren, ayther of them
10 nedyng other, and that one is not suffisant with-out that other.
And all thynges vniuersely ben created of Justice, and she is cause
of Intellect, for who-so putteth in beyng his operacion he is his
doer, and he is a rightfull juge. Therfor the beyng of Justice is his
root had of Intellect, and he is the wircher and brynger about
15 therof. He is his myght and operacion, he is his intencion, and he
is his speculacion of science. He is juge worchyng and resceyvyng
that þat is come of the act. In hym that resceyveth is that justice.
And it is double: open and privé. Open, it maketh the act wrought
with his condicions, and rightfull Justice peiseth and mesured by
20 that Intellect and iugement taketh hir name. Pryvé, for sothe, is the
feith or bileve of the juge worchyng his werk, and the certaynté
and confirmacion of his wordes. Therfor it apperith, as we said
before, that a kyng is likened in justice to the o God, and therfor
[f. 26] it sitte to hym þat he be stedfast and high | and all his werkes
25 propre and comvne. Who-so-euer therfor declineth fro propre or
comvne, it is no justice, for he most do after the justice of God and
His wille, and bileve fully that by his feith he executeth the law
that is the perfeccion of lordship. And as his werkes shewen, so
applien the hertis of his subgettis to hym. And such werkes as he
30 do, all such wolle his people do also, and therby the subgettes
wille deme by hym thair propretés. And the cominalté is in
dyuers grees, and trespassers of justice have difference therfro.
Sothly Justice is a novne relatif. But vnto a-noþer thyng it is correccion of wronge, and rightyng of weightes, and fourme of mesure,
35 and they ben names collectifes, and perteyneth to curialité, and
to the maner of largesse, and to operacions of goodnesse.

1 ordeyned] ordynat L.   2 of subgettes] of bestes and of subgett*es* L
3 remote] remoted (*indistinct*) L   5 seid] sayn L   6 kyng] kyng*es*
L   10 nedyng] nedyth L   suffisant] sufficient L   26 no] not L
31 cominalté] Comyns L   33 Sothly] for soþe L   it is] h*it* wull have L
36 operacions] op*er*acions L

Of the cercle and example of Justice

For sothe, Justice is had in 2 maners, and hath dyvysions. For
Justice perteyneth to jugement of juges, and ther is Justice perteynyng to man in reisonyng of hym-self, of that that is bitwene
hym and his Maker. Therfor stablissh Justice in this that ben 5
betwix the and thy peple, after commensuracion of thair maners,
and the setés of the reame. And Y shall exemplifie to the a laudable fourme, a philosophers sapiens full derworth, that shall shew
to the all thynge that is vniuersall in man that asketh gouernaunce
of subgettes, and shewith their degrees, qualitees and rootes, as 10
Justice most be handled in euery degree. It is diuided in 2 dyvysions circuler and rounde, and euery dyvysion is a gree. Therfor
begynne at euery of these dyvysions, and it wolle yeve the that,
that nothyng is precioser, and it is the cercle of þe firmament. And
when the vniuersall [r]egimen, oþer ordinacions, as wele byneth 15
as a-bove [be] to the conseruance of this world, me thynk that me
most be-gynne in such wise in this world, and this is the profite
of þis boke. And here is the figure: the world is a gardeyn or an
herber. His matir or substance is Jugement. Jugement is lordship
mvred with law. Law is the reame that the kyng gouerneth. The 20
kyng is þe pastour that is defended by his lordes and estates. His
lordes ben stipendaries susteyned with moné. Money is fortune
that is gadered of the subgettes. Subgettz ben seruauntes subiectes
to Justice. Justice forsoth is that is by hym|self intended, in [f. 26ᵛ]
the which is the helth of subgettes.   25

The 8 Boke, of substance simple, of speeris and of elementis

Understand that that first þat the almyghty glorious God
fourmed is substance simple and spirituell, in the ende of perfeccion and complement of goodnesse, in the which is the fourme of 30
all þyng, and is named Intelligence. And afterward of that substance goith out anoþer substance lesse in degree, that is called
the Soule Vniuersell[e]. And out of that soule is progressed out

3 of juges] of ius*tes* and Juges L   5 this] thys L   ben] byn L   7 setés]
Cites L   10 of] of h*is* L   12 and rounde] or rowunde L   gree]
degree L   13–14 that, that] þat L   15 regimen] vegimen AL   19 or
substance] and h*is* substaunse L   20 with] *with* þe L   23 the] h*is* L
26 L *resumes with this section on f. 108ᵛ, after section* Of takyng of medycynes
as on p. 64 above (*there entitled* Of yevyng of medecynes, *etc.*)   33 Vniuer-
selle] vniuerselly A vniu*er*sall L

anoþer substance þat is cleped Ile, before comensuracion that is
attended in length, brede and depnesse, in the which the body is
made symply. After that, the body hath a full noble figure that
ouercometh all fygures, and it is lesse in comparison and alder. It
5 abideth in the place of one of the speeris of the planetes for the
purenesse of it, sith it is sympler than the first. The rather therfor
of the speres is cleped the First Movyng, and ther ben 9 hevens
o[r] speres one ay within another. The first goth and closeth all.
After that is the sphere of the sterres fix, and than the spere of
10 Saturne, and the 5 other speres of the planetes, the mone lowest,
and with-in that the speres of the 4 elementes, of fire, aier, water
and erthe. So the erth is lowest of all the elementis, and is þikest
in substance betwix the assenciall bodyes. After whan, thes speres
were ordeyned one with-in other as it is before seid, after the wise-
15 dam and ordenaunce of the most highest and gloriosest God, in
disposicion mervelous and most ordinat fairenesse. And the speres
circulerly moven, and the planetis in thair cercles aboue the
elementes, and turnyngly ben ordayned vpon that, nyght and day,
wynter and somer, hote and cold. And comedled be some thynges
20 in some, and thynne is tempered with thik, and the hevy with the
light, the hote with colde, the moist with drye. Than componed be of
tham the length of tyme, vniuersell speces of componed bodies
that ben originall (o[r] mynerall), vegetable and anymal. They
ben therfor the originall of all thyng that is congeled in the bovell
25 of the erth, and in the depnesse of the see, in the holownesse of
montaynes, of fumositees inclosed, of vapours ascendyng, of
[f. 27] humyditees congeled in the holownesse of caves, in þe | which
erthly aier most lordshippeth, as gold, siluer, bras, iren, lede, tyn,
stones, margarites, corall, tutie, alum and such other, &c. Sothly
30 animal is all kynd that moveth, felith, and passith fro place to place
by hym-self, wherin lordshippeth most the aier. Vegetabill composicion is nobler than originall, animal more nobler than vegetable, and the man most noble in composicion of animal and of all
thynges lyvyng. And firenesse most lordshippeth in hym, and the
35 other 3 accorden in composicion, and ben found therin both
symply and componed. For man is of a body, thik or depressed

3 symply] si*m*pull L   5 for] and of L   6 rather] rath L   7 cleped]
callith L   8 or] L oo A   20 with thik] in thicke L   21 drye] þe
drye L   be of] he by L   23 or] of   29 tutie] tute L   30 felith]
and felyth L fro place] p *emended from another letter*   32 nobler] mor
nowbull L   34 firenesse] fairnesse L   36 For] and L   of a] of *om.* L

comesured, and of the soule, that is of symple substance and
spirituell. þerfor þu most, if þu be konnyng vpon sciences and
vertues in beyng, to take first vpon the the knowlechyng of thi
soule þat is next to the, above al other thynges, and so to know
afterward euery thyng in his kynde.   5

Of the soule

Understand therfor, þat þe soule vniuersell is light or strength
spirituell, had of intelligence þurgh God-is will, and hath 2
strengthes rynnyng in the body, as the light of the sone in parties
of þe aier. And eyþer of þese strengthes is a signe. The second   10
forsoth operant is lightned by the glorious God with 7 strengthes
þat ben cleped attractif, retentif, digestif, expulsif, nutritif, in-
formatif, vegetatif (and sensitif). The operacion of the strength
vegetatif in composicion of man-is kynd, is in reception of the
sperme in the woman-is priveté, and the disposicion þerof dureth   15
by 7 monthes. And whan this terme ordeyned of God and suffred
[is perfected] than chaungeth the soule animal sensitif, or sensible,
fro that, till he passe out of þat habitacle and geteth oþer gouernaill,
till 4 yere passe. Than the vertue resonable chaungeth the name
sensible, and gouerneth hym till 15 yere. And than the vertue in-   20
tellectif, and denunciatif of figures or likenesse, other of interpretacion of all sensible, gouerneth hym to 20 yeres. Than the strengh
judicial in prophecie or philosophie, that specialy medleth with
intellectual fourmes, hath the rule till 25. Than the vertue of kyndly
will gouerneth till 30 yere. And than þe roiall vertue explanatif,   25
þat is in kynges of thair originall, gouerneth to 40 yere. And þan
þe vertue legal, planted of and on his originall, gouerneth hym for
terme of his lyf. Therfor yf the soule perfet and complet be, be-|
fore his separacion fro the body, resceyved of the vertue animal [f. 27ᵛ]
vniuersall þat she hath highed and brought to the high perfeccion,   30
than it hath anoþer rule and gouernaunce, tille it come to the cercle
or firmament of Intelligence vnto whom it liketh it well. Truly
and yf the soule be not perfit, it slydeth into deppenesse byneth,
and than resceyvet gouernaill of hede [without] hoope.

---

6 L *displaces this section, to form it into conclusion of the work, occurring after
the Physiognomy fols.* 126ᵛ *f. At this point in* L, *the Physiognomy follows, as on p. 89
below*   11 by the] by *with* the AL   33–4 byneth, and] be nethe byndyth
and L   34 without] or of: *see n.*

Of man and of his 5 wittes, other of a kyng and of his 5 counselours

Whan God almyghty made man, and made hym noblest of bestis, He comaunded hym, He for-bade hym, He bihote hym,
5 and He rewarded hym and stablisshed his body as a cité, and his intellect as kyng in it, and sette it in the hyest and noblest place of the man, that is his hede, and made hym counselers to gouerne hym and to present hym all thyng that is necessarye, helpyng and kepyng hym from all noye. And he hath no hold neyther perfeccion
10 but by them. And he ordeyned euery of hem to have a propre dome, and seuerall fro other, and a propre maner of comunicacion from other, and that is gendred of gederyng and conveniences in beyng and perfeccion of thair werkes. Therfor tho 5 counselers forseid ben as 5 wittes that ben þese: the eye, the eere, the nose,
15 the tonge, and the hande. The eye that is sensat and visible hath 10 spices, þat is to sey, light, derknesse, colour, body, figure, place, remocion, and propinquité, movyng, and rest. The eeres sensat haue heryng of sownes, and ther ben 2 specis therof, animal, and not animal. The soune animal is double, that one resonable,
20 that perteyneth to man-is speche, and þat oþer vnresonable, as nyeyng of hors, chateryng of briddes and such other. The sowne forsoth not animal, is as brekyng of trees, and hurlyng to-gedre of stones, and such other vnto the which ther is no lyf, as thonder, tympane, or pipe, &c. Vndrestand wele therfor, that euery voise
25 or sovne, is whan the aier is moved and beryng hym, and with hym is moved the spirituell that ben nobill, so that the part be not medled with the part, till he come to the last, to the witte of his heryng, than þei ben deferred by the spirit vnto the vertue imagenatif. For-soth the tonge sensat is by tast and sauour, and therof
30 ben 9 sp[e]ces, þat is to sey, swetnesse, bitternesse, saltnesse, fatnesse, sovrenesse, dulnesse, fresshnesse, flatnesse, and sharpnesse. The wittes that ben in the handes ben 6, þat is to sey, touchyng, gropyng, course in hete and cold, rovgh, and smothe. |
[f. 28] The strength therof is conteyned and [planted] within 2 skynnes,
35 one of þe which is in the omest part of the body, and that other is that þat bilongeth to the flessh. Forsoth whan euery of these wittes ben had, the which God hath yove to His kyng, ther ryseth out of the rote of the brayn sotell skynnes and light, as webbes of

---

30 speces] spoces   34 conteyned and planted] insita et contenta B 133;
other possible readings in place of planted *include* implanted, fixed, infixed

areynes, and they ben as a vaill or a curteyn to this kyng. Therfor
whan euery of the 5 wittes presentith that that he hath to tho
skynnes that ben in þat substance of þe brayn, than ben gadered
all þe stappes of men sensat to the vertue ymaginatif, that re-
presentith, by that vertue cogitatif, that þat is in the mydell of 5
þe brayn, that he may se, gadre to-geder, and studie in their
figures and examples, so þat he may know þerby, þat þat anoyeth,
and that þat helpeth, and þat he may wirche after the mesure þat
cometh of tham. The constitucion and the existence of þe body
ben in the 5 wittes before named. The perfeccion of euery such 10
þing is in 5 thynges. The planetis, the luminaries except, vpon
the which moven the circuler speris ben 5. And kynde of bestis
ben 5, þat is to sey: man, volatile, and aquatik, crepyng and foure-
foted, and all thynge that crepeth or slydeth vpon the wombe. And
5 thynges ther ben without the which ther is no plant perfit that 15
waxeth in the erthe, and ther-in þei ben concurrant and accord
þere-with, þat is to sey: stok, braunche, lef, frute, and rote. And 5
ben comvsicall in songe, that without them the accord is nought.
And ther ben 5 portes of the see, &c.

Be therfor thy counselers in comprehension of thy werk, and let 20
euery of them be separat fro other, for than it is profitabler to þi
werk. Kepe therfor thy secret, and telle not to þem þe secretis
of thyn hert, and shew not to them of wheþer of hem þu haddest þi
counsel. And let them not wete þat þu beggist ony counseill of hem,
for yf þu do so, þei wille dispise the. Tempere þerfor in þi brayn 25
þeir willes, as þe brayn doth with þat that cometh to it of the wittes,
and declyne fro thair counsels þat contrarien to þi wille, so þat þu
be wele moved. And therfor Hermogenos seid, whan he was asked,
wheþer þe dout of hym is better of whom me asketh counseill,
þan of hym þat it is asked, he aunswered, 'The asker of counseill, 30
for his dome is sped be-fore, and of his wille passith a trew word'.
Therfor whan þu gadrest them for any counseill to be | yeve in thy [f. 28ᵛ]
presence, let none other mater be meved or handled with tham
but þat that þei come for. Here wher-in thei accorden, and y[f]
hastly þer þei accord and aunswere, than resist them, and shew 35
þem contraries, so þat þeir cogitacion may be prolonged and taried
to the last þat þei all be accorded. And whan þow perceyvest the

28 Hermogenos] o *possibly a badly formed* e *as elsewhere in this ms.: cf.* 26/38
78/6 *and contrast* 111/8: *cf. also* 74/30   34 yf] yeve

trouth of thair counseill, or of any of them by his word, þan put
þem to scilence, and let not them know wherin þi wille resteth,
till þu put it in act or experience. And considre diligently and sotelly
who most ledeth to trouth of counsaill, and after þe mesure of love
5 that he hath to the, and desire of thy prosperité and gouernaill,
resceyve his counseill. And be ware to put one before anoþer.
Make them even in yiftes, grees and werkes. What thyng is more
in cause of distruccion of a reame, and of kynges werkes, than in
slouthyng and lesyng of daies and of tymes, and in yevyng of more
10 honorificence to some than to others? For þei shold be peres and
egall in cherisshyng. And a yong man-is counsell is not incon-
venient. So þat it be holsome, after þat worche þu. And Y sey
þat jugement foloweth the body, and his genesis or burth is to
be considred in some thynges, for a man is disposed after þe
15 natures of the planetes þat had gouernaunce and strengh at his
generacion and burth. And peradventure his fader and his moder
wold teche hym or put hym to craft: the nature aboue full oft
draweth hym to art þat is convenient for hym. For it happeth in
like wise to certayn men that happeth to logge in a weowers hous,
20 and þat nyght he had a sone born, and þe men weren lerned in
astronomye and made a figure of the constellacion of his burth,
and founde Venus and Mars in Geminis and in Libra above the
erth. The contrary sterres and bad weren þan vnder the erth and
not risse. His burthe shewed that the child shold be wise, curious
25 of his hand, and of good and conuenient counsaill, and to be
biloved with kynges. They told to his fader no thynge þerof.
The child wax in prosperité, and his fader put hym to his craft,
and he coude not accord þerwith, neither to lerne it for no fair
spech ne foule, nether for betyng ne fleylyng. The child went
30 to scole with a konnyng clerk, and anon gate knowlechyng of
science so ferre that he knewe wele the cours and the tymes of the
[f. 29] bodies above, þe maners and the | gouernaill of kynges, and he was
made a counseller with the kyng and grew to grete lordship, myght
and power. The contrarye of this happeth of the mervelous wor-
35 chyng and disposicion of planetis and natures of them, in a kynges
sone. For whan he wax and grew vp, the fader wende to have had
hym konnyng in sciences, sende hym into Inde and into oþer
provynces, honourably, as it was sittyng, and he profited nought,
for his nature wold enclyne to no craft, save to be a smyth, wherfor

19 weowers] wedowers

the fader was gretly troubled. Therfor he assymbled his wisest
clerkes to wete the cause, and they declared that he was so disposed
and enclyned to at his burth. Such thynges in liknesse hath oft
happed bifore this.

How me shall chese a counseler, and how me shall take 5 counsell in all thynges, &c.

O Alexandre, dispise not litell stature in man, neþer none of
þem that þu seest love sciences, and habound in way of sapience
and of maners, and declyne and flee the pathes of vicious men.
Sothly such comonely be of good eloquence, is oft seyn, and 10
konnyng in stories. Therfor love such, and have them about and
by þe, and specially hym þat þu seest exercityng his wittes all
in vertues. And loke that þu do no thyng with-out his counseill,
and love his feleship, for such loveth trouth, and counseleth as it
sitteth to roiall magesté and removeth the contrary. Stedfast he is 15
in his inwit, constant in his hert, and trew and rightfull to thy subgettes. Vnderstand wele þat such conseil rectifieth counselers,
ordeyneth and augmentith the gouernaill of kynges, gouerneth
the reame. Neyther do no thynge of rasshnesse, puttyng before
that þat shold be put be-hynde, other his contrarye, neyþer in 20
maner no thyng doyng without counseill of philosophers. For
philosophres seyen that counseill is the eye of þynges komyng.
In bokes of Persiens it is rad that ther was a kyng in Inde, and he
asked of his barons and counselers counseill vpon a grete secrete
of love that he had to a quene. One of his counseilers answered, 25
that it was not necessarye to the kyng to aske an open counseill
vpon a grete secrete, but yf he dud it seuerely, for oft in such
privetees me may better and bolder telle it to one þan to many, |
prively than openly. So do þu, good lord. But I sey, not in all [f. 29ᵛ]
werkes but in some, consideracion had. Therfor it is convenient 30
þat þu calle them to thy presence in thair propretees, in byndyng
and losyng as Y have writ to the bifore. For a philosopher seid,
þat kynges wisedom is augmented by the counseill of good counselers, as the see is augmented by resceyvyng of flodes and waters,
and þat þurgh goode counseill and prudencie he myght gete more 35
þan by myght of fighters. And in a boke of Medes it was comended
to his sone seying, 'Sone, it is necessarye to the forto have counseill,
for þu art but one amonge men'. Therfor counseill hym that may

22 komyng] of komyng

delyuere the fro a mighty man. O Alexandre, spare not thyn
enemye, but, in asmoch as þu maist, whan euer þu have victorie
of hym, openly punyssh hym. And in all tyme be ware of the
myght of thyn enemye. Let not the habundance of thy witte,
5 neither þi bileve, neþer the highnesse of thy state, let the, but
[e]uer gadre oþer counseill with þyne, yf it like the, for it is to
be had and do, ay kepyng thyn owne counseill with the. And yf
they discorde fro the, than most þu see yf it be helpyng or profitable, and yf it be good, applye to it, and yf it be not, absteyn þerfro.

10   Of disposicion and nombre of counseilers

Besily and diligently Y warne the, and yeve the the best counseil,
that [n]euer þu ordeyne þe o counseler in gouernail of all thy
place. For his counseill myght destrue and corrupt þy reame, thy
wrecches and subgettes. For þei wolle attende their owne profites,
15 and thynk thy declinacion, and many oþer þynges þat were to long
to telle. For soth yf þu have not 5 counseilers þat pleseth the, as
Y have taught before, [let them be 3] and [no lasse], for grete profite
cometh therof, and specialy of 3, for but þe 3 with nethes shold
any þyng in counseil be wel canne. Therfor, þe first vpon whom
20 ben all kynges and all good thynges is þe Trynyté. And by the
nombre of 5 they ben halfed, and by þe nombre of 7 þei ben made
perfite, for þer ben 7 hevens, 7 planetes, 7 dayes in the weke, the
circuit of the mone 7, the dayes of pocion or of medecyne 7, daies
[f. 30] of perilles 7, and many oþer þynges | perteyneth to the nombre of
25 7 that were to longe to telle.

Signes and experience to prove a good or a bad counseiler by

O thyng ther is, wherby þu maist know thy counseiler, is þat
thow shew to hym that þu hast nede to money. And yf he induce þe
30 to destrue þyn owne tresour, feynyng hym pouer, and shewith þe
that it is expedient to the forto do so, vnderstond þat he putte no
prece to the. And yf he induce the to take by ravayne the money of
þy subgettes, þat woll be of corrupcion of gouernaill, and þei woll
hate the to moche. Truly yf he expone þat þat he hath, and sey that
35 þis is gate of grace and of your good lordship, and offer it to þe, he
is of right commendable and worth grete þank, for asmoch as he
chesith and wolle the confusion of his good for thy glory. Tempt

---

6 euer] ouer   17 let . . . lasse] sint saltem tres et non minus B 139

also thy counseilers in yiftes and rewardis makyng to tham. Whom
of them þat þu seest intendith and setteth his hert ouer moche
thervpon, trust that no good is in hym. And which of them
brethith in getyng of money and in makyng of tresours, trust hym
not, for his seruice is for gold, and he suffreth his money rynne 5
with wittes of men, and he is as depnesse out of ground, for
þere is no terme neither ende in hym, for the more his tresour
accreseth, the more is his wittes sette in besynesse of getyng. And
such a counseler myght cause the corrupcion of the reame by
many waies. And it myght happ that th[e] ardent love that he hath 10
to money myght induce thi deth, oþer his owne, for therto he intendith. And therfor it is convenient that thy counseilers be not
ferre fro thy presence. And comaund hym or them, that thei
have no treteis neþer havntyng of oþer kynges, or lordes houses,
and rede thair pistles or wrytyng, and write to them your privetés 15
and tydynges. And whan þow perceyvest any such, with-out any
tarying chaunge hym, and put hym a-way, for thair wittes [fall]
full sone and lightly to bihestes and to contrarie willes. And whoso
of thy counseilers inducith most of þi subgettis to thy love, he is
most profitable to þe, for he loveth best thy lyf and obedience.   20

Of good maners and vertues of a trew counseiler or seruaunt

Se at þe first he have perfeccion of lymmes, and accordyng to þe
werkes þat he is chosen for, and wherfor. Secondly, þat he have 24
godnes | of lernyng, and wille to vnderstonde þat þat is told [f. 30ᵛ]
vnto hym. Thirdly, þat he have good mynde of that þat he lerneth
or hereth, and for-yete not. Fourthely, þat he be consideryng and
perceyvyng whan any difficulté happeth, as Y taught you before.
Viftly, that he be courtly, faire spekyng, of swete tonge, and þat it
accord with his hert and cogitacion, and that he be sped in elo- 30
quence. Sixtly, þat he be lerned in all sciences, and specialy in
arsemetrik, that is an art full trew, makyng naturall demonstra-
cions. Seventhly, that he be trew of his word and lovyng trouth,
fleyng lesynges, of good makyng, of good maners and complexion,
softe, meke and tretable. Eghtly, þat he be not inordinat crapulous 35
in mete and drynk, þat is to sey, dronklew oþer stotlyssh, declynyng
from hasardrye and vnlefull pleyes. Nynghly, that he be of grete
hert in a good purpose and love honorificence. Tenghly, that he

10 the] thy   17 fall] declinant B 141

sette not his hert to moch vpon gold, siluere, or such oþer accidentes of þis world that ben contemptible, and þat is purpose
neþer his entencion be not sette but in thynges þat ben convenient to dignité and gouernaunce, and þat he love bothe his
5 negburghes and strangers. Eleventhly is þat he love rightfull men
and justice, hatyng iniurye and offence, yevyng to euery man þat
þat is his, helpyng oppressed men, and them that have suffred
wronge, removyng a-way all iniustice, makyng no difference in
persones [and] grees of men, for God created them all egally. Twelfly
10 is that he be stronge and perseuerant in purpose in þis, þat hym
semeth that he shold do, bolde with-out drede and pusillani-
mité. Thirtethly is þat he can all issues of expenses, and þat
no profite be hyd fro hym, þat shold bilonge to the reame, and
let not þi subgette have no cause to complayne in any thyng, but in
15 case suffred wherof profite may folowe. Fourtenthly is þat he be
not wordy neyþer to laughteryng, for temperance pleseth moch
men, yevyng hym curiously to men benyngly tretyng. Fyftenthly
is þat he be of the nombre of þ[em] þat loven not to moch wyne,
be his court open to all þat wolle come, and þat he entende to
20 espye and inquyre tydynges of all þynges comfortyng ay the subgettes, correctyng þair werkes, comfortyng þem in thair aduer-
sitees, omwhile deferryng and sufferyng þeir symplicité. |

[f. 31]   ## Of condicions of Man

Understande wele, that the most glorious God created never
25 creature wiser than man. And He sette neuer in oþer best þat He
sette in man, and þu shalt fynde [in] no oþer best consuetude or
maner, but þat þu shalt fynde it in m[a]n. For he is as bold as a
lyon, ferdfull as an hare, large as a cok, nygardous as a dogge,
harde and storne as a crowe, meeke as a turtle, malicious as a
30 leonesse, privé and tame as a colver, rogh and gylefull as a fox,
symple and meke as a lambe, swyft and light as a do or a pryket,
slowe as a bere, precious and dere as an elyfant, vyle and dulle as
an asse, rebell and clateryng as a lytell kyng, meke and humble
as a powe, wykked as a stork, profitable as a bee, dissolut and
35 vagabonde as a boore, wilde as a bulle, dombe as a fyssh, resonable
as an aungell, lecherous and malicious as an owle, profitable as a
hors, noyous as a movse. And vniuerselly ther is found no best,

9 and] in   18 þem] þat   27 man] men   33-4 rebell . . . powe]
see n.   37 movse] v ins. above

vegetable, originall (oþer mynerall), neþer hevene planet, neþer signe, neþer no beyng of all beynges havyng ony propreté, but þe same propreté is found in man. And therfor is Homo cleped the lytell world.

To have no trust in þe man that is not of thy law and profession 5

Never trust hym that beleveth not in thy law. And be ware þat it happe not to the as it happed by 2 men þat weren associed in a journé, of þe which one was a Cristen man, and that other a Jewe. The Cristen man rode vpon a mvle þat he hadde norisshed to his 10 plesure, þat bare his vitails, and oþer necessaries þat a travelyng man nedeth. The Jewe went a-foote, lakkyng vitails and all oþer necessaries. Thus sone þey talked, and þe Cristen man asked of þe Jewe what law and feith he had. The Jewe answered, 'I beleve that in heven now is God, whom Y worship, and abide to have 15 fro Hym the helth and goodnesse of my soule, and a reward to me and to them that accorden with me in my law, feith and bileve. And it is leefull to me whom Y fynde contrary to my feith and law to shed his blode, by-reve hym of his goodes, of wyf, childre, 19 fader and moder. Also Y am acursed yf Y kepe to hym ony | feith, [f. 31ᵛ] or yeve hym to lyve with, or do mercy to hym, or spare hym.' And consequently he seid to the Cristen man, 'I have shewed to the my law and my feith. Tell me certaynly þerfor of thy feith and of thi lawe.' To whom he aunswered, 'My feith, trust and law ben these. At the first I wille good be to my-self and to my childre and 25 their childre childre. I wolle do no wronge neþer harme to no creature of God-is, neþer to none þat kepith my law, other dis- cordeth þerfro. For Y beleve that evenes and mercy is to be obserued vnto euery lyvyng creature, and no wronge plesith to me. Me semeth that yf ought happe to a lyvyng creature, þat þat þyng 30 myght aswele happe to me, and that his hevynesse troubleth me. I desire also þat prosperité, helth, lustinesse and felicité happe to all maner of men vniuersely.' Than seid the Jewe, 'What yf offence or wronge wer do to the?' The Cristen man aunswered, 'I know wele that God is in heven and He is rightfull God and 35 wise, vnto Whom is no thyng hyd, secrete, neither vnknowen, of any thyng that is hid in His creatures, Who also rewardeth good- men for thair goodnesse, and bad and trespassours for þeir

5 þe] ins. above   30 a] followed by space containing erasure

trespas. Than seid the Jw, 'Why kepest not thy law, and why
confermest it not by dedes and werkes?' The Cristen man seid,
'What menest?' The Jw seid, 'Lo, Y am one of the children of thy
kynd, and þu seest me goyng a-foote bothe wery and hungery,
5 and þu art on horsbak, fed and in quyet.' The Cristen man than
aunswered, seid, 'It is trouth', and descended fro his mvle, and
losed his walet, and ete and dronk to-gedre as moche as suffised,
and made the Jw go to the mvle and ryde. And whan he was an
horsbak, he smote with the spores and hasted the mvle to rynne,
10 and left behynde hym the owner. Than the Cristen man called
and cryed, and bad hym to abide for he was wery. The Jw answered,
'Wost þu not wele how Y taught the my law? And now Y wolle
conferme it!' Than hasted the Jw his mvle and the Cristen man
hym, pantyng, brethyng and wery, folowynge, seid, 'O Jw, leve
15 me not in this desert, lest þat Y be slayn with leons and dye with
bad honger and dolourus thirst! Therfor have mercy vpon me, as
[f. 32] Y had vp-on the!' For all that, the Jw wold not loke bakward, | but
c[e]ssed [n]euer tille he passed his sight. Whan the Cristen man
was dispeired of helpe, recorded and mynded on the perfeccion
20 of his law and of his feith, and of that þat he had seid to the Jw
before, þat is to sey, how þat God is a rightfull juge, and fro Hym
is no thyng hid neþer prevé þat is in His creatures, dressyng vp
his hede vnto heven, [he] sed, 'My God, þu knowest þat Y have
bileved and bileve in The and in Thy lawe. And howe Y have
25 seintified Thy comaundement þu hast hedit. Therfor conferme at
the Jw my lavde in The.' These wordes seid, þe Jw went not moche
ferther, and the Cristen man come and found hym cast downe fro
the mvle, and his shynne broken, and his nek wreight. The mvle
stode stille a side-half, and the mvle, seyng his owne maister, went
30 to hym. The Cristen man toke his mvle, ascended and rode forth,
and left the Jw in jupparty of deth. The Jw þan cried, 'Moost leef
brother, for Goddes love have mercy vpon me, for Y am brosten
and in way of dying. Nede and pité rewe on me, and kepe thy
lawe that gaf the victorye, for thow hast ouer-come me.' Than the
35 Cristen man blamed hym, seying, 'Thow badly syndest in me.
Thow left me behynde the with-out any compassion oþer mercy.'
The Jw seid, 'Blame me never for thyng past, for Y told the
before my lawe and feith, wher-in I have be norisshed and
brought forth, accordyng to my parentil and aldres, þat euer

18 cessed neuer] cossed eu*er*

perseuereden in þat law.' Than had the Cristen man mercy vpon
hym, and brought hym ther as it was ordeyned, and put hym in
good kepyng. Natheles, sone after he died. Heryng þe kyng of þat
citee the werkes how the Cristen man did, dud calle hym to hym,
and made hym one of his counseilers, for his meke wordes and 5
goodnesse of his lawe.

How to chese writers to write thy secretis

Thow most chese to write thy secretes men that ben prudent, that
ben the st[r]ongist signe and myghtyest argument to shew the
quantité of thyn intellect and the sotelté of thy cognycion. For 10
significacion or interpretacion is [þe spirite], word [is þe body, and]
scripture is þe clothyng or garment. Therfor it behoveth hym to be
a man substanciall, faire chered and wele arraied. So it sitteth þat
þu chese thy scribes and writers þat have perfeccion in eloquence
ornat and in recordacion sotill, | as he is interpretator of thy wille, [f. 32ᵛ]
and is made privé to thy secretis and hid thynges. Therfor of nede 16
he oweth to be of good feith, of trew cognicion in thy wille, and
in all thy vniuersall werkes, and þat he intende þy profite and
honour, as it bihoveth. And yf he be not such, he shall do corrupcion. And he most be slighly and warly, þat no man se his prive- 20
tees neþer bokes. And Y graunt þat thow reward his werkis after
þe seruice þat he doth to þe, and after þe terme sette of thy wyll,
and after his besynesse in thy gouernaunce. Put hym þerfore in
degree of thy remvneracion, for thy prosperité is his, and his corrupcion is thyne. 25

Of privé messangers to be chosen, and who

Also vnderstand, that a messanger sheweth the wisedam of him
that he cometh fro, and he is eye in that þat he hereth not, and his
tonge in his absence. Therfor þu most chese the worthier of them
þat wolle happe be in thi presence, seyng honorabil, consideryng 30
trew, and declynyng, or fleyng, all filth or blame. And yf þu fynde
any such, calle hym to the, speke with hym, and telle hym thy wille,
and þan shalt þu fele yf it be in hym þat þu askest. For peraventure
it wille be with hym after none or toward nyght. And yf þu fynde
hym so, and not to thy determynacion, than send thy secretary 35
that is trew that wille not adde neþer dymynew in þat þat he is
sent with or for, but kepe thy comaundement and intendyng
to that that he hereth and make trew report vpon the answeres to

hym made. And yf þu maist fynde none such, let hym be trew in
beryng and presentyng of thy lettres to hym that they ben dressed
to, reportyng and bryngyng ayene an answere. And yf þu maist
know ony of the messangers besy about getyng of money or
5 beggyng it þere as he is sent to, se wele to hym, and thynk þat
he hedith not thy profite neþer worship. And send neuer no dronklew messanger and lover of wyn crapulously in message, for where-
euer he come in your bihalf þei wolle cherissh hym, and he may
bere no drynk. So shall þei know þat his lord þat sent hym is not
10 wise. Also, be ware þat þu send neuer þi priviest and grettest
counseller in message, and suffre hym neuer be long fro thi sight,
for þerof myght grow the destruccion of þi reame. Therfor preise
the qualitees of þi messanger[s], and reprove their infortunes,
[f. 33] as Y have taught to the | by-fore, by order, how þei shall be
15 knowen by trouth and good feith. Therfor, whan thy messanger
is not such, but setteth hym all to yiftes, rewardes and beggyngis,
he tresoneth the ther-in, and doth not as he was bid to do, and
sent for. And yf he [be] found such, and lacche in his occupacion,
I put no mesure, but Y wille þat þu put hym to infliccion and
20 affliccion.

To gouerne and to defende thy subgettis, and to make provostes vpon them

Now thow knowest þat þi subgettis ben the hous of the mooney,
þat is to sey, thy tresour, with whom is confermed thy reame. I like
25 therfor thy subgette to an herber wher-in be dyuers kyndes of trees
beryng fruyt, and have hem not as a place bryngyng forth wermode
and breres, and bryngeth forth no fruyt. For trees have in them
many braunches, bowes and stok erect, þat yeven fruyt and profitable sede to the multiplicacion of thair kynd, whan þei be wele
30 graffed and gouerned. Therfor, after the lytelnesse of thy tresour
is þe durabilité and defense of thy reame and thy power. In no
wise multiplie not to many dispensatours in makyng of grete
expenses, for þere-þurgh shall corrupcion rynne vpon the, for
euery of them, þurgh þe holdyng of grete company, trusteth to
35 ouercome his peere in corrupcion of his werk. And he wolle
streyne hym to shew hym trew to the and profitable, and þat
thurgh oppression of þi subgettes, and so wolle do euery of þi
counselers, euery of þyne estatis in thair offices mayntenyng and
for envie of other. And full many of them wolle sey oo thyng and

do anoþer, and corrupt many thurgh thair mayntenaunce and
defence.

The 9 Boke, in disposicion and nombre of astates other knyǵhtis, in and for ǵouernaill of the reame, and specialy in tyme of bataill

Worthy men in estatis ben the addicion and þe multiplicacion of
thy reame in thair degrees. þerfor þe best ordinacion and most
necessary is in thair degrees and thair disposicion, and that it be
not hid fro thair condicion, or ferre oþer neigh of þe nombre of
them, and þat is a full necessary ordinacion in propositure and
nombre, þat is referred and cleped nombre vnder nombre. Therfor
Y sey þat it is necessarie to þe forto have fourefold ordenaunce. For
euery place of the erthe is and hath fourefold difference, þat is to
sey, before, behynde, right, and left. And so ben þe specis of þe
world, þat is to sey, 4: est, | west, north, south. Therfor have þu
prouostes or comandours to gouerne euery quarter of thy reame or
host. And yf þu wolt have more than 4, lette them be 10 for [10 is]
perfit, for in that nombre is 1, 2, 3, 4, and this gadred to-gedre
maketh 10. The nombre of 10 is perfeccion of them þat complecten
4 and close it in nombre. Also let euery comandour have 10 vicaries,
and euery of them 10 leders, and euery of them 10 denes and euery
dene 10 men. The nombre of all wolle be 100,000 fighters. And
whan þu nedest the seruice of 10,000 men, sende for a comandour
or prouost, and ther wolle folow hym 10 vicaries, and euery
vicarie wolle bryng with hym 10 leders, and with euery leder 10
denes, and with euery dene 10 men. The somme of all wolle make
10,000 fighters. And yf thou nede 1,000 fighters, call i vicari with
his 10 leders, and euery of them with his 10 denes, and euery dene
with 10 men, and þere wolle be in all a 1,000 fighters. And yf þu
nede a 100 of fighters, comaunde o leder to bryng with hym 10
denes, and with euery dene 10 fighters, and the nombre of all
wolle be an C. And yf þu nede 10 fighters, comaund a dene to
brynge them. In this shalt þu be lighted in thy vitaill and expenses,
and have thy purpose, and lisse þi labour amonge thi astates.
For euery of them shall gouerne 10 lower than he in degre, and so
shal thy labour be lighted amonge them. But se þat thi prouostes or
comandours [be] sure, wise, and disponent. And it is full necessarie

22 100,000 fighters] C Millia hom*inium added above the line in the scribe's hand*
32 an C] 100 *added above in the scribe's hand*

to thy estate to have a good scribe or clerk, wise, witty, trew, and
consideryng, approved in chiualry, þat he see that your astate be
not corrupted with money. Enquere also diligently the wille and
thoughtis of them, and whan þu perceyvest any suche, remeve
5 hym, and gadre the remenaunt, and shew them the cause of his
remocion, and how þu haddest purveied for them. It is necessarie
therfor that he be treteable, curiall, not dispiser of oone for ferde
of a-nother.

Of a bataillous instrument helpyng the host,
10   and of the fourme þerof

Thow most of nede have with the the the instrument þat Themistius
[f. 34] made to þe help of thyn host, to distroye the enemyes. | And it
is a wonderfull instrument that is dyvyde in many maners. For it
may happe þe to visite a provynce or a reame, and þu most sodenly
15 gadre thy host in o day, or shortlyer, to-gedre. The sowne of that
instrument may be herd wele 50 myle. The which is a brasyn horn,
wrought with mervelous operacion, thurgh the sowne of the which
the worthy kyng Alexandre, whan he were in nede of destresse or
of bataill, sodenly fro 50 myle about in circuyte he wold gadre his
20 host. And the horne was gouerned by 50 men, for the mochnes
þerof and the inestimable workmanship, and it is full like þat
many kyndes of sovnyng metall ronne to-gedres in the makyng
therof.

Of gouernaill and disposicion of bataill, and of the fourme
25   to go to it.

Looke þu haunt not bataill[es] neþer expone þi soule and þe in
þem, but vse the counseile[s] of the worthiest of thy court, and
occupie the not in goyng to them as scomfited and shamles men
vsed forto do. Tempt not, neþer haunt not, bataill in thi persone,
30 but hold the worthiest of thy host about the. Occupie not, neither
noyse not, about such thynges as presumous bold men vsen for to
do in thair goynges to-gedre. For soth it is, þat þere strove neuer
kyng with kyng, but naturally þat one ymagineth how he may dis-
troye þat other. Therfor vnderstond þat envie is risen of body and
35 soule, oþer comyth of 2 repugnant contraries. And the spirit is
thair hope and trust of victorye of aiþer side, and thair bodies is the

11 Themistius] *four minims between* e *and first* s; *possible also to read as*
Thenustius   27 counseiles] counseiler

coniunccion of both parties. Therfor whan hoope faileth them they
dieth or yeveth vp the bataill, and as long as hoop perseuereth the
bataill dureth, for trust þat aither side hath. Therfor sette þi
strength and intencion in duryng and perseuerance of thyne, and in
stabilnesse and in sustentacion of þam þat beth of thy kynd, and   5
despise not þair persones as a dispiser, but here þem speke, bihete
þem yiftes and honours, and kepe þi promisses. Also wete wele þat
it is not sittyng to the to go in thyn host, but cooted oþer haber-
iovned, þat is to sey, harneysed, so þat þyne enemye sodenly fall
on the, oþer afray in þi men. þerfor be þi mynde and prouidence in 10
kepyng of thy self, þat, is | to sey, in armes, wardes [and] espies. [f. 34ᵛ]
And full necessarie it is to have wacche and ward both by nyght
and eke day. And make no bulwerkes ne strength of stone ne
tymbre but nye to hilles or waters. And see þat þu have a grete
market of vitaill with the, þeigh þu nede not half so moch. And   15
multiplie engynes to cast with, and þynges þat wille make grete
noyses and shoutes horrible, for þat wille cause strength and vertue,
durabilité and good purpose, of them þat ben with þe, and drede
and dyvysion of thyn enemyes: some with cast of dartes, oþer with
shot of arrowes and quarell, some in the foward, some in bataill   20
in the rereward, and some ordeyned forto rynne. And whan the
forward cometh forto fight, sette thaim in fair fourme and ordre,
and have towres of tre with men of armes þere-in, with shot fired
of arrowes quarell doudaynes. And yf þu se þem fals-herted and
faynt, comfort þem and induce them to perseuerance, oþer put   25
oþer better in thair places. Also ordeyne thy forward as it is writ
before and shall be hereafter. Stablissh at þi right side a kynd of
fighters and of smyters and aventurers, on thy left side a kynd
of spere men, in the myddes a kynde of shoters, and of casters of
wepen, shetyng fire and al-maner of shot, makyng grete noises and 30
terrible crying and sovnes, makyng many movynges. And yf þu
come to the place þere þat þu shalt with thyne aduersaries fight,
and whan þei perceyve þy comyng and ordenaunce, þei wille
stand first stille, and sone after cast sette on, than be ware of treson,
and specially yf þu se any part of thyn host out of array and vacil- 35
lant. Toward þat part dresse þi forward oþer bataill, sobirly,
actifly and manly, and euer haunte perseuerance and wisely settyng on, for ther-in lyeth the originall of victorye, wherfor it is
seid, þat victory may not come, till þat pusillamyté and feyntise

20 foward] *omission of* r *from* forward *perh. a slip: cf. ll. 21 and 26*

of hertis be ouercome with-yn tham-self. And than sette actifly on,
and multiplie thretynges, and ordeyn men to threten with terrible
noyses and sownes. And þat is of the nombre of ouercomyng and
victorying in the feld. And þer is a sleight and a cautile þat bryngeth
5 þe purpose about, to have victorye with, that þu have a determynat
[f. 35] place withyn the host stuffed with | vitaill to the su[c]course and
comfort of all the host. Mvltiplie also bestes beryng wardes and
castails of tree to fight vpon, as olyfantes þat ben terrible, and
have bestis swyft, as dromedaries, for at grete nede þei wolle help
10 as a castell. Yf þu besege any toure or castaill, ordeyne engynes
to cast stone with-all, and accordyng to nede multiplie þem. Vse
also instrumentes to thrill the wall with, and castyng wepynes.
And make stronge shot, and cast in piles venymed as gonne stones.
And yf þu maist, come to thair welles or waters and cast þere-in
15 poison and venyme, for so shalt þu destroye them. Obserue in all
perseuerance, for þat is full comendable, and bryngeth about thy
purpose. And folow neuer a man discomfited. And hast neuer in
none of þy werkes. And yf it be possible to þe, let all þy werkes be,
to be-gile treson and to ouercome þyne enemyes, and þerfor do
20 so þat bataill be last of thy werkes. For þe progenys of Jewes and
þe peple of Inde have ben ay traitours and begilers, and þat þei
hold for no reproof. Persiens or Tires, imperit and dull men,
natheles thei ben full hardy and of grete presumpcion. Therfor
fight with euery of thes folkes in suche wise as is conuenient to thy
25 werk. Make neuer a litell þynge grete, and do not bifore þat þat
shold be do behynde. And let þi werkes be after þe promyses, and
after the qualitees or disposicion of þe science of astronomye, as Y
have taught þe before, whan þu wilt have the suernesse of thy
purpos, after þe disposicion of þe bodies above. Se þat Leo be
30 ascendent, and se þat þe moone be in a good place of the cercle,
and þat he applie of frendlynesse to þe ascendent and to his lord.
And put þe lord of thascendent in þe houses of Mars, seying to
hym of a tryne aspect. Considre also all þyn operacion, whos
nature þu wilt have after þe strength of þe planetes and of thair
35 houses, and se þat þei accord in natures, for þat is þe hede of þe
werk. Whan þu wilt make a jorney, ordeyne the ascendent and the
third hous, oþer þe 9 hous, for þi jorney and for þe lord of tham,
the 4 hous for þe cité þat þu ert in or woldest wyn, the 7 hous for
[f. 35ᵛ] the place þat þu woldest go to, the myddell of þe heven, | that

6 succourse] surcourse   8 þat] *repeated*

is to sey the 10 hous, for jugement, worship, and profite of thy
werk, the 4 hous for the ende therof, wheþer it shall be good or
bad. Beware all-waies of the impedimentis of the moone, þat
she be not eclipsed, neither brent ne trouble with no bad aspect,
neþer in the brent waye, neþer in þe 6 hous, neþer in the 12 hous. 5
And yf a planet fortunat be in thascendent, it shewith prosperité,
good aventure happ, and specialy yf Mercury be without impediment in the mydle of the heven, it shewith accomplisshyng and
perfeccion of the werk, and yf he be in þe 7 hous, fortuned gladnesse, prosperité, and perfeccion of þi purpose. And yf he be vnder 10
the erth, in the 4 or 5 hous, and be fortuned þere, it signifieth
accomplisshyng of necessaries and prosperité of chaunces. And
beware all-waies, in the begynnyng of jorneys, þat þe moone be
not in a quartile aspect, oþer in opposicion to the sone. And yf the
lord of the ascendent be infortunat and be in the 7, þat is to sey 15
opposed to the ascendent, gif vp þi iourney. And yf he be þere
and fortunat, and specialy whan the lord of þe 7 hous is in the
ascendent, þu shalt sone sure and sauf retourne home, and thy
werk shall be accomplisshed. And yf þu wilt goo to bataill, put
þe hous of the moone in the myddes of the heven, and Mercury 20
frendly apperyng to þat hous and to the moone. And she fre fro
all impedimentes, in journeys is full profitable.

ꝫere begynneth the 10 Boke of Phisonomye, to know therby ꝫe qualitees of men after the outward parties of hym

Amonge all oþer þyng þu shalt not for-yete þe knowlechyng þat 25
þi soule may know and vnderstand by a full noble signe whan she is
with-draw fro carnell desires and concupiscens and is fre fro all
noyes. And þat division is knowen by þought, sithen forsoth the
soule of man is superans and lordshippyng vpon þe body and
preponderant to it, and the firy vertue þat is in the hert endith 30
not betwix hir and þe animal vertue þat is in þe brayn. þan is the
intellect, or vnderstondyng, su[b]ly[m]et, declared and augmented after mesure. Wherfor yf any aske the cause of prophetis,
þat have be proved in the world of pure intellect and of verray
vision, with myracles holpen bifore others, of þe premises [þat] 35

21 apperyng] e *written over* l   23 L (*f. 109ᵛ*) *resumes with Physiognomy,
immediately after the* 8 boke of substans simpull of Speris and of Elementes.
Phisonomye] Philosophie L   25 þyng] þyn*ges* L   30 to] vn to L
firy] furthur L   32 sublymet] sullynet A fullinet L sublimatur B 164
35 premises þat] premises A promisse þat L

[f. 36] comyth. And þis happeth of the | constellacion of the burth,
folowyng þe vertue generatif, as þu most aske signes and stappes
with fairnesse of nature. That is to sey, the science of phisonomy,
the which is a grete science, and by longevité of daies oure ante-
5 cessours and aldres have vsed it, and joyed in question þerof and
þe beauté of nature. The perfeccion wherof is attribuyd to þe old
Philemon, þat was an high doctour and maister of phisonomy.
And truly he sought, out of þe fourme and makyng of man, the
qualitees and the nature[s] of his soule. And in his story rynneth
10 a fair and straunge thyng: ordeyn þe þerfor vpon her, þat þu maist
vndrestond. I wolle establissh to þe of þis science of phisonomy
certayn rules and constitucions abbreuiat and sufficient. Be it to
the in grete price, of þe noblesse of thy nature, and þe purité of thi
substance. The disciples forsoth of the wise Ypocras peynted his
15 fourme in parchemyn and brought it to Philemon seiyng, 'Considre this figure and juge vs the qualitees of his complexion.' Who
biholdeth the composicion and þe disposicion of þe figure, and
comparet parties to parties, seiyng, 'This man is lecherous, a bi-
giler and loveth venerien actis and deliteth þer-in.' Wherfor þei
20 wold have slayn hym, seiyng, 'O fole, this is the figure of the most
worthi man þat is in the world.' Philemon corrected and pesid
hem, seying, 'This is þe figure of þe wise Ypocras. What aske
ye of me? Se þat after þis science I have shewed yow as Y felt in
hym.' Whan þei come to Ypocras, þei seid and told what þei
25 did and aunswered, and Philemon-is jugement. To whom Ypocras
seid, 'Certaynly, Philemon told you trouth and left behynd no lettre.
Sothly, sithen Y saw and considred þe foule and reprouable disposicion, I ordeyned and stablisshed my soule to be kyng vpon
my body and withdrow it fro the bad inclinacions, and Y had
30 victorie and put resistence ayens my concupiscence.' Therfor þat
is þe lavde and wisedam of þe werkes of Ypocras, for philosophie
is noþyng els but abstinence and victorie of concupiscence.

Of blode and colours and of thaire significacions

Ar we procede to jugementes or tokenes, it is to be vnderstand
35 þat blode, in þe which Lexus hath stablisshed þe sete of þe soule,

2 aske] take L querere B 164   4 is] ys called L est B 164   6 of]
þerof A (and, substant., L)   9 natures] nature A natures L investigabat . . . natu-
ras B 165   16 figure] signe L   26 told] sayd L   27–8 disposicion]
condicion L   28 ordeyned and stablisshed] ordenat to stabullet L
29 the bad] the om. L   35 stablisshed] stabullt L

sothly it is þe chere of þe body. It yeveth augmentacion | and [f. 36ᵛ]
strength and thiknesse of heere, fulsomnesse of witte and vnderstondyng, and sharpnesse of engyne. It constreyneth, it dulleth,
and it lettith. Yf þe blode be thynne and lytell, þe body is siklewe,
it deformeth his colours, all corporaltees it thynneth and maketh 5
leene, it lessith his mynd. It fauoureth his engyne, and yeweth
sharpnesse of inwitte, but it yeveth no mobilité neþer swiftnesse to
hym. Nathelesse all sensuell menbres þat in oure cheres ben constitut, o[r] sette b[y], eeres, eyen, and nastrelles, ben significatif
of blode. Wherfor mediocrité and temperance of body jugen and 10
shewen a perfit in-wit, and who-so hath a perfit inwit, he is egall
and even in vertue and wisedam, and so is his engyne, after þe
maner of temperance of the blood of þe which he toke his begynnyng. Therfor vnderstond þat þe matrix and moder is enbrion,
as a pot to boyle in mete. The colour redissh or rede, of the 15
blode, of hete it sheweth grete plenté. Paale colour, betwix
rede and white, meene and egall it sheweth complexion. Whos
cheres sheweth rede and clere, it signyfieth þat he is shamfast.
Whos colour is as a flame of fire, he is vnstable and suffreth
manyacy. Whitnesse with feblenesse, and yalow in colour, shewen 20
dymynucion of decoccion þerof. And yf þis hap in creature, dymynucion it sheweth, also lissyng of nature. Fle þerfor fro all men of
feble and yalow colour, for he is enclyned to vices and to lechery.
More-ouer, whos colour is grene or blak, it semeth þat he is ill
thewed. And whan þu seest oft any man beholden the, and whan 25
þu biholdest hym, he as a man scomfited or shamled, wexeth
rede and sigheth, or teres in his eyen appereth, dought not but
þat he loveth and dredeth the. And yf he do oþerwise he is envious,
bold vpon the, or despiseth þe. Be ware, and eschew fro, a man
infortunat þat failith ony lymme, as þu woldest be ware of thyn 30
enemy. Evener and more temperat is þe creature þat is accordyng
to meene statute, with blaknesse of eyen and heres, and with
gladnesse of chere, whitnesse forsoth medled with rednesse and
yalow colour, tempered with perfeccion of body and rectitude of
statute, and mediocrité, the hede betwix litell and moch, and seeld 35

---

3 engyne] yen L acumen ingenii R f. 89ᵛ   5 corporaltees] corpora-
lites L   7 yeveth] ȝeuyth me L   8 menbres] membris L   9 or sette by]
so sette ben A so sette byn L   14 moder] þe moder L   15–16 or rede, of
the blode] of red of blod L aut rubeus, sanguinis . . . innuit R f. 90   19 as
a] lyke L   21 creature] a creatur L   24 ill] euyl L   28 oþerwise]
oþer wayes L   35–92/1 seeld spekyng] spekyng sildyn L

spekyng, þat is to sey, with few wordes, but yf nede art it, and
þan meenly, and in þe sownyng of his vois sotell and not to
[f. 37] grete. And whan nature | declineth to blaknesse and carnosité,
þat signifieth good temperance and creacion. Lette þis plese the,
5 have þis with þe, and Y shall [in]terp[ret] and declar to the some
thyng by þe maner of separacion, and thou shalt tempere it in
rectitude of intellect and of vnderstandyng.

Of heres and thaire significacions

Understand of heres the most sure signes ben, þat ben with man
10 at his burth. The first forsoth ben the heres of þe browes, and of the
eyen. Therfor redissh colour of heeres is signe of dulnesse, and of
moch wrath and thretyng. Blak here sheweth rightfulnesse, and
love of justice. Who hath the mene betwix these both colours, that
is outward cleped bron, þat man loveth pease. Who hath heres
15 blak, foule, watrissh, or redissh fatty, he hath by disposicion a
violent and hasty inwit. Heres vnderblak, thynne, shewen good
thewes, so þat þei be not to moch depressed. Heres yelow and
whitissh vntechable and wild maners þei shewen. Heres vnder-
yelow, thyn and depressed, it sheweth good maners. Heres nessh,
20 and passyng thynne and rede, þurgh lakkyng of blode, it sheweth
womans witte. And the thynner þe heeres ben, the more gilefull,
sharp, ferefull, and of wynnyng covetous, it sheweth. Heres rough
and thynne, ferdfull and cold it sheweth the man to be. Playn
heres ben tokenes of fere. Heres forsoth playn and soft, ben sig-
25 nificacion of mekenes and of troublenesse of þe brayn. Crispe
heres omwhile manhode, omwhile fayntise it signifieth. Heres
depressed, to moch s[k]ewyng to þe forhede, it sheweth hym to
be declyned to a ferse or bestiall witte. Heres in þe myddell of þe
forhede sette, lokyng to þe brayn-ward, it sheweth a sligh, wise
30 man. Heres depressed, and wast abnut the temples and about þe
eeres, a curious and a lykerous man it sheweth. Heres by þe temples
thynne and fewe, a colde man with-out strength it sheweth. And
whan the last lyne of the heres sheweth to the forhede, it sheweth

---

5 interpret] deterpair A deterpar L et ego interpretor R f. 90ᵛ   12 moch]
to much L   here] eres L   14 cleped] þat ys L   Who] who so L   16 hasty]
a hasty L   17 to moch] much L   22 covetous] couetys L lucri cupidum
R f. 91   26 fayntise] fayntnesse L   27 skewyng] shewyng A squewyng
L iminentes fronti R f. 91   28 a ferse or] fers & a L   30 temples]
templers A tempull L   33 sheweth to the forhede] so., substant., L fronti
iminet R f. 91

þe man to be both lyfly and myserious, and whan it is gone fro the
forhede, hit sheweth hym to be sleighfull and of small intellect.
Whan þe last lyne of þe heres is long aboue fro the skull, it
sheweth hym to be slow, ferdfull, | femynyn and wrathfull. [Whan]   [f. 37ᵛ]
the last lyne of the heres of the bakhalf shadoweth, and is dyvided   5
by and þurgh the skull, and endeth above in the hight, a slygh
man with dull and luxurious inwit it sheweth. Multitude of heres
vpon the both armes foun[e]dnesse, madnesse, it signifieth. And yf
multitude of heres be vpon the nek and sholdres, wodnesse and
obstinacie it signifieth. Multitude of heres in the brest and wombe   10
sheweth horribilité and singularité of nature, and lyssyng of
lernyng, and founded love, and smalnesse of sapience. In the
wombe namly plenté of heres founde, it sheweth lechory. Vpon
the ribbes yf moch here appere it sheweth boldnesse. Here in all
places of the body founde, it shewith drede and fere. The skyn   15
of the hede yf it be ryveled or slak, a resolued inwitte femenyn
and nessh it sheweth. And yf þei be hard depressed or a-streigned,
a man askyng lavde and nygh-by a foole it shewith hym to be.

Of the hede and of his significacions

The hede omwhile, whan it is more þan oþers ben somwhat, it   20
sheweth and maketh more vertues and magnificence. A grete hede
with an high forhede and slow in chere, a meke man and omwhile
a man vntaught and a stronge man, it declareth. A to grete hede
sheweth a man to be dull, a foole and vntaught oþer vntechable.
A short hede is a signe of no wit neþer wisedam, a longe hede   25
sheweth the same to be imprudent, a pryk hede is a signe of sole-
ynesse. A moderat hede sheweth engyne, sapience, and thryvyng
inwit, omwhile ferdfull men and liberall. The hede swollen in the
for-part a soleyn man it sheweth. The hede in the forpart holow, to
gilis and anger he is enclyned. An hede like a flogge [both] before and   30

---

1 myserious] mis*erous* L   5 shadoweth] schewt L   dyvided] de-
lu*eryt* L desinit F 25.   6 hight] hed L: *see n.*   slygh] sle3th L
8 founednesse] founodnesse, *but vowel of* -od *may be badly formed* e A *om.* L
9 sholdres] þe schulders L   16 be ryveled or slak] reuylit or slak*ith* L
18 nygh-by] ny3th to L   20 The hede . . . is] When þe hed omquile ys L
22 an high] a he3th L   25–6 a longe . . . imprudent] a hede prolixe is a signe
of imprudencie, a longe hed shew*eth* the same to be imprudent A (*and, subst.*
L, *but with the opening words* I have hed prolixe)   30 anger] angery A
anger L (angery *conceivably the intended form?*)   30–94/1 both before . . .
sheweth] a redy man before and be-hynde it shew*eth* A a redy ma*n* boþe by-
hynde and by-for it scheweth L

be-hynde, a redy man it sheweth. An hede streight and in the myddes light and þerby playn, omwhile more ouer myddell image, he is myghty in wittes, and it declareth his magna[n]y[m]yté.

Of the forhede and of his significacions

5   A streyght and narow forhede, vntaught, vnclene and a devovrer
[f. 38] it signifieth. Who-so hath a litell forhede, he | is a foole. A sp[a]ciose forhede sheweth slow engyne. A large forhede signifieþ slouth. A l[on]ge forhede sheweth a man taught, and to preuaile in wittes. An humyl forhede is not manly. A croked forhede rounde and high
10 is a signe of dulnesse. A square forhede of moderat mochnes accordyng to the body and cheris, of grete vertue, wisedome and magna[n]y[m]yté is a token. A forhede contynuell and playn, it sheweth a man þat gretly chalangeth honour above his deservyng. Whos forhede is playn with-out ryveles or lynes, he is a stryver or
15 a mover of debate. A forhede [meu]yng neygh the hede, it sheweth a man to be soleyn. Whos forhede in the mydell is gadered to-geder, or streight in the mydell, he is wrathfull. Whos forhede is to full of ryveles vpon the brow, retract or with-draw, and specially who hath them so at þe ende of the nose, ben grete thynkers. Who hath slak or
20 diffuse skynne of his forhede, þei speken as laughters or flaterers and þei be in maner noious. Who hath a rogh forhede wyly they ben.

Of eyen lyddes and thaire significacions

Who in his eyen liddes hath moch heere, thair significacion [is] to be full of cogitacions and of moch hevynesse and his [speche] is
25 foule and grose. The eye liddes that hath moch heres signifieth hym to be vnapt to speke. And whan the eye liddes streynen to þe temples than is he envious. And who hath the eye liddes longe, he is provd and shamles. Whan the eye liddes be long and prolixe, bad and dull inwit it sheweth. The eye liddes whan they comen to-
30 gedre, a full sorowfull man and litell witte it sheweth. Croked eye liddes and litell, angustious mynde it sheweth. The eye liddes þat

2 omwhile more] oon while and L   3 it declareth his magna-
nymyté] it declareth his magnamynyte A   he declareth magnanimité L
5 narow] a narow L   vnclene and a] vnclenid and L   6 spaciose]
speciouse A (and, substant., L)   8 longe] large AL oblonga R f. 92
and] om. L   12 magnanymyté] magnamynyte A magnamite L
15 meuyng] supplied from L shewyng A: see n.   the hede] to þe hed L
17 to full] full L   20 laughters] lawthres L   23 thair . . . is] and thair
significacion A (and, substant., L)   26 streynen] strevyn L   30 litell] a
lytyl L

croken down to þe eyen signifien vpon envie. Whos eye liddes ben
thynne and comensured in length and shortnesse, and ben grete,
it is a signe þat is of light impression forto vnderstand. The heres
of þe liddes whan þei be fract to þe forhede-ward, vpon hard foly
and wrath it signifieth. Whos eye liddes descendeth toward þe 5
nastrell and þat oþer side is reised vp toward þe tymples, he is
vnclene, a foole, | shamles, insaciable, dull, for he is condicioned [f. 38ᵛ]
like a hogge. The lidde, and þat þat sheweth, and þat þat lieth
vndre the eye, more swollen þan full aboue, sheweth vpon þe
slomeryssh man and a violent.   10

Of eyen, aplis therof, brewys, and vp-on thaire significacions

The disputacion of eyen now is to swe, wher-in all the some of
phisonomye is constitut. For of oþer parties yf þe signes of the
eyen conferme them, þei ben þe more stedfast and certayn. Of þe 15
signes and tokens of þe eyen is gretly affermed in the sentence of
phisonomy, and here is all auctorité constitut. Sothly what we sey
now, and what we sey here-after, in jugementis of þe eyen, so þere
be no repugnance neþer ambiguité þurgh þeir sentences, it is þe
more ratified. Whos eyen be grete he is slowe, shamfast, envious, 20
inobedient, and namly yf þei be palissh. Whos eyen be litell, he is
bad or a foole. Yf one eye be more þan þe toþer, he is a mever of
malice and of foly. Whos eyen ben meene, declynyng to hevenly
colour, oþer to blaknesse, he is penetrable of intellect, curious and
trew. Forsoth eyen þat ben meene betwix blak and gray ben right 25
good, so þat þei be not radious, neþer þat white ne[þer] citrine
appere not in þam. These eyen shewen good nature. Tho eyen ar
worst þat haue about þem rede wemmes as blode, oþer white, oþer
blak, for þat signifieth þat he is a begiler, and worst of any, and
most reprouable. Whos loke is like to a womans loke, he is lecherous. 30
Who hath eyen like a cat oþer a ratte, it is a signe of wodenesse and
braynlesse. Who hath eyen like to an asse, he is dull and of hard
nature. Who hath eyen like to a gote or kid he is a foole.

4 fract] fractyd L   13 is] h*it* ys L   14 parties] p*artes* L   19 neþer]
and L   20 Whos eyen . . . slowe] *foll. by* Who hath grete eyen he is slowe
A   21 inobedient] Inobediens L   22 þe toþer] þe oþer L   23 de-
clynyng] and declynyng L   26 neþer²] ne *ins. above* A in þe L
28 wemmes] wemense L   32 an asse] a nasse L   33 kid] a kyd L

Of eyen lokynġ vp and downe depressed

Eyen lokyng vp, yf þei be rede and grete, þei signifien vpon a full
bad man, dull, a foole, and dronk-lewe. Eyen torned vp-ward
4 sheweth a maner of madnesse and a devovrer, and a man yove to
[f. 39] vices and venery. And yf any quakyng | be in them, tho vices woll
be stronger. And yf þei be pale, it sheweth vn-pacient and men-
sleers. Yf þei [ben] redissh and grete, þei ben violent; in women,
furious and vntemperat of þair tonges. Truly grete vnholsomnesse
and wodnesse in such maner is in such eyen. Eyen [þat] tourne
10 downward as þei were westerynges or goyng to glade, it sheweth
vn-meke and vn-plesyng folkes. And yf þei weren turned vp-ward
in any such spece, and yf quakyng be with-all, and þe eye liddes
ben vnderryveled, and þe breth be cold and thik, of þat it is pro-
nounced þat he hath epilency. Whan þe eyen ben sette in length
15 of þe body, þat sheweth hym to be sligh and a begyler. Whos
eyen ben extense with extencion of his chere, he is malicious and
wiked. Litell eyen tornyng to þe right side sheweth foly, and yf
þei declyne to þe left side, it sheweth hym to be yove with lust and
lykyng. Whan þe eyen ben litell and comen to-gedres by þe nose,
20 it is a signe of lechory, and þe more yf they be moist, and yf þe
browes joyne to-gedres. Also it sheweth hym to be venereus-kynd
and lovyng. And yf þe eyen be drye, þat sheweth inprudencie and
wikkednesse, and yf þei shake, they ben wikked, vnworthy and
bolde.

25 ## Of eyen depe and holowe

Eyen therfor full holow generaly as by rule have þe worst significacion. Sothly yf þe eyen be vnder-meued with water, þe eye
half full is moved, and þei ben grete and none oþer bad signe be
had, þei be not to be refused. Vnderstand þat holow eyen is a signe
30 of badnesse. Grete eyen and holow is a signe of envye and of deceit, and yf þei be dry, þei shew vntrouth, treson or sacrilegie to be
in hym. And whan þei ben sterne and holow, it sheweth wodnesse.
Also yf þei be holow and wepyng, of sorow and of malignité þei

---

4 yove] ȝevyn L   9 in such¹ . . . eyen] so, substant., L: perhaps
for is in such maner eyen   Eyen þat tourne] Eyen tourne A Eeyn tran L
10 westerynges or] westeryng and L   12 þe eye liddes] all þe yen liddes L
14 epilency] epilence L   14–15 in length of] ouer length oon L
16 malicious] malicolius L maliciosus R f. 94   18 yove] thewe (for
thewed?) L deditum R f. 94   19 to-gedres] to-gedur L   22 inpru-
dencie] inprudence L   29 holow eyen is] holow yen byn L

ben signes. Eyen þat in thair derknesse ben moist, þei ben fooles.
Eyen full holow of þe meene magnitude, drye and sterne, yf þe
liddes aboue be brode and emynent, and palenesse is about the
eye, it sheweth hym to be imprudent, wikked, vncertayn, and
neuer at rest. Whos eyen also be sette in depnesse, he is slightfull 5
and a begiler, and yf þei be litell and holow, it sheweth | vp-on [f. 39ᵛ]
sleight and bolnyng out.

Of eyen sette high and bolnyng out

High eyen and elate, þei ben bad in signes, and specially yf
swellyng be about them, þat sheweth wodnesse. Where þe goyng 10
about þe eye is holow as a dych, þat sheweth a gilefull mynd and
a thretenyng. Bolnyng eyen and sanguinolent, a man [dronkelewe]
it sheweth. Yalow in colour sheweth an vnrightfull man and a dull,
so þat þe liddes be charged or growed with any thyng. Yf they
bolne and be drye, it is a goode hope of good eyen, and yf þei 15
be fair and shewyng grete, moist and clere, it is a signe of a rightfull
man and of a lerner and of a prudent. Such eyen me troweth
that the sacred philosophers had, as Apollophicius þe prudent
clerk seith. Eyen moch bolnyng, rede and smale, it sheweth an
vnhelthfull mynde and a tonge bridilles and full vnstable of his 20
body. Whose eyen outward shynen, he is shameles, a clatterer and
a foole. If þe eyen be lytell, and bolnyng outward as þe eyen of a
[crevise], it sheweth folynesse and dulnesse, and a man folowyng
cupidité. Eyen whirlyng about sheweth impacientis without pité,
to women and belly plesaunce and lustis all yoven. Ther ben eyen 25
closed about with a yalownesse, and but if þu see þe better signe
with-in, take þem of þe worst part, for þei ben bolde and vnhappy.

Of eyen moche shakyng

A man havyng eyen moch tremelyng, he is bad. Who hath gret
eyen and quaueryng, he is slow and wandryng, and lovyng women. 30
Whos eyen ben small and tremlyng and varying, he loveth gretly
women. Qvaueryng eyen more blak þan yelow, þei ben full wroth-

3 palenesse] palynes L   5 slightfull] slowthfull L callidus
R f. 94ᵛ   10 þat sheweth] hit schewith þan L   11 dych, þat] dysch hit L
12 dronkelewe] *word omitted with blank space left* A *word omitted without blank
space* L temulentum S 49, R f. 95   16 fair and shewyng] swellyng L
is a signe of] signifeth L   17 me troweth] Y trow L   18 had] hase L
Apollophicius] pollophicius L   23 crevise] *word omitted, with blank space left*
A *word omitted with no blank left* L ut oculi cancri S 165 ut oculi canistri R
f. 95. *see n:*   31 tremlyng] tremulyng L

2550 C74   H

full. Eyen quakyng, shynyng and lepyng, þat sheweth giles and
deceytes, and yf þei be grete, foly and wodnesse. Eyen of moderat
magnytude and clere sheweth goodnesse and grete doyng, and of
grete þoughtis perfeccion, natheles omwhile wrathfull, vinolent,
5 and covetyng glory aboue oþer men. Some seith þat kyng Alexander had such eyen. Oþers seyn nay, but þat he had an eye parted
with rede and grey.

Of derke eyen

9   Eyen þat ben derk ben noyfull, and moch þe more yf þei be dry.|
[f. 40] But no force wheþer þei be grete or smale, but þat euer þe smaller
sheweth þe more wikkednesse. Derk eyen, holow, of temperat
mochnesse, so þat þei be stabill, shew a techer, and to teche and
lerne covetous, ripe, dredfull, and nygardous y-now, and full
chast. Eyen webbed or perled, þei ben lerned with bad craftes, þei
15 ben vntrew and intemperat. Wherfor me shall vnderstond þat þeir
contraries is best, þat is to sey, bright and clere, if þere happe none
oþer impediment. Such eyen seith Palamon Andor þat þe Emperour Adrian had, humble, egre, grete of light, and full. Sothly
the sight is good of bron eyen.

20   ### Of bright eyen

Coruscant eyen, yf þei be yelow and sanguinolent, þei shewen
foolehardynesse and nygh-by wode. Croked eyen, suspeccion
sheweth. Eyen glysteryng as yse, and shynyng, sheweth a gilefull
man, bolde, playn, a waker, a gatter of þynges by malice. Eyen þat
25 as dropis of shynyng liquour relusent, blissed and soft maners and
kyndly it sheweth. Blak eyen coruscant sheweth a dull and ferdfull
man. And whan þei ben medled with laughteryng, it is an high
þyng of imprudence and malice.

Of eyen sharply lokyng

30   Eyen sharply beholdyng, the Greke seith þat he is grevous. But
whan þei be moist it sheweth hardynesse, shame, and besy in his
doyng; redy and not noyous it is a token. Sothly who loketh sharp

---

1 quakyng] wakefull L trementes R f. 95ᵛ   4 vinolent] and violent
L violentum R f. 95ᵛ vinolentum S 167   5 some seith] men saying L
13 lerne] to lurne L   14 webbed] wewyd L   17 Andor] andor (or audor)
A om. L   32 loketh] lokes L

in the eye, be litil, dry and holow, ben olde, envious, [hardely and] prively noying, moch þe surer yf þe eye be light. It yeveth also by such eyen, the forhede to be gouerned with þe brewes, and to be exasperat by þe eye liddes. This is a circumstaunce of strength, of boldnesse and of hardynesse, and to be as a juge conseilles and 5 moch noying it signifieth. The eyen, the forhede, the browes, and þe liddes in rest, and tranquill and light, the sight with-yn sharp and gurchyngly lokyng, þat sheweth cruelté and grete ill wille and deceit to be juged þerby.

Of laughteryng eyen 10

With laughter delitfull eyen medled þei ben not laudable. For whan þei ben dry and vnder-laughteryn þei ben juges of malice. But holow eyen, whan þei laughteren, as to thretynges they ben sette, and moch þe more yf þe liddes of þe eyen twynkell | and the lippes [f. 40ᵛ] move. For such laughters, or ill thoughtes or bad conceit, other 15 sorow, it signifieth. And also with þese signes the browes amonge knytten to-geder, omwhile a-large and a-monge the eye twynkill, þei bewreyen ill and wikked þoughtis to be with-in. And yf the eye[n openen out] with laughter and knetten togedre, þat de- clareth joye after a wikkednesse done. þerfor the more the eyen 20 laugh and be drye, þat sheweth the laughter to be more perillous. And yf þei laugh feyntly, it sheweth þe man innocent in inwit, dull with-out effect or prudence oþer chastité. Whan þe eyen vnder- laughen softly and moistly, with all þe chere [in] [o]þ[e]n oþer absolute gladnesse, and þe browes, þe forhede, the liddes, soberly 25 or slakly in oo state of þe eyen, engyne, gretedoyng, rightfull, meke, religeous, kynde, wise and wele taught it sheweth hym þat doth so. Whan a man, as a child doth, loketh streightly with face and eyen and maketh chere of laughteryng, it sheweth gladnesse, and he shall [haue] his daily foode while he lyveth. 30

1–2 olde . . . noying] olde, envious, prively noying A old and envious, hardely and priuyly noyng L saevos, insidiosos atque ex occulto nocentes S 53: see n. 4 exasperat . . . liddes] experte with þe ye by þe ye lyddes L praestat . . . supercilia exasperari S 53 5 conseilles] consilees of L 7 liddes] ee lyddes L light] lightes A (and, substant., L): perh. the intended form 8 gurchyngly] gruchingly L 12 vnder-laughteryn] vnderlaw- teryng L 15 conceit] conseytes L 18 þoughtis] þoughteis A; thowȝtes L 19 eyen openen out] eye followed by blank space A ee with lawȝtur L propate- ant S 54 pateant R f. 96ᵛ 22 in inwit] in witt L 24–5 in open oþer absolute gladnesse] vpon oþer absolute gladnesse A þer apon absolute gladnesse L ubi totius vultus aperta atque absoluta laetitia fuerit S 55 cum tocius uultus apta atque absoluta leticia R f. 97 30 haue] supplied from L, om. A

Of hevy eyen

Hevy eyen sheweth alwey feere and feyntyse, and yf þei be
moist, in studie of grete artis or craftis þei be sette. And yf the
lyddes ben slak and þe forhede brode, with tranquyllité convenient,
5 and þe browes ben laudable, þat sheweth benigne engyne, trew,
and of grete þoughtis. And yf þei be hevy and dry and sharp in
lokyng, and þe browes vndre streight, noiyng-to-a-theef þei weren
eyen. And yf oft close and shit, bad maners, thretynges and noyous
it sheweth. The contrarie shewith a man to be occupied with good
10 art and science. And whan þei ben not moist but quaueryng, and
with pallour medled, þat sheweth appoplexie oþer suerly wodnesse,
neigh to whom such state abideth. And his brewes above-maners
knytten, þei ben smytte with vnhelth and wodnesse. Eyen þat oft
ben flowissh, þat sheweth grete þought. Grey, whaþer it be good
15 or bad, draw it out of þe qualitees before. It is open þat grete,
profunde and nessh eyen ben best of thought and of contennance.
And in þat other side, dry, derk, smale and holow, direct and hard
eyen, ben significatifes of bad cogitacions.

Of eyen shewyng and open

20 Open eyen sheweth a man vayne and astonyed. Staryng eyen, |
[f. 41] shynyng and lightly intendyng, as tham þat be contumacied and
askyng grace it sheweth. Eyen þat oft closeth and shitteth, it declareth a man to be feynt and ferdfull. And yf with that þei ben
dry, he thynketh gile and to privé manaces he [in]tendith. And yf
25 þei be peruerse or pale, foly it sheweth. Also who terribly putteth
his sight, he is vexed with ill thoughtis. Yf the state of his eyen
have any moistur, and meke and soft, tho ben studiant, sobre and
lovers. And yf immobill, pale or rede, with drynesse ben the eyen,
tho ben signes of wrath, wodnesse and of dyuersité. And yf with
30 tho signes they rollen about as a-writh, it sheweth a full grete
wodnesse to be appropred to hym. Also who-so-euer lightly
moveth his browes and knytteth them vnder dyuers movyng of
þe apple of the eye, and closeth lightly his eye lid, it is a signe of
feyntise. Who also that one of his browes lightly depresseth and
35 lightly reuokith, and dressith tham, desiryng fairenesse therby,

---

3 þei] that L   7 noying-to-a-theef] A *and, subst.*, L feri S 56 & fieri
R f. 98ᵛ: *see n.*   11 appoplexie] appexen L   24 manaces he intendith]
mana*ces* he attendith A maners he *yntendyth* L ex occulto insidias tendere
declarant R f. 99   28 or rede] and red L uel R f. 99   29 tho] that L

that sheweth them vnchast and avowterers. Omwhile the ouer browe is deduct to the myddell, and meveth theder and theder; in like wise doth the eye vnder-neth: these ben open signes of lechours and of avowtrers.

Of eyen standyng

Eyen with humour standyng, of feyntise ben juges. Whos eyen with drynesse standen, and pallen, they ben not hole, but ben astonyed in thair mynde. Who also with stabilnesse liften vp the liddes of thair palled eyen and drawen thair breth violently, impacient, vnwise, cursed and wrath-full it sheweth them to be. Eyen vnder-rede standyng, likerous and devowrers it sheweth; short eyen standyng, a nygard, covetous and appetiter of wynnyng. Standyng eyen, smal and moist, with a slak forhede and browes movyng, that sheweth a lerner, a techer, a thynker and a naturell disputer. This is þat one spece þat is approved in stabill eyen.

Of eyen lightly movyng

Whan the eyen lightly moveth and the sight is sharp, that shewith a man fraudelent, a begiler, vntrew, slye and a thef. And whan litell eyen ben moch movyng, openyng and shittyng, and þe browes moveth also, þat shewith a faynt ferdfull, a manyak and worst. Eyen that ravently and swiftly moven, that | shewith [f. 41ᵛ] a man troubled in inwit and suspected, and slow in his doynges. Who-so-euer browes and eyen meven y-like swift, they ben hardy and sure men. Vagabond and whirlyng eyen aboute and derk, intemperance of lechernes it shewith. Quakyng eyen and grete, whan þei ben derk and erren it shewith devowryng, and vntemperance of wyne and women, and appopelixé.

Of slowe eyen and late movyng

Whose eyen ben immobill as a stone, he is sleightfull. Wete eyen and hote and stabill, shewen þem redy in venerien lecherousnes. Whos eyen late meveth, he hath slow and sloggissh wit, hard and

---

1 Omwhile] oon wile L   6 juges] iugesse L indices R f. 99ᵛ
18 shewith] *for* -ith *expansion from here to end of text, see n.*   20 ferdfull]
ferefull L   21 ravently] rauenly L   22 doynges] goyng L in rebus agendis
R f. 100   23 meven y-like] meuyng in like L   27 appopelixé] appolesie
L apoplexiam R f. 100   29 sleightfull] slewthfull L   30 lecherousnes]
lecherouse L

loth to begynne any thyng and so to leve it, wherthurgh it is open
knowen, þat no mevyng resonable is attemperance and best maners
apropred.

Of eyen glavk or whitissh

5   There ben many maners and spices of glauk eyen. For some ben
tany, gallish grey, and of dyuers colours and dry. Forsoth drynesse
shewith bestiall maners. Tany moist ben better þan drye eyen.
Glavk and white, a faynt and fleyng man it shewith. Litell glavk
eyen, it shewith a man to be with-out shame and without feith
10 and justice. Grey eyen havyng a litel of cityrne colour, as a safred
cercle goyng about it, shewith tham þat hath worst maners. Therfor above all other, the best kynd of eyen ben the glavk spice, whan
they ben somwhat moist, tranquill, grete and bright. Vnderstonde
wele that in that spice is hardynesse and engyne. Ther ben oþer
15 grey, half glauk. But first of glauk in the which is variaunce, talk
we, as litell dropis in the applis is seyn, as it were a corne of myle,
some rede, some blak goyng about it. It shewith a troublous in-wit,
envious and feynt. Also whan they ben glavk and grey, þat
shewith madnesse. Therfor ther ben blak [dropes] in the eyen,
20 as cornes of myle vnder lightyng in-signed, the which litell dropes
have many colours, for they ben pale tany, or rede as sparkles of
fire, and of colour sanguyne, blak, or white, and euery of the kyndes
of these colours after thair clernesse, or more or lesse. Ther is a-
nother maner of variaunce, of the coloure of the cercle that cir-
25 cuyth the appill. And tho cercles ben variantly ordeyned. For
[f. 42] omwhile | the vtter cercle is blak, and that with rede, and omwhile
whitter. Where the dropes ben rede (not expresse rede, but redissh)
that shewith a gentill inwit, a rightful, worthy and engenyous.
Where the dropes ben right rede, or quadrat, and other lighteth
30 as fire, and with-yn other dropes full pale medled, and other glauk,
the cercle with-out the applis gone about sanguynolent or tany,
and the eye be moch and clere, and the appill moveth as angry
and his browes also, in such men is an inwit passyng the wildnesse
of bestis. For what-euer wikkednesse, such an eye he purposeth
35 to do it. Therfor the more of rede dropis be there, the more it
shewith hym to be wrathfull and avovtrer. The more and the

21 sparkles] sp*erkes* L   25 tho] þes L   29 or quadrat] and quadrant
L quadrate R f. 101   31 gone] go L   32 eye be] eye ben A yen ben L
magnitudo sit oculo R f. 101   moveth] mouyng L

derker that the eye be, the more the vices ben alleviat. Dropes of
blode-r[e]de or pale, in blak applis, other beth medled to-gedre,
it shewith il doers and v[e]naries. But if it be paled and derk, in
wikkednesse and deceit he gretly studieth. And they be sanguynos,
it shewith manhode. The high o[b]seruacion herof is this, the more   5
surer and the gretter and the clerer the colours be of the droppis,
it shewith the vices to be gretter. The lift cercle, yf it be rede in
moist eyen, and none other sharpnesse come bitwene, it shewith
grete wit and wisedam, a rightfull and an engyneous man. Yf that
cercle be blak, it signifieth a begiler, a theef, and a wrongfull man,   10
sette all in getyng of money, and foule to medle with women. Ther
ben also eyen variant as Iris the rayn bow, and yf that happe in
dry eyen it shewith wodnesse, also yf thei be not ferre fro insanie.
More-ouer it yeveth them magnificence and wisedome and vertue.
Natheles, omwhile it shewith vpon full angry, mynles-manered   15
men. Whan truly the eyen ben with-out variaunce, good and
certayn state it shewith. Eyen as rede as fire, it shewith a bad man
and an obstinat. And yf eyen be rede, it shewith strength, hardynesse and myght to the haver. Grey eyen with yelownesse raiyng
as a grene stone, that shewith a bad man. Who hath grey and grene   20
eyen, he is ill fortuned and a theef, wherfor all men havyng such
wemmes in thair eyen, as rede as blode, or white, of all men ben
worst and most begilers. |

Of the applis of eyen

The applis liyng streight shewith vanyté. Short applis wikked-   25
nesse detectith. With these 2 signes bestis ben reproved. For where
in bestis is a moderat orbe of the applis, stronge bestis it shewith.
Serpentis, apis and foxes have litell applis. And whan o appill is
more than that other, it is wikked and shewith wikkednesse. Whos
applis done as a wheel honged about, and that vniformely, witte   30
wele that they shall be in hold with wikked hondes. Sothly, whos
applis now wrappen and rynneth, now theder and theder, and now
interrestith, that shewith the badnesse that he ymagyneth not to

2 blode-rede] blode brode A brod bred L; Guttule sanguinolente vel pallide
R f. 101: cf. 95/28 and l. 22 below   3 venaries] vernaries A veneris
L   5 obseruacion] conseruacion A (and, substant., L). herof] þer for L
9–10 yf . . . blak] si niger (var. lect. Sinister) S 44   10 blak] darke L
11 medle] bemedilt L   12 Iris] is L   13 thei . . . ferre] hyt be nott
sayd L   17 shewith. Eyen] scheweth vpon. Full angry ien L Oculi qui in
rubore igni assimilantur homo pessimus est R f. 101ᵛ   28 o appill] þe oon
appull L   29 that other] þe oþer L   32 applis now] een L   33 that¹] it L

be brought a-bout, but he þynkith how he may it do. And yf fro
these applis a derknesse as a clovde circuyteth the liddes, that
shewith a man to be a-fire and meved to do an angerious dede.
The applis lenying a-side or doun, the state of the eyen in the same
5 wise, it shewith an vnkynd man. Whan glauk and grey variant be
the applis, it shewith wodnesse. Whan the applis is blak and hath
citryneté, and shewith as it were gylded, that signyfieth vpon a
bad man, a man-sleer, and vpon a sheder of blode. If the appill
be blak, it shewith a slow and a dull man. Whos applis is moche
10 departed with blaknesse, he is feynt. The applis in the brynk of
whos circuyté shewith apperances, that signyfieth an envyous,
janglyng, ferdfull, and bad man. Wemmys about the applis in the
eye apperyng, it shewith an il man, and worst yf the eye be grey.
Who hath his appil shewyng, as it were with-out þe eye, and so
15 doth the substance of all the eye [pass] in bolnyng, he is mad it
signyfieth.

Of the browes of the eyen

The browes that full oft and contynuelly closeth and openyth,
so the eyen ben smale and litell, he is feynt and full bad, suffryng
20 a siknesse. With whom the browes and the eyen y-like swyft
moveth, they ben hardy and sure. Who also vncertaynly moveth
thaire browes, and joyneth tham, vnder dyverse movynges of the
[f. 43] applis, and the lyddes nesshly closeth, þei ben feynt. | Who so
euer depresseth one of his browes lightly, and nesshly reuokith it
25 and dressith his sight on a thyng, tho delyten in faire thynges, and
ben entriked with lechory and with avovtry. Amonge also the
ouerbrowe is lad to the myddes, and moveth theder and theder,
and the eye lithe to an angle, and meveth his browes vncertaynly:
the same also is a signe of lechours and of avovtrers. The heeris of
30 the browis, whan they ben blak and thykke, it shewith a goode
and a stronge inwitte. Fewe, thynne and redissh, sikenesse of inwit
it shewith, and hastyng to age, but thy heres abiden not longe.
Whan the heres of the browes croken downe-ward, and in oone
naturelly worchen, that shewith a lyer, a sligh man and a foole.

3 angerious] ennoryous (*for* ennioryous?) L   6 is] byn L   14 his]
þe L   þe] *ins. above* A   15 doth . . . bolnyng] qui autem pupillam
foris prominentem cum [*v.l.* cuius] totius oculi substantiae latitudine habet, est
amens S 166   28 lithe to an angle] lyke an egill L   his] the L
33 croken] þem crokyn L

Of significacions of the noose and of the nostrelles

Whos nastrels ben grete and grosse, he is a man of full litell
sapience. The more the nastrell be, the better is the signe. For
litell nastrell is assigned to old men and engyneous men, to thefis
and scomfited men. Who so hath a longe noose strecchyng nygh 5
to his mouthe, he is bothe worthy and hardy. And suche a noose
is yoven to hasty men. The extremyté of whose nastrelles ben
longe, he is suttill, hasty, light and founed. Whos noose is brode
and in the myddell declynyng to the height, he hath many wordes
and is a lyer. Whos nastrels ben brode, he is lecherous. Whos noose 10
is thynne and sotill, his owener is full angry. The extremytees of
whos nastrels is thynne and sotill, he is a man that loveth debatis.
The endes of whos nastrelles ben sharpe, that shewith a man
lightly moved to wrathe. Fat nostrelles shewith an envious man.
Croked nostrelles is yoven to grete herted men, and to meeker 15
than to lecherous. Perverse nostrelles shewith peruerse mynde.
Direct nostrelles shewith vntemperance of tonge. Open nostrels
of fredome and of strength is a signe. And whan they ben narow
and rounde and closed, of foly is a token. Nastrill hole [thikke and
playne] and round shewith a stronge man and grete herted. Who 20
have the nostrill of grevous and of harde oppenyng, he is angry. And
in like wise, who | so hath them full open he is wrothfull also. [f. 43ᵛ]
The part of the nastrell that is by the forhede, yf it honestly joyne
to the forhede, it disposith a man to be manly and prudent. And yf
that part be discrepant, it shewith fooly and a faynt inwitte, and it is 25
a signe femynyne. His nose is most egall that is meene of lengthe and
of brede to his extremyté and that his hooles be not full moche.

Of significacion of the movthe, lippes, and of teth

Who so hath a grete mouth he is glotenous and bold. A litell
mouthe is womannyssh, and his cheres and inwit accordeth with 30
them. Who so hath a wyde mouth, he is batellous and hardy. The
best state of mouth is not to be humyll, for the mekenesse therof

---

1 nostrelles] nose thrylles L   2 litell] grete L   4 is assigned] byn
assigned L   old] wold L levibus R f. 103: see n.   8 light] and lygth L
founed] sownded (for fownded?) L stultus R f. 103   10 noose] nostrelles
L   13 endes] ende L   14 moved] y-moued L   19 Nastrill hole]
nose thrillis hole L   19-20 thikke and playne and round] cum imae nares
solidae tanquam obtusae et rotundae sunt S 70   20-1 Who have the
nostrill] whose nose thryllys   23 The part] also þe part L   nastrell] nos-
trellis L   honestly joyne] be honestly joyned L   29 A litell] and a litul L

is an argument of badnesse and of feyntise. The spice of malignité, of envye, and of vntemperance, is shewed by a drye mouthe and holowe as a dyche. Aristotles such maner of men with holow mouthes gretly he juged likerous. And whan the mouthe to moche
5 is, and to grete, it shewith a gloton, an impacient man, and a wyked, for such mouthes have whales of the see. Whan the mouth shewith moch and is rounde, with thikke lippes and broken, that shewith envious, a gloton and a foole. Of full fewe tho signes ben. Whos lippes ben grete, it shewith a dull man and a foole. Who
10 hath grosse lippes he is a foole. Thynne lippes in a moche mouthe, yf the omyst lippe be rody as sette ouer the lower, that shewith a stronge man, and a grete-herted. Thynne lyppes with a lytell mouth, a faynt, ferdfull, vnhappy man it shewith. If the lower lippe lolle outward, Lexus seith that it shewith an il-tonged man,
15 and imprudent. Whan the lippes excedit and the mouth be smale, it declareth a man to be besy to gete laude and honour. Whan the lippes ben not wele died, he is sikelewe. Lippes consolut, dependent, is a signe of hevynesse. In assis, horsis and olde men that is a signe. Whan lippes grynnen and leven the tethe bare, that shew-
20 ith cursed, wrathfull, and crying men, and for to do wronge redy: that spice is next to the kynde of dogges. Whos teth ben febill
[f. 44] and fewe and litell, all his body is febill. Whos ben longe | and stedfast, he is badde and glotonous.

Of voice and of his significacions

25   Whan the voyce is grosse it shewith the man to be bolde and hardy. Who hath grete voice and shrylle, he is batailous and eloquent. Whos voice is meene betwix grete and smale, he is wise, redy, trew and just. Who hath an hevy voice, he is seruaunt to his wombe. Whos voice is rough, he is envious, and hath hid bad-
30 nesse in his hert. Whos speche with hastynesse is swift, he is hasty, wrathfull and of bad maners, who is hasty in wordis, and specially yf he have smale voice, vnworthy, founed, importune and a lyer. If his voice be grosse, he shall be angry, comandyng, and of bad nature. Who hath a swete voice, he is envious and
35 suspecious. Fairenesse or flateryng of voice shewith plenté of

1 feyntise] feyntes L   spice] spices L   3 maner] a maner L
4 likerous] lecherous L   11 omyst] omast L   13 ferdfull, vnhappy] a
ferdefull a vnhappy L   14 an il-tonged] a euyl tongyd L   25 the man] a
man L   26 shrylle] chirley L   27 betwix] be twene L   28 an
hevy] a hevy L   34 bad] a bad L

founednesse and of dulnesse. A faire voice, foly and litell science
shewith. Whos brethe is longe, he is vile of condicion or nature.
Who movith oft, and speketh with mevyng of his hondes, envious,
eloquent and a begiler he is. And who holdeth his hondes stille
whan he speketh, he is perfit and [in] intellect wele disposed, and 5
of holsome counseill.

Of laughter and of [his] significacions

Who, laughyng moch, is benygne, in all thynge he shall be convenient, for nothynge to moche hevieth neþer besieth hym. Who
laugheth litell, he is contrary to hym, for all men dedis displesith 10
hym. Who laughteth with high voice, he is shamles and a foole.
Who also whan that he laugheth, cowghith, or with difficulté
bretheth, he is shameles and badde, &c.

Of the chynne and of his significacions

The larger the chynne be, the more troubled inwitte it shewith, 15
and omwhile it shewith hym to be piteuous. Me most be ware of
them that have smale chynnes, for above all others they ben most
impacient and envious. If the chynne be rounde, womanyssh
maners and femynyne condicions it shewith. A man-is chynne is,
or oweth to be, ny-by square. Also yf the chynne be full longe and 20
prolixe, with gilis his mynde is occupied. And yf that, nought to
moche, the half of the chynne | be depressed, of venerien plesaunce [f. 44ᵛ]
and of graces it is a signe.

Of chekes and of thaire significacions

Who hath chekes crasse, ydiotis and drounklew they ben. Who 25
hath them to leene, ben wykked. Whos chekebone shewen abscised
fro the eyen and ben full and peisyng and greued and round, that
shewith envie. And whan they ben light and prolix, that shewith
an importunat claterer. All chekes whan they ben full and fatte,
an idel likerous man it shewith. And the contrary shewith begilyng 30
and feyntise. Of lippes, jawes and forhedes, yf the cheris ben
sorowfull, it shewith madnesse and foly. Yf the cheres ben glad,

7 his] *supplied from L*   8 laughyng] *possibly for* laughith   11 Who]
who so euer L   15 troubled] trebuller L   17 chynnes] chynne L
18 womanyssh] womans L   19 shewith] signifieth L   20 ny-by] neȝth L
Also] & also L   21 gilis] gile L   23 graces] gracius L   26 ben]
þey be L   abscised] abysed L   28 that] hyt L   31 feyntise] fayntesy
L timidum R f. 105   cheris] chekes L, vultus S 69   32 cheres] chekes
L vultibus S 69

kykyngnesse and likerousnesse it shewith. Ferre of, me may know
an hevy or a lusty chere, a liberall, a derk and a wikked cheere,
a waker and a slomerer, &c.

Of the face and of his significacions

5   Whos face is passyng moche, he is slowe. Whos face is full litell
and small, he is [a gloser] and a flaterer. Who hath a litell face
declynyng to yelownesse, he is vicious, a begiler, a dronklew and
full bad. Who hath an oblonge face, shamles and envious he is.
Who hath a sclender face, he is bifore-seen in his werkes and sotill of
10 intellect. Who hath a sotill face, he is of many thoughtis. Who hath
a meene face, in chekys and in templis turnyng to blaknesse, trew
he is, lovyng, vnderstondyng and wyse, servisable, wele-made and
engyneous. A playn face lakkyng feere signifieth a stryver, a bad
lerner, a wrongfull, and an engyneous man. Whos face is not moche
15 faire, it is seeld that he hath good maners. Whos face is to moche
glad, he is a foole. Whos face is flesshly, he is not wise. Importune, slowe, and lyer he is. Whos flessh of the jawes ben grete,
he is of grosse nature. A dronklewe face shewith a dronklewe
man, an angry man an angry face, a shamfull man a shamfull faace.

20   ### Of significacion of tymples and of the eeres

Who hath inflate tymples, and the pryncipall veynes grete, and
full chekes, he is full angry. Full grete eeres, of foly and of imprudence ben signes, and small and lytell, of malignyté. Who hath
[f. 45] full grete eeres, he is a foole. | Neuerthelesse he is retentif of mynde,
25 and is like to be of long lyf. And who hath passyng smale eeres, he
is dulle, lecherous and thevyssh. Eres passyng short ben referred
to foly. Oblonge eeres and narowe have signyficacion of envye.

Of the nodell and of his significacions

Whan the nodell is thynne and longe, it signyfieth a man thynk-
30 yng evell. A wast nodell with prolixité shewith anymosité. A short
nodell, in beyng and in example knowen it is, þat his begynnyng is
with foulehardynesse. A rounde nodell shewith the vertue of the

1 kykyngnesse] lykyns L   5 full] to L   6 a gloser and a flaterer]
slowe and a flaterer A a flaterrer and a gloser L malus est callidus et adulator
R 105ᵛ malus est et calidus et adulator S 168   14 an engyneous man]
a large-man L inmundum R fols. 105ᵛ–106   18 shewith] hit shewith hym to
be L   27 have] hathe L   30 anymosité] a man with animosité L
animosum significat R f. 106   31 his begynnyng] see n.   32 with
foulehardynesse] with-owt full hardines L

inwitte, and approveth and shewith the abilnesse of the body. The
nodell yf it enclyne in the left side, it signyfieth in maner a foole
and a ferefull man. Whos nodell declyneth to the right side, Aristotle gaf it to cinedes, that ben men castrat. Wha[n] the nodell is
stabill and temperat, it shewith full good thewes. A nessh nodell   5
and inflixible, not out of heere, but a lernyng man it shewith. A
harde nodell, a bad lernyng man it shewith. The nodill sharp, not
only dull, but soleyn it shewith a man to be. A nodell hole and
soled and wast and that lightly boweth it sheweth rapaces. A nodell
that is louse and not worth, noyers and envious it signifieth. Who 10
hath to wast a nodell, angry and not lernyng þei ben. A nodell
deflixe or bond doun, vntaught and soleyn, and vpon fooles
omwhile it signifieth. Also whan-euer the nodell is broken, open
it is that he is other a foole after, other effemynat. A nodell above
not even, an impacient, a soleyn, a foole, and an idel man it   15
signyfieth. The nodell whan it is bende in, his inwit to be occupied
with thoughtis it shewith, or by symony, or by il tonge and
malignyté. Whan betwix the joynyng of the sholdres and nodell-is
begynnyng shewith a litell tournyng, and the knottis superficie
þere be sharp, proude and soleyn they ben. The nodell that hath   20
interest with the sholdres shewith vpon an vnapt man to lerne, and
omwhile wikked: after the rarité of the sholdres thow shalt | pro- [f. 45ᵛ]
novnce. But and the veynes ben clere, grete, and wele woven to
the nodell, the same to the sholdres shewith.

Of the nek and throte and of thaire signyficacions   25

Who hath a grete nekke, he is founyssh and a grete eter. And
who hath a grete hard nek, he is stronge, angry, and hasty. Who
hath a long, sclender nek, folissh, clateryng and feynt he is. Who
hath a short nek, he is gilefull, sleightfull, sotill, engenyous and a
deceyver. A rough and sharp throte, lightnesse of inwitte, and   30
many wordes to have, it shewith. And yf a grete knotte be on the
throte, in maner it shewith lightnesse, nought hardynesse neyther
il-seiyng.

3 ferefull] ferdeful L   4 Whan] what A when L   6 out . . .
man] see n.   but a] but of L   6–7 A harde] an herde L   9 rapaces]
rampanes L rapaces S 77: see n.   13 broken, open] see n.   14 is other
a foole] is a foole L (perhaps correctly)   18 nodell-is] þe nodull-is L   31 on]
in L uertex gutturis tanquam nodus eminet R f. 107   32 nought] not L

Of the signyficacion of flessh

Flesshe in plenté and harde, grosse witte and intellect it shewith.
Light flessh signifie[th] vpon good nature and vnderstandyng. The
subtilité of the body shewith moche delyuernesse and full many
5 conceytes.

Of the shuldres and of thaire signyficacions

The thiknesse of the sholdres and of the bak, with a brode brest,
shewith worthynesse, hardynesse and retencion of vnderstandyng,
and of sapience. The brede of sholdres shewith ay good witte. And
10 thaire sclendernesse shewith the contrarie. Thynne sholdres and
streight in sharpnesse, shewen a man to be douted. Sholdres not
fatte but wele sette shewen vertue in a man. Slak sholdres of in-
firmité is a signe and of feyntise. The reisyng of sholdres is a signe
of sharp nature and of vntrouth, and omwhile of fooly.

15 ## Of armes [and] cubitis, and of thaire signyficacions

Whan the armes ben so longe that with his hand he may touche
his kne, worthynesse with largesse and noblesse of inwit it doth
signyfie, and omwhile pride and covetise to reigne and gouerne
others. And whan the armes ben full short, it is a signe of discorde
20 of love, and ignorance, and a faynt man and a bad it declareth.
Thynne cubitis, feynt and bad lerners it signyfieth. Whan they
be mene, it shewith them that have articles of felicité. And yf the
[f. 46] brawne be good, it declareth a strong inwit, | and ben refourm-
yng of an able body.

25 ## Of handes and palmes and of thaire signyficacions

Whan thy hondes ben so streyght that whan thy body vp-right
stondyng may reche to the knees, able men and stronge it shewith.
And whan to the hippe, other to the myddell therof they rechen,
they declaren an il-willed man, that joyeth in other men-is harmes.
30 Handes full short shewith fooly. Full litell handes and stronge,
shewith wisedame, sklender and full long, a tyrant and foly de-

2 and harde, grosse witte] & grose, harde inwitt L   3 signifieth] L
signifien A   7 sholdres] schulder L   9 ay] a L   11 streight]
schorte L erecti R f. 107   shewen] schewi*th* L   12 shewen] schewi*th*
L   13 feyntise] fayntenes L   reisyng] rising L   15 and cubitis, and of]
cubitis, and of A cubitis & L   18 covetise] couetnose L   21 bad
lerners] badnesse L   29 il-willed] ille wyckyd (? *indistinct*) L   31 long]
lytyl L

claren. Soft and nessh handes shewen a lerner. Light handes and
sotell, moche wisedome and good intellect they shewen. Fatte
hondes, yf the fyngres ben short, a comerous man, a threter, and
a theef, it shewith. Who in etyng of [mete] bondith hede and
mouth, and rynneth to mete with the hand, yf the hand be smalle, 5
il-willed they ben, and joyen on other men-is harme. Longe
palmes with longe fyngres, it shewith a man to be wele disposed
to many artis, and specially to m[e]chanyk craft, and a wise man
in his werkes, and to be of good gouernaunce.

Of the signyficacion of fyngres and nayles   10

Grete and short fyngres shewith dulnesse and madnesse. The
closyng and joynyng to-gedre of them shewith a man envious.
Whan they ben gadred to-gedres, and closen to-gedres as a cliew,
it shewith a wiked and a nygardus man. And yf thei ben in certeyn
fyngres knotted to-gedres, it is referred to foly. White nailes and 15
vnder-rede of full good engyne ben signes. Nathelesse passyng
short or paale, other blak, shewith a wikked man. Narowe and
oblonge nailes, of sollidité and of wildnesse is a signe. Sharp and
rounde nayles to venerien actis ben redy. Croked and reflixed
nailes, imprudent men it signifie[th] and raveners. Who hath them 20
impressed and moch broken, ben foles and theves. These signes
that ben yoven to the nailes of them-self, without other accordance
of other signes be-fore in other chapiters rehersed, have no myght. |

Of the significacion of the sholdres   [f. 46ᵛ]

Of shuldres, the strength and multitude of flessh vpon them 25
founednesse they declaren. Sklendernesse and soteltè of them
declareth debilité of hert.

Of the brest, wombe and bak, and of their significacions

The brede and grossenesse of sholdres, and of baak the worthynesse, shewen hardynesse, with retencion of witte and of wisedome. 30
A sotill baak shewith a man of discordant nature. Mediocrité,

---

3 yf] and iff L   comerous] *conmerouse*   4–5 of . . . mouth] in etyng
who bondysch h*i*s hed and much L: *see n.*   6 il-willed] ille wyckyd L
on] of L   8 mechanyk] mochanyk AL: *contrast note to 75/28*
10 and] & of L   13 closen] clos*eth* L   14 nygardus] nigard L   thei
ben] h*i*t be L   17 other] or L   20 signyfieth] signifieth L signyfien A
22 the] his L   24 significacion] significac*i*ons L   25 strength]
strenkyth L   31 discordant] discordyng L

sothly, of bak and of brest is a sure and a proved signe of vnderstandyng and of good counseill. Who so hath a grete wombe, he is
like to be vndiscrete, folissh and proude, and lovyng venerie.

Of the rybbes and of thaire signyficacions

5   The brede and strenght of rybbes shewith proude and moch
wrath. Thaire crokednesse declareth malice. Thaire egallité is
a full goode signe.

Of significacion of the hanches and of the thies and botox

Sclender hanches shewith lovers of women. Buttox, whan in-
10   ward they have moch flessh, inbecillité of strength, and slaknesse, it
shewith. Whan the bones of the buttox shewen out, that declareth
manhode and multitude of strength.

Of signyficacion of knees and of shynnes

Plenté of flessh in the knees, vpon nesshnesse and febilnesse of
15   vertue it signyfieth. Grossenesse of shynnes shewith boldnesse and
strength. Of them subtilité shewith a man ignorant. The brede of
shynnes and of heles signyfieth vpon strength of the body.

Of significacion of fete, anclees and sperlyng

Grosse fete and flesshly, founednesse and love of iniurie it
20   shewith. Fete havyng moch flessh and harde, it declareth a man to
be of bad intellect. Litell fete and light, signyfieth vpon hardnesse.
Faire fete and smale shewen a mery man and a fornycatour. Whan
the anclees and the thies ben grosse, that shewith a dulle, shamles
[f. 47]   man. Whan the sperlonge is grosse and | stronge, it shewith a myghty
25   man. And whan they ben sklender, a ferdfull man it declareth.

Of ingoyng and out-goyng, other of movyng of stappes and of pases, &c.

A slow movyng shewith dulnesse, an hasty movyng lightnesse.
Who goth hevyly, he is slow. And who goth hastily and trip-
30   pyngly, he is hastif and besieth hym for thyngis that he can not

8 significacion] significacions L   botox] botockes L   13 signyficacion]
significacions L   15 boldnesse] badnes L audacians R f. 108ᵛ   18 sig-
nificacion] signyficacions L   anclees] ankyls L   sperlyng] sperlynges L
21 of bad intellect] bad of intellect L   23 anclees] ancles L   26 other of]
& L de motibus R f. 108ᵛ   29 hastily] hastyngly L   29–30 trippyngly]
tripp|pyngly, *divided by line-ending as indicated* A tryppingly L   30 hastif]
hasty L

dispose. Whos pases ben brode, they ben slow: nathelesse they
speden thair purpose. Whos pases ben short, they ben hasty,
suspecious, impotentis, and of il wille in thaire werkes.

Of the egalité and good disposicion of a man

He is of goode mynde and wele made in nature, that hath soft 5
flessh and moist, meene betwix rovgh and smoth, not to longe
neither to short, white declynyng to redenesse, plesaunt in looke,
heres playn and meene, with grete eyen declynyng to roundnesse,
of meene and mesured hede, egall in mochnesse of nek and wele
disposed, sholdres somwhat bendyng, lakkyng plenté of flessh 10
in thies and in knees, of clere voice with temperance betwix sotill
and grosse, with longe palmes and longe fyngres declynyng to
sotilnesse, of smale laughter, derision or feynyng, and his cheres
medled with gladnesse and plesaunce. Forsothe thow shalt not
fasten thy jugementis vpon one of these signes neither sentence, 15
but gadre the witnesse of all. And by dyverse signes and tokens
speke, not puttyng hym to be suche or suche of nede, but so
enclyned and disposed. And euer remembre on Philemon-is jugement vpon Ypocras, and vpon Ypocras-is most assured aunswere, &c.
                                                              20

Explicit

1 nathelesse] neuertheles L   10 of flessh] in flesch L   11 with
temperance] in temperaunce L   17 hym] þem L

IV

þE PRIUYTÉ OF PRIUYTEIS

English translation
by
Johannes de Caritate

From a MS. probably written *c.* 1484, now the property
of Mr. Robert B. Honeyman, Jr., of Rancho Los
Cerritos, San Juan Capistrano, California.

[þe Fyrst Boke]

[Capitulum i]

[f. 4]   . . . a meruulus wytt, þat bothe he was a nobyl werryur of knightly
prowes alle the dayis of this present lyfe, eke a nobyl phylysophyr,
5   in alle prouydens and moral vertuys, bothe of practyk and elo-
qwens, hos name men clepyd Sir Milis Stapylton, þe qwyche lyuyd
in dayis of Henry þe Syxte, Kynge of Englond. þe qwyche notabyl
knyght, for vertu, and to profyte hem þat schuld come aftyr hym,
dyd me to translate thys boke owte of Latyne in to Englysch.
10   Qwyche boke þe prince of phylysophris, Arystotyl, compylid at þe
preyer of Alysaundir conqwerour. And thowe thys phylisophyr purposyd on alle wyse to kepe secrete thyse materys her folowyng, yit to
þe petycion of so gret an emperour he thowgh[t] he myght make no
contradyxcion. þer-for, makyng a-seeth in parte to þe emperour and
15   also hydyng in parte þe priuyté of sundry craftys, he compylid
thys boke, spekyng in it be clos conclusyounys, be examplis, and
figuratyf spechys, techyng owtward, lettyrly, phylosophyk doc-
[f. 4ᵛ]   tryne | longyng to þe lord of lordys, to kepe the helth of þe body of
man and woman and to profytabylnes inefabyl, be þe qwyche þe
20   knowlech of heuynly bodyis be gotyn. And myne autor in Latyne,
aftyr þe ende of hys pystil sent to þe seyd byschop, þe qwych he
puttyth in þe begynnyng of hys boke as a prolog, he notyfyyth

---

3 *f. 3, containing opening of text, is missing*   13 thowght] thowgh *perh. intended form: cf. 121/3, 127/26*   18 to kepe] *the words separated by blank space*

þe chapituris seriatly, þat is as to sey in ordyr, to fynde qwat
mater a man wul loke vppon þe more esyly. And fyrst he makyth
a gret comendacion of Arestotyl, how many of þe olde phylisophris
held hym of þe noumbyr of prophetys, and odyr sundry op-
pynyownnys of Aristotyl, þe qwyche nowdyr longyth to þe matyr 5
of thys boke ner soundyth to trwth, qwerfor at þe substauns of thys
mater I begynne be ordyr, be þe help of owr Lord Iesu to procede.

18 Arystotil] i corrected from o   26 and how a kyng] repeated

[f. 6] **The ende of þe capytillis of þe fyrst boke and þe begyninge**
35 **of þe secunde**

3 custom] relygiosite   31 promotyng] g *corr. from* d   tweynti] tweyti *perh.
intended form*

36 to] *with interlinear ij above: roman (or arabic) figures regularly written above ordinal and cardinal numbers in this text: this will not normally be recorded hereafter.*

3 twenty] *altered from* thwenty

Thende of þe capy[ti]llis of þe thyrd boke

---

13 þer] *inserted above the line*   16 counsillouris] mesyngeris   21-2 *heading omitted in body of text in ms.*   23-4 *omitted in body of text in ms.*
25 xj] *numbered* xviiij *in body of text, in ms.*   26 twelthe] *headed* nynghte
in body of text, in ms.   28 thyrdtene] *headed* tenthe *in body of text, in ms.*
31 fourtene] *headed* eleuynth *in body of text in ms.*   32 attendauns]
medial a *ins. above an* e *which has not been crossed through*

And conceyue qwat sum euir he be þat schal rede þis boke, he schal
30 fynde mor merwullus and mor plesaunt materys, also mor of substauns, within thys boke than is expressyd in thyse chapytyrrys. For
þise chapytillis serue but for to dyrecte a man in to qwat mater he
wul rede of, &c.

34 **Her ende þe titillis of þe capitillis of this boke.** |

[f. 9] Prolongyng þe tytil of þe secunde chapytir, I brynge to remem-

---

1 fyftene capytil] *headed* twelthe *in body of text, in ms.*   4 The syxtene]
headed thi[r]dtene *in body of text, in ms.*   8 seuyntene capitil] *headed*
fourtene *in body of text, in ms.*   18 thwenty] *cf.* 118/3, 132/21
19 propyrté] p̄pyrte *second contraction presumably a slip*   24 propyrteis]
p̄pyrteis *second contraction presumably a slip*   26 ingenerally of] of ingenerally
of   29 And conceyue] *run on on same line as last words of list of contents*

brauns be qwat mene þei þat wul labour in þis boke to vndyrstond
þe phylisophyr, qwer he specifiyth of vertuys moral, of prudens in
demenawns, or of execucion of ryghfulnes, it must be takyn as
a parabyl or as an exampyl.

Digressio expositoris   5

And qwer as þe fylysophyr remembryth of þe makyng of
medycynes, me semyth best to wryte hem after þe gyse and maner
þat þe physycyens wryght qwan þei make ther byllis to send to
potecaryis to haue made ther medycinys to recwr þe seke. þe
qwyche wrytyng stondyth be figuris and wordys abreuyat, þat 10
no man can vndyrstonde ner rede but physycienis, to kepe þe
craft clos. For vndyrstondyth [it] wele, þat þer gone many sundry
thyngis to medycynis, and oftyn sqwyche thyngys, þat if men
knwe qwat thei wer, þei wold noȝt receyue hem. Qwer-for be gret 14
wysdam, phylisophris of olde tyme made her | bokys and wrytyng [f. 9ᵛ]
in sqwyche maner wyse þat no man schuld rede but clerkys
stodying in þe same syens. For in medycinys ther go very poysonnys, þat if tho poysonnys wer taken or receyuyd alone, þei
schul sle hem þat vsyd it. Qwer-for, be wysdame and gret vndyrstondyng in natur, phylisophrys þat made bokis of medycinys, þei 20
ioynyd sqwyche spycys as were conuenyent to destroy þe qualiteis
of þe poysonnys, and eke to make natur strong ayens þo sykenes.
Ther be put in medicynis pycche, wax, arsenyk, syndyrris of yrin,
cassia fystula, manna and sqwyche odyr. Qwerfor the medicinis
be wrytyn mor clos, as doctourys of physik wryte in þer bokys. 25
Anodyr cause qwy thyse byllis be wrytyn closly and also bokys
of physyk: for if þei had be wrytyn opynly, so þat gramaryens
myght vndyrstonde ther bokes, þe most part of þe pepyll schuld
a ben physyciounis, and so þe syens noȝt schuld a ben had in
reputacion, þat philisophris for a specialté labourryd. Now to þe 30
tityll of capitill [two.]|

[Capitulum ii] [f. 11]

... Thys phylisophir, as I seyd be-forn, beyng in age, thys emperour, qwan he had co[n]queryd the empire of Percys, seyng þe
disposycion of þe pepyl of þat countré, wrote to hym a pystil 35

---

3 ryghfulnes] *intended form perh.* ryghtfulness, *but cf.* 122/30, 127/26, 144/22
and see also 114/13, 122/5   6 And] A And, *the first A being in red, separated
from the word* And   12 it wele] wele it.   13 medycynis] *followed by space
containing erasure*   18 þei] *prec. by* it *with uncompleted* t   31 f. 10
missing   35 countré] r *ins. above*

conteyning this sentens, 'O grete doctor, reuler of ryghtfulnes, I
sygnifye to thy wysdam þat I haue foundyn in þe cuntré of Perce
certeyn pepyl, þe qwych habunde in resun and sotel vndyrstondyng, þat stody to haue vndyrstondyng in sotel materis, and also
5 to haue lorchyp abouyn odyr nacionis and to gete a kyngdam be
conquest. Qwerfor I purpose to slee hem alle. But how that thow
appoyntyst and decreyst in þis mater, sende me an ansqwer be
wrytyng.' Thys phylisophyr, be gret wysdam consyderyng þe
constellacion ouer that cuntré, conceyuyng þat thow þe wurthyiest
10 of þat region had ben slayne, þer schul a left as wyse and as
sotel, and alle he coude naȝt a slayn, he ansqwerd on thys wyse:
[f. 11ᵛ] 'Nobil emperour, if | thow mayst chonge þe eyr and þe watyr
of þat cuntré, and also þe disposicion of þe cyteis of þat londe,
fulfylle þi dysyr and slee hem. And if it be so noȝt þat thow
15 mayst chonge þise seyd thyngis, lorchyp ouir hem as a conquerour
with goodenes and feyr behauyng, and her her petycionys gracy-
usly with benygnyté and goodly cher. And if thow do thus, haue very
trost that þer alle hertis and wyllis schal be soget to þe, be þe help
of God, and redy to fulfyl þi dysir and comaundement, euyn at
20 thy wille, for loue þat þei scal haue to þe. And be thys mene schalt
thow lordechyp ouir hem with victory.' Alisaundyr, redyng thys
pystil, fulfillyd Aristotyllis counsel dyligently, and thyse men of
Perce aftyr that tyme wer mor obeyng to hys commaundement
than ony odyr nacion of alle hys conquest. Be thys maner of wys-
25 dam eueriman may haue cler vndyrstondyng þat þe frowardnes
of men be goodenes and feyr speche is euir ouircomyn. |

[f. 12]   [Capitulum iii]

Aftir þis forseyd pystil, Arystotil wrote anodyr to Alisaundyr,
conteynyng this sentens folowyng: 'O glorius sone, Emperour
30 most ryghful, God conferme and make þe strong in þe wey of
knowyng tho thyngis þat be nescesary to þe, and also in þe path
of trewth and vertue, and represse fro þe alle bestyal appetitys
that repreue manhod and be dysworchypful a kyng to vse,'
(⁋ Vndyrstonde her: lecchery and odyr vicis.) 'and eke mut strenght
35 thy kyngdam and illumyne thy wytte to his only seruyse and wurchyp. And, myghty Emperour, þe pystyl þat thow sentyst me, I

---

5 lorchyp] cf. 125/19 and see 121/3   a kyngdam] a ins. above   17 beny-
gnyté] benyngnyte with abbreviation for n before g   18 be soget] be ins. above
23 aftyr] prec. by expuncted wer   30 ryghful] cf. 121/3

receyuyd it with wurchyp as was conuenient, and plenarly vndyr-
stode it, qwat desir thow hast to haue me personally, meruellyng
how I may absteyn, or be fro, þi presens, qwer also thow
repreuyst me, that I schuld make no fors of thy werkys ne how
thow dydyst, be wysdam or odyr wyse. And for thys opynyoun   5
þat thow hast as be thy wrytyng of me, I haue | purposyd and   [f. 12ᵛ]
hastyd me to make a decré to thy buxumnes, þe qwyche schal be
to the as a balauns, be þe qwyche thow mayst discusse and pondyr
alle thy werkys, and se qwat thow schal do to thy wurchyp and
profyte, and qwat thow schalt leue, þe whyche canon or decré schal 10
fulfylle my stede. Than, euyn as thow haddyst recours to me to axe
counsel of me, qwan thow stondyst in dowghtis of straunge materis,
on þe lyke wyse thow schalt haue recours to thys booke in tyme of
nede, and a rewle it schal be to þe most certeyn, to alle thyngis þat
thow wult and of tho in specyal þat I schuld schewe the and I   15
were present with the. Thow owyst noȝt than to repreue me,
sythyn thow knowyst, or owyst to knowe, that I leue noȝt to come
to thy most excellent and clerest welth and glory for þat I haue therof despyte, but þat onweldynes of age and febylnes of body haue
comyn abought me, and yoldyn me, or made me, so heuy, sterke   20
and onweldy þat I am on-abyl to go. Furthermor, that thow axyst
| and desyrist to know, it is so gret a priuyté þat mannys brest may [f. 13]
scarsly bere or soffyr. How than owteward may it be expressid
be wrytyng? In mortal skynnys how may it be depeyntyd,' (þat is
to mene be þe skynne þat is vtter parte of body) 'ignobyl folk to 25
vndyrstond?' (As ho seyth, how may thys be wrytyn expressly þat
is so grete a mystery, euery man to vndyrstond it be my wrytinge?
❡Forth now in þe texte:) 'Qwerfor', seyth Aristotyl to Alisaundyr,
'to þat qwyche is conuenient, and semyth þe to axe and inquire,
and it is leful and semyth me to trete of, I am bowndyn and be-   30
holdyn to ansqwer of dwe, as thow art boundyn of dwe of dyscrecion
nowt to require of me mor of thys priuyté þan þat I haue wrytin
the in þis boke and youyn þe to þe dysir. For if thow wysely and
sotelly and stodyusly rede thys boke and vndyrstonde it, and fully
hast knowyng and kunne þat is wrytyn and conteynyd þer-inne,   35
I beleue withowte dowght, þat þer schal be none obstakyl be-twene
the and þat þi disyr is to knowe. For qwy God | hath youyn the   [f. 13ᵛ]

---

3 or] *corr. from* ob   4 how] *prec. by letter partially formed, and canc.*
7 make] *ins. above*   9 thy werkys] thys werkys   11 as] *prec. by*
canc. h   15 and I] & I

so gret grace in vndyrstondyng and in redynes of wytte and in
lettyratur of kunnyng or syens, also be my doctrine that of yought
thow haddyst befor, qwyche I toke the, þat now be thy self thow
mayst take, and fyguratyfly vndyrston, alle that is wrytyn in thys
5 boke, þe qwyche thow askyst of me to be taught of. For þe dysire
of thy feruent wylle schal opyn to þe and help the now for to
opteyne thy purpos, and schal brynge þe to þat ende and purpos
qwyche thow dysiryst, owr Lord grauntyng. The cause is ground
on to wysis: one is owteforth, anodyr inforth. The cause owteforth
10 is þat thy tresur of gold and syluyr gotyn be this syens, in tyme of
nede, be compassyon, hauyng mercy of thy sogettys, to releue
hem. The cause [in]forth is thys gret priuyté of olde phyliso-
phyrris and ryghtful men, qwyche glorius God chase and comendyd
14 to hem, and taught hem. And I comende to þe [þe] same secrete
[f. 14] with sondry odyr in þe qwyche, owteward, | thow schalt fynde þe
grettest phylosophy and doctrine, withinforth þe fynal cause
qwych is intendyd and purposyd, for ther is alle þe pryncypal
purpos and fynal. And qwan thow hast perceyuyd þe betokynnyng
of dyuysyounys, and þe clos fyguris of examplys, than plenerly
20 and perfyghtly thow schalt purswe thy purpose desyrid. God than,
that is most wyse and most gloryus, illumyne thy reson and puryffye
thyne vndyrstondyng, to perceyue þe sacrament of thys syens, that
thow mayst meryte þerin. The cause is ground qwy that I fynytely
reuele fyguratyfly my priuyté, spekyng to þe be clos examplys and
25 tokynnys. For I fer gretly þat þe boke of þise priuyteis schul come
in to þe handys of ontrwe folk,' (þat is to sey, wrecchys), 'þe
qwyche fere noȝt God, or þat it come to þe power of dyssolute folk,
and so þei schuld come [to] this last priuyté qwyche is Goddys
[f. 14ᵛ] secrete, to qwyche priuyté God hath dempt hem on-|abyl and
30 onwurthy. And I, if I schuld wryte þis gret priuyté opynly, I wer
þe transgressour of þe grace God hath sent me, and breker of
heuynly priuyté and of hyd reuelacion. Qwerfor I sqwer to þe
vndyr attestacion of Goddys dome, þat I detecte thys sacrament or
priuyté to þe vndyr þe same maner þat it was reuelyd or schewyd
35 on-to me, and I wul þat thow knowe þerfor þat he þat detectyth
priuyteis and tellyth owte or makyth knowyn hys counsellis, ther
schal folow hym sone many infortunes, qw[e]rfor thow mayst noȝt

---

8 cause is ground] ground is cause *with interl. letters* b *and* a *above* ground *and*
cause *respectively*   12 inforth] outeforth   26 of] *repeated*   30 And
I] *prec. by canc.* I   32 I sqwere] *followed by second* I, *canc.*

be sur of casual casys betydyng and euyllis þat be to come.
Owr Lord þerfor kepe þe fro alle lyke casys of infortune, and fro
euiry dysonest verke.' Thus endyth þe secunde pystyl of Arystotyl
þe grettest phylysophyr.

Capitulum iiij

Aftyr thys pystil the phylysofyr, procedyng in hys boke, begynnyth
vndyr þis wyse:

O Alysaundyr, aftyr þat I haue expressyd my conceyte in þis
pystil | I brynge now to thy remembrans þat most holsum doc-   [f. 15]
tryne, þe qwyche I was wunte alwey to expugne to þe, in formyng
thy nobyl vndyrstondyng. And þat same doctryne of wysdam schal
be þi solas and a myrour of helth. It behouyth of necessyté to euiry
kyng to haue to helpys, be þe qwyche hys kyngdam must be
susteynyd. And one of hem is strenght of men, noȝt of her bodyis
only, but stronge in wylle, þat þei be redy to help þe in tyme of
nede. And be þe strenght and multytude of swyche maner of men
a kyngdam is defendyd and comfortyd. But thys wul noȝt be but
qwan þe hede and gouernour of þe kyngdam is ryghtful, and
reulyth be ryghtfulnes, and as a lord hath lorchyp ouir hys sogettys,
and þo sogettys withowte ony rebellyon obey to hym þat is lord.
For knowe wele þat for inobedyens of sogettys þe power of þe
kynge is febyllyd and sette at nowght | and þe sogettis haue lordy-   [f. 15ᵛ]
schyp and take þe reule, if justyse or wysdam fayle in hym þat is
an hed. And I schal telle þe cause be wyche, and for qwyche,
sogettys be inducyd to obey her lord. And conceyue þat þe cause
is on tweyne weyis. One cause is owteforth, anodyr is inforth.
þe cause owteforth I told in þe pystyl beforn, þat is to sey, þat
a kyng dyspende hys ryches be wysdam qwan he seth nede amonge
hys sogettys, yeuyng iche of hem aftyr her deseruyng. And with
alle this a kyng must haue a-nodyr wyle þe qwyche I schal expresse
to þe in þe chapityrris folowyng, qwer-as I schal trete of ryches and
of help and conforte a-yen hys sogettys. The secunde wey is to
enduce thy sogettys wylle to be ocupyid. And thys is chef and in þe
fyrst degré, for þei þat be onocupyid, þat do but jangyl and carpe,
þei wul dyscusse be-twene hem al thy dedys, bothe bad and
goode, and hem-self ydylnes bryngyth to gret wrecchydnes. And þis

---

9 I] *prec. by space containing erasure*   17 is] *prec. by canc.* is   But thys]
prec. by þa *cancelled by expuncting*   19 lorchyp] *cf. 122/5*   27–8 þat
a kyng] *followed by* tho *canc.*   34 onocupyid] *medial* o *ins. above*
36 wrecchydnes] *first* c *ins. above*

[f. 16] secunde help hath tweyne causys, one owteforth, | a-nodyr ınforth.
[. . .] þe inforth cause is þat þe kyng excercyse justise abowght
hys possessciounis and in exaccionys of money, to be in hem as a
trwe eyer and a ryghtful successour. For if it be so þat be extorcion,
5   or mor þan justyse requyryth, or to oftyn, þe pepyl be taskyd for
þe kyngys propyr vse, thys meuyth þe pepyllis hertys and withdrawyth hertys of hem fro þe kynge, and causyth hem to be mys-
lyuirys and to reprehende þe amonge þem self, and prey God for
hys deth þat her gode may be restoryd, for in sqwyche gotyn gode
10   þe kynge is neuir trwe eyr. Qwer-for a kyng schuld spende and
schuld lyfe of hys owne, and so dyspende hys gode be wysdam
þat he schuld neuir nede. And þan grace wul folow, and þe gode
Lord schal help, þat to wyse men þat stody for grace He yeff hem
goode plentevusly, and to knowe her dysire, with-owte Home is
15   impossybyl to possede owte owdyr of tresur[i]s or kunnyng.

[f. 16ᵛ]   **Of four maner of kyngys** | **Capitulum v**

Ther be four maner of kyngis, þat is to sey, dysposid on four
wysis: one þat is large to hym-self in expens and large to hys
sogettis, anodyr qwyche is a nygard to hym-self and a nygard to
20   hys sogettys, the thyrd þat is a nygard to hym-self and large to hys
sogettys, the fourth þat is large to hymself and a nygard to hys
sogettys. The nacion of Ytalyaunis þei hold þis opinion, and sey
þat it is no vice in a kyng to be a nygard to hym-self, and to be
large to hys sogettys. Men of Inde sey þat he is most comendabyl
25   of kyngys þat is a nygard to hym-self and to hys sogettys. The
Peercys sey and afferme þe contrary bothe to Italyunis and men of
Ynde, seyng þat þe kynge is nought wurth þat is noȝt bothe large
to hym-self and also to hys sogettys. But, seyth þe phylisophyr, be
my dome he is werst and most to be repreuyd of very deseruyng,
30   þat is large to hym-self and a nygard to hys sogettys. For he þat
is demenyd so, is kyngdam be lykelynes sone must be destroyd.
[f. 17] þan it behouyth | vs to enquyr sotelly of thyse vertuys and vicis,
and to expresse qwat largenes is and eke qwat nygardschyp is, and
qwer þat errowr is in largenes, and qwat hurt fallyth and folowyth
35   of abstynens of largenes. It is opyn and pleyne inowgh þat qwalytés
be gretly to be repreuyd qwan þei dyscord fro a mene.

---

3 as a] as As *with final* s *canc.*   10–11 and shuld] & *ins. above*   15 tresuris]
tresur*us*   29 be] *ins. above*   34 hurt] *followed by canc.* e   36 qwan]
second minim of n *written with long downstroke*

(Conceyue þat þe phylysophyr clepyth largenes and nygardy qwalyteis. And eke he seyth:)

We knowe wele þat þe obseruaunz of largenes (þat is to sey þe behauyng in largenes), is pasyng hard to demene as it owyth to be. And as sone, or as esy, is þe transgressyon of larges, for þe excesse 5 þat fallyth þer-of. And it is esy and lyght inowe nygardy and wast-fulnes to be exersysid of euiry man, and it is as hard to reteyne largenes. And conceyue þat moderat larges is a profytabyl vertu as to a kyng or a reuler. And if thow wult haue þis vertu, conceyue 9 fyrst thy power, and | qwat thow mayst do sauyng þi-self. Con- [f. 17ᵛ] syder also þe tyme of nede, and þe merytis or deseruyngys of þi sogettys. Thow schalt þan yefe aftyr þi power to them þat haue nede, qwyche be honest personys and haue deseruyd to haue reward. And he þat yefth on odyr maner of wyse he synnyth, and pasyth þe rewle of largenes. For he that yefth yiftys to þem qwyche 15 haue none nede, he schal no preysyng haue þerby. And alle þat euir he yefyth to wastourys or mysrewlyd men, he lesyth it. And he þat lyghtly with laues spendyth or yefth owte hys goode, he schal sone come to þe wrecchydnes of byttyr pouirté. And sqwyche one is lykenyd to hym þat yef hys enmyis victory ouir hys owne 20 persone. He þerfor þat yefth in tyme of nede of hys goode to nedeful honest folk, is clepyd a vertuus large kynge, þe qwyche is bothe wyse to hym-self and large, and eke to hys sogettys, and sqwyche a kyngis | kyngdam schal contune in prosperyté, and hys [f. 18] commaundement schal be obseruyd. Olde wyse men preyse 25 sqwyche a kynge, for ryghfully he may be clepyd vertuus, large and mesurabyl. And he þat lauessyth owte þe godys of hys kyng-dam inordynatly and withowte mesur to þem þat haue no nede, or ellis to onwurthy pepyl, sqwyche one is as a destroyer of þe comun welfar, a spyller of þe pepyl, a destroyer of þe kyngdam, 30 onabyl to haue gouernaunz. Qwerfor a-monge þe pepyl he is clepyd a wastur, inasmyche as prouydens and polycie be fer fro hys kyngdam. The name of nygardy dysworchyppyth gretly a kynge, and dyscordyth gretly to a kyngis magesté. If he be notyd with owdyr of thyse vicis, þat is to sey, with nygardy or of wastfulnes, 35 if he wulle þanne wysely counsel to hymself, he owyth with hye diligens to prouyde on trosty manne þat is trwe, discrete, and wyse,

---

18 he þat] he *ins above*   26 ryghfully] *intended form perh.* ryghtfully, *but cf.* 121/3 *and see also* 114/13   34 If] if owdyr   35 or] *ins. above*

[f. 18ᵛ] chosyn a-monge many be hys | sadnes, to home þei schuld comytt þe
dysposicion of þe comun, and to gouerne þe ryches of þe kyngdam.

The sexte capitil begynnyth   Capitulum vjᵐ

The phylisophyr seyth furthermor to Alysaundyr on thys wyse:
5 O Alysayndyr, I telle þe stedfastly þat qwat kynge sumeuir ber
sqwyche a kowntenauns in expens þat is mor þan hys lyuelod
drawyth, sqwyche a kynge destroyith and is destroyid. For, as I
haue told þe oftyn, þe exclusyon, or declyne, or bowyng from
nygardy and wastfulnes, and þe adquysycion of largenes, is þe
10 glory of a kynge, and þat thyng qwyche maketh euir tendur
a kyngdam. And this is qwan a kynge restreynyth or withdrawyth
hys hande or hys power fro þe possesciounys of hys sogettis.
Qwerfor it is wrytyn in þe doctrine or commaundement of þe gret
14 doctour Hermogynes, þat þe most hye and trwe goodenes, clernes
[f. 19] of vndrystondyng, and fulfyllyng | of þe lawe, and owteward
tokyn of perfeccion in a kynge, is þat [he] absteynyth fro þe
possessyounys of hys sogettys, and also fro her money, for þise
be cause of destruccion of a kyngdam. Knowyst þou noȝt, þat
for as myche as þe wastful expens of kyngys pasyd þe receyte of
20 her cyteis, and on thys maner þe receytis faylyng and þe kyngys
expensys [contynuing], þei extendyd be extorcion her power and
takyn away odyr mennys goodys and þe receyte of her sogettys
lyfelodys, and þat þe soget, for her trowbyl and wronge, haue cryid
to God for help. And God, heryng hem, hath sent a brennyng
25 wynd and scorgyd hem (þat is to sey haue sofyrid mennys hertys
to ryse ayens hem), þat at þe last, for vengauns, þe pepyl haue
rysyn to-gyddyr ayens hem, and made an ende of hem, þat if God
had noȝt an-holpyn and defendyd hem, alle þe kyndam had ben
vttyrly destroyd. Knowe þer-fore, þat ryches is cause of duryng
30 of manhod and prosperyté. For manhod may noȝt endur, if
[f. 19ᵛ] sqwych | as is requyryd fayle or be destroyd. Iche þer-for, lord,
gretly must be-war of superfluyté and ouirdone aboundauns in
expensys or yiftys. That than temperauns of largenes, þe qwyche in
euery lord is gretly commendabyl, may be gotyn, onwyse and
35 lauesse yeuyng must be schonyd. And it is of þe substauns of
largenes and of vertu to lesse of, and noȝt to inquyr of, þe hyd
materys of priuyteis, ner to reduce to mend yiftys, as of þe kende

---

1 many] n *ins. above*   17 also] *prec. by downstroke as of incomplete* I
27 ayens hem] hem *ins. above*   ende] *prec. by canc.* ayens   35 it is] *ins.*
above canc. sumtyme

of þiftis. Also it is of þe substauns of vertu to reward þem þat
deserue reward, and also to foryef a wrong done ayen the, and to
wurchyp þem þat of gouernaunz and godys be wyse and wurchypful, to help þem and supporte þat be sympyl and mene wele, to
fulfyle þe defautys of innocentis, to ansqwer goodely to þem þat 5
salute [þe], to represse þi tonge fro alle euyl speche, bothe be-forn
folk and be-hynde hem, and if it be so þat thow be wrongyd owdyr
of þi persone or þi name, sofyr for þe qwyle | tyl tyme oportune be, [f. 20]
and to fle foly and noȝt to knowe foly. And now (seyth Arystotyl)
þat I haue told þe now, it is breuely phylosophyk or prophetyk 10
wysdam. And if þou had be-forn þis tyme neuir a-lernyd þe odyr
doctrine but þis, it wer innowghe for þe, bothe in thys world and
in þat qwyche is to come.

Here begynnyth þe seuynth capitil   Capitulum vij^m

Know þan þat vndyrstondyng, qwyche is be wysdam, is hed of 15
alle gouernaunz, helth of soule, keper of vertu, sercher or ouer-
loker of vicys. For be þis resun of vndyrstondyng we behold or se þo
þingys þat be nessescary to fle, and be þat we chese þo thyngis þat
be neccesary to be chosyn. þis is þe begynny[n]g of alle vertu, rothe
of all gode thyngis preisabyl and honorabyl. And þe fyrst instru- 20
ment of intellygens is dysir of goode fame. For he þat trwly disiryth
be menys conuenyent to haue gode fame, he schal be bothe famus
and | also gloryus. And he þat feynydly dysiryth fame and folowyth [f. 20ᵛ]
noȝt þe menys to gete it, be infamy schal be confoundyd. Fame
þer-for is chef and princypal þat is desyryd in gouernauns. For 25
a kyndam is noȝt desyryd for þe self but þe fame, as þe glory and
plesauns of a kynge in hys conqwest is to be famed a wyse, manly
and wurthy werryor. The begynnyng þer-for of wysdame and
vndyrstondyng is dysir of gode fame, þe qwyche be reule of remys
or ellis lordchyp is gotyn. But conceyue þat if for [oþer þan] þis 30
cause gouernauns or lordechyp be dysiryd or ellis gotyn, it schal
noȝt be þe getyng of fame, but of enuye. Inuye gendyrith lesyngis,
þe qwyche is rote of repreuabylnes and mater of vycis. Inuye
gendryth detraccion, and detraccion gendryth hatered. Hatered
gendryth wronge. Wronge gendryth pertynacy, þat is to sey fro- 35
ward boldnes. And þis froward boldnes gendyryth angyr. Angyr

6 þe] hym   9 noȝt] *prec. by* ig: *see n.*   18 nessescary] *altered from*
nessecary   20 preisabyl] i *ins. above.*   25 þer-for] *ins. above*
29 reule] *corr. from* reuly: *cf. 134/29*

[f. 21] gendryth stryfe. | Stryfe gendryth enmyté. Enmyté gendryth werr.
Werre destroyth lawe and also cyteys. And thys is ayene þe lawe
and ryght of natur. And þat qwyche is repugnaunt to natur destroyth þe body. Stody þer-for and loue þe desyr of goode fame,
5 for-qwy resun be þe dysyr of gode fame dryuyth or sokyth owte
[un]trwthe, and [un]trwthe is rote of alle perysabyl thyngis. And
[trwthe is] grounde and mater of alle gode thyngis, for it is contrary
to lyinge, and gendryth dysir of ryghtfulnes, and thys justyse or
ryghtfulnes gendryth confydens. Confydens gendryth largenes.
10 Largenes gendryth famyliaryté or homlynes. þis homlynes gendryth
frendchyp. Frenchyp gendryth counsel and help in euery nede.
And be thys þe world was ordeynid, and eke þe lawe of man, for þis
acordyth bothe to resun and natur. Than is it opyn in owghte
þat þe dysir of gouernanz for goode fame is goode, lawdabyl and
15 durabil. |

Capitulum viij

[f. 21ᵛ] O Alysaunder, declyne and sette asyde þe bysynes of bestyal lustys
or inordinate wyllys or desyrys of þe flesche, for-qwy þei be
coruptybyl. And trwly carnal appetytis inclyne þe wylle and
20 sensualyté to dysyris coruptybyl of a bestly dysyr or a bestyal in-
clynacion, þe qwyche is of þe spyrite of lyfe in bestys, þe qwyche
dysyris be noȝt forbydin be dyscrecion. Qwer-for, qwan carnal
lustys be fulfyllyd, þe coruptibil body is glad, and þe vertuus
intellygens, or þe soule, is trowbyld and sory, þat is incorruptybil.
25 Thanne thow must knowe þat þe bysines abowght þe lustys of
þe flesche gendyr carnal loue. Carnal loue gendryth couetyse.
Couetyse gendryth dysir of ryches. Desir of ryches gendryth on-
schamefulnes. Onschamefastnes gendryth presumcion. Presum-
29 cion gendryth ontrwth. Ontrwth gendryth bryburry. And bryburry
[f. 22] bryngith | forth schame and repref, of qwyche is born and brought
forth thraldam, þe qwyche ledith or bryngyth to þe detryment
bothe of Goddis lawe and lawe of man. It is also destruccion of
famyliarité and confusyon of alle vertuus verke and eke of manhod,
þe qwyche is contraryus to natur.

35 **The nyghte capityl**   **Capitulum ix**

Than fyrst and formest chefly it is conuenyent to a kynge, as to
hym-self, þat þe fame of hys name, as in laudabyl wysdam, be in

---

6 untrwthe (*twice*)] *initial* t *canc. in revision, to give* rwthe: *see n.*   13 owghte]
nowghte   26 Carnal loue gendryth] gendryth *written twice; the first* gendryth *canc.*

ryfe pupplyschyd or dyvulgate, and þat he with hys men, bothe in
communicacion and in hys gesturis schew dyscrecion and wysdam.
And for þat he is wurchyppyd and hys fame spred. And for þis
he is feryd of hys men, qwan þei se hym eloquent in hys wysdam
and is prudent in hys conceyte and hys dedys. But lyghtly it may 5
be knowyn qwydir þer be wysdam in a king or of onwysdam, be
odyr to kynnys. For qwat kynge sum-euir subdwyth his kyngdam
vndyr þe fer and lawe of God is wurthy | to regne and wurchypfully [f. 22ᵛ]
to haue lordchyp. But he þat onprofytabyly bryngyth hys owne
lawe in-to seruyté, and puttyth or throwyth vndyr hys kyngdam 10
and empyr, is transgressour of weyis or menys of trwth. As ho
seyth, he þat makyth lawes for hys pepyl and byndyth to obserue
þo lawys, þe qwyche lawys he makyth aftir hys carnal dysyr and
noȝt aftir þe lawys of God, he followyth noȝt þe veys of trwthe,
and is despyser eke of hys owne lawe, þe qwyche is cause þat 15
hys pepyl hath no confydens in hym. And conceyue þat wyse
phylisofrys, as seyth þis doctourr, qwyche wer inspyryd of God,
seyd þat it semyd a kyngis magesté to obtempyr hym-self to lawful
ordynawuns be þe lawys of God made, noȝt to make nwe lawys
hym-self, and be þe fyrst þat brekyth hem. But lete a kynge at 20
þe lest wey so demene hym þat hys pepyl may haue þat conceyte
þat he feryth God a-bouy, and hys subiecte to Hys godly power.
For | þan men fere hym and do hym gret reuerrens, qwan þei se [f. 23]
þat he feryth God. And if it be so þat only in apparens owteward
he schew hym-self religius, and is in hys werkys euyl-doyng, 25
sythyn þat it is herd for to couir werkys off wykkydnes but þat
þe pepyl on sum maner schal know yt, þan schal he be repreuyd of
God and condempnyd of men, and hys dede schal be infamyd, hys
empyr or hys dygnyté schal be mynwsyd, and þe dyademe of hys
glorye and excellens schal want wurchyp. For þer is non pryce, 30
reward ner tresour þat may bye ayen goode fame, if it be fully lost.

þe tenthe capitil   Capitulum xᵐ

Mor-ouir, it semyth a kynge to haue in wurchyp þem þat haue
þe lawe in kepyng, to wurchyp relygius men, and to enhauns wysemen, and forto talke with hem, to meue also to hem dowghtful 35
qwestyonnis, and to make interrogacion honestly, and to þer
resounys to ansqwer dyscretly, and þem þat be most wyse and

---

6 or] *ins. above*   11 of trwth] *added in margin*   18 obtempyr] ob-
temperyr

[f. 23ᵛ] most nobyl, to haue hem | most in reputacion and reuerrens, euiry
man aftyr þat hys state is in dygnyté or byrth, or in wyse gouernauns.

þe elleuynth capitil   Capitulum xj

5   It behouyth mor-ouir a kyng to thenk of þat qwyche is to come,
and to casuel chaunchys þat he perceyuith schal come and be-tyde
be lykelynes, to ley to hande befor be menys of wysdam, þat þe
chauns may þe eselyer be born. It acordyth also a kyng to be com-
passyf, and wrath and þe meuyng of þe sensualyté to restreyne,
10   lesse þat he, meuyd withowte avysement, fulfyllyd hys angyr in
dede as in smytyng or odyr vengauns doyng. And it is vertu in
a kyng to know hys owne errowr be þe dyscussyon of hys owne
reson, and qwan þat he is meuyd to do amys, be wysdam to reuoke
hys mocion, for it is gret wysdam in a kyng to gouerne hym-self.
15   Qwan þerfore a kynge ony proffytabyl thyng seyth to be done, þe
[f. 24] qwyche is goode, he owyth | to haue þat dyscrecion in hys doying
þat it be nowydyr to late done, nor to sone, for if he be to hasty
in hys dedys, þe pepyl wul sey he is impetuus. And if he be
slowe, þei wul sey þat he is sclugye, feynt and remysse. Qwerfor
20   a mene is necessary.

þe thuelthe capitil   Capitulum xij

It acordyth gretly to a kyngis dygnyté to be clad in solempne aray,
noȝt in nyce aray, but in solempne garmentis of valowr, þat he may
alwey schewe hym-self, qwan he must apper be-for hys pepyl, to
25   seme mor excellent, þe mor goodely and þe mor onorabyl. For it is
acordyng to a kyng in þat prerogatyfe to pase odyr, þat is to sey in
hys aray. For be aray þe dygnyté of euery state is made þe mor
semly, and mor had in reuerrens, þat dwe reuerrens be noȝt with-
29   drawyn for febyl aray. It is conuenyent to a kynge to be portly in
[f. 24ᵛ] hys behauyng, to be gentyl of speche, | eke þat hys voys be cler,
for þat profytith myche in tyme of bateyl.

þe thyrdtene capitil   Capᵐ xiij

O Alysaundyr, how specyus and how wurchypful it is in a kyng
to absteyne fro myche speche, but if it be so þat nede askyth it.

---

7 be lykelynes] be *ins. above*   11 doyng] *ends with flourish, possibly*
for doyngis   17 nowydyr] *possibly slip for* nowdyr   18 impetuus]
-us over a cancellation   21 thuelthe] *cf.* 120/18 *but see also* 118/3

For it is bettyr þat mennys erys hauyn longyng to her a kynge
speke, þan þat þe erys be repleschyd of myche speche of þe
kyngys talkyng. For qwan þe erys be fulfyllyd, þe affeccion or
dysyre of þe spyryt be fulfyllyd, and þan þei charge noȝt myche
of hys talkyng. It is also conuenyent and syttyng to a kyng, to 5
absteyne hym, and noȝt come to oftyn in-to þe felyschyp of hys
sogettys, and in specyal amonge þem þat be folk of none reputacion. For ouir-myche homlynes a-monge sogettys gendyrrith contempte of worchyp, and causyth þem to sett lytil by hym. Qwerfor
þe custom of men of Yinde is preysabyl, in dysposycion of þe 10
kyngdam and in despensacion, eke in makyng ordynauns for her
kynge, þe qwyche is þis: | þat þe kynge schal apper but onys [f. 25]
in þe yer be-forn hys men in kyngly aray, and alle hys wer-
ryourys abowght hym armyd, and he hymself syttyng vppon a stede
armyd in gold and precyus stonys on þe most semly wyse. And þan 15
þei make þe communnys to stonde alange or abak far fro þe kynge,
in sqwyche a dystauns þat þei may se þe kynge, and þan þe
statys of þe reme and hys baronnys a-bowght hym. And þat day
þei wer wunt to spede hard materis and to declar þe chaunsys of
thyngis done be-for, as in batell or odyr notabyl cassys. Than 20
schuld he telle hys charge and hys bysines þat he hath abowght
þe profyte or welefar of þe communys, or qwat daungeris in bateyl
he hath had for hem. And þat day he was wunt to yef yiftys to hys
lordys and to hys mene, and to delyuer prysonneris fro prison,
grauntyng þem perdonnys, and þat day to releue grete chargys of 25
hys sogettis, and many dedys of mercy to put in excersyse. | And [f. 25ᵛ]
qwan þe kynge hath spokyn, one of hys most notabyl princys, þat
hath most wysdam in vttyrrauns of materis, [schal speke] and þis
prince schal make a processe in comendacion of þe kynge, yeldyng
also preysyngis to God þat hathe so wele prouydyd to þe kyngdam 30
of Yinde to sende to þat pepyl so wyse an hed to gouerne þe kyngdam be justyse and mercy, and eke þat hath confermyd þe pepyl
of Yinde to be obeying and a-cordyng with one wylle. And aftyr
þe preysyngis of God and recommendacion of þe kyng, he schal
turne hys speche to þe preysyng of þe pepyl, commendyng her 35
goode maner, inducyng hem be examplys and resunnys to humilyté,
obedyens and reuerens, and to loue þe kynge. The qwyche speche
endyd, alle þe pepyl stodyith tenhauns þe kyngys [name] with

3 be] *prec. by canc.* is   18 and hys] *prec. by canc.* a   38 with] *ins.*
above

preysyngis, and to comend hys werkys, and to prey God for þe
kyngis lyfe, and be alle cyteis and hows-holdys to telle þe kyngis
dedys and hys wysdam. For þis þei lern her chyldyr of yought
[f. 26] tenduce to þe kyngis wurchyp and to loue | hym, tobey hym and
5 to drede hym. And be þis maner of wey þe goode fame of a kynge
princypally is pupplyschyd and incresyth bothe in priuyté and
opynly.

The fourtene capitil   Capitulum xiiij

The kynge þan was wunt to command þe malefactourys, þe
10 qwyche be þe commune voys of þe pepyl wer wurthy to dye, þat
day to make delyuerrauns, þat alle presumptuos pepyl schuld feer
and be correctyd be exampyl of hem. And þan also he was wunt
to reles or to lesse trybutys, and of marchauntys of odyr londys
and eke of hys owne reme, to dyspense with hem, and to reles
15 a parte of þer trybute, and to kepe hem and defende her personys
and her goodys. And þis is cause qwy þat countré is so ryche, for
þat marchauntys haue no wronge þer, but be onestly tretyd, and
þat equité is kept in bying and sellyng to ryche and por, straunger
and odyr, qwerfor þe kyngys tributys and resceytys be augmentyd.
20 Therfor it owyth to be stou[d]yd þat merchaundys comyng fro fer
[f. 26ᵛ] countré | þat þei be noȝt troubyllyd, ner haue no wronge, for þei
be bererrys of fame thorow-owte þe world, qwerfor straungerys
þei wold be tretyd be trwth, and be þis mene þe kyngis receyte is
incresyd, and cyteis be defensyd and incresyth bothe þe kyngdam
25 and þe wurchyp of þe kynge, and for þe fame and gode report þe
enmyis of þat kyngdam wax aferd. And þus lyuyth þe kynge
pesybilly and swrly and be this mene hath hys desyre.

The fyuetene capitil   Capitulum xv

O Alysaundyr, dysir noȝt þat qwych[e] is coruptybil and tran-
30 sytory, and þat qwyche thow must sone forsake. Ordeyne ryches
incoruptybyl, þat is to sey Lyffe onchongeabyl and euirlastyng
Kyngdam, þe qwyche is glorius and durabyl. Dresse þer-for thy
thowghtys to goode, yeldyng thy self gloryus and manly. Schone
þe weyis, in lustys of þe flesch, of bestis and lyonnys, and þer
35 onclennes. Be noȝt crwel, but sparyng þem þat thow hast victory |

---

4 tenduce] & tenduce   13 or] *prec. by canc.* &   22 fame] *prec. by*
canc. be   27 swrly] ly *over canc. final flourish* (*i.e.* -e *contraction*)
29 qwyche] qwychy: *cf. 129/29*   30-2 Reade/Take heade *in margin, in later hand*

of. Thenke of þat qwyche is to kome, and of accydental casis, for [f. 27]
thow knowyst noȝt qwat þe nest day schal brynge forth, qwydyr
trowbyl or ese, lyfe or deth. Folow neuir nor fulfyl þe dysyris of
þe flesch, as in etyng, in drynkyng, in lying with women, nor in to
longe slepe, for þise hurt natur.   5

The sextene capitil   Capitulum xvj

Buxum Emperour, inclyne þe noȝt to lying with women, fort
haue do with hem fleschly, for þat vyce is a propyrté of sqwyne.
Qwat glory is it to þe to exersyse þe vice of bestys onresonnabyl
and þe vice of brutis? But beleue me withowte dowght, þat oftyn 10
carnal comyxtyon is destrucion of þe body and schortyng of þe
lyfe, and corupc[i]on of vertuys, transgressyon of þe lawe, and
it gendryth womannys condycionys and at the last it bryngyth in
þat I spake of be-forn, þat is to sey, schortyng of lyfe.

The seuyntene capitil   Capitulum xvij | 15

It is conuenient to an emperouris magesté to haue in hys hows- [f. 27ᵛ]
old priuat seruauntys, þe qwyche be men of wurchyp, and trwe in
kepyng of priuyteis, with þe qwyche he may be myry in hys
chambyr, and eke to haue honest personys þat can harp and lwte
and pley at orgynnis qwan þat he fyindyth hym-self tedius, þat 20
is to sei irkesum or onlysty. For mannys spyritis hath delectacion
in sqwyche naturally, and hys wyttis restyn for þat tyme, and also
stody and curyosyté wansen awey for þe tyme, and alle þe body
is strenghyd þer-with. And if thow wult haue delectacion in myrth
of musyk, at þe most endur thre dayis in sqwyche maner of sportys, 25
or ellis contune four days, aftyr thow se yt expedyent, with honest
myrth in a priuat place. And qwan thow art in þat solas, absteyne
þi self fro drynke, but sette þi pece to þi mowth, as if thow drankyst
oftyn, and soffyr þi meny þat be in þat myrth with þe to drynke 29
oftyn of myghty wyne, | and make þi-self as thow thow were wel [f. 28]
forth, and feyn þiself as if thow wer takyn with myghty wyne.
And þan waite wysely at þi mennys langage and at her behauyng,
and than schalt thow her many secrete materis and her and per-
ceuye myche thyng, and make as thowghe þow heedyst hem noȝt.

7–8 fort haue] *written as one word* fforthaue   13 womannys] *corr. from*
no-mannys, *the* w *by error covering* o *as well as* n   at] *followed by second* at, *canc.*
26 se yt] seyt   28 þiⁱ] þei *conceivably intended form*   30 thow thow]
run together, separated by stroke in revision   31 thow wer] thowre were
32 waite] i *ins. above*

But lete thys maner of reuel no3t pase thryis in a yer. And thow
must haue a-bowght þe þi specyal menne þat schal telle þe al
þat euir is done and seyd thorow owte þi kingdam. And qwan þat
thow art amonge thy barownys, wurchyp þem þat be holdyn wyse
5 men and sad men, and þo þat haue deseruyd to be wurchyppyd.
Hold yche of hem in hys state. Comawnde one to dyne with þe þis
day, and anodyr to-morow. Yef þem rewardis on þe lyke wyse,
settyng þem after þer degré be in wurchyp. And lette þer be no
wurthy man longyng to þe, nor with-inne þi kyngdam, but lette
10 hym fele þi largenes in yiftys. And lete alle men knowe þe buxumnes
[f. 28ᵛ] of þi magesté, and the | nobylles of thy lyberal herte.

þe eghtene capitil   Capitulum xviij

It syttyth also a kyng to haue dyscrecion and contynens, and
for to absteyn fro myche lawghyng. For oftyn lawghyng takyth
15 a-wey reuerens, and causyth also þat a man of wurchyp is no3t
sett by, for it is a token of a wantown hert. Also oftyn lawghyng
gendryth age, makyng a rympyld face.

The nynetene capitil   Capitulum xi[x]

Mor-ouir, thow must knowe þat men be bowndyn mor to do
20 reuerrens to þe kynge, and þe kynge to do wurchyp to þe pepyl
with-in hys palyce and hys consystory, þan in odyr placys. For þer
it syttyth þat he þat hath done wronge be ponyschyd aftyr hys
degré be, þat odyr þat be present schuld feer and absteyne hem
fro wrongys doying. But conceyue þat on one maner of wyse
25 a wurthy man that hath offendyd schuld be ponyschyd, and on
anodyr maner of wyse he þat is an abiecte persone, a man of none
[f. 29] valwr. It is þer-for good | rygourr and also to kepe or to obserue
contynens, þat þer be betwene þe kyng and hys sogettys a dystyn-
cion of personys. For it is wrytyn in þe boke of Esculabyis, þat
30 sqwyche a kynge is laudabyl and to be louyd þat is lyke to an egyl
hayng lorchyp a-monge byrdys, and no3t he is to be preysid þat
is as a byrd sogette. If ony persone þer-for in þe kyngis courte, or
in þe presens of þe kyngis magesté, presume any wronge to do, or to
brynge in ony offens, or to offend ayens any man, lete it be con-
35 sydryd to qwat entente he do hit, qwydir it be done of myrth for to
plese þe and to prouoke odyr to sport, or if it be done in despyte or

13 It] *Illuminated initial* I *followed by* it *written out in full*   18 xix] ixi
32–3 or in] or in in   35 do hit] *run together*

contempt of þi dygnyté. And if it be for þe fyrst cause, lette
hym be esyli corectyd. And if it be for þe secunde cause, lette
hym dye þer-for.

Þe tweynti capitil   Capitulum xx^m

O Alysaundyr, obedyens of a lordchyp or of a lordchypper 5
stondyth on four wysis: þat is to sey, in relygiosyté, | in loue, in [f. 29^v]
curyalyté, and in reuerrens. O Alysaundyr, turne to þe the hertys of
þi sogettys, take fro hem wrongys and onryghtys, yef no man mateir
nor cawse for to speke amys of þe, for þe comun pepyl is redy to
gangil. Conteyne so þi-self þat þei haue no mater to speke ayens þe, 10
and be þat schalt þu schone her bysynes: þei may noȝt do ayens
þe. Mor-ouir, knowe þat sadnes is þe glory, þe enhaunsyng or
þe wurchyp of euery dygnyté, and þe feer of a lordchyp and þe
enhaunsyng of a kyng. Than is it þe most hye wysdam þat þi
reuerrens abyde in þe hertys of þi sogettys rather þan þi loue.   15

Þe one and tweynti capitil   Capitulum xxj

It is wrytin þat a kynge schuld be in hys kyngdam as þe reyne
to þe erth, þe qwyche is þe grace of Good and þe blyssyng of
heuyn, þe lyfe of þe erth, and þe help of alle lyuyng thyng, for be
þe menys of reyne in þe oryent, marchauntis ordeyne her jorneys 20
in qwenchyng sondys, help also to bylerris in stabylischyng þe erth.
| And yit vmqwyle in reynys þer falle thundrys and lyghtenyng, [f. 30]
and ryueris and spryngis bolne, and many hurtys be-tyde þer-of,
be qwyche hurtys lyuyng thyngis perysch; but neuirþeles þise
accydental thyngis lette nowght but þat men preyse gloryus God 25
in Hys magesté, consyderyng þe tokynnys of hys Grace, and yiftis
of Hys mercy. For be þe reyn þe frwtys of þe erthe be multiplyid,
and gresse and herbis, treis and vynnys, increce and burgyn, and
for þis cause men yef preysyng to Good and foryet þe hurtys þe
qwyche þat be-tyd be reyne. And exampyl of a kyng is acordyng 30
to þe exampyl of wyndis, þat glorius God sendith owte and exten-
dyth fro þe tresur of [H]is mercy, and be þo wyndys bryngith forth
cloudys and makyth cornys to growe, and rypyth þe frutys of treis
and þe spyrytis alle of lyuyng thyngis be qwekynnyd. Watir
dysirid be wyndys be had, for wyndys lyftyn watrys beryng hem 35
houyng ouir þe erth. | It helpyth eke schyppenne to seyle for lukyr [f. 30^v]

8 mateir] mate*ir*   27 be þe] *prec. by canc.* þe   32 His] þis
35 lyftyn] f *ins. aboue*   36 houyng] g *ins. above*

in-to fer londys, and many gode thyngis be causyd be wyndys.
And yet, neuir-þe-lesse, many hurtys be causyd of wyndis, many
gret perellis, and many lettyngis bothe on þe lond and on þe ssee,
and owteward trowbyllis with sygingys þei brynge to þe hert.
5 Mennys goodys in tempestis þei brynge to losse and to spoyling,
and be hem þe corruppcionys of þe eyr be gendyrd, dedly venym
is noryschyd, and many grete hurtys falle of wyndys. And qwan
creaturis þat be on þe erth besechen Hym þat makyth alle þingis
to take a-wey fro þem thys hurtys, He soffyrryth neuir-þelesse þe
10 wyndis to haue her propyr cours and her accion of propyrté
youyn to hem. For alle thyngis be Hys wysdam be equal weght,
nowmbyr and order He hath ordeynyd, and as a lawe hath ordeynid to Hys seruaunt to serue tho, and þat yede owte of Hys
[f. 31] inenarrabyl goodenes and Hys gret mercy. | Thys parabyl also
15 may be [l]ykenyd to wyntyr and to somir, þe qwyche God hath
ordeynyd to generacion and refresschyng and to nwyng and also
dwrabyllyté of temporal thyngis, and eke of thyngis natural. And
yit many inconuenyentis, perellis and mortalyteis betyde, bothe
of hete and of cold, bothe of somir and wyntyr. And on þe lyke
20 wyse, in a kyng it betydith, for þer comyth many grete profytis be
hym, and also tho thyngis þat be heuysum and dysplesyng to hys
sogettis, qwan in hem þe abieccion of mysery be þe kyngis correccion neghyth.

Þe to and tweynti capitil   Capitulum xxij

25   O Alysaundyr, inquir and serche of þe pouerté and necessyté of
þe por, þat be hard be-stad, and help to þo nedy folk in tyme of þer
necessyté. And of þi buxumnes þu schalt chese sqwyche a man þat
knowy[t]h her talkyng, þat louyth justyse, þe qwyche can far with
29 hem and inquyr qwat þei nede, þat þis man may fulfylle þi stede,
[f. 31ᵛ] and mercyfully loue hem and gouerne hem. And in þis | maner
obseruauns of þe [kyngis duetis is fulfyllyd and the pe]pyl is
gladyd and Godde is plesyd.

Þe tre and twenty capitil   Capitulum xxiij

       O Alysaundyr, ordeyn be þi wysdam dyscrete personys, þe
35 qwyche in tyme may stuffe þe with alle maner of greynys, noȝt
for þi owne howshold only, but for to help þi communys in tyme
of nede. For in yeris of derth þi pepyl þat is poor schal perysch,

15 lykenyd] kykenyd

but if þei haue relef. Þan þi prouydens myche schal be comendyd, if þu haue qwer-with to releue hem. Þis is a gret sleyght and defens of þe kyngdam, þe helthe of þe pepyl, and þe kepyng of þi cyteis, for þan þi commaundment schal thyrl þi pepyllis hertys, and þan þi chef glory schal be, qwan þe pepyl haue cler vndyrstondyng þat 5 þi prouydens was so gret to prouyde be-forn of sqwyche a gret necessary casualté, and men seeyng þi wysdam, þei schal feer þe, loue þe, and do þe gret reuerrens.

The four and tweynti capitil   Capitulum xxiiij

O Alysaundyr, oftyn I have warnyd þe, and yit I warne þe, þat 10
þu kepe | my doctryne, and if þu obserue it þow schalt haue þi [f. 32]
purpose, and þi kyngedam schal be stablyschyd and abyde or
contynw. Fear þan þe schedyng of mennys blode, for þat longith
to God, þat knowyth þe priuyté of euiry mannys hert. Qwer-for
neuir of crwelté, but he be dempt be lawe, sle hym noȝt qwat-sum- 15
euir he be. Take noȝt vppon þe Gooddys offyce, for it is noȝt
youyn to þe to knowe Goddys priuyté. For if God ponysch be deth,
it is to suppose þat He is grettly offendyd. Bewar þan of schedyng
of mannys bloode, for þe gret doctor Hermogynes wrote seyng
þus, 'Qwan a creatur sleeth a creatur lyke to hym, þe vertuis of 20
heuyn' (þat is to sey, aungelys), 'þei crye to Goddys Magesté,
seyng, "Lord, Lord, þi seruaunt wul be lyke to þe!" And if he be
slayne onryghtfully, the hyest Maker abouyn ansqweryth, "Soffyr
hym þat sleth, for he schal be slayne. Þe vengauns is to Me, and I
schal reward it." And so oftyn þe vertuys of heuyn schal represente 25
hys deth þat is slayne, tyl vengauns be | fallyn vppon þe man-sleer. [f. 32ᵛ]
þe qwyche mansleer schal be one of þo þat schal abyde in euirlastyng peynys.'

Þe fyue and tweynti capitil   Capitulum xxv

O Alysaundyr, in alle peynis thow hast knowlech, for many 30
kendis of peynis and harmys thow hast had in experyens. Brynge to
remembrauns þin owne stok, þinke on þi fadir and þi modyr, and
dyscysse her lyfe, and þow mayst fynde and drawe owte many
goode examplys. For þe done dedis of þem þat wer befor, is a
certytude of lernyng of þo þingis þat be to come. Dyspyse neuir 35

7 feer þe] þe ins. above   11 þu obserue it] ins. above   31 thow hast]
thow s hast   32 on] followed by canc. interl. insertion (beginning wu?)
35 certytude] certydtude, with otiose d expuncted

hym þat is lesse þan yow in dygnyté, for oftyn it betydyth þat
ryght pore be made ryche and come to wurchyp, and þan hath
he myght to noye þe. Be war þat þu breke neuir þi promysse ner
þi feyth, ner no bonde of frenchyp qwyche þu hast promysid, for
5 disworchyp folowyng, for þat acordyth to ontrwe and onstedfast
yong folk and also to comune women. Kepe þer-for trwly þi
[f. 33] feyth promysyd, for to alle ontrwthe þer folowyth an euyl | ende,
þow it be so þat gret profyte myght falle in brekyng of þi promysse.
For it is an euyl tecche and a repreuabyl exampyl, and of þe kende
10 of euyl dedys and onuertuus. Knowe þat be trwth and feyth [be] þe
congrecion and gadryng of men in felyschyp and trost: cyteis
þer-by be inhabytid, þe communyon of men, þe domynacion of
a kynge. Be feyth castellis be kept, cyteis be gouernyd. For trwly,
take awey feyth and alle men schal retorne to þe fyrst state, þat is
15 to sey lyke to brutis, and in symilytude to bestis. Most trwe
kynge, bewar þat þow breke noȝt þi feyth þat þu hast made, ner
þi promisse nor thyne othe. Knowyst noȝt, þe gret clerk Hermogines beryth record þat þer be to spyrytis kepyng þe, one on þi
ryght syde, anodyr on þi left syde, kepyng þe and knowyng alle
20 þi werkys, makyng relacion to þe Maker abouyn alle þat euir
þat þu art purposyd to do? In trwthe, and þer war ryght noȝt ellis
but þis, yt schuld withdrawe þe and euery man fro euery dishonest
[f. 33ᵛ] werk. Ho comst | [þu] streynyth þe so oftyn for to sqwer? Truly
þu schuldyst noȝt do þat with-owte gret necessyté. A kynge, but if
25 he were myche preyid and oftyn requyrid, he schuld noȝt sqwer.
Knowyst noȝt þat sqweryng is dysconuenyent to þi dygnyté, and
þat þu doste derogacion to þi wurchyp qwan þu sqwerist? And if
þu wold serche þe cause qwy þe kyngdam of Ambayenis and Scytis
wer destroyd, I schuld ansqwer to þe, þat þe kyngis of þis nac[i]-
30 ounys vsyd sqweryng to fraude and to disceyt of men, brekyng
þat feyth, þo boondys and þo kumnauntys þat þei made with odyr
nacionys, be sleyghtys to ondo hem and to destroy hem, qwerfor
be justyce and equité of þe almyghty Rewler, men of Iinde destroyd þem. O best taught Alysaundir, I wul þat þu knowe þat in
35 ordynauns of þi kyngdam and gouernaunz of þine empyr, þer be
certeyn specyal techyngis ryght moral longyng to þe as to þin owne
howsold, and also to þe comun peplys gouirnauns. But her is noȝt
[f. 34] þe place qwer | I am purposyd to wryte hem, but I schal yef hem to

þe in a certeyn place of þis boke, and þei schal be holsum techyngis
brefly expressyd and ryght profytabyl, in þe obseruyng of qwyche
þu schalt be in prosperyté, owr Lord grauntyng.

Þe syx and twey[n]ti [capitil]   Capitulum xxvj

Forthynke þe neuir of þinge þat is past as of trowbyl or heuynes, 5
for þat is þe propyrté of feynt wommen. Kepe euir opyn manhod,
kepe euir curyalyté of gode tecchys and gentyl, excersyse goodenes.
For in þise is þe proteccion of þi kyngdam and þe destruccion of
þin enmyis. Ordeyne and spede chyualry placis, and ordeyn stodyis and scoolys in þi kyngdam. Soffyr and comaunde to þi sogettys 10
to do lern her chyldyr in alle honest syens, and in specyal in þe
seuyn lyberal syens. And to por folk þat may noȝte, þat haue
chyldyr lyckely to lernne, þi prouydens schuld help to þer fyndyng.
Make a prerogatyfe in dygnyté to alle goode stodyerris, to þem þat 14
profyte in þer stody, þat be þat enhaunsyng | þei may haue a lyst [f. 34ᵛ]
and a zele to stody and to lerne. And to þem þat be wele lettryd
þu schalt behaue þe thus: qwan þei beseche þe of ony boone þat
is leful, þu schalt graunt y[t] frely, þu schalt with benyuolens yefe
attendaunz to her lettris þat þei wryght on to þe, and preyse þem
þat haue deseruyd presyng, and reward hem þat haue deseruyd 20
to be rewardyd. And if þu do þus, thow schalt excyte lettryd men
for to enhaunse þi nobyl deedys, and to wryte þi gestys to an
euirlastyng remembraunz. Thys maner of doyng is comendabyl,
and þis prudens is to be preysid. And in þis þine empyr is wurchyppyd, þi kyngdam is made semely, and þin courte is illumnyd, 25
alle causualteis and nobyl dedys þat longe to þi persone be
comendyd to mende. For ho sublymyd þe kyngdam of Grekis
as be fame? Ho wrote her deedys and perpetually be alle þe world
dyfamyd hem? For trwth it was þe bysy stody and þe pregnaunt
wytte of sad wyse men þat passyngly louydyn konnyng, and for 30
þat þei deseruyd | sqwyche preysing. And trwly I sey, a maydyn [f. 35]
dwellyng with an husbond-man þ[er] be gret stody knwe þe cours
of þe yer and þe constellacionys and þe cours of alle sterris, and
þe meuyng of alle planetis, and qwan þe festys schuld falle of hem,
and þe solempnyté of euiry monthe, þe causys also of þe schortyng 35
of þe day and þe nyght, the sterrys also of destynyis, qwat schuld
betyde, and infynyte thyngis be-syde, þe qwyche syens causyd þe

10 scoolys] one o ins. above   18 graunt yt] grauntyd   32 þer] þat

world to magnyfye her, to wundyr of her wysdam. Qwerfor þe
grownde of preysyng spryngyth of gouernauns.

Here endyth þe fyrst boke of þe Priuyté of Priuyteis.

Parisiensis

5 **Explicit primus liber de Secretis secretorum, secundum
translacionem Johannis de Caritate.**

[þe Secunde Boke]

[The fyrst capytyl]   [Capitulum i]

[f. 37] . . . of yougthe and browght vp with venym, þat þe natur of þat
10 mayde was turnyd in-to þe natur of serpentis. And had noȝt I þe
same owr beholdyn her dyligently and be my kunnynge dempt how
sche was dysposid, qwanne þat I saugwe her þat sche with-owte
schamfastnes so boldly and so orybyly behold in to euiry mannys
face, I sawe veryli þat sche schuld a-slayne as many men as sche
15 had bytyn, as thow lernydyst in experiens aftyr-ward. And had I
noȝt a-youyn þe warnyng at þe fyrst tyme þat thow haddyst
aloyne by her, þu hadist bene starke dede.

The secunde capitil   Capitulum ij

O Alysaundyr, kepe þi nobyl angelyke soule, for it was com-
20 mendyd to þe, noȝt to be dyshonestyd, but þat it schuld be glory-
fyid. Be noȝt of þe nowmbyr of onclene lyueris, ner of her kend,
but of þe nowmbyr of wysemen. O buxum kynge, if it may be be
ony wey, ryse noȝt, ner sytte noȝt, ner ete noȝt, nor drynke noȝt,
[f. 37ᵛ] nor | do vttyrly ryght noȝt, with-owte þe counsel of an experte
25 man in þe kunnyng of sterris. Know þer-for for certeyn, þat
glorius God made ryght noȝt in veyn nor ydil to natur, but alle be
made of a cause prouabil, and of a reson most certeyn. For be
þis wey and inquisycion, Plato, owr most excellent doctour, knwe
þe partis of þingis compownyd and of contraryus qwalyteis and
30 of colourys in her kendys, in comparyson to þingis compounyd,
and be þat he had þe kunnyng of sterris formyd to deme by. Trost
neuir in onwyse mennys seyingis, as þei þat seyne þat þe kunnyng of sterris is hard to be knowyn, and also þe cours of planetis,

---

8 *f. 35ᵛ blank; f. 36 missing.*   9 yougthe] t *ins. above*   20 but] t
indistinct   25 Know] *prec. by canc. capital* S *and the sign for a new section*

and þei sey þat no man may cum þer-by. But sqwyche pepyl þei
knowe noȝt qwat þei sey, for to þe power of mannys vndyrstondyng
þer is no thyng hard, for alle þingys be knowabyl in vey of resun.
And odyr folys þer be also, þat sey þat God prouydid and ordeynyd
fro þe beginnyng euirlastyng, qwerfor þei sey þat it profytith noȝt   5
to know before qwat | schal be-tyde aftyrward, sythyn it is so þat it   [f. 38]
is necessary þei schuld falle and must nedys be: qwat is wurth þan
þe kunnyng of sterris? I ansqwer and sey, þat thow sum thyngis
schal come necessaryly, yit if þei be knowyn be-forn þei schal be
þe mor esyly born, and be wysdam, in maner sette a-syde. And þus   10
þei be schonyd for in as myche as þei be for to come, and þat I haue
knowyng of hem, I receyue þo chaunsys be wysdam and prouydens, and so þei pase with-owte ony gret heuynes or gret hurt.
As be exampyl, qwan we se be owr syens þat wyntir schal falle of
gret vttyr cold, and long endur, men may puruey of sqwyche stuff   15
þat þei schal with-owte ony grete anoyauns scape þat wyntyr. On
heete of þe same wyse. And qwan a derth schal falle, if men knowe
it be-for, þei may make prouydens of qwete, of wyne, and of odyr
thyngis necessary, so þat þei schal scape þise hard | yeris of   [f. 38ᵛ]
hungir and nedfulnes. Þer-for it is myche wurth to know þat schal   20
be-tyde, for be þat knowlech men may be war and schonne þat
euyl þat schal falle. And also, mor specially, qwan þei se þat
sqwyche a thyng schal be-tyde, þei may pray God, þat hath alle
thyng in gouernanz, þat of Hys hye goodenes He wul turne fro
hem þat euyl chaunz, or dyspose it odyr wyse. For þ[e] good   25
Lord diffinyd neuir thyng so streytly þat be þat He dyd derogacion
to Hys power þat He may reuoke aftir He seeth cause qwy to reuoke.
For men may be-seche þe buxumnes of God with orysonnys,
deuocionys and preyeris, with sacrifisis, fastyngis and elmes, and
odyr goode dedis, axyng foryefnes of þat þei haue done amys,   30
forthynkyng hem of her gilt. And be thys mene almyghty God wul
turne fro hem þat vengauns, trowbyl, or heuynes þat þei fer of.
Lete vs þan now turne ayene to owr | fyrst entente and exortacion.   [f. 39]
It owyth to be knowyn þat astronomy is dyuydid in to þre partis,
þat is to sey in þe ordynacion of þe ix heuynnis and of þe speeris   35
and þe dysposycion of planetis, and þe dyuision of þe sygnys, þe
elongacion also of hem, and of þe maner of þer werkynkys. And þis
parte of astronomy is clepyd þe syens. The secunde parte is of þe

25 þe] þat   30–1 in margin in later hand: The Protestor wanteth these
dedes of Charité

qwalyté and þe maner of knowyng þe meuyng of þe fyrmament, þe
rysyng or þe spryngyng of þe sygnys, vppon thyngis neghyng þe
celestyal speris or euir þei come to knowlech be vysual appeirryng.
And þis is þe secunde parte of astronomye, or þe konnyng of
5 domys. And þe thyrd parte, þe qwyche is most wurthy, specyfiith
of thre thyngis, þat is to sey, of speris, planetis, and sygnis. Knowe
þan certeynli þat planetis þat be fyxe, þe nowmbyr of hem is a
thousaund and nyne and tweynti, of qwyche in a certeyn parte of
9 þis boke I schal schewe þe my doctrine.

[The thyrde capitil]   **Capitulum iij**

And now fyrst and formest I schal yef þe my doctrine of
medecynys and odyr priuyteis þat be necessary to kepyng of þi
helth, þat thow schalt nede no leche. For þe kepyng of helth is
bettir than ony medycine, and þis doctrine and þise secretis be
15 ryght necessari to þe gouernanz of þis world. But it must be knowyn
þat þer is no wey to do ony thyng by, or to gett ony syens, but only
be clernes and power of vndystondyng. And þis power is noȝt
but be helth. And helth is noȝt withowte equalyté of complexcion.
And þer is no complexcion but be temperaz and equalyté of
20 humoris. And glorius God hath ordeynid a mene and a remedy to
þe temperauns of humoris and to þe conseruyng of helth, and to
gete many odyr þingis þerby, þe qwyche God schewyd to holy
[f. 40] profetis, and to ryghful men, and to sondry odyr qwyche þat
He chase and ill[u]mynyd with þe spyryte of godly | wysdam, and
25 hath yiftid hem with þe yiftis of kunnyng. And of þise seyd men
phylysofris had þe begynnyng and þe princehed of fylosofye, and
men of Yinde, Peercis, Grekys, and Latynis of þise haue drawyn
owte and wrytyn þe byginyngis and priuyteis of craftis and syensis
lyberal, for be-cause þat in fylisofris wrytingis þer was founde no
30 thyng fals ner no thyng repreuabyl, but appreuyd of wyse men.
He trwly þat is cause of hys owne lesyng, myche mor þan schal yeue
occasyon or cause to odyr men of lesyng, for þat thyng þat we loue
we chese, and we seke þat thyng þat we ar purposid to knowe.
But þu owyst to knowe, þat among alle odyr fylisofyris, glorius
35 God hath inflamyd Grekys with kunnyng most specially to þe
serchyng of syens, and to knowe þe begynnyng and grownde of
causis and thyngis natural, and of þat we haue made remembranz

1 sygnys] *followed by canc.* s *or* f   4 wurthy] onwurthy; dignior B 6
10 I schal] is schal   15 to gett] to to gett   19 hath ordeynid] *prec. by*
another hath ordeynd, *canc.*   22 ryghful] *cf. 121/3*   23 illumynyd] illimynyd

in odyr placis. And nowe aftyr þe sentens of fylysofris in þis booke
I purpose sentencyusly to procede.

The fourthe capitil | Capitulum iiij [f. 40ᵛ]

Alle wyse men and natural philysofris acorde, seyng how man
is made of opposytis and contrarius elementis, and of sqwyche 5
humorys þat alle-wey nedyth noryschyng and fedyng and pocyon-
nis, qwyche if he fayle or lak, hys substauns must corupte. And if
so be þat he vse þise metys and drynkys in superfluyté, doyng
excesse, or ellis he withdrawyth hem to myche be abstynens, he
must nedly falle into grete sekenes or febylnes. And if he vse hem 10
temperatly, he schal fynde help and comfort to þe lyfe, strenght of
body, and helth of alle hys substauns. And furthermor, þei acorde
in one, þat he þat pasith þe dwe mene in fulnes or in voydenes,
in slepe or in wecchyng, in meuyng or in reste, in laxing hym
or constypacion of hys wombe, in withdrawyng or holdyng hys 15
veynal blode, may not escape þe woodenes of sekenes and heuysum
troubyl of infyrmyteis. Of alle qwyche vndyr congruent schortnes |
I yefe þe my doctrine most certeyn, of þe kendys of sekenes and [f. 41]
remedyis of þo sekenessis. Alle þise wyse men þan acord þat he þat
is war of superfluyté, and of to myche indygens or abstynens, 20
kepyng equalyté and temperauns, þat manir of man þat vsyth
þis schal perceyue and possede þe most holssum helth and lenght
of dayis, þat is to sey lyue longe. And I trwly fond neuir no fylisofyr
dyscordyng fro þis sentens, but þat alle þe delectabyl thyngis
of þis world, qwedyr þei be of lustys or lykyngis, or ryches, or 25
melodyis, or wurchyppys, alle be for duryng, or durabylité. He
þanne þat desyrith to lyue and to endur longe in helth, he must
renounce or forsake hys owne wylle, þat he hast noȝt o mele or on
etyng sone aftyr anodyr. For I hard sey of Ypocras þat he kept
sqwyche a maner of dyete þat hys body semte febyl and i-weykyd 30
þer-of, qwerfor hys dyscypyl seyd to hym, þat if he wold ete wele
hys body schuld noȝt be so febyl. To home Ypocras ansquerd,
'Sone, I wul ete on sqwyche | wyse þat I may lyue, and noȝt [f. 41ᵛ]
lyue forte ete, puttyng my lust in etyng rather þan in longe lyuyng'.
Nurchyng must be dysiry[d] and vsyd to þat entent to durabylnes, 35
to lyfe longe, and noȝt to desyr longe lyfe to hawe lust of metys.
And trwly I knw many þat lessyd of fedyng, absteynyng fro her
appetitis, sparyng her belyis, and lyuid temperatly, dietyng

16 not] o *ins. above*   35 dysiryd] dysiryng

þem self, and þer-for þei had heyl bodyis of bettyr dysposicion, of
lenger lyfe, and of goode appetite, beyn and lyght in meuyng. And
þis is experte and opyn in men of þe cuntré of Arabe and also be
hem þat oftyn vse to go be desertys and for jorneys, þat labour,
5 and ete but lyghtly. Qwerfor it is an opyn argument þat to absteyn
fro gret etyng, and to porge þe stomak be summe labour to confort
þe natural hete, is most chef medycyne.

The fyfthe capytil   Capitulum v

9   O Alysaundyr, in medycine is conteynyd þe most certeyn and
[f. 42] trwest lernyng, þat þe kepyng of helth stondyth | in tweyn thyngis
chefly. The fyrst is þat a man vse metys acordyng or conuenyent
to hys age, and to þe tyme in þe qwyche he is inne, and to þe
custum of hys natur, þat is to sey, þat he vse metys and drynkys
with þe qwyche he hath be wunt to be norchyd with, and with
15 sqwyche as þe substauns of hys body hath most be refreschyd with.
The secunde is þat he purge hym-self of þo thyngis þat be gen-
dyrrid of superfluyté and corupte humourrys, as is vryne and
egestyon, &c. [Aftir] that it owyth to be knowyn, þat þe bodyis
of men, qwych be receptaclys of mete and drynke, þei be mynucyd
20 and resoluyd, bothe þe bodyis receyuyng, as wele as þo alymentis
þat be receyuyd, in qwyche þei be resoluyd, fyrst be natural hete,
qwyche dryith þe moystur of bodyis, and nurchyth and labouryth
and is febyllyd for þe tyme, and aftir confortyd be slep and browgh
24 to equalyté. þe body is also resoluyd be þe hete of þe sonne and
[f. 42ᵛ] be wynde, þe qwyche dryith þe moystour of bodyis | and be fed
of moystur as wele of bodyis as of flodys. Qwan þan þe body is
hot vaporabyl, þat it stemyth of myghtynes, noȝt of labour, for
sqwyche a dysposyd persone grose metys be norchyng, for þat
qwyche is sent owte of sqwyche a dysposyd body is of grete
30 quantyté, and of gret substauns and grose substauns, for gret hete
and vaporis of þe body, sicut veneria. And qwan þe body is depressyd, lene and weyke, or ellis drye, and þe stomake of no scharp
appetyte, þan be goode to vse sotel metys þat be lyght of dygestyon,
as be hennys and partrychis, and þo þat gendyr moystur, as veele
35 and kyddys, for þat qwyche is dyssoluyd fro sqwyche a body so
dysposyd is but of lytil quantyté, for þe streyt passagis of þe
wombe and of pooris. And þis is þe certeyn wey of doctrine to
kepe helth, þat a man euir vse metys acordyng to hys complexcion

5 an] *ins. above*

in hys helth. As thus, þei þat be of hoote natur and myghty sof-
fycyently, hote metys in temperauns acord to hem. And þei þat be |
of cold natur, þo thyngis þat be cold in temperauns acorde to þe [f. 43]
norchyng of þat dysposicion. And on þe lyke wyse of moyste or
drye bodyis, to vse metys aftir þer dysposicion. But þanne if þe 5
hete of þe body be aumentyd and inflamyd, or fyrid be grete in-
flammacion, owdyr for hote metys, or a casuel or a straunge hete,
þe qwyche ouircomyth and hath lordechyp ouir þe body, þan [is]
it necessary to vse metys contrary, as colde metys, pork, and
sqwyche odyr. And qwan it is so þat þe stomak is myghti and 10
goode, to sqwyche one acordyth best myghty and stronge metys.
For sqwyche a stomak is lyke to a myghty fyr, þat hath power to
brenne myghty and grete treys, and þow þei be many. And qwan
þe stomak is febyl and colde, to sqwyche one sotel metys and
lyght of dygestyon be most acordyng. For þe werkyng of sqwyche 15
a stomak is lyke a fyr þat on ese may brenne rede spyris and
ruschys. And þe tokyn of a goode stomake is þis: lyght-|nes of [f. 43ᵛ]
body, and clernes of wytte, and goode appetyte. The tokynys of
a febyl stomak and of febyl dygestyon be þise: slugynes of þe
body and starkenes, slownes in alle dedys, but in specyal in gate, 20
and also softnes, bolnyng of þe face, and oftyn gapyng with þe
mowthe, heuynes of þe eyn, reysyng of wynde at þe mowth, qwyche
is clepy[d] bolkyng, and in specyal qwan þer rysith sowr or byttyr
mater, or fleumatyk, fro þe stomak, with þat wynde, and for þat be
gendryd wyndis and bolnyngis of þe wombe, and þe appetyte is 25
mynucyd and febyllyd. And if þis febylnes and indygest mater be
habundaunt, þer comyth þer-of streykyng owte of þe armys and
þe body, and þe bak bowyth, and þe nek, and many odyr thyngis
besyde þat be contrarius to helth, destroy[u]s of þe body, and
coruptifis of natur. Qwerfor, buxum Emperour, þu owyst to kepe 30
þe fro sqwyche dy[s]conuenyentys, be goode dyetyng and be þisse
folowyng medycinys.

The syxte capitil | Capitulum vj [f. 44]

Syth þe body of man is coruptybyl, and corrupcion betydyth of
opposycion complexcionary, and humourys þat be in þe body, as 35
sanguyne, rede coler, flewme, and malencoly, qwyche is blak
coler, I am avysid in þis present werk to wryt to þe profytabyl

9 contrary] second r ins. above   23 clepyd] clepyng   37 wryt] wyt
ins. above with r ins. above this

thyngis, and on alle wyse to þe necessary, as of þe priuyteis of þe
craft of medycine, with þe qwyche thow schalt be contente, sythin
it is to þe gretly honest, and most conuenyent, þat alle þe sekenes
of a kyng or a lord be noȝt wust of hys leche. And if thow exemplarly
5 and prudently beholdyn þat kunnyng in medycynis, and be
þat wysdam þat I haue wrytin to þe, and þis syens put in vse and
experyens, thow schalt nede no leche, except casualteis, þat is to
sey hurtys of batellis, and odyr þat on no wyse may be schonyd.

þe seuyth [capitil]   Capitulum vij

10   O Alysaundyr, qwan thow art rysyn fro slepe, þu schuldys
walke esyly a lytil in þi chambyr toward and froward, and alle þi
[f. 44ᵛ] membrys with þi body euynly to strech | and streyn owte euynly
on lenght, and to kembe þine hed. For þe strecchyng owte of þi
membris strenghyt alle þi body, and makyth dygest humoris to
15 ascende and to fylle alle partys, and þe kembyng of þine hede
bryngyth owte vaporys and fumys of noyus humorys, þe qwyche
in tyme of slepyng ascendyd fro þe stomak to þe hed. And
in somyr wasche þe with cold watir, for [it] constreynith and
reteynyth þe hete of þe body and of þe hed, and þis excytith a dysir
20 to mete. And aftir clothe þe with godely clothys, þe qwyche be
ryche of clothe, goodely of colour and of facion, for þe appetyte
and þe wylle and þe spyrytis be confortyd and delytid in þe consyderacion and þe beholdyng of fresch aray. And aftyr þat þu schalt
drye and rubbe thy tethe with þe barke of a tree qwyche is drye and
25 hoote of natur, and byttir of tast, as is þe barke of aloes and of þe
[f. 45] pynet-tree and þe fyrre tree. And þis rubbyng helpith | myche,
for it clensyth þe teth and kepith hem fro rootyng and fro wurmys,
and þe flewme of þe mowth it lyqwefyith and bryngyth owte, it
scharpyth and clensyth þe tunge and claryfyith þe speche and
30 þe voys, and it excytith dysir of etyng. And aftyr þat, in tyme conuenyent, þu schalt porge þi-self be egestyon and wynde, for þis
profytith gretly. It opynnyth þe stoppyngis of þe brayne, it
makyth fulle and fleschy þe nek and þe armys, it claryfiyth þe face
and þe syght, it strenghyth þe wytte, and it slowyth and make
35 age to tary. And þan vse precyus vnguentys, as stybyn in somir,
rose in wyntir, and mastyk and myrte, þe qwyche be delytesum
of tast. For þe spyrite is noȝt refrescyd but only be delytesum tast,

---

2 sythin] *at end of line, with* in *repeated at start of next*   3 it] *ins. above*
sekenes] sekenens   17 stomak] stomamak   20 clothe þe] þe *ins.*
above   31 egestyon] *otiose abbreviation mark above medial* e

and alle [sqwete] odyr[is] is [hys] mete, and þe spyrite is made
stronge and refreschyd and opynnyd, þe body is confortyd, þe
herte joyth, and þe blode þanne begynnyth to renne into þe
veynys, of gladnes of þe spyrite. And | aftyr þat þu schalt take [f. 45ᵛ]
aeltrod, þat is to sey, þe lectuary of þe wode of aloes, þat is clepyd 5
ligni aloes alectuarium, as it is wrytyn in bokis of medycinys, and
with þat of aronde, þat is to sey, rubarbe, þe weght of four fer-
thyngis. And thys profytith gretly, for it withdrawyth flewme fro
þe mowth of þe stomak, and it excytith þe hete of þe body, and it
excludyth ventosyté of þe stomak and of þe wombe, and yeldyth 10
a sqwete tast. And aftyr þis, thow schalt talke with þi lordys and
with wyse men as is acordyng to a kyng, and do þat is syttyng
þe to do.

(But conceyue þat in þo dayis Crystyn feyth was noȝt, qwerfor he
remembryth noȝt of þe seruyse of God, þat men schuld fyrst serue 15
God, and aftyr do þat qwyche is conseruyng of helth of þe body.)

Þe eght capitil   Capitulum viij

Qwan þe owr is comyn and þi appetyte forte ete, aftyr þine vse
and custum, vse a lytyl labour be-forn, owdyr in rydyng or walkyng
or sqwyche a-nodyr werk doying, for þat helpyth myche þe 20
body. | It excludyth and puttyth a-wey ventosyteis, it dysposyth [f. 46]
þe body, confortyth it, and makyth it leght, and it settith a-fyr þe
hete of þe stomak, it constreynyth and strenghyth þe joyntis, and
it lyqwefyith off þe superfluyteis of humorys ondygeste, and makeþe
flewme to descende bothe fro þe hede and þe stomak, and it 25
helpyth þe stomac dryid with grete hete, makeng humoris to descende þer-oppon. Than lete þer be sett be-forn þe many sondry
metys, and chese þat most noryschyth to the aftyr þe desyr of þi
stomak, equaly etyng with lyght bred wele labouryd. But ordyr
aftyr nortur and aftyr þe gyse of seruyse þine etyng, so þat þu 30
begynne noȝt atte last cours and aftyr retorne to þe fyrst. But if þu
wult kepe þe to o cours fede on þe last in þe begynnyng and retorn
noȝt. Allso to þe helth of þi body haue consyderacion, settyng one
be-forn anodyr of þi metys, as þus: if þu take at þi mele a potage, 34
þat þe kende þer-of be forto lose þi | wombe, and aftyr þat anodyr [f. 46ᵛ]
potage of qwych þe kend is to make constipat, if þe molyficatyf
go beforn, it makyth lyght and esy digestion and eke egestyon.

1 sqwete odyris is` hys mete] hys odyr is sqwe mete   24 makeþe] make
þe: cf. 163/27 and see also 160/9   28 to] ins. above

And if þe constipatyf potage be etyn first, and aftir þat þe molyficatyf, þei be consumyd both with effecte of losyng. And if it be
so þat a man take many sondry potagis or metys qwyche be lyte
of dygestyon, it behouyth þat somme mete be etyn be-forn þo, þe
5 qwyche is substancial of abydyng, þat it make resydens in þe
bottom of þe stomak. For þe deppest part of þe stomak is most
myghty for to dygest, for as myche as þer be in þe bottum fleschly
partis, and also þat it is ner þe lyuir, of qwyche hete of þe lyuir
alle metis be chefly dygestyd. And note þis in special: þat at euiry
10 mele and euiry etyng, sese euir with appetite, and þan þu schalt lyfe
longe, for of superfluyté of mete þe stomak is anguyschyd, the
[f. 47] body is noyd and heuyid, or greuyd, and the | spyrite is hurte, and
þe mete abydyth in þe bottum of þe stomak, heuy and noyus.
Reuoke þi wylle fro drynkyng of kold drynkys in mete tyme,
15 but if þu hast had hem [in] vse þe mor custommabylly, for cold
drynkis in mele time qwenchyth þe hete of dygestyon, and con-
foundyth þe mete, and gendryth many lettyngis to dygestyon, and no
thyng hurtyth mor þe body. If cold drynke be had in vse, and if it
be so that þu haue a gret appetite [t]o drynke watyr or anodir cold
20 drynke, lette be clene and pure and cold, noȝt het with no fyr, and
drynke but lytil.

The nynghe capitil her beginnith   Capitulum ix

And qwan it is so þat þu hast etyn, walke softly a thousand
pacys, or ellis stonde ryght vppe, þat þe mete may descend
25 fully to þe bottum of þi stomak fully, þan vppon a soft bed ley
þe to slepe, and rest one hour vppon þi bedde on þi ryght syde,
and þan torne þe on þi left syde and fulfylle þe resydw of þi slepe
[f. 47ᵛ] on þat syde. For þe left syde is cold, and hath nede of | hetyng,
qwerfor þe lengest slepe owyth to be on þe left syde. And þan if
30 þu fynde peyn or warkyng in þi stomak or in þi wombe, or ondygestyon, þan þe best medycine is for þe to ley on þi wombe a schet
warmyd, on many fold, or to hold in þi armys mayde þat is
bewteuus and hote. And if it be so þu þikvs and reise wynde, with
qwyche wynde þer rysyth a byttir and a sowr matere fro þe sto-
35 make, yt betokynnyth a cold stomak. And þe remedy is þat anone
þu drynke a byttir syrippe as is centory þe siruppe, and þe syruppe

---

8 of þe lyuir] of þe lyuier (*contraction for* er)   19 to] do   28 and]
ampersand ins. after following word had been written   30 warkyng] r *ins. above*
33 reise] i *ins. above*   36 as is] *prec. by cancellation consisting of & and of
two letters of another word, the first letter being* i, *and the second left unfinished.*

of wurmewode, and sqwyche odyr, with a cold watyr, as is endyue,
borage, and sqwyche odyr, and be þis mene to prouoke a vomyte,
for þat enprisonnyng of mete in þe stomak is vtter destruccion to
þe body.

The tenthe capitil of þis boke　　　　　　Capitulum x 5

Than, meuyng beforn mete and labour excityth þe hete of þe
stomak, and makyth þe fir myghti, but aftyr mete it is noyus, for
fast goying and labour makyth þe mete soudenly with-owte dyges-
tyon to falle in-to bottum of þe stomak, | of qwyche be gendryd [f. 48]
stoppyngis-inne of wynde, and many odyr hurtys. Than be-war 10
þat þu slepe noȝt be-forn mete, for þat wul drye þe and make
þi body and þi face leene and owte of lykyng. And aftir mete it
dothe euyn þe contrary, makyng þe stronge, and nurchyth þe
and makyth þe in lykyng, for qwyll þat a man slepyth, þe naturalle
hete dyffusely rennyth fro alle partys to þe stomak and to þe iner 15
partis of þe stomak. And þan is þe stomak made stronge to seeth
þe mete þat is with-inne, for þan þe vertu racional sekyth reste,
and alle þe spyritis be in qwyete. Qwer-for sum fylisofris sey þat
þe sopir profytith mor þat i[s] etyn at euyn, þan þat mele þat [is]
etyn at myd-day. For þe myd-day mele receuyuth þe hete of þe 20
day, and þan þe wytte of a man is in laboryng, in ymaginyng, and
in speche, and þe spyrite is vexid bothe be heryng and be speche,
and many odyr thyngis, þat be labour and be hete, and meuyng
and bysynes, þat at mydday þe natural hete is dyffusyd and spred 24
abroode be | þe vtter partys of þe body, and þerfor þat tyme þe [f. 48ᵛ]
stomak is myche febyllyd and is on-myghty to sethe þe mete. But
atte þe euyn sopir i[s] alle þe contrary, if it be so a man hath noȝt
etyn to myche at none. For at euyn þe body goth to rest, labourys
be sesyd: þan be þe spyritis and wyttis in rest, and þan comyth
vppon þe [þe] coldenes of þe nyght, qwyche dryuyth þe myght 30
and hete of natur to þe inner part of þe stomak, and þat causyth
good dygestyon.

Thow schalt also haue knowlech þat he þat is wunt to ete twyis
on þe day, and aftyr chongyth þat dyete and takyth hym to o mele,
it is very certeyn þat it schal turne hym to noyauns. For in lyke as 35

15 iner] e *apparently corr. from* i　　19 is¹] it　　22 in speche] *in ins. above*
23 many] *ins. above*　　27 is] it　　33 Thow schalt] *prec. by headings for
a chapter* þe elleuynth (elleuynth *prec. by canc.* tenth) *and* cap[itulu]m xj. *Initial
T of* Thow *illuminated as though initial of chapter.*

he þat is wunt to ete but onys on þe day, and chongyth on-to twyis, hys stomak may noȝt dygest it esyli, but þe n[u]triment abydith ondygest. And he þat is wunt to kepe a certeyn howr of

4 etyng and chongyth þat owr in-to anodyr, schal sone fynde þat

[f. 49] it schal hurt | hys natur. For euir take þis for a rewle general, þat a costum is as a natur. Than if ony nede qwyche hath no lawe compelle a man to þat, þat he must chonge hys custom or hys vse, þat must be done dyscretly and wysely, þat he chonge nowt alle at onys, but be lytil and lytyl, and so with Goddis help it schal

10 be wele.

And bewar in specyal þat þu ete neuir tyl þat þu knowe surly þat þi mete qwych þu etyst be-forn be ful dygest, and þat þi stomak be voyde. And that mayst þu sone know be þine appetyte, and be þe sotelté of þi spatyl, qwan it is as fresch watir, noȝt towghe. For he

15 that takyth mete withowte necessyté of þe body, he schal fynde þe natural hete euyn cold and onmyghty in maner. And if he ete qwan þat he hath goode appetyte, he schale fynde þe hete of þe stomak as a brennyng fyre. And as sone as euir thow hast dysir

[f. 49ᵛ] to ete, þu schuldyst ete a-none, for | but þu ete sone at þat tyme

20 þe stomac is a-none repleschyd with noyus and euyl humoris, þe qwych it drawyth to yt fro alle þe body of superfluyteis, qwyche werkyng trowbyllyth þe brayn, sendyng vppe euyl vaporis to þe hede. And qwan þat mete is receyuyd aftyr þat, it fyndyth þe stomak lewke and weyke, and noȝt dysposid to dygestion, for

25 a cloyauns of euyl humoris receyuyd be-forn, qwer-for it profytith noȝt to þe body, but turnyth to corrupcion.

My purpose is her to determyne of þe four tymys of þe yer and of þe qualyté and quantyté and þe propyrté of iche part, and of þe varyacion of hem.

30 Þe eleuyth [capitil]   Capitulum xj

Ther be four tymys of þe yer the qwyche þat be dystyncte, þat is to sey in-to ver, into somyr, in-to heruest, and in-to wyntyr. Ver begynnyth qwan þe sonne entryth þe sygne of Aryes. þan is þe

34 begynnyng of ver, and i[t] enduryth be nynety and thre dayis and

[f. 50] thre and tweynty | hourys and þe fourthe part of an hour, þat is

---

2 nutriment] *three minims for* nu   5 it] *ins. above*   11 And bewar]
prec. by headings for a chapter: þe twelthe capitil *and* cap[itulu]m xij. A *of* And
illuminated as though initial of chapter   15 fynde] *ins. above*   31 be¹]
prec. by canc. þu   34 it] in   35 þe fourthe] þe *ins. above*

to sey, fro þe [one and tweynty] day of Marche goyng owte to þe
four and tweynty day of June. And in þat tyme þe nyght and þe
day be euynnyd in her regeounys, þe tyme waxith plesaunt and
sqwete, þe aer is puryfyid, spryngis boyle owte of þe erth, þe
moystur þat in wyntyr abode in treis rotys ascendith vp in-to þe 5
croppys, bestys and foulis renwe her kendys, and þe erth and alle
thyngis þat ber lyfe be frescyd and nwyd.

Þe tweltht capitil   Capitulum xij

Ver is hot and moyst, and it is temperat lyke to þe aer. þe blode
of man is qwekynnyd, and sterys a-brod to alle odyr partys and 10
membrys, and it profytith in that: þat it is equal of complexcion,
þat is to sey temperat. And in þat tyme of ver thou schuldyst ete
hennys chykynnys, curlewys and soft eggis among, þat is to sey,
seldum, and letwse wylde, þat is to sey, rampsys. Drynke and ete
gootys mylke, for it restoryth gretly natur. þer is no tyme of þe 15
yer þat is mor | bettyr or mor profitabyl to bledyng, and in þat [f. 50ᵛ]
tyme labour and meuyng is goode to þe body, and also batthys,
and to prouoke sqwete, to drynke syryppys made of spycis and
herbys, and to take purgacionys inne, for þat beforn in odyr tymys,
owdyr be ondygestyon or be mynucion, be tyd to þe hyndrauns 20
of þe bodi, thys tyme be moystur restorith.

Þe thyrdtene [capitil]   Capitulum xiij

Somir begynnyth þan qwan þe sonne entryth þe fyrst degré of
þe Crab, þat is to sey, signi Cancri, and it conteynyth to and
[n]ynti dayis and thre and twynti houris and þe thyrd part of an 25
howr: þat is to sey, fro þe thre and tweynti day of June to þe four
and tweynti day of Septembyr. And in þis tyme þe days be lenghyd
and þe nyght is shortyd. In alle regiounys hete growyth, þat is to
sey, encresyth, wyndis be inflamyd be hete and depressyd, þe
see is pesybil, serpentis be gendryd, venym is dyffusyd, þer is 30
clernes in þe aer, corne waxith rype, and þe world is þan lyke a
spowse complete of body and of perfyte age, | inflamyd with hete. [f. 51]
The tyme of somyr is hote and drye, in þe qwyche rede coler is

---

1 one and twenyty] tenthe   2–3 þe day] þe ins. above   3 her
regeounys] run together; separated by vertical stroke in revision   7 be] ins.
above   11 þat it is] þat and is ins. above   12 is to] followed by second is to
canc.   20 be mynucion] run together; separated by vertical stroke in revision
25 nynti] twynti   32 and of perfyte age] repeated as first words of f. 51

reysid, excytid, and haboundyth in bodyis dysposyd. And it behouyth to be war in þat tyme of euiry mete þat is drye and hote
of complexcion, for þat excytith rede coler. Absteyn þat tyme
of replecion, bothe of mete and drynke, les þe natural hete be
5 qwenchyd, but ete þan euiry thyng þat is of moyst and cold complexcion, as veele with vynegyr, cucurbytis, and fatte chykynnys and
capounnys. þi potage schuld be made with þe brenne of barly frute,
qwyche is of sour sauur or tast, and sour applys. þat tyme hurtyth
lest þe body to begete chyldyr. And spar þat tyme fro letyng bloode,
10 meuyng of þe body, and also fro bathis.

Þe fourtene capitil　　　　　　Capitulum xiiij

[f. 51ᵛ]　Haruest begynnyth þan qwan þe sonne entryth þe fyrst degré of
þe sygne of Lybra, or þe sygne of þe Weghtis, and it conteynith
four scor days and eghte | and seuyn[tene] houris and iij fyfte
15 partis of an hour, þat is fro þe four and tweynti day of Septembre
tyl þe to and tweynty day of Decembyr. In þat tyme þe day and þe
nyght be euynnyd, and þe nyght begynnyth to growe and takyth
a part of þe day. þe aer begynnyth to wax cold, þe wyndys blowe,
þe tymys be chongyd, flodys decrese, wellis be mynucyd, grene
20 thyngis begynne to seer, frutis falle, þe bewté of þe erthe fatyth,
foulis flye to hoote regyoynys, wyld bestys seke her dennys and
serpentis her dychys, qwer þei gadyr foode to susteyn þem in
wyntir. þe world is þan lykenyd to a womman of ful age, þat hathe
[n]e[e]d of clothys, for yought is departyd fro her, and age hastyth
25 on. Haruest is a tyme þat is cold and drye, in qwyche tyme blak
coler arysith. þer-for it behouyth þat tyme hote and moyst metis,
as be chykynnis, lambys, dowys yonge, with poudir of gyngir, olde
[f. 52]　wyne of depe colour, and sqwete | wyne, and sqwete grapys.
Absteyne fro alle metis þat gendyr malencoly, as bef, porpeys,
30 grapes, sel fyscys, elys, and sqwyche odyr. Put þan in excercyse
þe meuyng of þe body mor and rather þan in somir. Bathys þis tyme
if nede be and laxatyfis vse. And if a man nede to haue a vomyte,
lete yt be done but a lytil, and in þe hettest hour of þe day, for in
sqwyche houris superfluyteis be gadryd in a man. þe purgacion of
35 þe wombe is gode to be had þat tyme, be pylettys clepyd auree,

---

4 bothe] *repeated*　　14 seuyntene] seuyn & tweynti　　15 an hour] *ins. in
top margin*　　15–16 *ordinal numbers here, exceptionally, not surmounted by roman
figures*　　21 foulis] u *corr. from* l　　24 need] eld *ins. above*　　27 be
chykynnis] *run together; separated by stroke in revision*

electuarium rosarum, lapis laizuli, and armenium, and sqwyche
odyr þat drawyn blak coler and repressyn humoris.

þe fyftene [capitil]   Capitulum xv

Wyntir begynith qwan þe sonne entryth þe fyrst degré of þe
Capricorne, and it conteynith threscor dayis and nynetene, and 5
fourtene hourys, that is to sey, fro þe [on]e and twynti day of
Decembyr, to þe one and tweynti day of Marche. In þat tyme þe
days be schortyd | and þe nyght is lenghyd, colde waxith myghti, [f. 52ᵛ]
wyndys waxe scharpe, þe leuys of treys fallyn, alle grene þinge for
þe most part deyith, þe most part of bestis þat be wylde in cauernys 10
and depe placys of þe erthe hyde hem, þe aer waxith derke, bestys
bothe wyld and tame quake and tremyl, þe vertuis and streynghys
of bodyis be febyllid. Than þe world is lykynnid to an old woman
ner nakyd, neghyng to deth. And þe tyme of wyntir is cold and
moyste, in qwyche tyme it behouyth to chonge þe dietyng and to 15
retorne to hote metis and hote substanscis, as be chykynnis, and
vse of rostis, gootis, and hogge, lambis, and alle hoote wynis,
figgis, notis, and red wyne, and hote letwaryis. Absteyne þe fro
medycinis þat lose þe wombe, and fro mynucion of blode, but if
gret necessité constreyn þe, þan chonge þe aer, þat is to sey, drawe 20
in to warme and to closse placis fro þe aer. Vse noȝt þat time gret |
habundauns of metys so þat dygestion be febyllid. Anoynte þi [f. 53]
body with precyus and hote vnguentis, and vse temperate bathis.
Myche meuyng nor dedis of Venus nor sadde etyng noyith noȝt
þanne so myche as odyr tymis, for þat tyme of feruent cold, þe 25
natural hete is gadryd to-gydir and entrith þe inner parte of þe body.
And þer-for in wyntyr is best digestyon. And in ver and in somyr
þe stomac is colde, for in þise tymys þe poris be opynyd and þe
natural hete is dysceuerid in to alle þe partis of þe body, and for
scantnes of hete þe digestyoun of þe stomak is lettyd, and humoris 30
be meuyd to þe extremyteis. Than take hede and knowe wysely
thys doctryne and kepe it, and owr Lord kepe þe.

Þe sextene capitil   Capitulum xvj

O Alysaundyr, þis precyus dyete prefyxid to þe, loke þu kepe,
conseruyng þe natural hete of þi bodi, for as long as natural hete is 35

---

5 nynetene] *surmounted by indistinct* ixi (?) *for* xix   6 fro þe one] fro þe
thre   17 gootis] *altered from* gottis   18 red wyne] *run together; separated
by vertical stroke in revision*   28 stomac] *corr. from* þ wynde   35 is] s
written over another letter

temperat in a man, helth induryth and a man is longe lyuyd and
[f. 53ᵛ] kept | in helth. And conceyue þat on tweyn wysis a manne waxith
olde or aged, and dyith. On wyse be deth natural þat no man may
scape, þat qwan very age comyth, þe qwyche is cold and drye, þe
5 body is destroyd. And a-nodyr wyse qwan þat be mysdyetyng or
odyr mys-rwle sekenes fallyth, and be þat euyl cause þe body is
weykyd and destroid. Conceyue þan þat þo thyngis þat make þe
body fatte be þise: rest, and surenes, and þe vse of sqwete metis,
and to chonge delycasyis, and þe drynkyng of sqwete mylke, and
10 sqwete wynis þat be hote, and also slepe aftir mete on a soft bedde in
a chambyr þe qwyche smellith sqwete, and þe bedde is leyd a-
bowght with sqwete spycis or sqwete herbis couenyent to þe tyme
of þe yer, and to entir þe bathys of sqwete watris, and lytil taryng in
hem, for longe abydyng in a bath weykyth þe body. And vse þe
15 tast of sqwete herbys qwyllis þu art in þe bath in euiry tyme as is
conuenyent, as, in wyntir, worme-wode and fedyrfoye, and tansey
[f. 54] and sothyrnwode, | and in somyr, rosis and violeettis, and sqwyche
þat refresch be þe mene of colde. And in euiry monthe loke þat
þu haue a womyte onys, but in specyal in somir. For a vomyt
20 wascyth þe body and þe stomak, and porgyth hym fro corupte and
noyus humoris. For þe fewer humoris in þe stomak, þe mor þe
natural hete is confortyd, to make goode dygestyon, and þe body
is þe mor moyst, and in specyal if þise folowyng thyngis be had:
þat is to sey, joye and myrthe in hert and spyritis, victory of þin
25 enmyis, and to haue delectacion in melodyis and pleyis, and to
be-held bewtewus personys, to her rede plesaunt bokys, and to her
sqwete songis, and to lawghe with sqwyche folk a[s] þu louyst,
and to go frescly arayid in ryche clothis, and to anoynte the with
sqwete smellyng onymentis conuenyent to þe tyme of þe yer. And
30 as þise seyd thyngis confort myghtyli þe body, on þe like wyse þise
thyngis folowyng drye þe bodi and make it febyl: that is to sey,
[f. 54ᵛ] lytil etyng | and drynkyng mykyl, and to myche labour, and to
stonde oftyn, and to walke owte of mesur, and to slepe be-forn
mete o[n] hard beddis, to walke in desolate and hard placis, to haue
35 gret stody in mend, and to be in ferr and drede, and to entyr
watyrris or bathys qwych be made be sulfur, and to ete ony maner

---

3 aged] d *written over two canc. letters, second of which is* m   22 goode]
repeated   27 as] & (*poss. intended reading*)   31 to] *ins. above*
32 drynkyng] *prec. by canc.* lytil   34 on] or (dormire ante prandium supra
stramenta dura B 82)

of salt mete, and to vse myche olde wyne, and to drynke myche,
and to vse to myche purgaciounys, and to blede to oftyn, and to
haue heuy and sory thoughtis. And be-syde þise, Ypocras seyth
þat he þat is replete of mete or drynke, or ellis constipat of wombe,
and entryth in to a bath, he fallyth in-to ylica passion, or þe 5
colik, or þe stone, or odyr greuus sekenes, or he þat lyith with
a woman, hauyng to do with her, qwyll his stomak is fulle, oftyn
fallyth in-to þe same. A man schuld noȝt renne aftyr, nor ryde
forth-with aftir, hys mele. And be war of þis: þat þu ete noȝt
fysch and mylke togidyr, for it wul cause þe sekenes of lepyr. And 10
wyne and mylke etyn or dronkyn togydyr be processe | causyth [f. 55]
þe same.

Þe seuyntene capytil   Capitulum xvij

Knowe now how þe body is dyuidyd in-to four partis. The first
part is þe hede. Qwan it is so þan þat superfluyteis be gadrid in 15
þe hede, þu mayst knowe be þise signis: þe eyn waxin dymme, þe
browys be heuy, þe templis werke, þe erys synge and gyngil, þe
nose is also stoppid. Qwatsum-euir he be þat hath þis sekenes,
lette hym take gencyan and sethe it in sqwete wyne, and with þe
rotis of peletir, and lette hem sethe to þe half, and lette hym hold 20
þat decoccioun in hys mowth euiry morow, tylle þat he fele þat
he be holpyn. And lete hym vse myghti mostard sede with hys
mete, and lette sethe a peny weghte þer-of with powdyr made of
twelue vnguentis, and þat lete hym vse beforn he ley hym to slepe,
and anoynte and bynde to hys hede. And he þat refusith þis 25
medicyne may falle in-to perlyus sekenes, þat is to sey, sekenes of
þe eyn, sekenes of þe brayn, and odyr many, fro qwyche God kepe
þe. |

[Þe eghtene capitil]   Capitulum xviij [f. 55ᵛ]

The breste is þe secunde part of þe body. And if in þis parte þer 30
be foundyn superfluyteis, þei be knowyn be þise tokynnis: þe tonge
is heuy, þe mowth is salt, and in þe mowth of þe stomak þe mete
þat is etyn sauiryth byttyr, and with þat a dysposicion to þe
koughe. Thus schalt þu recur it: þu must lesse þi etyng, and vse
vomytis thre days, and aftir þi vomyte take and ete sugir roset and 35
incorperent it with ligno aloes and mastyk, and aftir þi mele ete

---

4 or ellis] *prec. by &*   5 in-to] in *ins. above*   21 euiry] *prec. by*
canc. letter   35–36 and incorperent] & *ins. above*

as myche as a walnot of þe grete letuary clepyd amissous, þe
qwyche is made of þe tre of aloes and of safirroun. And he þat
dyspisith to do aftyr þis doctryne may lyghtly falle in-to þe peyn
of þe syde, and peyne in þe renys, and many odyr sekenes.

5   **þe nyntene capitil**   **Capitulum xix**

The eyn be þe thyrd part of þe body. And it behouyth hym þat
wul haue helth on hys eyn, þat he defend hem fro dust, fro al maner
[f. 56]   of | smoke, and fro alle aerys þat excede temperatnes of equalyté,
owdyr in cold or hete, and fro euyl wyndis. Let hym noȝt beholde
10   bysili sqwyche a thyng of qweche he is noȝt auertyd, ner vse noȝt
to loke vppon smale thyngis ner sotel wrowght thyngis, and schunne
myche wepyng, and oftyn hauyng to do with women, and implecion
of drynke and mete, and in specyal of drynke and of þo metis
þat gendyr grose humoris, sendyng þem vppe to þe hede, as
15   lekys wurtis and myghti ale, ner slepe noȝt qwylis þu art replete.
And þo thyngis þat confort þe syght and þe eyn be kendis goode
confortatif, and þe watyr or þe juse of fynkel, of verueyn, of rosis,
of celydony, of rwe, and oftyn, þe eyn opyn, to dyppe hem oftyn in
cold watyr and to loke on þe watyr. The tokynnys[or]cause of dyspo-
20   sicion of þe eyn conuenyent or dysconuenyent is knowyn be eght
rewlys: of þe towche, of þe veynys, of þe fyguris, of þe warkyngis
[f. 56ᵛ]   propyr, | of þe colouris and qwantyté of þo passyounys þat go owte
of hem, and of owteward thyngis occurrent, þat is to sey cold or hete,
and also if þer apper gret veynnys replet with humoris. The multitude
25   also of sekenes is cause qwyche is knowyn be colour of þe eyn
and þe peyn: þat if he þat hath seke eyn, his sekenes comyth of
blodys habundawns, he felyth oftyn prykkyng in hem. And if þe
cause be of coler, bolnyng and extencion schewyth, þat is to sey,
þei be powtyng owte, repleschyd with mater. Flewme maketh þe
30   eyn heuy and onweldy, sor and ondysposyd to beheld ony thyng.
And if þe cause be of malencoly, þe eyn be wattry and twyn-
kyllyng oftyn. Also þe hede fulle of wynde stofyth þise materis
in-to þe eyn. And odyr tokynnys þer be many, þat euiry wyse
man may be reson deme. Than febylnes is knowyn besyde þise,
35   þat if þe fygur of þe eye, qwyche schuld be rownd in þe cyrcuité, if
[f. 57]   it fayle þat. And þe | werkyng of natur of þe eyn be knowyn be þis

---

3 may lyghtly] *corrected from* malyghtly   8 of equalyté] *prec. by* in l
expuncted   22 þat] *prec. by canc.* f   29 powtyng] *prec. by canc. letter*
(r ?)

dysposicion: tho eyn þat meve fast be of hote natur; late of meuyng,
colde; þei þat be ful of humoris, and qwan þei lawghe, ful of watyr,
þei be moyst. Than be þer sum eyn þat her dysposycion is to se
a thyng a-ferr, and ner hem þei may noȝt see. And sum þat may
se ner and noȝt ferr. Thei þat may se nye and noȝt ferre, þei haue 5
a cler and vysibil spyrite of syghte, but it is smal, for qwyche
smalnes þei be impotent to se a-ferr. Thei þat may se fer and noȝt
ner, þei haue a myghti and myche of þe spyrite of syghte and of
vysual vertu, þe qwych is grose, moyst, and perturbate, qwer-for,
or þe syght may haue very knowlech of þat þing, it nedyth gret 10
dystauns to depur it, þat þe grose vapowris be departyd fro hem.
And of hete þei be knowyn qwan þe colour schewyth þe humoris
þat hath lordchyp, | as red, yelow, bloo, dunne. And of quantité, [f. 57ᵛ]
for þe gretnes of þe eyn, with proporcion of þe werkyng and
multytude of substauns schewyth þe gode and wele dysposyd 15
mater of qwyche þe eyn wer made of. And hos eyn be grete and
powtyng owte, is onschamefast, clataratif and foltysch. And he þat
hath eyn depe with-in hys hede is sotel and a deceyuur. The cur
þan of yche febylnes is in vj thyngis with gode demenauns, þat
is to sey: to bewar of þe aer and contynual labor, ydylnes in sted- 20
fast beholdyng, in mete and drynke, wecchyng, lying with women,
and þe accidentis of þe spyrite. And loke in þise sekenes and
euiry sekenes þe wombe be laxe.

Þe tweynti [capitil]   Capitulum xx

The priuyté of manne is þe iiij part of þe body. And qwan it is so 25
þat superfluyteis be gadryd in þat part, þise tokynnys folowe: þe
appetite is febyl and weyke. He þan þat felyth þat dysposicion, he
must take þe herbe clepyd | grete ache, and walwurte, and of þise [f. 58]
rotys, and putte þe herbys and þe rotes to-gydir in sqwete wyne
þat is qwyte of colour and tempyrryd with watir and hony, and 30
absteyn fro myche etyng. And he þat is necclygent to do þis, may
lyghtly falle in-to þe apposteme of þe codde, sekenes of þe longis,
and peryl of þe strangury.

Þe j and tweynti [capitil]   Capitulum xxj

It is red in þe story of olde fylysofris þat þer was a myghti kynge 35
þat dyd gadyr þe best lechys of Inde, of Meedys, and of Grekys,

6 is] *ins. above*   9 vysual] u *corr. from* y   15 of substauns] of
substauns of   17 clataratif] ti *ins. above*   30 qwyte] *corr. from* sqwyte

and þis kyng comaundyd to yche of hem synglerly to stody to
make sqwyche a medycine þat it wer suffycyent to a man to vse
þat medycine alone ayens alle sekenes. The leche of Medys seyd
þat it profytid to an heyl man most qwyllis þat he is fastyng to ete
5 of þe clustir of rype sqwet grapis vj drammis. But I sey þat he
þat slepyth so myche þat he felyth in hys stomak none heuynes
[f. 58ᵛ] ner ponderusnes ner | rawnes lette hym neuir fer of þe gowte.
And þe Grekys sentens was þis, þat he þat wold take euiry morow
twyis fulle hys mowth of warm watyr, it make an heyl man swr
10 fro all vnkowth sekenes, þat he nedyth to vse none odyr medycyne.
And he þat euery morow wul ete seuyn drammys of a clostyr of
sqwete grapys, or of reysyng sqwete, and in þer propyr kende,
nedyth noȝtis to dowght of none infyrmyté þe qwyche is causyd
of fleme. And be þe vse of þis medycyne, þe vertu memoratif is
15 a-mendyd, and þe vndyrstondyng is illumyd, and he þat vse þis
in tyme conuenyent to hys complexcion, he [sc]ha[l] neuir fer þe
feuyr quarteyn. And he þat etyth be þe morow notys and fyggys
with a few leuys of rwe, þer is no poysun þat þat day may noy
hym, nowdyr in drynke ner mete nor ony odyr wyse. Qwer-for be
20 noȝt with-owte reysyngis nor þise odyr necessary. |

[f. 59] **The to and tweynt[i] capityl**   **Capitulum xxij**

O hye and nobyl Kyng, on alle wyse stody to conserue þi natural
hete, for as longe as þat is temperat in a man, so longe helth con-
tynuyth, and a man is strong, wele colouryd, and myghti. For þe
25 helth of man stondyth in tweyn thyngis þat I haue rehersyd, and
þe corupcion of þe body or destruccion, comyth of to causis: one
is natural, anodyr is ayens natur. The natural cause comyth of
repugnaunz and contradyccion of contraryus qualyteis, þat is to
sey, qwan drynes hath lordchyp in þe bodi þan must it nedys fayle.
30 Corupcion or deth þat is ayens natur comyth of summe accydental
cause, as if a man be dedly woundyd in batel, or odyr causys
soden, or of sekenes, or be euyl counsel.

---

3 alone] *followed by canc. vertical stroke as of* I   5 vj drammis] *ins. in*
margin as vjȝᵃ   8–9 take . . . mowth] *prec. by canc.* euiry morow take twyis
ful hy [*sic*] þat wold   11 a clostyr] *prec. by canc.* o *and canc. downstroke.*
14 memoratif] if *ins. above*   15 illumyd] *between* ill *and* yd, *three minims;*
possibly illiumyd *or* illumiyd   16 schal] thar   32 counsel] cou
with two contraction marks

Þe thre and twenti [capitil]   Capitulum xxiij

Knowe þan þat þer be of metys sondry kendys aftir þe qualyteis.
Summe be sotel and summe groose, and summe in a mene. Sotel
metys gendryn sotel blode, þe qwyche is cler | and goode, as qwete, [f. 59ᵛ]
henys chykynnis, and eggis soffte. Grose metys be þise (and þo be 5
goode for myghty, hote stomakis, and to þem þat labour in fastyng,
and to þem þat slepe aftyr mete) as: beff and porpes, grapes, and
alle salt metys. þat mete qwyche is inne a mene gendryth none
inflacion nor superfluyté, as is lambes flesch, and wedrys flesch,
and alle flesch qwyche is hote and moyste. But yit in þise folk 10
be dysceyuid, þei þat rost þise fleschys. For þan þei turne
noȝt to þer noryschyng, but if it be so þat þei be etyn forth-
with fro þe spyte, for ellis þei cause hardnes of dygestyon, inordynat hete, and dryenes. Than be þer summe metys þat
in specyal gendyr malencoly, as þe flesch of buglys, þe flesch of a 15
cowe, and olde schep, for þise haue grose humoris drye and scharp.
And if ony of þise maner of kendis schuld be goode, be þei þat be
pasturyd in moyst pasturys, and þe flesch of sqwyche be mor holsum
þan þo þat be pasturyd on | hethys. Knowe wele also þat fyschys [þat] [f. 60]
be smale of substauns, hauyng thynne skynnys and esy of chowyng, 20
þat be noryschid in sondy rennyng watrys, be bettir, mor norchyng,
þa[n] see fyschys and odyr norchyd in odyr fresche watrys. It
be-houyth þan to be war of alle fyschis þat haue grete bodyis and
thyk skynnys, for sqwyche maner of fysch is venemmus to natur.
And þis her of fyschis is suffycient for in my boke of naturis þu 25
maiste fynde alle odyr kendis.

Þe foure and tweynti [capitil]   Capitulum xxiiij

Thow owyst also to knowe þat watrys be profytabyl to euiry
lyuyng thyng, noȝt only to bestys, but also to alle vegetabyl thynge.
And haue mende þat I haue taught þe sofyciently of watrys. And 30
I haue taught þe þat alle watrys, bothe sqwete and salt, þei had
her begynnyng of þe see, and of þis I haue made þe an opyn
demonstracion. But now more-ouir knowe þis, þat þe most helth-
sum and lyghtest watrys be þo þat renne nere | cyteys. And qwan [f. 60ᵛ]
þat þe erth is pure and withowte rochys (or rokkys), þat haboundyth 35
noȝt of fumosyteis, þe water of sqwyche a sprynge is best and

---

4 as qwete] as s qwete   12-13 forth-with] r *ins. above*   22 þan] þat
26 maiste] i *ins. above*

most to be preysid, and lyght. Watyr þat comyth fro a stony
grownde þat haboundyth of fumositeis is febyl and noyabyl, and
þo in specyal þat froschys, todys or snakys haue delyte to abyde in,
as þise polkys and al-stondyng watrys. The tokynnys of goode
5 watrys be þise: þat is lyght, cler, and drawyng to qwytenes,
sqwete-tastyd, qwan þei wul be lyghtly hoote and lyghtly colde.
In sqwyche natur delytyth. And note þis, þat salt watrys and
byttyr or moddy watrys be cleped fumos, for þise dry the wombe
and dyssolue it. Poole watrys, and alle stondyng watrys, þei be
10 hote, heuy and grewus, for þei stonde and haue none meuyng,
and for þe sonne abydith vppon hem longe and many dayis,
qwerfor þei gendyr coler, and make þe splene to growe, and þe
longis to gret hurt. Watrys þat comyn in to one ryuer fro to sondry
14 spryngis, of to sondry soylis, þei be hote and febyl, for þei haue
[f. 61] inne hem of erthly partys. | And þe drynkyng of cold watyr qwyllis
a man is fastyng noyth to þe body, and qwenchyth þe natural hete
and þe hete of þe stomak. And aftyr mete it makyth warm þe body,
and gendryth flewme, and if a man drynkyth myche it coruptyth
þe mete in þe stomak. Thow schalt þan drynke kold watyr in
20 somir and hote watyr in wyntir, and noȝt þe contrary wyse as
folys seyn þat haue no grownd qwat þei sey. For þe drynkyng of
hote watyr in somir mollyfyith and makyth febyl þe stomak, and
destroyth þe appetite. And cold watyr in wyntyr qwenchyth þe
natural hete, and destroyth þe instrument of þe brest, and noyth
25 to þe longis and causyth many noyauncis.

Þe fyue and twenti [capitil]   Capitulum xxv

It is also to be knowyn þat wyne of qwyche þe grape is browght
forth on an hylle ayens þe sonne, þat þe sonne lyith þer-vppon alle
day, is of mor drye natur þan þat qwyche growyth in lowe valeys
30 and moyst and pleyn placys. þan þe fyrst wayne is goode for ollde
f. 61ᵛ] men, þe qwyche haue myche flewme and myche moystor, | but
it noyth to yong and to hote men. þan þis fyrst wyne makyth hote
and delyuerith of superfluyteis and fro colde and grose humoris.
And wyne, þe mor rede þat it is and þe mor thykke, so myche þe
35 bettyr it gendryth blode. But qwanne it is myghti and of myghti
scharpnes, þan it is clepyd þe fyrst blode and þe fyrst nutriment,

5 qwytenes] *altered from* wytenes   13–14 *numerals, exceptionally, not*
surmounted by roman figures   30 wayne] *poss. slip with* wyne *as intended*
form: see n.   31 *Bottom margin of f. 61 bears signature* John Harcourt

and it hath bothe naturis in hym, bothe of drynke and eke of
medycyne. But yit if a man vse þis stronge drynke contynually, it
noyth gretly. But qwan sqwyche is dowcet and sqwete in tast i[t]
do[th] noyaunz to þe stomak, gendryth ventositeis and inflacionys.
But þe most preysabyl and most [sotel] of euiry wyne is þat 5
qwyche comyth of grapys growyng in pleynys be-twene mown-
teynis, þe qwyche grapys be of sqwettnes in a mene and of fulle and
perfyte rypenes, sotel, þat be noȝt gadryd tyl þe vigorrus myght be
tryid owte be þe werkyng of þe sonne, þat is pressyd myghtyly
at þe most vttyr maner, þat [þe] skynnys, þe pypiounys and þe 10
tendrauntys fully be avoydyd of her moystour, of qwych | þe [f. 62]
colour is lyke gold, þat is to sey, a mene be-twene rede and lyghte
yelow, and hath a scharp and a delectabyl tast, þe qwyche is ful
puryffiyd or fynyd. And þ[u] fyndyst sqwyche a wyne, drynke
þer-of temperatly, aftyr þe age is of þi body, and þe qwalyté 15
of þe tyme of þe yer. And þise be þe qwalyteis of þe yer: þe hete,
þe colde, þe moystenes, þe drynes, and as it is expressyd be-forn of
þe foure tymys of þe yer. For þis seyd wyne, dronkyn mesarably,
confortyth þe stomak, it strenghith the hete natural, it helpyth
dygestyon, it kepith fro corupcion þe mete þat is etyn, and it 20
sethyth þe mete with-in þe stomak, and bryngith it to norchyng of
alle partys be þe veynis of þe body and be þe porys, puryfying þe
mete, and hym-self also, in-to blode þat is sotel and substancialle.
And aftyr, it ascendith vppe to þe nek with temperat hete, and it
makyth þe hed strong and a-myghty ayens alle caswel sekenes. 25
Also it causyth þe hert to be mery, it maketh þe face wele colouryd,
it make[th] þe tonge | clene and wele dysposyd to talke, it maketh [f. 62ᵛ]
a man to forget pensyfhed, it maketh a man bold and hardy, it
excytith þe appetyte, and many odyr goode thyngis it dothe to
kende. But þan wyne, qwan it is dronkyn owte of mesur, it dothe 30
harm, and þise hurtys folowe: fyrst, it makyth dulle þe vndyr-
stondyn[g], and it lettyth þe wytte, and it trowbyllyth þe brayne.
It makyth febyl þe vertu natural, it makyth a man foryetful, it
hurtyth alle hys fyue wyttis with þe qwyche he is gouernyd
and dysposyd of alle þe bodyly werkyng. It flemyth þe appetyte, 35
febyllyth þe synowys and joyntis, it gendryth þe pallsy in þe

3–4 it doth] in do   5 sotel] preysabyl; suavius B 92   14 þu] þe
23 substancialle] altered from substanciaulle   27 maketh¹] ms. make perh.
intended form: cf. 160/9, and see also 163/4, 149/24   31–2 vndyrstondyng]
vndyrstondynd

membrys, it gendryth sekenes in þe eyn, hurtyng þe syte. It
brennyth coler. It destroyth þe lyuir, for it makyth þe blode mor
grose. It makyth þe blode of þe hert to chonge fro pur and clene
blode to blak and malyncolious blod, and of þat comyth fer, drede,
5 dowghfulnes, heuy dremys, spekyng in þe slep.

[þe Thyrd Boke]

[The fyrst capityl]   [Capitulum j] |

[f. 64] . . . and vsyth þise temperatly, that absteynith hym fro gret and
hasty etyng and drynkyng, and also fro lying with women and fro
10 labor, how may þer þan ony sekenes betyde to sqwyche a man?
And it behouyth hym þat is dysposid oftyn to be dronkyn, þat
he wasche hym with hote watyr, and þat he haue a sege vppon
rennyng watrys, and þat he haue a-bought hym salow leuys, and
odir leuys beyng refrygeratyf in werkyng. And he must anoynte
15 hys body with confecte salt, and to vndyrsmoke hym with colde
encensys. And þis [is] a souerrey[n] medycine ayens dronkeschep.
An chonge neuir sodenly fro an hot drynke to a cold.

The secunde capitil   Capitulum ij

There be þanne summe thyngis þat make þe body fatte and
20 stronge, and summe þat make þe body lene and weyke, and summe
þat þe bodi dryen, and summe þat make it moyst, and summe þat
yef strenght and beuté, and summe þat gendyr slowth and
sloggynes. Tho þat strenghte the body and make it in goode
24 lykinge be sqwete metys þat be esy of dygestion, and tho þat be |
[f. 64ᵛ] metys acordyng to þe complexcion, and þe drynkyng of sqwete
wyne þat is takyn in tyme qwan natur nedyth. And þo thyngis þat
make þe body moyst be þise: rest of þe body, gladnes of hert, and
mery felyschyp, and metys þat be hote and moyst, as vele and
sqwyche odyr, and þe drynkyng of sqwete wyne, and þe receyuyng
30 of hony þe qwych is made in wodys, in rotys, or holle treys
schadowyd fro þe sonne, and, in-especyal, slepyng aftyr mete
vppon a soft bedde in a colde place, and to be bathyd in hote bathys,
and to stonde but lytil qwyle in hem, þat þe moystour of þe body
be noȝt dyssoluyd in to-gret qwantyté, for þe bodi is þe bettyr þat

---

1 sekenes in] sekenes & in   4 blak] l ins. above   6 At least one leaf
missing   10 may] many   14 anoynte] a noynte   29 sqwete] medial e ins.
above   31 in-especyal] written inespecyal   34 to-gret] written togret

it hathe sumqwat of moystur and wetenes of þe bath þan þe contrary. And also to haue þe tast of sqwete thyngis þat make þe
spyrite myri, but euiry thynge owyth to be done in tyme conuenyent: and, in somyr, to haue þe tast of rosis and vyolettys, and,
in wyntir, odyr conuenyent. And in somyr to excercyse vomytis   5
twyis | or thryis in a monthe, for a vomyte waschyth þe stomak fro   [f. 65]
euyl and corupt humorys, and qwan þe corupt humorys be expulsyd
þe natural hete is aumentyd and confortid to dygeste þe alymentys.
Gouerne wele þan þi body if thow wult þat it be in hele, and
obserue my counsel, for þat is to þe chef solas. And reuerrens   10
comyth with ryches, and vyctory of þi enmy teh, and to lyue in
lykyng, and to excludyt alle heuynes and stody. Vse amonge instrumentis musical to her myri songis, and to vse alle odyr plesaunsis
and as I haue her beforn in thys boke taught þe. And þo þat lene
þe body be thyse: myche abstynens fro mete and drynke, þe vse of   15
dayli labour and excersise in ony werk with contynuauns in hote
placys and in þe sonne, longe wecchyng, slepyng be-forn mete
vppon herd beddys, for so þe hete is lettyd for grete habundauns of
moystour qwyche is in þe body, to be bathyn in brunston watrys   19
and salt, and to ouir-hote watris, | hungyr, þe drynkyng of olde   [f. 65ᵛ]
wyne, to haue oftyn purgacion of þe wombe, oftyn bledyng and vse
of lecchery, pouerté, thowght, fer, euyl thowghtys and angyr,
oftyn sorow betyding, and euyl chawnsis, þise cause þe body to
be lene.

þe thyrd capitil   Capitulum iij   25

A bath is one of þe mervellis of þis world, for it is edyfyid aftyr
þe tymes of þe yer. For a cold bath is attribute to wyntir, a lewke
bath to ver, an hot bath to somyr, a dry bath to haruest. Of hye
prudens a man schuld ordeyn in a bath thre or fowr mansyounys
dystyncte aftyr þat I haue her rehersid, þat he þat wul be bathyd   30
may stonde fyrst a qwyle in þe cold bath, and aftyr in þe lewke, and
so forth, and in hys goyng owte on þe same wyse tabyde a qwyle
in yche of hem, þat he chonge noȝt to sodenly fro gret hete to gret
cold. It wold þer-for be ordeynnyd i[n] a plase qwer myche
comyth of wynde, and to haue gret furneyssis and fresch and   35

---

11 enmy teh] enmyteh; victoriam super inimicos adquirere B 95: see n.
19 brunston] u *surmounted by contraction; perhaps* brumston   28 an hot] ahot
*run together, with a surmounted by indistinct horizontal stroke overlapping marginal
decoration, and presumed to be contraction sign. Perhaps* a hot *intended*   34 in]
it   35 of] *ins. above*

[f. 66] sqwete | watyr and þer a man schul vse sqwete odowrys conue-
nyentys to þe tyme, as, in ver and somyr, þo thyngis þat be sqwete
of tast and colde confort, and in odyr tymys as is conuenyent, as I
haue her beforn expressid. And þan sytte on a sete vndyr qwyche
5 þer is sette a vessel with rose watyr made warme, þat þe fumys
may smyght in to þe body be ascencion, and aftyr, lette hym be
wypte with clene lynen clothes. And aftyr alle thyis is done, lete
hym go in to odyr chambrys, and vse as I haue lernyd þe in this
booke. And if it be so þat he be ouir-comyn of hete, lette hym
10 kembe hym and lett hym vse a puryfyid vnguent þat is conuenyent
to þe tyme, for in ver and somyr he must vse þe oyl confecte of
sandel and enylege, and in haruest and wyntyr to vse vnguentys
of myrre, and with þe juse of þe herbe clepyd bletys, and to cast
14 vppon þe hed watrys dystyllyd. And aftyr þe anoyntyng he must be
[f. 66ᵛ] rubbyd and wascyn clene. And yf it be so þat he hath | thyrst, lete
hym drynke of þe syrip made of rosis and of þe letwary muscat,
þat is to [say] þe letwary made with muschre. And þan lete hym
strecche owte hys armys somqwat, and a lytil qwyle aftyr þat,
qwan hys appetyte is comyn, lette hym ete a lytil, and drynke
20 myghty wyne þer-to, and with þat quantité of watir þat he was
wunt to vse, lytil or noȝt, and aftir þat to vndyrsmoke hym with
incensis conuenyent to þe tyme. A[nd] aftir þat, lett hym rest hym in
a delycat bedde and lett hym take a gode slepe, for þat helpyth
gretly, and þe todyrdele of þe day to spend it in myrth. And þis
25 is þe gouernauns of þe ordyr of helth and of norchyng of þe body.
And he þat is olde and ouercomyn of cold and moystur, lette hym
be war how he taryith in a bath. And no lengir he schuld stond but
tylle þe bath hath made hym wete. And þan let hym throwe vppon
[hym] as myche of temperat watyr as he wulle, and as sone as he
30 wulle. And he þat is flewmatyk, it behouyth hym to come in no
[f. 67] bathe but if he be fastyng, | and anoynte hym with hote vnguuentis.
And he þat is of hote natur, lette hy[m] d[o] as is wrytyn her-
beforn.

þe fourth capitil   Capitulum iiij

35 O Alysaundyr, qwuan þat þu hast fulle knowleche of þis doctrine,
and þan þu hast fullfyllyd it in dede, þu schalt nede none odyr leche
alle þe dayis of þi lyue, with þe help of God. But it is to be knowyn

18 somqwat] *altered from* somwat   29 as myche] s *ins. above*   32 hym
do] hyd   36 fullfyllyd] fuᶠllyd

þat greuus infyrmytés, qwyche be gendryd of hete, or of þe dayis
termynd, and þe cours of þe mone, be knowyn, qwedyr þei be
longe of abydyng or schort. And of sygnys procedyng, it is
knowyn to qwat ende þei owe or schuld come. And I haue trwly
taughte þe, and I haue schewyd þe schortly, þe dyuysiounys and 5
þe knowleche of þe sekenesis. And in watir also is a prouyd tokyn
in þise thyngis. But þe sygnys gooyng beforn be bettir and trwer,
as I haue determynid in þe boke of watrys. And þise sygnys be
syffycyent to hym þat holdyth wele in hys mende þe doctrine of 9
þat boke, also as it | [is] conteynyd in þe boke þat [I] made þe of [f. 67ᵛ]
medycynys compounyd and of crafty watrys and drynkys, in confecte vnguentys and plastrys, aftyr þe o[r]dyr and craft of Grekys,
Ytalyenys, menne of Inde (or Indyciennis) and men of Persis,
in qwyche þer is none experyment ontrwe ner dysceyuabyl. And
for be-cause alle þise wer priuyteis and byryid, or hyd, and no-qwer 15
foundyd in þ[e] commune place, qwer-for I thowght noȝt wurthy
þat þei schuld be hyd fro þe. And it is wurthy þan þat þu knowe
þat gret medycyne qwyche is clepyd þe tresour of phylysofris, and
namyd, or seyd, þe glory inestymabyl. And I trwly kowde neuir
yit fynde, ner neuir knowe nor perceyue, ho fonde þis medycyne. 20
Summe sey þat Adam was þe fynder þer-of, and summe sey þat
Esculapydes, and Hermogynes þe leche, and Hyrssos, and Donas-
tyes, and Vacyleos, and Hebreos, and Dyerys, and Taranus,
gloryus phylysophris qwyche be in nowmbyr viij, to home it was 24
youyn to knowe þe secrete of siencis þe qwyche | wer hyd fro alle [f. 68]
men. And þise wer thei þat made inquysicion, and dysputyd of
þo thyngis þat be abouyn natur, of fulle and of voyde, of fynyte and
infynyte. And concordyngly þei accordyd in þis medycyne inestymabyl, the qwyche is dyuydid in to viij partys. And summe sey
þat Ennok knwe þat secrete be a vysyon, but þei mene and sey þat 30
Ennok was Hermogynes, home þat Grekis myche comende and
preyse, to home þei ascryue alle secrete and heuynly syens.

Þe fyfte capitil   Capitulum v

Take with þe blyssy[n]g of [God of] þe jwse of sqwete pome
garnettis xxᵗv rotis, and of þe jwse of sowr pome garnettis x rotis, 35
and of þe jwse of sqwete applys x rotis, and alle þe cler jwse of
a clustir grapis, and of qwyte swgyr þat is clene x rotis. Putte alle

3 of abydyng] of ins. above   13 menne] m corr.   16 þe] þo
34 blyssyng] blyssyg altered from blyssyd

this in a vessel so þat it be but half fulle, a[nd] lete it boyle with
dyscrecion with a cler fyr with-owte smoke, and skymme it allwey
as it rysith, and lette it sethe to þe haluyndel. And lett it boyle so
[f. 68ᵛ] longe þat it be as thykke as thykke hony, but ster it, for | brennyng,
5   to þe bottum. And þis is that best hony with þe qwyche medycinys
owyn to be made with.

The sexte capitil   Capitulum vj

Take, with þe helpe and blyssinge of God, of rede rosis one rot,
and of vyolettys þe fourthe parte of a rot, and putt[e] alle þis in tenne
10   rotyis of fresch and cler watyr. Aftyr þat haue be, putte in thys
seyd medycine of þe watir of elcorenge half a rot and of þe watir
of grene mynte half a rot, and of watir as is specyfyid. þan alle
thyse, þus proporcionyd, lette hem stonde on þe fyr a day and
a nyght, tylle alle þe strenght be gone owte of þise seyd thyngis.
15   And aftyr ordeyn a cler fyr, and sette þis medycyne vppon yt, tylle
þe thyrd part of þe watyr be sodyn inne. Than take it off, and cole
tylle it waxe cler, and aftyr putte þer-to of hony arayid, and of þe
seyd hony thre rotis, and lette it sethe so longe tylle it be thycke.
19   And aftir þat put þer-to a dramme and half one of goode muske, |
[f. 69]   and one dramme of ambre oryental, and thre drammys of þe tre
of aloes, þat is moyst and betyn smalle. And thys is þe fyrste
medycyne, of qwyche þe vertu is to conforte þe brayne and þe
hert myghtyly, and also þe stomak.

The seuynth capitil   Capitulum vij

25   Take of merablonys, galengan, of cabely with owte þe barke,
and take of þe mary and pytthe of caroblys of Babylon þe fourth
parte of a rotyle, and of lyquoryse with-owte þe barke, þat is of
yelow colour, tweyne vncys, and of rype kernellis of decynotis
tweyne vncis. Alle þise lete hem be brokyn to-gydir, and put in
30   a vessel with tenne rotis of watyr a day and a nyght, and aftyr
þat sethe hem sokyngly to þe half. þan take hem fro þe fyre, and
stere it wele to-gydir tyl it be alyke thykk, and þan clense it oftyn
tylle it be cler, and þan putte þer-to of pr[epar]at hony, qwyche is

---

1 and] At   6 owyn] y *surmounted by contraction sign and apparently foll. by*
blurred downstroke: perhaps owyin.   9 putte] putty   18 thycke] c *ins.*
above   19 dramme] *with symbol* 3 *above it: this feature not recorded here-*
after   30 a day] *article a corr.*   32 tyl it] it *above canc. three minims*
33 preparat] *priuat*

hard, tweyn rotis and sethe it a-yen tylle it be thykk. And qwan it is
takyn off, putte þer-to | of mastyk betyn to powdyr an ownce, and [f. 69ᵛ]
of rebarich þe fourth parte of an ownce. And þis is þe secunde
medycine, of qwyche þe propyrté is to make stronge þe stomak,
and to porge euyl and corupte hymorys þat be gadryd in þe 5
stomak, with-owte ony vyolens or lothelynes, and with-owte ony
hurte. Mor-ouir it makyth stronge þe chyne and alle joyntis, and
þe brest and þe brayne.

Þe eghte [capitil]   Capitulum viij

Take of emleg a pece, and parte it, and of dymide and of elyleg 10
of Yinde half a half part of a rot, and of darsainy, caryell, and
tekelenge galangale, [and] notys muscate, one ownce. And lete
alle thys be brokyn to-gydir noȝt to smalle, and putte hem in
fresch watyr ten rotys, and lette it lye in þat watyr a day and a
nyght. And aftyr in þe same watyr sethe it with a soft fyr to þe 15
half, and þan lete it be steryd myghtyli to-gydir, and aftir þat
clense it tylle it be clere, and putte þer-to thre rotis of hony
of qwyche I remembryd in þe begynnyng, | and lete hem sethe [f. 70]
to-gydir tyl thei be thyk. And thys is þe thyrd medycine, of home
þe propyrté is to conforte alle þe spyritual membrys inforth.   20

[Þe] nynght capitil   Capitulum ix

Take, with þe blyssyng of God, of þe watyr of palmys, and put
þer-to of tendris þat beere wylde applis a pounde, and of salt watyr
oftyn clensid a l., and of watyr of salicenne wele clensid a l., and
putte þise to gidyr, and putte hem in a qwarte of vine-egyr so þat 25
alle may lye fletyng þer-inne, and lete it stonde a day and a nyght.
And aftyr clense it and putte þer-to thre pounde of hony, and lete
it sethe with a soft fyr tylle it be thyk. And thys is þe fourth
medycine, of qwyche þe propyrté is to help þe appetite and þe
longis and þe instrument of þe brest.   30

Þe tentht capitil   Capitulum x

Take fresch estynes and grene trifera, vndyr þe weyght of
a pounde, and putte it [in] a quantité couenyent of watyr, and adde
iij partis of comyne, and lete hem stonde a day and a nyght, and 34
aftyr sethe | hem to þe half. Þan take four partys of hony and putte [f. 70ᵛ
þer-to, and sethe hem tylle þei be thyk. And thys is þe fyfthe, of
qwyche þe propyrté is to putte awey malencoly, and to dyssolue

flewme, and to consume superfluyteis of humoris, to tempir þe
stomak, to dyssolue hym þat is constipat, and to dyssolue wynde.

The elleuynth capitil   Capitulum xi

Take with þe help of God, of decolayis, asenyis, contrariores, of
5 yche half a rote, and of degeneris arabyk [thre] vnce and of þe
kyrnellis of þe pynet one vnce, and lete alle þise be brokyn in watyr
of rose, and putte þer-to of hony preparate iij rotis, and sethe hem
on þe fyre, and stere hem tylle it be thyk. And þis is þe syxte
medycine, of home þe propyrté is to make smothe þe breste, and
10 to conforte in refreschyng, and it restoryth þe brest, and puttyth
awey þe peyn of þe tethe.

The twelthe capitil   Capitulum xij

Take with þe help of God of spyca indica thre owncys, and of |
[f. 71] arecyn, and as myche of amome, and of cubellis thre drammys, and
15 lete hem be putt in v vncys of fresch watyr. And aftyr þat lete it
stonde tylle þe vertu and myght be encresyd, and þan clense it,
and putte þer-to of hony preparat and claryfiyd an owunce, and
lette it boyle with a soft fyr tyl it be thyk. And þis is þe seuynth
medycyne, of home þe propyrté is to repare þe stomak and to dys-
20 solue and putte awey ventosyteis.

Þe thirten [capitil]   Capitulum xiij

Take of grene rubarbe þat is sad thre owncis, and of declanucis
a dram, and brose hem to-gydir, and putte þer-to ten owncis of
fresch watyr, and lete hem stonde tylle þe vertu be gone in to þe
25 watyr, and þan ster hem to-gidyr and clense hem. And putt þer-to
iij owncis of hony preparat and boyle hem with a soft fyr tylle it be
thyk. And thys is þe viij medycine, of home þe propyrté is to
amende þe lyuir and to repayr þe hert, and to confort þe body.

[Þe fourtene capitil]   Capitulum xiiij

30   Than take and gadyr alle thyse medycinys to-gydir, and þus
[f. 71ᵛ] schal be made | [þe] nynthe and þe last medycine. And þan take
and putte þe quantyté of an egge of datys with-owte stonys, and
lete it be dyssoluyd as it is wrytin be-forn, but þat date melyte is
best, qwyche is qwyte and softe with-in as þe brayne is. And qwan

---

5 thre vnce]: ⁱⁱⁱⁱ/an vnce; uncie .iij. B 102   17 owunce] *between* w *and* c,
two minims surmounted by horizontal stroke

þei be brokyn in watyr tyl þe strenght be owte þer-of þan gadyr
alle to-gydir, and putte in vj powund of rose watyre, and þan
lete it sethe tyl it be thyk. And þan take it off and lete it kele, and
þan putte þat to þe vnguent klepyd belesan. And put þer-to of
ambre oryental, or ellis beletan, or orengis, of þise thre drammys 5
(ℨ iij), and putte þer-to of margarytis brokyn to powdyr half
a pounde, and of poudyr of precious stonys, þat is to sey rubyis,
safyris, topasys, jacynctis, ℨ i, or to vncis of yche of hem, and of
þe jwse of narde thre drammys (ℨ iij), and of powdyr of gold viij
drammys. And þan put alle þe forseyd medycinys to þis thyngis, 10
and putte þem in a vessel | of gold þat is smokyd with þe tre of [f. 72]
aloes, and sette it viij dayis vndyr a rofe qwer pur eyer is, þat
spyritual vertuys may entir in to it, and lete it stonde þer none
nyght qwan þe mone is in froward dysposicion and faylith þe
ouir cowrs, or ellis hys bemys. And qwan it is complete vndyr þis 15
seyd forme, it schal be to þe as one of þe grete tresouris of þis
world. Take þan þerof be-forn mete and aftyr mete one dramme.
For þis is þe summe of alle medycinys, and chef ende of alle
mydicynal entencion to fle flewme, coler, malencolye, peyne in þe
renys, to putte away emerrowdys and alle bolnyng, to dygest þe 20
mete and to tempir þe complexcion, to clere þe syte, to sese werkyng of þe templys, and, brefly to conclude, it helpyth alle maner
of sekenes bothe inforth and with-owte. But it hath one specyal
thynge, þat it causith a man to haue a cler wytte and a goode brayne.
Qwerfor, o Alysaundyr, if þu vse this thow schalt vse none odyr, 25
for þis suffysith. | Nor þu schalt neuir blede nor be boystid but be [f. 72ᵛ]
þe consel of a man þat is experte in astronomye, and for þis
cause þe profytabylnes of medycinal kunnyng is exaltyd in þat,
and þe natural wylle is enclyned and claryfiyd in þat.

The fyftene capitil   Capitulum xv 30

Bewar Alysaundyr, þat þu opyn no veyn be þe maner of
bledyng, nor take no medycine, but be þe lycens of an astronomer.
And thow schuldyst algatis attempt be þine owne rede, do it noȝt
tylle þe tyme þat þe nwe moone be growyn so myche þat it be
pasyd fro þe sonne. And be war þat þe mone be noȝt in Cancro nor 35
in Pyscibus. And be war of þe beholdyng or respecte of þe sonne

4 klepyd] l *ins. above*   5 orengis, of þise thre drammys] thre orengis,
of thise thre x drammys   13–14 lete . . . dysposicion] non permittatur . . . in
illa nocte in qua Luna erit malignor B104   19 fle flewme] fleme flewme
30 capitil] *foll. by second* capitil, *canc.*   34 þat it] þat h. it

ascendyng to þe mone, and also qwan þe moone is in coniu[n]x-
cion with þe sonne in a quwattry sygne, as Pysces or Capricorne or
sqwyche anodyr. Be war les þat Mercury be in constellacion
4 ascendyng, and also of Saturne. And þe most profytabyl of owrys
[f. 73] in opynnyng of veynis is in þe myddys of þe mo[n]th lunar, | þat
is, qwan þe mon[e] begynith to wane, and þat it be in Libra or
in Scorpyone, and qwan noying sterris be-holde it noȝt, þat is to
se be noȝt dyrecte þer ayens, for þan þe mone is werst and noyabyl
in werkyng. And as for boyistyng, only it may conuenyently be
10 done in þe waxeng of þe mone, qwan þat noyabyl sterris behold it
noȝt, schewyng her bemys directely þer-vppon. But qwan it is
euyn ayens Mercury, and þat þe mone and þe planete of Venus be
in one sygne, or ellis þat Venus and Mercuryus behold þe mone,
and qwan it is so þat þe moone is in constellacion ascendyng, þan
15 hath it power and rewle ouir þat same place in þe Scorpyon.
Qwerfor, qwan þu wulte take a laxatyfe, loke þat þe mone be in
Scorpyon or in Lybra or in Pyscibus, but bewar of neghyng nere
of þe mone to þe planete of Saturne, for þan it makyth humorys
[f. 73ᵛ] and also þe medycine to congele in þe body. And | þe mor þat þe
20 [mo]ne elongid is fro Saturne, so myche þe bettyr, and þow it be
with [þe] planete of Mercury it is noȝt to be feryd. Lete þan þe
begynnyng and chef of his body be aftyr þe goode constellacion of
þe mone, and þe absens fro noyus sterris, and his prosperyté in
hys ascens or goying vppe. And qwan þu wulte yef a medycine, loke
25 in qwat sygne be þe mone and þe sonne, þe qwyche þu mayst know
be [þe] monthe qwyche þu art inne, and if þu beholde dyligen[t]ly
þe sygnys and þe monthys descryuyd in þis present spere. And
if þe mone be in þe sygne þat is coleryk, þu must make þat medicyne
the more scharp. And if it be in a malycoly sygne þu must make it
30 ryght stronge, and if it be in a flewmatyk sygne, but esy and soft,
aftyr þe qwalyté of þe sygne and aftyr resun, for qwan þe sonne
is in þe decens, þe natur of þe wombe is made sad and also losyd.
[f. 74] Qwerfor dyligently it owyth to be consy-|dryd qwydir þe moone
be in a coleryk signe or in a malencoly sygne or in a flewmatyk
35 sygne. And if it be so þat bothe lumynaryis, þat is to sey þe sunne
and þe mone, be in colerryk sygnys, or ellis þat þei neghe or

---

2 a quwattry] aqua wattry   as Pysces] as s pysces   6 mone] month
18–19 makyth . . . congele] makyth the medycine to congele humorys & also
þe medycine to congele   20 mone] sonne *canc., with* luna *ins. above*
28 must] *prec. by canc.* ma

beholde sqwyche maner sygnys, dowght noȝt þat a medycyne þan
schal lytyl profyte as to losyng of þe wombe but if it hurt gretly
natur. And if it be takyn in a melancolyk sygne, owdyr it schal
profyte ryght nowght vttyrly, or vttyrly to myche it schal lose þe
receyuur. And if þe sunne and þe mone be in a flewmatyk sygne, 5
þe laxatyfe þat is youyn warkyth esyly, and namely if þe mone
be in waxyng, for as Doctour Plynyus seyth þat, þe moone waxyng,
alle humorys þat be in a man encrese, and also, decresyng þe mone,
humoris mynwse or decrese, experyens schewyth.

Here endyth þe thyrd boke of secretis. 10

[Þe Fourth Boke]

[The fyrst capytil]   [Capitulum j] |

· . . present werk. But [þ]ow owyst to knowe, Alysaundyr, euyn [f. 76]
as in plantis þe dyuerse naturys and dyuerse strenghys [be] youyn
be Goddys grace, on þe lyke wyse in stonys þer be foundyn sondry 15
kendys and sondry vertuys, of qwyche þe bewté and profytabylnes
is inestymabyl of price, for þei acorde most to a kyngis magesté.
þe kyngis crownys and dyademys be arayid and mayd þe most
gloryus and semly with precyus stonys, be hos bewté þe syght is
confortyd and holpyn, þe wylle, þe se[n]ssualyté and þe hert be 20
delityd, þe dygnyté of astate is adornyd, or arayd, and be þe
vertuys of hem greuus sekenes be putte owte of men and wom-
mennys bodyis, with-owte qwyche is [n]one medycine profytabyl
or effectuus. Qwer-for lechys and physicyens vse hem to þe
puttyng owte of þe most greuus sekenes in man or woman. And 25
conceyue trwly, þat passyng grete vertu is bothe in plauntys and
in stonys, youyn be natur of God, but þei be hyd onknowyn
to man-kende. But in | þe boke qwyche we compylyd of stonys, we [f. 76ᵛ]
haue fully tretyd and schewyd þe propyrteis and vertuys of hem.

And now fyrst and formest, seyth þe fylisophir, O Alysaundyr, 30
I wol now take þe, or lerne þe, of alle priuyteis þe most priuyte and
secrete counsel. And Goddys counsel schal help þe to performe
þi counsel and purpos, and to hyde or couyr þi priuy purpos.

(Conceyue þat now þe fylisofyr inducyth þat blynde mater þat
I spake of, qwyche begynnyth þus:) 35

3 a melancolyk] *run together; separated by vertical stroke in revision*   11 *f. 74*
blank; f. 75 missing   13 þow] yow   16 of qwyche] *prec. by* i   17 inestymabyl of] of *foll. by canc.* o   23 none] ony *with* n *surmounted by two*
small irregular strokes, perhaps accidental

Take þe bestly stone vegetabyl and myneral, þe qwyche is no
stone, nor hath þe natur of a stone. And þis stone is lykynnid in
somme maner to þe stonys of mownntys, myneralis or mynis,
and plauntys and bestys, and it is foundyn in euiry place and in
5 euiry tyme and in euiry man and it is conuertybyl into euiry
colour, and it conteynnith in it alle four elementis, and it is clepyd
þe lesse world. And I schal clepe it þat name þe qwych þe comun
pepyl name it, þat is to sey, þe terme of an egge, þat is to sey, þe
[f. 77] egge of philysophris. | Diuiyde þan þat in to four partis: euiry
10 part hath on nature. þan compownne hym equaly and proporcion-
ably so þat þer be no dyuysion nor repugnans, and, owr Lord
grauntynd, thow schalt haue þi purpos. This is þe vnuyersel
maner, but I schal dyuide it to þe to specyal werkyngis. It is
dyuydid trwly in to fowr, and on tweyn manerys it is made wele
15 and withowte corrupcion. Qwan thow hast þer-for watyr of þe
eyr, and eyer of þe fyr, and fyr of þe erthe, þan thow schalt haue
plenerly þe craf. Dyspose þer-for þe aery substauns be dyscrecion
and dyspose þe erthly substauns be hete and moystour tyll þei come
to gyd[ir] and be conioynyd, and þat þei dyscord noȝt nor be noȝt
20 dyuydid. And þan conioyne to hem to werkis, operatyf vertuis,
watyr and fyr, and þan thy werk schal be complete. For if yow
menge watyr alone it schal make qwyght, and if thow putte fyr
it schal make rede, owre Lord grawntyng.

24 **Þe secunde capitil**   **Capitulum ij**

[f. 77ᵛ]   And owr fadir Hermogines qwy[che] | is threfold in filosophye,
on þe most best wyse filosophying, seyd þat þe trwthe is so, and
þat it is no dowght, þat lower thyngis to hyer thyng, and hyer to
lower be corespondent. But þe Werker of myraclis is on Godde
alone, fro Home descendyth euiry meruulus werk. And so alle
30 thyngis be creat of one only substauns, be an only dysposicion, of
home þe fadyr is þe sonne, and þe mone þe modyr, qwyche bar her
be the wedyr in þe wombe. þe erthe is priuyd fro her-to. This is
clepyd or seyd þe fadyr of enchauntmentis, tresur of myracclys,
þe yessuer of vertuys. Be a lytil it is made erthe. Depart þat
35 qwyche is erthly fro þat qwyche is firy, for þat qwyche is sotel is
mor wurthy þan þat qwyche is grose, and þat rar, porous, or lyght,

---

2 þe natur] þe h nature   7 I schal] ischal   9 egge of phily-
sophris] *in margin*, ouu*m* phi*losophorum*   13 but] & but   20 to werkis] to,
as regularly with numerals, surmounted by ij   24 Capitulum ij] Capi*tulum* iiij

is mor bettyr þan qwyche is thyk of substauns. þis is done wyseli or
dyscretly. It ascendyth fro þe erth in-to heuyn and fallyth fro heuyn
in-to erth, and þer-of it sleth þe ouyr vertu and þe nedyr vertu, so it
hath lorchyp in þe lowe thyngis and | hye thyngis, and þu lord- [f. 78]
schyppist vppeward and downward, and with þe is þe lyght of 5
lyghtys. And for þat alle derkenes schal fle fro the. þe ovyr vertu
ouircomyth alle, for euiry rar thyng werkyth in to euiry thyk thyng.
And aftyr þe dysposicion of þe mor world rennyth thys werkyng.
And for þat Hermogines is clepyd threfold in filosophye and of
þe meruellys of þe world. And þat stone is þat fyghtyth with 10
watrys and wyndis. þu seyst it a-ryse abouyn watrys qwan watrys
renne with wynde, and it is born in þe see of Mydyl Erth, and þe
propyrté þer-of is þis: if þu take þis stone and putte it in anodyr
stone and ber it with þe, it is noȝt possibyl þat ony oste may
dwr ayens þe or withstonde þe, but þei schal flee myscheuusly 15
be-forn þe.

Of two precyus stonys meruul

Ther be also tweyn precious stonys of meruulus vertu, þe
qwyche be foundyn in derk placys, of qwyche one is qwyght and
þe odyr reede, and þei be foundyn in grauell and sonndy watrys. 20
And the | werkyng of hem is this: the qwyght stone begynnyth to [f. 78ᵛ]
apper vppon watrys in þe downgoyng of þe sunne, and it abydith
abouyn vppon þe facis of þe watyr tyl mydnyght, and þan it
begynnyth to descende bakward, and in þe sprynging of þe sunne
it schal come downe to þe depe. The rede stoone hath werkyng in 25
contrary, for it begynnyth forto apper in þe sprynging of þe
sonne, tyl þe howr of mydday, and it is in fallyng downne to þe
downe-goyng of þe sonne. And þe propyrté of þise stonys is this:
þat if þu hange of þe rede stone half a dramme vppon one hors of
of þi[n] hoste, all þe horsis of þine host schal neuir sese of neying 30
tyl þu take a-wey þat stone. And þe werkyng of þe qwyght stone
is þe contrary. Qwer-for þei be myche wurthe to þe help of þine
host and to slegytis of werre. And þe propyrté of þis stonys is thys:
if tweyn stryue togydir, put þe qwyght stone in þe mowthe of one
of þe stryuerrys, and if þe ryght of þat þei stryue for longe to hym, 35
[he] schal speke spe-|dyly in his mater, and ellys he may noȝt [f. 79]
speke a word mor as longe as it is in hys mowthe. And þe reed
stone hath þe contrary werkyng. And I schal determyne to þe þe

30 þin] þis   36 he¹] &

propyrteis and vertuys of stonys in enchauntementis and of summe
[plawntis] in þe folowyng tretyse.

And þu fully hast knowyn, of my tretyse gooyng before, qwer I
haue tretyd of natural thyngis and priuyteis of creaturis, þat þe
5 degré of pla[un]tis, and þe dysposicion, is aftyr þe degré and þe
dysposicion of mynerallis aftyr her beyng, and þat þei receyue
a propyr forme aftir her begynnyng and natur of hyer naturys, þat
is to sey ouircomyng and lordchyppyng in h[e]m. And ouircomyng
in plauntis is a wattry natur, and in myneral stonys is an erthly
10 natur. þer-for þe naturis of plawntis resceyuith of þe natur of
watris a bolnyng or encresyng, as þe same receuyith watyr be
meuyng and impulsion of wyndys in his place. And as euiry
[f. 79ᵛ] watrys be of sondry figurys, for þer-inne | be many figuris, so it
fallyth in pla[un]tys. Alle figurys be foundyn in pla[un]tis, sythyn
15 þan þat watyr is ouircomyng in plawntys and it is noȝt extendyd
but be dyfusyon, and sythyn þe werker of dyssolucion of watrys
is euirlasting, verkyng withowte sesyng to hys heuyn, þat is to sei,
Mercuryus. For it is vnyuersally trwe, þat euiry planete gouernyth
and dysposith and acordyth and is assimiylid to his natur, as, be
20 exampul, Saturne kepyth þe erth, Mercury þe watyr, Jubyter þe
aer, þe sonne, fyr. And þis conuenyens is noȝt foundyn in the
[changeabyl] werkys of planetys, but in þe werkyngis of planetys
qwyche þei haue contynwally and perpetuyally be þe ouyr vn-
uersal vertu, þe qwyche is abouyn þe verkyngis of alle þise vertuys.
25 But here is no place to schewe þise hard materys. But for þis I
haue made to þe mencion, for it is gretly necessary and profytabyl
to þe for þe folowyng tretyse, in qwyche we schal determyne of
[f. 80] synguleris and þingis indyuysibyl, | of sondry vegetabyl, and also
of pla[un]tis. The knowyng of þis longith to filysophris, and þe
30 knowleche of natural werkyngis longith to lechis. And I wul noȝt
þat it schal be hyd fro þi wysdam, þat þu schalt vndyrstonde þat
euiry thyng wantyng lyght of þe nombyr of vegetabyllis is attribute
to Saturne and gouernyd of Saturne. And qwat þing of vegetablys
is floryschyng and luminus is youyn to, and gouernyd be, Mercury
35 þe planete. And qwat sum-euir of vegetablys is floryschyng and
beryth no frwte is attribute to Mars and gouernyd be Mars. And

___

5 plauntis] planetis (plantarum B 119)   and þe²] *prec. by canc. is as*
8 hem] hym   12 as] *added in margin, without precise indication of point at
which it should be inserted*   13 be²] f be   14 plauntys] planetys plauntis]
planetis   29 plauntis] plane*tis*   34 youyn to] youyn to Saturne: *see n.*

euiry vegetabyl floryschyng and beryng frwte or seede is gouernyd
be þe sonne, and to þe sonne attribute. Than compowne and
conioyne þise dyuysiounys, and sey þat eueri vegetabyl beryng
frwte and noȝt flowryng, as is an appyl, is att[r]ibute to Saturne
and to þe sonne. And euiry floryschyng thyng beryng no 5
frwte is causid of Mercuri and Mars. Also sum vegetable | be [f. 80ᵛ]
plaunty[d] be bowys, and sum be here sede, and summe be born or
sprongyn with-owte seede, and sum with-owte plauntyng. Than
it is opyn and cler inowe of þise forseyd, þat euiry kende of vegetabyllis or growyng thingis hath a propyr dysposycion, þe qwyche is 10
complexcionat, and folowyth þe vertu of a planete, and is assimyld
þer-to and attrybute or youyn. And it hath a-nodyr vertu, qwyche
is assocyat or felyschypd and attribute to þe vertu of tweyn planetis
or of many, aftyr þat it may take, and it helpyth yche propyrté þat
is youyn to þat vegetabyl, þat is to sey, þat natural vertu þat 15
dysposith hys kende in hete, in smellyng, in tast, and in schappe.
And a natural soule gadryth alle þis propyrteis and vertuys natural,
for þei be concurrent fro it, and it folowyth be it, and it makyth
it to dwr as myche tyme as is dyfynyd to it, and betokynnid of þer
vertu. For þer is no dede with-owte meuyng, and þer is no werkyng 20
with-owte God. And þus schalt þu fynd sum kende of vegetabyllis
qwych | be noyabyl, and sum kende þat is helsum and helyng, [f. 81]
and summe þat gendyr myrth and joye, and sum þat cause
loue, and summe þat cause hatred, and sum þat to þem þat bere
it yeuyth reuerrens and wurchypp, and summe abiection and 25
contempt, and sum þat makyth a man to see fals dremys, and
sum þat cause a trwe vysion. Summe gendyr manfulnes and
strenght, and summe slawght and febylnes. Summe kepe þe body
fro dedly venymmis, and summe corupt þe body and bryng in deth.
And I schal make þe a mencion of alle þise kendis with argumentis 30
and opyn prouyngis. That kend of vegetablys qwyche gendryth
reuerrens and wurchyp is a certeyn tree qwyche hath conuolute
leuys. þe schap þer-of is rownde, and also þe frwte. þe brawnchys of
þat tre be tendyr and moyst, and of sqwete tast. He þat pluckyth
vpp þat herbe in hys name, and beryth it wyth hym, for certeyn 35
he adquirith (or getyth) reuerens and wurchyp be þat. And þer is
a-nodyr tree þat spryngith vppe on heyght þe lenght of a mannys
arme, qwyche hath longe, moyst leuys, qwyche leuys | haue [f. 81ᵛ]
withinne hem qwyght veynys. And he þat beryth with hym of

6 be] qwy be   7 plauntyd] plauntyl   32 is] Haui is   35 wyth] corr. from wuth

þe substauns of þat tree schal be exaltyd aftyr hys degré be. Ther
is a-nodyr hauyng gret leuys, and þe brawnchys of þat tre be extendyd vppon þe herthe, of qwyche þe smelle is sqwete. And he
þat beryth þis with hym is lyght, manful and hardy. And it is noȝt
5 goode to fyght with hym þat beryth þis vppon hym, for he ouircomyth euir hys aduersary in euiry cause. Ther is anodyr of þe
kende of treis þat hath prykyllis þer-vppon, and it is plauntyd,
and it hath anelong leuys, and þe leuys falle or euir þe flowrys
sprynge, and it beryth thre flowrys anelong, qwych be reede of
10 colour and of sqweete sauour. And he þat etyth þo flourys, it betid-
yth to hym joye and lawghyng. And he þat pullyth vppe þe flourys
with þe leuys and prykyllis, and þan sokyth þe flourys thynkyng
on ony woman, it settyth her afyr in hys loue. Ther is a-nodyr
14 herbe clepyd adrasinon, and it spryngith in þe cuntre of Sin, and
[f. 82] it hath currlyng leuys, smale and | drye, and þe seed þer-of is
rownde and very lyghtyl, qwyght withinne. If þu take of þe seede
of þat herbe vij kernel in name of ony persone, and breke hem in
þat personys name in þe rysing of þe sterre clepy[d] Lwcyfer þe
morow sterr, and of þe planete of Venus, so þat þe bemys of þo
20 planetis towche þe sedys, if þu yef þat persone to drynk þo seuyn
kernellis brokyn or brosid, or ellis to ete in ony mete, þi loue schal
abyde in þat personys hert, to obey to þe alle the dayis of hys
lyue. And of þe kende of plauntis þer is a certeyn plaunt qwyche
gendryth sekenes, of hom þe tendraunt or crop is plawntyd, of
25 qwyche þe brawchys growe owte þe lenght of an arme, of qwyche
þe flouris be qwyght, spryngyng be-for þe leuys, beryng neuir
frwte. þe propyrté þer-of is of Mars and Mercuri, þe nature is fyri
and aery. He þat beryth þat erbe with hym schal neuir be with-
owte sekenes tyl he throwe it fro hym. Ther is also of þe kend of
30 plawntys an holyng herbe of qwyche þe sedys be sowyn, þe bowyis
[f. 82ᵛ] þer-of be | four sqwar, þe leuys rounde, þe flourys þer-of be lyke
þe fyrmament, þe sede is rede, hauyng sqwete sauyurr, and of
goode werkyng. He þat drynkyth þer-of, or hath þe tast þer-of,
schal be made hole of malencoly, or of pensyfhed, or of dreede,
35 or of þe frenesy, and of many odyr sekenes. And þer is anodyr
qwyche is clepyd macynsson, þe qwyche is myghty to geete booth
loue and reuerrens. O Alysaundyr, I haue fynyschyd perfyghtly

---

16 take] *repeated*   18 clepyd] clepyl   25 brawchys] *intended form per-*
haps brawnchys: *see n.*   34 of dreede] of *foll. by second* of *begun and left*
unfinished

þat I promysid to trete to þe. Be þerfor euir vertuuus, and gloryus
God euir gouerne þe and directe þe and kepyth þe, Hos goodenes
euiry creatur perceyuith or takyth part.

(The tretyse is þus complete of tokynnis and natural maneris of
men, to þe ryght nobyl kyng Alysaundyr, and conqwerour grettest, 5
þe qwyche was lord vndyr Good of alle þe world, clepyd þe
monarke in þe septentrion, kyng, in þe world, of kingis.)

Aristotil:

O Alysaundyr, now þu hast knowyn þat qwyche I haue tretyd 9
and expounyd, þat is to sey, þe substauns of þis | world, as is to þe [f. 83]
necessary. þerfor vse vertu, and prosperyté schal folow.
(Now folowyth of enchauntementis qwyche Holy Chyrche hath
forbodyn, qwerfor of þat it suffisith.)

The thyrd capitil   Capitulum iij

Ryghfulnes, or justyse, is þe preysabyl comendacion of þe pro- 15
pyrteis of Hym þat is hyest gloryus One in beyng. Qwerfor þe
kyndam of þis schuld be of Hym as in gouernauns be symylitude.
For God chesith and ordeynith a kyng to gouerne þe pepyl be
equyté, þat þei as seruauntis schuld gete and labour to hys
sustynauns and to herris, and he to defend her goodys, posses- 20
sc[i]ounis and her lyffys, and dresse alle nedeful euyn as her good.
And in þis a kyng is lykynnyd to Goode, therfor it behouyth a kyng
aftyr þat he is lykenyd, to folow Hym þat is hyest in alle hys
werkys. God is wyse and kunnyng, and þe precony and Hys
namys be gloryus in Hym, and þe grettenes of Hys lordchyp is 25
abouyn Hys comendacion myche mor þan His | wysdam. þe con- [f. 83ᵛ]
trary to Hym be wrongis, for þe contrary to wronge is ryghfulnes.
In ryg[h]fulnes þer-for heuynnys wer creat and ordeynyd abouyn
erth. In ryghtfulnes also holy prophetys wer sent. Ryghtfulnes
þan is a foorme, or a schap, of vndyrstondyng, þe qwyche gloryus 30
God hat creat, or made, and browght Hys creaturis to þat. And
be ryghfulnes erth was bylyd, and kyngis wer ordeynyd, and
sogettis obey, and soulis be sauyd and delyueryd fro euiry vyce,
and ayens her kyngis fro euiry corrupcion. And þerfor seyden In-
dyciannis þat the ryghtfulnes of hym þat regnyth is mor profytabyl 35
to hys sogettis þan þe plenteuusnes of alle temperal goode for þe
tyme. And þei seid, mor-ouir, þat a ryghtful lordschypper is bettir
þan a sesonnabyl reyn. It was also foundyn wrytyn in a ston in

11 vertu] vertu & vertu

Caldé tonge, þat a kyng and vndyrstondyng be bredyris and iche
of hem hath nede of odyr, for þe tone suffysith noȝt with-owte
[f. 84] þe todyr. And alle thyngis in vnyuersel be creat | of ryghfulnes, and
sche is cause of vndyrstondyng, þe qwyche puttyth in her beyng,
5 abyding beyng or werkyng. Thys is His dede, He is a ryghtful
juge. Qwerfor þe beyng of justice and þe rote þer-of descendith
fro vndyrstondyng. It semyth þat ryghfulnes is on tweyn wysis,
þat is to sey, opyn and hyd. Opyn justise is clepyd qwan iustise is
schewyd be werkyng in deede abouyn condiciounys, qwyche is weyd
10 and mesuryd be cler vndyrstondyng, and dome takyth name of þis.
Hid iustise is þe trwnes or þe ryghtfulnes, cruelnes of þe domysman
werkyng þe verkis, and a certitude or confirmacion of hys seyingis.
Qwerfor it apperith, as we seyd beforn, þat a kyng is lykenyd in
ryghfulnes to God abouyn, qwerfor it is conuenyent to hym to be sted-
15 fast in his werkis, and in þe werkys of hys communnys. He þan
[f. 84ᵛ] þat declynith fro propyr or comun justise, he folowyth noȝt | þat
ryghtfulnes qwyche is in God. For if þu be ryghful, þi sogettis
schal fer þe and comende þe, and þu schalt plese hym þat is hyest.

[The fourth capitil]   Capitulum iiij

20   Ther be to maner of justisis, one þat longith to jugis in yessuying
domys, and þer is justice þat longith to euiry man in gouernauns
of hym-self, gydyng hym be resun and concyens betwene God
and hym. Qwer-for, Alysaundir, ordeyn ryghfulnes in tho thyngis
þat be betwene þi pepyl and þe, þat is to sey, mesuris of maner in
25 ordeynyng a lawe to be kept, in domys, in behauyngis, in taskys,
in þi lyuyng. And ferthermor þan ryght requirith, extende neuir
þi power, for alle þat pasith justyse is but oppression. And now
wul I trete to þe of world, how, be a figur longyng to þi gouernauns,
sotelly þu schal constrw be symylitudis. The world is a gardeyn
30 or an herber. Of it þe matyr or þe hegge is dome. [Dome] is
lordechypper defessid with lawe. Lawe is þe kyngdam, and
[f. 85] specyally þe gouernaunz of þe kinge | þat gouernyth. þe kynge is
herdeman qwyche is defendyd of hys lordis. þe lordis be feid folk
born vppe with money. Money is þe fortune qwyche is gadryd of
35 sogettis. Sogettis be seruauntis þat justise hath subdwyd. Justise
is þat qwyche is intendyd be þe self, of fer of God and resun, in
qwyche is þe helth of sogettis. Knowe þan þat þat fyrst thyng þat

---

11 trwnes . . . cruelnes] *see n.*   16 noȝt] *repeated as first word of f. 84ᵛ*
20 Ther be] *does not begin new paragraph in ms.;* Capitulum iiij *in margin.* T *not
illuminated nor otherwise distinguished in ms.*   36 be] p be

gloryus God formyd or made, is a sympil spiritual substauns, in
þe ende of perfyghnes, and þe complement or fulfillyng of goodenes,
in qwyche is forme of alle thyngis, and it is clepyd Intellectife.
þan of anodyr substauns þer yed owte, a substauns lower of degré,
qwyche is clepyd þe Soule. þer was þan of þat Soule anodyr   5
substauns clepyd Yle, beforn þe commensuracion, qwych is at-
tendyd in lenght, brede and depnes, in qwyche was made a sympyl body. þan þat body, beforn þe most nobyl fygur, þe qwyche
ouircomyth alle figuris, elder and trwer comperatifly, it abode in   9
þe place | only, þat is to sey of speris and planetis, þat qwyche was   [f. 85ᵛ]
more þer-of and þat qwych in þe begynnyng was most sympil, the
fyrst þer-for of speris goyng abowght, or closyng, to þe terme of
þe sper of þe moone. And þer be nyne heuynnis, one in erth and
anodyr amonge hemself. þe fyrst þer-for, and þe hyest, of sperys,
is þat qwyche encludyth alle odyr, and with-ine þat is þe sper of   15
sterris, and aftyr þat þe sper of Saturne, and so forth to þe sper
of þe mone, qwych is benethe, within qwyche sper be þe four
elementis, þe fyr, þe aer, watyr, and erth. Qwerfor þe erth is in þe
myddis of alle elementis, and it is þe mor thyk substauns and
sadder essencially. And aftyr þise speris wer ordeynyd aftir þe   20
ordynauns of God, þe speris had her meuyngis rowndly in
her partis and planetis, vppon þe four elementis and be sundri
qwyllis þe nyght and þe day, wyntir and somyr, hete and cold.
And sum be comyxte or medyllid | in summe. And contemperat is   [f. 86]
þat qwyche is rare, thynne, porose or sotel, with þat qwyche is thyk,   25
and þat qwyche is ponderus in hem, with þat qwyche is lyght. Of
lenght of tyme, vnyuersal kendis of bodyis compounyd, þat be
oryginal[lis], or mynis of metellis, or vegetablis and bestis. Tho be
clepyd oryginallis qwat thyngis sum-euir be congelid in þe
bowellis of þe erth, and in þe depnes of seeys, and in þe hollenes   30
of hyllis, and in bolnyd materis includyd, and of vaporis ascendyng, and of congelat moystouris, and in þe holues of cauernys, in
qwyche erthly aer hath most lordchyp.
And þise be tho qwyche he spekyth of, as gold, siluir, yryn, lede,
bras, tynne, stonys, margarites, coal, vitriole, alumme, and   35
sqwyche odyr qwyche be sene and knowyn.
And euerythyng þat meueth fro place to place, and hath felyng, and
goth or meueth ony vyse be hymself propyrly, is clepid beste, and

þe aer hath lordchyp in þem. And þe composicion of vegetablys |
[f. 86ᵛ] is mor wurthi þan þe composicionis of originallis, þat is to sey, of
þe speris, for þe lyf incresyng in hem. The composicion of bestis
is mor wurthi þan þe composicion of vegetablys, for þe[i] haue
5 bothe lyfe and also felyng. But þe most nobil is man, in composicion
pasyng al bestis, þe qwyche lyuyth, felyth, vndyrstondyth, and hath
abilté of gouernauns. And in man fyrines hath most lordchip. And
in hym and his composicion, or makyng, alle elementis be concurrent. For man is of a thyk body commensurat, and of a soule
10 qwyche is sympil of substauns spirytual. It behouyth þan the, if
þu be knowyng abouyn syencis and trwthis of beyng and abyding,
þat þu begynne fyrst at þe knowyng of þine owne soule, qwyche
is mor ner to þe þan ony odyr thynge, and aftyr þat, to haue kunnyng and knowyng of odyr. For knowe þat þe natural soule is þe
15 spyritual strenght sprongin of inteligens be þe wylle of God, and it
[f. 87] hath tweyn strenghys concurr-|ent in bodyis, as þe lyght of þe sonne
in partis of þe aer. One of þe qwyche þevise of strenght is [tokennyng],
and [þat] odyr is werkyng, þe qwyche gloryus God hath indwyd with
vij strenghis, þat is to sey strengh retractyf, and attractyf, dygestif,
20 and expulsif, nutritif, and informatyf, and vegetatif. And þe
strenght in werkyng of þis strenght vegetatif, in þe makyng of
mannys body, is in þe receyuyng of mannys seede in þe womannys
wombe, and in þe dysposicion þer-of, qwyche endwryth vij
monthis. And aftyr þat it hath abydin þat tyme in waxing þat God
25 hath ordeynnyd, þan He infudyth þe bestly soule sensibyl, tylle þe
pasyng owte or þe departyng, and it getyth a-nodyr gouirnauns to
þe fyllyng of tyme of iiij yeris. And þan he yeldyth hym to resun-
nabyl vndyrstondyng, þe qwyche is clepyd vertu resonnabyl, þe
qwyche chongith þe name of sensibyll, and þan he gete a-nodyr
30 gouirnauns tyl þe complement of xv yeris. And þan entryth þe
[f. 87ᵛ] strenght intellectife qwyche | is denuncyatyf of fyguris or simy-
litudys, or interpretac[i]ounys of sensibilys, and þan he geteth
a-nodyr gouernauns to þe complement of xxv yeris. And þan
comyth þe strenght judicial or phi[lo]s[of]ical, þe qwyche be-
35 holdyth intellectual formys, and þan he getyth anodyr gouernauns
to þe tyme of xxx yeris. And þan betydyth þat vertu or strenght
qwyche is namyd þe kyngly strenght voluntary, and þan it hath

---

5 þe most] is þe most   7 And²] *prec. by canc.* e   17–18 is tokennyng,
and þat odyr] is anodyr þat   24 And aftyr] *repeated*   32 geteth] th *ins.*
above   34 philosofical] phisical; philosophica B 131

a-nodir gouernauns to þe complement of xxxv yeris. And þan
komyth þe strenght clepyd legal, þe qwyche is plantatyf of orygy-
nallis, and þan it getith anodyr gouernauns to þe complement of þe
lyfe. And vndyr þis maner of forme is þe soule complete be-forn
it departyth fro þe body. And þan it schal be receyuyd of þe   5
animal vertu natural, qwyche is receyuyd be her and browght to
þe hye perfeccion, tyl he come to þe cerkyl or firmament of in-
telligens, to qwych he hath deseruyd. And if þe soule be no3t
perfyght, it descendith to þe sqwolow | of hell, and þan he re-   [f. 88]
ceyuith a gouernauns fro þe hede with-owte hope of wellfar.   10
Qwan þer-for almyghti God made man, He made hym wurthyest
of alle bestis. He yaf hym a comaundement and forbad hym, He
ponyschyd hym and rewardyth hym, He ordeynith hys body as a
cyté and hys vndyrstondyng to gouerne in þat cyté, and He en-
closid hym in þe most nobyl place of man, þat is to sey þe hed, and   15
hath ordeynid hym v masyngerys to gouerne hym, and to represent
to hym alle thyngis qwyche þat be necessary to his help and confort,
qwyche kepe hym fro euiry thyng þat is noyabyl to hym, and he
hath no perfyght knowlech withowte hem. And God hath youyn
to yche of þise v masengeris a propyr dome be þe qwyche he   20
dyferensith and is departid from odyr, and þis[e] v masyngeris be
the v wyttis, qwyche be in þe eyn, in þe erys, in þe nose, in þe
tonge, and in þe hand. Than þe kyndys of vysibil thyngis þat | be   [f. 88ᵛ]
conceyuyd be þe yen be x sondry kendis, þat is to sey lyght and
derknes, colouris and body, figuris and beyng, fernes and nernes,   25
and meuyng and rest. The wytte or propyrté þat longith to þe eris
is heryng of soundis, or thyngis soundyng, and þer be tweyne
kendys, one is bestly and a-nodyr is no3t bestly. þe sounde þat
we clepe bestli is on tweyn maneris, one is racional, qwyche is
longing to speche, and þe sound onresunnabyl is þe neyng of an   30
hors, þe krying of a crowe and sqwyche odyr. þe sound qwyche is
clepyd no3t bestly is as þe ruscyng of treys, þe clascyng of stonys,
þe tramplyng of fete, and sqwyche odyr, and of þo þat ber no lyfe
as a thondyr, a tympan, an harp, and sqwyche odyr. Knowe þan
þat euiry voyse in hys ordyr vnyuersally, qwan it meuyth be   35
vyolens, þe aer meuith þer-with, beryng it, and þat spyritual
nobylles is meuyd þer-with, beryng it vndyr þat forme þat no
part is medyllyd with | odyr part, tylle it come hole to þe last   [f. 89]

---

1 yeris] y *at end of line,* yeris *at beginning of next*   17 thyngis] g *altered
from* k   21 þise] þisi   35 ordyr] *medial* r *ins. above*

strenght, or to þe herers vndyrstondyng, and þan be hym it is
born to þe vertu ymaginatyf. Than þat wytt qwyche longith to þe
tonge is made be þe wey of tast and sauour, and þer-to longyn ix
spycis or kendys, þat is to sey: sqwettnes, byttyrnes, saltenes, fat-
5 nes, sournes, weryschnes (or onsauerynes), sauyrines (or sqwetnes),
scharpnes [and] dryischnes. And þe wytt qwych is in þe hande
is in þe strenght of towchyng or gropyng, and þe cours þer-of
is in hete or cold, scharp and soft, and it is þe strenght
conteynid be-twene tweyn skynnys, qwyche one is in þe vttyr-part
10 of þe bodi and þe todyr in þat qwych longith to þe flesch. Quanne
þer-for ony of þise wyttis be gotyn qwyche God hath youyn to þis
seid kyngis vndyrstondyng, þer sprynge owte fro þe roote of þe
brayn sotel skynnys, lyght as þe webbe of an arenne, and tho be as
14 coueryngis or corteynis to þis kynge. Qwan þerfor is presentyd þat
[f. 89ᵛ] euiry wytt | hath, and þat comyth to þo skynnys qwyche be in þat
substauns of þe brayne, þanne be þe steppys gadryd of þe wyttis
of man to þe vertu ymagynatyf, qwyche representyth þo thyngis
to the vertue cognytif, or of knowlecchyng, qwyche is in þe myddis
of þe brayn, þat þei schuld gadyr and stody in þe figurys of hem,
20 and examplis, to know in hem þo þat helpe and þo þat noye,
and þat he schuld werk a mene qwyche comyth to hym of hem.
þer-for þe ordynauns and þe beyng of þe body is in þise v wyttis
namyd be-forn. The perfeccion þer-for of euiry thyng is in v
thyngis. The planetis o[f] qwyche þe speeris meue cerkylly be
25 v, and þe kendys of bestis be v, þat is to sey: man; foule; fysche;
four-fotyd bestis; monstris, dragounys and alle þo þat gon on tweyn
feete, be þe v kend of bestis. And þer be v thyngis with-owte
[f. 90] qwyche v þer is no plaunt | þat growyth owte of þe ertht perfyght,
that is to sey, þe stok, þe braunchis, þe leuys, þe frwte, and þe
30 roote. And þer be v tunys mysical with-owte qwyche þer is no
songe consonaunt, that is to sey, an vnyson, a thyrd, a v.ᵗᵉ, a vjᵗᵉ,
and an eght (viij). And þer be v þe most nobyl dayis of þe yer, in þe
lastt part of May. Therfor, Alysaundyr, lete þi masyngeris and thi
counsellouris be v in þe comprehension of þi werkis, and lete yche
35 be sondryd fro odyr qwan thow wult axe owght, for þan it is so
most profyghtabyl to þi werkis.

---

1 herers] second r ins. above   4 sqwettnes] prec. by canc. sau[yrines]
4–6 saltenes ... dryischnes] cf. B133/22–23   6 and dryischnes] or dryischnes
18 cognytif] ti ins. above   20–1 margin, in later hand: intellec[t]   24 of] vppon
27 þe] þer   31 vnyson] surmounted by i, as with numerals regularly in this ms.

The fyfte capitil   **Capitulum v**

Kepe þi secrete with-in þe, and telle noȝt to hem fyrst qwat is in
thyne hert, nor telle to none of hem hos counsel semyth þe best,
nor telle to none of hem how thow woldist borow her consel. For
þan þei schal despyse þe, wenyng þu haue no wytte. Tempyr þan, 5
qwan thow hast herd hem, with-in þi soule, her wyllys, | euyn as [f. 90ᵛ]
I rehersid þe dysposicion of the brayn of þo thyngis þat come fro
the fyue wyttis. On þat lyke forme gadyr in thy wytte her seyngis,
and declyne fro her counsellis in þat þei contrary to þi wylle.
[And] for this seyd Hermes, qwan he was axid qwy þe dome of hym 10
þat yefyth counsel is bettyr þan hys þat axith counsel, he ansqwerd,
'For þe dome of hym þat sekyth counsel is robbyd or drawn owte
of wylle.' Therfor, qwan thow gadryst þi consel to yeue ony ver-
dyth of counsel in thy presens, yef hem no counsel nor medyl noȝt
thy counsel with herris, but yef goode audyens to hem in qwat 15
thynge their acorde. If þei yef an ansqwer in hast and acord, make
resistens and obieccionys ayens her seyngis, that her wyttis and her
stodyis and thowghtis may be prolongid, and þat þei may stody
for wytte. And qwan þan þat þu hast perceyuyd þe very trwe wey
of þi materis, and þat her counsel is goode, or þat ony of hem seyth 20
þe | trwth, make hem sese with sum word, and telle none of hem [f. 91]
alle, nor schew be no cher, that thow wult do aftyr ony of hem,
tylle þe dede be putt in expperyens.

[The sexte capitil]   **[Capitulum vi]**

And consider wyselé qwyche of hem drawyth to trwth and ryght 25
of counsel. Consider also þe loue þat he hath ayens the, and þe
desir of thyne welfar, and þe zele þat he hath to þe prosperyté of
þi gouirnauns. Take, if þu fynde sqwyche one, hys counsel, but
loke of alle tho v þat þu preferr none be-forn odyr, but make hem
lyke in yiftis and in alle thy werkys. For þe destroying or hyndrauns 30
of a kingis werk in many dayis is þat he wurchyppyth sum and
preferryth be-forn sum. And it is noȝt inconuenyent to a kyng, as
for þe age of a man, thow he be yong and he be wyse, for þe
dome is chongyd aftyr þe body, for qwan þe dome is febyl, þe
body is febyl. And the natur or complexcion is to be considŕyd, for 35

---

5 Tempyr] temp*eryr*   10 And] Et   23 expperyens] *first* p *unclear;*
possibly experyens *badly written*   24 *chapter heading om.*   25 And consider]
run on without chapter heading or new line   27 zele] *prec. by canc. minim*
30 þe destroying] þe of destroying

he þat is generat (or born) oftyn is dysposid aftyr natur of planetis þe
[f. 91ᵛ] qwyche | be in þe regyon of his byrth. And if it betyde happly
þat þe progenytourys teche sqwyche one ony manuel craft, þe
natur þat he hath of bodyis abouyn drawe hym to þe craft qwyche
5 is conuenyent to hym.

[The seuynth capitil]   Capitulum vij

As be exampyl, for lyke to this betyd, certeyn clerkys wer on
a tyme harborowyd at a websterris hows, and, þat same nyght, of
þe hostis wyfe þer was born a sone. þe natur and dysposicion aftyr
10 þe owr of byrth of þe chyld þei ordeynid. And hys planetis and hys
natural dysposicion was in Venus and Mars, in his gree beyng
Geminus with Libra, and no contrary sterris wer noȝt that tyme
sprongyn. þan þe natur of þat chyld be þe dysposicion of planetis
in þe owr of his byrth schewyd þat þe chyld schuld be in tyme
15 comyng wyse, courtly, and delyuir of hand and of goode counsel,
and to be fortunat to haue loue of kyngis. But þise seyd clerkys
[f. 92] seyd noȝt of alle | þis to þe chyldis fadyr. And aftyr þis chyld grwe
in waxyng, and þis childis fadyr atemptid to lern þe child his craft,
and sondry bysinessis of husbondry. But for feyr speche or re-
20 bukyng or betyng he myght lern ryght noȝt alle þo craftis. And att
þe last, qwan þei sey it wold noȝt be, þei lete hym aftyr hys owne
dysposicion to do qwat he wold, and þe chyld a-none drwe hym
to wele lernyd men and wurchyppful men and his [wit] was redy
to receyue clergé and wysdam, þat with-in schort tyme he k[n]we
25 þe cours of sterris, and þe tyme of bodyis abouyn, and was both
perfyght in astronomy and eke in astrology. He knw also þe
maneris and gouernanscis þat longe to kyngis and his fame and
wysdam spred abrode. He was made a counsellour and a priuy
masynger with þe kyng.

30 [The eght capitil]   Capitulum viij

But it fille contrary of meruelus werkyngis of planetis and þe
[f. 92ᵛ] dysposicionys of hem, as it fille of tweyn | sonnys of þe king of
Inde. And qwan one of thys kyngis sonys was waxyn, þe kyng sent
hym wurchyppfully to þe chef stodyis of his reme to be lernyd in
35 sondry syens, but none, lytil or myche, myght synke in hys hed,

6 Capitulum vij] *written in margin*   7 As be exampyl] *run on without*
starting new line   10 þei ordeynid. And] & þei ordeynid   14 schuld
be] *ms. has this both before and after* in tyme comyng   26 astrology] ro *ins.*
above   30 Capitulum viij] *in margin*   31 But] *begins line, but B not*
illuminated or otherwise distinguished as chapter initial

saue only smythis craft, to þe qwych be his dysposicion he was. Qwer-for þe kynge, heuyid gretly, sent for clerkis to knowe þe cause. þei serching þe cause be þe constellacion of hys byrth, þei founde how þe bodyis abouyn wer so demenyd þe hour of hys byrth þat it myght none odyr wyse betyde to þat child. And þus it fallith in sondry personys. Despyse neuir þerfor þe lytil statur of a man, for þu knowyst noȝt hys konnyng, and in specyal if þu se he hath a wytt and konyng, and dysposid to vertu, fleyng vicis, but sqwyche kepe hym with the. And loke þu do neuir thyng of substauns with-owte counsel. For a sad man | þat euir fleyth [f. 93] vicis and is trwe in word and deede is to be chyrischid. Loue his felychyp, for sqwyche a man louyth þat qwyche [is] conuenyent to a kyngis magesté. Putte neuir a matyr þat may abayde be-forn a matir qwyche is necessary to be sped, ner in contrary do neuir ryght nowght with-owte þe counsel of a philisophir, for wyse men sey þat counsel it is þe eye of þingis þat schal come. And it is wrytyn in þe boke of Persis how a kynge axid onys counsel of hys reporturis, and counsel of a gret priuy mater, qwyche was told to a qwene belouyd of þis kynge. þer-for one of his counsel seyd, 'It behouyth noȝt a kynge þat he schuld axe ony counsel of vs of ony priuy dede but separatly of one in a priuy place, for in priuy placis sqwyche thyngis schul be seyd'. But I sey, þowge it be þus in one case, in alle it may noȝt be so. A consideracion must be had aftyr þe mater be. | But it acordyth wele þat thy conselouris be gadryd [f. 93ᵛ] in euiry mater þat longith to charge of byindyng or onbyndyng, as I haue seyd beforn, for elde filysofris seyn þe wysdam of a kynge is aumentyd be þe counsel of his counsellouris or masyngeris, as þe see is aumentyd be flowyng of flodys in-to it. For a kyng may get mor be prwdens and wysdam excersisid be goode consel, þan with an oste of armyd men. And it is wrytyn þat a lorde of þe region of Meedys wrote to his sone seyng, 'Sone, consel is to þe necessary, for one is in alle men.' Consel þer-for with hym þat his wysdam is sqwyche it may delyuer þe fro a myghti man. And spar neuir thyn enmy, but qwan thow mayst preuayle myghtili, take þine auauntage. But yit be war of þe power of þin enmy. Be ne[ui]r þe habundauns of thy wytt in þi crwelnes or þe hythe of þi state of þi owne persone, lette but | euir þat anodyr mannys [f. 94]

3–4 þei serching . . . þei founde] *canc. & followed by* þei serching . . . & þei founde (*perhaps for* þei serch[ed] . . . & þei founde: *see n.*)   13 abayde] *form intended perhaps* abyde   16 And it] *prec. by* E   32 is] *see n.*   36 crwelnes] *see n.*

counsel loke that thow gete beside þine owne. And if it be for thy
wurchyp, do þer-aftyr, and þi owne counsel lete it abyde withinne
þe. And if þi consellouris dyferens fro þi sentens, consider þe wey
in þat mater þat may turne most to þi wurchyp. But I charge þe
5 sadly and counsel þe, ordeyn neuir supportur or consulour of þine,
be he neuir so gret a state, in þi stede to haue gouernauns of þi
kyngdam. For hys wytt and counsel may destroy thi kyngdam and
þe lordys, þe sogettis also, and turne þe profyte þat longith to þine
vse to hys propyr vse, and atte þe last, qwan he is sett in pride,
10 ymagyne thy destroccion and many odyr harmys. And if it be so
þat þu mayst noȝt haue v supportouris or counsellouris, as I haue
schewyd the be-forn, loke þat att lest þu take iij, for grete gode
comyth þer-of, for withowte þe thirde nothyng is knowyn.

[The nynghte capitil]   [Capitulum ix]

15   The fyrst þer-for vppon qwych alle þingis be is a Trynité and
[f. 94ᵛ] be | þe nombyr of v and seuyn it is perfyght. For þer be vij heuynnys,
and þe circuit of þe mone goyth be seuyn, and the dayis in qwyche
medycinis schuld be receyuyid be vij, and þe dais dysemolle be vij,
and many odyr longen to þe nombyr septenary þat wer longe to
20 reherse. And o maner how thow schalt assay þi counsellour is þis:
telle hym how þu algatis nedyst money, and if he counsel þe to
make distraccion of þi tresor to sel owght, or to ley to wedde
owght, or ellis to spende þat qwyche þu leydis vpp to maynteyn
thyn owne oste, knowe veryli þat he puttith none hed price in the,
25 þat is to sei, he chargith noȝt þi worchyp. And if he induce þe to
receyue money of hys sogettis be taske or odyr mene, he hatith
þi welfar. But if it be so þat he profyr his owne goode, and sey
þus, 'Lord, sqwyche as I haue, it is yowris: i[t] [I] haue gotyn
[f. 95] vndyr yowur | lordchip and grace', he þat seyth thus deseruyth
30 to be comendyd and is wurthy alle preysing, for sqwyche one chesith
his owne confusion and his owne hurte, for-be cause of þe and
þi wurchyp. Thow schalt also tempte þi counsellouris in yiftis

14 *Chapter-heading omitted*   15 vppon] vppon on   16 þe nombyr]
*prec. by fainter z-shaped sign, possibly incomplete &, but apparently intended to fill
gap left at beginning of line*   18 dysemolle] *in body of text the reading is*
determinabil, *inserted in narrow space, apparently over erased shorter word. In
margin, in scribe's hand* dysemolle *is added without erasure of* determinabil.
See n.   20 counsellour] counsellouris   22 distraccion] *prec. by canc.* o
23 leydis] leydis *with contraction sign apparently inserted in narrow space after
writing of following word*   28 it I] if   30 preysing] si *ins. above*   31
cause] for be cause

yefyng, for qwyche of hem þu seist puttyth alle his attendauns to
take yiftis, haue no goode trost in hym, for his seruise is for gold,
and he letith money renne with mennys wyttis, and sqwyche one
is a depnes with-oute a grounde and þer is none ende in hym, for
allewey þe mor mony komyth to hym, þe mor is his labour to gete. 5
And sqwyche a vise in one of þi consellouris is cause of hyndrauns
of þi kyngdam, and happy the cause of þi owne deth, or to þat
harme qwyche he purposith. Qwer-for sofir neuir none of hem
to be longe fro thy presens, and yef hym in comaundement þat 9
he drawe to none odyr kynge, | ner þat he sende no wrytingis to [f. 95ᵛ]
[hem], no pystil nor no tydyngis. And qwan thow perceyuyst ony
sqwyche thyng, send for hem with-owten ony taryinge, for þe
hertis of men be chongabil redyli to feyr behestis. And he is most
profitabil of alle þi counselleris, þat louyth trwthe and is obbeyng,
and inducyth odyr men to loue þe, and he þat puttyth his lyfe and 15
gode for þe, and he þat besyde þise hath þise þat I schal reherse þe.
First, þat he be perfyght in alle hys membris þat be necessar to
werkis for qwyche thow chesest hym. And þat he haue a wytt to
take lyghtly, and a wylle to vndyrstondyng, of þo thyngis þat be
seyde. And þat he haue a retentyf wytte, þat he be noȝt foryetful. 20
And þat he be consideryng and perceyuing qwan any hard mater
be meuyd. And þat he [be] courtly and gentil of speche and
eloqwent. And þat he be sotel in euir[y] syens, but in special in ars
metrik. And þat he be trwe in wordis, louyng trwthe, fleyng lesyngis, 24
wele demenyd in maneris and of gode | complexcion, tretabyl and [f. 96]
meke and soft. And þat he be notyd with no spyse of gloteny. And
in special þat he be noȝt dronkelewe, and þat he be noȝt leccherus
and þat he sett asyde pleyis and delectacion. And þat he be myghti
hartid in hys purpos, and louyng wurchyp. And þat gold and
seluyr and odir accidentallis of þis world be to hym in no reputa- 30
cion, and þat hys purpos and entente be but in þo þat acord to
wurchyp. And þat he loue hys neygbour and allso alle vertuus folk,
þow þei be absent. And also þat he loue alle þo þat loue ryghtfulnes,
hatyng alle wrongis, yeldyng to euiry man þat is his, helpyng þem
þat be oppressid wrongfully, exceptyng neuir mannys persone in 35
ony jugement, sythyn þat God hath formyd alle men equalle. Also
þat he be myghti and perseueraunt in tho thyng þat he seyth owe
to be done, hardi withowte fer or discomfortabylles, and that he
knowe þe vttrest of þine expensis, and þat no profitabyl þinge be

22 meuyd] *perh.* menyd   37 he seyth] he se seyth

onknowyn to hym qwyche longith to þe gouernauns of þi kyng-
[f. 96ᵛ] dam, | þat þi sogettis on no wyse compleyne, but in sqwyche casis
as he may profyght. Also þat he be noȝt fulle of wordis, or to myche
lawghyng, for temperauns myche plesith men, and þat he be gentil
5 and courtely. And also þat he be famos in kepyng howsold to
comeris in resonnabyl tyme, and þat he [be] tendaunt to enqwyr
and seke nouelteis, confortyng [þ]i sogettis, corectyng þe werkys
of he[m], and confortyng þem in aduersyteis, beryng sumtyme
and sofryng her sympilnes.

10 **[The tenthe capitil]** [Capitulum x]

Knowe þan þat God made neuir a mor wyse creatur þan man,
and He gadryd neuir in ony best þat He gadrid in hym. For þu
schalt noȝt fynde in ony best manir or custum qwyche þu schalt
noȝt fynde in man. For he is hardy as a lyon, sum ferful as an
15 har, in largenes as a kok, a nygard as a dogge, hard and scharp
as an harte, and meke as a turtyl, malycious as a leenes, homely
and socyal as a dowe, sotel and slegti as a wulfe, sympil and meke
[f. 97] as a lombe, lyght and sqwyft as a kydde, slow and sloggi | as a
beer, dereward and precyus as an elefant, dulle and foltysch as an
20 asse, rebelle as a kyng, obeyng and meke as a pekok, foltysch as an
ostrych, profytabyl as a bee, wantoun and vagabunde as a bor,
ontame as a bole, domme as a fysche, resonnabyl as an aungelle,
leccherus as a sqwyne, malycious as an owle, profytabyl as an hors,
noyabyl as a mouse. And vniuersaly þer is foundyn [noȝt] ony best
25 or vegetabyl or original or myneral, nor heuyn or planete ner tokyn,
nor no thyng þat is, of alle thyngis beyng, hauyng ony propyrté,
but þat propyrté is foundyn in man. And for þat is he clepyd þe
lesse world.

[The elleuynth capitil] Capitulum [xj]

30 Trost neuir in man þat belyuyth noȝt þi lawe. And be war þat
it be-tyde þe noȝt þat betidyd to tweyn men þat wer felychyppyd
to-gidir in a iorney, of qwyche one was a wyse man or a wycche
of þe Est, and þe todyr was a Jwe. þis oryental wycche, or wyse

7 þi] his   10 *chapter heading om.*   11 Knowe] *word begins
line, but* K *not illuminated nor otherwise distinguished as chapter initial*   13 in
ony] *prec. by canc.* o[ny]   29 Capitulum xj] Capitulum viij, *in margin*
30 Trost] *prec. by canc.* And (*with its* d *ins. above) but not distinguished in any way
as chapter-heading*   32 wycche] *first* c *ins. above*   33 wycche] *first* c
ins. above

man, rode vppon a mwle, qwyche | bar hys vitaylis and alle thynge [f. 97ᵛ]
necessari to hym. þe Jwe yede on hys feet, hauyng nowdyr mete
nor odyr necessariis. And qwyl þei wer talkyng, þe wyse man of
þe Est seyd to þe Jwe, 'Qwat is thyn lawe?' þe Jwe ansqwerd, 'I
be-leue that in heuyn is o God Qwyche I wurchyp, and abyde 5
or troyst to reward my soule wele, and alle þo þat lyue as I do in
þe same lawe and feyth. And my beleue is allso þat he þat dyferensith fro my law it is leful to me to take, if I may, his lyf and hys
gode, hys wyf and his childyr. And allso I am a-cursid if I kepe
promysse to ony sqwyche, or help hym, or if I schewe ony mercy 10
to hym. Now,' seid þe Jwe, 'I haue teld þe my lawe: tel me now
thyn'. And þis wyse man ansqwerd, 'My feyth and beleue is this.
First I wul wele to my-self and to alle my kynne, and I wul to no
creatur of God ony harm, ner þo þat folow my lawe, nor to tho 14
that be ayens my lawe. And I beleue þat equité | and merci owyth [f. 98]
to be schewyd to euiry lyuyng man. No wrong is plesauns to me,
and me semyth if ony hurt betyde to ony lyuing creatur, it be-
tidith to me, and trobyllith me. I dysir prosperyté, helth and
felicité schuld betyde to alle men vynuersally'. þan ansqwerd þe
Jwe, 'Qwat if an offens or wronge be donne to þe?' To home þis 20
oriental, 'I knowe that God is in heuyn, Qwyche is ryghful, goode
and wyse, to Home no thynge is hid, no priuité nor ryght, nowght
vttyrly in no creatur, þat rewardyth goode men aftyr her goodnes,
euyl men and transgressouris aftir her euyl dedis.' To hom þe Jwe
ansqwerd, 'Qwy kepyst þu noȝt þi lawe? And qwy confermyst 25
nowght þi lawe in dede?' þe qwyse man ansqwerd, 'Qwer schuld
I execute it?' To hom þe Jwe seyd, 'I am comyn fro þe childryn
of thi kynred, and þu seyst me walke vppon my feet, hungry and
wery, and þu rydyst wele att ese, hauyng habundauns of vitayle.' 29
To home þis oryental, 'þu seyst trwthe.' | And with þat word he [f. 98ᵛ]
descendyd fro hys mule, take forth hys vyteillis, and fedde þis
Jwe wele, and yaf hym drynke, and aftyr sette hym on hys mule,
and putte his sporis vppon his helis, and dyd hym to ryde forth.
And þis Jew, as sone as he was vppe, he toke þe mule with hys
sporis and rode awey, leuyng þis odyr man alone. And thys 35
oryental cryid aftyr hym, 'Abyde me, for I am scomfytid!' But þis
Jwe rode forth, and seyd, 'I haue told þe my lawe, and þe con-
dycion ther-of, and I schal conferme it in dede as thow hast done
thyne.' And forth þis Jwe rode in hast, and yit þis oryental cryid

14 to] *ins. above*   16 lyuyng] lyueryng   36 scomfytid] d *corr. from* l

and seid 'O, forsake me no3t in this desert, lest I be storuyn for
hungir and thirst, and þat I be no3t þis nyght slayn with lyonnys!
Schewe me now mercy, as I haue schewyd to þe mercy!' But
þe Jwe toke no hede to his wordis, but rode as fast as he coude, tyl
5 he was owte of hys ey-syght. And þis odyr man in vttyr despeyr, at
[f. 99] þe last he remembryd of God and His lawe, for qwych he | had
done þat good dede, and seyd, lyftyng hys eyn toward heuyn, 'My
God, Thow knowyst þat I haue trostyd in Thi lawe and in Thy
commaundementys. I haue halowyd The. Conferme þan þe
10 Jwe may haue knowyng þat I schewyd hym mercy for The!' And
as he yede forth no3t longe aftyr, he perceyuid qwer þe Jewe
lay, þat be vengauns fylle fro his mwle, and brake his arme, and ner
his nek, and eke his legge. And þe mule stod bye hym stylle, but
as sone as he sey hys mastir he cam renneng to hym, and þis
15 oryental, rydyng vppon hym, forsoke þe Jwe. And qwan þe Jwe
sawe hym depart, he cryid aftyr hym and seyd, 'Goode brodyr, for
God haue mercy on me! For I am loste, and now I dey, hauyng
nede of þi compassyon. Haue mercy and kepe thi lawe, for God
hath youyn to þe þe vyctory of me, in þat þu hast ouircomyn me!'
20 And þan þis oryental, or man of þe Est, began to vndyr-nyme hym,
seyng, 'þu hast gretly synid ayens me qwan þu forsokyst me in þis
[f. 99ᵛ] wyldirnes alone, with-owte | ony mercy.' To home þe Jwe an-
sqwerd, 'Repreue me no3t of a thyng þat is past, for I haue schwyd
þe þat it is my lawe and my feyth, in qwyche I was norchid, and I
25 fond my fadyr and modyr, and odyr agid folk many, perseueraunt
in thys lawe.' And this wyse man had mercy vppon hym, and
browght hym to hys place, and delyuerid hym to hys pepil, qwyche
aftyr fewe dayis deyid. And the kynge of þat cyté, heryng þe dedys
of compassyon þat þis wyse man had done, dyd hym to be clepyd
30 to hym, and made hym a chef counselour of hys, for hys goode
werkis. Preysyng to God and an ende of þis tale.

þe [twelthe] capytil   Capitulum [xij]

It behouyth þe to chese to wryght thy priuy thyngis wyse men
qwyche be as a tokyn and as a myghti argument to schewe þe
35 qwantité of þi degré and þe sotelté of thy knowlech. For þe
tokynnyng or þe interpretacion of hys word is þe spiryte þer-of,

---

4 no] *whole word surmounted by horizontal stroke; form intended possibly* non
12 lay] h lay   25 odyr] o *corr.*   29 dyd] & dyd   31 Preysyng] s
prec. by two minims   32 twelthe] nynghte   xij] ix

þe dystyncciounys be as a bodi, þe wryting is þe clothyng of þe
word. And | euyn as it behouyth þe to be a substanc[i]al man, and [f. 100]
wele and semely arayid, to seme gloryus, so on þe lyke wyse it is
conuenyent to þe to haue a wryter qwyche hath þat perfeccion in
eloquens and in sotel endyghting, to expres thi wylle, and sqwych 5
one þat þu make hym þi secretary. But loke beforn, þat he be
juste and trwe, and of sotel wytt to take þin menyng, and þat euir
he yeff attendauns to þi wurchyp, for if he be non sqwyche, he may
harme the, and þat he be war þat no man, frend nor fo, come in
to þat place qwer þi priuy wrytyngis be kept. Lett sqwyche one be 10
euir ner the, and sett hym in a dygnité þat þer may grow profyght
to hym, and reward þou hym besyde.

Þe [thyrdtene capitil]   Capitulum [xiij]

Know þan veryli, þat a masenger schewyth þe wysdam of hym
þat he is sent fro, and is in a maner as an eye [in tho thyngis] þat 15
[he] seyth noȝt, and his er in tho thyngis þat he herith noȝt, and
hys tonge | in hys absens. Chese hym þat is mosst wurthy of þo þat [f. 100ᵛ]
be in þi presens, þat is wyse, circumspecte, and wurchypful, trwe,
and fleyng fro alle foule and dysonest thyngis, in qwyche no blame
is foundyn. Tempte hym if þise be in hym. Clepe hym and comun 20
with hym in sqwyche thyngis as he knowyth noȝt þi wylle nor þi
menyng, and þan þu schalt a-none fynde in hym þat þu sekyst,
þat is to sey, wysdam. And if þu se hym sotel and wyse, kepe hym
with þe, and if he be pleyne, noȝt proferryng of doubylnes, make
hym a secretary, for he schal noȝt pase þi byddyng in hys wrytyng. 25
And þou fynde hym noȝt scharp of wytt, but only trwe, make
hym a masenger to ber letteris and to report þat he heryth and
seyth. And if it be so þat ony of þi masengeris be bysi to take
rewardys to hys profite, in þo placys to þe qwyche he goth on þi
masege, sett hym a-syde, and lett hym no lengir do þe seruise. And 30
if þu haue a masenger þat louyth, and puttyth his lust in, dryn-|
kyng of wyne, sett hym asyd, for þe condicion of Percys is þis: [f. 101]
to asay a masenger, yeuyng hym plenté of myghti wyne, and if þei
sey þat he dranke myghtili wyne, so þat he pasid hymself, þei
coniectid anone þat his lord was noȝt wyse. Be war þat þu send 35
noȝt þi chef counsellour and chef mesenger on no masege, nor

---

7 þat] þᵗ, *with* t *corr. from* e   12 þou] þo *with* u *ins. above*   13 thryd-
tene capitil] tenthe   xiij] x   26 þou] *written* þᵒ   33 a masenger]
article a *ins. above*   36 mesenger] g *corr. from* d

soffir noȝt longe him to be absent fro þe, for þat is destruccion of
þi kyngdam. And of qwat condyciounis þi masenger schuld be, I
haue wrytyn to þe. But if it be so þat thow fynde hem noȝt of þat
kondicion þat I haue teld þe but is redi to take rewardis and to
5 make him-self ryche, and lesith þi mesagis þat þu inioynist hym,
do hym sorow i-now, and sette hym asyde.

The [fourtene] capityl   Capitulum [xiv]

I haue told þe beforn þat þe suggettis of þin house be expensis,
or þi tresur, be þe qwyche þi kyngdam is defensid. Make euiry thi
10 sogettis to an ortyard in qwyche be dyuerse frutis, and haue hem
noȝt as greyn or sedis þat brynge forth wurmewod and thornys,
[f. 101ᵛ] and ber no-thyng fr-|uteful. And gode treis haue in hem many
bowys and brawchys, frute and carnellis, with þe qwyche þei
may be multipliyd be þe mene of a werke-man. And so may þi
15 sogettis if þei be wele take hed to and goode. Of hem-self þei
schal encrese thy tresur be many vertuful menis of ocupacionys
profitabyl, if þei be tendyd. And it behouyth þat a myghti man reule
hem, and thow also se to her necessiteis, and I haue told þe residwe
in odyr placis. But take heed þat þei haue a gouernour þat takyth
20 heed to þe kepyng of hem and noȝt to þe destroccion, qwych be
a wele dysposid man, þat þei haue noȝt cause to compleyn. For he
þat is noȝt vertuus and wyse, men be redy to rebel a-yens hym and
hys gouernauns, and þei þat be wele dysposid, þei schal deme
amys of hym. But make noȝt many rewlerris in þine hows, for
25 jche of hem schal assay to ouircome hys felaw, and euir þei schal
make talys yche of odyr, jche of hem to schewe hym-self profitabil.
[f. 102] And þat wul jche of hem do, þe lenger tyme | to abyde in þi seruyse
and in þat ocupacion. And yit haue uery knowyng þat sqwyche
pykethankis thei make ryche hem-self and oppresse þi sogettis.
30 And thow schalt fynde many sqwyche þat sey one and do a-nodyr,
and sqwyche folk þei corupte myche pepyl, þat þei may hold hem
on hand, and þatt þe[i] lyst defende.

The [fyftene] capytil   Capitulum [xv]

Nobyl men ben þe addicion and multiplicacion of þi reem, for

---

3 so] *followed by short empty space, perhaps containing an erasure*   7 four-
tene] eleuynth   xiv] xj   13 brawchys] *cf. 178/25*   16 many] n
ins. above   vertuful] *prec. by* w   22 men] *prec. by indistinct first letter of*
a word begun and left uncanc.   27 *f. 102 upper margin, later hand:* thes
31 þat] & þat   32 þei] þer   33 fyftene] twelthe   xv] xij

be hem þi court is honourryd, and iche gouernauns is ordeynid
in hys degré. þe best ordynaunsis nessesari in her disposicionis is
þat þu be noȝt ignoraunt to knowe þe dysspo[si]cion of hym þat
is fer, as wele as he þat is neer. And þe ordynacion of hem is fourfold. For euiry place in hys differens is fourfold, þat is to sei, be- 5
hynde and befor, on þe ryght hand and þe left hand. And so be þe
dyuysiounis of þe world iiij, þat is to sey þe est, þe west, þe north,
and þe sowth. Ther-for lete yche of þi most noby[l] lordis, qwyche
be most stronge, to haue a part of þi lond in gouernauns vndyr the,
and if þu wult haue moo make ten. For ten is four perfight, for in 10
þe nombyr of four þer is | one and too and thre and four, and so [f. 102ᵛ]
makyth þis nombir tenne. þer-for þe nowmbyr of [ten] is þe perfeccion of þo qwyche knytt four. Than in þine osste lett euiry
lord at þe lest haue ten vikyrris and lette euiry vikyr haue x
personis or ductoris, and euiry ductor x denis and euiry dene x 15
men. Ther-for qwan þu hast neede of x thowsend men, send for
o lord or preceptor, and his vicaryis and ductoris with alle odyr,
as I haue rehersid, schal fulfille þe nombir of x (ten) thowsend.
And if þu haue nede but of o thowsend, þu schalt commaund to
one of þi vicaryis and þer schal come with hym ten ductoris, and 20
with euiry ductor x (ten) denis, and with euiry dene x (ten) men,
and þe summe of thyse is a thowsend. And if þu nede an hundrid,
send for o ductur, and lette hym bryng x (ten) denes, and euiry
dene his ten men. And if þu nede but x send for o dene with hys
men. And þis schal spar thy vitaylis and þu schalt haue redili thi 25
purpose, and þi labour schal be lessid, and thi lordis labur also.
And it is necessary to thy lordis to haue a wyse scribe, qwyche be
approuyed in chi-|ualry, þat he take hed þat þei be noȝt corupt [f. 103]
with no yiftis. [þe]r-for make oftyn inquirauns, and if þu perceyue
ony sqwyche, remeue hym fro þe rewle þat he hath in thyne hous. 30
And qwan þu hast done so, gadyr alle þe todyr lord[is] his felawys,
and telle hem that in his remeuyng þu prouydyst to her all welefar. þu must þer-for be wyse and redi in sqwyche materis, and
despise noȝt summe for þe compleyn of summe. And þu must haue
þat instrument þat Cerustius þe nobyl werryour made, to þe helpe 35
of his osst. It is a ferful instrument, qwyche is dyuidyd on many
maneris, and for happyli þu must gadyr þine oste on o day, qwyche
instrwment may be herd eny wey xl myle, qwerfor it is necessari.

---

2 ordynaunsis] ordynauns is   29 þer-for] For for   38 instrwment] in
instrwment

Þe [syx]tene [capytil]   Capitulum [xvj]

Use noȝt myche batellis, ner putt noȝt þi body to oftyn in
juberté in batellis, but haue euir counsel of þe grettest lordis in þi
4 court. Nor be neuir ocupiid in sqwyche thyngis as þei be þat
[f. 103ᵛ] haue | be scomffitid in bateyl, ner assay noȝt a synguler bateyl in
þi owne persone, for knowe veryli þat neuir kyng wul fyght with
odyr but if he cast hym to myscheue hym þat he fyght with. Knowe
wele þat invye is decendyng fro þe body and spirite, qwyche
comyth of tweyn contraryis repugnaunt. þe manly hert of [þem]
10 is þe trost of þe victory, and loke hym þat is feynt-hertyd dyith and
so sesith þe bateyle, for a bateyl euir lastyth as longe men trost
to haue þe victory. But lette þi stabylnes be in prolongacion of
prosperyté and vertuus lyfe, and in sustentacion of þi kynne. And
of thi sogettis despyse neuir þe personys, but in tyme promyse
15 hem yyftis, and kepe þi promys. And for no plesauns of þi-self
be neuir in ost ondefensid or on-armyd, for þe asspyis of thin
aduersary. Qwer-for, bothe be day and nyght, haue wecchis in
euiry ost, and haue abowght redy euir men of armys. And pycche
neuir þi tentis but ner an hyl or ner a watyr, and euir be befforn
20 of vitayle, and euir make in þin [oste] to be schet gunnys, and
hydus noysis to sonde euir, for þat confortyth þi men and con-
foundyth þine aduersaryis. And lete þi gentyllis haue sondri |
[f. 104] manir of fyghtyng wepyn, sum sperys, and sum crosbowys, and
sum mastris of engynis, and sum with sqwerdys to renne amonge
25 þe osste. And qwan it comyth þat þei schal fyght, send in forme
a gret apparayle, with eleuauntis hauyng towris on her bakkys,
and in þem archerris schetyng brennyng qwarellis. And if þu se
þi men ferful or dredyng, anone be redy a-mong hem and confort
hem, and induce hem to perseuerrauns. And ordeyn thyne oste,
30 as I haue taught þe, in-to thre partis or four, aftyr þe place be, and
on þe rygh-hand men of armys and fyghterris on foote, and on the
left hand speris, and in þe myddis archeris, and som þat make orybil
noysis, and throwyng brondys of fir. And loke in euiry batel
sqwych a place for þin host as is most avayle, her bakkys to þe
35 sonne. But bewar of tresun, and most in special qwan þu seyst
þi men ony thyng slakeryng, and anone hast þe thidir with þo þat
be with þe in þi ward, and schew þi manhod in wordis and also in

---

1 syxtene capytil] thirdtene, *with medial* t *ins. above.*   xvj] xiij   26 a] *ins.*
above uncanc. &

dede. And haue ner þine oste | a conuenyent place to ber to lordis [f. 104ᵛ]
if þei happe to be wondyd, in qwyche þer be kept wyne and odyr
drynkis, and also harnes and al maner of weypyn. And if it be so
þat þu ley a seege, vse day and nyght engynis. And loke if þu canst
aspye qwer ony wellis be, or kondyghtis, þat serue þine aduersaryis 5
of watir, and poysun that, for þat schal sle myche pepyl. And be
euir perseueraunt þat a begunne þu leue noȝt onperfight, nor
folow neuir þine aduersaryis qwan þat þei flee. Haue neuir gret hast
in thy werkis, and haue consideracion to þe condicion of the pepil
þat þu fyghtist with, for sum haue euir þe victori with sotelteis and 10
sleyghtis of wer, and sum be perseuerauns and manhod, qwer-for
on alle wyse knowe þe dysposicion of þe nacion þat þu schalt fight
with-alle, for þat is a chef thing. But, alwey þat þu may, haue
myghtily þi purpos in euiry werk. Haue with þe an [a]sturonomere
to yef counsel, þat þe dysposicion of þe bodyis abouyn help þe, and 15
be acordyng to þat werke. Ordeyn þe ascendent vppon þe oryent
in | þe Lyon. And bewar, begynne neuir no werk qwan þe mone is [f. 105]
clypsid, or troubyllyd, or felichyppyd with an euyl planete. Qwerfor
to knowe alle þi werkyng of þe planetis euir þu must haue astro-
nomeris. But yit be war þi-self, þat in þe begynnyng of none of þi 20
werkis þat þe mone be dyrectly ayens the bemys of þe sunne, nor
þat it be in þe sixte or þe twelth degré, or goyng bak, but euir in
þe ascendyng schal thi werkis be prosperus. Qwerfor do neuir gret
materis but be þe counsel of an experte astronomer. And know
þat þe mone is þe most helpyng planete in alle jorneys. 25

The [seuyn]tene capitil   Capitulum [x[vi]j]

How necessary it is to þe, and allso gloryus and preysabyl,
sythyn I haue told þe to knowe þe dysposycion of plauntis and
odyr, þat þu now haue knowenge of þe most nobyl creatur in erth,
qwyche is manne, how natur werkyth be dysposycion complex- 30
cionary. þe qwyche gret knowlecch or syens, olde philisophris put
myche in practic, and as | to þe most chef experimental man, we [f. 105ᵛ]
ground vs vppon þe mosst famus of alle elde doctouris, clepyd
Philemon, and hou þis man in his siens was asayd we bryng to remembrauns. Tweyn dysciplis of Mastir Ypocras depeyntid his figur 35
in a perchemen schyn, and bar it to Philemon, seyng, 'Considir

---

3 weypyn] e *ins. above*   14 asturonomere] st*uronomere, with abbrevia-*
tion sign for ur, *but perhaps for* astronomere (*Possibly,* an st(u)ronomere *is*
written for ast(u)ronomeres)   26 seuyntene] fourtene   xvij] xiiij

þis figur, and telle vs þe qualiteis of his complexcion.' Qwyche
mastir made comperison of alle partis of þat figur to-gydir, [and]
seyd, 'þis man is leccherus, louyng þe likyng of þe flesch, and a
disceyuabyl man.' And quan þise men herd thys, þei wold haue
5 slayn hym, seyng þus, 'O foole, þis is þe figur of a wyse man and
a wele reulid man, and as wurthi a man as ony in þe world!' And
þis doctor pesid hem and seyd, 'I knowe noȝt to hom it longit.
But ye axid me aftyr my craft to sey þe trwthe, and be my craft
9 I haue ansqwerd yow.' þan þei seid no mor, but toke her leue, and
[f. 106] keme to Mastir Ypocras, and told hi[m] how þei had done, | and of
þe doctor Philemonis ansquer. And Ypocras yaf hem this ansqwer,
'Trwly, that doctor seyth soth and wysely, and he pasid noȝt
himself in o word of my persone. But qwan I came to mannis age,
and conceyuid þat my natural disposicion was to þo visis, I with
15 vertu and gret labour ouircam hem, and so att þe last I had þe
victori, and be labur am comyn to þis plyght of vertue.' And þis
is þe preysing and þe wysdam in ouircomyng of vicis of þis Mastir
Ypocras. For þe filosofie of filisofris is right noȝt ellis but abs-
tyne[n]s and victory of þe concupiscens of þe flesche.

20 [The eghtene capitil]   Capitulum xviij

And, Alysaundir, I yef þe rewlys abreuyat. And first knowe, þat
þe modyr is [to] þe embrion as a pott is to þat qwyche is sodyn
þer-in. Qwyght and blo colouris medylid, þat turnyth to yelownes,
is a tokyn of ondygestion. And if þis betyd in a creatur, þe natur
25 of þat creatur is dymynusid. Fle þan fro euiry yelow-blo man, for
sqwyche be redi to vicis and to leccheri. And qwan þu seyst a man
loke oftyn vppon þe, and qwan þu lokyst vppon hym he is aferd, |
[f. 106ᵛ] and if he sighe causeles and in his eyn þer apper terys, he louyth
þe and dredyth þe. And if it be the contrary wyse, he hatith þe
30 and despisith þe. Be war þan from euiry infortunat qwyche is
dyminuit or mynusid in ony membyr, euyn þat as þu schuldist
be war fro þine enmy. þe best-dysposid men and most euyn in
natur [be þo] þat be of mene statur, with blake eyn and blake her,
and a rownd face, and qwycht of colour, medyllid with reed, and
35 a browne color with euyn dysposicion of þe body, and vppryght

9 þan] corr. from þi or þat   10 him] his   20 Capitulum xviij] in
outer margin   21 And, Alysaundir] begins line, but without further dis-
tinguishing as start of chapter   24 þe] þ corr. from n   31 euyn] euyn þat
or euyn þu, with the second word indistinctly canc.   32 fro] in ony membyr fro

statur, þat hath a mene hed, noȝt to gret nor to lytil, and few wordys
but qwan nede is, and þe byggenes of hys voys in a mene. And
qwan þe natur declynith to brownes and yelwnes þan is it most
preysabyl. And þi[s] maner statur and complexcion lette dwelle
with þe. And I haue tolde þe be interpretacion þe maner of þe 5
disposicion: assay þu hys wytte.

[The nyntene capitil]   Capitulum xix

Plenté of pleyn heris betokyn mekenes and coldnes of brayn. And
many herys vppon þe scholdris betokyn foltyschnes. And multi- 9
tude of heris | on þe brest and þe wombe betokyn horybilnes [f. 107]
and syngulerté of natur, and dymynucion of vndyrstondyng,
and louyng of onryghtis. A red colour is a tokyn of onwysdam, and
of myche wrath, and of watyng and dysseyuabylnes, and of a
sspyer. And blac her betokynnyth ryghtne[s] and loue of trwth and
justise. But a mene be-twene bothe colouris signyfiith a louir of pes. 15

[The tweynty capitil]   Capitulum xx

Men þat hath gret yine is inuyus, onschamfast, slow and inobe-
dyent, and most in specyal if þe colour turne to blones. And of
home þe eyn turne to blones or to blacnes and be of a mene gretenes,
is of scharp wytte, courtely and trwe. And qwan þe eyn bolne 20
owte, with a bolny[n]g face, þei betokyn malic[i]ousnes and wykkydnes. And he þat hath eyn lyke þe eyn of an asse is foltysch and
of herd natur. And he hos syght is scharp, and hys eyn meue fast,
sqwyche one is a dysceyuur, a thef and ontrwe. And if þe eyn be 24
redysch, it betokynnyth | is strengh, manhod, myghtines. But [f. 107ᵛ]
tho eyn be werst þat haue qwyght spottis, or blake spottis, or reed,
rounde abought, for sqwyche one is werst of men.

[The one and tweynty capitil]   Capitulum xxj

Browys þat haue myche her betokynnith on boldnes of speche.
And qwan þe browyis be so longe þat þei come to þe templis, it 30
betokynnith onclennes of complexcion. And he þat hath browys
thynne-herid, and wele demenyd in lenght and breede, and þei
be greete, sqwyche one hath a redy wytt to vndyrstondyng.

1 to gret] to to gret   8 Plenté of] *does not start new line; runs on from
previous words, preced. by canc.* he þ[at]. P *not illuminated, but distinguished by
overlapped doubling*   13 watyng] g *altered from* d   16 Capitulum]
capᵐ *prec. by canc., perh.* lj[ber]   xx] *prec. by expuncted* xv

The [to] and tweynty capitil   Capitulum xxij

A nose þat is longe and smalle, it sigynfiyth gret angir. And he
þat hath a longe nose crokyng doune to his mowth schul be dysposid to be hardy. And a fnatyd nose betokynnith impetuusnes.
5 And he þat hath nose thyrllis wyde schuld be angri. And sqwyche
a nose þat rysith in þe myddis is fulle of wordys and a lyer. But þat
nose is euir most comendabil þat is equal and in a mene of lenght,
[f. 108] and þe nose thyrllis proporciond | in a mene, with a pleyn face
þat is noȝt bolynd, [for þa]t betokynnyth a stryuer, a wrongful
10 man and extorcionner. And he þat hath a face in a mene, nowdyr
to fat, nowdyr to lene, is trwe, and louyng, and wyse, and seruisabil
and wel wyttid.

And he þat hath a gret wyde mowth schuld [be] bold and hardi.
And he þat hath gret lyppis schuld be foltische. And he þat hath
15 myche flesche in hys face is nowȝt very wyse. And he þat hath
a sclendir face is circumspecte in his werkkys and sotel of vndyrstondyng. And he þat hath a litil yelw face is vicious, a dysseuyir
and dronkelew. And he þat hath an-long face is a doer of wrongis.
And he þat hath bolnyd templis and ful chekis is pasyng hasti.
20   And he þat hath smalle erys is foltisch and leccherus. And he þat
hath ryght grete eris is a veri fole, but he schuld a-haue a retentyf
wytt. And he þat hath a gret voys schuld be hardi and eloquent.

The thre and tweynti [capitil], of þe voys   Capitulum xxiii

24 And he þat hath a vois in a mene, nowdyr to gret, nowdyr to smal,
[f. 108ᵛ] is wyse, prouydent, and ryghtful. And | he þat spekyth thyk, and
hath a smalle voys, is inportune, a lyer, bysi and ontrwe. And he
þat hath a veri gret voys schuld be angri and vengabil. And he þat
hath a sqwete voys schuld be inuius and susspicius. A fayr voys
betokynnith onwysdam and grettehertydnes. And he þat meuyth
30 oftyn with ony parte in his talkyng, he is inuyus, eloquent and
disceyuabil. And he þat absteynith fro meuyng of handis he is wele
disposid and of goode connsel. And he þat hath a longe, smal nek,

---

1 to] thre *expuncted and surmounted by* ij   9 for þat betokynnyth] it be-
tokynnynnyth   13–19 *numbered* Capitulum xx *in margin*   23 *Left-
hand chapter-heading placed above matter of l.* 20, *but marginal indication gives
correct position; right-hand heading with roman numerals in correct position in
margin*   25 prouydent] *prec. by tall downstroke of unfinished letter*
(l?)   And] *followed by* & *as first word of next page*   28 A fayr] *prec. by canc.*
&, *and followed by* f

he [is] ful of noyse and foltisch. And he þat hath a schort nek is disceyuabil, sotel, and ful of tresun. And he þat hath a gret nek is foltisce and a gret eter.

[The four and tweynty capitil]   Capitulum xxiiij

And he þat hath a gret bely is indiscrete, louyng lecchery, and 5 prowde. A mene bely and a streyght brest betokynnyth hye vndyr-stondyng and goode counsel. Largenes of þe brest, and grettenes of scholdris and also of bak, betokynnyth manhod and hardynes and a retentyf wytt. And a smal bak betokynnith a man to be of a discordaunt natur. And a mene bak is a tokyn of equalyté 10 and a passing goode tokyn. And lyftyng of þe scholdris tokyn-nith scharpn-|nes of natur and of ontrwthe. And qwan it is so [f. 109] þat þe armys be so longe þat þei may be extendid to þe kneys, it betokynnith hardines, manhod, and larges. And schort armys þe[i] signifie discordis and ignorauns. Handis þat be longe, with longe 15 fyngeris, betokyn disposicion to many vertuys, and in special craftis mecanyk, and wyse in werkis it signyfiyth, also goode gouernauns. Gret fyngris and schort signyfi foltischnes and onwysdam.

Feet þat be gret and ful of flesch betokyn folyschnes and loue of 20 wrongis. Smale feet and smote betokyn hardnes of wytt. Smale leggis signyfye ignoranz and gret leggis betokyn manhod and strengh. Gret helys with rownd leggis betokyn gret strenght. Miche flesch vppon þe kneis betokynnyth softenes or tendyrnes of complexcion, and fayling of vertu. He þat hath wyde pasis in 25 his gate and slow schal be prosperus in hys werkys, and he þat makyth schort pasis in hys gate is suspicious, impetuus and on-myghti and euyl-wyllyd in hys werkis.

[The fyue and tweynty capitil]   Capitulum xxv

But he in natur is best disposid, of best memory, | þat his flesche [f. 109ᵛ] is soft and moyst, þat is a mene be-twene hardnes and softnes, noȝt 31 of hys statur to longe nor to schort, qwyche declynith of cher to reednes, meke in beholdyng, hauyng pleyn her in a mene, þat hath

---

4 *Chapter-heading in margin. Text run on without starting new paragraph*
5 And] *written over* & *at start of line, but not otherwise distinguished as chapter initial*   6 brest] r *ins. above*   8 betokynnyth] betokynith betokynnyth
13 kneys] n *ins. above*   20 Feet] F *written, exceptionally, as single f, of normal size, prec. by small double* ff. *This probably indicates start of new section or, possibly, is attempt to corr.* S   26 and he] Et he   31 soft] s *corr.*

eyn of a goode bygnes, turnyng to largenes, and þat is hed be wele
mesuryd in a mene, and hys nek proporciond to hys hed in
mychenes, hos scholdris be declyning, hauyng but lytil flesch in
his thyis and kneis, þat hath an hoole voyce, in temperauns of
5 hythe and gretenes, and hath a longe palme and longe fyngirris
declyning to sotelnes, þat lawghith but lytil, þat is no scorner,
and þat his cher is medyllid with gladnes and myrth. But for alle
thyse þat I haue rehersid of tokynnis judicyal þu schalt noȝt
ȝeue soden jwgement of one tokyn, but of many, acordyng
10 qwedyr it be to gode or euyl, and euir enclyne to þe bettir part in
euiry dome. And now, preysind wurchyp and reuerrens be to owr
Lord Jesu Cryst now and euir, þat hath holpyn me in part to
fynysch þis boke, Amen.

Finis Secretorum

15   **Her endyth þe Boke of þe Priuyté of Priuyteis.**

Explicit liber quartus Secretorum, Deo gracias.
Amen

6 declyning] ni *written with four minims as though* nn *but with diagonal
overstroke indicating* i (*perhaps for* declyniing)   7 for] *repeated*

sylyche pyisyng : And treuly y say a man
syu dwellyng w͛ an husbond man y͛ be
gret stody! knwe y͛ cours off y͛ yer & y͛ ystu
llacomys & y͛ cours off alle sterris &
y͛ menyng off alle planetis : and qwan
y͛ ffestys schuld ffalle off hem : And y͛
solempnyte off euy monthe : y͛ cansys
Also off y͛ sthortyng off y͛ day & y͛ nyght
The sterrys also off destynys qwat
schuld betyse And m͛yntyme thyngf
be doe : y͛ qwyche spens cansys y͛ wor
ld to magnyffye her to wondyr off her
wysdam : quer ffor y͛ grodnese off þy
syng : spryngyth off goimannys wyt.

Here endyth y͛ fferst boke off y͛ pryute
off prynces.

prscensys

Explicit pmus liber de secretis secre
torum secundum translacionem johis de caritate

This booke made for the rule & gou-
naunce of mans body to kepe him
in helth & goode disposicon off body /
was sent fro þe grete philosophir ——
aristotill to the nobill prince kyng
alexander . off the which begynnith
here begynnith the prologe .

nobil kyng, if thou wilt
diligently rede and vnder
stonde this litil booke and
tretice: and rule thi selfe
aftir the doctrine. rulis &
precept[is] in this booke or tre-
tice writtin: thou shalt kepe thi selfe in helth
and goode disposicon of body. and haue conti-
nuance of longe life. Yitt notwithstanding
the doctrine of this booke: thy life may be
shortid by othir chaunce of warre. or othir
perellis. To preserue the fro the deth happyng
by such meanis: this booke helpith not. but

II. Bodleian MS. Rawlinson C.83, f. 2

myghtyer than opposed And contrarye metes þen þan / that is to sey coolde
for grosse metes and stronge ben good to a stronger and an hota stomach
for it fareth as a stronge fire that hath myght to brenne grete wode
But whan the stomach is cold and feble than vse he sotell and light metes
for that stomach is likened to a fire that brenneth but redely, tendre
and sotell wode / The tokens of a good stomach ben lightnesse of the
body clernesse of vnderstandyng ledyng and good appetite / The
signes of a bad stomach is that is feble of digestion by hevynesse of
body neshnesse of flessh swelling of face / oft apenyng of
the mouth gref of even fonte and bad rechyng and the savor to be
sowre sol bitter ariseth with other stynkyng And therof ben engendred wyndes and swellynges in the wombe / And the appetite is lost
If the thynges be in grete quantite therof cometh fretyng and swellyng
of the emytres reflexions of thynes quakyng of the body happyng of
the mouthe and many other harmes that ben contrary to helth / and
ben distruction of the body and corruption of nature / Therfor most
clement emperour and kyng thow sholdest full diligently kepe the fro
the forseid mischeuaunces

here foloweth a full profitable epistle of full grete price / yevyng
a rule to lyve for conservation of helthe / In the whiche ben many
necessaries of the secrees of medicyne / Some clepen this epistle
a book by hym self / And it hath the glose of John of Spayn
that translated it out of grewe and arrabik into latyn and
sende it to Dame Theophayne Quene of Spayn vndre yis
fōrme / To Dame Theophayne Quene of Spayn / John
of Spayn sendeth gretyng or helthe ₢c

O   Alexandre sith the body is corruptible and corruption happeth
    thertes of opposicion of complexion and of humors that ben
    ther yn / It is sittyng to me by this present werk to wryte
vnto the some maner of profites / and at all necessary / and of
secretis of the art of medicyne with the whiche be gretly contented
sithen it is vnhonest that a leche sholde know all the infirmites
of thynges / If diligently thow beholde this examplar / and after
the order of this full precious book whiche thow hyvest shalt nede

1.

Here begynneþ þe boke made of þe governance of þe governance of Princes compyled by þat renomed Philosophre Aristotiles and sent to þat excellent Emperour and Prince invincyble Alexandre of Macedonie þe whiche is clepe and called þe secrete of secretes and tresore incomperable.

Armaduke þe sone of Danyelle þe fayre of alle laughtes fonde in þe Regioun of Grece with inne þe temple of þe solarye þis boke in þy Lepte þe whiche þat famous and gret Philosophre Custakabine made þe whiche he lete calle þe boke of Aristotle secretes and he translated it oute of greke in to Caldee and affter þe request of þe kyng of Calde nay but of Arabie he translated it oute of Arabeske in to Latin and sent it to þe ful reverent fader and ful noble persoun Guy de Valence þe Busshop of Triple as þat a renomed Philosophre cleped Aristotle whiche Alisaundre hade with him bereþe record whome he cleped his maistre by whos wisdam and console he obteyne alle hoos enemys þe whiche Aristotle Alisaundre desired to hane with him but he wrote him tres of expense and wrote him tres howe he shonlde maynteyne him to his gret honnoure and worship And þis was þis boke translated in to Latin noust al but such as is moste profitable and gode manis understonding for þe state and governaunce of Princes þe whiche boke with þe content is nonst to shewe to commune ne to rede to every man openly but secretly to kepe it and to rede it to fore þe state ly Princes of þe worlde þat may be to hem a mirrour to loke and a dirrecte forme for hem and for alle þeire lieges worship to contynue And repon þis Alisaundre wrote an Epistle to Aristotle his maistre howe.

V

DECRETUM ARISTOTELIS:
ÞE SECRETE OF SECRETES,
AND TRESORE INCOMPERABLE

Around 1448, in hand of John Shirley
(The 'Marmaduke' version)
From Bodleian MS. Ashmole 59, ff. 1–12ᵛ.

Here begynneþe þe boke made of þe governance of princes com- [f. 1]
pyled by þat renommed philosophre Daune Aristotiles, and sent
to þat excellent emperour and prince invincyble, Alexandre of
Macedoyne, þe whiche is cleped and called þe Secrete of Secretes
and Tresore Incomperable.   5
MArmaduke þe sone of Patryke, þe sage of alle langages, fonde in
þe regioun of Grece with-inne þe temple of þe Solayle, þe whiche
þat famous and gret philosophre Euscalabinis made, þis boke,
surely kepte, þe whiche he lete calle þe Boke of Aristotle Secretes.
And he translated it owte of Greeke in-to Calddé and, affter þe   10
request of þe Kyng of Arrabie, he translated it oute of Arrabeske
in-to Latin, and sent it to þe ful reuerent fader and ful noble persone Guy de Valence, þe Busshop of Triple. And þus was þis
boke translated in-to Latin, nouȝt al, but such as is moste profitable and gode [to] mans vnderstonding, for þestate and gover-   15
naunce of princes. þe whiche boke, with þe content, is nouȝt to
shewe to comvne, ne to rede to every man opunly, but secretly to
kepe it and to rede it to-fore þestatly princes of þe worlde, þat
may be to hem a mirrour to lyve, and a directe fourme for hem and
for alle þeire lieges, wysely to contynue, as þat a renomed philo-   20
sophre cleped Aristotle, whiche Alisaundre hade with him, bereþe
record, whome he cleped his maistre, by whos wisdam and conseile

1 of þe governance] *foll. by canc. of the* governaunce   8–9 þis boke ... kepte]
between Solayle *and* þe whiche þat   8 Euscalabinis] *four minims between* b
and s; *one over-stroke for* i   11 of Arrabie] of Calde nay but of Arrabie: *see n.*
13 Triple] *ms. (f. 1, ll. 14–20) continues with matter of pp. 203/20–204/4 below:*
As þat a renomed philosophre . . . honnour and worship. *I transpose these lines
and place them after ll. 13–20 here*: And þus was þis boke . . . wysely to contynue
(*f. 1, ll. 20–27*): *see n.*

he overcame alle heos enemys. þe whiche Aristotle Alisandre desired to haue with him, but he wrote him lettres of excuse, and
wrote him lettres howe he shoulde mainteyne him to his gret
4 honnour and worship. And vppon þis, Alisaundre wrote an epistle
[f. 1ᵛ] to Aristotle his maistre, howe | he shoulde resceiue hem of Perce,
wheoche wolde þane submitte hem to him for his gret and imperial
magnanimitee.

Capitulum j

Off þe firste epistle þat Alisaundre wrote to his maistre
10 **Aristotle, of his conquest of þe royal revme of Perce**
ARistotle, ful noble techer of rightwysnes, I signefye to þi prudence þat I have founden in þe lande of Perce one maner of folke
of gret raison and of perceuerant vnderstonding, studying for to get
reavmes and for [to] haue gret domynacions and lordshippes above
15 oþer. For þe whiche cause we haue purpos for to sleo hem alle. For
it is saide by þe olde and wyse naturiens for a gret pollecye, 'Love
and lordship wolde haue no feliship.' But sende þowe to me sen-
dently þy wille, whiche we wol filowe and fulfille.

[Capitulum ij]

20 **Howe Aristotle makeþe aunswere to Alisandre by lettres**
BOvntevous and glorious Emperour Alisaundre, if þou may
moeve þe eorþe, þe water and þe ayer and disposicions of þe
citees in Perse þanne fulfille þy pourpos hardely. And if þou may
not do so, slee not þe people, but governe hem in goodnes, and
25 encresce hem benignely and graciously. And if yee do soo, haue
gode affiance þat with þe helpe of God þey shoulle alle be þy
subgettes, for to perfourne þy wille and þy comaundementes. For,
fore þe love þat þey shul haue to þee, þou shalt haue þe lordship and
þe victorie of hem in pees and in reste. þe whiche lettre resceyved,
30 Alisaundre did folowe þe counseyle of Aristotle, and by þis meene

---

1 Alisandre] corr. (indistinctly) from Aristotle   5 howe] repeated as first
word on f. 1ᵛ. This, as all opening words on pages of this text, has capital initial
6 submitte] subimitte (see n., and cf. 212/19, 215/18, 218/11,, 222/4 and 5)
8 Capitulum j] this and all later chapter numbers in outer margin. Initial C
partly removed by cutting of edges of ms.   19 Outer margin nota per Shirley
(n partly removed in cutting)   21 Bovntevous] later (early modern) hand
crosses through second v   23 þanne] later hand crosses through e   25 gra-
ciously] foll. in ms. by virgula which later hand alters to colon   26 shoulle]
later hand alters to shall   27 subgettes] later hand alters to subiectes
29 pees] later hand underlines and substitutes peace (in outer margin)   lettre]
lettre   resceyved] later hand crosses through s : see n.

weere alle þey of Perce more obeissant to Alisaundre þane any
oþe[r] nacions þat he hade to-fore wonne or conquerde. |

Capitulum [i]ij [f. 2]

How Aristotle wrote an epistel to Alisaundre excusing him [of his absence] frome his so imperial [pre]sence 5

COnsider, Alisandre, feyre sone, glorious and precious Emperour, ho[m]e God for weledoing conserve, conferme, and sende
þe counsance to fele trouþe and vertue, and wol represse and putte
doune frome þy alle þy bestial desyres, and wol stablisshe þy
reavmes, and lighten þy witte to his wirching and honnour, and to 10
resceyve alle gode spirites honurabully as it þe tyme and cas
appertteneat. And as I have vnderstonden, glorious lord, þat
I were with þee by þi gret desire and wille, and þat þou merveylest
þee howe I may absteyne me from þee and þi presence, and þat
I am nought tendre ne desirous for to here of þe gode spede of 15
þine so honurable conquest and prudence þe wheoche þou haste
emprysed and thenkest to perfourne, for þe whiche cause I purpose
to make þee a litell boke canonet, þat shall yif þee myn avise inne,
þe which shall muche helpe for to enhaunce, and beo vaillance for
to instructe þee tacomplisshe alle þyne enperiale desirous courages, 20
and suffisaunte excuse for me þat I come not to þyne hye emperial
presence, þe whiche shal beo to þee opun and verray instruccion
of alle þy doutes and demandes as þaughe I were in persone
eche houre with þee. Wher-fore, Alisaundre, dere Emperour, me
semeþe þou shouldest not of right so reherce on me by þyne 25
epistilles none vnkyndenesse ne despite. But wit þou it
weele, incomperable conquerrour, þat I let not for none yvell
wille þat I bere to þine conqueste and enhexaltacion of þine honnour, but by cause in especiall boþe of gret age þat I am charged
with, and feoblesse of my weyke persone, haue made me hevy and 30
ful vnable for to goo any longe weye. And þat þou desirest for to
knowe and haste desired of me, to wit, þe moeving of | þe sterres, [f. 2ᵛ]
þe crafft of þe lowe thinges, þe crafft to constreine nature, and of
oþer thinges diuers, certes þat were thinge þat vnneþe any mortal
spirit shoulde vnderstonde. But þat at longeþe for þee tenquere of, 35
and man shoulde medle off to seye, I lete þee wit of right, and

3 iij] ij 5 presence] absence 7 home] howe
13 by] *see n.*

aunswere þee, þat frome hensforþe it longeþe not to þy raison
more for to demaunde me, ne to þi raison discretly avysed, þa[n]
I haue and shal put in þis boke, wheoche beon my so dere and
secrete, þe which if þou rede and eke vnderstande hem and canste
5 hem hollye, I leve þat bytwene þee and þat þou desirest of me to
witte, þere shoulde be none obstacle, for God haþe given þee
plenier and gret witte sotyle, and gret vnderstonding. By my doctrine and discipline þat þou haste herde and leorned to fore þis,
þou maist weele comprehende al þi desire brennyng and opneþe
10 þee þe weye streght to þy pourpos, þe whiche shal bring and leede
þee to gode eonde by þe wille of God. And vnderstonde wele, þat
by þe moyene of two thinges þou maist come [to], and acheeve,
þyne hole entent. þe first is for to haue miseracion, pitie and mercy
of þy subgettis, and despise and leve þeire godes and possessions.
15 And also þe knowlegge and þinvestigacion of gode dedis and þe
olde secretes and doctrines of olde worþy men, philosofrus, and
juges, þe wheoche God haþe chosen, and given hem sapience for to
introduce oþer. And vnderstande þou þat þe cause why I reherce
and renuwe to þee my secretes figurativement and a lytel derkly,
20 and þat I speke to þee derkly by strange examples and figures, þis
is þe cause: for I haue gret doute and feere lest þis boke may
come oft syþes in to þe handes of yvel and of vntrewe arguwers,
þe wheoche beon not worþy to medle with any suche thinges. And
24 with-oute fayle, if it so betyde, by myne assent or knowlege,
[f. 3] and in my defaute, I were a gret and yvel | tresspassour ageinst
God, and outragious breker of þe hevenly secretes. And þer-fore,
Alexandre, in þis maner I charge þee vppon þe attestacion þat I
may recorde ageinst þee to-for God, þat þou kepe al þat I shal
shewe þee, by worde or be wryting, secrete. For þou shalt wele
30 knowe þat a secrete diskouerd, tolde and discoverde, ne may not
fayle with-oute gret wronge or sorowe to some partie. And so
God sendeþe it and makeþe al þe werke deshonneste in mo
maniers þane herte cane thenke, til it come to þe point. But at
þe begyning remembre þee what I haue saide to-for þis tyme to þee,
35 and let þat by þi mirrour. For it behoveþe of necessité þat every
king have thre aydes for to susteine his reavme and comfort [it].
þe first ne may not beo hade with-oute þe secounde, I let þee wit,
þe whiche oone is þat þer beo a trewe governour and iuste to þe

---

2 ne . . . avysed] *see n.* þan] þat   3 my] *see n.*   11 *Outer margin* nota
per Shirley   35 *Outer margin* nota per Shirley   36 comfort it] comforted

subgitz of þe kinges, by þe which þat þey alle obeye þe kinge
truly and faste, þat is to sey in oone maner. For alle reavmes
beon destrude and brought to þe desolacion outrely by inobedy-
ence and rebellion of þe kynges sugitz, by þe which þe kynge and
heos lordes may beo calde vnwyse and fooles, and þeire subgitz 5
regnen and governe. And also, in þe same wyse, kynges and þeire
reavmes beon replenisshed in habondant goodes and riccheses
durables by þe due and goode obeysaunce of þeire subgettes to
þeire souereine lord, wysely advertysed by his trewe approbate
acustumable counsayle, so þat þe prince resceiue, governe, depart 10
and despende heos ricchesses wysely, for he shoulde largely and
conveniently give to heos subgetz affter þe place, þe tyme and
þeire desertes, yche one affter his estate and degree. Also þat oþer
is, þat þe prince sholde exorte and charge heos saide subgetz, and
chaunge þeire courages, as þe cas requireþe, to gode maniers and 15
condicions, by þensaumple of þe prince living, and of his vertuous
condicions, of his propre persone and estat, alweys | in his [f. 3ᵛ]
conuersacion priué and appert, to þe counssaunce of heos subgetes.
For þe prince shulde do alweys iustice egales bytwene him and
heos people, and bytwene alle his people and subgez, ech of hem 20
with oþer, affter equytee and raison in alle cause, boþe of þeire
persones, of þeire godes and possessions, money in any maner
goten or hade by hem in tyme passed, and of þe truwe and humble
behaving with al þeire duwe obeissaunce to þeire prince, and
principally to gif hye thanking to God þat sendeþe his subgetz 25
suche quiete living and encresce, with haboundaunce, vnder þe
domynacion of þeire prince, for al þat gode comeþe of God, withoute whome no man may no weele do.

Capitulum iiij

Aristotle wryteþe to Alisandre of [fou]re maner of kynges 30

DO nowe þy diligent vnderstonding, dere Emperour, for to
vnderstonde affter my wryting to þee þat þou shalt weele perceyve,
þat þere beon foure maners estates and condicions of kynges. For
one condicion is of him þat is large and liberal til him-self and to
heos subgetz. þe seconde is of þat kinge þat is tyl hym-self 35
coveytous, and large to heos subgetz. þe thridde kynge is he þat
is coveytous to him-self and to heos subgctz also. And þe feorþe

---

1 obeye] beo obeye   15 þeire courages] *repeated*   18 priué] *later*
hand adds question mark above   30 foure] thre

king is large to him-self and to heos subgettz in mesurable
avaricious by tymes oportune. To þe which þe Ytaliens affermen
þat it is no vice to a king if he be to him-self avaricious, and large
to heos subgetz. And þey of Perce seyne þat þe prince is not
5 comendable but if he beo large to him-selff and to heos subgetz.
But to my jugement, seyþe Aristotle, I halde him moste noble
kyng perseuerant, þat he þat is large to him-selff and to heos servantz, he is moste worþy and beste liche to to-longe endure, for
many causes þat beo likly and raisonable, as it shall be shewed here
10 more evidently in þis same chapitre towardes þe eonde. But þe
[f. 4] prince þat is avaricious to him selff and in þe | same wyse to heos
servaunte, his reavme, his puissance, his domynacion, may not
longe stonde perseverant and weele endure by no raison. For of
avarice þere fallen so many inconveniencyes likly and proveable,
15 which defaiteþe and fordoeþe alle maner of raisonable and goode
governaunce and rightfull and semblable, or convenient, largesse.
And þer fore, noble Emperour, consider þe maner of alle þy so
noble tryvmphes, conquestes, and victories in þy werres, þat
beon acheved offt syþes by provident and honurable acquestes,
20 and so revolve in þine advertence þonnour of covenable largesse
in alle laudable and gode governement of princes, and þe vnrightfull avaricious fait in werre, for þeire ambission and reprovable, sore inybit, avarice. For þis is clere thing: þe qualitees of
largesse and of avarice beon reprehensible, of booþe inordinately
25 folowed and vsed, whane þey beon withdrawen longe and fare
frome a convenient moyene. For, Alisaundre, it is knowen in alle
prudence þat it is a gret charge and harde thing for a prynce for to
kepe in his noble estate largesse, and a light thing and esy for to
passe largesse. For every creature may lightly beo foole-large or
30 avaricious, bytwene þe wheoche twoo every man enspired of
raison can thenke to fynde or ymagyne a moyene. And if þou
beo disposed, Alisandre, to knowe or seche þe vertue of largesse, it
behoveþe þee to kepe threo thinges. First þy powaire þat þou haste,
and þe secounde þan þe necessitee þat þey þat haue til do, haue.
35 And þanne þe meryte or þe desert þat þy men haue done to þee,

---

1-2 large to him-self . . . avaricious] large to him-self and large to heos subgetz nay but to heos subgettz in mesurable avaricious   1 mesurable] *corr.*
reading perh. mesurablé *or* in mesurable[nes]   11 *f. 4 upper margin, later*
hand liberalitie *and* covetousnese   17 *outer margin* nota per Shirley
21-2 and þe . . . werre] and þe . . . werre *and between* largesse *and* in alle *see n.*
31 *outer margin* videte per Shirley

to whome þee most give of right. And þeos three thinges considerd,
þowe shalt weel so vndrestond þe beste weye to chese þe maner of
þi governance, of largesse or of avarice, to attempre þee affter þy
mesurable pouair of þy gifftes to þy men þat haue deserved it. And
who þat oþer-wyse giveþe, he doþe wronge, and brekeþe þe rule 5
of largesse. For he þat giveþe to him þat haþe nouȝt ne nouȝt
deserved haþe, he is not to | beo preised ne thanked. And to gif [f. 4ᵛ]
to any persone þat is not able to resceiue þy gifft, or ellis haþe
deserved no gifft, he leeseþe his gifft. And who-so giveþe over þe
might of his ricchesse or þe substance of his gode, he leseþe his 10
ricchesse, and bringeþe him-selff to nought and to yvel arrivage,
and is wele resembled to him þat giveþe his enmy victorie above
him. And þer-fore I sey, þe prince þat giveþe affter his powair,
in tyme and in place, to hem þat ben worþy, or þat haue neode, or
have deserved gifft or rewarde, he is large to him-self and to heos 15
subgetz, and þe lordship of his reavme is durable, and men shal
wele kepe heos comaundementz. And suche a lorde haþe alweys
beon preised, loved and obeyed of þe olde wyse faders, for he is
vertuous and attemperate. But þe lord þat dispendeþe or giveþe
his gode desordinately of his reavme to hem þat haue not de- 20
served it, and to suche as haþe nouȝt [neode of] it ne [beon]
worþy to haue it by suche vnresonable moyens, he is a depopy-
lai[t]ou[r] and destroyer of þe peple and alle þeire godes, and
right vnable for to be called lorde, or to have any lordship, or to
have þe domynacion of any royalme, or see royale, for suche a 25
prince is sayde a foole-large governour, for by him is al gode
providence exyled oute of his roiaume. And in þe cas semblable,
avarice of þe prince is thing ful descovenable to royal magestee, and
if any kynge or prince be envolupte with any of þeos twoo vices,
if he, knowing hem wele in his rete[n]tyf and approbate expert 30
raison, [be] wel disposed to leve and eschuwe hem at þe tyme of his
neode, and putte remedie, him behoveþe by perfite diligence effec-
tuel, and suffisant counsaylliers, comitte þe charge and governaunce of his reavme to suffisant persones, to suche as cane be
thought necessarie and byhovely for him and for þunyversell gode 35
of his persone, of his reavme, with heos subgitz.

21 neode of] deserved   22–3 depopylaitour] depopylairous   31 þe]
repeated

Capitulum v

Howe þat princes shoulde eschuwe foole largesse and coveytyse |

[f. 5]   EVer drawe to þis, to þy memoratif rayson, Alisaundre, for
5 ferme governaunce and doctrine: þat þe prince þe whiche trusteþe
and estemeþe heos domynacions beon of gretter value and
revenue þane þey may bere or be charged with, he may lightly
bring al to desolacion with-outen þat he purveye gode and convenyent remedy by ful weele avised provysioun. And þer-fore
10 I sey to þee, þat for to flee largesse and avarice is þe opun erudicion
and doctryne to conquerre covenable largesse, and to flee foole
largesse, and live in þe worldely glorie perdurable, with hye glorie,
by whiche moyene if þe prince absteyne him, and with-drawe heo[s]
ambissious hondes frome þe felonous and þe vnrightful ravyne,
15 frome þe truwe goten godes of heos subgetz. And þer fore seyþe
Ermogines, þat if þe king absteyne him and with-holdeþe him
frome violent rape of þe moneye of heos subgettes, þat is a certaine
token þat in hyme is verraye and gret bounté of vnderstonding
and plenté of perseuerant lawe, and pleine parfeccion. For þou
20 maist wele suppose þat whane in any cuntrey or regioun þe gret-
nesses of despenses do surmount or excede þe revenuz of þe
same, þe princes þan spreden þeir handes to gete and haue weye to
þe goodes of þe comvnes. For þe whiche þe poure subgetes, for þe
gret wronge and extorcion þat þe princes raveynously surmitten
25 vppon hem, preyen to þe glorious God almighty to sende some
vent subtyle or chaude mellee amonges suche irraisonable lordes
and souereynes, þat þey falle nyhande al to adnichilacion of alle
þeire godes and hyenesse sodainly, with-oute duwe repentaunce
and þe hye misericorde of God Which chargeþe every raisonable
30 creature with þe duwe and charitable rule of living, for to so surely
atteyne and conquere þe everlast and perdurable lyff of His blisse,
[f. 5ᵛ] ordeinde for man. And wit þou wele, mighty and | ful noble
Alexandre, take it for certeine and ferme discipline, þat ricchesse
lefully goten beon þe cause of þabbyding and of þe dower of þe
35 soule, and also partie of it. For þe soule may not dwelle in þe
bodye, which is duwe herbarowe, but if alle wrongful causes be
vtturly destrued. And þer-fore every man in himself shoulde

---

1 Capitulum v] *in outer margin of f. 5, placed after the title on f. 4ᵛ*
7 *Outer margin, later hand* Exactions   18 hyme] *corr. from* his
31 everlast and] *perh.* everlastand

eschwe large dispenses, foolelargesses and outrageous gifftes, and
holde þe attemporance of largesse, for þere is no thing þat exorteþe
a lorde to tyranye as þe superfluyté of gifftes and despenses. And
wit þou weele þat þe substance þat man shoulde leve of largesse,
and gete þe derke secretes celestialles. Man cane not bring to   5
mynde al þat he haþe excessively given. And suche deedis beon
gode and vertuous to gif hem þat haue neode and þat haue deserved. And eke forgive þou a wronge done to þee, or iniurie or
villanye, and worship hem þat beon worþy, and enhawce hem
þat beon worþy. Helpe þe suffratous and supporte þeire angwys-   10
shes, aunswere courteysely to hem þat saluwen þee, and kepe þy
tonge of villaynous langage fromc hem to seye or dissymyle, to-fore
or þowe haue founde dede or tyme covenable, and shewe hem
þat it is to sette at nought, but wisdame to flee sottye or ignorance.
Nowe þeos thinges þat I have writen to þee, right noble Emperour,   15
I preye þee to here hem, and ententyfly leorne to folowe my doctrine in hem. And þanne have I certaine and ferme affiaunce þat
in þy werkes, in þy weyes, and in þy deedis, þou shalt have þy
charité haboundantly, suffisaunt scyence for [to] governe þee al
þy lyve. Nought for al þis, solempne Emperour, I shal seye þee   20
here-affter a philosophye abregged, þe whiche shale suffise þee
to alle þy werkis þat þou shalt haue til do in þis worlde or in þat
oþer, alle þe dayes of þy lyff, þe wheoche I exorte þee fermely to
reteyne in þy memorialle herte closed and sette.

Capitulum vj   25

Howe þat prynces shoulde labour for to gete gode renommee |

FOr als muche, feire sone Alexandre, right excellent Emperour,   [f. 6]
and my chosen nourre and right weele lernde desciple, þat þou
desirest to here of myn avyce touching þe provident behaving of
[þ]y persone, and in especiale, more desirously, of þy so noble   30
conquest and þavaunsing of þy renommed estate and of þy
werres, for þe first þat þou shalt vnderstande, þat [vnderstonding is
þe keper of] þe persone of man and his þe hole governement of þe
heele of þe soule, and is þe keping of vertues and þaspye of vices.
For by vnderstonding man vnderstondeþe and knoweþe þe yvelles,   35
and cheseþe þe goodes. And by þat cause þe entendement is norissher

---

2 *Outer margin, later hand* Giftes   3–6] *see n.*   20 Nought . . .
þis] *see n.*   25 Capitulum vj] *in outer margin of f. 6*   30 þy¹] my

of vertues, and þe roote of alle thinges lowables and honurables.
þe first instrument] of þe mans vnderstonding is desyre of gode
renommee. And with-oute any doute, he þat desireþe in trouþe for
to have gode counseyle, he shal have it, and he þat in flaterie for to
5 have yvel counsayle, and also subtyle and fraudelent, by yvel
renommee [is confounded]. And is and shoulde beo þe principale
to haue domynacions and seignuries, for to enhance laudable
renommee. For reaumes and lordshippes, ne shoulde not beo
rightfully desired ne possessed for a mans propre plaisaunce and
10 persone, but for by þat moyene to gete hem goode fame and
rightful renovne. And þer-fore þe comencement of sapience and
vnderstonding is of goode fame and loos, þat is goten by þe gode
governance of his lande and cuntrey, with þe lordshippes adiacent.
But in lordshipes gotun vnlawfully by þe odyble werre of wronge,
15 of coveityse, and of tyrannye, þe which ne may not longe persever
in tranquyllité, þoo desires beon goten al in oþer maner moyens.
For þat is none geting of gode encresce, ne first engendred in
mans conceyte but by lesinges and oþer fals ymaginacions, þe
19 whiche beon roote and begynniyng of all maner of vyces envyous.
[f. 6ᵛ] For envye engendreþe detraccion, and | þat same engendriþe hate,
þe which engendreþe iniurie and he repugnaunce and rebellion,
þe whiche engendre and makeþe enemys. And þey causen
battayles, þe wheoche destroieþe þe lawes and citees, all ageinst
kynde and nature. And of right þat at is ageinst þe right of þe
25 kynde destroyeþe mans bodye. And þer-fore I rede and fully
avyse þee, noble emparour, þat þou studye ne muse þee not to
gretly to gete by suche labours oþer mens pocessiouns or richesses,
in eschuwing þe gret inconveniences þat folowen þus by my
simplesse here-to-fore reherced to þee. And also by-cause of þat
30 gret desire þat man haþe for to enhance his goode fame, his raison,
his witte, his vnderstonding, he ymagineþe and degestiþe by alle
inwardes gode thoughtes and willis ymaginaries, and induciers
to holly and feithful raisouns. þe whiche shal consequently
[induce] to gode publyque and is full contrarious enemye to alle

2 *Outer margin, later hand:* Consilium rectum   6–8 principale . . . renommee]
principale of þe contrarie to enhance laudable renommee for to haue domynacions
and seignuries; Fama ergo est quod principaliter . . . appetitur in regimine B 45:
see n.   10 hem] *at end of l. Curved horizontal stroke over minims prob. indicates
that they represent* m. *Word ends with long downstroke, perh. as flourish or filler:
alternative possibility is to read* heim   19 begynnyng] *see 218/11 and n.*
25 destroyeþe] o *badly formed, resembles* e

subtilletees and fraudilent purpos, and norissheþe justice and
raison. þe whecche twoo engendre evidently conscience and
foyaltee, þe wheche engendreþe largesse raisonable, þat engendreþe
famuliaritee, þe which þane engendreþe frenship fyable and
lawdable, þat engendreþe counseile, comfort, and principal helpe. 5
And by alle þeos vertuous meenes þe worlde was establisshed,
and þe beninge [lawes] so sette by þe souerein Lord. And þis
acordþe with alle raison and nature, þe whiche was first doctrine
to alle þe constant and laudable naturiens. And þus full digne
Emperour A[lexandr]e, þe sone of þe noble kynge of þe royaume of 10
Macydoigne (and some tyme wrote him so in heos epistilles of his
subiugacion of þis worlde, and some tyme also he reherced him in
heos writynges to heos subgetz, 'Alexander filius dei Amonis,' and
an oþer tyme, by conquest and his connyng calde him-self 'Alexandre sone of þe gret kynge Phelip of Macedoygne'), þus, by þeos 15
ensaumples of my doctryne, saide Aristotle to Alexandre, with
þe surplus filowing, þy wysdame shal lede þee þe righ[t] weye.

Capitulum vij
Howe þat þeorþely prynces shoulde eschuwe luxurye | 19

GLorious Emperour Alexaundre, and my ful precious nurre [f. 7]
and dere desciple, eschuwe þowe vtturly þe gret thoughtes enforcementz, þenchaysouns of voluptuous loustes and bestialles and
carnelle synnes, for þey beo corumped and of lytel tyme enduring,
for þappetyte and þe charnel desire of man courages beo so corump-
tible, and to vicious wille so sore enclyned to þe bestial delectacions 25
of þe bodye, þat is soroufull and hevy. And þer-fore þou shoulde
þou wit and deeme, þat þe yvel enforcementz of delectacions vnclene
engendren carnelle love, þe whiche engendreþe avaryce and
ricchesses, þe which makeþe a man litel shamefaste, þe whiche
affermeþe decepcions, þe which engendreþe presumpcion, þe 30
vntrouþe, desloiaulté, and infidelité, þe whiche engendreþe rob-
berye, theffte and all pillages, and bycompþe blame, of þe which
comeþe kaytivytee and wrecchednesse, þat bringeþe man to his
destruccion of al famuliarité and by [þ]inde of alle gode and ornate
werkis, þe which is expressely ageinst alle nature and gode thewis. 35

---

1 subtilletees] *long faint downstroke through medial* e *extends above to* t *of*
consequently, *here on* 212/33, *and is prob. accidental, or due to later hand*
10 Alexandre] Aristotle   17 right weye] righweye: *perh. intended form*
18 Capitulum vij] *in outer margin of f.* 7   34 byþinde] by hinde. *Alternative*
possibility transcribing of by hende *from prototype ms: see n.*

Capitulum viij

What sapience þe princes and ġret lordes þat ġoverne and haue ryal possessyons shoulde have

HOnurable prynce and Emperour incomparable, it is ful con-
5 venyent and ordinate regyment [to] a gret lord, þat his renomie
and glorie be puplisshed in sapience and comended, and þat
wysely and avisyly he speke til his famulier servantz and officiers,
and in lyche wyse to all heos subgetz estately and lawfully as þe
tyme and þe mater requereþe. Fore þe which governaunce he shal
10 [be] þe more preysed, honoured, allowed and dred. And take þis
for certaine, Alexandre, þe people shal lightly vnderstande and
knowe by certaine signes, if þe princes have sapience or in-
sapience. For what-so-ever lorde or kynge þat subduweþe his
[f. 7ᵛ] reavme or his propre | godes to devyne governaunce service, he is
15 worþy to regne and have honurable service of heos subgettes and
seruauntz, and hye renomee and domynaciouns of alle heos
domynacions and seignuries. But þe lord þat putteþe Goddes lawe
in-to servage is a traitour and passer of trouþe, and despitous him-
self of his lawe. And who þat despreiseþe þe lawe, he is despreised
20 of alle men, and condampned in þe lawe. And þer-fore seyne þe
olde gret philosophurs, þat al first at þe begynning it longeþe
to a gret lorde þat he vse his lawe with-oute any vanyté with-
outeforþe, but þat in dede men may knowe þat in his werkis and
dedis he is subgette to God and douteþe Him, and is humble, and
25 subget to God to his power. For þanne gode men wol drede þeire
kynge and governour, and love him. And if it beo so þat þe
princes shewe hem outewardes in apparence to þe people þat they
beo religious and gode men, and doone and live wrecchedly in þeire
wirkinges and seyinges, al þaughe þei do hem secretly, yitte it may
30 not fayle but at þe laste þe people shal knowe þe sooþe al opunly.
And douteþe not but suche a prince shal beo condempned of God,
and by þat weye his regioun shal beo defamed and reproved
vniuersalli to destruccion, and brought to nouȝt by his desclaun-
derous governaunce of þat vicious lyving. What wolt þou þat I

---

2 What] Alexandre what *see* p. xxxiv *and n. and cf. l. 4 below*   4 in-
comparable] *displaced* Alexandre *of heading (see l. 2 above) perh. intended to
follow here, being either omitted or so postponed for sake of serial anagram of chapter
initials: see pp. xxxiv ff.*   14–15 he is worþy] *repeated*   25 þeire] *repeated*
30 but . . . people] but þe people but at þe laste þe people   33 vniuersalli]
five minims between the v *and the* u

seye þee more? Fore þere is no tresoure ne ricchese þat may bye
þat ageine to þe kynge, but for to rekover his gode fame. Afftir þis,
noble Emperour Alexandre, þowe shalt clerely vnderstant þat it is
thing ful convenient til a kynge or a gret prince þat he worship
heos juges, deputés, or any of heos oþer officiers þat governe his 5
lawe and putte it in execucion, and to love alle gode religious
peple, and giff lavde and honeste rewarde and gret thanking to alle
heos wyse counseylliers and vertu[o]s subgetz, and offt comvne
with hem and moeve hem in questyouns and comvnycacions
lowables and doutables. But þe prince shoulde deshonestes inter- 10
rogacions [eschuwe], and discretement to aunswere in þeire ques-
tyounes demaundables, and [graunt leve] to alle heos | oþer [f. 8]
subgettes, ordinaries and licensated, to approche þeire princes presence. And þe prince shoulde alweys thenke and remembre of his
wyse easy comunyng with boþe heos lordes, heos officiers, heos 15
counseylliers and truwe subgites, þat at þe disolving of heos parle-
mentz and counseylles þer betyde not none incydent inconvenientz,
troubles vnleofull, but if þey touche þuniyversale honnour and welfare of hem alle in generall, and prerogatyffly to þeire prince.
And eke to bee wyse and debonaire, withoute yre or male-talent, 20
to holde feythful promesses, for þe whiche comynycacion sodaine
ne doþe not come offte to þe point of þe fait of þe deliberacion
with-oute þe knowlegge of his errour to whom þe right belongeþe,
þat by þe moyens of gode discrecion where þat neode is þe cas
may beo wysely and soignously repellede. For þe soueraine 25
sapience in an hye prince is to governe him-self wysely. And þer-
fore þe gret prince whane it komeþe to his knowlegge any gode or
any proufit þat is longinge to him, þat he may weele do by him-selff,
do it wysely and descretely in his propre persone, nought to
hastely, þat men holde him not to besye folelye, ne neyþer to 30
slowe ne to desirous in besinesse þer-abowte, lest þat he beo hurte.

Capitulum ix

Whate hornament gret lordes shoulde haue, and whate habyllementz gret princes shoulde haue for hem

I Notefie to þy roial excellence, imperyal Alexandre, þat it is con- 35
venyent to þine estate and to alle princes for to beo honurablement

4 til a] til a a   7 lavde] v over a corr.   8 vertuos] ms. vertues may
in fact be vertuos with badly formed o   18 touche] repeated   þuniyversale]
intended form perh. þunyversale, but cf. 204/6, 212/19, 218/11, 222/4 and 5

and richely cloþed and eke apparaylled, þat shoulde beo more
apparissant and noble þane to oþer of lower estate of beauté
and ricchesse, for þe nobley of his estate roiale, and hyenesse. þe
whiche by þat moyene of strange and ryche ornamentz, þat to þe
5 peple, boþe heos subgetz and non-subgetz, may seo and knowe
[f. 8ᵛ] him, | heos dignytees impariales in alle wyses aboute his persone to
magnefye his hyenesse, and þat hye reverence and honnour shoulde
[be] more done to him, and nought empaired ne withdrawen, but
muche raþer enhaunced and encreced. þat þe prince haue a feire
10 voice, and discrete in his langageing, with manly sitting and gode
countenance and behaving of his persone, with alle heos visaige,
hede, hondes, armes, leggis, body, with alle heos oþer membres
corespondend, þe whiche adhorneþe muche þe prince and doþ
him gret profit. And, by especiall, to comforte, moeve and haban-
15 don his chiualleris at þe tymes of heos bataylles for to do wele.
O noble Emperour Alexaundre, what it is a noble and a precyous
thinge for a prince to beo moderate, and absteene him frome
muche speking, but if þat necessité ne requereþe it not. For it is
more convenient þat þe people eeris beo alweyes dresset to here
20 comandementz and þe decrees of þe prince þat he wol seye, þane
þey þat beon sawled and plentyvously, with mete and drynke,
wheche haue þanne gret courage to outragiously inordinate tyme,
to speke vn-to þe hyenesse of þeire prince, and eke par aventure
þe people desire not so offt to come in þe presence of þe prince.
25 And also it is not appertenent þat he acompanie his hyenesse ne
his persone offt with þe rude or þe villaines people. For to miche
famuliarité norissheþe despite (or, priuee companie amenuseþe
honour). And þer-fore þey of Ynde hade a ful noble and feire
coustume in þe disposicion of þeire royavme and þeire kynge,
30 and of þcire gifftes, þat þey gif to þeire kynge, whome þey should
not see, ne appere in his presence, but in oone tyme of al þe
longe yeere. At whiche tyme þe people shal beo þer assembled,
every man his best arraye armed, a-boute þeire kinges persone,
34 þe prince vppon a feyre whyte steede armed boþe man and horsse,
[f. 9] koverd of þe ricchest cotez, trappures, and | withe alle oþer ryal
apparaylles longing to þe kynges estate, embrowded of fyne golde
of Arrabye, fretted and kowched with alle maner of moste orientale

---

13 prince] princes   14–15 habandon] habandonþe, *perh. for* habandon
to: *see n.*   24 not so] not to so   35 cotez, trappures] *apparently altered
from* cote trappures

perree, and stoones of charboncles, of rubyes, of dyamandes, of
saphires, of emeraudes, of amatystes, with þe fynest and þe derrest
and moste precious perrye þat may be hade by see or by lande.
And þe comvne people innumerable firther frome þe kyng. And
þat daye þe wysest, þe worþyest, þe moste acceptable, shale speke 5
to þe kynge, and have agreable and plesante langage in þe name of
alle þe saide people, giving hyely thankinges duwe and digne to
glorious God, þat hade so ordeinde þe reavme of Ynde so noble
a kynge, with so gode governaunce, and so lowly obyssance to
þeire kynge, of oone hert and wille. And in preysing of þe people, 10
þe kynge rehersseþe to alle heos subgetz þeire humble obeissaunce,
þeire truwe and feythfull governance, þeire gret gifftes, þeire gode
maners and dedis, and chargeþe hem so contynuc of bettur, with
mieeknes, honour and feyth to þeire souerain prince. þe people,
for þe ioye þat þey haue of prudencye of þeire prince, þey offre to 15
him þeire godes and persones to heos hye comaundementz, and
hertely preyen to almighty God, 'Preserve his so hye persone, his
nobley, and his reavme, with þenhabitantz subgitz in reste and
tranquyllitee!' þe kynge entreþe in to his palays, of paleys richest
and feirest, þe lordes, þe gentylles, þe marchandes, and þe re- 20
menaunt of þe kynges subgitz, eche man to his owen cuntrey and
masyouns, þe whiche rehercen and tellen to þeire wyves, þeire
children, and þeire servantz, and given hem pleine ensample and
clere instrucc[i]on of þeire kynges noblesse, and by þis introduc-
cion encressen honoures, graces and gode gouernances in re- 25
giouns.

[Capitulum x]

Howe þe princes shal puinisshe þe wrong and kepe þe truwe |

KYnge Alexaundre, it is appertenyng to your estate imperial [f. 9ᵛ]
for to punisshe þe yveldoers, boþe by ioust iugement and be right, 30
to execute justice affter þe fourme and tenure of þe suggestion
veritable of þe compleynant, and in many cas to respite þe duytees
of heos subgetz and perdounes, and fynde þe ease covenable to
alle heos subgitz. Which shal beo þe supportacion and þe famous
glorie of þemperour excellences, by þensaumple of þe reavme of 35
Ynde, þat is so wyse, so iustely, and so prudently governed, þat
þe lande is so replenisshed of al maner of marchandyse, by þe

---

4 innumerable] u *and first minim of* m *over corr.* o   5 acceptable] acceptable þat daye   30 be] beo

renomee of þe princes governaunce, þ[ourʒ-ou]t þe coursse of alle
parties adiacens, what of people, what of godes, so many, so noble,
and so ryche, and so raisonable pryce bought and solde, by þe
reporte of merchandes þe wheoche so honurabully blasen þe hye
5 polecye of þe prince, of alle maner of rule and governement by
trouþe and right, þat þeire goodes, þeire estates, all maner of
worldely suffisaunce þer haboundeþe, encresceþe and multe-
plieþe, þat woundre is to be thought. þe whiche þinge palpabully
sheweþe þe hye polecye of þe prince consell, and first of gode en-
10 sample of him-self, causeþe all, and is þe first spring and welle,
and begynniyng principal, þat alle þe rentes and þe revenuz
royalls beon waxen, groven, and in any wyse multeplyed. And
þer-fore þeos eorþely princes shoulde with alle favourable moyens
forbere and suffur in supportacion and in þe help of alle þeire
15 subgitz, by whome þeire seignuries beon so labourde and borne vp.
þer it proveþe wele, þat þe cuntrey is gode þat haþe gret recourse
of marchandes, with þeire marchandyse, þe kynge is more worshiped, þenmys beon troubled and tremble, and peysible quiete,
concorde and love [haþc] þe prince at his ease.

20   [Capitulum xj]

Howe þe princes shoulde kepe justyce and beo mercyfull |

[f. 10]   LEove and moste glorious Emperrour, for þe love þowe owest
souerainly to þe eternal God and Maker of alle thinges, holde
justice, and take þou none hede, ne reche þee nouʒt, to encresce
25 þy noble estate in geting of thinges corumpable. And þou shalt
weel vnderstande, þat þyne nobley, þy prudence, þy trouth, þy
gret imperial estate, stondeþe principally, by doctrine and clere
inspeccion of alle maner instruccion of alle oþer fadere þat man
haue herde of, or ellis cane rede off, first in foure thinges þat
30 beon ful rightfull and raisonable, prudent, ioust, and covenable
for þe renommee of þe prince, for his enduree moste laudable to
alle heos subgetz and þe oþer, of þe worlde in his circuyte. þat
is to thenke, in þe first vertue of þe foure, of þe princes encresce,
and exaltacion of his fame and honnour, [þat] is to seye, obedyence
35 and loyale religion; ferme and truwe loving, for þe secounde; for
þe thridde, circumspecte and honestee in alle thinges; and, for

---

1 þourʒ-out] þat   7 haboundeþe] doþe haboundeþe   11 be-
gynniyng] *intended form perh.* begynnyng, *but cf.* 212/19, 215/18, 222/4-5
19 haþe] &

þe feorþe, duwe reverence and clene, in duwe places, to hem þat
hit belongeþe to, and tyme acustumed and necessarie. O Alexandre,
tourne þy duwe benyvolence to þe soules of þy subgites. Take
awey þe iniuries and þe vnrightwysnes frome hem. Give no mater
of oblocucion to þe people of þi governaunce, for litel thing of þy 5
desires, for þe noys of þe people lightly boþe loveþe and spekiþe
amysse, and þer-fore contene þe alweyes so þat no maner man
may seye reproche ageinst þee, and þerby þou shalt eschuwe þeire
ymagin[a]cions to þy reproche. And knowe þowe, discrecion of þy
prodommee is glorie of dignytee, reverence of lordship, þe whiche 10
is þe exaltacion of þemperour and al his empeyre. And þy moste
souereine prudence is, and may beo, þat þy reuerence of þy
subgetz dwelle to-geder in þerthes of þy subgetes to-fore love.

Capitulum xij

Off þe fynal entencion of emperours, kynges and prynces | 15

MOste excellent and redouted precious Emperour, remembre þe [f. 10ᵛ]
neode and þe miserable necessité and feble indigence of þy poure
subgetz, and of þy comfortable clemence supponayle hem. Chese
one of þy wel-loved servauntz, or officer þat cane speke þe langage þat þey beon off, and of gode eloquence, loving rightwysnes, 20
and þat is wele willing to fullfille þy wille and desires, mercyfully
to governe and perfourne, to helpe and execute, and in suche
thinges, and oþer semblables werkis of vertue and of charité, is
þe kinges comandementz, gladnesse of þe peple, and þe plesaunce
of þe Creatour of alle thinges eorþely. And whane any famyne, 25
necessité, or indigent derth or scarcesité, fortuneþe or falleþe in
þyne empyres landes or regyouns, amonge þy subgittes, wherby
gret hungre or thrust or pouerté emperissheþe, destroieþe, or
makeþe hem destroied or lost in any wyse, or in defaute of money,
victayle, or of any oþer godes, to þeire hele or releve opun þane 30
þe coffres of þy tresore or richesses of golde, of silver, of iouayles,
þy garnners of greynes, of cornes, þy bernes [of] heye and forages,
þy celliers of þy diuers wynes and drinkes, þy warderobes of þy
cloþes for borde and backe to were, þy parkes, þy pastures, with

---

1 feorþe] f (*written* ff) *over a corr.*   2 *Outer margin* nota per Shirley
4 awey] awey frome hem   9 ymaginacions] ymaginecions   11 of
þemperour] of *repeated*   14 Capitulum xij] *in outer margin of f.* 10ᵛ
15 emperours] emper*ur*os   23 is] is is   31 iouayles] y *corr. from*
another letter, apparently i

alle þyne oþer necessaries, for þy subgettz to live by. In helpe
and sustentacion of þyne subgettes, and of þy charité, with gode
wille departe it with him. For þe love of þy verraye Creatour so
departeþe to þee so largly of Heos glorious haboundaunce, and
5 leueþe it to þee. þus þine royal and imperial magnifisence shal
beo mainteynde in prosperitee. þus þy name and þine excellent
wisdame shal be knowen amonge þe peple, þe whiche shal vniuersally gif þee laude, and ever obeye, love and drede þee, and ever-
more shoule feere to displese or disobeye þee, or any of þyne,
10 in tyme comyng.

[Capitulum xiii]

Of þe vertuous and holly clemence of þe prynces |

[f. 11]   NOwe glorious and excellent Emperour, full offt syþes I haue
taught and warned þee, and yitte ageine I counselle, teche, and
15 warne þee, þat þou observe and kepe my doctryne, þe whiche if
þou kepe and observe, þou filoweste streght þyne owen wille, and
þy kyngdame shal durabully last, videlicet, þat is to seye, spare
þe blode of man-kynde to shedde, for þat longeþe to God alloone,
þat knoweþe þe secrete and þe hidde thinges of mans herte. Ne
20 take þou not to þe þoffice of God, for it is not given to þee to knowe
þe priuee counseyle of God. And þer-fore eschuwe þou, in als-
muche as þou canst, to spille mans bloode. For þat solempne
doctour Hermogines wrote, seying, 'Whane þe same thing created
sleeþe þe creature lyke to him, þe vertues of heven shoule crye
25 to þe Hye Magesté, seying, "Gode Lorde, þi servant and bondeman
wol beo lyke to þee." For if he slee vnrightfully, þe Hye Maker shal
leve him þat sleeþe and forsake him. And þane þe Hye Maker,
"For he haþe sleyne, and þer-for is [vengeaunce to] Me, and I
shal quite it." And ever in alle þy[r] lovinges þe vertues of heven
30 shal represente to þee Lord þe deth of him þat is sleyne, til þat
He haþe done and take vengeance of him þat is sleyne, þe whiche
shal beo condempned to þe everlasting peyne of helle.' Firþermo,
Alisaundre, I haue taght þee to-fore þis, þou knowest weele, alle
þe knowlegge of alle yvelles. Drawe to þy knowlegge þe behaving
35 of alle þy forþebringers, and departe of yvell thinge frome þat
oþer, and þer-of þou may drawe ful many gode ensamples. þe
dedis þat beon passed shal give þee teching. Despice þowe never

18 shedde] *first* d *corr. from* e   28 is vengeaunce to Me] Mihi vin-
dictam B 56

þe lower þan þy-self, for þe pouer man may by fortune come to gret
ricchesse and become worþyer þane þowe, to desese þee. Bewar,
Alisandre, to breke þy feyth, for þat longeþe to yonge folkes and to
yvel governed wymmen. For by feyth and trouþe is assembled of
peple þe multytude, enhabiting of citees, comvning of vertues, 5
lordship of þe princes. By feiþe, castelles and citees beon holden
and kepte, and by feith men beo knowen frome wylde beestes.
And Hermogines, þat doctour, seyþe | that þere beo two spiritis [f. 11ᵛ]
þat kepen þee, þat one on þy right syde, þat oþer on þy lifft syde,
þat knowen alle þy werkis and decreve[n] hem to þi Creatour, al 10
þat þowe haste wele governed þee inne. And do þou þy peyne
to with-drawe al þy reaume frome alle thing in-honeste, and þat
þou resteine hem offt for to swere, but if it beo by force of gret
neode, and principally þat þou kepe þe behestes of þy mouþe
and of þy seel. For breking of covenantz of princes, with þer 15
adiacentz, haþe beon þe desolacion of hem-self by þeire alies and
gode freondes. And also, noble Emperour, studye to ordeine
vniuersitees, studies, and scoles, for to leorne of þe noblest
sciences to enriche þy reaumes by þeire conninge, and beo to hem
þeire prerogatyff and support. For þe gret gode þat shal filowe by 20
þensaumple of þeire besye and honneste ocupacion, give hem of
þi gode, to-fore oþer scoliers. For by hem also þy governance shall
be in memoire perpetuata by scriptures in þeire librarijs. þis
maner is to be preised, for it was first þe vp-areysing of alle Grece,
by þe meene of þat vniuersal cité of Athenes, of þeire sciences þere 25
so studyed.

Capitulum xiiij
Of þe gode regiment of þe princes for þeire bodely hele

O Alexandre, I wol not hyde ne kepe frome þee my medecinal
doctrine, but I shal shewe to þee some secretes þat shal suffice to 30
þee, þat þou shalt neode no leeche. For þe conservacion of þy body
is better þane any medecyne. For it is to wit al-so, þat þer is no
wey to knowe any thing, or to do anything, but if it beo by þe
power of clere vnderstonding. And power of mans persone cane
not be hade but by might of heele. And heele cane not beo hade 35
but by equalité of complexiouns, and þer may be no manere of
compleccion but by temporance of humours, and conservacion of

---

8 two] tw *corr. from* th   10 decreven] decreved, *perh. intended form or*
slip for decrevet(h)

hele, and oþer thinges to beo hade, þe whiche God shewed by
reuelacion to Heos holly prophetis and rightwyse, þe wheche He
chase before and shewed by þe spirit of þe devyne sapience, and
endowed hem with þe dowers of conniyng. Ab istis, philosofres
5 þat folowed philosoficalli þe principal begynniynge haden, Per-
[f. 12] syanes, Juwes, Grekes and Latynes. | Of þeos nacions conyng
þey dranke, and wrote sciences crafftes, and of many oþer thinges
neodfull to man in þis worlde. For in þe scriptures of hem was
founden no falsede, none vnkunnyng, no reproef of frivoles, but
10 ever of wyse and vertuous men, ever sich approved, taughte,
and byleved. And who þat so beo, þat is cause of his owen losse,
muche raþer he shal leeue til oþer þe cause of losse, for þat at we
haue chosen, þat same we love, and þat we desiren and entenden.
Never-þe-leese, we shal wele wit and vnderstande, þat God al-
15 mighty amonges þe Grekes enflawmed to þe seching and leorning
of sciences and of þe kyndes, þe natural sciences to beo koned
more to hem at þe begynnyng of þe worlde þane til some oþer
nacions, affter [þ]influwence of þe heven. And if inspiracion of
þe celestial hevens with devyne influence affter þe disposicions
20 of þis lowe eorþe, might not be holden approbate, and also
beleved and taught by þe truwe remembraunce of scriptures lefft
here amonges vs, what cane mans wit thenke þat is folowing
credible?

Capitulum xv

25 **Of þe consecracion of sapience of heele for mans persone**

PEople were assembled and come to-geder of þe moste naturale
and renomed philosophre[s] þane beeing on lyve, for to determyne
for a principal conclusion medecinable. þe wheoche of one assent,
by congruence of þeire studye, þat at þey hade leorned or herde,
30 [acorded] þat þe worþyest creature of þis midel eorþe, vnder
Criste, made affter His ymage, is man, composed of þellementes, of
þe foure contraire humours, þat ever nedeþe norisshinges and
passiones and moystours. þe whiche if þey wanted, þe substance

---

4 conniyng] *intended form perh.* connyng, *but cf.* 212/19, 215/18, 218/11, *and*
l. 5 below   5 begynniynge] *cf. l. 4 above*   18 þinfluwence] *ms. indistinct:*
apparently jinfluwence, *but poss.* þūfluwence   32 humours] elementis,
nay but humo*u*rs

shoulde be corupte, and if in þees were vsed superfluité or dymini-
cion, þane it should renne in-to infirmitee, feoblenesse and many
oþer gret inconveniences. And if medecine were temporately [take]
þer shoulde beo founde helpe, reformacion of þe pacient body,
and of al his substance, heele. And þerfore þey acorded to-gedir þat 5
he þat passeþe þe duwe maner | of Aristotle in þe fulle or in þe [f. 12ᵛ]
voyde, in slepinges or wakinges, in moevinges or in restis, in leting
þe bloode, in dissolucion or withholding of þy wombe, in with-
drawing or withholding of blode, he may not escape seeknesse of
seeke furores, hevynesses, and many oþer incidences of seeknesses 10
and of some intollerable, inportable, or incurable firmitees and infirmitees. Alle þe saide philosofres acorded also þat he þat eschuw-
eþe and kepeþe him frome superfluytate and excesse, and of
indigence, keping moderatly equalité and temporance, he shal haue
heele hollye, and longe dayes. And I, forsoþe, fonde noone of þe 15
philosophor[es] þat blamed þees sentences, þat is to sey, þat alle
þe delitefull thinges wheþer þey beo delites or ricchesses, honoures
or loustes, alle þey beo desired and coveited of mankynde for þe
durabilité of þe man. And þer-fore who-so þa desireþe for to haue
longe lyffe and ioyous, late him studie and thenke to gete þat 20
thinge þat acordeþe durabull and convenyent to preserve holsome
and longe lyff, and forsake his owen propre appetytes and
never putte mete vppon mete withe full stomake, but wit gode
appetite and degestioun of voide stomake. I haue herde of Ypocras
þat he conserued by gode mesure heos dyetes, for þe which he 25
kepte his body feoble. To whome oone of heos desciples saide,
'O noble doctour, and þowe wolde weele ete, þou shouldest not
sustene so muche feobulnes of þy body.' To whome Ypocras
aunswerd and seide, 'I wol ete to lyve, and not to lyve for to ete.'
Norisshing for feobulnesse is for to seche, but no feobulnesse for 30
norisshing. I haue knowen many hole þat lyteld of þeire foode and
[made] abstinence of þeire appetytes, sparing glotonye and living
temporately by dyetes, þat by þat moyene were ful hoole of bodye,
of longer wirching of lyff, of gode appetyte, and lighter. þe which
is proeved in Arrabyens walking by desertes and longe weyes. For 35

7–9 in leting þe bloode, in dissolucion or withholding of þy wombe] in
dissolucion of his wombe, in leting þee bloode, in dissolucíon or withholding of
þy wombe   10 seeke] seekee   16 philosophores] philosophorum
perh. form intended. Outer margin Nota per Shirley'.   17–18 ricchesses,
honoures or loustes] ricchesses, honoures or ricchesses loustes   22 appetytes
and lykinges] appetytes and appetites

þat is soþe thing and manifeste argument, to abstene þee frome
to miche eting and superfluité is þe souereine medecyne generally.
Et sic explicit Decretum Aristo[te]lis.

3 *Explicit followed by* And begynneþe þabstracte Brevyaire compyled of diuers
balades &c. *Catchword* xiij *crossed through and* I *substituted, although next leaf in
fact f. 13*

VI
VIa
VII
VIII

VII

THE BOOKE OF THE GOUERNAUNCE OF KINGES AND PRINCES CALLED THE SECREET OF SECREETES

Translation from a French version of the
Abbreviated Tripolitanus text;
second half of the fifteenth century.
From University College, Oxford MS. 85,
fols. 36–68 (pp. 70–134)

Numbering in this manuscript is by pagination, not foliation; page-numbers are therefore here given in the outer margins immediately below the folio-numbers. Where necessary for distinctiveness, readings from the manuscript are designated in the footnotes by the sigil U

VIa

The opening pages of
LE LIURE DU GOUUERNEMENT DES ROYS ET DES PRINCES, APPELLE 'LE SECRET DES SECRES', LEQUEL FIST ARISTOTE AU ROY ALIXANDRE

From Cambridge University Library MS. Ff.1.33 (fols. 3–10); this French version of the Abbreviated Tripolitanus text is the presumed basis of John Shirley's translation (VI), *The Governance of Kynges and of Prynces*

With corrections and variants supplied from:
H British Library MS. Harley 219
R British Library MS. Royal 16.F.x
V text printed by Vérard, Paris, 1497
G text printed in Gilles de Romme, *Le mirouer exemplaire*, Paris: Guillaume Eustace, 1517, sig. P5r–S1v

Where necessary for clarity of distinction in the footnotes, the reading of MS. Ff.1.33 is designated by the sigil F. Readings from the later pages of this manuscript are also occasionally given in the footnotes to texts no. VII and VIII.

VIII

ROBERT COPLAND, THE SECRETE OF SECRETES OF ARYSTOTLE
Printed 1528

From the unique copy in the Cambridge University Library (STC 770)

With a selection of variant readings
taken from the unique copy in the Folger
Shakespeare Library, Washington, D.C., of Anthony Kitson's
reprint, *The Secrete of Secretes*, 1572 (STC 770(a)) and from the
unique copy in the British Library of Robert Wyer's fragmentary
reprint, *The dyfference of astronomy* (STC 6837)

W= Wyer, *Dyfference*
K = Kitson, *Secrete of Secretes*

Where necessary for clarity of distinction in the footnotes,
Copland's readings are designated by the sigil C

VI

THE GOVERNANCE OF KYNGES AND OF PRYNCES CLEPED THE SECRETE OF SECRETES

Translation by John Shirley, about 1450, from a French version
presumed to be that in Cambridge University Library MS. Ff.1.33

Transcribed from British Library MS. Add. 5467, ff. 211–224ᵛ

[*THE SECRETE OF SE-*/CRETES, CONTAINING THE /
most excellent and learned instructions / *of Aristotle the prince of
Philosophers:* / which he sent to the Emperour, King A-/lexander:
very necessarye and profitable / for all maner of estates and
degrees. / With some instructions in the / ende of this booke, 5
touching / the iudgment of Phi-/sognomie.

> Lordes and maisters, wise and honourable,
> Of this said booke make oft a loking glas:
> For ye shal find it good and profitable,
> With wisedome to bring your nedes to passe: 10
> Make your entent, as the auc[toures] was,
> Which grounded it on right hie grauiti[e],
> Counselling you to lyue in equytie.]

1–13 *Supplied from* K, f. A1, *which continues*: IMPRINTED AT LON-/
don by VV. VVilliamson for An-/thony Kitson, dwelling in / Paules
Churchyard at / the signe of the / Sunne. 1572. A1 *missing in* C
10–12] *bracketed portions illegible* K

    And thus here endeth the boke cleped Les Bones Meures [f. 211]
and [begynneth] the boke named The Gouernance of
Prynces, seyd The Secrete of Secretes, the whych Arestotle
made, and direct hit to Alexandre the grete conqueroure of
the worlde.   5

[H]ere begynneth The Gouernance of Kynges and of Prynces, in
this boke filowyng, cleped The Secrete of Secretes, which Aristotle
wrote to Kynge Alisandre. And then nexst foloweth the ordenances
of the titles of the chapitres of this boke. And first the prologe of
the doctour that translated this same story oute of Grece into 10
Frensh. And out of Frensh into oure moders tonge by youre
humble suget and seruyture Johan Shirley in the last | dayes of his [f. 211ᵛ]
grete age, so as his ignorant feblesse wolde souffise, which recom-
mendeth and submittetth to the noblesse and the supportacion of
youre excellent discression to correct, adde and amonuse, there 15
as youre fauourable gentylesse best liketh. The which first doctoure
and translatoure recommandeth Aristotle that was full worthy

    6 and of] *prec. by* seid, *crossed through*   12 *From this page onwards
recurs the running title* The governance of kynges and of prynces, *the first section
of the phrase on the versos, the second on the rectos*   15 amonuse] *intended
form perh.* amenuse

The table		Page in this edition	[f. A2]

❡ The prologue of a doctour in recommen-
dacyon of Arystotle the prynce of
phylosophres   a.   253   5
❡ An epystle that Alexander sent to Arys-
totle   b.   261
❡ The answer of the sayd epystle   c.   263
❡ The prologue of a doctour named Phylyp
þat translated this boke in to latyn   d.   265   10

1 *Table at end of book, sig.* L3 f. K

	Number of chapter in list of contents	Chapter no. in actual text, where this differs from no. in list of contents	Page in this edition
forto be recommaunded as for oone of the most and best philosophre and astrologien that euer was tofore this day.	j	ii	253
First an epistel that Kyng Alexandre wrote to Aristotle, that solempne clerk	ij	iii	261
Then the aunswere of that epistle fro Aristotle to Alexandre	iij	iv	263
The prologue of the doctoure Philip that translated this boke into Latyn	iiij	v	265

(line numbers 5, 10 appear in right margin)

6 Aristotle] Alexandre **nay** bot to Aristotle: *see n.*

5 et²] *supplied from chapter-heading in text; see 292/4*

b.] *this sigil re-used thus in body of text*

[f. 212]

1–2 *item om. in list of contents; heading here supplied from body of text*
5 avarice] avarices

5

2 ɀ] *rounded* r C   3 ʃ] *long* s C

5

10

3–5 xviij *and* xix] *in margin,* xx *and* xxj, *respectively, beside each; below:*
cunc*t*a cap*i*tula ord[ine] obiret.

5 y.] *no punct.* C

Number of
chapter in
list of
contents

Of the mercy, grace and perdon   [f. 212ᵛ]
   of the kynge   xxiij
Of the peyns, ponysshementes
   and imprisonmentes of the
   kynges   xxiiij   5
Of the ful knowyng of all thoo
   gouernances   xxv
Of the feyth and the trewe as-
   surance of the kynge   xxvj
Of the vniuersitees, studies, and   10
   scoles of the [reavme]   xxvij

1 mercy] *preced. by canc.* mer, *to the* r *of which a long curling downstroke had
erroneously been added*   8 Of the] the *repeated*   11 reavme] studies

	Number of chapter in list of contents
De la garde du roy	xxviij
De la di[f]era[nc]e d'astronomie	xxix
De la garde de santé	xxx
Du gouuernement des mallades	xxxj
5 En quantes manieres on peut garder sa santé	xxxij
Des diuerses viandes	xxxiij
De l'estomac	xxxiiij

2 diferance] diseraine F; *chapter-heading, fol. 16, is* De la diference du roy; difference HV

2–4 *In place of letters, compositor has here used as sigils the ampersand, the abbreviation sign for* -orum, *and the abbreviation for* et cetera: *but in body of text the signs used are, respectively, the ampersand, the rounded* r, *and the abbreviation for* -orum

---

10 Of how] *prec. by canc.* Over: *see n.*

	Number of chapter in list of contents	Number of chapter in text in manuscript, where different from number in list of contents
Des signes pour congnoistre l'estomac	xxxv.	
Une espitre de grant pris	xxxvj	
De la maniere de trauailler	xxxvij	
5 [La maniere de mangier		xxxviij]
De abstinence	xxxviij	xxxix
De non boire eau pure	xxxix	xl
De la maniere de dormir	xl	xlj

5 *Chapter-heading supplied from position in text, f. 19ᵛ: omission in the table of contents causes discrepancy thereafter between numbering of the chapters in it and in body of text.*

9 f. 213 *begins with matter of* 241/12–243/4 *repeated, canc.*

	Number of chapter in list of contents	Number of chapter in text in manuscript, where different from number in list of contents
De garder sa coustume	xlj	xlij
Comment l'en doit garder et changier coustume	xlij	xliij
Des quatre temps de l'an	xliij	xliiij
5 De prins temps, quel il est	xliiij	xlv.
De [esté temps] et quel il est	xlv	xlvj
De [auptonne] et quel il est	xlvj	xlvij
De yuer et quel il est	xlvij	xlviij
De la challeur naturelle	xlviij	xlix
10 Des choses qui engressent le corps	xlix	l

6 esté temps] auptonne   7 auptonne] este temps

5

10

2 *This is last item in* K *as extant*: f. L3ᵛ *ends with this, and catchword* Of *of next item.* L4 *is missing*

5

10

9 hete] hete And knowe the soth: *see n.*

	Number of chapter in list of contents	Number of chapter in text in manuscript, where different from number in list of contents
[Des choses qui amaigrissent le corps]		liij
[De la premiere partie du corps]		liiij
De la seconde partie du corps	l	lv
5 De la tierce partie du corps	lj	

1 *This chapter omitted in list of contents; title supplied from chapter-heading in text, f. 24ᵛ; in the text this chapter and the two following occur out of place, on fols. 24ᵛ–25ᵛ, following chapters li and lii (on fols. 23ᵛ–24ᵛ): hence they are there numbered liij and lv.*

	Number of chapter in list of contents	Number of chapter in text in manuscript, where different from number in list of contents
De la quarte partie du corps	lij	
Des manieres des poissons	liij	lvj
De la nature des yauues	liiij	lviij
De la nature du vin et du bon et		
5 du mauuais qui s'enssuit	lvj	lix
Du siropt	lvij	lx

5 qui s'enssuit] *these two concluding words of the chapter-heading occur on a separate line from the words preceding, and this chapter has been accorded two separate chapter numbers:* De la nature ... mauvais *is numbered* lv, *the words* Qui s'enssuit *are given the number* lvj. *I omit the number* lv *rather than altering all following numbers, which refer to chapters not included in this ed., and which, furthermore, do not correspond to the actual numbering in the body of the text*

4 *numbered* Y *in body of text* 5 *numbered* A *in body of text*
6 *numbered* B *in body of text* 7 *numbered* C *in body of text*

	Number of chapter in list of contents
Of the foure partie of mans body	lj
Of the maner of fisshes and of their naturs	lij
Of the nature of divers waters	liij
Of naturs of wynes, of the gode and of the badde	liiij |

1 partie] parties *prec. by canc.* pati

	Number of chapter in list of contents	Number of chapter in text in manuscript, where different from number in list of contents
De la fourme et maniere de justice	lviij	lxj|
[f. 4] Des secretaires du roy	lix	lxij
Des massaiges du roy	lx	lxiij
5 Du gouuernement	lxj	lxiiij
De la phi[z]o[n]omie des gens	lxij	lxv
Du liure de santé	lxiij	

4 massaiges] *body of text, fol.* 30^v, *has* messaigiers; messagiers HV (*both with* messagers *in body of text*); R *has no list of contents, but in body of text reads* messagrs *for* messagers   6 phizonomie] phinozomie F; *chapter-heading in body of text, fol.* 31^v, *reads* phisonomie; phizonomie V; R (*in body of text, f.* 20ra) *has* philosomie.

Thus endeth the table. |

1 A] numbered D in body of text   *2 B] numbered E in body of text*
3 C] numbered F in body of text   *4 D] numbered G in body of text*

[f. 36]   Here begynneth the Booke of the Gouernaunce of Kinges
p. 70 and Princes, called the Secreet of Secreetes, whiche was
first made by Aristotle to Kynge Alexander.

The prologe of a doctoure recommending Aristotle

5   GOd allmighty preserue oure kynge and the prosperité of his
true subgites, and stablissh his reame to the perfeccion of the feith
of Criste, to reigne and endure to the exaltacion, laude and worship
of the kynge and alle the lande. I that am seruaunt to the kynge
haue put his commaundement to effectuell execucion and haue
10 yiuen cause of oparacion to geete the booke of good and vertuous

---

Cy finent les reb[r]iches du liure du gouuernement des
roys et des princes

☾ Prologue du dotteur en recommandent Aristote   .j.

Dieu tout puissant vueille garder nostre roy et la gloire de ceulx
5 qui croient en lui, et conferme son royaume pour prendre la loy
de Dieu, et le face regner a la exultacion, louange et honneur des
bons. Je qui suis seruiteur du Roy ay mis a ex[e]cuscion son commandement, et ay donné euure d'aquerir le liure des bonnes meurs

---

1 rebriches] rebeliches F; *cf. 228/4*

[a.] ❡ The prologue of a doctour in recommendacion of Arystotle [f. A3]
the prynce of phylosophers.

GOd almyghty saue our kynge/ & the glory of all his frendes, and
conferme his realme in the faythe of god. And cause hym to reygne
in thexaltacyon, prayse/ and honour of his people. I whiche am 5
seruaunt to the kynge haue put in execution the werke of his
commaundement/ in getynge a boke of good maners to his

And thus here endeth the rubriches of the chapitres of this
boke of the Gouernance of Kynges, with Prologe of the
doctour translated it, &c., recommaundyng Aristotle.

Capitulum ij^m

Almighty God kepe oure souerain lord Kyng of England and 5
of Fraunce, and of all his trewe and humble subgettes, that they
live in prosperité and ferme pece, and graunt to his excellent and
noble estate, and all hem vniuersally and singulerly to confourme
hem lastyngly ever, vnder humble and perfite obeisaunce vnder
the Cristen faith of oure dere Lord Criste Jhesu. The which make 10
and graunte to oure said souerain Lord to reigne and governe
to the exaltacion, lovyng and honoure of all gode. I that am servant
of the kyng have here put in execucion his hie commaundement,
and have putte in warke to sech and rede the boke called | 'Of [f. 214]

4 *This, and all subsequent chapter-numbers and -headings, in side margins.*
5 Almighty] *guide-letter* a *in space provided for decorated initial. So with opening
word of subsequent chapters, no decorated initials being inserted. In one case, indicated below, space provided is left blank, and opening word given in entirety after
this space. In another two cases indicated catch-letter omitted*   9 vnder
humble] vnderhumble

condicions to the gouernaunce of his royall persoone, whiche was
made by the prince of philisophers Aristotle, to the noble emperoure Alexandre, sonne to Kynge Philipp of Grece. And this
[f. 36ᵛ] booke ma-|de the seid Aristotle in his olde age and debelitee of
p. 71 his persoone, be-cause he might nat laboure to perfourme the
6 commaundement that Alexander had yiuen him in charge. For
Alexandre loued him, and made him maistre and gouernoure aboue
all othir, because he was a man of grete wysdome and noble wy[tt]e.
The whiche Aristotle laboured all-wey withoute cessing to vnder-
10 stand and knowe the vertuous condicions and spirituell wysdomes
contemplatiue and charitable. And also he was right wyse and
lowelye, and loued reson and justice, and rapoorted euer reson
and trouth. And therfore diuers of the philosophers reputed him

8 wytte] wysdome

---

au gouuernement de lui, lequel liure est nommé 'Secret des secrés'
et le fist le prince des philosophes Aristotes filz de Mahommet de
Macedomniere [a] son disciple l'empereur Alixandre [lequel] eut
deux couronnes. Et ce liure fit le dit Aristotes en sa viellece et en
5 sa feblece de son corps pour ce qu'il ne pouoit trauailler ne
cheuauchier ne faire les besougnes que Alixandre lui auoit en-
chargiés. Car Alixandre l'auoit fait maistre et gouuerneur par
dessus tous, et l'amoit moult pour ce qu'il estoit homme de tres
bon conseil et de tres grant charge et de soubtil entendement et
10 tousiours estudioit sens cesser les bonnes et gracieuses meurs et les
sciences espirituelles et contemplatiues et charitiues. Et si estoit
moult saiges et humbles et amoit raison et justice et touziours
rapourtoit verité et loyauté. Et pour ce plusieurs philozophes le

3 Macedomniere] *six minims between* o *and the following* e F Macedoine GR
Macedoyne H Macedone V   a] et FG *and substant.* R a HV lequel] *om.* F
lequel RVG *and, substant.,* H

gouernaunce. The whiche boke is called the secrete of secretes/
made by the prince of phylosophres Arystotle the sone of Mahon-
net of Macedony/ to his dysciple þe emperour Alexander sone of
Phylyp kynge of Macedony the which Alexandre had two crownes.
This sayd boke Arystotle compyled in the oldenesse of his body/ 5
bycause that he might no more trauayle nor ryde to do suche
besynesses as Alexander had put in to his charge. For Alexandre
had made hym gouernour and mayster aboue all other bycause he
was a man of veray good councell/ of grete clergy/ and subtyll
vnderstandyng. And incessantly studyed good & gracyous maners/ 10
& scyences spyrytuall/ contemplatiues/ and charytables. He was a
wyse man/ & meke/ louynge reason and Justyce/ & euer reported
ryghtwysnesse & trouthe. And therfore many phylosophres repute

---

13 ryghtwysnesse] righteousnesse K (*regular substitution, not indicated
hereafter*)

God Maniers' vnto the kepyng and governance of hym, the which
boke is named 'The Secrete of Secretes', the which [made] the
Prynce of Philosophres, cleped Aristotle, the sonne of Maheuwe-
met of Macidomnere, and his disciple the emperoure Alexandre,
which bare two corones. And this boke made that Aristotle in his 5
age and feblesse of his body, bicause that nature souffised not
in hym to take the peyn of laboure, ne to ride ne for to perfourme
such thynges as Alexandre had charged and gyven to hym in commaundement. For Alexandre had made hym governoure and
maister above all other, and loved and trusted hym full much, 10
bicause that he was a man of gode counseile and subtile vnderstondyng, and all his live put hym-self to studying, and noght
cessed, vpon gode and gracious maners, and vpon the science[s]
spiritualle[s] and contemplatives and charitablez. And he was full
wise and meke, and loved reison and rightwisnes, and ever more 15
he reported all trouth and sothnes. And therfore many philo-

---

3 cleped Aristotle] *blank space separates these two words*   16 many]
prec. by canc. may Phi.

of the nommbre of prophetes, saying that they had founde in
diuers bookes of Greekes that oure Lorde sent to him His moost
excellent angell whiche seid that God wolde make him to be called
by the world more angell than man. And wite ye well that Aristotle
5 in his lyving made divers tokenys and signes right merueilous
whiche shulde be longe to reherce. And also in his deth he made
many straunge werkes. For the whiche a religious companye of
peeple called Pipatike seid and heeld oppinion that he was rauiyssht
vp to heuen in the semblaunt of a dowe of fyre. And during the lyf
10 of the seid Aristotle, Alexander thrugh his good counseill submised
and conquerid alle landes, and had euer the victorie ayeinst his

1 nommbre] *intended form perh.* noumbre

reputerent du nombre des prophetes et disoient qu'il auoit trouué
en plusieurs liures des gres que Dieu lui auoit enuoié son tres
excellent aignel qui lui dist, 'Je te feray nommer par le monde plus
[f. 4ᵛ] angle que homme'. Et saiches que le dit Aristote fist | en sa vie
5 moult de signes, estranges euures et miracles qui seroient longues
a racompter et auxi en sa mort si fist moult d'estranges euures
pour ce que vne religion et compaignee de gens qui se appeloient
paripatique disoient et tenoient ceste oppinion qu'il auoit esté
monté ou ciel en fourme d'une columbe de feu. Et tant que le
10 dit Aristote vesqui, Alixandre par le conseil dudit Aristote
subiuga toutes terres et eust vittoire contre tous et aquist seigneurie

5 de signes ... miracles] designes ... miracles F (*articles, etc. joined to following nouns: see vol. ii*) de signes les quieulx durent estranges œuures et miracles
R des signes lesqueux furent estranges oeures & miracles H de choses & de
signes qui furent ouurages moult estranges, comme miracles V de signes,
lesquelz furent estranges oeuures, et miracles G   7 ce] *inserted above line*
8 paripatique] par ipatique F; paripatique R *and, substant.* H perypathetiques V

hym of the nombre of prophetes. And say þat they had founde
dyuers bokes of the grekes which god had sent hym by his moost
excellent aungell/ saynge to hym. I shall make þe to be called in
þe worlde more an aungell than a man. And wyte ye þat Arystotle
dyde in his lyfe many sygnes whiche were straunge in werkes & 5
mer-|uayles/ whiche were to longe to be accompted. Before his [f. A3ᵛ]
dethe he dyde many straunge werkes. Wherfore a relygyon &
company peryadyc sayd & helde opynion that he had ben in heuen
in lykenesse of a douue of fyre. And as longe as he lyued Alexander
ouercame all þe worlde through his councell. And all landes by the 10

3 hym.] *cf. 265/5, 325/12 and 17, 363/31 and n., 369/28, 377, 36; but see
299/7, 369/10, and 371/16*   9 fyre.] *no punct. (at end of line)*

---

sophres reputed hym of the noumbre of profettes, and seid that he
had foundon in many bokes of Grece, of Egipt, and of the
Ebrayeux, that God had sent hym his glorious aungel that said to
him, 'I shall | make the called by all the worlde more aungel then [f. 214ᵛ]
man'. And wit ye well that this Aristotle made in his live many 5
stronge sygnes, warkes, and miracles, that sholde be longe forto
reherce, and att his deyng did right stronge and grete dyuersitees.
Bicause that, a religion and a companye of folk that cleped hem
'Paripatik' said and helde this opynion, that he had passed to
heven in the fourme of culuer of fure. And whilst that Aristotle 10
lived, by his counseil and his excellent propre chiualrous corage,
he surmounted, and subdeuwed in conquest, all the circuyte of
this world, and of all landes had soueranité, and victories above

enmyes, so that he gate the lordshippes of alle the worlde. And
alle reames and nacions he subdued vnder his emperiall commaundement. And the seide Aristotle made many faire pistles for
4 to yive Alexander knowlege of the secreetes. And whan Alexandre
[f. 37] had conquerid the reame | of Perse, and sett alle the grete lordys
p. 72 of the lande in prison, he sent a pistle to Aristotle in the fourme
folowinge.

---

de tout le monde. Et par toutes terres, a la renommee de lui, et de
toutes nacions, furent soubmises a son imperilité et a son commandement, mesmement de ceulx de Peresse [et] Arable, ne ne
furent gens nullez qui osassent resister en-contre lui ne en dit ne
5 en fait. Et fist le dit Aristotes maintes belles espitres pour l'amour
qu'il auoit eu a Alixandre. Et vne de ses espitres est cy desoubz
escripte laquelle il enuoya au dit Alixandre. Car quant Alixandre
eut subiugé ceulx de Peresse et mis les plus haulx hommes du pais
en ses prisons, i enuoya vne espitre a Aristote en la fourme qui
10 s'ensuit.

---

3 Peresse et Arable] Perse et d'Arabe R *and, substantially,* VG

fame of hym/ were put vnder the imperyall commaundement/ & in lykewyse they of Perce/ & Araby. And there was none þat durst gaynsay Alexander/ in worde nor dede. And þe sayd Arystotle made many goodly epystles for þe loue þat he had to Alexander/ & for to cause hym to knowe all þe secretes/ he made an epystle 5 here vnder wryten/ þe which he sent to Alexander. And whan Alexander had ouercome þe realme of Perce & set þe moost of them in his prysons/ he sent an epystle to Arystotle whiche foloweth.

2 And] and   3 Arystotle] arystotle

all other erthly criaturs, and his passyng renomme[e] spradde above all nacions and mans re[gi]ou[ns], and subduwed at his hie commaundementez and imperiall imperialitté. And they of Persse, of Ynde, of Arabie, ne generally none other, durst neyther in worde ne in wark withstond hym in no wise. And for the entire, 5 speciall and pryncipall love that he had euer to Alexander, he made many solempne, faire and fructuous [epistles] to the kyng Alexandre, of the which one seweth next folowyng, that he wrote and sende to his lorde Alexandre. For when Alexandre had subdewed 9 hem of Perse, and the grettest | of the lordes of hem had in his [f. 215] prison, he wrote an epistle to Aristotle, this epistle folowyng.

1 renommee] reno*mm*es   2 regiouns] creato*u*rs : *see n.*   5 withstond]
prec. by canc. wis   10 hem] *prec. by canc.* hym   grettest] *form
intended possibly* grettes*tes* : *cross-stroke of* t *foll. by long downstroke as of contract.*
-es *but word is at line-division and at foot of page, and the sign is commonly otiose
in this ms.*

Epistle sent by Alexander to Aristotle

DOctoure of justice and moost noble rectoure, we certifie to thy
grete wysdome that we haue founde in the reame of Perse diuers
men whiche ben of habundant wysdome and reson, and of grete
5 and subtile vndirstandinge. And they weene to haue dominacion
a-bouen alle othir, and to conquere alle landis. For the whiche
cause we purpose to put thaim to deth. Natwithstandinge, sende
us woorde by writinge that thou seemyst best and moost expedient
to doo in the premisses.

Vne espitre que Alixandre enuoya a Aristote   .ij.

Dotteur de justice et tres noble recteur, nous segnifions a ta grant
saigesse que nous auons trouué ou royaume de Peresse plusieurs
homs lesquelz habondent tres grandement en raison et entende-
5 ment soubtil et penestratif. Et cuident par dessus autres auoir
seigneurie et acquerir tous royaumes pour qui nous auons tous
entencion de les mettre tous a mort. Toutes fois, ce que bon t'en
semblera nous vuilles par tes lettres signifier.

b. ⁋ An epystle þat Alexander sent to Arystotle.

DOctour of Justyce & right noble phylosopher we sygnyfy to thy hygh wysdome/ þat we haue sen[e] in þe realme of Perce many men, whiche habounde gretly in reason/ & vnderstondyng/ subtyl & penetratyfe. Wherfore al we haue intencyon to put them to deth. 5
Howbeit as thou semest best sygnyfy vs by thy lettres.

1 Alexander] alexander   3 sene] sent CK

Capitulum iij^m
This epistil Alexandre sende to Aristotle

Doctoure of justice and full noble gouernoure, we do signifie to thy grete wisdome that we have found in the reavme of Percy many men the which habundon gretely in reison full subtill and 5
p[e]n[e]stratyf, and wene to have lordeship above other, and to gete all reavmes. For the which cause we haue full entencion and clere purpos forto put all to deth. But by any wise all that there semeth gode in this mater signifie hus by your lettres with all godely possibull hast. 10

6 penestratyf] prenostratyf   wene] *ins. above canc.* wennen

The answere of the seid pistle

IF thou may chaunge the aire of the erthe and watirs and
ordinaunce of the citees, than fulfill alle thyne desire. And yf thou
may nat doo it, cesse thy-self and refrayne thy desire, but reule
5 and gouerne thaim in thy goodnesse, and exalte thaim in thy
benignitee. And yf thou doo so, I trust by the grace of God that
they shall be alle thy true subgites for to perfourme all thy pleasires
and commaundementes. And for the loue that thei shall haue to
the, thou shall reigne vpon thaim pesiblely in grete victorie. And
10 whan Alexandre had seen this pistle, he founde thrugh the counseill of Aristotle the reame of Perse more obeisaunt to him than
ony othir nacion. |

La responce d'icelle espitre   .iij.

Se tu peus changier et muer l'air de ta terre et l'iaue et l'ordon-
nance des cités, acompli tout [t]on desir et se tu ne le peus fere
cesse toy et n'en fay riens. Maiz les gouuerne en ta bonté et les
5 excaulce en ta begninité. Et se ainsi le faiz i'ay esperance a l'aide
de Dieu que tous seront tes bons subgiés a tous tes bons plaisirs et
commandemens. Et pour l'amour qu'ilz aront en toy tu regneras |
[f. 5] sur eulx paisiblement en grant vittoire. Et quant Alixandre eut
10 veue ceste epistre il fist second le conseil de [Aristotes et] ceulx de
Peresse [furent] plus obeissans a Alixandre que autre nacion.

---

3 acompli] et acomplir F; *so, substantially*, V; acompli R *and, substantially*,
HG. *The different version represented in B.M. Additional MS. 18. 179 reads*
(f. 5) adonc accomplie ton pourpos hardiment, *but the* e *of* accomplie *is written
over an* r   ton] son   9–10 Aristotes et ceulx de Peresse furent] le
conceil de ceulx de Peresse F, ceulx de Perse & furent V, ceux de Perse plus
obeissans H *and, substantially*, R

c. ❡ An epystle þat Arystotle sent to Alexander.

YF thou can/ moeue & chaunge the ayre frome þe erth/ & water/
& þe ordynaunce of thy cytees to accomplysshe thy pleasure. Yf
thou can [not] do it ceas of & | do it not/ but gouerne them in thy   [f. A4]
goodnesse/ and exalt them in benygnyte. And yf thou do thus I   5
hope with the grace of god that they all shall be thy frendes to all
thy good pleasures and commaundementes. And for the loue that
they shall haue in the/ thou shalt peasybly reygne ouer them in
grete vyctory. ❡ And whan Alexander had red this epystle/ he
dyde after his councell/ and they of Perce were more obedyent to   10
hym than to ony other nacyon.

---

2 *No initial woodcut, but* Y *supplied as catch-letter*   can/] *no punct.*

Capitulum iiijᵐ
Thanswere of Aristotle made to Alexandre, vpon the [receite] of this lettre

[A]lexandre, yf thou maist chaunge and meve theire of thy
land, the water and thordenances of citees, and fullfille and ac-   5
complissh all thy desires well, then thou maist be avised, and elles,
cesse of thy surquydous pruyde and vnstaunchable coveitise, but
governe the peple of thyne obeysaunce in benygnité, and enhance
hem with thy bounté. And yf thou thus dowe, I have hope that
by the grace of God that all they shalbe thy trewe subgettes, to   10
all thy gode pleisours and commaundementes. And for the love
that they sholde have [thee] in, thou shalt reigne above hem
peisibully with grete | victorye. And when Alexandre had seen   [f. 215ᵛ]
this answere, he made the peple of Percy more obeisant then any
other nacion, thus doynge by the avise and counseile of Aristotle.   15

3 receite] answere   4 Alexandre] *guide-letter* a *missing*   7 vnstauncha-
ble] *prec. by canc.* vnstable   15 doynge] *prec. by canc.* doyg

[f. 37ᵛ] **The prologue of a docture callid Philipp whiche translated**
p. 73 **this booke in to Latyn**

PHilipp which translated this booke was sonne to Parys and was
right wyse interpretatoure, and vnd[i]rstandinge all langages.
5 Which Philipp seide in this wyse: I haue nat knowen nor redde
nothir temple nor othir place where the philosophers haue accustumed to doo and vndoo all thaire operacions and secreetes, but I
haue sought it, nor I haue herd of no wyse man that had vndirstandinge in the science of philosophye but I haue visited him,
10 vnto such tyme as I had knowledge [of] the Sun which made
Exculapideos. And at the last I fande a solitarye man full of grete
abstinence, and kunnynge in philosophye, wham in right lowly
wyse I besought that he wolde shewe me by writinge the knowlege

---

Le prologue d'un dotteur appellé Philipe qui translata ce
liure en latin   **.iiij.**

Philipe qui translata ce liure fu filz de Paris. Et fu tres saige
entrep[r]eteur et entendeur de toutes langues et dit ainsi: Je n'ay
5 sceu ne lieu ne temple ou les philozophes estoient acoustumés de
faire toutes euures et tous secrés que je n'aie serchié ne n'ay nul
saige homme par qui ie seuce qu'il eut congnoissance des escriptures des philozophes que ie n'aye visité jusques a tant que ie
vins a la congnoissance du souloil laquelle fit Exculapidos, et
10 trouué vn homme solitaire plain de tres grant abstinence et tres
saige en philozophie auquel me humiliay diligemment et sup-
pliay deuotement qu'il me monstrat les escriptures de la congnois-

¶ The prologue of a doctour named Phylyp that translated this
boke in to latyn. d.

PHylyp that translated this boke in to latyn was a chylde of
Parys/ & was a veray wyse interpretour & vnderstander of lan-
guages/ & he sayd thus. I haue not knowen nor seen tyme that the 5
phylosophers haue holpen/ or haue ben acustomed to helpe or to
make all werkes or all secretes but that I haue sought/ nor haue
knowen by no man by whome I knewe that he had knowlegyng
of þe scryptures of Phylosophers/ but I haue vysited hym vnto
þe tyme þat I came to þe knowlege of councell/ þe whiche was 10
Estulapideus/ & a man solytary & of grete abstynence/ and veray
wyse in phylosophy/ to whom I meked me dylygently, requyrynge
hym that he wolde shewe to me the scryptures of the knowlege
of the sonne/ the whiche he gaue vnto me/ with a ryght good

2, 3 in to] into K   5 tyme] *so also* K: *see n.*   6 holpen] holden K
10 councell] *so also substant.* K: *see n.*   11 Estulapideus] *ins. in narrow*
space in small roman print K

Capitulum v^m

The prologue of the doctoure cleped Philip that translated
this boke out of Grece into Latyn : beholde and rede it.

Philip that translated this boke, was borne and norisshed and
fedde in the famous cité and vniuersité of Paris, and was a full and 5
discrete interpretoure, and did [vnderstand] all maner of langage,
that said thus: I have not knawen ne red in the temple where the
philosophres were accustumed to rede to make all werkes and all
secretes, but that I have sought ne founde, no wiseman by whome
I wist that [he] had knowlege of the scripturs of philosophres, but 10
that I have viseted hem, vnto the tyme that I saugh the counsance
of the sonne, the whiche made that connyng philosophre Estula-
pides, where that I founde a man full solutarie, of full grete
abstenence, pleyne and full wise in philosophye. To the whome I
humbled me full diligently, and besought hym full devoutly that 15
he wolde shew me the scripturs and the knowleges of the sonne, the

of the Sun, which thinge he deliured vnto me right gentilly.
Wherynne I founde all that I sought, according to my desire. And
whan I had all myn entent, I went home to my hous, thankinge
and hertily yiving graces and laudes to my Creatoure. And aftir
5 that, at the request of a moost noble kinge, with grete studie and
laboure I translated this booke out of Greeke in to Latyn, whiche
booke was made by the right wyse philosophre Aristotle, whiche

sance du souleil, lequel les me bailla tres voulentiers. Et saiches que
ie trouuay tout qua[n]que ie desiroie et tout ce pour quoy je estoie
alé au dit lieu et tout ce pourquoy ie auoie lonc temps trauaillé.
Et quant ie eus ce que ie auoie tant desiré ie m'en tourne a mon
5 hostel a tres grant joye et en rendi plusieurs graces a mon Creatour,
et depuis a la requeste d[u] tres noble roy en grant estude et en
tresgrant labour ie translaté ce liure de grec en caldee et depuis de
caldé en langue arabique lequel liure fist le tres saige Aristote qui

5 graces] *repeated*   6 du] de FHR de ce V du G

travaulled fore And when that I had that
I had travauled fore or desyred then I went
me home to myn house with full grete ioy
and yolde many thankynges to god my
creatoure And aftr that at the request and
the full the comaundement off the nobul
kyng with grete study and diligent besynes
us I fonith I have translated this boke out
of the literal language off Calde nto Ebrede
out off Ebredre into Greke Out of Greke
nto Arabesk out off Arayeke into latyne
out of latyne nto frenssh and out of franssh
ndr it is translated into oure vendelosigh
vies modevs tonge by yor humble servonte
in this laft yeves and febull age John Churley
dev submyttyng both hym and this his
symple boke to yor fashonable correccion
suportacion And Amende where yor wisdom
and gentlesse anne thynke ther is nede ffer
that Englissh is so boistous and harde
to deplie in all off the curiosite off the
fayre and language off franssh which
Amonge the multitude of this worlde is
moste vendned and desyred the latyne in
his congruytees above all other praysed
and comended this sime which late dam
Aristotles furst studied made and compiled

wyll: | And surely I founde as moche as I desyred/ & all that I [f. A4ᵛ]
had ben about a hole yere/ & wherfore I had longe tyme trauayled.
And I thus hauynge my desyre retorned home with grete ioye/
yeldyng thankes to god my creatour. ⦅ And than at the request
of the moost noble kynge with grete study & labour I translated 5
this boke out of Greke language in to Caldees tongue & syth in to
the speche of Araby. The which boke the moost wyseman Arys-

which he toke hem me with gode will. And witteth well that I founde
that all that I desired, and all that for which I was so comen vnto
that place, and thynge that I had longe | travailled fore. And when [f. 216]
that I had that I had desired, then I went me home to myn hous
with full gret ioy, and yolde many thankynges to God my crea- 5
toure. And after that, at the request and the full hye commaundement of the nobul kyng, with grete study and diligent besynes, as
I kouth, I have translated this boke out of the literal langage of
Caldee into Ebrewe, out of Ebrewe into Greke, out of Greke into
Arabesk, out of [Arabesk] into Latyne, out of Latyne into Frenssh 10
(and out of Franssh now it is translated into oure reude volgaries
moders tonge by your humble servitoure, in his last yeres and
febull age, John Shirley, ever submyttyng both hym and this his
symple warke to your fauourable correccion [and] supportacion:
and amende where your wisdom and gentilesse cane thynke ther 15
is nede, sith that Englissh is soo boistous and harde to applie in
all, after the curiosité of the fayre said langage of Franssh, which
amonge the multitude of this worlde is most renommed and desired, the Latyne in his congruytees above all other preised and
commended), this same which boke Daun Aristotles furst studied, 20

4 desired] travailed fore or desired   10 out of Arabesk] out of
Ebrayeke

answered alle-wey to alle the requestes of Kynge Alixandre, as
more at large ye shall see here-aftir by ordre.

Most gloriouse sonne and right just Emperour, allmighty God
stablissh the to haue knowlege of the wey of trouthe and vertuous
5 disposisions, and yiue the grace to refreyne the from all flesshly
[f. 38] desires and bestialles, and | conferme thy reame to His moost
p. 74 digne seruice and worship. Latinge the wite, moost deere son, that
I haue resseyued thy pistle with worship and reuerence, and haue

8 with] whith, *altered from* which

respondoit touziours a toutes les requestez du roy Alixandre que
plus a plain pourries cy desoubz veoir par ordre.

Cy nous dit aprés :

Tres glorieux filz et tres [iu]stes Empereur, Dieu te conferme en
5 la uoie de congnoissance et les chemins de verité et de vertus, te
vueille demoustrer et te refraigne des desirs charnelz et bestiaux
[f. 5ᵛ] et conferme ton royaume a son | seruice et a son honneur. Saichiés
tres chiers filz, que i'ay receu ton fait reueraument et honnourable-

4 iustes] vistes F justes R *and, substant.* HVG; *cf.* vigle *for* rigle 270/7
8 fait] *ins. above*

totle made/ whiche answered alwayes to all the requestes of kynge
Alexandre/ as more playnly appereth in this present boke.

b. ❡ An epystle sent to kyng Alexandre by Arystotle.

RYght glorious sone and ryghtwyse/ god conserue the in the
walke of knowlegyng the wayes of trouthe & vertues/ and with- 5
drawe thy carnall and beestly desyres/ & conferme [thy] realme
to his seruyce/ & to thy honour. Letynge the wyte deere sone þat
I haue receyued thyn epystle reuerently & honourably as it

3 b.] *sigil shared with section bearing similar title, on p. 261 above*   6 thy]
his CK

made, and compiled | at the request of Alexandre the Grete, for [f. 216ᵛ]
naturall disciplyne of hem that list to here and rede, as it sheweth
filowyng by the ordre of the chapitours.

Capitulum vjᵐ

Aristotle nowe thus writeth to that glorious Prince Alex- 5
andre

Full glorious sonne and full avised emperoure invyncibull,
God conferme the in the waye of counsance, and the path of trouth
and of vertuwes. I woll shew the and restreyn the from flesshly
and bestely desires, and conferme thyne hie empire, thy riale 10
reavmes and larges landes and provynces to His service and
worship. Witte thou, dere sonne, that I have receyved thy lettres
and thy doynges reuerently an honourabully as it apperteyneth,

clierly vndirstande the grete desire that thou hast that I might
dayely be in propre persoone in thy noble presence, hauing the
grete meruaile how I may so longe absent me from the, repreeuing
me, saying I reke litle of alle thy besinesse. For the whiche cause I
5 haue disposed me in all goodly hast to make a booke the whiche
shall conteyne all my werkes, to the excuse of myn absence and
defautes, which schall be a moost certeyn reule and doctrine to
alle thy needys as well as though I were there present. Right diere
sonne, thou shuldist nat put me to blame. For thou knowyst well
10 that I wold fayne come to the, alle excusacions laid aparte, sauf
that I am so greef and heuy with age and so grete feblenes of my
persoone, that I in no wyse may come to the. And for suche thinges
as thou hast all-wey desired to knowe, thei ben suche secreetes
that mannys wytte with grete peyne may conceyue nor compre-
15 hende thaim. How may they than in the hert of a mortall man be
vndirstande, which thinge aught nat to be knowen nor publissht,

---

ment si comme il appartient et ay plainement entendu le grant
desir que tu as que ie feusse personnelment auecques toy, et te
merueilles comment ie puis tant moy tenir d'aller par deuers toy.
Et si me repreues moult et dis qu'il me chault pou de tes besougnes.
5 Et pour ceste cause i'ay ordonné et me suis hasté de fere vn liure
pour toy lequel pesera et contiendra toutes mes euures et suplira
mon obstance et mes deffaux et te sera [r]igle et dottrine a toutes
les choses que tu vouldras et lesquelles ie te mostreroie sy ie
yestoie present et auecques toy. Treschier filz, tu ne me dois
10 blasmer ne reprendre car tu ses bien que ie ne lairoie pour nulle
chose du monde que ie ne venisse a toy sy n'estoit ce que ie suis
tres grief et pesant d'aage et en grant foiblece de ma personne,
pour quoy nullement ie ne puis aller a toy. Et saichez que ce que
tu m'as demandé et que tu desires tant santir sont tieulx secrés

---

7 obstance] absence HV abscence R   rigle] vigle F rigle V regle RH reigle
G; *cf.* vistes *for* iustes *268/4*   11 ie suis] *two minims, smaller than usual,*
between ie *and* suis: *possibly mere filler for gap accidentally left*

apperteyneth/ and playnly haue vnderstande the grete desyre that
þu hast that I were personally with the. Meruaylyng how I can
absteyne me fro the. Reprouynge me of þat I care but lytel for
thy besynesses. For þe which cause I haue ordeyned & hasted me
to make a boke for the/ the which shall weye & conteyne all my   5
werkes/ supplyenge myn absence & defautes/ and shall be to the
a ryght certayne rule & doctryne in all thynges þat thou wyllest.
The whiche I will shew as I were presently with the. Dere son
thou ought not to repreue nor blame me/ for thou knowest well   9
þat for no thyng of | the worlde/ but that I wolde go to the/ and yf   [f. B1]
were not þat I am so sore greued/ and laden with aege & weykenesse
of my persone/ wherby in no wyse I can go to the. And wyte thou/
that þe thynge which thou hast demaunded of me/ and that thou
so moche desyrest to knowe & haue is þe secretes that nature
humaynes thought scantly can compryse nor susteyne. How than   15
may in the hert of mortall man be wryten or vnderstande that
thynge that he ought not to knowe. And that thyng that is not

6 defautes/] defautes.   11 were] it were K

---

and pleynly vnderstond the grete desire that thou haste that I shold
be personelment with the, and that thou merveilest the gretely
that I may kepe me so longe fro the. Of the which reprevest me
much, and seist that I rech but litell of thy grete warkes. And
therfore I hast me, and purpos to make a boke for the, the which   5
shalbe more worthy to the [than] all myn other warkes or con-
[f]ectes, besechyng the that notwithstondyng my defautes of
vnkunnyng or of absence, that thou may take my boke and | my   [f. 217]
gode will in gree. For it shalbe rule and right doctryne lovable
to thee of all thynges that thou most aye desirest, the which shall   10
opunly and pleynly be shewed to thee as that I were ever present
with the. Right dere and glorious Kyng and sone, thou shalt not
blame me ne answere, for thou wost well that I wolde for no
worldely thyng have been so longe fro thee, but that I wolde have
comen to the, ne had been that I am in grete age, and feble of my   15
person, for the which I may in no wise com to the. And witte it
well, that [thou] ha[st] asked of [m]e, and that desirest all forto

3 me²] *repeated*   6 to] *ins. above canc.* for   6–7 confectes] con-
sectes   17 thou hast asked of me] I have asked of the

nor it is nat my parte to declare it. Neuerthelesse, I am bounde by
right and dutie to answere to thy demaundes. And also thou art
bounde by thy wysdome that thou shall neuermore aske more than
is conteyned in this booke. For yf thou reede it diligentlye, and
5 cleerly vndirstande and knowe all that is comprehendid therynne,
withoute any doute thou shall haue al thy desire. For God hath
yiven the suche grace of vndirstandinge, with notable wytt and
discrecion, and also through the doctrine that I haue yiuen the
[f. 38ᵛ] before this tyme, | that by thy-self thou maist vndirstande and
p. 75 knowe all the perfeccion of thyn entent. For the grete and feruent
11 desire that thou shalt haue, will open the the weye forto come to
thy purpose, and shall guyde to the effectuell conclusion of thy
desire. And the cause why that I open the my secreetes by derke
exaumples and figures is this: I dreede that in tyme comyng this

---

que humaine pensee a grant poine les pourroit aprandre ne soub-
tenir: comment donc peut il ou cuer d'omme mortel estre de-
primés ne entendu ce qui n'a-partient assauoir ne qui ne soit licite
ne conuenable a traitier? Toutes fois, ie suis tenus par droit deuer
5 de respondre ad ce que tu me demandes. Et auxi tu es tenus par
saigesse que tu ne me demandes jamais nulle chose fors ce qui
est contenu en ce liure. Sans nulle doubte tu auras ce que tu as
desirés. Car Dieu te donne telle grace, tel entendement et sub-
tillece de grant engin et de sience et auxi par la dottrine que ie
10 t'ay autres fois donnée, que par toy mesmes pourras conceuoir et
entendre tout ce que tu desires et demandes et le sauoir. Car le
desir de la grant voulenté que tu yas te ouura la voie que tu auras
[f. 6] ton propos et te merra | a l'aide de Dieu a la fin que tu desires. Et
saiches que la cause par qui ie te reuelle mon secret finiatiuement
15 et vng petit obstinnament et que ie te baille par obscurs exemples

2–3 deprimés] deprimez HR de exprimer V   4–5 par droit deuer de res-
pondre] par droit deuoir de respondre H par droit deuoir respondre R de
droit de respondre V par droit devuoir de respondre G   14 finiatiuement]
see n.; figuraument R, figuratiuement HVG   15 obstinnament] obscure-
ment HRVG

behouefull nor couenable to be spoken of. Howbeit I am bounde by
veray duety to answere to that/ that thou demaundest. I shall neuer
other thynge shewe the/ but that whiche is wryten in this boke.
For yf thou rede it dylygently/ and vnderstande it playnly/ and
that thou mayst knowe þat is conteyned in it/ without doubt thou 5
shalt haue all that that thou desyrest. For god shall gyue þe suche
grace/ suche vnderstandynge/ and subtylte of grete wyt and scyence/
and also by the doctryne þat I haue gyuen the afore tyme/ that by
thy selfe thou mayst knowe & conceyue that whiche thou desyrest.
And þe cause why that I haue opened and related my secretes 10
fyguratyuely & somewhat derkly/ & that I haue put obscure
examples/ and by fygures/ is that I doubt/ & feare moche that this

---

1 couenable] conuenient K

---

knowe, wit and fele, been such secretes that mans witte vnneth
without grete payne may knawe, lerne, ne comprehend, ne susteine. How may hit then in the hert of mortall man be conceived
neyther vnderstonden such thyng as is not couenable ne apper-
tynent to be so knowe, and that it is not lefull forto trete of? And 5
yit I am by the right of God beholden to that thou askest of me. And
also thou art all beholden so much by wisdom that thou demaunde
me never no thynge but that at is conteined in this boke. And with-
out doute | then shalt thou have that at thou hast desired. And [f. 217ᵛ]
graunte the such grace, such vnderstondyng, and such engynous 10
subtilité and science also and by the techyng that tofore this I have
taght the, that by thy self thou may conceyve and vnderstond all
that at thou desirest and askest forto witte and knowe. And know
that wherfore that nowe I shew to the the my secret fynatively and
a litill obstynatly, and that I woll by dirk ensignes and by figures, 15

---

1 witte] witte shall   6 And] *prec. by* And also thou art beholden to that
thou askest of me.   11 science also] *see n.*   14 nowe] nowe that
15 by dirk] -e *at end of* bye *crossed through*

booke might come to the handys of vntrue men, and in the power
of thaim that ben of ill disposicion, which shuld vndirstande and
knowe my secreetes, to the whiche they ben vnworthy. Wherfore,
truly, I doute me that I haue trespaced ayenst the will and pleasire
5 of God, for to open and declare to the His noble secreetes. Nat-
withstanding, by the pleasire of His mooste digne grace I shall
declare the this thinge at this tyme, lik as here-before He hath
declared bothe to the and to me. Lating the wite, yf thou discouere
and open theise secreetes which aught to be kept priuee, thou shalt
10 hastely haue many ywell fortunes, and thou shall nat be sure of
the grete myscheeuys that may growe to the-warde, whiche God
defende. And aftir alle this, haue in thy remembraunce this noble
and profitable doctrine, whiche I make the redy and intende to
expounde to the, and it shall be thi grete solace and mirroure of
15 saluacion.

RIght deere sonne, euery kinge most haue needes iiij thinges for
to susteyne him-self and his reigne. But he may nat well haue

---

et par figures si est car ie doubte qu'i-cilz ne vienne au mains des
juuenceaux et a la puissance des arrogans et des mauuais et pour-
roient sauoir les grans secrés de Dieu. Et Dieu scet bien qu'il n'en
est mie dignes. Certes je fais doubte que ie n'entrepasse la vou-
5 lenté et la grace de Dieu pour toy descouurir et reueller ses secrés,
mais saiches que par la voulenté de Dieu te reueleré et discipré
ceste chose ainsi comme il a esté autres fois de Dieu reuellé a
toy et a moy. Saiches donc tres chiers filz ie te descripré les choses
qui sont a seler et, les secrés reuellez, tu auras asses de mauuaises
10 fortunes et si ne pourras estre seur des grans maulx qui te sont a
auenir. Mais Dieu tout puissant vueille garder toy et moy de telles
choses et de toutes euures deshonnestes. Aprés toutes ses choses
ayes en memoire ce noble et proufitable enseignement que ie t'ay
aparaillé et entens a exposer et ton noble cuer enfermer, et ce sera
15 ton grant soulas et mi[r]ouer de salut. Il conuient, tres chier filz,
que chascun roy ait deux choses qui soubstiennent lui et son
royaume. Mais il ne les peult fermement gouuerner se n'est quant

6 reueleré et discipré] reuelle et desceure R *and, substant.* HVG
15 mirouer] misouer F miroueur H mireur R mirouer VG

boke sholde come to the handes of infect persones/ & in the power
of arrogant & euyll folkes/ which myght knowe þe secretes of
god. And god knoweth wel that they be not worthy. Certaynly I
make grete doubt/ þat I in this trespace not þe wyll and þe grace
of god. I do relate & dyscouer this thynge/ as it hath ben reuelate 5
of god (or now) vnto [m]e. Wyte thou then ryght dere sone that I
haue dyscouered to þe/ the | thynges that ben to be hyd. And yf [f. B1ᵛ]
thou dyscouer these secretes/ thou shalt haue shortly euyl fortunes/
and mayst not be sure frome grete harmes that shall be comynge
towarde the. But almyghty god kepe the & me from suche thynges/ 10
& from all dyshonest thynges. And after all these thynges haue in
thy mynde this noble & prouffytable doctryne/ þat I make redy
to the/ & intende to expose thy noble hert/ to informe it to thy
grete solace/ as myrour of helth yf thou wylt apply þe therto.
Moost dere sone it behoueth euery kyng to haue [t]wo thynges to 15
susteyne hym & his royalme. But he maye not stedfastely haue

1 to] into K   6 me] þe C (and, substant., K)   7 ben] be K (regular
substitution, not indicated hereafter)   15 two] owo C .ij. K

---

it is for I doute me that they ne com not to the handes of yonge
folkes and the puissance of aragans and of yvel [that] may not
knowe the grete secretes of God. For God knoweth well thay
be not worthy. Certes, I doute me that I entre not in to the will
of God and His grace, forto discover to the, and shew the, His 5
secretes. Bot witte thou well that by the will of [God], I renovell
and discouer to the tho thynges that been helde an-kepe, and
discouer the secrete thynges. For thou shalt have ynowe of yvell
fortunes, and thou may not be sure of grete aduersitees and
yvelles that been comyng to the. But God almyghty so kepe the 10
and me of such thynges, and of all other dishonestees. After all
thees thynges, have in mynde this noble techyng that I have taght
the, and intende yit forto tech the, and thy noble hert confourme
it, the which shalbe to | the grete solas and hele. It behoveth, dere [f. 218]
sonne, that every kynge have ij thynges that shall sustene hym 15
and his reavme. But he may not fermely governe hem and he that

8 discouer] to discouer   14 to] repeated

thaim but whan he is obeied of his subgites, and that the subgites
egally and holl with oon assent ben obeisaunt to the as to thaire
lord. For thrugh the disobeisaunce of the subgites is the might and
4 power of the prince greetly lessid and weyked. And yf the subgites
[f. 39] reigne | the gouernoure may no thinge doo. And I shall shewe the
p. 76 cause why the subgites ben moost meeuid in thaire corage to
obeye thair lord. There is ij causes. Oon is inwarde and a-nothir is
outward. And as for that outward, is whan the prince dispendith
wisely his richesse amonge his subgites, rewardinge euery man as
10 he is worthy. And therwith the kinge most haue a wyle wherof I
shall make mencion hereaftir in the chapter of the vices and aides,
that is to wite, the kynge aught to laboure to haue the hertes of
his subgites by good operacions. And this is the first fundacion of
his welfare which may be doon ij weyes, oon outward and the

---

le gouuerneur est auec ceulz qu'i doit gouuerner, et celui qui resne
est obeys des subgiés et que les subgiés soient egaument du courage et par vne mesme forme obeisans au seignieur. Car par la
desobeissance des subgiés est moult afebliee la puissance du
5 seignieur. Et ce les [subgiés] regnent, le gouuerneur ne peut riens
fere et ie te monstreray la cause pour quoy les subgiés sont emus
et encouragés d'obair a leur seignieur. Il [s]ont ij. choses, l'une
est dedans, l'autre est dehors, et ie t'ay nagueres desclairié celle
[f. 6ᵛ] de hors, c'est assauoir quant le seignieur dispence | saigement de
10 ses richesses a ses subgiez. Et qu'il ait euurés eu eulx en largesse
en donnant a chascun selon ce qui sera dignez et auecques ce il
conuient que le roy ait vne cautelle de laquelle ie feray mencion cy
desoubz ou chapistre des vices et des aides. C'est assauoir que le
roy se doit efforcier d'auoir les cuers de ses subgiés par bonnes
15 euures. Et ce cy est le premier degré et fondement de son fait et
ce cy se peut faire par ij. choses, c'est assauoir l'une dedans et

5 ce les subgiés] celles *poss. for* ce iceles F se les subgez R *and, substantially,* HV   7 sont] font F

it/ but yf he haue good & grete gouernaunce of them that ought to
gouerne. And he þat reygneth so is obeyed of his subgectes. And
his subgectes egally with one courage/ & by one selfe forme shalbe
obedyent to þe lorde. For by þe dysobedyence of þe subgectes
þe power of þe lorde is gretly feblysshed. And yf þe subgectes 5
reygne/ þe gouernaunce may nothyng do. And I shall shewe the/
þe cause wherfore þe subgectes ben styred & couraged to obey
theyr lorde. Two thynges ther is. The one is outwarde & þe other
inwarde. It is not longe syth I declared to the þat that is outwarde.
That is to wyte/ whan þe lorde spendeth wysely his rychesse 10
amonge his subgectes/ and þat he in them worke lyberalyte &
þat he gyue to echone as they be worthy. And therwith þe kynge
behoueth to haue a wyle/ wherof I shall make mencyon in þe
chapytre of vyces & helpes. That is to wyte that þe kynge ought
to enforce hym to get þe hertes of his subgectes by good werkes. 15
And this is þe fyrst degre & foundacyon in doyng of his dedes by

3 egally] equally K (*this regular substitution, together with* equal *for* egal,
not indicated hereafter)   4 to] vnto K   8 lorde. Two] lorde. two
12 echone] eche one K

---

is above is obeyd of his subgettes, and that his subgittes be egaly
of will and corage, and by one same fourme, obeisant to theire
lorde [What that the subgettes governe, the lorde ne can no
thynge dowe. And I shal shew to the that cause wherefore the
subgettes been moeved in theire corages to been obeisant to theire 5
lorde.] They be two thynges, that one is withynne, that other
is without. And I have noght longe gone declared to the that
without, that is to saye, when the lorde dispendeth wisely of his
ricchesse till his subgittes, and that he have also anenst them
largesse in gyvyng to everich one after his desert and worthy[nes]. 10
And herwithal hit behoveth to have a cautele of the which I shal
make mynde here-after in the chapitre of vices and of aides, that
is to saye, that the kyng shall enforce hym forto have the hartes of
his sugettes by gode werkes. And this is the first degree and
grounde of his warke. And that may he dowe by two thynges, that 15

othir inward. That is outward, that the kinge shall kepe and
mayteyne justice aftir the possessions and richesses of his [s]ub-
gites and that he be piteefull and mercyfull. The cause inwarde
is that he worship and haue in his tendre recommendacion the
5 grete clerkes, philosophres and wyse men. For oure Lord God hath
yiven His noble science in-to thaire disposicion. And I recommend
the this secret principally, with many othir whiche thou shalt finde
hereaftir in this book, wherynne is conteyned by grete science and
doctrine the finall conclusion of the principall purpose. For aftir
10 that thou hast vndirstand the significacions of the woordys, and the
derknes of the ensaumples, than shalt thou haue hooly and per-
fitelye alle thy desires. Beseching oure Lord moost gloriouse and
moost souerayne Kynge, that He will enlumyne and endue thi
reson and vndirstandinge, so that thou may clierly conceyue the

2–3 subgites] bubgit*es*   7 secret] secret*es*

l'autre dehors. La cause dehors est que le roy face et maintienne
justice selon les pocessions et richeces de ses subgiés et qu'il soit
pitieux et misericors. La cause de-dans si est que les grans philosophes, clers et saiges il honnoure et les ait pour recommandees.
5 Car Dieu leur a commandé la sience. Et ie te recommande cestui
secret principalment auecques plusieurs autres que tu trouueras
en plusieurs et diuers chapistres de ce liure, que tu trouueras en
iceulx tres grande sience et dottrine et aux quelz est contenue la
cause finable pour qui tu trouueras la cause de ton principal
10 propos. Car quant tu auras aperceu lez significacions des paroles
de l'oscurté des exemples, lors auras plainement et parfaittement
ce que tu desires. Cy pry a Dieu, tres saiges et tres glorieux roy,
qu'il vueille enluminer ta raison et ton entendement affin que tu
puisses et saiches aperceuoir les secrés de ceste sience et que en

.ij. thynges. One inward & þe other outwarde. The cause out-
warde is þat þe kyn|ge do/ & mayntene Justyce/ [over] þe pos- [f. B2]
sessyons & rychesses of his subgectes/ & þat he be pyteous &
mercyfull. The cause inwarde is þat he honoure grete lerned men/
& þat he haue them for recommended. For god hath recommended 5
them theyr scyence. And I recommende þe this secrete pryncypally
with dyuers other/ whiche thou shalt fynde in other chapytres of
this boke/ wherein thou shalt fynde grete wysdome & doctrine
& þe content of þe fynal cause wherby thou shalt fynde thy pryncypall purpose. For in it thou shalte lerne þe sygnyfycacyons of 10
þe wordes/ & obscurytees of þe examples. Than thou shalt playnly
& perfytely haue that/ þat thou desyrest. Wherfore pray to god
moost wyse & gloryous kynge þat he wyll lyghten thy reason &
vnderstandynge to thende þat thou mayst knowe & perceyue þe
secretes of this scyence. And in þe same thou mayst be myn heyre 15

3 rychesses] riches K (*a regular substitution, which is not indicated hereafter*)
10–11 sygnyfycacyons of þe wordes/ &] sygnyfycacyons/ of þe wordes & C
significations of the wordes, and K   14 thende] the ende K

is to say, that oone withynne, that other without. The cause without is that the kynge dowe and mayntene justice after the possessions and the richesses of his subgittes, and that he be pitous
and mercifull. The cause withynne is this, that the grete philo- 4
sophres, clerkes | and wise, that he honoure hem, and to have hem [f. 218ᵛ]
specially for recommended, for God hath sent hem theire science.
And I recom[m]aunde to the, Alexandre, this secrete principally,
with many other that thou shalt fynde her-after in many dyuers
other chapitres here folowyng in this boke, in the which thou shalt
fynde grete science and doctryne, and in the which is conteyned 10
the cause fynable for which thou shalt fynde the cause of the
pryncipall purpos. For when thou hast perceyued the significacions of the wordes of the derkenes of the ensaumples, then shalt
thou pleynly and perfitely [have] that at thou desires, praying
God the wise and the most souerain Lorde and Kynge, that He 15
will enlumyne thy reison and thyne vnderstondyng to that ende
that thou may and can apperceyve the secrete of this science, and

7 recommaunde] recommaunde   14 desires] *prec. by canc.* desartes

secreetes of this science, and that thou may be myn heire and
successour.

Of the maner of kinges touchinge largesse |

[f. 39ᵛ]   THere is iiij diuersitees, he that is large to him-self and large to
p. 77 his subgites, and a kynge that is skars to him-self and large to his
6 subgites, and there is a kinge that is large to him-self and skars to
his subgites, and som kynge is [skars] bothe to him-self and to his
subgites. The Italiens seyn there is no vice in that kynge that is
skars to him-self and large to his subgites. The Persiens seyn the
10 contrarie, for he that is skars to him-self and to his subgites, his

3] *wording of chapter-heading perh. intended to be repeated as opening words of
body of chapter*

---

ycelle tu puisses estre mon hoir et mon seul successeur, et si te
vueille ottroyer icellui Dieu qui ces richesses alargist et donne
abondanment a la vie des saiges et aux estudians donne congnoissance de ce qui est fort et d'estre dificile a nature, et sens lequel
5 riens ne peut estre fait.

De la maniere des roys touchant largesse   .v.

Il sont quatre manierez de roys. Il est roy qui larges est a soy et
larges a ses subgiés. Et est roy qui est auers a soy et larges a ses
[f. 7] subgés. Et est roy qui est larges a | soy et auers a ses subgiés. Et
10 est roy qui est auers a soy et auers a ses subgiés. Les Ytaliens dient
qu'il n'est nul vice ou roy qui est auers a soy et larges a ses subgiés.
Les Judeans dient que le roy est bon qui est auers a soy et ses
subgiés. Les Perssiens dient tout le contraire et tiennent cest
oppinion, que le roy ne vault riens qui n'est larges a soy et a ses
15 subgiés. Mais entre tous les roys dessus diz celui est le pire et ne
doit estre riens prisiés qui n'est larges a soy et a ses sugiés. Car s'il

& successour/ & þat he wyl graunt þe largenesse of goodes/ to gyue
haboundaunce to þe lyuyng of wyse men & studyentes/ with grace
to knowe þat whiche is dyfficyle/ & without the same nothyng can
be done.

e ❡ Of þe maner of kynges as touchyng largesse.   5

THere be .iiij. maner of kynges. There is a kynge þat is lyberall
to hym selfe/ & lyberall to his subgectes. There is a kynge þat is
lyberall to hym selfe & hauyng to his subgectes. The Ytalyens say
þat it is no vyce to a kynge þat is hauynge to hymselfe/ & lyberal to
his subgectes. The Indyens say þat þe kyng is good þat is hauyng to 10
hymself/ & to his subgectes. The Percyens say þe contrary/ & ben of
opynyon þat þe kyng is not worthy þat is not large to hymselfe &
hauyng to his subgectes. But among | all þe kynges aboue sayd he [f. B2ᵛ]
is the worst/ & ought in no thynge to be praysed þat is not liberall

13 aboue sayd] abouesayde K

---

that in the same thou may be myne heire and my soole succes-
soure. And that [graunt thee that] God That enlargiseth His
ricches, and giveth habundantly to the wise and to the scolers
and the studiantes konnyng and knawlege to that that is stronge
and harde to nature and witte, without Whiche no thynge may 5
be done.

Capitulum vijᵐ

Of the maner of kynges of their largesse

[O]f kynges ther be thre maners. First, ther is a kynge that is 9
large to hym-self and to his subgettes. And there | is a kynge that [f. 219]
is large to hym-self and averous to his subgettes. And there is a
kynge that is averous to hym-self and to his subgettes. The Ytaliens
saye it is no vice to a kynge that is auerous to hym-self and to his
subgettes. The Parcians saye all the contrarie, and holden this
opynion, that the kynge will not acheve, that is not large to hym- 15
self and to his subgettes. But yitte amonge all thees iij kynges
here-aboue spoken of, is the worst and lest worthy forto be preised,

9 Of] guide-letter o missing

reame shall soon be destrued. Wherfor we most curiously enquere
of the vertues and vices before seid, and declare what thinge is
largesse, and what thinge is auarice, and wherynne is the erroure of
largesse, and what mischeeuys may enswe for faute of largesse.
5 It is to be knowen that alle thinge that is out of meene is reproue-
able. And it is a greet thinge to kepe well largesse, and as litle thinge
to passe it. And it is light to be couetous and foule-largesse. Than
yf thou will haue largesse considre thyne owne power, and the tyme
of neede, and the merites. Than aughtyst thou to giue aftir thy
10 power, mesurablely, to thaim that ben worthy and hauen neede.
For he that yiueth othir-wise he passeth the reule of largesse. And
he that yiveth his good to him that hath noo neede, he aught to
haue no laude therfore. And all that is yiuen to thaim that ben

6 as] *perh.* a *intended*   7 foule-largesse] *poss. slip for* foule large, *but cf.*
283b/11 and 284a/10 and 13: see n.

---

estoit auers a soy et a ses subgiés, son royaume seroit tous destruis.
Il nous conuient doncques soubtiuement ancquerir des vertus et
des vices dessus diz et monstrer quelle chose est largesse et quelle
chose est auarice, et en quoy est la difiction de largece et que[lz]
5 ma[u]l[x] s'en ensuiuent de non auoir largece. Il est clere chose que
les qualités sont a reprouuer quant elles se alongent du moien, et
sauons bien qu'il est forte chose de garder largesce et legiere chose
de la trespasser, et est a chascun legiere chose d'estre auaricieux et
folz larges. Se tu vieulx doncques acquerir largesce, regarde et
10 considere ton pouoir et le temps de la neccessité et la merite des
hommes. Tu doiz doncques donner selon ton pouoir par mesure a
ceulz qui en ont neccessité et qui en sont dignes. Car qui donne
autrement il peche et trespasse la rieulle de largesse, et auxi qui
donne ses biens a celui qui n'a nulle neccessité il n'en acquiert nulle
15 louange, et de tout ce que l'en donne a ceulz qui n'en sont pas dignes

2 anquerir] enquerir HRV   4 difiction] lerreur HRV *and, substant.,* G
5 clere] *both preceded and followed by cancelled* clere   maulx s'en ensuiuent]
mal sen en suiuent F mal sensuit RHV *and, substant.,* G   9 *outer margin:*
nota per Shirley   10 merite] *followed by a stop, with, apparently, an*
attempt to erase it

to hym selfe & to his subgectis. For he þat is hauynge to hym
selfe & to his subgectis/ his realme shall be clene destroyed. Than
it behoueth vs to enquere of þe vertues & vyces abouesayd/ &
to shew what thyng largesse is/ & wherin the errour of largesse
lyeth/ & what harmes come for lacke of largesse. It is euydent that   5
the qualytees ben to be reproued whan they go fro þe meane/ & be
auarycyous [or] folysshe lyberall. But yf thou wyll enquere or seke
largesse/ regarde & consyder thy power/ and þe tyme of the neces-
syte/ & þe merytes of men. And than thou aught to gyue as thy
power wyll (by measure) to them þat haue nede/ & be worthy   10
of it. For he þat gyueth other wyse he breketh þe rule of largesse &
synneth. And he that gyueth his goodes to hym that hath no nede/
he getteth no thankes. And al þat he gyueth to them þat be not

---

2 shall be] shalbe K *(regular substitution, not indicated hereafter)*   4 wherin]
line division between wher *and* in C wherin K   6 fro] from K
7 auarycyous or folysshe] auarycyous ꝛ folysshe C auaricious, foolishe K
9 aught] oughest K   12 synneth.] *no punct.*

---

he that is not large to hym-self ne to his subgettes. For yf he were
avarous to hym-self and also to his revme, he and hys lande
sholde sone be destroyd. Then it behoveth hus sotelment to enquere of the verteus and vices here-aboue saide, and expressely
to shewe what thynge is largesse and what thynge is avarice, and   5
in what thynge is the diffinyssion of largesse, and eke what yvell
foloweth yf the kynge hath no largesse. It is clere maters that the
qualitees therof been to be repreved, that when they drawe alonge
the moyens. And yitte we wot well that it is a stronge thynge to
kepe largesse, and light thynge to passe it. And it is a light thynge   10
for every man forto be avaricious and foole-largesse. Yf thou
wilt then what is largesse honest, | take hede and consider thy   [f. 219ᵛ]
poiar by mesure, and the tyme of the necessité, and the desart
that it shalbe given to. Then shalt thou gife after thy power and by
grete discrecioun to hem that haue nede [and that be worthy of   15
your giftes. For who that giveth in other wise, he dothe wrong and
breketh the reules of largesse, and he that giveth his godes to hem

---

7 foloweth] ol *in ligature together, inserted in narrow space over canc. letter,*
apparently a   11 foole-largesse] *cf. 282a/7, 284a/10: see n.*   15–285b/1 and
that . . . acquireth] it requireth: *see n.*

vnworthy is lost. And he that dispendith his goodis out of reason and mesure, he shall soone come to the bitter cost of pouertee, whiche is likenyd vnto him that yiueth victorie vnto his enmyes vpon himself. The kynge [that] yiueth his good to them that ben
5 worthy and in tyme of neede, he shall reigne in grete prosperitee, and his commaundementes shall be fulfilled. And the kynge that
[f. 40] dispendith the goodes of his | reame out of reson and yiveth theym
p. 78 to thaim that ben vnworthy and haue no neede, suche a kinge shall destrue both his peeple and his land and he is nat worthy to reigne,
10 for he is called foule largesse. The name of couetyse is foule in a kinge, and bycometh right ylle to the magestee roiall. Than yf a kynge will reigne worshipfully, he may haue noon of theise ij vices, that is to sey that he be nat foule largesse nor couetouse. And yf the kyng will haue good counseile, he most diligently pur-
15 veye him of a man of wytte and discrecion and politique, to whom he shall committe the reule of his estate and weele of his reame, and the gouernaunce of the richesse of his land and how thei aught to be dispendid.

4 The kynge that] That the kynge

---

est perdu. Et qui despent ses biens oultre mesure il viendra toust ou tres amer riuaige de poureté, et est ainsi comme celui qui donne sur lui vittoire a ses annemis. Qui donne donc de ses biens en temps de neccessité a ceulz qui en ont besoing, tel roy est larges a soy et a ses
5 subgiés et vennra son royaume a grande perfeccion et prosperité, et
[f. 7ᵛ] sez commandemens seront acomplis. Et qui despent les | biens de son royaume sans ordre, et donne a ceulx qui n'en sont pas dignes et qu'il n'en ont nul besoing, tel roy destruit son peuple et la chose publicque et son royaume, et n'est pas dignes de regner.
10 Car il est appellé foulz larges. Et le non d'auarice e[s]t trop lait au roy et auient trop mal a la royalle maiesté. Donc se le roy veult regner honnourablement il conuient qu'il n'ait ne l'un ne l'autre de ses .ij. vices, c'est assauoir qu'il ne soit folz larges ne auaricieux. Et ce le roy se vieult conseillier, il ce doit pourueoir en tres grande
15 diligence d'un saige homme lequel soit esleu entre plusieurs autres auquel il commette tout son fait et soit de son royaume et ait le gouuernement des richesses de son royaume, comment elles se doiuent dispenser.

10 est²] et F est HRV est trop infame et G: *cf. 310b/6*   14 se] *ins. above line*

worthy/ is lost. And he þat spendeth his goodes outragyously/ shall
soone come to þe wylde brymmes of pouerte/ & is lyke hym þat
gyueth victory to his enemyes ouer hym. But a kynge þat gyueth
his goodes mesurably to them þat haue nede/ is lyberall to hym
selfe and his subgectes. And his realme shal come to grete pros- 5
peryte/ & his commaundement shalbe fulfylled. And he þat
spendeth þe goodes of his realme without ordre/ & gyueth to them
þat be not worthy/ & to them þat haue no nede/ such a kynge
destroyeth his people/ & þe comyn welthe/ & is not worthy to
reygne as a kyng. And þe name of auaryce is an ouer foule name 10
to a kyng/ & to moche harme cometh to his regall mageste. Therfore yf a kyng wyl reygne honourably/ hym behoueth not to haue
þe one nor the other of these vyces/ þat is to wyte/ that | he be not [f. B3]
to lyberall/ nor to coueytous. And yf þe kyng wyl be counceyled/
he ought with grete dylygence to pouruey hym of a wyse man/ 15
whiche shall be chosen amonge all other/ to whome he shall
commyt his doynges of þe realme/ & the gouernaunce of the
rychesses of the same as they ought to be spent.

    5 and¹] and to K   subgectes.] *no punct.*

---

that have no nede ac]quireth no preisyng. And of that, all men
give to such that be not worthy, that is laste. And who that dispendeth his godes ouer mesure, he shall come anone to pouerty.
For it fareth by hym as it doth by a capitaigne that wolde give his
enemye victorie. And who that giveth his gode in tyme of neces- 5
sitee to hem that haue nede, such a kynge is large to hym and to
his subgettes, and his reavme shall soo encresse to grete perfeccion
and prosperité, and his commaundementes shalbe fulfilled. And
he that dispendeth the godes of his reavme without mesure and
ordre, and giveth largely to hem that be not worthy, or that have 10
no nede, that kynge destroyeth his peple and his reavme, and all
the gode ensaumple to other, and is not worthy to reigne, for he
is called foole large. And the name of auarice is full yvell and
foule. And yf the kynge will counseile hym, he sholde purvey
hym of full grete diligence of a full profitable man, the which may 15
be chosen amonges | many other, to whome he shall committe [f. 220]
and gife power of his reavme how to dispende it.

    2 laste] *intended form poss.* loste, *but cf. warldes 303/15*   10 or] *prec. by*
canc. ot   11 that kynge] that the kynge   14 he] *prec. by canc.* s

Of largesse and couetise, and othir vertues and vices

KYng Alexandre, right deere sonne, I telle the certainlye, yf
a kinge dispende more than his land may bere, he most needys
enclyne to foule largesse and couetise. Suche a kinge withoute
5 doute shall be destroied. But yf a kinge enclyne him-self to largesse,
he shall reigne in perpetuell glorye, and this is to vndirstand that,
whan a kinge restreineth him from takinge the goodes and pos-
sesions of his subgites. And wite ye well, that I haue founde in the
writinge of the moost noble doctoure Hermogenes, saying in this
10 wyse, that the right grete and souereyne bonté, and true cliernes
of vndirstandinge, and habundaunce of feith and science, and signe
of perfeccion is whan the kynge withdraweth of takinge of the
[f. 40ᵛ]   goodys | and possessions of his subgites. And this was the principall
p. 79   cause of the destruccion of the reame of Ingland. For diuers princes
15 of the said land made so outragious dispences, that the rentes and
possessions of the reame might nat suffise thaim. And for to
mayteyne that grete and outrageous dispence, they tooke the

1 vices] s *ins. above*

De largesse et auarice et de plusieurs vertus   .vj.

Roy Alixandre, tres chier filz, ie te di certainement que se aucun
roy vieult faire plus grans despens que son royaume ne peut
soustenir, ne peut muer qu'il ne s'encline a celle largesse et auarice,
5 tel roy sens nulle doubte se destruit. Maiz se il s'encline a largesse
il aura gloire perpetuelle de son royaume. Et ce cy sentent quant
le roy se retrait et n'a cure de prendre les biens de ses subgiés ne
leurs pocessions. Et saiches, tres chier filz, que ie treuue en escript
au commandemens d'un tresgrant dotteur Hermogenes qui dit
10 que la tresgrant et souueraine bonté et vrayc clarté, doucement et
planté de loy et de sience est signe de parfeccion de roy quant il se
retrait de prendre les biens et lez pocessions de ses subgiés et ce
fu la cause de la distincion du royaume d'Engleterre. Car plusieurs
roys d'Engleterre faisoient si grans despens et si oultrageux que les
15 rantes du royaume n'y pouoient souffire. Et ainsi pour soustenir
leur oultrageux despens, ilz prisent les biens et les pocessions de

13 distincion] dinstincion F destruction HVG *and, substantially,* R: *see n.*

f. ⁅ Of largesse and auaryce/ and of many other vyces.

KYnge Alexander moost dere sone I tell the certaynly that yf
ony make greter expence than his realme can susteyne/ that he en-
clyneth to folysshe largesse & auaryce. Suche a kynge without
doubt shalbe dystroyed. But yf he inclyne to lyberalyte/ he shal 5
haue perpetuall glory of his realme/ yf he drawe hym fro takynge
þe goodes & possessyons of his subgectes. And wyte thou dere
sone that I fynde wryten of a grete doctour named Hermogynes
whiche sayth that the gretest & souerayne goodnesse/ bryghtnesse
of vnderstandyng/ & plente of lawe/ scyence & perfeccyon of a 10
kynge/ is þat it behoueth to kepe hym fro takynge of the goodes and
possessyons of his subgectes. It hath ben þe vndoynge of many
realmes. For dyuers kynges haue made greter & outragyous expences than þe stynt of theyr realmes coude extende/ wherfore they

---

Capitulum viijᵐ

Kynge Alexandre, dere sone, I saye the certeynment that yf
any kynge will make grete dispenses that his reavme may not
susteyn, [ne] meve hym but that he will enclyne to such largesse
and auarice, such a kynge withouten any doute he destroyeth 5
hym-self. But yf he enclyne hym to largesse, he shall perpetuall
ioye of his reavme. And yf the kynge dispose hym to rescure vn-
duewly, to take the godes of his comons with vnreisonable and to
grevous imposicions, he may not longe governe, neyther by
Goddes lawe ne by mannes lawe. And witte ye well, dere sonne 10
Alexandre, that I fonde it writen by the doctrine and commaundement of a full solempne doctour Hermogines, that the
grettest and moste souerain bounté and veray clerenes certeyn is
swetely sette and pleynted of lawe and of science, the which is 14
perfeccion of the kynge when he with-|drawethe hym to take the [f. 220ᵛ]
godes and the possessions of his subgettes. And that hath be the
discrecion of that honnourable reawme of England, all thynges

11 fonde] o over y (or, conceivably, vice versa: unclear)

considred, the manhode, ricches and commoditees, both above
therth and in the bowelles of the erth, of men, of wymmen and of
all maner of bestes and foules, of all kyndes of fisshes, bothe of the
fresshe waters [and of the salt waters], of all maner of cornes and
erbes for mannes sustenance, of trees and woddes for bildyng, and 5
fynally of all metalles and thynges mynerall, that is to say, of gold,
of siluer, of coper, of tynne, of quik siluer, of sulphur, of alablaster,
of secole, of wheston, of freston, of milneston, of marle, and
specially of the grete richesses of wolles, pereles, and of salt, of
faire welles, of geete and of many other comoditees which cometh 10
not to mynde forto reherce. Consideryng also the litilnes of the
circuyte and the grounde of this said litill and honnourable reavme,
in all the compas of this mydell erth ther is none lich ne comper-
able therto that any man knaweth, ne that the gode of the sayntes 14
[and] the holy churche is so reuerently and | devoutely served [f. 221]
inne. And that I reporte me both to gentilmen, marchandis and
pilgrymes, to hem all that most have seen, and yit noght reherced

10 geete] *see n.*   16 gentilmen] *second* e *over* a

goodes and lyuelode of thaire subgites, which caused thaim to crye to oure Lorde for socoure, Who sent His vengeaunce vpon the seid prynces in suche wyse, that the comons rebellid agains thaim, and destrued thaim all, and thaire name sett to nought.

5 And had nat be the mercy of the gloriouse Lord that susteyned and kept the peeple, the land had ben clierlye destrued. Than thou aughtist to kepe the from outrageous dispence and giftes out of

leurs subgiés, laquelle chose est jniure, et le peuple cria a Dieu lequel enuoia sur yceulx roys sa vengence tellement que le peuple

[f. 8] se rebella contre | eulx et furent du tout destruis et leur nom mis au neant. Et se ne fust le grace de misericorde du glorieux Dieu qui

5 soustint le peuple, le royaume eust esté du tout destruit. Tu te dois doncques garder de foulz et outrageux despens et des dons ou-

---

1 jniure] *stop preceding the word but none following it*

toke the goodes and landes of theyr subgectes. For þe whiche
iniuryes doynge þe people cryed to god/ whi[c]he sent vengeaunce
on the sayd kynges. In suche wy[s]e that theyr people rebelled
agaynst them & put them to destruccyon. And without the grete   4
mercy of god that | susteyned them, þe realmes shold haue ben   [f. B3ᵛ]
vtterly dystroyed with þe people. Thou then oughtest to absteyne
þe from outragyous expences/ & ought to kepe temperaunce in

2–3 whiche, wyse] whishe, wyce (*letters interchanged; the words begin con-*
secutive lines).

---

of marble, besechyng almyghty God so to preserve it to his hie
pleasaunce, and [in] humblesse and grete devocion preye and seye
after Daun John Lidegate, late monke of Bury,

> Lord God, preserve vnder thy myghty honde
> Oure Kynge, oure Qwene, theire pepull, and this lande.   5

For as is redde in dyuers autentike and credible cronycles, ther
have been such kynges of this reavme that have done so grete and
outragious dispenses, and so charged and oppressed their poure,
trewe subgectes, that theire rentes and revenuz myght not souffice
to bere hem, the which charges is opun iniure, that the comvne   10
peple cried to God, the Which sende vpon the kynges such vengeance to theire chastisement, that hi[r] peple rebelled and aroos
aganst hem. And in the same wise did they in Fraunce, and were in
poynte outturly forto be destroyed, wittensyng in England, Jak
Strawe, and semblabully in Fraunce, Jak Bon-homme. And nad   15

4–5 *Written as prose, continuous with the text*   11 sende] *preced. by*
canc. charges   11–12 sende ... vengeance] sende such vengeance vpon the
kynges such vengeance   12 hir] his

reason and mesure, and kepe well temperaunce and largesse, and be nat to besy to enquer the derke secreetes, and reproche neuyr the giftes that thou hast yeuen before, for it longeth nat to a good man.

5   **Of vertues and vices and the doctrine of Aristotle**

THe substaunce of alle vertues is to reigne, yeue [to] the nedy, and forgiue iniuries, and doo worship and reuerence to thaim that ben worthy, and cherissh thaim that ben lowly, and amende the defautes of such as ben of symple condicion, and to be liberall
10 in salutacions to the peeple, and be nat to full of langage and be

6 to the] the to   7 doo] doo to

---

trageux et dois garder atrampance en largesce. Et ne vueilles en- querir les oscurs secrés ne reprouchier le don que tu auras fait, car il n'a-fiert pas aux bons.

Des vertus et vices et de la dottrine Aristote   .vij.

5 La substance de toutes uertus est regner, donner les biens, et pardonner jniures, et honnourer ceulx qui sont a honnourer, et porter reuerance a ceulx qui sont dignes, et soustenir aux humbles, et amender les deffaux des simples, et de saluer voulentiers les gens, et toy garder de trop parler, et laisse passer les jnuires

1 atrampance] attrempance VG; atemerance H: *see n.*

lyberalyte. And gete not the derke secretnesse & reproches that
thou shalt haue/ for it belongeth not to them that be good.

g. ℂ Of vertues & vyces/& of þe doctryne of Arystotle

THe substaunce of all vertuous reygnyng is to gyue to them þat
be good/ & perdon iniuryes/ honoure & bere reuerence to them   5
þat be worthy/ & haue mynde of them þat be meke/ & amende þe
defawtes of them þat be symple/ & with good wyl saue þe people/
& kepe þe fro to moche spekyng/ let iniuryes passe tyll thou se the

they not founden the grace and | the mercy of God almyghty,   [f. 221ᵛ]
Which that supported bothe reavmes in the tymes of theire nede,
bothe thoo regions had finally destroyed. Therfore þe wisemen
shold alway kepe you fro outragious dispenses and giftes. And
have a temperance in your largesse, ne that ye enquere not after   5
darke secretes ne reproch not the giftes that ye have given, for it
is not conuenyent to folkes of gode estate, &c.

Capitulum ixᵐ

Of [v]ices and vertues after the doctryne of Aristotle

The substance of all vertues is to reign and to gife of thy gode dis-   10
cretely and wiseli, to perdon iniuries and wronges, to worship hem
that bene honourables, and forto do reuerence to hem that bene
worthy, to susteyne humble folke, and to amende the defautes of
the simple folke, and salue gladdely the peple, and kepe the fro
grete spekyng, and lete the iniuries passe vnto the tyme, and feyne   15

9 Of vices] Of offices   10 The substance] **To here** the substance
11 wiseli] *prec. by canc.* sadly

nat [hasty] to reuenge the iniuries doon to the. And fayne that
thou vndirstande nat the folye of thaim that ben foolys. Dier
sonne, I haue taught the, and shall teche the, many thinges
4 whiche thou most kepe in thyne hert, trusting verily that while
[f. 41] the seid doctrine shall be with | the in alle thyne operacions and
p. 80
besines, thou shalt [a]llwey haue cheevinge brightnesse and suffisaunt science in thy reule and gouernaunce during thy lyuing
dayes. And also I shall teche the the science of phisik in breeue
termys, which I wolde neuer haue doon had nat ben that science,
10 with othir doctrine folowing, aught to suffise in this worlde, all
thinge considred.

Of the vndirstandinge

RIght diere sonne, I lat the wite that vndirstandinge is the key of
gouernaunce of man, and saluacion of the soule, keper of uertues
15 and meroure of vices. For by vndirstandinge we may knowe tho
thinges that aught to be eschewed, and folowe that that aught to

6 allwey] llwey, *with first* l *elongated, rising to top of page, forming part of
decorative scheme (see vol. ii)*

---

jusques a temps, et faindre que ne saiches pas la folie des foulz.
Chier filz, ie t'ay enseigné et enseigneray encores plusieurs choses
lesquelles tu retendras en ton cueur, et ferme sience que tant
comme iceulx enseignemens seront tousiours en toutes tes voies
5 et en toutes tes euures, tu auras touziours clarté luisant, et souf-
fisant sience en ton gouuernement tout le temps de ta vie. Toutes-
foiz ie te aprendray la sience de fisique abregee, et jamais ne t'en
eust rien dit ce n'est ce que icelle sience auec les enseignemens qui
s'ensuiuent te deuront souffire en toutes euures en cest siecle et
10 en l'autre.

De l'entendement   .viij.

Saiches, treschier filz, que l'entendement est chief du gouuernement de l'omme et salut de l'ame, et garde des uertus et miroer des
vices. Car en celui entendement nous regardons les choses que
15 l'en doit fouir, et eslisons se que l'en doit eslire et en-suiure. Il est le

2 choses] *stop preceding* choses, *but none following*   5 en] *inserted above
line*   6 tout] *final* t *inserted above line*   15 que] *abbreviation for* que
inserted above line

tyme of defence þat thou knowe not þe foly of foles. Dere sone I
haue taught þe & shal teche þe many thynges þe whiche thou shalt
kepe in thy hert. And I ensure þe þat þe sayd techynges shall
always be there in al thy doynges & werkes. Bryght & suffycyent
scyence of physyke shortely comprysed thou shalt haue. And I   5
wolde neuer haue shewed the ony thynge/ but þat þe sayd scyence
with þe techynges þat folowe ought to suffyse the & thy werkes in
this worlde and in the other.

h. ℂ Of the vnderstandynge.

DEre sone knowe thou þat þe vnderstandynge is þe chyef of þe   10
gouernaunce of man & helth of the soule/ keper of vertues/ & of
vyces. For in þe sayd vnderstandynge we beholde the thynges þat be
to be chosen. It is þe key | of vertues/ & the rote of all laudable   [f. B4]

---

the that thou knawe not the foly of foles. Dere Kynge Alexandre,
I teche the, and yit I shall teche the, many thynges that thou shalt
kepe in thyne herte for ferme science and trewe disciplyne. The
which yf thou kepe hem aye well and treuly, vnchangeabully, that
in all thi dedes and thy warkes thou shalt euer have clere sight and   5
sufficient connyng in all the gouernance all the dayes of thy life.
For I shall | teche the the science of fisike abreged. And I wolde   [f. 222]
neuer have tolde it the, but that the same science with thabrege-
mentes and the techynges that here folowne, they shall suffise the
in all thy besines and warkes, in this warlde and in that other.   10

Capitulum x^m
How Aristotle writeth to Alexandre of entendementes

Witte thou fore sothe, dere sonne, that entendement is the
souerain and chief of the gouernance of man, and the hele of his
soule, and kepyng of vertues, and lech to eschewe all vices. For [in]   15

be chosen. For it is the keye of alle vertues, and root of alle goodnesse laudable and worshipfull. And the first instrument of it is
good renoun and fame. For he that with good entent desireth to
haue good fame, he shall in euery place be glorified and honeured.
5 And that desireth it feyntlye and ypocrytlye, he shall shamefully
come to confusion through his euill renoun and fame. The kynge
aught principally labour to haue good fame, more for his land
than for him-self.

5 that] *intended reading perh.* he that

chief des uertus et la racine de tous biens louables et honnourables.
Le premier jnstrument d' icelui est desir d'auoir bonne renommee
car qui desire par tout auoir bonne renommee il sera par tout
[f. 8ᵛ] glorieux et honnourés. Et qui faintement et ypocrite-|ment le desire,
5 il sera en la fin confundus par mauuaise rennomee. Le roy doit
principalment querir a auoir bonne renommee plus pour le bon
gouuernement de son royaume que par lui.

goodes. And the best instrument therof is to haue good fame. And yf it be contraryly done/ it shalbe confounded at the last by yll fame. A kynge ought pryncypally seke to haue a good fame/ more for the gouernynge of his reame than for hymselfe.

3 fame/ more] fame. More

---

that same entendement we rewarde thoo thynges that man sholde flee, and eschewe they[m] that been forto flee, which is the souerain thynge of all vertues, and the rotes of all thynges that been to be praysed and moste honoureable. And the first thynge of that desire is forto have a gode name and renommee, for in all places he shalbe 5 honoured and glorified. And he that by fait and ipocritement be-haveth hym, at the ende he shalbe confonded by yuell renommee, for the gouernance of a kynge shold be principally to seche and to have gode renommé, more for the gouernance honourable of his region then of hymselfe.   10

2 theym] they, *perh. intended form: see* the *in* O.E.D., *s.v.* they, *II. 4b*
3 and] *followed by* souerain thyn *repeated and canc.*   8 for] more for

Of the intencion finall that the kyng aught to haue

THe begynnynge of wisdome and vnderstandinge, it is to be of good fame, by the whiche lordshippes and reames ben conquerid
4 and purchaced. And yf thou desire to haue reames and lordshippes
[f. 41ᵛ] thrugh envye, [it] is no good | fame. Lating the wite, that enuye
p. 81 engendreth lesinges, whiche is root and causer of alle vices. Envye engendrith yuell tunges. Yuell tunges engendreth hate. Hate engendrith shame. Shame engendrith wrath. Wrath engendrith diuision. Diuision engendreth faute of justice. Faute of justice
10 engendrith bataile. Bataile breketh any lawe and destrueth reames, and is contrarie to nature, and destrueth the man. And therfore,

---

De l'entencion finable que le roy doit auoir   .ix.

LE commancement de saigesce et d'entendement est d'auoir bonne renommee par laquelle sont les royaumes et les grans seignieuries aquises. Et se tu aquiers ou que tu desires royaumes ou
5 seignieuries ce n'est pour auoir bonne renommee, tu n'aquereras ia a la fin aultre que enuie. Et saichies que enuie engendre mensonge, laquelle est matiere et racine de toutes vices. Enuie engendre mal parler, mal parler engendre haine, haine engendre vilenie et si engendre rancune: rancune engendre contrarieté, contrarieté en-
10 gendre jniustice, jniustice engendre bataille, bataille ront toute loy et destruit cités et est contraire a nature et destruit le corps de

---

8–9 *outer margin:* nota per Shirley   8 et si] *ins. above*   9 *virgula*
after second contrarieté *but with no punctuation after the first*

i. ⊂ Of þe fynall intencyon þat a kynge ought to haue.

FOr the begynnynge of largesse that a kynge ought to haue/ is to
haue good fame/ wherby the grete realmes & grete lordysshyppes
be goten. And yf thou desyrest to get realmes or lordysshyppes/
yf it be not by good fame/ thou shalt gete none other thynge but 5
enuy. And enuy bredeth lesynges/ whiche is mater and rote of all
vyces. Enuy bredeth yll speche/ yll speche bredeth hate: hate
bredeth vniustyce/ vniustyce bredeth batayle/ batayle breketh all
lawe/ dystroyeth cytees/ and is contrary to nature. Than thynke

2 For the] *corr. reading perh.* The   largesse] *so also* K: *see n.*   7 yll
(twice)] euyl K

Capitulum xj^m

**Of the commandement and the entencion of wisdam, and
of entendement fynable of a kyng, by Aristotle**

Aristotle writeth to [Alexandre] the commaundement of wisdam | 4
and of entendement [by] the which fynabully forto have gode [f. 222ᵛ]
renommé, by the which the reavmes and the grete lordes[hippes
be] goten and soght.

And yf thou seche or desire reavmes or grete lordeships, that is
no-but forto have grete renommee, thou shalt have noght elles
therof at the ende but envie. And witte well that envie engendreth 10
lesynges, the whiche is the rote and brynger-forth of all vices.
And envie engendreth wronge, the which norissheth bataile, the
which destroyeth the lawe and breketh hit, the which is contrary
to nature, and destroyeth mannes body, and maketh dissolacion of

4 Aristotle] *initial* A *not in space for decorated initial, which is left blank*
Alexandre] *blank space left at end of one line and beginning of next*   6–7 and
the grete . . . goten] *canc. or* grete lordeshippes *foll. by* and the grete lordes goten
12 engendreth] engrendreth   14 dissolacion] i *ins. above*

diere sonne, remembre thy-self and doo thy diligent laboure to
haue good fame. For the grete desire that thou shalt haue to haue it,
shall drawe to the-warde the trouth of alle thinge, latynge the wite
that trouthe is principall root of all goodnes, as it is seid. It en-
5 gendreth familiarité. Familiarité engendrith loue. Love engendrith
counseile and socour, and vndir this fourme was all the world
made, and the lawes constitued and couenables to reson and nature.
Than it apperith well that good fame is lyf worshipfull and perdurable.

l'omme. Pense doncques chier filz que tu puisses auoir bonne
renomee. Car par le grant desir que tu auras d'auoir bonne renommee tu tireras a toy la verité de toutes choses. Et saiches
que verité est racine de toutes choses qui sont a louer et matiere de
5 tous biens. Car elle est contraire a menconge laquelle est racine et
matiere de toutes vices comme dit est. Et saiches que verité engendre desir de justice, justice engendre bonne foy, bonne foy
engendre largesse, [largesse engendre] familiarité, familiarité engendre amitié, amitié conseil et aide. Et par ses choses fut tout le
10 monde ordonnés et les loys faittes, et sont conuenables a raison et a
nature. Il appert donc que desir d'auoir bonne renommée est
pardurable vie et honnourable.

8 largesse engendre] *missing in* F, *supplied from* HRV

dere sone & set thy desyre to get good fame/ and thou shalt haue in the trouth/ and all thynges laudable/ for it is cause of al welth. For it is contrary to lesynges/ whiche is mater of all vyces/ as it is sayd. And trouth engendreth the desyre of Justyce. Justyce engendreth good faythe. Good faythe engendreth famylyaryte. 5 Famylyaryte engendreth frendshyp. Frendshyp engendreth councel and helpe. And for this cause all the worlde was ordeyned/ & the lawes made which be couenable to reason and nature. It appereth than that the desyre to haue good fame is honourable and perdurable lyfe.   10

8 couenable] conuenable K

castelles, citees and cuntrees. Thynke then, dere sonne, to gete the gode renommee. For by the grete desire that thou may gete the grete renommé, thou shalt drawe to thee the trouth of all thynges. And witte well, on that other partye, trouth is the veray rote of all thynges that oght to be praysed and matiere of all godes. For it is all 5 fully ageynst lesynges, the which is matier and rote vniuersally of all vices, as it is said here-to-fore. And witte you well that verité desireth rightwesnes and justice, the which desireth and engen- dreth largesse, the which engendreth familiaritee, the which en- 9 gendreth frenship, the which | [engendreth] gode counseile and [f. 223] helpe. And therfore, dere Emperoure Alisaundre, Kynge and my sonne, aboue all other erthly thynges ordeyne that the lawes be done suche and soo truly and wisely, that they be covenable grounded, and accordyng to reason and to nature. Thus by Aris- totle it is fully determynde and concluded that gode renommé is 15 lastyng life and honnourable.

3 grete renommé] by grete renom*m*e   5 it] *preced. by canc.* is   10 en- gendreth] *missing from text; supplied from position as catch-word on f. 222ᵛ.*

Of the mischeeuys that growen thrugh flesshly desires

ALexander, dier sonne, thou moost leeue all flesshly desires and bestialles, for thei ben full of corrupcion. The flesshly desires enclineth the hert to delectacions and perdicion of the soule, hauyng
5 no discrecion, reioysing the body corruptible, and destrueng the vndirstandinge of man. Lating the wite that such desires engendreth carnall loue, whiche loue engendrith couetyse. Couetyse engendrith desires to richesse. Desire to richesse makith a man shameles. He that is shamelesse most be proude. Pride makith
10 man withoute feith. Man withoute feith is a theef. A theef is
[f. 42] openly shamed, growing to an | vtter mischeef and finall destruc-
p. 82 cion of his body.

1 desires] *final* s *ins. above*

Des maulx qui s'ensuiuent de charnel desir   .x.

ALixandre, chier filz, laisse tes desirs bestiaux du desir charnel, car ils sont corumpables. Les desirs charnelz enclinent aux desirs
4 de corumpacion de l'ame bestiale sens nulle discrecion auoir, et ses
[f. 9] iouissent en corps corrumpable et corrompent l'en-|tendement de l'omme. Et saichies que tous desirs engendrent amour charnelle, amour charnelle engendre auarice, auarice engendre desir de richesse, desir de richesse engendre souuent homme sans vergoigne, et homme sans vergoigne fait homme orguilleux, et orguil-
10 leux homme est sanz foy et est larron; larrecin est incl[ig]né a vitupere et puis a chetiueté et a la finable destrucion de son corps parvient.

1 s'ensuiuent] s'ensuient H, sens *unfinished and with blank space left* R 4–5 ses iouissent en] *so in* FV; & for es ioissent en R, et si ens [*unfinished and followed by space left blank*] en H   10 larroncin est incligné] larroncin est incljoné F larrecin met homme V Larrecin met homme G larcine met homme H larron met homme R

k. ⟨ Of euylles þat folowe flesshely desyre. |

ALexander fayre sone leue thy beestly desyres of thy flesshly [f. B4ᵛ]
appetyte/ for they be corruptibles. The flesshely desyres draweth
thy hert to beestly corrupcyon of þe soule without ony dyscr[e]cyon/
& dryeth þe body of man. Wotest thou what flesshely loue bredeth? 5
It bredeth auaryce/ auaryce bredeth desyre/ desyre bredeth rychesse
and maketh a man without care/ to be a proude man/ without
lawe/ and a thefe. Theft bryngeth a man to shame/ and fynall destruccyon of his body.

5 man. Wotest] *no punct.* (*line division*)

Capjtulum xijᵐ
Of the yvelles that conveniently folowne of carnal desires

Dere sonne, O Alisaundre, lese all thi bestiall desires that been
flesshely, for they corrupte. Thy flesshely desires been enclyned
to corrupcion of bestiall life, without any discrecion had. And they 5
enioyen hem in bodies corrumpable, and corumped vnderstondyng
of men. And witte thou it well, that all desires carnalles engendre
flesshely delectacion and love, the which [engendre] avarice and
coveitise, that engendre the concupissence with riches that desireth oft men to have no shame, the which maketh man to be 10
orgeyllous and proude, and ferre oute of hym-selfe. And man
without hym-selfe engendreth thefte and larcine. Larcine maketh
men forto stele, the which is much to be blamed and sore in-
prisoned, and bryngeth his | body to fynabull distruccione and [f. 223ᵛ]
warldes shame.   15

Of the wysdome and ordinaunce of a Kynge

IT is needfull and couenable that the good fame of a kinge be in
laudable science, and good and honest lyf of his body, whiche shall
be knowen and cast abrode in alle the parties of his reame. And
5 that he kepe noble parlamentes and discreet counseilles with his
owne peeple. And whan his subgites heere him speke sadly and
discreetly, and see him doo alle his besines with wysdome and
policie, they will bothe worship him and dreede him. Latinge the
wite that the wysdome or folye of the kinge may easely be vndir-
10 stande, for whan he lyueth in good and parfite luf to God-warde,
he is worthy to reigne and to haue worshipfull dominacion, but
the kinge that is of ill lyf, and settith his reame in ill custumes, he
trespaceth greetly, and leuyth the wey of trouth, and despiseth
the good wey and the feith of God, and in the ende alle men shall
15 despise him.

De [s]a[i]gesse et ordonnonce du roy   .xj.

IL est chose juste et raisonnable que la bonne rennomee du roy
soit en louable sience et preudommie espandues par toutes les
parties de son royaume. Et qu'il ait parlement souuent et saige
5 conseil souuent auecques les siens, et par ainsy il sera loués et
honnourés et doubtés de ses subgés quant ilz le verront parler et
faire ses besoignes saigement. Et saichies que par le gouuernement
se peut acongnoistre la saigesse ou folie du roy. Car quant il se
gouuerne en preudommie vers Dieu il est digne de regner, hon-
10 nourer et seignourier. Maiz celui qui met son royaume en seruitude
et en mauuaise coustume trespasse la voye et le chemin de verité.
Car il mesprise sa bonne voye et la loy de Dieu et il sera en la fin
mesprisé de tous.

1 saigesse] largesse: *cf. chapter-heading 234b/1*

1. ⁋ Of the wysdome and ordynaunce of a kynge.

IT is behouefull & ryght that þe good fame of a kynge/ be in
honourable scyence and worthynesse (thoroughout al realmes) to
be shed frome his realme/ and haue communycacyon of theyr
wyse councel with his. And therby he shall be praysed/ honoured/ 5
& doubted of his subgectes/ whan they se þat he speketh and doth
his werkes wysely. For easely is perceyued the wysdome or foly
of a kynge/ for when he gouerneth hym in worthynesse towarde
his subgectes/ he is worthy to reygne honourably. But he that
putteth his realme in seruytude or thraldom/ of euyll customes/ 10
he breketh the way of veryte/ and dyspyseth the good way and lawe
of god. And at þe last [shal] be dyspraysed of all folkes/ as he hath
deserued.

8 hym] him selfe K   11 veryte/ and] veryte. And

Capitulum xiij^m
Of largesse and of the kynges gode ordenance

It is juste cause and reasonable that gode renommé of the kynge be
preised, science and predonommee spradde, by all the [parties] of
his reavme, and that he have oft parlement and wise counseiles 5
with his subgettes when that they will speke to-gidders, and do his
besynes wisely. And therby he shall [be] preised and honnoured
with grete doute. And witteth it well that by this gouernaunce they
shold knawe the wisdom of the kynge. For when the kynge
gouerneth hym in predonommé aganst God he is worthy to reigne, 10
to be honoured, and to gouerne as in lordeshippe. But he that
putteth his kyngedam in seruitude and in yvell custums passeth
the right way of charité. For yf he misgouerne and mistake hym
fro the righte waye of God and of the lawe, at the laste he shalbe
mistaken of alle other subgettes, fremde and knawen.   15

3 cause] *prec. by* reason *in the bold chancery hand of chapter-openings, canc. by*
underlining   gode] *prec. by canc.* kynge   5 his] *prec. by canc.* the   wise] e
foll. by letter begun and canc.

2550 C74   X

Of the religiouse lyf and holinesse of a kinge

EFtsones I pray the to doo as the philosophre hathe spoken,
saying in this wise: it perteyneth that the moost royall magesté
be gouerned aftir the lawe and rightwisnesse, and nat by a feynt
5 shewing outwarde, but bi pure deede, to thentent that is subgites
may clierly see and knowe the good lyuing of the kynge, and that
he dreedith God and demeenyth him aftir His Lawe. Than the
[f. 42ᵛ] kinge shall be worshipped and | dredde of his peeple. And yf he
p. 83 shewe him-self outward feynyng to be of vertuous and religious
lyf, and that he be yll to his subgites, for yll operacions will nat
10 longe be hidde but that the peeple shall vndirstand it, than shall
he be dispraysed and diffamed both of God allmighty and of alle
men, and the worship and dignitee of his corone shall faile. What
shuld I sey more? There is no richesse nor othir thinge in this
15 worlde so grete of value as the good fame. And on the othir partie,

---

De la preudommie du roy, religiun et sainteté   .xij.

DE la preudommie du roy, religiu[n] et sainteté ie te prie derechief
et de ce que les saiges philosophes ont parlé et dit. Il appartient que
la royalle maiesté soit gouuernee selon les droiz et les lois, non
5 proferees et apparences, maiz de fait, affin que chascun voie et
congnoisse clerement la preudommie du roy et qu'il doubte Dieu,
quar qui se vieult gouuerner selon Dieu lors sera doubté le roy et
aimé quant on verra qu'il doubte Dieu. Et se il se monstre sainte-
9 ment preudomme et religieux et il soit mauuais a ses subgés, les
[f. 9ᵛ] mauuaises | euures ne se peuent celer et ne peut estre que le
peuple ne les congnoisse. Et pour ce il sera mesprisés de Dieu et de
toutes gens diffamés et de son fait en serra mendres et abaissiés et
fauldra l'onneur de la couronne de son royaume. Que te diré ge
plus? Il n'est tresor ne autre chose en ce monde qui vaille bonne
15 renummee. Et d'autre part, chier filz, il affiert que tu honnoures

---

2 religiun] religium F, religion HRV   5 proferees et] pas par fainte-
14 tresor] prec. by canc. trest

m. ☾ Of the worthynes/ relygyon/ and holynesse of a kynge. |

ANd yet agayne well beloued sone I tell þe that the phylosophres [f. C1]
haue spoken and sayd. It behoueth that þe royall mageste be
gouerned by ryghtwysnesse/ & not by faynt apparence/ but in dede/
to thende þat euery man may se and knowe clerely the goodnesse 5
of the kynge/ and that he feare god. And wyll be gouerned in godly
wayes/ than shall he be honoured & doubted. And yf he shewe
hym selfe faynynge to be good/ and is nought to his subgectes/
his yll werkes can not be hyd/ nor it may not be but his people
shall knowe it. He shall be dyspysed of god & shamed in the 10
worlde. And his dedes shalbe lessed/ & the honoure of the crowne
of his realme shall fayle. What shall I tell þe more? there is no
tresure in this world to good fame. And moreouer dere sone/ it

1 m.] *no punct.*   5 thende] the ende K (*expansion of apocope regular, not*
indicated hereafter)   13 to] *see n.*

Capjtulum xiiij^m

Of the kynges religioune and his hele

Of the kynges prodonomee, of his hele and religion.

I pray the yit agayne, and of that at the wise Philosophre[s] have
spoken and said, I[t] behoveth that the roial maiesté be gouerned 5
after the lawes and rightes before muche approued | and preferred, [f. 224]
but to that entente that eche man may knawe the prodonommee
and the wisdam of the kynge, and that he love and doute God. For
yf he will doute and loue God, then he shalbe douted and loued of
all men. But yf he shewe hym a gode man, holy and religious, and 10
is contrary in werkes and all his dedes til his subgettes, and that the
peple do well apperceyve [it], it may not faile but that he shalbe
disprased of God and of all his peple famed, and of his estate he
shalbe lassed and made lowe, and the honoure and the corone of
his reavme lasse taken hede offe and obeyed. For ther is no richesse, 15
wisdom ne puissaunce in this warlde, so vailable to the grete

6 before] *prec. by canc.* s   8 kynge] *prec. by canc.* prynces   9 of]
prec. by canc. god   12 apperceyve it] apperceyvede

deere sonne, it is nedfull that thou worship thi knyghtes, and doo
reuerence to men of religion and exalte thaim that ben purueid
of grete wysdome, and speke oft with thaim, makynge thaim questions and doutes, and also worship the nobles of euery man as he is
5 worthy.

Of the purueaunce of a kinge

THe wyse kynge most oft tymes thinke vpon the thinges that
may falle, to thentent he may wysely purueye agains that may be
to him contrarie, and so shall he bere the more lightly the aduer-

---

les clers et portes reuerance au proudommes de religion et exauces
les saiges et parlement auecques eulx, en leur faisant doubtes et
questions de leur demandes. Les honnoure ainsi selon ce que vn
chascun en sera dignes.

5 De la proueance du roy   .xiij.

Il conuient que le saige roy pense souuent des choses qui sont
a aduenir affin qu'il puisse saigement pourueoir ad ce qu'il lui
puit estre contraire et qu'il puisse plus legierement porter les

---

1 exauces] *foll. by stop*   6 choses] chos *followed by short vertical stroke,*
presumably abbreviation for es-, *at end of line.*

besemeth þat thou worshyp clerkes/ and pouerte of good men of
relygon/ and exalt wyse men and speke oft with them. And questyon
often of doubtes with them. And demaunde many thynges of
them. And answer wysely to theyr questyons. And honoure noble
men as eche of them is worthy.   5

n. ❡ Of the pourueyaunce of a kynge.

IT behoueth that a wyse kynge thynke often of thynges to come
that he may prouyde for suche thynges as be contrary to hym. And

---

estates of this warlde, as is the predonommé vniuersally of the
pepull. And on that other side, thou glorious Emperoure, it behoueth and longeth to thy roiall excellence that thow honnoure the
clargie and bere reverence to the well lernyng men occupied ver-
tuousli in scoles, in studies and in vniuersitees, and of clene and   5
deuoute religions, to helpe and enhance hem the wise, the well
willed men and counsailers and officiars of thy parlamentes,
makyng theire questions and demaundes, with the redy remedies
and absolucions, | pro republica, to the honoure, worship and   [f. 224ᵛ]
profete of thyn estate roiall and of thyne vmbill true subgettes.   10

Capitulum xvᵐ

**Of the ǥode purveiaunce of the kynǥ to the ǥode of his
reavme**

It behoveth the wise kynge to remembre and thynke on thynges
that bene conuenient and oportune for the prosperité and the 15

3 roiall] *prec. by canc.* g

sitees and sodeyn aduentures. And the kinge aught to be merciable,
and to bere his ire and angir couertly, and wysely refrayne, to that
entent he fulfille nat his purpose withoute sad deliberacion. And
he aught wysely to knowe how he shuld be gouerned. For the
5 moost souereyn wisdome and vertue that the kyng may haue [is]
discrecion to demeene him-self wysely and sadly. And whan he
vndirstandeth any thinge that may be to him good and profitable,
8 he aught to labour it diligently and discreetlye, to thentent men
[f. 43] shall nat sey that the kinge | dooth his thinges slauly and necli-
p. 84 gentlye.

aduersités et les contraires aduentures. Et si doit estre le roy
piteux, et son yre et son courros doit saigement couurir et re-
fraindre affin que sa[ns] deliberacion il ne vienne ou fait qu'il a en-
pensé et son courroux doit raisonnablement congnoistre sens
5 esreur et rapeler saigement. Car la plus souueraine saigesce et
vertus que le roy puisse auoir e[s]t de lui saigement gonuerner. Et
quant il voit aucune chose qui lui est bonne et proufitable, il se
doit fere en grant diligence et discrecion affin que les gens ne dient
qu'il fait ses besoignes trop soutement et trop negligemment.

3 a] *ins. above*   4 doit] *prec. by canc.* et   5 et²] est   6 est] et F
est HRVG, *cf. 284b/10*

þat he may the easlyer bere the aduersytees and contrary aduentures. And the kyng ought to be wysely hyd & refreyned/ to
thende that without | delyberacyon he come not to the dede that [f. C1ᵛ]
he purposed in his anger. And he ought reasonably knowlege his
anger and errour/ and appease hym selfe easely. For the moost 5
souerayne wysdome and vertue that a kynge maye haue/ is to rule
himselfe wysely. And whan he seeth ony thynge that is good and
prouffytable for hym to be done/ he sholde do it with grete
dylygence/ & dyscrecyon bycause þe people shal not say þat he
hath done his besynesse folysshely/ or to neglygently.   10

4 And] And that K   knowlege] to knowledge K

---

welfare of hym and his reavme, and to withstond all that may
be contrarie to hym, that he may the lightlier bere the aduertise of
his enemyes and theire harde aventures. A kynge also shold be
pytuous, and his ire and his furious wrath he sholde couuertely
restreyne, to that ende that his deliberaciones and his warkes 5
come not to that his vnauysed and inordynate ireous thoght. For of
reason he sholde thynke that it is wisdom to restreyne an irous
witte. For the moste soueraynst wisdom is vertue that a kynge
may have to gouerne and rule hym. And when that he saith any
thynge that may be to hym profettable, he sholde dowe it with 10
grete diligence and discrecion, to that ende that his peple say ne
deme not that he doth his warkes to folily ne to necligently.

4 couuertely] *prec. by canc.* thenke   5 deliberaciones] *contraction-sign*
for -es: *intended form perh.* deliberacions

Of the clothinge of the kynge

IT longeth to the roiall magestee that the kinge be clothid
worshipfully and shewe himself in riche and noble clothinge,
passing all othir mennys clothinge. And he aught to haue good,
5 faire, straunge clothinge whiche in prerogatyf dignitee shall passe
all othir. For the whiche his highnesse and power is the more
exalted and dredde, and the more reuerence is doon to him.
And it is needfull that the kinge be a fair speker and louinge, and
that he maynteyne himself in graciouse langage, and in especiall
10 in tyme of werre and bataile.

Des vestemens du roy   .xiiij.

Il afiert moult que le roy en sa maiesté royalle soit vestus honnourablement et qu'i tousiours se monstre en beaux et riches
[f. 10] vestemens et doit en beauté de | robes seurmonter tous autres
5 vestemens. Il doit donc vser de beaux, chers et estranges vestemens et qui en grant pr[er]ogatiue et dignité apparent et tous
autres seurmontent. Car pour [ce] sa dignité en est plus hon-
nouree et sa puissance plus exaulcee et plus grant reuerance lui
[es]t faite et randue. Et si affiert bien que le roy soit beaux parleur
10 et doulz et aimables et en gracieuses paroles et par especial en
temps de guerres et de batailles.

[Manuscript continues]

6 prerogatiue] prologatiue F, prerogatiue HRG, preeminence V   7 ce]
om. F ce HVG se R   9 est] ait

o. ❡ Of the vestymentes of a kynge.

IT besemeth well to þe mageste royall that þe kynge be clothed
honourably. And that he shewe hymselfe alway in fayre and ryall
clothes. And ought in beaute of robbes to surmount all other
clothynge. Also he ought with grete prerogatyf & dygnyte vse 5
fayre/ deere/ & straunge vestures. For therby is his dygnyte more
excellent and his myght more exalted. And more reuerence is made
to hym. And also it besemeth a kynge to be fayre spoken/ with
softe and kynde wordes/ specyally in tyme of warre.

Capitulum xvi^m

Of the vestures and clothynges of the kynge

Right conuenient and thynge appurtenaunt to the roiall estate of
the kynges maiesté, that his hie person be honnourabully clothed,
and that euermore he shewe hym in riche vestures and clothynges 5
to his peple, and that . . .

[Manuscript breaks off]

5 that euermore] that euermore that   6 that] *supplied from position as*
catch-word

Of the countenaunce of a kynge

ALexandre, dier sonne, it is a preciouse thinge and worshipfull,
that the kinge speke litle, but yf it be for greet neede. For it is
bettre that the earis of the peeple be feruently desiringe to heere
5 the woord of the kynge, than that they shuld be full and annoied
to heer his langage through the spekinge to miche. For whan the
earis of the peeple ben full of the kinges wordis, the hertes ben
weery of the sight of him. And the kinge aught [not] to shewe
him-self to oft to his peeple, nor to haunte the felauship of his
10 subgites, and in especiall the comons and olde peeple, for thrugh
the grete familiarité he shuld be the lasse preised. And therfore
the Judiens haue a good custume in the ordinaunce of thair kynge
[f. 43ᵛ] and of the reame. Thaire kyng sheweth neuyr him-self | openly
p. 85 before his peeple but onys in the yere, at whiche tyme he shewyth
15 him-self in royall apparaile. And all his lordes and knyghtys ben
armed aboute him, and him-self vpon a destrier, armed and araied
as it perteyned in the magesté royall, and his peeple beinge a certeyn space from the lordys and nobles, spekyng and declaringe to
the kyng highnesse the grete and chargeable maters of the land,
20 shewing him the cases and perillis that ben past, and how notablely
he and his counseill haue ben demeenyd and guyded therynne.
And is the kinge accustumed to gyf grete giftes, and to forgyue to
diuers thaire trespaces, and to light the greet charges of his peeple,
with many othir good deedys. And whan thaire speches been
25 ended, the kinge sitteth downe in a cheyer. And than ryseth oon
the wyse princes, spekinge to the peeple, laudinge and recom-
mendinge the noble wisdome and good gouernaunce of the kynge,
yiuing graces to allmighty God that hath so loued and worshipped
the Judiens as to sende thaim so noble and wise a kynge, and hath
30 confermyd the peeple alle with oon assent to the obeisaunce of the
kynge, and in the benigne lowlynesse, and worship and pleasire
of his highnesse. And whan the wyse prince hath thus spoken,
[th]an the peeple doon thaire power to exalte the laude and
honeure of the kinge, recommending his good and vertuous opera-
35 cions, praying to God for him. And by this meene is the god
deedys and vertuous wisdome of the kynge raported by citees
and townes thrugh-out the reame. And so ben thaire children
endoct[r]ined and taught, whiche causeth thaim aftir to owe thaire

10 olde] *see n.*   26 to] *repeated*   33 than] and

p. ☾ Of the countenaunce of a kynge.

SWete sone Alexander it is a goodly thyng precuous/ and
honourable whan þe kynge speketh but lytell. But yf ouer grete
nede requyre it. It is better þat þe eeres of þe people be wylling
to here þe wordes of a kynge/ than to be wery of his to moche 5
spekyng. For whan | þe eeres be glutted with the kynges speche [f. C2]
theyr hertes be wery to se hym. And also þe kynge ought not to
shewe hymselfe to often to his people, nor haunt to moche þe
company of his subgectes/ & specyall of vylayns. And therfore
the Yndyens haue a good custome in þe ordynaunce of theyr 10
realme. For theyr maner is that theyr kynge sheweth hymselfe
but ones in the yere. And than he is clothed in vesture royall. And
all þe barons & knyghtes of his realme ben rychely armed and
arayed about hym. And he is set vpon a stede þe ceptre in his
hande armed with ryche armures royalles/ and all his people a good 15
way before þe barons & other noble men. And ther they shew þe
dyuers perylles & aduentures þat be passed. And how þat he & his
councell is well ordred. And þe kynge as than is wonte to pardon
grete offences to some of them. And whan þe parlyament is ended
þe kynge setteth hym in a chayre & anone ryseth one of þe moost 20
wysest men & speketh to þe people/ praysyng & commendyng þe
wyt & good gouernaunce of þe kynge/ in yeldynge thankes to god
þat hath so well ruled and mayntened þe Yndyens kynge/ & þat
they are pourueyed of so wyse & honourable a kyng to reygne &
guyde them. And than he confermeth þe sayd people in one wyl & 25
courage to þe obedyence of þe kynge. And then he commendeth
þe people & aloweth them gretly of theyr good maners & condicyons which [h]e reporteth to them. And sheweth them goodly
wordes & examples/ þe better to put them in grace & obeysaunce/
with mekenesse in the good wyll of the kynge. And whan this 30
wyse prynce hath thus spoken/ the people enforce them to exalte
the praysynges/ and commendacyons/ and good maners of this
sayd kynge/ in prayenge god hertely for hym. | And by this meane [f. C2ᵛ]
by theyr good maners/ and wysdome of theyr kyng they cause
countrees and cytees to be obedyent to them. And thus ben the 35
chyldren brought vp in theyr youth/ & taught in the honoure and

9 specyall] specially K; cf. 383/15   22 kynge/ in] kynge. In C
25 them.] no punct. (at end of line) C   28 he] be C he K

loue and feith and obeisaunce to the kynge. And his vertuous name
[f. 44]   and good fame is openly shewed and declared in all | the parties of
p. 86   the lande. In the whiche tyme is justice kept and punicion executed
vpon thaim that haue deserued it, to thentent that they that ben
5   willinge to doo yll, refrayne and correct thaim-self. And also the
kynge shewyth graces to the marchauntes in thaire tributes, and
preserueth thaim in rightwisnesse and justice. And that is the
cause that the lande is soo full of peeple and grete richesse. For of
all the parties of the world the marchauntes resorte to Judé for
10   thaire grete availe. And there ben both riche and poore susteyned,
whiche causeth the tributes and rentes of the kinge continuelly
to encreece and amende.

Of the kynge[s] justice

THe kynge most beware that he doo no wronge nor vilanye to
15   the marchauntes. But he aught to loue thaim and cherissh thaim,
be-cause they goo in to diuers parties of the world, where they
make thair repoortes as they haue cause. And the kinge aught by
right and justice see that euery man haue his owne good. And so
shall his lande, citees and townes be fully replenyssht with goodys,
20   and his rentes and reuenues shall encreece and multiplie, and his
might and power be dred of his enmyes. And thus shall the kinge
lyue and reigne pesiblye and suerly, according to his pleasire and
desire.

Of the worldly desires [of a kynge]

25   ALexander, dier sonne, coueyte nat the worldly thinges whiche
[f. 44ᵛ]   ben transitorie and corruptible, and remem|bre that thou most
p. 87   needys leue all tho behynde the. Than desire to haue the richesse
that is nat transitorie nor corruptible, and the lyf that may nat be
chaunged, that is, the reame of euerlastinge joye and glorye. Than
30   direct all thy thought and will to good perfeccion, and leue the lyf
of the beestes whiche lyuen in thaire foulnesse, and be nat redy
alle-wey to beleue alle that is tolde the. And be nat to hasty to
pardone all such as haue ben agains the, and thinke wyselye on
alle thinges that may falle. And sett nat thy desire to miche in
35   meyte and drinke, or in sleepe, nor in flesshly desires.

Of the chastité of a kinge

MOoste noble emperoure, enclyne nat thy-self to the luxury of

37 enclyne] en clyne

reuerence of the kynge. And the good fame of the kyng secretly and
manyfestly is spredde and knowen. And the ryche and poore ben
therby susteyned thoroughout the realme of Ynde. And the
kynges possessyons and trybutes encreaseth therby.

q. ℂ Of the Justyce of a kynge. 5

A Kynge ought to ordre hym soo that he do no wronge/ nor
harme to marchauntes/ but ought to cherysshe them. For they
go thoroughout all the worlde/ and by them is reported the good
and all renownes of lordes & prynces. And a kynge ought by veray
Justyce to yelde euery man his. And so his landes and cytees shal 10
be garnysshed with all welthes. And the kynges werkes shall multyply to his honoure and glory/ and shal be the more redoubted of
his foes/ and shall lyue & reygne at his wyl & desyre in quyetnesse.

r. ℂ Of the worldly desyres of a kynge.

ALexander ryght worthy sone/ coueyt not always wordly 15
thynges/ for they be corruptyble. And thynke that thou must leaue
all. Demaunde than suche thynges as can not be corrupte. That is
the lyfe that | can not chaunge and the realme perdurable. And [f. C3]
reyse thy thoughtes in goodnesse/ and therin kepe þe stronge &
gloryous. And leaue the lyfe of bestes þat alwaye lyue in theyr 20
fylthynesse. Beleue not lyghtly al thynge that is tolde to the.
And be not enclyned to pardon them/ agaynst whome thou hast
had vyctory. And thynke on the tyme & of thynges that may
happen. For thou knowest what is to come. And set not thy desyres
in meates & drynkes/ in lechery/ nor to moche slepe/ nor in carnall 25
desyres.

ı. ℂ Of the chastyte of a kynge.

SOuerayne Emperour enclyne not to lechery of women/ for it is

2 knowen. And] *no punct.* (*at end of line*) C   9 veray] very K
12 and shal] et en sera F f. 11   14 r.] *no punct.*   15 wordly] worldly K
24 desyres] desire K

the wommen, for it is an hogges lyf. What lif is that for the, yf thou
gouerne thy-self after the vices of the beestes vnresonable? Dier
sonne, beleeue me, for luxurie is destruccion of the body, shor-
tinge of lyf, corrupcion of alle vertues, and trespacinge of feith,
5 and in conclusion, ledith man to all yll disposicions.

Of the kynges disportys

IT is needful at some tyme that the kynge take his disportes with
his felawes and princes, and that he haue mynstrellys with many
diuers instrumentes, with daunsinge and singinge, for, whan a man
10 is anued and wery, suche delectable disportes comforteth nature
[f. 45] and yiueth | to the body strength and vertu. And yf thou delite
p. 88 thy-self in suche dispoortys, be ware that thou drinke nat, and
feyne the that thou art to hote to drinke, and let othir drinke who
so will, and than shalt thou heere many secreetes. And take suche
15 disportes but ij or iij in the yere. More-ouer, it is good that thou
haue nygh to thy persoone som true and secreet familiares that
shall rapoort the alle thinge that is seid and doon in thy reame.
And with thy barons and subgites, worship the wyse menne, and
doo reuerence to thaim that therof ben worthye. And kepe iche
20 of thaim in his estate, and at som tyme make thaim to eite with
the, now som, and anothir tyme som, and gyue thaim gownes, yche
of thaim aftir thaire estate and as they ben worthye. And see that
there be noon of thy knyghtys, familier counseilers, but that they
feele thy largesse, and soo shall appeere to alle men the noblenesse
25 of thy corage.

Of the kynges discrecion

DIere sonne, it is expedient that the kinge with his wysdome
haue good and faire countenaunce, and in especiall that he laugh nat
to miche, for through to miche lawhing is the man lasse praysed
30 and worshipped. And the kinge aught to make of his men [more]
in his owne courte or counseile, thann in othir parties. And yf any of
his men doo hurt or shame to any othir, the kynge aught to punissh
him aftir his deserte, in exaumple of alle othir. And thou aught in

a swynysshe lyfe. And no glory shall be to the yf thou gouerne the
after þe lyuynge of bestes without reason. Dere sone beleue me/
for without doubt lechery is destruccyon of the body/ the abrege-
ment/ & corrupcyon of all vertues/ the deth of a man self/ and
maketh the man feminyne. And at the last bryngeth hym to all 5
euylles.

[ʃ.] ⟪ Of the sportynge of a kynge.

SOthly it is besemynge to a kynge to take his pastyme and sporte
with his prynces and lordes. And that he haue many and dyuers
maners of mynstrylles/ and syndry instrumentes/ daunces and 10
songes. For the humayne creature naturally anoyeth. And in suche
instrumentes and pastymes nature delyteth & | the body taketh [f. C3ᵛ]
force & vygoure. Than yf thou wylt delyte in suche thynges/ do it
þe moost honestly & secretly that thou mayst. And whan thou arte
in thy pastymes beware for drynkynge of wyne. And let þe other 15
sporte them as longe as they lust. And than thou shalte haue many
secretes dysclosed. And make not this pastyme often/ but twyse or
thryse in þe yere. Also it behoueth þe to haue nyghe to the some of
thy famylyer seruauntes that shal tel and reporte to þe what is sayd
in þe realme. And whan thou arte amonge thy barons & subgectes/ 20
honoure wyse men & bere reuerence to euery man as they be
worthy. And euery man in his estate/ mayntene & let them ete with
þe somtyme/ one after another. And gyue gownes somtyme to one
& somtyme to another/ after theyr estate/ and as they be worthy.
And in ony wyse se þat there be none of thy knyghtes & famylyers/ 25
but þat he fele of thy lyberalyte & of thy grace. And thus ouerall
shall appere thy largesse & gretnesse of thy courage and honour.

⟪ Of the dyscrecyon of a kynge.

MOst worthy sone it is good that a kynge haue lyberalyte/
goodly gesture/ and countenaunce/ & that he laughe not to 30
moche. For ouermoche laughyng causeth many to be lesse set
by/ and to be lesse honoured. And fynably ouermoch laughyng maketh a persone to seme older than he is. Also a kynge
ought to loue his people in his courte and of his councel more than
in other partyes. And yf ony do vylany to another/ he ought to 35
punysshe hym as he hath deserued/ that | other may take example [f. C4]
therby/ and eschewe them from yll doynge. And in þat punys-

7 ʃ] s C (*but cf. 237/3 and 7, 323/14*)   10 mynstrylles] minstrels K
syndry] sundry K   32 fynably] finally K 37–321/1 in þat punysshynge] in
punishyng K

thy punisshinge to considre the persoone that hath trespaced, and
[f. 45ᵛ] a[s] well aught to be punissht an high and | noble man as oon of
p. 89 the common peeple. And at som tyme it is good to doo justice
with rigoure, and at som tyme with fauoure to thentent to make
5 a difference be-twixt the persoones. For it is vriten in the book
of Macabees, that the kinge aught to be loued and worshipped that
is likenyd to the egle whiche hath dominacion ouer alle birdys, and
nat to be likenyd to a-nothir birde subgite to the egle. And therfore,
yf any man doo vilanye to othir in thy presence, thou aught to
10 considre yf he haue doon it in dispoort, to do solace and mirth to
thy persoone and othir, or yf he did it in despite of thy royall
magestee. For the first cause he aught to be correctid, and for the
secunde he aught to dye.

Of the reuerence of the kinge

15   ALexander dier sonne, the obeisaunce of the kinge groweth by
.iiij. sundry weyes. First, through the vertuous lyving of the kinge.
An othir weye, that he yiueth his subgites cause to loue him, and
for-by cause he is jentill and curteyse, and for the worship and
reuerence that he dooth to thaim that haue deserued it and been
20 worthye. Diere sonne, doo soo miche that thou may haue the
hertes and corage of thy subgites and kepe thaim from alle wronges
and iniuries. And be ware that thou yive thaim no cause to speke
ayenst the, for thrugh the vois of the peeple may lightly growe
greet harme and damage. Latinge the wite, that the wysdome of
25 the kinge is the digne glorie of his reuerence, and exaltacion of his
reame. It is founde in diuers hooly scriptures, that the kinge is
in his reame as the reigne is in the erthe, which is called the grace
[f. 46] of God, the bles|sing of heuyn, lif to the erthe and to alle crea-
p. 90 tures lyuing. For thrugh the reyne all othir thinges encrecen and
30 frutifyen, how be it that at som tymes with gret reyne [cometh]
greet wedir, thundyr and tempest, both by see and by land, which

2 as] a *followed by blank space sufficient for one letter and gap between two words*
30 cometh] *om.* U viennent F, f. 13

shynge thou ought to regarde þe persone þat hath done amysse.
For elles sholde a hyghe & noble man be punysshed as another.
And yf thou do so thou shalt not be alowed of þe people. And it is
good somtyme to do rygorous & strayt Justyce/ & somtyme not/
to thende [þa]t þ[e] dyfference of þe persones be knowen. For it is   5
wryten in the boke of Machabees that a kynge ought to be praysed
& loued/ yf he be lyke þe eygle/ which hath lorshyp ouer all fowles.
And not as he whiche wyll be lyke another foule þat is subgecte
to the eygle. Wherfore yf ony do vylany to ony other in the presence of þe kynges mageste/ it ought to be regarded & consydered   10
yf þe offence were done in game or for to cause the kyng to laugh/
or to make hym or other glad of it/ or yf he dyde it in despyte/ &
shame of the mageste royall. For þe fyrst dede he ought to be cor-
recte/ and for the seconde to suffre dethe.

⦅ Of the reuerence of a kynge.   15

WOrthy kynge Alexander dere sone the obedyence to a kynge
cometh by iiij. thynges. That is for þe vertuous lyuynge of the
kynge. Bycause he maketh hym to be beloued of his subgectes.
Bycause he is curteys. And for the honoure and reuerence/ that he
dothe to them that be moost worthy of it. My dere sone do so   20
moch that thou mayst drawe to the þe courages of thy subgectes/
and auenge them of all wronges & iniuryes done to them. And beware that thou gyue not to thy subgectes cause and mater to speke
agaynst the. | For speche of people many tymes may do hurt. Than   [f. C4ᵛ]
haue in thy mynde suche wyse that nothyng may be sayd agaynst   25
the. And so thou shall eschue the yll wyl and dedes of them that
had yll wyll agaynst the. And forsoth the largenesse of the glory
of thy dygnyte and reuerence, and exaltacyon of thy realme, and
that reboundeth moost to thy honoure is to haue the hertes of thy
subgectes. It is founde in holy scryptures, þat the kyng is ouer a   30
realme as the rayne is ouer þe erth which is the grace of god and
blyssynge of the heuens and cometh on the erthe/ and all lyuynge
creatures. For the rayne is called the way of marchauntes/ and
helpe of buylders. How be it that in the rayne falleth somtyme
thondre and lyghtnynge/ swellynge of the see/ and floodes with   35
tempestes and many other euyls cometh therby, wherwith medowes

---

5 þat þe] not þat C *and, substant.*, K   7 lorshyp] lordship K
17 iiij.] foure K   23-24 to thy ... agaynst the.] *corner of page torn off:*
o *of* to, e *of* the, *and full stop missing*   24 hurt. Than] *no punct.* C

causeth grete hurt to the peeple. Natwithstandinge, the peeple
thankyn oure Lord of His grace, consideringe that the reyne
comyth of His mercy. Suche anothir ensaumple thou may finde of
wynter and somyr, in the whiche ceasons oure Lorde, of His moost
5 divine grace, hath ordeyned the sharpnesse of coolde, and grete
hete, to thengendring and norisshinge of alle thinges naturell.
Neuerthelesse, grete harmys and mortall perilles growen and
comen of greet feruent coolde of wynter, and of heete of somyr.
And soo it is of the kinge. He most at som tymes doo greuaunce
10 to his subgites, whiche contrarieth greetly the hertes of the comons.
But whan the peeple seeth and knowyth that by the grace and good
gouernaunce of the kinge the[i] ben kept in vnitee, peas and justice,
than they forgete alle the harmes that ben passed, thanking allmighty God of His high grace that He hath purueide thaim of so
15 noble a kynge.

How the kinge aught to see to the pouerté of his subgites

I Pray the, deere sonne, enquere of the necessité of thy poore
subgites, and that thyne habundant grace preuaile to thy poore
subgites in thaire greet neede. And also thou aught to cheese and
20 ordeyne a good man that louith good justice and vndirstandeth the
langage of thy subgites, and committe him the reule and gouer-
[f. 46ᵛ] naunce of | thy peeple, and that he kepe thaim in rightwisnesse,
p. 91 with loue and pitee. And so shall thou performe the pleasire of
God to the conseruacion of thy reame and of thy subgites.

25 ## Of the misericorde of the kynge

DEere sonne, I pray the and counseile the, that thou make grete
prouision of cornes and of all maner vitailes, to thentent yf the tyme
of derth and hungre falle in thy reame, that than thou maist helpe,
socoure and counforte thy subgites in thaire necessitee. And sende
30 vitailes to the citees and townes in alle the parties of the land and
of thyn habundaunt grace releeue thy peeple. And this is a principall wile and wisdome to the conseruacion of thy reame and
saluacion of thy subgites. Than will they haue grete desire and
corage to fullfille alle thy pleasirs and commaundementes. And
35 shall thou reigne in grete pro[s]perité, and thei shall reioyse gretly,
and the wysdome meruailing of thy ferre-casting wytte, which

27 vitailes] s *ins. above* (*at end of line*)

and verdures hath perysshed. For god made it so of his grete
goodnesse/ benygnyte/ and grace. The whiche selfe example ye
may fynde in wynter and somer. In the whiche the souerayne
largesse gyueth and ordeyneth coldenesse and heate/ engendrynge
and encreasynge of all newe thynges. How be it many euyls &   5
perylles cometh by the rygour of grete coldenesse of wynter/ &
grete heates of somer. In lyke wyse dere sone is it of a kynge. For
many tymes the kynge doth many grefes and euylles to his sub-
gectes/ and maketh them to beare grete herte agaynst hym. But
whan the people seeth that by the grace and good gouernaunce of   10
þe kynge they be in peas and well ruled they forgete the abouesayd
euylles/ and thanke the gloryous god that hath pourueyed them of
so wyse a kynge. |

[s.] How the kynge ought to remembre his subgectes.   [f. D1]

I Requyre þe swete sone that thou of thy goodnesse thynke and   15
inquyre oftentymes of thy poore subgectes/ and knowe theyr
necessytees. And set amonge them suche men as be vertuous and
that loueth god and Justyce and that knoweth theyr maners/ and
vnderstandeth theyr speches/ and can gouerne them peasybly
and in loue. And yf thou do thus/ thou shalt do the pleasure of thy   20
creatoure. And it shall be saufegarde to thy realme/ and gladnesse
of the and thy people.

t. ⅭⅠ Of the mercy of a kynge.

DEre sone I councell the that thou make grete prouysyon of
corne and vytayles in suche wyse that thy countrees may haue   25
haboundaunce/ in eschewynge (as it chaunceth often) to haue
scarcyte/ and famyn. In so moche that by th[y] grete prudence
thou mayst saue and maynteyne thy subgectes. And thou ought
to haue thy garners stuffed/ and to proclayme thrughout all thy
realme and cytees/ how thou hast gadred and stored the of greynes   30
and other vytayles. And that thou kepest them to the prouysyon of
thy realme/ and to vtter them with plente to the saluacyon of thy
subgectes. The which doynge wyll cause thy people to be coragyous
to do thy commaundementes. And so thou shalt prospere/ and euery
man wyll meruayle of thy grete lyberalyte/ & of þe prouydence   35

14 s.] *om.*   21 saufegarde] safegarde K   25 vytayles] victuels K
27 scarcyte/] scarcyte ʃ   thy] the CK ta F f. 13ᵛ   28 subgectes. And] *no
punct.* C   31 vytayles. And] *no punct. (at end of line)*

shall cause thaim to gyue laude and preysing to thyne approued manhode, and yche man shall dreede to displease the.

Of the perill of murdrye

ALexander, deere sonne, I haue oft desired the, and preyde
5 the, to kepe my doctrine, for if thou kepe it trulye, thou shalt with-oute doute come to thy purpose, and thy reame shall endure in
[f. 47] good estate and prosperité. That is to | say, that thou be ware aboue
p. 92 alle othir thinges as miche as thou may of shedinge of the blood of mankinde, for that longeth alle oonly to God. And therfore pre-
10 sume nat to take vpon the that longeth to God Himself. For it perteyneth nothir to the nor to no man to desire and enquere the pryuetees of God. Than be ware of murdrye. For the moost noble doctoure Hermogenes seith that he that sleeth or put to deth the creature like to him-self, alle the vertues of heuyn ben withoute
15 ceessing beseching and cryenge to the high Magesté of oure Lorde, saying thus, 'Sir, Thy seruaunt will be egall to Thy-self!' And oure Lord answerith to the vertues, saying thus, 'Let be, let be! For the uengeaunce longeth to Me, and I can yeelde to him agayn.' Latinge the wite that who that euyr sleeth a man, and in
20 especiall withoute a resonable cause, God will take uengeaunce. And the uertues of heuyn ben euer afore God presentyng the bloode and death of him that is slayne, till the uengeaunce be taken.

Of the knowledge of the seid perilles

25 DIere sonne, of alle paynes and perilles see that thou haue knowlege, for I haue had and knowen in my tyme grete harmes and perilles. And also haue in thy remembraunce the deedys of thy forefadirs, and how they haue lyued. And therby shalt thou see and lerne many good ensaumples whiche shall yeue the vndir-
30 standinge of diuers thinges that may falle in tyme comynge. And also I pray the that thou will nat greeue nor disprayse him that is lower than thy self. For it falleth oft that he that is lowe may
[f. 47ᵛ] hastily growe | to grete worship and richesse, and than he is
p. 93 mighty to helpe him-self.

afore hande in thy besynesses. And they wyll repute the | as [f. D1ᵛ]
holy/ and lawde and magnyfye thy worthynesse. And euery man
wyll feare to dysplease the.

v. ❧ Of paynes and punysshementes.

MY dere sone Alexander/ I admonysshe/ and also praye the to 5
kepe my doctrynes and thou shalt come to thy purpose. And thy
realme shall be durable and in good estate. That is to wyte/ aboue
all thynge that thou kepe the frome shedynge of mannes blode. For
it belongeth onely to god/ whiche knoweth the secretes of men.
Than take not on the/ the offyce that belongeth onely to almyghty 10
god/ wherfore as moche as thou mayst withdrawe thy hande
therfro. For the doctour Hermogenes sayth. That who that sleeth
the creature lyke vnto hym/ all the sterres of the skye ceaseth not
to crye to the mageste of god/ lorde/ lorde/ thy seruaunt wyll be
lyke vnto the. For surely god wyll take vengeaunce on hym that 15
sleeth a man/ and specyally without reasonable cause. For god
answereth to the vertues of heuen saynge. Leaue ye/ for in me lyeth
the vengeaunce/ and I can yelde it. And wyte thou that the vertues
of heuen without cease do present before the face of god/ the dethe
and blode of hym that is deed/ tyll that god hath taken vengeaunce 20
for it.

u. ❧ Of the knowlege of the sayd paynes. |

O Moost louynge sone/ of all suche paynes with the knowlege [f. D2]
therof/ wyte thou that I haue sene moche harme/ and many euylles
oftentymes come therby. Do soo that thou mayst haue in thy mynde 25
the dedes or werkes of poetes. And thynke how they haue lyued.
And therby thou mayst se and lerne many goodly examples. And
theyre thoughtes shal gyue the grete documentes in tyme comynge.
And also I pray the my dere sone, that thou greue nor dysprayse
none lesser than thou. For it happeneth often that the small 30
estate ryseth ryght soone in to grete rychesses and honoures/ and
may be so myghty that he maye endomage the. Many examples
therof hath ben seen as phylosophres reherse.

12 therfro. For] no punct. (at end of line)   sayth.] see 257/5n. and 363/31n.
17 saynge.] see n. to l. 12   26 poetes] tes peres F f. 14   30 that the] the K

To kepe his feith

DEere sonne, be ware that thou breke nat thi feith that thou hast
promysed, and the aliaunces that thou hast made, for that longeth
to common harlottes and peeple withoute feith. And therfore kepe
5 well thy feith and promyse. And yf thou doo othir wyse, harme
and in-conuenientes shall enseue, and, in the ende, yll conclusion.
Latyng the wite, that through good and stable keping of the feith
and promyse is the good felauship of men assembled, and the
citees and townes in-habite with peeple, and the kinge reigne and
10 perseuere. And yf thou breke thy feith, all men shall liken the to
the childe or beest vnresonable. Beware than that thou breke nat
thy feith, and kepe truly the promisses and aliaunces that thou hast
made, how be it that parauentur [falleth] the greeuouse domage.
Hast nat thou vndrestandinge that thou hast ij spirites, wherof
15 oon is in thy right side and the othir in the lefte, whiche knowen
alle thy deedys, and repoorten to thy Creatoure all that thou hast
doon? And me seemyth this all only aught to yeue the cause to
withdrawe and leeue all dishoneste and yll operacions. For thou
aught neuer to swere but yf grete nede cause it. And if thou wilt
20 knowe, the cause why the reame of Ymbre and Assiriens were
destrued was this: the kinge made many fals othis and promisses
for to deceyue the menne and citees that were next to his lande,
[f. 48]   and breeke the aliaunces and promisses | that he had made, by-cause
p. 94   it was to the profite of his lande and him-self. And in the same
25 wyse, the wyse men of his lande made many fals othis to begile and
deceyue thaim that were thaire next neighbours. But the divyne
sapience and the moost souereyn and high Juge might no lenger
suffre thaim. Right dier sonne, I will that thou wite, that for the
reule and ordinaunce of thy lande I haue made morall doctrine
30 and speciall techinges and profitable, whiche perteyneth to the
and to the gouernaunce of thy reame, and of thy propre familiar
householde, and of thi peeple. But it is nat yit tyme to declare
thaim to thee, but thou shalt fynde thaim in a certayne place of this
book heere-aftir. And yf thou kepe and obserue my said doctrine,
35 thou shalt by the mercy of God haue alle thy desires. And, deere
sonne, be nat repentaunt of thy good deedys passed, for that

x. ⟨ How a kynge ought to kepe his fayth or othe.

ABoue all thynge (dere sone) beware that thou breke not thy
faythe and othe that thou hast made. For it is belongynge to
strompettes/ and also to people that kepe not/ nor do not care
for theyre faythe and othe. Wherfore kepe thy faythe that thou 5
hast promysed/ for and yf that thou do otherwyse/ it wyll come
to an euyll ende at the last. And yf by aduenture or fortune/ it
chaunceth that ony welthe cometh by faythe brekynge/ the trust
therof sholde not be good/ but veray euyll & reprouable/ and suche 9
a man | is put in the nombres of them that be nought. Wyte thou [f. D2ᵛ]
than that by kepynge of faythe is made þe goodly assemblynge of
men. Cytees ben inhabyted with comyns/ and soo is the good
sygnouryes of kynges. By kepynge of fayth castelles ben holden and
kepte in lordshyps. And yf thou breke thy fayth thou shalt be reputed of euery man as a chylde or a brute beest/ than beware 15
therof. And kepe also the othes/ and alyaunces that thou hast
made/ though that they be greuous and domageable to the. Wotest
thou not þat thou hast two spyrytes alwaye with the/ one on the
ryght syde and the other on the lyft syde/ whiche knowe and kepe
all thy workes. And reporte to thy creatoure al that thou hast 20
done. Of a trouth thou ought onely to absteyne þe frome all
dyshonest workes. And constreyne none to swere/ but yf ouer
grete nede requyre it. A kynge ought not to swere/ but he be moche
requyred and prayed. And yf thou wylt wyte what was the destruccyon of Nubye/ and of the Assyryens/ I certyfye the that theyr 25
kynge made othes gylefully/ to deceyue the men and cytezens
next by. And brake his alyuances and promysses that he had made/
bycause they were profytable to his realme. And also to his subgectes he made many fals othes to destroy theyr next neyghboures.
The ryghtwyse Juge coude susteyne nor suffre them no longer. 30
Moost dere sone I wyll that thou knowe/ that for the gouernynge
and ordynaunce of thy realme I haue made the some new doc-
trynes/ the whiche specyally is for the profyte of thyn owne
famylyers and the. But as yet it is not tyme to gyue them to the.
I wyll gyue the them in a certayne place of this boke shortly 35
abreged. The | whiche yf thou kepe for thy selfe prouffytably/ with [f. D3]
the helpe of god thou shalt haue prosperyte/ and that that thou
desyrest. Swete sone repente þe not of thynges that be passed/ for

1 or] and K   12 comyns] commons K   15 beest/ than] beest than C
beast, than K   25 Assyryens/ I] assyryens. I C

longeth to wommen that ben feble of condicion. And doo so that
thy goodnesse, trouth and jentilnesse be manifestly knowen and
vndirstande, and that shall be the conseruacion of thy reame and
destruccion of thyne enmyes.

5   **Of the studies and scolys**

DOo so miche that thou may haue studies and scoles, and commaunde that thy subgites put thaire children for to lerne the lettres
and noble sciences. And thou aught to helpe and socoure the
gouernaunce of the scolys and of the poore clerkes, and yeue som
10 auauntage and prerogatyf to the grete and notable clerkes, and so
shalt thou gyue thaim cause to studie and laboure to haue the high
[f. 48ᵛ] perfeccion of science. And | gyue laude to thaim that ben laudable,
p. 95 and worship thaim that ben worshipfull, and giue of thy good to
thaim that haue deserued it, and so shalt thou exalte the clerkes
15 and stire thaim to gyue the laude and pryse, and to make faire
and plesaunt scriptures of the and of thy deedys, whiche shall be
by thaim had in perpetuall recommendacion.

                  Of the sauf garde of the kynge

ALexander deere sonne, sett nat thyne affiaunce in no womman
20 nor in her dedys nor seruise, nor vse nat thaire companye. And
yf it be nedfull that thou haue the companye of woman, take suche
on as men may beleue she be true to the. For whan a womman
hath thy persoone betwix hir armes, thou art like to the jewell
that is leid in the kepinge of a marchaunt, which abideth the
25 jupartye of the see. For than she hath thy lyf in hir will. Beware
than of suche mortall venyme, for it is no newe thinge that men
han ben put to deth with venyme. More-ouer, deere sonne, trust
nat a [s]oole phisician alone for oon phisician might likly doo grete
harme. And therfore, to escheue the perilles, yf thou may, take
30 diuers phisicians, and that they ben alle of oon accorde. And yf

                   28 a soole] afoole

that belongeth to women whiche ben weyke of condycyon. Let thy
goodnesse, thy faythfulnesse/ and conscyence be all hoole, and
manyfest. And they shall be saufegarde of thy realme and destruccyon of thyn enemyes.

y. ❡ Of studye.   5

TAke hede that thou haue studyes and scoles in thy cytees. And
cause all thy people to lerne theyr chyldren lettres and noble
scyences/ and vse them to studye. For thou ought to helpe and
socoure the gouernayle of studyes and poore scolers. And gyue
auauntages and prerogatyues to good studyentes that proufyte to   10
theyr lernynge, and this wyse thou shalt gyue an example to them
that be laye/ exalte theyr prayers and receyue theyr wrytynge
mekely/ prayse them þat ought to be worshypped. Gyue thy goodes
to them that be worthy. Cherysshe clerkes and styre them to
prayse the. And put the and thy werkes in goodly wrytynges/   15
which by them shalbe perpetually praysed.

z. ❡ How a kynge ought to kepe his body.

MOst beloued sone kynge Alexandre/ trust not in women/ nor
in theyr werkes/ nor seruyces/ and company not with them. | And   [f. D3ᵛ]
yf necessyte were that thou must haue company of a woman/ do so 20
that thou mayst knowe that she is true to the/ and holsome of her
bodye. For whan thy persone is betwene the armes of a woman/
thou arte as a Jewell/ put/ and restynge in the handes of a mar-
chaunt/ that careth not to whome it is solde. And beynge betwene
her handes/ is the poyson of thy welfare/ and also the destruccyon 25
of thy body. Beware therfore dere sone/ of suche women/ for
they be venymous and deedly. For it is no newe thynge to knowe
that by theyr venym many men haue dyed. Thou knowest well
that many kynges haue forthered and shortened theyr lyues and
haue dyed by poyson. Also dere sone Alexander beware that thou   30
put not thy trust in one physycyen onely. For one physycyen maye
hurte the/ and shortely do to the moche harme. And therfore yf
thou mayst/ do so that thou haue many physycyens. And that they
be of one agrement. And yf thou wylt haue ony medycyn/ take
it not but by the councell of them all. And that they be such as   35

1 whiche] that K   8 ought] oughtest K   9 studyes] studyens C
students K estudes F f. 15   11 an example] example K   20 woman/
do] woman. Do   32 harme. And] *no punct.*

thou take any medycyne or receyte, that it be made of a certeyn
weight and mesure as the sekenesse may require. And remember
whan thou ware in the parties of Inde, where many grete giftes
and presentes ware presentid the, amonge the whiche presentes
5 was sent to the a faire mayde whiche was of childehode brought
[f. 49]   vp with venime and serpentes, wherof of | hir nature was [she]
p. 96   conuerted and turned to the kynde of serpentys. And than I tooke
grete kepe of hir, and with sad deliberacion auised hir countenaunce. And whan I sawe her straunge looke and bolde coun-
10 tenaunce withoute shame, I perceyued that with a soole bit she
might put a man to dethe, as more pleneurly aftirwarde it was
preuide before the. And had nat ben that I vndirstande hir nature
at the begynnynge, at the first touchinge that thou shuldist haue
had with hir, thou haddest ben dede withoute remedye. Deere
15 soone, remembre thy noble soule whiche is yeuen the from the
felauship of heuen, and put hir nat to endeles perdicion, but kepe
hir soo that she may be glorified in the nombre of thaim that ben
notable and wise.

Of the difference of astronomye

20   ALexandre deere sonne, I pray the, and it may be, that thou
nothir ryse nor sitte, nor eite nor drinke, nor do no thinge, withoute the counseill of som notable clerke that hath the perfeccion
of the science of astronomye. Lating the wite for certayn, that the
gloriouse God hath mad no thinge withoute cause and grete reson.
25 And by this weye the noble doctoure Plato laboured to enquere
and vndirstand of alle thinges that ben made and composed of the
f[ou]re qualitees and humors contrarye. And so he had the knowlege of alle thinge that is create. And more-ouer I pray the, gyue
29 nothir feith nor credence to som foolys that seyn that the science
[f. 49ᵛ]   of constillacions of the planetes | may nat ben vndirstande, for
p. 97   truly they wote nat what they seyn. Latinge the wite, that to the

6 she] *see n.*   21–2 withoute] withtoute   27 foure] faire

knoweth the qualyte and nature of the thynges that ben put/ and
necessary in the medycyne. And that it be of a certayne weyght and
measure/ as the medycyne requyreth it. For by equall porcyons of
weyght and measure the arte of physyke is compownded.

℃ And thynke on dere sone that whan thou was in the partyes of 5
Ynde, many people made to the grete presentes and fayre. Amonge
the whiche was sente a fayre mayden whiche in her chyldheed had
be nourysshed with venym of serpentes/ wherby her nature was
conuerted in to the nature of serpentes. And than yf I had not 9
wysely beholden | her and by my artes and wyt knowen her/ [f. D4]
bycause that contynually/ and without shamefastnesse euer she
loked in the faces of the people/ I perceyued that with ones bytynge
she wolde haue put a man to deth as sythen thou hast seen the
experyence before the. And yf I had not knowen her nature/ at
the fyrst tyme that thou had medled with the sayd mayden thou 15
haddest ben deed without remedy. Fayre sone kepe thy noble
soule/ whiche is gyuen to the and sent from the company of aun-
gelles the whiche is taken to the of god for to kepe. Not that thou
soyle & marre it/ but þat it be put amonge the wyse & gloryfyed
spyrytes.   20

        & ℃ Of the dyfference of astronomy.

ALexander fayre sone/ I praye the/ that yf thou mayst do it/ that
thou ryse not/ nor eate/ nor drynke/ nor do ony other thynge/ but
by the councell of some that knoweth and hath the scyence in
knowlegynge the sterres and astronomye. And thou shalte wyte 25
my dere sone that almyghty god hath made nothynge without
cause/ but hath done euery thynge reasonably. And by certayne
scyences and wayes/ the wyse phylozopher Platon sought and felte
the operacyons of all thynges composed of the foure elementes/
and the humoures contrayres. And hadde also the knowlege of 30
the thynges created and formed. And also my dere sone Alexander
I praye the beleue not such fooles which say þat þe scyence of þe
planettes is so harde to be knowen/ & that none maye come therto.
Surely they be fooles and wote not what they say. | It is a noble [f. D4ᵛ]
thyng to knowe thynges whiche be to come. Yf thou knowest the 35

2 medycyne.] *line-ending not justified*   5 ℃ And thynke] C *does not start
new line for such sections beginning with paragraph marks, but runs them on*   was]
wast K   13 sythen] sithens K   15 had] hadst K   21 &] *used as
sigil for chapter* C   Of . . . astronomy] *text of Wyer's* Dyfference of astronomy
starts here   23 ony] any   WK (*regular substitution, not indicated hereafter*)
31 formed.] *no punct.*

vndirstandinge of man is no thinge impossible. There ben othir
that ben litle wyser, that holden oppinion that [at] the first making
of all thinges oure Lorde ordeyned of euery thinge what shall falle
in conclusion, and by this means astronomye shuld nat be nedefull
5 nor profitable to no man. Suche men ben foolys, and wote nat
what they seyn. For yf a thinge most nedys falle, thou shalt the
more easely bere it and the more temperatly suffre it with lesse
greuaunce. And by this ensaumple, whan thou vndirstandyst that
wynter is comyng, thou makyst thy purueaunce of woode, cole,
10 and othir nedfull thingis, wherby thou suffrest the more easely
and with lesse peyne the feruent colde and sharpnesse of wyntyr.
And in the same wyse of somyr, to eite colde meytes, and ordeyne
for the grete hete. And also whan a grete famyn and hungre shuld
come, to make thy purueaunce of corne and of all othir vitailes,
15 for to passe it more lightly, and suffre the bittyr perilles of hungre.
Than it is behouefull and expedient to knowe the thinges that
may falle. And yf thou vndirstande a perill comynge, wherto thou
can finde no remedye, than with thy good peeple make deuoute
prayer to oure Creatoure that so hath ordeyned, that of His diuine
20 grace He may turne the perilles to an othir weye. And thinke nat
that God hath ordeyned the destinyes of alle thinges in suche
wise but He may breke thaim as Hym liketh best. Right dere sonne,
[f. 50] I lat the wite that the good peeple may | so please oure Lorde with
p. 98 deuoute prayers, fastinge, oblacions, and allmes-dede with othir
25 good deedys, that He will of His habundaunt grace turne and
reuoke the perillis that the peeple douted so miche. Than turne
we agayne to oure first purpose. Lating the wite, that astronomye
is diuided in iiij. parties. That is to sey, in the ordinaunce of the
secrees, in the disposicion of the signes, and of lenghthinge and of
30 the meuing of the sonne, and this parte is called science of
astronomye. The othir is to vndirstande the qualité and the maner
of the meuing of the firmament, and the berthe of the signes vpon
suche thinges as ben vnder the firmament of the moone, and this
parte is called the more digne parte of astronomye, and is sciences
35 of the sterres, planetes, and signes. And wite ye well that there
be .M!xxviij. planetes fixed and stabled, wherof we shall make
mencion hereaftir.

24 allmes-dede] all mesdede

thynges whiche be to come/ thou and other persones may put remedy by good prayers. And requyre the creatoure that hath ordeyned them to retourne theyr malyce/ & ordeyne them otherwyse. Thynke not dere sone that god hath ordeyned & predestynate such thynges/ but that by his power he may chaunge them otherwyse whan he pleaseth. Wyte thou dere sone þat þe good people pray to our creatoure with orysons & deuout petycyons/ by fastyng & sacrefyces/ by almesse & other maner/ axyng of pardon of theyr synnes/ & doynge penaunce/ þat our lorde may retorne & remembre suche predestynacyons whiche other do feare so moche.

℃ Retorne we dere sone to our fyrst purpose. Wyte thou þat astronomye is deuysed in .iiij. partes. That is to wyte in ordynaunce of sterres. In þe dysposysycon of sygnes/ & of theyr elongacyons. Of the moeuynge of the sonne. And this partye is called scyence of astronomy: The oth[e]r parte is of þe knowlege of the moeuynge of the skyes & of the mone. And this partye is called astronomy. And is þe worthyest/ of sterres/ planettes/ & sygnes. And there is .M.xxviij. planettes sygned/ and formed/ of þe whiche we shall speke more playnly.

[ƺ] ℃ Of the gouernayle of helth.

HElthe amonge all thynges is to be goten and hath more than ony myght of rychesses. For þe kepyng of helth is by vsynge of equal thynges conioyned to the body/ as by attemperaunce of humoures. | For the gloryous god hath ordeyned them/ and gyuen [f. E1] dyuers remedyes to the attemperaunce of the humoures to the kepyng of helth. And hath shewed it to his holy men and prophetes/ & to many other Just men whiche he dyde chuse and enlumyned with the holy goost/ in his sapyence dyuyne/ and myghty. And hath gyuen them the gyftes of the scyence/ of these thynges here after folowynge. These phylosophers put the begynnyng of it. That is to wyte they of Ynde/ of Grece/ and of Athenes. Whiche phylosophres were Just and perfyte/ and theyr wrytynges were the begynnynge of scyence & secretes. For in theyr wrytynges is nothynge founde to be reproued nor spylt/ but approued of all wyse men.

8 axyng] axynge W asking K   pardon of] pardon for K   11 purpose. Wyte] purpose/ wite C (and, substant. WK)   14 moeuynge] mouyng(e) WK 15 other] othtr   18 .M.xxviij.] a thousande and eight and twenty K 20 ƺ] rounded r, abbreviation sign for q[uia], but cf. List of Contents, p. 241a used as initial for chapter C here   22 rychesses] riches K   27 Just] CW iust K 31 Ynde] CW Iude K   32 Just] CW iust K

Of the gouernaunce of thaim that ben seeke

DIere sonne, I lat the wite that alle the wyse and naturall philosophirs sayn that man is made and fourmed with .iiij. elementes
contrarye, whiche most all-wey be susteyned with meyte and
5 drinke. And yf the nature of man be nat fedde and susteyned with
meyte and drinke, the substaunce most nedys be corrupt and failled.
Neuerthelesse, yf he shulde eite and drinke alwey he shuld be the
weyker and falle to seekenesse and grete inconuenientes. But yf
9 the man eite and drinke temperatly and by reson, he shall finde
[f. 50ᵛ] therynne grete helpe, strengthe and helthe of his body | and
p. 99 membres. The wyse philosophers seyn all of oon accorde that
yf the man passe the cours of nature and temperate maner of
lyuinge by, in etynge or drinkinge to miche, slepinge or wakinge
to miche, or going or restinge to miche, or going to miche or to
15 litle to pryuee, or in latinge bloode to miche or litle, he most
needys falle into grete seekenesse. And the philosophirs seyn of
oon accorde that he that kepith him from etynge and drinking
to miche, with the circumstaunces aboue rehercid, kepinge temperaunce, he shall haue hele and longe lyf. And for certayn, I finde
20 no philosophre but he kepith this oppinion, saying that all the
delites of this world, be it in delicious meytes, in richesse, worship,
or in flesshly desires, ben nat ordeyned but for to endure and lyue
lenger, and sith it is soo that man desireth longe to lyue and endure,
he most diligentlye doo and perfourme that that longeth therto,
25 with mesurable temperaunce. Also I haue herd of Ipocras, that
kept certayn dietes to lyue and endure the lenger, nat to lyue
and endure for to eite and drinke. And it is holsum at som tymes
to pourge the superfluitees and ille humours that ben with-ynne
the body.

30 ## In how many maners helthe may be preserued

DEre sonne, I lat the wite that helthe is kept principally by .ij.
weyes. First, that the man vse of such meites and drinkes as he
hath ben norysht and brought vp with. The secunde is, that he
purge him of the yll humors and corrupcions whiche greeuyn
35 him inward.

---

4 meyte and] *followed by full stop (at end of line); the first of several occasions,
not subsequently indicated, where a full stop is used at the end of a line apparently
merely to make the margin less uneven*   26 nat] *and nat*

[&c.] ❡ Of the gouernayle of seke people.

ALl wyse and naturall phylosophres say þat man is made and
composed of foure contrary humours/ the which haue alway nede
to be susteyned with meate and drynke. The substaunce wherof
behoueth to yssue and be corrupte yf ony do alway eate and drynke/ 5
and he sholde waxe weyke and fall in grete dyseases/ and haue many
inconuenyences. But yf he eate and drynke temperatly and reason-
ably/ he shall fynde helpe of lyfe/ strength of body/ and helth of all
the membres. The wyse phylosophres saye that yf any man trespace the god of nature/ and the good maner of lyuynge/ be it in 10
to moche eatynge and drynkynge/ or to moche slepynge/ or
wakynge/ in to moche walkyng or restynge/ beynge to laxatyfe/ or
to moche letynge | of blode or to lytell/ it can not be but he must [f. E1ᵛ]
fall in many dyseases/ and greues. Of the whiche dyseases I haue
bryefly founde/ and therin wyll I shewe the my councell/ & remedye 15
for the same. All wyse phylosophres accordeth in one sayeng. Who
so kepeth hym fro ouermoche eatynge & drynkyng & frome þ[e]
excesses aforesayd & kepeth temperaunce/ he shal be helthfull of
his bodye/ & lyue longe. For I can fynde no man but he is of this
opynyon/ & wyll saye þat all delectable thynges of the worlde/ be 20
it in pleasure of þe body/ it is but for to lyue þe longer in them.
But for a more secrete ye ought to enforce you to do suche thynges
as ben belongynge to longe lyfe/ & not to folowe the appetyte/ þat
is to wyte/ not to lye meate upon meat. And dere sone I haue herde
often spoken of Ypocras which kept many tymes dyete to thende 25
þat he myght lyue & endure the longer. Not for to lyue and endure
for þe meate & drynke. Also dere sone it is grete holsomnesse to be
purged of superfluytees & euyll humours whiche ben in þe body.

A ❡ In how many maners a man may kepe his helthe.

GOod sone I praye the haue in thy mynde stedfastly these cer- 30
tayne instruccyons and kepe them. Knowe thou that helth is chyefly
in two thynges. The fyrst is lete a man vse suche meates & drynkes
as he hath ben nourysshed with. The seconde that he purge hym of
yll humours that be corrupte & greue hym. For þe body of man is 34
fedde with meates & drynkes whiche nou|rysshe it by naturall [f. E1]
heate that dryeth/ nouryssheth and fedeth þe moystnesse therof.

1 &c.] *rounded* r *with cross-stroke, abbreviation sign for* -rum, *used here as initial
for chapter: but cf. List of Contents, p. 241a*   14 greues] CW griefes K
17 þe] þat C that W the K   24 lye] put lye CW laye K   32 is lete]
CW is, let K

Of diuers meytes |

[f. 51]
p. 100 WHan the body is hoot and full of hoot fume, than grete meytes
ben good and profitable. And that that is norissht in that body
shall be mykyll and of greet quantité, thrugh the grete hete of the
5 body. And whan the body is slendre and drye, than smale and
subtile meytes ben good. And that that is norisht in that body
shall be of litle quantité, be-cause the condytes ben streight. And
it is a grete wisdome, whan a man vsith good meytes accordinge
to his complexion. That is to sey, whan a man is of hoot nature,
10 that he vse temperately of hoot meytes, but yf the heete of the
stomac be bolden and growen with superfluitees of hoot meytes
and hoot wynes, or by othir cause, than is best and profitable coold
meytes for him.

Of the stomac

15 WHan thy stomac is good, stronge, and hoot, than vse grete and
hoote meytes, for than thy stomac is likenyd to the grete fire
that with his might brennyth a loode of woode. But whan thy
stomac is coold and weyke, than vse smale and subtile meytes.

The tokenys to knowe the stomac

20 THe signes of the stomac coold and of feble digestion ben
suche: whan the body is ill at ease, heuy, and full of slaugth, and
the face bollen and gape often, and is yien [ben soore and he
bolkethe] for[th]e right foule, avoiding ill sauoured wynde by
24 the whiche ben engendred wyndy bollnes of bely, and with-
[f. 51ᵛ] draweth | thappetite of meyte. And theise signes betokne an yll
p. 101 stomac, therfore be ware of alle suche meytes and drinkes as ben
contrarie to thyne hele.

Epistle of grete pryse

[D]Ere sonne, hou be it that mannys body is corruptible, and
30 often fallith in to corrupcions and sekenesse by-cause of the contrarye humors that ben in him, we therfore haue purposed to write
in this booke som thinges that shall be to the needfull and profitable, whiche I haue drawen out of the secrete medicyne whiche
shall be to the plesaunt and agreable. For at som tymes may falle

22–3 yien . . . forthe] yien fore U a douleur des yeux et rote F f. 18ᵛ
29 Dere] Here

B. ⟪ Of dyuers meates for þe stomake.

WHan þe body is fat & full of vapours grosse meates is good
for it. & of þe nourysshyng of suche a body/ þe dygestyon is grosse/
& of grete quantyte for þe great heate/ & vapours of þe body. And
whan the bodye is skl[en]der & drye/ subtyll & moyste meates be 5
good for it. And þe dygestion therof is of smal quantyte for þe
streytnesses of þe conduytes. And it is grete wysdome & scyence
for a man to vse suche meates as ben good & appertenent to his
complexyon/ that is to wyte yf he fedde hym with hote meates
temperatly. But yf the heate be to greuous & brennynge within 10
the body by ouer stronge wynes & hote meates/ or other accydentes/
than contrary meates & drynkes wyl do grete ease & prouffyte/
þat is to wyte suche as ben colde.

⟪ Of the stomake.

⟪ Yf thy stomake be to hote than hote & cours meates be good. 15
For such a stomake is lyke a myghty fyre for to brenne gret
weyght of logges. But whan þe stomake is colde & feble than it is
good to haue lyght & subtyle meates.

⟪ The sygnes to knowlege þe stomake.

⟪ The sygnes of a stomake þat is of an yll & weyke dygestyon is 20
whan þe body is vnlusty/ heuy/ & slouthful, þe face is swollen/ &
yaneth often/ & hath payne in his eyen/ & bolketh often & rudely/
& þe bolkyng is sowre & vnsauery/ watry & stynkyng/ & therby is
bredde wyndes & swellynge of the bely & þe appetyte of meate is
marde. Therfore swete sone beware of meates and drynkes þat 25
may hurte or be contrary to thy helth. |

⟪. C. An epystle of grete value.   [f. E2ᵛ]

MOost dere sone Alexander sythe it is so that the body of man is
corruptyble by dyuersyte of complexyon/ & of contrary humours
that ben in it/ wherby often there cometh corrupcyon to it/ I 30
thought to delyuer the some thyng þat shall be necessary & prouffytable to the. In the whiche I wyll treate of the secretes of
physyke whiche shall please the. For certayne dyseases come to a

---

5 sklender] sklneder C   9 hote] whot K (*regular substitution, not in-*
dicated hereafter)   10 brennynge] burning K (*regular substitution, not in-*
dicated hereafter)   12 & proffyte/] &/ proffyte   14 *Title not given*
separate l., but printed to right of preceding words CK *separate title in* W   15 cours]
CW course K   19 *title printed to right of preceding words* C *separate l.* WK
25 marde] CW marred K   31-2 prouffytable] profetable W profitable K

seekenesse to a kinge whiche is nat honeste to shewe to the
phisicians. And yf thou wilt cleerly vndirstande and considre my
doctrines, thou shalt haue no neede of phisike, but yf it be in cace
of bataile. Alexander, diere sonne, whan thou rysest from sleepe,
5 goo a litle weye, and strecche out thy membres egally, and kembe
thy hede, for the strecching of the membres yevith strenght, and
the kembing taketh vp the fumous smoke that is comen vp to the
hede in thi sleepe. And in somyr wassh thyn hede with colde
watyr, and that shall kepe ynne the heete of the hede, and yiue
10 appetite to meyte. And than see that thou be clothid in faire and
preciouse clothinge, for the lyf and the herte taken grete delite
and counforte in the sight of faire clothinge. And aftir, rubbe thy
teeth with som barke or othir thinge that is hote and drye with
14 a bitter sauoure, for it is profitable for to kepe thaim cleene, and to
[f. 52] take awey the stenche of the | mouthe, and to make the voice more
p. 102 cleere. And also vse oft to doo rubbe thyne hede and thy body,
for that is holsom, and causeth the sparring of the brayne to open,
and encreecyth the nekke, and maketh the face the more cleere,
and amendith the blode, and causeth that the man is [nat] so sone
20 balled. And see that thou be annoynted with good and sweete
smellyng oynementes, for in the swete sauoure takith the hert
grete pleasire, lating the wite, that alle thinge that is swete sauour-
ing is to the herte meite norisshinge and grete delite. And whan
the hert hath taken his refeccion in the good sauoure, than the
25 blode rennyth in grete myrth in alle the veynes of the body. And at
som tymes thou shall take a lectuarie of a woode called aloe, whiche
thou shall finde writen in the booke of medicines, and also of
reuballe, whiche is a precious herbe, to the weight of .iiij. pens,
and this shall take the fleume from thy mouthe and stomac, and
30 yiueth hete to the body, and driueth awey the wynde, and yiueth
good sauoure. Moreouer I counseile the that thou comon often
with the noble and wise men of thy reame, of alle suche maters as
thou hast a-doo, and gouerne thaim graciously aftir the custumes.

The maner to trauayle

35 WHan thyne appetite comyth to eite, and the houre accustumed
is come, than take a litle trauayle before thy meyte, that is to sey, in
walkinge or dooyng som occupacion, and that helpeth well the

26 a lectuarie] alectuarie

kynge whiche be not honest to shewe to physycyens. And yf thou
wylt obserue this lesson/ thou shalt haue no nede of physycyens/
except in causes þat may come in batayle/ the whiche may be
exchewed. Alexander fayre sone/ whan thou rysest frome thy slepe/
walke and stretche thy membres egally and combe thy heed/ for 5
stretchyng of the lymmes gyueth force/ and combynge reyseth the
vapoures that ben come in slepynge and putteth them frome the
stomake. In somer wasshe thy heed in colde water/ whiche shall
yelde the naturall heate/ and shall be cause of appetyte to meate.
Than clothe the with goodly and ryche apparell. For the hert of 10
man delyteth in the beholdyng of precyous meates & clothyng.
Than rubbe thy tethe with some cours lynnyn/ or other thynge
that is hote and drye of compleccyon/ and swete of smell for it is
holsom for the tethe/ and kepeth them clene/ clenseth the stenche
of the mouth/ and clereth the voyce/ and gyueth appetyte to eate. 15
And rubbe thy heed often in the same wyse for it openeth the
claustres of the brayne/ and thycketh the necke and other membres/
and clenseth the face and the syght/ and prolongeth stowpynge of
of aege/ and amendeth the blode. | Also anoynt the somtyme with [f. E3]
swete smellynge oyntementes/ as the tyme requyreth/ for in suche 20
swetenesse thy hert taketh grete pleasure/ & is nourysshed therby.
And þe spyryt of lyfe taketh refeccyon in good odoures: and the
blode renneth meryly thrugh þe vaynes of the body. After that
take somtyme an electuary of a wood called Aloes/ and of Rubarbe
whiche is a precyous thynge, to the pryce of foure pens. Which 25
thou shalt fynde wryten in the boke of physyke/ and this shall do
the moche good/ for it voydeth the heate of the mouth of the
stomake/ and warmeth the body and wasteth wyndes/ and maketh
good taste and sauoure. After this I councell þe that thou be often
with thy noble and wyse men of thy realme/ & speke to them of thy 30
besynesses that thou hast to do. And gouerne them sadly accordynge to theyr good customes.

D. ☾ Of the maner to trauayle.

OR euer thou eate or thyn appetyte cometh at thyne houre accustomed do som trauayle/ that is to wyte walke or ryde a lytell/ or do 35
some other worke/ for it helpeth þe body moche/ it voydeth all

---

1 physycyens] physycyons W phisitio*n*s K   4 exchewed] CW
eschewed K   8 stomake.] *no punct. (at end of line)*   14 stenche] stinke
K   15 the mouth] thy mouth K   23 meryly] merely W merily K

[f. 52ᵛ] body, and dryueth | a-wey the wyndynesse, and maketh the body
p. 103 mightier and lighter, and counforteth the stomac, and wasteth
the yll humours of the body, and causeth the fleume of the stomac
to descende.

The maner to eyte

DEre sonne, whan the meite is before the, eite of that that thou
desirest mooste, with brede that is resonable laken with leueyn,
and eite first the meite that aught to be eiten first. And yf a man
haue ij. maner of meites, that is to sey, of harde digestion and of
10 soft, he aught first to eite the meyte of hard digestion, and after to
eite of that that is of soft digestion, for in the botome of the stomac
is gretter hete to digeste the meyte, for the hete of the lyuer is
nygh, which causeth the meyte to boile in the stomac.

Of abstinence

15 WHan thou eytist, halde the streight vp, and eite by layser,
though thou haue grete appetite to thy meyte. For yf thou eite to
hastilye, the humours multiplie and ouercharge the stomac, to thy
grete hurt, and greuaunce of the body, and the more abideth in
the botome of the stomac.

20   ### Of drinkinge of pure watyr

ALso d[r]inke nat pure watyr, and in speciall after that thou
hast eyten thy meyte, but if thou haue vsed i[t] custumablely, for
[f. 53] the colde wa|tyr that is drunken aftir thy meyte coldith thy
p. 104 stomac, and qwenchith and lettith the hete of digestion, to the
25 greuaunce of the body. And yf so be, for the grete habundaunce of
hete in thy body or stomac, or through hote meytes, thou most
needys drinke colde watir, than take it temperatlye and as litle
as thou may.

The maner to sleepe

30 AFter that thou hast taken thy refeccion, than slep[e] vpon a soft
bedde temperatly. And first slepe an houre vpon the right syde, and
than turne vpon thy left side and slepe alle that is resonable, for the
lift side is colde. And yf thou feele any soore in the baily or in thy
stomac, than, for a souerayne and counfortable medycyne, take
35 a warme shert and ley it vpon [thy stomac], or elles take in thyne

22 it] in   30 slepe] slept

ventosytees/ and maketh the body lyghter/ stronger and lustyeth
the stomake/ and waste[th] euyll humoures of the body and maketh
the flewme of the stomake descende.

❡ Of the maner of eatynge.

❡ Fayre sone whan thy meate is set afore the/ eate of suche as thou 5
desyrest moost/ resonably/ with well leuayned breed. And eate
[fyrst] of such as ought to be fyrst eaten. For there be two maners
of dygestyon of meat | in a man that is to wyte/ softe/ & harde. [f. E3ᵛ]
For in the botom is moost heat for to make [dygestion of] meat/
bycause it is moost flesshly/ and nyghest the heat of the lyuer 10
wherwith the meate is soden and dygested.

E. ❡ Of abstynence of meat.

WHan thou eatest/ eate by leasure/ though thou haue grete
appetyte to eate. For yf thou eate gredely noughty humoures do
multyply/ the stomake is laden/ the body is greued/ the hert is 15
hurte/ and the meate remayneth in the stomakes botome un-
dygested.

F. ❡ How pure water ought not to be dronken.

ALso beware dere sone that ye drynke no pure water/ specyally
whan thou haste eaten meate. But yf thou be wont therto. For as 20
soone as the water is vpon the meat/ it coleth þe stomake/ and
quencheth the heate of the dygestyon and comforte of the meat.
It letteth dygestyon and greueth the body. Yf thou must nede
drynke water alone/ take it the moost temperately/ and as lytell
as thou mayst. 25

G. ❡ Of the maner to slepe.

WHan thou hast taken thy refeccyon and hast luste to slepe/ lye
downe on a softe bedde and slepe temperatly. A[n]d fyrst lye
downe on the lyfte syde/ and slepe theron a reasonable space/ for
the lyfte syde is colde and hath nede to be warme[d]. And yf thou 30
fele ony payn in thy bely or in thy stomake/ than | lay therto a [f. E4]
souerayne medycyne/ that is a warme lynnen cloth layde theron.

---

2 wasteth] wasted CW wasteth K   4] *title run on immediately after*
prec. words CK   15 laden/] *no punct.* (*at end of l.*)   28 And] Aud C
And K   30 to be warmed] to be warmeth C of warmeth W

armes a faire maide and holde hir surely. Latinge thi wite, that
trauayle before meyte is good, and yiveth heete to the stomac, but
aftir meite it is contrarie, for than the meite abideth in the botome
of the stomac, vndigeste, wherof ben engendred diuers seekenesse.
5 And wilt thou wite that slepe before meyte is nat good, for it
maketh the body lene and dryeth the humors. But the slepe aftir
meite is good and holsome, for it filleth the body, and yevith it
strenght and norisshing. And whan a man slepith, the body
restith, and the naturall hete that is a-brode in all the membres
10 draweth and resorteth to the stomac, and yeuith it strenghth of
digestion vpon the refeccion of the meite. And than the naturall |
[f. 53ᵛ] vertu askith his quiete rest, wherfore som philosophres han seid
p. 105 that it is bettyr to eite at evyn than in the mornynge, and for this
reson: the meite that is taken in the mornynge greuith the stomac,
15 be-cause of the hete of the day, and maketh the body the more
weery. And, in the othir partie, a man cha[f]ith himself with
goinge or dooinge som othir occupacions. And for the grete hete
that apperith in the noon tyde, the naturall hete of the body is en-
weyked, and enpeireth the might of the stomac, and causeth it
20 to be wors of digestion. But for to take his refeccion at euyn, the
body is the bettyr at ease, and lesse greeuid of the laboure of the
day, and the hert and membres of the man ben in more rest, because of the colde nyght, whiche yeuith naturall heete to the
stomac.

25   **Of kepinge of mannys hele**

THou aught to vndirstande, that he that custumablely takith his
meyte at .ij. tymes in the day, and than brekith his custume and
eiteth but onys in the day, it is yll and greuous to the body. And in
the same wyse, he that is vsed custumablelye to eite but onys, and
30 chaunge it, and eite twys. For than the stomac hath no vertu to
digeste the meite, and [it] abideth in the stomac vndigeste, withoute any norisshinge. And that is accustumed to take his refeccion at a certeyne houre, yf he chaunge that houre and take it at
an othir, he shall in breef tyme apperceyue that it dooth him hurt
35 and greuaunce, for custume chaungeth nature.

13–14 this reson] *run together in ms.*   16 chafith] chasith

Wyte þou dere sone that trauayle is good/ and gyueth heate to the
stomake. But after dyner it is a noughty thynge/ for the meat
abydeth vndygested in the botome of the stomake/ and therof be
bredde many dyseases. And slepe before fedynge is not good/ for
it maketh the body leane and dryeth the humoures. But slepynge   5
after fedynge is good/ for it fulfylleth þe body & gyueth force/ &
nourysshyng therto. For whan þe body of man resteth/ than þe
natural heat draweth þe heat þat was spredde in all þe membres
in to þe botom of þe stomake/ & gyueth strength therto vpon þe
refeccyon of þe meat. And heat requyreth rest. Therfore some   10
phylosophres haue sayd þat it is better & holsomer to eat at nyght
than in the mornyng/ for the eatyng in þe mornynge bycause of
þe heat of þe day greueth þe stomake/ & þe body is more trauayled
therwith. And moreouer þe persone chauffeth in trauaylyng
doynge his besynesse/ in goyng & spekyng/ & many other thynges   15
þat belongeth to þe body of man/ by þe which heat þat is outwarde towarde none/ þe naturall heat þat is inwarde is weyked &
appeyred/ & þe meate is harde to dygest. But at nyght it is more
easy & lesse greued with þe heat of traueyle. And þe hert &
membres of man ben more in quyet by þe coldnesse of þe nyght/   20
that gyueth naturall heat to the stomake.

H. ❡ The kepyng of custome or wont.

THou shalt vnderstande my dere sone that he that is wonte to
eate but one meale often is dyseased/ for þe stomake is without
dygestyon & þe body hath smal nourysshyng. And he þat is acus-   25
tomed to eate at one time ones | another tyme twyse he shal [f. E4ᵛ]
lyghtly perceyue that it doth hym harme/ for custome chargeth
nature.

27 chargeth] CWK change F f. 20v

How a man aught to chaunge his custume |

[f. 54] ANd yf nede constreyne the to chaunge thy custume, doo it
p. 106 wysely, that is to wite, to chaunge it by litle and litle, and so by
Goddys mercy thy mutacion and chaunge shall be good and nat
5 greuous. And beware that thou eite no meyte tyll thou knowe for
certayn that thy stomac is void, and that he haue digestion of the
firste meite. And th[i]s shall thou vndirstande by the desire that
thou shall haue to thy meyte, and thy spatill shall subtilye stire
in thy mouthe. And yf thou eite thy meite withoute neede and
10 appetite, it will cause the hete of thy stomac by processe to be as
colde as the glas. And yf thou take thy meite with good appetite,
the naturell hete of thy stomac shall be as the fire, and make
good digestion. And whan thyne appetite is come, loke that thou
take thy meite without longe taryenge. For yf thou make taryinge,
15 thy stomac takith his full refeccion of the yll humors that ben in
the body, whiche shall trouble the brayne, and enwyke the stomac,
and the meite shall doo no profite to the body. And, in cace be thou
maist nat take thi meite so soone as thy appetite is come, and that
thi stomac be full of yll humors, do so that thou may haue a vomyte
20 or thou eite, and than a lectuarye or othir thinge that is counfortable. And than eite surelye.

Of the .iiij. seasons of the yere

OVre intencion is to declare in this book the .iiij. ceasons of the
24 yere, and the qualité and propirté of yche of thaim, and the con-
[f. 54] trarieté and difference | of the same. Whiche ceasons ben diuided
p. 107 as here-aftir folowith, that is to sey: vere, somyr, autumpne, and
wynter. Veer begynneth whan the sun entrith in the signe of Aries
and endureth .iiij.^{xx} xiij dayes, x[x]iij. houres, and the fourth parte
of an houre, that is to wite, fro the xth. day of the ende of Marche
30 vnto the xxiij^{ti} day of June. And in this ceason ben the nyghtys and
the dayes egall in thaire regions. The tyme is swete, the wyndes
risen, the snowes meltyn, the ryuers enforcen thaire cours, and the
humors of the erthe taken heete, whiche ascendith to the height
of trees, and causeth thaim to florissh. The medues refresshen
35 thaire verdure, all maner seede and corne springeth and groweth,
alle maner floures taken thaire fressh colours. And the birdes
renwen thaire fressh clothinge, and payn thaim to vtter thaire

7 this] thus   26 as here-aftir] ashere *run together*   28 xxiij.
houres] xviij houres

J. ⅭHow one ought to chaunge custome

ANd yf nede constreyne the to chaunge thy custome/ do it wysely/ that is to wyte by lytel and lytell. And so by the grace of god thy chaungynge shall be good. But aboue al thynges beware that thou eate not tyl thou fele thy stomake empty and that it hath 5 made good dygestyon of the fyrst meale. And this thou mayst knowe by þe desyre that thou shalt haue to thy meate: and by thy spatle that tornyth subtylly in thy mouthe. And yf thou eate without nede or appetyte the heate of thy stomake shall be made colde as yse. And yf necessyte be þat thou must eate/ & haue an 10 appetyte therto/ þe kynde heate of thy stomake wyll be as hote as fyre/ & of good dygestyon. And beware þat whan thy appetyte cometh that thou eate not forth with/ for it wyll gadre yll humours of thy body in to thy stomake/ whiche wyll hurte thy brayne. And yf thou tary ouer longe or thou eate/ it wyl feble thy stomake/ & the 15 meate wyll do thy body no good. And yf so be þat thou mayst not eate as soone as thy appetyte requyreth/ and þat thy stomake be ful of yll humours/ do so þat thou mayst vomyte or thou eate/ & after þe vomyte take an electuary/ and eate surely.

K. ⅭOf the foure seasons of the yere. | 20

OUr intencyon is to treat in this boke of þe foure seasons of the [f. F1] yere/ with the qualyte/ propryete/ contraryte/ and dyfference of eche of them. And they ben certayne seasons of the yere deuyded as foloweth. That is to wyte [fyrst] prym tyme or vere. And in this season the dayes & nyghtes ben egall of length. The wether is fayre. 25 The warme wether cometh. The snowes melte/ ryuers renne swyft and clere & waxe warme/ the moystenesse of the erthe ryseth to þe heyght of trees/ and causeth them to smel swete. Medowes and graynes sprowte and corne groweth/ & all floures take coloure/

---

13 gadre] gather WK   24 fyrst prymtyme or vere] prymtyme or vere begynneth whan the sonne entreth in the sygne of Aries/ and lasteth foure score & xiij. dayes/ and .xiij. houres/ & the fourthe parte of an houre. That is to wyte frome þe .x. day in the ende of Marche, to þe foure and twenty day of June C and, substant., K: see n.   25 length.] no punct.

swete and melodious songes. The trees ben spredde with greene
leuys and floures, beestes engendren, and alle thinges taken might
and vertu. The erthe taketh beauté, whiche is like to the faire
spouse that is clothid in riche and precious clothinge, which
5 causeth to seeme miche fairere.

Of the ceason of veer and what it is

WEer is hote, and temperate with humor. In this ceason mannys
bloode meeuith and spreedith in all the membres of the bodye, and
the body takith perfite compleccion. And in this ceson shuld be
10 eiten chikenys, kyddes, and egges till .vi. and no moo at onys, and
eite letuse that is egre, whiche is called in som cuntree karioles.
Eite also gotes mylke. And in this ceason is bettir to be lat bloode
[f. 55] than in | any othir ceason. And allso it is good to trauayle, and to
p. 108 haue the bely softe, and to swete, and walke, and to bath him-self,
15 and to eite suche meites as will purge well the baily, for all the
wastinge that thou shall haue through bleedinge or digestion is
soon recouerde.

The ceason of somyr and what it is

SOmyr begynneth whan the sun entreth in the first pointe of the
20 signe of the Crabbe, and endureth iiij^{xx}xij daies, xxiij^{ti} houres, and
the iij^d parte of an houre, that is to say, from the xxiij^{ti} day of
June vnto the xxiiij^{ti} day of Septembre. In this ceason ben longe
dayes and shorte nyghtys. And in all regions the hete encrecith, and
the wyndes swage, the see is pleasaunt and meeke, the aere is swete,
25 the cornys drien, the serpentes growen and cast out thaire venyme.
The vertu of mannys body is fortified and perfourmed, and alle
the worlde is replenysht with goodys. And this ceason is likenyd
to the spouse that is faire and plesaunt in hir parfite age. And this
ceason is hoot and drye. And beware of all thinges that ben of hote
30 and drye compleccion duringe this tyme. And be ware also that
in this ceason thou eite nat, nor drinke nat, to miche. And eite
suche meites as ben of hum[ide] and colde compleccion, as the
flessh of calf, mylke with vineger, potage made with barly mele,
frutes that ben of egre sauoure, and pome garnadys. And drinke
35 but litle wyne, and dele but litle with womman. In this ceason

32 humide] humour (*poss. intended reading*)

byrdes ben clothed with newe robes/ and enforce them to synge.
Trees ben decked with leues and floures/ and the landes with
sedes. Beestes engendre and all people take strength & lust. The
erthe is arayed goodly/ & is as a fayre bryde clothed with
Jewelles of dyuers coloures bycause she sholde seme the fayrer 5
at her weddynge.

L. ⁋ Of prymtyme/ and what it is.

THe prymtyme is hote & moyst temperatly as the ayre. This
season þe blode moeueth and spredeth to all the membres of the
body/ and the body is parfyte in temperate complexyon. In this 10
season chekyns/ kyddes/ and poched egges ought to be eaten/ with
letu|ses & gotes mylke in these thre monethes. Prymetyme be- [f. F1ᵛ]
gynneth whan the sonne entreth the sygne of Aryes and lasteth
.xcii. dayes/ an houre and a halfe fro the .x. day of Marche to þe .x.
day of June. In this season is the best letyng of blode of ony tyme. 15
And than is good to trauayle and to be laxatyfe. And to be bathed.
And to eate suche thynges as wyll purge þe bely. For all dyseases
that cometh/ eyther by purgyng or bledynge/ retorneth anone in
this prymetyme.

M. ⁋ Of somer and what it is. 20

SOmer begynneth whan the sonne entreth þe fyrst poynt of the
creuyce/ & lasteth .xcii. days/ & an houre & a half. That is to wyte
fro þe .x. day of June to þe .x. day of september. In this season þe
days be longe & þe nyghtes short. And in al regyons encreaseth
& abateth theyr heate & þe see is calme/ & þe ayre meke & fayre. 25
The flours wyther & serpentes encrease & shed theyr venym/ &
sprede theyr strength. The myghtes of mannes body be fortyfyed.
And al þe world is ful of welth/ as þe fayre bryde þat is [of] goodly
stature & in perfyte aege. The season of somer [is] hote & drye/&
than coler is moeued. And in this season is good to beware of all 30
thynges þat be hote & drye of complexyon. And take hede of to
moche eatyng or drynkynge for therby is þe kyndly heate quenched.
In this season eate meates of colde & moyst complexyon/ as veale/
mylke with vyneygre/ & potages made with barly meale. Eate
fruyt of eygre sauour/ as pommegarnets/ & drynke small wynes/ 35
& vse not the company of women. In this season lete the not

14 .x.²] tenth K (*so regularly with numerals; this substitution not indicated hereafter*)   23 september. In] *no punct.* (*at end of line*)   28 of] *supplied
from* K   29 somer is hote] some hote CW sommer, whot K   35 pom-
megarnets] Pomgranates K

be nat let bloode but yf grete neede cause it, and vse litle trauaile |
[f. 55ᵛ] and litle bathinge.
p. 109

Of the ceason of autumpne, and what he is

[A]Utumpne entreth whan the sonne entreth in the first degree
5 of the Leon, and lasteth .iiij.ˣˣ and viij. dayes, and .xxvij. houres,
that is to sey, from the xxiiij. day of Septembre vnto the xxijᵗⁱ day
of [Dec]embre. In this ceason, the nyghtes and the daies ben egall
of lenght. The aire troubleth, the wyndes entren in thaire region,
ryuers and springes discreecyn, the gardyn drieth, the frutes
10 waxen ripe, the beauté of the erthe fadith, the birdes seekyn the
warme cuntreis, the beestes axen the cauys and warme places, the
serpentes seekyn thaire repaire, where they gete thaire liuinge for
wynter. The erthe is as the olde womman that is naked, and passed
youthe, and age draweth neere. The tyme is colde and drye. And
15 therfore, this ceason, eite hoote meytes, as chykenys, lambys, and
drinke olde wyne and eite swete reysons. And beware of all thinges
that engendreth blac colour, as to walke to miche, or to mich
leying with womman. And take no bathe, but yf it be grete nede.
And yf a man haue grete nede of a vomyte, take it at noon tyme,
20 for that is the warmest houre of the daye. And at that houre superfluitees and humors gadren in the bodie. And also it is good in this
ceason to purge the belye with a medicyn called asmon and as-
macon, and by alle othir thinges whiche withdrawyth the blac
24 coloure and refrayneth the humours. |

[f. 56] ## Of wynter ceason, and what it is
p. 110

WYntyr begynneth whan the sun entreeth in the first degree of
the signe of Aries, and endureth .lxx[x]ix. daies and xxiijᵗⁱ houres
from the xxijᵗⁱ day of [Dec]embre vnto the xxᵗⁱ day of Marche. In
this ceason, the daies ben shorte and the nyghtes ben longe, the
30 colde is grete, the wyndes ben sharpe, the leuys fallyn downe, and
alle thinges lose thaire verdoure for the moost parte. And the
bestes rasoorten to cauys or dykes for the grete colde, the aire and
the tyme waxeth blak, and the erthe is like to a womman of grete
age, naked, and in decrepitude nygh to deth. And by-cause the
35 wynter ys colde and moist, it is good to vse of hoote meytes as

4 AUtumpne] IUtumpne   5 viij. dayes] dayes and xviij dayes (*first*
dayes *poss. intended reading*)   7 Decembre] Nouembre   28 Decembre]
Nouembre Nouembre F.f. *2 2ᵛ: English presumably reproduces error in its original*

blode/ but yf grete nede compell the. Vse lytell trauayle/ & seldome
bathynge.

N. ❧ Of Autumpne/ or heruest. |

HEruest entreth whan þe sonne cometh in to þe fyrst degre of [f. F2]
the balaunce & lasteth xci. dayes & an houre & a halfe. That is to 5
wyte fro the .x. daye of Septembre to þe x. daye of Decembre. In
this season the day & nyght be of one length. And than þe dayes
waxe short & þe nyghtes longe. The ayre is derke/ & þe wyndes
entre the northen regyons or septentryon. The wether chaungeth/
& þe ryuers & sprynges waxe lesse. The orcheyardes & fruytes 10
wydreth. The beaute of erthe fadeth. Byrdes cease theyr syngyng.
Serpentes seke theyr holes wher they assembled theyr lyuyng in
somer for þe tyme of wynter. The erthe is as an olde naked woman
þat gooth fro youth to aege. This season of heruest is colde & drye/
this tyme blacke coler is moeued. In this season is good to eate 15
meates þat be hote & moyst as chekyns/ lambe/ & drynke olde
wynes/ eate swete reasyns. And kepe þe from all thynges þat brede
blacke coler/ as lyenge with women more than in somer/ nor bath
þe not but yf grete nede requyre it to be done. In this season yf
a man haue nede of vomytynge/ do it at none in the hotest of þe day. 20
For at þat tyme al þe superfluytees of mannes body gadreth togyder. Also it is good to purge þe bely with a medycyn ordeyned
therfore & other thynges þat ben to expulce blacke coler & to
refrayne humoures.

O. ❧ Of wynter and what it is.   25

Wynter cometh whan þe sonne entreth þe fyrst degre of þe sygne
of Caprycorne & lasteth lxx. dayes & an houre & a halfe. And begynneth þe .x. day of Decembre/ and contynueth to þe .x. daye of
Marche. In this | season þe nyghtes be longe & þe days short/ [f. F2ᵛ]
it is veray colde. The wynes be in þe presse/ & þe leues fall/ & 30
herbes leeseth all theyr strength/ or the moost parte. All bestes
hydeth them in caues and pyttes of hylles. The ayre and the wether
is darke. And the erthe is lyke an olde decrypyte persone/ that by
grete aege is naked and nygh to the deth. Wynter is veray colde
and moyst/ & than behoueth the vse hote meates/ as chekyns/ 35

---

10 orcheyardes] orchards K   11 wydreth] widereth W withereth K
erthe] the earth K   21-2 togyder] togyther KW   22 ordeyned] ordeynen W

chikenys, hennys, moton, and othir hote flessh and fatte. Also vse figges, nottes, and rede wyne. And beware that thy belye be nat softe, nor blede nat. Also hurt nat thy stomac thrugh eytinge and drinkynge to miche, or with hawntinge wommen to miche.
5 Neuyrthelesse, in that ceason the felauship of wommen is good, to take it temperatlye, and bathinge is good. Lating the wite, that through the grete colde the naturall hete gadreth in the body, and therfore the naturall digestion in the stomac is bettre in wynter ceason and in veer, than in the othir .ij. ceasons. For in
10 somyr and autumpne, the bely is colde, and the naturall hete of the body is spred abrode, so that the stomac hath litle parte therof, whiche causeth the wors digestion. |

[f. 56ᵛ]
p. III

Of the naturall heete

ALexander, deere sonne, I pray the, aboue all thinges, kepe well
15 the naturall heete of thy body. For as longe as the kyndelye and temperate heete is in thy body, thou shall haue good heele and longe lyf. Doing the to wite, that a man dyeth by .ij. sundry weyes. Oon is bi kyndely nature of age, whiche werith oute and ouer-throueth the man. And an othir weye is through accident casuel-
20 tees, by glayues, seekenesses, or by som othir aduenture.

Of the thinges that maken the body fatte

DEre soone, that thinge that makyth a man fatte is whan a man takith his rest, and filleth him with diuers swete meytes, and drinkes swete wyne and mylke, and than slepe vpon a softe bedde,
25 and smelle alle thinge that is [swete, and in especiall take bathes of fresshe water, in the which be] swete smellinge herbys. And tary nat longe therynne, for longe tarying enweyketh the man. And drinke no wyne but if it be sufficiently temperate with watyr, or of an herbe called alchemyn. And put som in thy wyne for it is of
30 hoote nature. And in somyr vse of violet floures, of malowes, and othir thinge of colde nature. And take a vomyte onys in a moneth, and in especiall in the somyr, for the vomyte wasshith the body, and purgeth him of the ylle and stinkinge humours beinge with-ynne. And yf they be but litle humors in thy stomac, it will
35 counforte thy naturall hete. And whan thou hast had a vomyte
[f. 57] withoute violence, the | body shall take his fillinge of good fatnesse
p. 112 and humiditee, and the stomac shall be well dispoosed of diges-tion. And if thou reule the vndir this forme thou shall haue joye

25–6 swete . . . be] *see n.*

hennes/ motton/ and other hote & fatte flesshe/ eate fygges/ nuttes/ and drynke grene wynes. And beware of to moche laxe and bledynge/ & eschewe company of women/ for it wyll feble thy stomake/ and bathes be good. And for the grete colde the natural heate entreth in to the body/ and therfore the dygestion is better 5 in wynter than in somer. And in heruest the bely is colde/ and than the poores ben open by heate of the season/ and reproueth the naturall heate of all the partes of þe body. And therfore the stomake hath but lytel heate/ wherby the dygestyon is febled/ and the humours assemble there.   10

P. ℭ Of naturall heate.

SOne Alexander I pray þe kepe the kyndly heate of thy body/ and thou shalt haue longe helth. For the body of man dyeth in .ii. maners. One is by grete aege the which ouercometh the body and dystroyeth it. The other is accydentally/ as by wepen/ sykenesse/ 15 or other aduenture.

Q. ℭ Of thynges that fatteth the body.

Ryght dere sone these ben thynges that fatteth the body. That is [f. F3] to wyte ease of the body and fyllynge it with deynty meates and drynkes/ & mylke/ and than to slepe on a soft bed. All swete smell- 20 ynge floures in theyr season/ and bathynge in fresshe waters. But yf thou bathe the/ tary not longe in it/ and haue swete smellynge thynges in þe bath. And neuer drynke wyne but it be well tem-pered with water. And specyally in wynter make water of floures called Assynini and put it in to thy wyne/ for it is hote of nature. 25 And in somer vse vyolettes and floures of malowes & other thynges that be colde/ & vse to vomyte ones in a moneth specyally. For vomytes wassheth the body and purgeth it of wycked humoures and stynke that is in it. And yf there be but fewe humoures in the stomake/ it conforteth the naturall heate. And whan thou hast 30 vomyte wyllyngly/ the body wyll fyll it with good humydyte and be of good dysposycyon to dygest. And yf thou gouerne the thus/ thou shalt be mery at thy hert/ lusty with reasonable helth and

and mirthe, good heele, reson and vndirstandinge, with glorye,
worshippe, and victorie of thyne enmyes. Moreouer, I will avise
the at som tymes to take delite and disporte and playe, and to see
goodly menne and faire wommen, and to rede bookes that ben
5 plesaunt and delectable, and were faire clothinge aftir the ceason.

Of the thinges that maken the body leene

THere ben certeyne thinges that causeth the body to be leene
and drye and the weykere: that is to say, to eite and drinke to
miche, to miche trauaile, to longe beinge in the sun, to miche
10 going, to miche sleepinge before dyner, to be full of melancolye
and pencyfnesse, and to be bathid in watirs that ben of sulphur
kynde, to eite salt meytes, drinke olde wyne, to miche goinge to
pryué, to miche bleedinge. Latinge the wite that he that bathith
him the bely full, he shall haue seekenesse in the ynner parties
15 of the body, and in the same-wyse cace, he that lieth with a
womman the bely full, and also that aftir his meite rennyth or
rideth or trauaileth to miche. Therof will enswe a grete sekenesse
called paralatike. And he that often etith fyssh and drinketh mylke
and wyne to-gedir, Ypocras seith he shulde be a lepre by lyklyhode.

20 ## The first parte of the body |

THe body is diuided in iiij. parties. The first parte is the heede,
wherynne gadreth superfluités and yll humors, whiche thou shall
feele and knowe by theise signes folowinge: the yien waxen
troubelous and dymme, the browes swellyn, the nosethrilles ben
25 straight. And yf thou feele any of theise signes, take an herbe called
aloyne, and lay it in swete wyne, and make it to boile with a roote
called pugilchiny, so longe that half of the wyne be wasted. Put
som therof in thy mouthe, and kepe it longe ynne, all-wey wasshing
thy mouthe, till that thou feele that it doo the good. And allso eite
30 with thy meite the seede of whight mustarde, beten in poudre,
and it [shall] ease the greetly. And yf [thou] doo it nat, it may
folowe grete seekenesse in thyne yien and brayne, and in othir
parties of the body.

The secunde parte of the body

35 THe breste is the secunde parte of the body. And yf seekenesse
come therynne, thou shall knowe it be theise signes folowing:
thy tunge shall be letted, thy mouthe shall be salt and byttyr, or

good vnderstandyng/ glory & honour/ & ouer al thyn enemyes
vyctory. Also I wyll that thou delyte in the beholdyng of goodly
persones/ or in redynge of delectable bokes/ or in weryng of precyous garmentes/ and goodly Jewelles/ as the tyme requyreth.

R. ℂ Of thynges that leaneth the body.   5

THese ben the thynges that maketh the body to be leane/ weyke/
and drye/ to moche eatynge/ to moche trauelynge/ to moche
walkynge in the | sonne/ to moche goynge/ to moche slepyng afore [f. F3ᵛ]
noone/ melancoly/ feare/ to bathe in water of the nature of brym-
stone/ eatynge salt meates/ to moche drynkynge of olde wyne/ to be 10
to laxe/ and ouermoche letynge of blode. For Ypocras sayth that
he þat batheth him with a full bely/ or lyeth with a woman shal
haue sykenesse in his entrayles. And also to renne/ or to ryde/ or
to moche trauayle after meat bredeth a grete dysease called palsey.
And moche eatyng of fysshe, or mylke and wyne togyder Ypocras 15
sayth it wyl make one lazar.

S. ℂ Of the fyrst parte of the body.

OF þe .iiij. partes of þe body the head is þe fyrst. For in þe heed
gadreth all superfluytees/ and euyll humoures/ whiche thou shalt
fele and knowe by these sygnes folowyng. The eyes ben troubled/ 20
the heryng is thycked & þe nosestrylles ben stopped. Yf thou fele
suche a dysease take an herbe called wormwood/ and sethe it in
swete wyne tyll the halfe be wasted/ than holde it in thy mouth &
wasshe it many tymes therwith tyl thou fele þat it dooth þe good/
& eate whyte mustard sede powdred with thy meate. And yf thou 25
do not thus thou mayst happen to haue som dysease/ & specyally
in thyn eyes/ in thy brayn/ & in other partes of thy body.

T. ℂ Of the seconde parte of the body.

THe seconde parte of the body is the bulke. Yf dysease come
there thou shalt knowe it by these sygnes folowynge. The tongue 30
is lette/ þe mouthe is salt/ bytter/ & vnsauery. The mouth of the

9 noone/ melancoly] *no punct.* (*at end of l.*)   12 batheth] Bathe W
17 S.] *no punct.*   21 stopped.] stopped/   29 bulke.] bulke/   31 vnsauery.
The] *no punct.* (*at end of l.*)

ellys swete, the mouthe of thy stomac shall be egre, and thy
membres shall be sore. Thou most eite litle, and haue a vomyte.
Take a litle sugre rosett with aloe and mastic, and alle that eite
to-gedirs. Or elles take som good spice confortatif. And aftir this
5 thou shall eite with good appetite. And aftir thy meite take
a lectuarye clepid dionision, whiche is made with aloe, galingale,
and grasegrinte. And yf thou doo it nat, there may folowe doloure
[f. 58] and seekenesse in the hede, and feuers, | with impediment of the
p. 114 tunge and othir diuers seekenesse.

10   **The thryd parte of the body**

THe third parte of the body is the belye. And yf yll humors
come therynne, thou shall vndirstande it by theise signes folowinge:
thy bely shall swelle, and thou shall haue doloure and sterkenesse in
the knes, and thou shall goo heuily. Thou most be pourged bi som
15 light and subtile medicyne, like as I tolde here-before in the
gouernaunce of the breste. And if thou doo it nat, thou may
lightlye haue doloure in thyne hip bones, in the splene, and in the
bak, and in the jointes, and seekenesse in the bely and in the lyuer,
with ill digestion.

20   **The fourthe parte of the body**

THe fourthe parte of the body is the genitories. Whan superfluitees and ill humors gadren therynne, thou shall vndirstande
by theise signes: thin appetite shall appeire, and a reednes shall
come to the stonys and vpon the share. Thou most take an herbe
25 callid apium, and fenell sede, and the roote of archemese or of an
othir herbe called smallache, and ley thaim alle in good whight
wyne. And of that wyne euery day drinke a litle in the mornynge
with a litle watir and hony. And eite nat to miche. And yf thou doo
29 it nat, it will enswe seekenesse in the bladder and in the lyuer, and
[f. 58ᵛ] thou nat pisse | easely, and so shall thou haue doloure in the en-
p. 115 trailes and longys, and thus may it engendre the stone. Deere
sonne, I haue red an historye that there was a mighty kinge
whiche was assembled to the best phisicians that were in Inde
and in Grece. And he desired of thaim to make him suche a
35 medicyne that he shulde neuer neede othir hele. The phisicians of
Grece seid that it is good and profitable to drinke euery mornynge
twys his mouth full of hoote watyr. He shall be hole, and haue no

12 it] if it   26 whight] wihight   31 engendre the] engendreth the

stomake is sowre with | grefe in all thy membres. It behoueth þe [f. F4]
to eate but lytel & to vomyte/ than eate a lytel sugre of roses
with aloes & take good comfortyng spyces & eate an electuary
named Dionisium. And yf thou do not thus/ thou mayst fal in
dysease of þe syde/ of þe raynes/ & feuers/ & specyally of þe tongue 5
wherby þu shalt not properly speke/ & dyuers other maladyes.
Decoccyon of ysope is good.

V. ℂ Of the thyrde parte of the body.

THe thyrde parte of the body is the wombe [.Y]f it be combred
with euyll humoures þu shalt knowe it by these sygnes. The bely 10
wyll swell with payne & styfnesse in þe knees goynge a slowe pace.
It behoueth to vse some subtyle & lyght meates/ as is sayd before
with the gouernynge. And yf þu do not thus there wyl folowe
ache in the hyppes/ in the mylte/ in the back/ and other ioyntes/
and in the lyuer/ with yll dygestyon.   15

X. ℂ Of the fourth parte of the body.

THe fourth parte of the body ben þe genytours. Yf superfluyte
& noughty humoures gadre in them þu shalt knowe it by these
sygnes. The appetyte wyl waxe colde/ & reednesse wyll appere
vpon them & vpon þe share. Than must þu take a sede called 20
Apij with fenell sede & þe rote of mugwort/ & of another called
Acham/ & atracies. And with these herbes put þe rotes in good
whyte wyne/ & drynke a quantyte of it euery mornyng with a lytell
water & hony & eate not moche after it. And yf þu do not thus þu
shalt haue payne in þe bladder/ & lyuer/ & shalt not pysse/ & 25
shalt haue grefe in þe intrayles and lunges with bre[d]ynge of the
stone. Swete sone Alexander I haue rede also the hystoryes of
a myghty kynge/ whiche assembled all the best phylosophres |
that were in Ynde and Grece. And commaunded them to make [f. F4ᵛ]
a medycyne so prouffytable that he sholde nede none other for his 30
helth. The Grekes sayd he that drynketh euery mornyng twyse
his mouthfull of warme water shall haue a good ende/ and shall

5 þe syde] that syde W   raynes] reignes K   9 wombe. Yf] wombe/ yf C
and, substant. K   specyally] especiallye K   7 ysope] Tysope W   16 X.]
no punct.   18 noughty] naughtie K   26 bredynge] brekynge CW
breakyng K ⟨se pourra⟩ engendrer ⟨la pierre⟩ F f. 24: *see n.*

neede of othir medycyne. The phisicians of Inde said that it is good
and profitable to eite euery mornynge, fasting, certeyne cornes of
whete myle and nasturcij. And me seemyth that the man that
sleepith sore shulde haue no seekenesse by reson in his bely, ne nor
5 he aught nat to dreede the palsye nor goute nor doloure in the
jointes. And who that eiteth euery day alibi aurei, vij dragmes, and
with oo[ue] passes and of swete reysens, he shall be sauf for fleume,
and he shall haue the bettir memorye and the more cliere vndirstandinge, and he shall be sauf from the feuers quarteyns. And
10 that eiteth nuttes and figges, with a fewe leuys of rue, he is that
day sauf from all venyme. Moreouere, I pray the to kepe well
the naturall heete, with humiditees in mannys body. He shall haue
heele. Latinge the wite, that the destruccion of the body comyth
of .ij. soundry causes. The first is naturall. The secunde is ayenst
15 nature. That is naturall is for the contrarieté of the compleccion of
man. And whan age ouercometh the body, than he most nedys
dye. The othir, that is ayenst nature, comyth by casuell auenture
[f. 59] with glayues | or seeknesse, through ill gouernaunce. And on the
p. 116 othir partie, it is good to haue knowlege of the nature and kynde
20 of meites, for som ben subtile and som ben grete, and som is
a meane betwixe bothe. Latinge the wite, that subtile meites engendreth good bloode and chere, that is to sey: good whete, hennys
chikenes, eggys. And grete meites ben good for him that is hoote,
and vseth laboure, and trauaile after meite. The meite that is small
25 and in meene engendreth noo swellinge nor superfluitees of alle
humors, that is to say, lambe, capons, and othir suche as ben hote
and moiste. How be it that at som tymes suche flessh, whan it is
rosted, makith the bely harde, hote, and drye, yf suche meite be
taken temperatlye, whan it is hoote, it is good and profitable to
30 the body.

---

1 good] *second* o *ins. above*   4 sore] *see n.*   7 ooue] oon *with
curved sign over* n *as normal in this ms. for* oon: *see n.*

nede none other medycyne. The physycyens of Ynde sayd that it
is good to eate euery day fastyng a quantyte of greynes of whyte
hony. And me semeth that who so taketh one of these sayd medycynes by reason shall not haue payne in his wombe/ nor ought not
to feare palsey/ nor gowte/ nor ache in his Joyntes. And who so 5
eateth euery mornynge .vij. dragmas of clustres of swete wyne
grapes/ shall not feare þe dysease of flewme/ and it wyll amende his
mynde/ and claryfy his vnderstandynge/ and he nedeth not to
doubt feuer quartaynes. And who so eateth in the mornynge a
fygge with nuttes and a quantyte of leues of rue, þat day shall not 10
nede to feare venym.

❡ Of naturall heate.

❡ Moost myghty kynge I requyre the to study the maner to kepe
the naturall heat of thy body/ with þe moysture therof/ in the
whiche two thynges lyeth the helthe of thy persone. And knowe 15
thou that the destruccyon of the body cometh in two thynges/
one is naturall/ and the other agaynst nature. And for þe contraryte
of the complexyon of man/ and whan aege surmounteth þe body
it behoueth for to dye. Other wyse vnnaturally by aduenture/ as
by wepen/ or stones/ or by sykenesse and lacke of helpe/ or by 20
venym/ and other chaunces.

❡ Of the qualytees of meates.

❡ Forthermore it is good that thou knowe the natu|re of meates/ [f. G1]
for some ben grosse/ or cours/ & some ben lyght & subtyle. The
subtyle bredeth thynne blode/ & good/ as pure wheate/ chekyns/ & 25
new layde egges. Grosse meates ben good for suche as ben of hote
humours/ labourers/ fastyng/ and þat slepe after meales. Meane
meates bredeth no hote nor superfluous humours/ as the flesshe
of lambes/ yonge porke/ & other that ben hote and moyste/ but
suche meates chaunge often in rostynge to hardnesse/ to heate/ 30
and dryenesse. And they ought to be eaten forthwith after the
rostynge/ and ben good yf they be so taken with good spyces. Some
meates brede melancoly/ as befe/ cowes flesshe/ and all flesshe
that is cours and drye. Other that brede and fede in moyst and
watry/ & shadowy places ben more subtyle/ better and holsomest. 35

6 .vij. dragmas] sixe drams K   22 qualytees] qualytes W qualities K
26 egges.] *no punct. (at end of l.)*   31 dryenesse. And] *no punct. (at end of l.)*
34 drye.] *no punct.*   brede and fede] feede K   35 *End of text of Wyer's
Difference of astronomy*

Of the maners of fysshes

THe fyssh that is litle and of tendre skynne, and light in the mouthe, and that is norisshed in swete watir and rennynge, is bettir and more holsom than is the fissh that is norisshed in dede
5 watyr nat rennynge. But the fissh of the see is bettir and more holsom than the fressh watyr fyssh. Beware of othir fisshis that ben grete and of harde skynne, for [s]uch ben yll and wyndye. And take this poynt suffisauntlye as for this tyme.

9   ## Of the nature of watyrs |

[f. 59ᵛ]   THou aught to wite that watyr is profitable to all creatures, and
p. 117   to beestes resonable and unresonable. And alle maner of watirs, bothe swete and bittre, comyn fro the see. And the best and moost holsom watirs and lightest ben tho that ben comynge by a pure ground and cliere, nygh the hilles, and that it touche no fumositees
15 nor muddy grounde, for that watir is heuy and nat holsom, and there-ynne ben frogges, serpentes, and othir venyme beestes. And also watyr that is slepinge is nat good nor holsom. The good signes of watir is whan it is light, cliere, and of good sauoure, and that is soone hote and sone colde. In this watir is naturally delite. Othir
20 watirs that ben salt, bitter, and muddy, dryen the bely, and causeth it to be of yll disposicion and ille digestion. The watir that is in lowe cuntree is nat holsom, and by nature and kynde they ben hote and heuy and causen the splene and longes to growe. The watyr[s] that rennyth thrugh many cuntrees ben greuous hote and heuy,
25 and ben nat holsom, be-cause they haue parte of the kynde of diuers landys. And he that drinketh colde watyr fastinge be-fore diner, it hurtith the body and destroieth the naturall heete of the stomac. And drinking of watir aftir meite, it warmeth the body and engendreth fleume. And if thou drinke mykell watyr with thy
30 meite, it corrupteth and wasteth the meite in the stomac. In somyr drinke colde watyr, and in wyntyr leuke warme. For colde watyr in wyntyr wasteth the hete of the stomac, and destroyeth the in-strumentes of the body, and hurteth the lunges, and engendreth
[f. 60]   diuers seekenesses. And also hote watyr in somyr | doth harme,
p. 118   and enweyketh the stomac, and destroieth the appetite.

7 such] fuch

Y. ℂ Of the nature of fysshe.

Fysshes that ben of small substaunce/ & thynne skynnes/ easy of eatynge/ bredde in rennynge waters nyghe the see ben better & lyghter than they that bredde in þe see or fresshe ryuers. But fysshe that bredeth in þe see is holsomer than fresshe ryuer fysshe. 5 Therfore beware of fysshe of grete substaunce with harde skynnes for suche ben comynly venemous.

A. ℂ Of the nature of waters.

THou ought to knowe þat clere rennynge waters that ben nyghe to cytees in pure grounde as small brokes be the best and lyghtest. 10 Water that co|meth out of stony erthe where as is moche fumo- [f. G1ᵛ] sytees is heuy/ contagyous/ & noysom. Water of puddles or fenne full of frogges/ addres/ and other venymous wormes be vnholsom. The sygnes of good water is to be clere/ lyght/ & of good colour/ þat lyghtly dooth sethe and lyghtly coole. In suche waters nature 15 delyteth. Salt water of þe see is fumysshe and laxeth þe wombe/ & water of þe see is hote and heuy bycause it moeueth not/ & the sonne is dayly ouer it/ and it bredeth coler/ and creaseth the mylt and the lunges. The drynkynge of waters with a colde stomake fastynge afore dyner greueth the body/ and quencheth the heate of 20 the stomake. But drynkynge of water after dyner warmeth the stomake and bredeth flewme. And moche of it corrupteth the meate in the stomake. Thou oughtest to drynke colde water in somer and warme water in wynter/ and not contrary wyse. For warme water in somer mollyfyeth and weyketh the stomake/ and 25 wasteth the appetyte. And in wynter colde water quencheth the heate/ and destroyeth the instrumentes of the brest/ it noyeth the lyghtes and lunges and bredeth many greues.

---

11 moche] to much K   16 delyteth. Salt water] delyteth salt. Water

Of wyne, and of the good and yll that folowyth

DEre sonne, I late the wite that the wyne made of the reysen
growinge in hilles agains the sunne is of driere kynde than is the
wyne made of reysen growinge in playne cuntree and moiste. The
5 first wyne is good for olde peeple, and to thaim that ben moist
and fleumatike, but it is nat good for thaim that ben hote and
yonge. The first wyne is hote, and deliureth the man from superfluités of colde humors, and maketh him mighty. And the wyne
that is of rede coloure and thikke, engendreth blood. But and thy
10 wyne be mighty and stronge, ant that it be taken to often, it will
hurt the body. And whan the wyne of this condicion is swete it
hurtith the stomac, and causeth it to swelle, and engendrith
wynde. But the wyne that is moost comon for alle maner com-
pleccions is that that groweth in large landes nygh to hilles and
15 vales, and that the raysen be of good swetenesse and ripe, and that
it be nat gadred till the substaunce of the might be goon, with the
humiditee of the barke. And that the wyne and the raysen be
som-what faded. And this wyne aught to be of coloure betwixt
golde and rede, and of sauoure egre, bitinge and delectable, and
20 that the lyes be thikke in the botome of the pipe, and that it be
pure and cliere aboue. And whan thou hast suche wyne, drinke
therof with temperaunce, aftir the ceason and ease of thy body,
for it yiveth might to the stomac, and counforteth the naturall hete
[f. 60ᵛ] of the body, and helpith the di|gestion and ledith the meite to
p. 119 alle mambres, and kepith thaim withoute corrupcion, till it be
26 conuertid in-to good blode, and driveth awey ill humors, and
restorith the brayn, and reioysith the hert. It yevith good coloure,
and byreuith from the man melancolye, and maketh him the more
hardy, with othir good thinges. And whan the wyne is taken out-
30 rageouslye, out of reson, it causeth theise harmys folowinge: it
troubleth the brayn and vndirstandinge, and yiveth impediment to
the wytte, the tunge and memorye, and enweyketh the hete and
naturall vertue of the body. It makith a man to lese all remembraunce, and hurteth all his membres. It withdraweth the appetite,
35 it maketh the yen foule and yll-farynge, it shewith the coloure
dedly and destroieth the lyuer, it maketh ill bloode, grete and blak.
It wastith the stomac, it maketh the man to speke to miche and
slepe to miche, and fantasyes to come in his slepe. It causeth the

1 and of] *arabesque decoration to right of horizontal stroke of* d *resembles
suspended* e   13 wyne] *corr. from* wynde

B. ℭ Of the nature of wyne.

THe nature of wyne that groweth on mountaynes nygh to þe
sonne is dryer than that/ that groweth on the playne grounde/ in
moyst places/ & shadowes. Wyne is good for aeged people/ and
suche as be moyst & flewmy. And enoyeth them that be yonge and 5
hote. And wyne warmeth & delyuereth colde and cours | super- [f. G2]
fluytees. The reeder and thycker that wyne is the more it bredeth
blode. But yf it be stronge and bytter/ than it is called the fyrst
blode and the fyrst nourysshyng/ and hath the nature of drynke
and medycyne. And often dronken it noyeth the body and nourys- 10
sheth it not. And whan wyne is naturally swete/ it noyeth the
stomake with s[w]ellynges and wyndes/ but such wyne is comynly
swete of complexyon/ and suche as groweth in large feeldes
stretchynge towarde the mountaynes and valees hauynge swete
clustres/ & rype/ and be not gathred tyll the myght of the sub- 15
staunce of the bery is gone with the moystnesse/ and þat the vyne
and the grape be somwhat wydred. And thou shalt knowe that
wyne ought to be of an eygre taste sharpe and pleasaunt/ and haue
thycke lyes on the botome of the vessell/ and fayre and clere
aboue/ & whan thou hast fayre and good wyne drynke tem- 20
peratly therof to þe ease of thy body/ as the tyme requyreth. For it
strengtheth the stomake and the heates of þe body/ and helpeth
dygestyon and kepeth frome corrupcyon/ and rypeth the meate in
the membres/ puryfyeng it/ & worketh in them tyll it be coniunct
in good blode/ & nourysshynge/ and trauayleth & reyseth the heat 25
of the body temperately/ and kepeth a man sure of wycked
humours. It gladdeth the hert/ & maketh fresshe colour in the
face. It quyckeneth the mynde & soupleth the tongue/ & destroyeth
all melancoly/ & make[th] a man bolde/ & to haue good courage &
appetyte. And hath many other good propryetees. But yf wyne 30
be outrageously taken many inconuenyences come therby. It
troubleth þe brayne/ þe mynde/ þe wyttes/ þe vnderstondynge. It
maketh the vertue of natural | heate wylde/ & causeth forgetful- [f. G2ᵛ]
nesse. It combreth the tongue & weyketh all þe synewes & lymmes

4 shadowes. Wyne] no punct.   8 it is] is it K   10 medycyne.
And] no punct. (at end of l.)   12 swellynges] smellynges C swellings K
14 towarde] towards K   15 &] repeated   16 þat the] the K   18 eygre]
eager K   26–7 temperately/ and . . . humours. It] temperately. And . . . hum-
ours/ it   29 maketh] make C maketh K   30 propryetees] properties K
33 wylde] prob. slip for weyke: afoiblist la chaleur et la vertu naturelle F f.
26ᵛ: see n.

mouthe to stynk and [maketh] the knees and leggis the weyker. It
destroieth the seed of man and his good compleccion. And, briefly
to sey, it destroieth clierly the body, and engendreth meselrye.
Be ware than that thou drinke nat out of mesure, sith that he
5 chaungeth his nature as doth an herbe callid reubarbe whiche
yevith [lyf] to the lyuer and [hath] many grete vertues, and so
hath the wyne, as more plainly is founde in the booke of medicynes.
Natwithstandinge, the rubarbe is mortall venyme in him self for
him that takith it out of mesure, and so it is of the wyne whan it
10 is taken outrageouslye out of reson, for therof ensweth grete
mischeeuys and inconvenientes.

Of the sirupe |

[f. 61]   ALexander, deere sonne, I counseile the that thou take at som
p. 120 tymes of the sirupe aigre, that is to sey fastinge, and in especiall
15 whan thou feelist the humors and fleume habunde to myche, for it
is right good and profitable. And I shall telle the a thinge. I meruaile
gretly how a man may dye or be seeke, that eiteth brede made of
good whete, and good and holsum flessh, and drinketh good wyne
with temperaunce, and that kepith him from to miche etynge and
20 drynkynge and trauaile. And whan suche a man fallith in secke-
nesse, he most be helid subtilye, as he that is drunken of wyne. That
is to sey, that he be wasshen with watyr, and that he be sett vpon
a rennynge ryuere, and that he haue greene garleke aboute him,
and that he annoynt his stomac with an oynement called assandale,
25 and he shulde smell the smoke of frankencesse and othir good
spices. And that is right profitable. Than gouerne thy body
wysely, yf thou wilt haue longe lyf. Latinge the wite, that theise
thinges folowinge ben counfortable to nature, that is to sey, good
spoortes, to see richesse, to haue grete reuerence, to haue victorie
30 vpon his enmyes, to eite good mettes, to heere mynstrellys and
instrumentes of musike, to see faire thinges, to were plesaunt and
precious clothinge, to heere often tidinges, to speke with thaim
that ben wyse, and to enquere of tho thinges that ben passed and
for to come, and at som tymes to take delite with faire wommen.

of þe body. It maketh the eyes reed & blered. It chaungeth þe
colour/ & destroyeth þe body/ & maketh cours & noughty blode.
It marreth dygestyon. It causeth to many wordes/ & to moche
slepe. It maketh þe mouthe stynkynge. It letteth þe goynge/ &
dystroyeth þe sede of man & bredeth lepry. Beware therfore þat 5
thou drynke not wyne outrageously/ but moeue & chaunge þe
nature therof with rewbarbe whiche causeth þe lyuer to lyue. And
wyne with Rubarbe hath many vertues as is founde playnly in
bokes of physyke. Howbeit Rubarbe & wyne be bothe deedly
venym yf they be outragyously taken. And surely all euyls cometh 10
of wyne vnmeasurably dronken.

C. ⦅ Of goodnesse & harme þat cometh of wyne.

NOble kynge Alexander/ forgete not to take tarte syropes in þe
mornyng fastynge whan flewmatyke humours habounde to moch.
For it is proufytable & wasteth them moche. Also I meruayle þat 15
ony man may dye or be seke that eateth breed of clene and good
wheat/ holsome & good flesshe/ & drynketh good wyne of grapes
temperatly. And yf he kepe hym fro to moche drynkyng/ eatyng/ &
trauayle. Yf sykenesse ouercome such a man he must be healed
as a dronken man. That is to wyte he must be wasshed with 20
warme water/ and than set ouer a rennyng water betwene .ii.
grene wylowes/ & his stomake anoynted with an oyntement of
sandres/ or sandalles/ & haue a fumygacyon of frankensence: &
other swete spyces/ & it wyl do hym moch good. And yf ony man 24
wyll forsake holly þe drynkyng of wy|ne he ought not to leaue it [f. G3]
sodeynly at ones but lytel & lytell/ & to mengle it euery day with
water more & more/ tyll at the last there be nothynge but clere
water. And so he may kepe his helth & good complexyon. Thus
gouerne thy body yf thou wyll lyue longe. And kepe my doctrynes/
& consydre these thynges folowynge wherein nature conforteth 30
gretely. That is to wyte: Goodly pastymes/ syght of grete rychesses/
grete reuerence/ vyctory ouer enemyes/ fedyng on good meates/
noyse of mynstralsy/ syght of precyous garmentes/ often herynge
of good tydynges/ speche of wyse men/ to enquere of thynges past
and to come/ and communycacyon with fayre gentylwomen. 35

2 noughty] naughtie K   3 (twice) to] two K   5 lepry] the lepry K
12 C.] *headed* Y. *in List of Contents*   23 frankensence] francomsence K
24 good. And] *no punct.* (*at end of l.*)   29 wyll] wilt K   31 wyte] *foll.*
by full stop, not colon as regularly in C's introductory clauses: cf. 257/3, 265/5,
325/12 *and* 17, 369/28, 377/36; *but see* 369/10 (*and* 299/7)

Of the fourme and maner of Justice

[f. 61ᵛ]
p. 121
DEre sonne, Justice may nat be praised to miche, | for the moost
gloriouse God made it, and ordeyned it vpon his seruauntes and
vpon alle his werkes, for to reigne in all landes. And Justice aught
5 to kepe, preserue, and defende the blood, the richesse and possessions of the [s]ubgites in rightwysnesse. And so doth oure
Lorde, and therfore [that lord] that kepith well justise, he is in
that cace sembleable to God. Diere sonne, Justice is the fourme of
vndirstandinges whiche God made and ordeyned, and sent it to
10 his creatures. And by Justice was erthe made and edified, and the
kinges were made, and ordeyned to kepe and maynteyne justice,
for justice causeth the peeple to be of good disposicion and
obeisaunt, and it maketh the proude lowlye, and saueth the good
peeple from hurtes and wronges. And therfore the Judiens seyn
15 that the justice of a good lorde is bettir to the good peeple than
any habundaunce of goodes. And yit more, they seyn that the
lorde that is juste and resonable is bettir than the swete reyne
that fallith at evyn. And it was onys founden in a ston writen in
langage of Caldee, that a kynge and Justice ben brethren, and
20 nothir may reigne withoute the othir. For the thinges of the worlde
ben made and ordeyne to maytayne and kepe justice, whiche is
saluacion of the subgites. Diere sonne, whan thou hast any grete
thinge to doo, aske counseill, for thou art a man soole. And telle
nat to thy counseillours thy corage nor what thou purposist to
25 doo, but suffre yche of thaim to declare his oppinion, and heere
what they shall sey. For yf thou vttir thy purpose at the begynnynge, it will be to the a disprayse. Than tempre thyne hert, and
heere thair counseill, and whan thou feelist the counseile good and
[f. 62]
p. 122
fruituouse, kepe thy first | purpose pryuee to thy-self, till thou
come to thyne effectuell execucion, but considre well euery mannys
31 counseill, and who hath best spoken, and yiven the most freendly
counseill. And than seeth, withoute taryinge, the execucion be nat
delaied, for it is grete losse to a kinge to lose the tyme, and parill
to make tarying and delay in his besinesse and needys. And yf so
35 be that a yonge man and of lowe degree yive the good counseill,
disprayse him nat, for it is possible that a man shall be borne in
suche constillacion that he shall haue wysdome. As it felle onys

6 subgites] bubgite*s*   7 that lord that] that U quant un seignieur le fait F f. 27ᵛ

D. ❡ Of the fourme of Justyce.

O Moost dyscrete kynge Justyce can not be praysed to moche/ for it is of meruaylous sharpe nature/ lyke to the moost gloryous god. And he ordeyned it ouer his aungels/ ouer his werkes/ & ouer al realmes. And thou ought to kepe Justyce/ and defende the 5 wyttes/ the rychesses/ & possessyons of thy subgectes and all theyr werkes/ for so dooth almyghty god. And ony lorde doyng in lyke case is lyke to god. For by maynteynyng of Justyce he foloweth god/ and thou ought to folow hym in all nedefull werkes. And this is the fourme of vnderstandynge the whiche god created/ and 10 graunted to his creatures. By Justyce the erthe was made/ and kynges ordeyned to kepe and maynteyne Justyce/ for it maketh subgectes meke and obedyent/ prowde men lowly/ and kepeth all persones in saufe fro wronges and domages. And therfore they of 14 Ynde saye that the Justyce of a good lorde is better to | good sub- [f. G3ᵛ] gectes than the plentyousnesse of the erthe. And also they say that the Just and reasonable lorde is better than the rayne that falleth in the euenyng. And there was ones founde wryten in a stone in the speche of Caldee that wyse kynges ben bretheren hauynge nede eche of other/ and one maye not be without the 20 other. For all the kynges of the worlde be to rule/ and maynteyne Justyce/ whiche is the helthe of [subgectes]. Therfore yf thou hast ony thyng for to do aske councell/ for thou arte but one man. And shewe not all thy courage to thy councelers nor lete them not knowe what is in thy wyll to do. For yf þu shew thy mynde at þe 25 begynnynge þu shalt be dyspraysed. Than attempre thyn herte/ and thy wyll/ but here councel fyrst. And manyfeste not that/ that lyeth at thy herte tyll thou come to put it in effecte. Consydre well the councell of euery man/ and whiche of them hath Juged thy mater and counceled þe best for the/ and with the best loue 30 that he hath towarde þ[e]. And whan thou hast thus recorded thy councell/ put thy mynde in effecte without delay. For the gretest destruccyon that may come to a kynge is to be slowe in his werkes & to lese tyme. And yf so be that a yonge man of small estate gyue the good councell/ dyspyse it not/ for it is possyble that a man may be 35 borne in suche constellacyon þat naturally he shall haue wysdome.

1 D.] headed A in List of Contents   4 aungels/ over] no punct. (at end of l.)
20 hauynge] hauyynge C hauing K   22 subgectes] Justyce C and, substant.,
K   24 thy courage] the courage K   29 man/ and] man. And   31
þe] þat C thee K

in the parties of Inde, that a childe was borne in an hous wherynne
were logged certeyn wyse clerkes, which founde that the childe
was borne in suche constillacion, and vnder suche planete and
signe, that he shulde be wyse, curteys, and lovinge, deliure of his
5 membres, and full of good counseill, well beloued with kinges and
lordys, whiche thinge the clerkes tolde no woorde therof to the
fader. And whan the childe was waxen of resonable age, the fadre
and the modre sett him to crafte, whiche he might neuer lerne,
for no betinge nor techinge that his maister might doo to him.
10 And the fader and the moder sawe this, they let him alone and doo
his owne will. This childe enclined his hert to lerne the science
and the cours of the firmament, and of vertuous condicions, and
the maner and gouernaunce that longeth to kinges. And finally, to
say in conclusion, thrugh his wisdome and science, he was aftir
15 gouernour and reuler of the kynge of the lande. And the contrarie
by-fell of a kynge of Inde whiche had .ij. sonnys. And whan the
[f. 62ᵛ]   oon | was of age, he was sett to lerne science with the best maisters
p. 123   that were in alle the lande, and he was endoctrined and taught
in the best and most easiest weyes that might be, and as it aper-
20 teyneth to a kinges sonne. But alle thaire diligence, laboure, and
techinge was in vayn. For the childe might neuer enclyne his hert
nor his nature to lerne no science nor arte, sauf oonly to the forge.
Wherof the kynge was heuy and gretly troubled. For the whiche
cause he assembled alle the noble clerkes and wyse men of the
25 lande, and askid thaim how it might be that his sonne might lerne
no science nor othir thinge saue forgeinge. And they answerde and
seide, that the nature of the childe was of suche constillacion that
he might enclyne all-only to that arte and noon othir. Therfore
disprayse nat the man of lowe degree nor of litle stature, whan
30 thou seest in him habundaunce of science and wysdome, with
vertuous condicions, for suche a man thou aughtist to loue. And
doo no thinge withoute counseile. And I pray the loue him that
loueth trouth, and that yiveth the true counseill, and that at som
tymes contrarieth thyne oppinions. For suche a man is ferme and

10 And] *intended reading perh.* And when

¶ Example.

¶ There was vpon a tyme a chylde borne in the partyes of Ynde.
In the hous where this chylde was borne were certayne wyse men
lodged/ whiche founde that the sayd chylde was borne vnder
suche a constellacyon/ planet/ and sygne that he sholde be wyse/ 5
meke/ courteys/ amyable/ fresshe of wytte/ and shol|de be loued of [f. G4]
kynges & grete lordes. Whiche thynge they wolde not shew to þe
fader which was a weuer. Whan þe chyld came to aege þe fader
& moder set hym to theyr occupacion/ but he coude neuer lerne
for ony beatyng nor chastysement. At þe last they lete him do as he 10
lyst/ & he set his mynde to lerne scyences/ & þe moeuynges of þe
skyes/ & of all thynges aboue nature. Also he lerned good condycyons & maners to þe gouernaunce of prynces & kynges. And
fynally by his wytte & wysdome he was ruler of all þe countre.

Another example.   15

¶ In þe realme of Ynde were .ii. chyldren. Whan one of them
came to aege þe kyng set hym to scole for to lerne scyence/ & all
þe studyes of Ynde & had þe best techers in all þe prouynces for
to teche hym in all þe spede þat coude be possyble as to a kynges
sone belonged. But all the dylygences of his fader and other techers 20
auayled nothynge nor coude make hym enclyne neyther by his
mayster nor by his nature to lerne ony scyence nor arte but onely
forgynge or smythes crafte/ wherof the kynge meruelyed/ and sore
troubled sent for all the wysest of his realme/ and demaunded of
them how it myght be that his sone wolde lerne nothynge but onely 25
smythes craft. And they answered that the kynde of the chylde
was of suche complexyon/ and that he was inclyned to that arte
and to none other. Therfore dere sone Alexander dyspyse no man
of lowe byrthe nor of small stature yf thou se ony scyence or ony
wysdome in hym/ and that he haue also good condycyons and 30
maners in hym/ and [d]ooth exchewe vyces. Suche one so wel
manered is w[or]thy to be loued of prynces and kynges. And thou
ought for to do nothynge without councell. And I pray the dere
sone that thou | loue hym þat loueth trouthe & þat counceleth þe [f. G4ᵛ]
faythfully & somtyme contrary to thyn opynyon. For suche a man 35

1 *title not on separate l.* CK   2 partyes] partes K   14 of] ouer K
15 *title not on separate l.*   16 chyldren. Whan] chyldren/ whan   20
dylygences] dilligence K   31 dooth] booth C doth K   exchewe] eschewe
K   one] a one K   32 w[or]thy] wrothy C worthy K

stable in his corage, and juste and true to the and to thy subgites.
And the counseill of suche a man is good and profitable, for it
yiveth ordre of gouernaunce to the kinge and to all the lande. And
good counseill encreecith the wisdome of the kynge, through the
5 whiche counseill thou shall conquere more than by bataile. There
was a mighty man onys in the reame of Medee that wrote a lettre
[f. 63] to his sonne in this fourme: | 'Deere sonne, it is needfull that in
p. 124 alle thy werkys and needes, that thou haue good counseill.' And
take it of him that can yeeue the good counseill. And aboue alle
10 thinges, spare nat thyn enmye, but, as thou may, shewe thy might
and victorie vpon him. And, on the othir partie, be ware of the
power of thyne enmye, and trust nat so miche in thyne owne witte
and in the height [of] thyn estate, but that thou take awise and
counseill of othir. And yf it please the to, take it. And yf it doo
15 nat, leue it. More-ouer, deere sonne, I pray the, exorte the, and
counseill the, that thou yive neuir thy might and puissaunce to
oon man alle-only to reule and gouerne all thy lande and thy
subgites, but make many officers. And thou will preeue any of thyne
officers, lat him wite that thou hast grete neede of siluer. And yf
20 he counseill the to take of thyne owne tresoure, or of thy juelles,
that man loueth the and is feithfull and treue to the. And yf he
counsaile the to take the good of thy subgites and put thaim in
pouerté, he is nat true to the, nor he loueth the nat. And yf so be
he profre the such good as he hath of his owne, rather than to
25 destroye thy subgites, suche a man thou aughtist to loue and trust,
and haue him in thy tendre recommendacion. And also thou maist
preeue thyne officers and seruauntes by the diligente labour that
they doon in exercisinge thaire occupacions. And if a seruaunt doo
more than perteyneth to his occupacion, to thy worship, suche
30 a seruaunt thou aught to cherissh and trust. And trust nat him
that is holly sett to make tresoure, and gadreth good, for he serueth

is stedfast of courage/ faythfull & Just to þe & thy subgectes. And
þe councel of such a man is good to þe gouernayle of þe kynge &
of his realme. Forthermore lette not thy besynesses þat sholde be
fyrst done be þe last. &c. But do euery thynge by councell & ordre.
For councell is þe shewer of all thynges to come. It is behoueful 5
therfore þat þu do all thy werkes by councell of faythfull & secrete
councelers. For thy wysdom by þe councell of them shall encrease/
as the see encreaseth by þe ryuers & floodes þat fall in to it. And þe
better þu mayst wynne by þe myght of warryours. It is founde wryten
þat a grete wyse man of Ynde wrote lettres to his sone in this wyse 10
❧ My well beloued sone/ it is behouefull þat þu beleue councell
in all thy besynesses/ for þu arte but one man. Take councel therfore of suche as þu knowest can gyue the good. And aboue all
thynges spare not thy enmy/ but whan þu mayst shew thy vyctory
ouer hym. And euer be ware of þe power of thy enmy. Trust not 15
in thy owne wytte nor in þe grete heyght of thyn estate/ but euer
take councel of other/ which yf thou seme good & prouffytable
accepte it/ & elles not. And also I admonest þe & councell þe
chefely þat thou neuer make none of thy offycers thy lyeftenaunt onely/ nor gyue hym thy myght/ for his coun[cel] may 20
destroy þe/ thy realme/ & thy subgectes. And seke alway to his own
prouffyt & thy vndoyng. But thou ought to haue dyuers offycers/
& yf þu wyll assay and proue ony of them thou must fayne þat
þu hast grete nede of money. And yf he councel the to take of thy
treasure & Jewelles for to spende he loueth þe and is faythful to þe. 25
And yf he councell the to take þe money of thy subge|tes to make [f. H1]
them poore he is corrupte & hateth the moche. But yf he be such
one that wyl offre the his own goodes and say. Syr by the gyfte and
grace of god I haue goten some goodes I gyue them to the/ suche
ought to be praysed and loued best/ as he which had leuer to gyue 30
his goodes away than the poore subgectes sholde be taxed and
destroyed. Proue also thy offycers and yf thou se that ony of them
dooth his offyce dylygently/ and more for thyn honoure than he is
commytted/ thou ought gretly to trust in hym. And yf there be ony
that delyteth in takyng of gyftes and gapeth for promocyon/ & to 35

3 besynesses] businesse K   4–5 ordre. For] ordre For *perh. for* ordre for
6 faythfull & secrete] secrete & faythfull K   8 see] seas K   11 *On same
l. as preceding words* CK   13 the] thee K   18 admonest] admonish K
20 councel] cou*n* (*at end of l.*)   23 wyll] wilt K   25 to þe] vnto thee K
26 subgetes] *probably for intended* subgectes   28 one] a one K
2550 C74   B b

[f. 63ᵛ] nat for loue but for his owne | singuler auayle. For suche a man is
p. 125   likenyd to [an] abyme with-oute botome. For the more good that
he gadreth, the more wolde he haue. And suche an officer may be
cause of the destruccion of the and of thy reame. For the grete
5 and feruent desire that he hath to good, he may perauenture doo
som grete mischeef, or to slee thy persoone for good. And yf thou
haue any suche seruaunt, beware that he haunte nat with noon
othir grete lorde, that he make no writinges ne enquere tidinges.
And yf he doo, put him awey from the withoute taryinge in es-
10 chwinge alle perilles. Deere sonne, thou most loue that officer that
loueth the, and exorteth and sterith the hertes of thy subgites to
loue the, and that puttith his persoone and his goddes in thy
seruise. And that he haue the condicions folowing: that is to sey,
that he be perfourmed in his membres for to exercise truly his
15 office, and that he haue good vndirstandinge for to conceyue his
charge. That he be curteys, amyable, and speke faire, and that his
woordys accorde to his hert. That he be lettred and true in woorde
and dede. That he loue no lesinges. That he be of good condicion,
tretable, and temperat of his mouthe with meite and drinke. That
20 he be nat lecherous, nor dyse plaier, nor noon othir dishonest
games. That he be a man of grete vndirstandinge and corage, and
that he loue aboue alle othir thingis worship. And that he sett
nat his hert all-oonly in golde and siluer, nor in othir erthly thinges
saue that that toucheth the good gouernaunce of thy worship and
25 well of the reame. And that he loue both pryvee and straunge. That
he hate iniurie. And that he be perseueraunt in his purpose with-
[f. 64] oute | dreede, doinge his operacions touchinge thyne highnesse.
p. 126   And that he be nat to habundaunt in spekinge or laughinge, but
temperate. And that he be to thy subgitys graciouse and jentill.
30 That he entende diligentlye to enquere and knowe tidinges of all
the parties of thy lande. That he counforte thy subgites in thaire
aduersitee, and that he supporte the trouthe in the pouer peeple
and correcte the rebellys. Deere sonne, I lat the wite that God
made and fourmed man right wise creature, and He made neuer
35 kinde in no beest but parte is founde in man. Man is hardy as lyon,
cowarde as an hare, kynde as a dogge, harde and sharpe as a bore,
jantill as turtill dowe, dispitouse as a lyonesse, pryvé as a dowe,
full of malice and barat as a foxe, meke as a lambe, light as roo,
resemblinge a goote in many condicions, heuy and slaughfull as

27 touchinge] thouchinge

gadre treasure/ put not thy trust in hym. For suche a man is lyke
a hurle pytte without botome/ for the more that he hath the more
he coueyteth to haue. And suche one is the destruccyon of a realme
many wayes. For peraduenture the brennynge desyre that he hath
to gete rychesses maye moeue hym to do many euylles/ and maye 5
chaunce the procuracyon of thy deth. Yf thou perceyue suche
an offycer/ lete hym not be ferre frome thy presence. And suffre
hym not to make treaty with straunge lordes nor prynces/ nor
wryte no newes to them. And yf thou doubt that he dooth the
contrary/ chaunge hym without ony delay. For the courage of 10
many men be soone chaunged/ and lyghtly inclyned to do contrary thynges.

℩ Also dere sone thou ought to cherysshe þe offycer that loueth
& moeueth thy subgectes to loue the. And that putteth his persone and goodes to thyn honoure/ and that hath these propryetees 15
folowynge. that is to wyte that he be parfyt in his lymmes for to
trauayle in his offyce that he is chosen to. That he be courteys/
lowly/ and eloquent/ and that his wor|de accorde with his hert. [f. H1ᵛ]
That he be a clerke wyse & well condycyoned/ laborous & sober
of mouthe in eatynge and drynkynge/ not lecherous/ nor player 20
at dyce and other dysordynate games. That he be hardy/ and set
not his mynde on golde nor syluer/ nor other thynge of the worlde/
but that/ þat belongeth to the gouernaunce of the/ and the realme.
That he loue the welth of his neyghbours as of them that be ferre.
And that he hate all wronges/ and by Justyce yelde euery man 25
his owne. That he be angry with them that do iniuryes & extor-
cyons/ & that he greue no man wrongefully. And that he be perseueraunt & stedfast in his purpose which is behouefull. That he be
without feare and in good wyll. That he knowe the stynte of his
expences. And that he prolonge nothynge that may be prouffytable 30
to the realme. And þat gyueth not thy subgectes cause to complayne
of hym in doynge agaynst þe comyn wele. That he be not ful
of wordes/ nor a grete laugher. That none be refused comyng to
his hous. And that he be dylygent to here & enquere of newes
and tydynges. That he comfort the subgectes and correct theyr 35
werkes/ & helpe them in theyr aduersytees.

2 hurle pytte] whirle pit K   13 ℩ Also] does not start new l. CK
15 propryetees] properties K (regular substitution, not indicated hereafter)
16 folowynge. that] see 257a/3 and note.   34 hous. And] hous And (And
beginning newl.) C house and K   35 tydynges.] no punct.

a bere, preciouse and deere as the olifaunt, foule-made and rude
as an asse, obeisaunt and lowly as the pecok, meeuing as the fyssh,
luxurious as an hogge, foule as a bugle, faire as an hors. And shortly
to sey, there is no beest, birde, nor planete, ne signe in the worlde,
5 nor othir kynde, but it is founde in man. And the profecies callen
man the litle worlde.

Of the kinges secretaires

DEere sonne, thou most haue wyse men to write thy secreetes
and to vndirstande and knowe thy will and purpose, whiche most
10 be faire langagiers for to make thy writinges ordinatly in faire
langage. For like a faire and preciouse gowne honowreth the body
of the kinge, so doth the faire and plesaunt langage to the writinge. |
[f. 64ᵛ] And ther-with a secretaire aught to be of good feith and true, and
p. 127 that he can conceyue clierlye thy will and entent, and that he take
15 good kepe to alle thy needfull thingys. And that noon othir man
come in the place where he writeth and leith the secretes and
writinges. And, deere sonne, see that thy seruauntes be gretely
rewarded for thaire seruise, and exalte thaim so that they be allwey
diligent and willinge to doo the true seruise. For in thaim lieth
20 thy worship, thy lyf, and destruccion.

Of the kynges messangers

DEre sonne, I lat the wite that the messangere shewith the wysdome of him that sendith him forthe. And the messangere is the
yie, the eare, and tunge, of the lorde. Than thou most cheese
25 to thy messangere the moost suffisaunt man in trouthe, wysdome,
and worship, that thou canst gete in thy courte. And that he loue
thy honeur and hate thy dishoneure. And yf thou finde suche oon,
discouer him thyne entent of thy corage. And yf thou can fynde
noon suche, at the leest gete oon that will bere a lettre trulye and
30 bringe the answere. And yf thou finde any of thy messangers
couetouse, and that they desire to haue giftes of thaim that they
ben sent to, trust thaim nat, but auoide thaim in alle haste. And
make neuer thy messangere of a man will be drunke, for by him
shall be tolde and knowen that his lorde is nat wyse. And also
35 make no messangere of thy grettest officer, and suffre him nat to
be fer from thee, for it may be cause of thy destruccion and of |
[f. 65] thy reame. And yf thou haue any messangere that doth any treason
p. 128

11–12 body of the] *repeated*   25 messangere] messangeres

E. ❡ Of kynges secretaryes.

DEre sone it behoueth to chuse the a secretary for to wryte &
knowe thy secretes/ he must be a man of grete wysdome and well
lerned/ for to vnderstande thy mynde. He ought to be trusty and
eloquent and that can speke dyuers languages for to put thy 5
besynesses in goodly ordynaunce and semely speche. For as | a [f. H2]
fayre garment honoureth þe body of a kynge/ so goodly speche
arayeth and indeweth a lettre. And also he must be trusty to hyde
& kepe close thy doynges. And þat he suffre none to come to þe
place where thy wrytynges be & þat none se them. Swete sone 10
such persones ought to be cherysshed & well rewarded for theyr
seruyces. And exalte them in suche wyse þat they be always
dylygent in thy necessytees & nedes. For in them is conteyned thy
glory and honour/ or thy lyfe & destruccyon.

F. ❡ Of a kynges messagers. 15

MYghty emperour þe messagers alway sheweth the wysdome
of hym þat sendeth them. They ben þe eyes/ þe eeres/ & the mouthe
of theyr lord. It behoueth for thy messagers or ambassadours to
chuse suche as ben moost suffycyent/ of clere vnderstandyng/
wyse/ honourable/ & trusty/ which loueth thy honour/ & hateth 20
thy dyshonour. (For in thy court þu mayst finde them bothe). And
yf þu fynde suche discouer & shewe thy courage to them. And yf
þu fynde none suche or better/ fynde one þat wyll trustely bere thy
lettres/ & brynge the an answere of them. And yf þu fynde þat
messager be coueytous to do his owne prouffyte & to gete gyftes/ 25
truste not in hym/ but entyerly forsake hym. And also make no
man thy messager þat wyll be dronke/ for by suche one it shall
be sayd & knowen þat þe lorde is not wyse. And ferthermore make
not thy messager of thy gretest offycer/ & lete hym not be ferre
from the/ for it may well be the vndoyng of the & þe realme. And 30
yf þu sende messagers by whome ony treason come to the/ I tel

1 E.] *headed* **B** *in List of Contents*   15 F.] *headed* **C** *in List of Contents*
messagers] Messengers K (*this, substant., a regular substitution: not indicated
hereafter*)   17 eyes/ þe] *no punct.*   18 lord. It] *no punct.*

to thy persoone, I telle the no mesure that he is worthye to suffre.
But doo as thou seemyst beste.

Of the gouernaunce of the peeple

DEere sonne, thou knowyst well that thy peeple and subgites
5 is the hous of thy memorye, and the noble treasoure whiche confermeth thy reame. For thy subgites arne as thy gardyne, wherynne
ben diuers trees, whiche beryn frute and seed, and multiplie to
th[y] ease and to thy pleasir. And so is the peeple thy might and
power and durable treasoure, and defence of thy lande. Than thou
10 most curiously see that thy subgitys be well gouerned, and haue
regarde of thaire necessitees, and kepe thaim from vilanye and
alle wronges, and reule thaim in rightwisnesse aftir the custume of
the cuntree. And ordeyne suche an officere as will gouerne thaim
justlye be reason and goodnesse, and that he be wyse and pacient
15 and full of vertuous condicions. And yf thyn officer be of yll disposicion, the subgites that were good and treue will be yll, and redy
to rebell agains the and him bothe. And also see that thou haue
juges and true notaries, to thentent the juges be nat corrupte with
gyftes as it is often seen. And aftir this, I pray the and exorte the
20 ofte to sett thy self in bataile. And take [nat example of] thaim
that thrugh envie and grete presumpcion madly entre in bataile.
And take often the counseil of thyne owne housholde famuliers.
[f. 65ᵛ] And blame nor dispray|se nat thy menne of werre, but yiue
p. 129 thaim faire langage, and promitte thaim good and worship. And
25 beware that thou entre nat in bataile but that thou be armed of
euery peece that needith. And whan thou seest thyne enmye, renne
nat vpon him sodeynly vnauised and vnpurveide. And see allwey
that thyne hoste be surely warded. And logge euyr thyne hoste as
nygh as thou maiste to hilles, watirs, and woodes. And that thou
30 haue euer with the plenté of vitailles. And also that thou haue many
trumpettes and mynstrellis, for thei yeue vertu and norisshinge to

8 thy ease ... pleasir] the ease and pleasir to thy pleasir

the not þe measure of payne þat they ought to suffre/ but do therin
as | thou semest best. [f. H2ᵛ]

G. ℂ Of the gouernaunce of the people.

FAyre sone thou knowest þat thy people & subgectes ben þe
hous of thy mynde/ & þe treasure wherby thy realme is conforted. 5
For thy realme & subgectes ben as an orchyarde wherin ben dyuers
trees berynge fruyte/ the which trees haue dyuers rotes & sedes
for to bere/ growe/ & multyply þe fruyte/ & be þe defence &
durable treasure to thy realme/ & of thy myght. It behoueth than
that thy subgectes be well gouerned/ & þat thou take thought and 10
care to that/ that is nedefull for them/ and to beware that no
vyolence nor wronges be done to them/ and after theyr condycyons
and wontes to ordre them. Than gyue to them a good offycer
that intendeth not to theyr vndoynge/ but that intendeth to rule
them well/ Justly and in quyete. And se that suche an offycer be 15
wyse/ full of good maners/ well condycyoned/ and pacyent. For yf
he be not suche one/ wyte thou þat the wyse men that were good
before/ wyll become euyll and rebell agaynst the. Also se that thou
haue good and dyscrete Juges/ and þat shall be worshyp to the/
and encrease of thy court/ and of thy reame. And that the sayde 20
Juges be not corrupte with gyftes and mede/ and that they haue
good notaryous scrybes/ and egall sollycitours & aduocates þat
wyll not take brybes as it happeneth seldom. Dere sone I pray the
and admonest the that thou put thy selfe often in batayle/ and
take oftentymes the councell of them of thy court. But put the not 25
with them that onely by enuy and couetyse entreth presumptuously
in batayle. And blame not nor dyspyse thy men of warre/ but
vse | fayre wordes amonge them/ and often promyse them gyftes [f. H3]
and honours. And in no wyse put thy selfe in batayle tyll thou be
pourueyed of al necessary armes and other thynges therto belong- 30
ynge. And whan þu seest thyn enmy renne sodaynly vpon hym/ and
not slowly/ and euer haue good outryders and watches about thyn
hoost. And lodge the alwayes as nyghe as thou mayst to hylles/
woodes and waters. And haue alway more haboundaunce of
vytayle than nedeth. And aboue al thynges grete quantyte of 35
trompettes/ tabours and other mynstrelles. For they gyue force/

3 G.] *headed* D *in List of Contents*   17 one] a one K   25 thy court]
the Courte K   26 couetyse] couetous K   32 watches] watchers K
33 nyghe] neare K   35 nedeth. And] *no punct.* (*at end of l.*)   36 trom-
pettes/ tabours] *no punct.* (*at end of l.*)

thy peeple, and cause thyne enmyes to be ferde. And be nat allwey
armyd with oone armys but with diuers. And be well purveide
with archers and crosse bowes, and put thaim in good array. And
ordeyne som of thyne horsmen to stire the cuntree, and the re-
5 manent stablelye to abide in array in bataile. And whan thou entrest
thy self in bataile counforte thy peeple with faire wordes, and yive
thaim hert and corage to perseuere in hardynesse. And of alle
thinge be well ware of treason, and haue spies in alle suspecious
places. And yf thou see thyne enmyes flee, chase thaim nat
10 hastilye, but kepe stablely thy menne in arraye as miche as thou
may. And if thou will saute any castell or towne see that thou
be well purveide with gunnys and engynes to breke the wallys,
and that thou haue kunnynge maisters to make mynes, with grete
multitude of archers and crosbowes. And laboure to withdrawe
15 thair watyr, or elles poysone it. And yf thou may, haue spyes
amonge thyne enmyes to vndirstande thaire purpose. And yf
[f. 66] thou may | ouercome thyne enmyes by any othir weye than bataile,
p. 130 take it. For bataile is the last conclusion whan there may be noon
othir weye. And doo no thinge withoute counseill and good de-
20 liberacion.

Of physnomye

AMonge all othir thinges erthly, I will that thou vndirstande and
knowe a parte of the noble science callyd phisonomye, wherby thou
shall haue vndirstandinge of the nature and condicions of the
25 peeple. Whiche was founde by the right noble and wyse philosophre Phisonomias, whiche made a cerche of the qualitees and
nature of the creatures. And in his daies reigned the wyse doctoure Ypocras. And be-cause there was grete fame in that cuntry
of Phisonomias and of his grete wysdome, the familier seruauntes
30 of Ypocras toke pryuely the figure of thaire maister, and bare it to
Phisonomias, and prayd him to juge the qualitees and condicions
of the figure. And whan Phisonomias had seen the figure, he
seid, 'This man is luxuriouse, barateuse, and rude.' And whan the
seid seruauntys harde him sey soo, they were gretely displeasid
35 with him, and said thus, 'A, foole, this is the figure of the best and

7 to] to to (*line division*)

myght/ and reioyce them that be with the/ and make dyuysyon
& feare to thyn enemyes. And be not alway armed in one harneys/
but with dyuers. And be well stored with archers & handgonnes.
And ordeyne some of thy men to renne/ and other to stande stedfastly in thy batayles. Conforte thy men with fayre wordes and 5
gyue them courage/ & herty them to fyght. And aboue all thynges
dere sone beware of treason with all thy power/ and haue euer
good knyghtes about the well & swyftely horsed that yf chaunce
happen that thou must nedes flee/ that by them thou mayst saue
thy persone. But yf thou see ony of thyn enemyes fle haste the 10
not to chase them but kepe thy folke alway togyder the moost
that thou mayst. And yf thou wylt assawte castelles or townes haue
grete quantyte of gynnes/ and artyllery for to breke the walles.
And pouruey the of connynge myners/ and grete nombre of archers
and crosbowes. And do soo that thou mayst take away the water 15
from them of the fortresse. And euer kepe some of thy enmyes
for to knowe theyr doynges within. And yf thou can not haue it
but by ba|tayle doo it. For alway the last ende of thy werkes ought [f. H3ᵛ]
to be batayle. And this ought to be done whan thou can not haue
them otherwyse. And doo all thy werkes by councell and not 20
hastely.

❦ Of the physonomy of people.

AMonge all other thynges of this worlde I wyll that thou knowe
a noble and meruaylous scyence that is called physonomy by the
which thou shalt knowe the nature and condycyon of people. And 25
it was founde by a phylosophre named Physonomyas/ the whiche
sought the qualytees of the nature of creatures.

❦ In the tyme of the sayde Physonomyas reygned the moost
wyse physycyen Ypocras. And bycause the fame of Physonomyas
and his wysdome was so gretely spredde/ the dyscyples and 30
seruauntes of Ypocras toke hys fygure secretly/ and bare it to
Physonomyas to here how he wolde Juge and say by þe sayd fygure
of Ypocras. And bade hym say and tel the qualyte therof. Whan
Physonomyas had well beholden it/ he sayd. This man is a wrangeler lecherous and rude. This herynge the dyscyples of Ypocras 35
they wolde haue slayne Physonomyas/ and sayd to hym. Aa fole

4 renne] runne K   5 Conforte] comfort K   14 myners] moiners K
18 thy] theyr CK   20 otherwyse] otherwayes K   21 hastely] hastilye
K   22] *chap. headed* E *in List of Contents*   physonomy] Phisiognomy K
(*regular substitution, not indicated hereafter*)   27 creatures] *no punct.* (*at end of l.*)
29 Physonomyas] physonomyas   33 hym.] *see 257/5n. and 363/31n.*

wysest man in the worlde!' And whan Phisonomias sawe thaim
so meeuyd, he appeasid thaim with faire langage, sayinge thus,
'I knowe well that this is the figure of the noble doctoure Ypocras.
And I haue tolde you what I knowe by my science.' The whiche
5 seruauntes went home ageyne and tolde thaire maistre what
[f. 66ᵛ] Phisonomias hath tolde | [thaim. Than Ypocras seid, 'Truly
p. 131 Phisonomias hath tolde] you the playn trouthe of my compleccion,
wherynne were alle the seid vices.' Deer sonne, I haue breefly
drawen out the reules of this science, wherby thou shall haue noble
10 wysdome. If thou see a man of feble colour, vse nat his companye, for he is enclyned to luxure and to ill disposicion. And yf
thou see a man, whan thou blamest him for som-what, that he
looke vpon thee in fere and shamefastnesse, that waxeth rede in
the face, that sobbeth, and his yien watir, that man loueth and
15 dreedith thy persoone. And be ware as of thyne enmye, of him
that is nat perfourmed of his membres, and that is marked in the
visage, and also of him that is ill fourmed. Latinge the wite that
the best compleccion that is, is he that is of meene stature, and
that his here of his hede, and his yien, ben blake, the visage
20 rounde, the colour medilde betwixt rede, white, and browne, and
that is body be holl and right vp, the hede in a meene, nothir to
miche nor to litle, that he speke litle but yf neede be, and the voice
of his woorde sweete. Such a man were good and necessarie to be
aboute thy persoone.
25   Whan the here of the hede is playne and softe, the man is curteys
and jentill, and his brayne is colde.
     Whan a man hath the here of his hede harde and thikke, it is
a signe that he is a foole and nyce. And whan he hath mykell here
on the belye and on the brest, that man is of right good complec-
30 cion and singulere nature, and he is louinge and kepith longe in his
herte the shame that is doon vnto him.
     Yf a man haue the here of the hede blak, he loueth justise and
reson. And yf they been reede, he is nat wyse, and lightly wroth.
[f. 67] And yf they ben of meene coloure betwixt rede and | blac, that
p. 132 man is well disposid and l[o]ueth pease.
36   Whan a man hath grete yien, he is envious. And yf they be in
a meene, and of coloure betwixt yelow and blac, he is of good
vndirstandinge, curteys and true.
     ANd he that hath the yien longe, and the face longe, suche a man

35 loueth] leueth

this is the fygure of the best man of the worlde. Whan Physonomyas
sawe them thus moeued/ he appeased them the best waye that he
coude with fayre wordes saynge. I knowe well that this is the
fygure of the wyse man Ypocras. And I haue shewed you by
scyence as I knowe. Whan the dyscyples were come to Ypocras 5
they tolde hym what Physono|myas had sayd. And Ypocras [f. H4]
sayd, Truely Physonomyas hath tolde you the trouthe, and hath
left nothynge of my complexyon in the whiche ben all my vyces.
But reason that is in me ouercometh and ruleth the vyces of my
complexyon.   10

⁋ Dere sone I haue shortely abreged to the/ the rules of this
scyence of Physonomy/ the whiche shall infourme the gretely.

⁋ Yf thou se a man with salowe coloure/ flee his company/ for
he is inclyned to the synne of lechery/ and to many euylles. Yf thou
seest a man that smyleth lyghtly/ and whan thou beholdest hym 15
he wyll loke shamfastly and wyl blusshe in his face and sygh/ with
teeres in his eyes yf thou blame hym for ony thynge/ surely he
feareth the and loueth thy persone. Beware of hym as thy enmy
that is tokened in his face/ and of hym also that is mysshapen. The
best complexyon that is/ is he that is of meane coloure with 20
browne eyes & heere/ and his vysage betwene why[te] and reed/
with an vpryght body/ with a heed of metely bygnesse/ and that
speketh not but of nede be/ with a softe voyce/ suche a complexyon
is good/ and suche men haue about the.

⁋ Yf the heeres be playne and smothe the man is curteys and 25
meke/ and his brayne is colde. Harde heere and curled is a token
of foly & lewdnesse. Moche heere on the brest and on the bely
betokeneth very yll or very good complexyon naturally and is very
amerous/ and kepeth in his herte the iniuryes þat hath ben done to
hym. Blacke heere betokeneth to loue reason & Justyce.   30

⁋ Duskysshe eyes betokeneth fooly/ & lyghtly to be angry. Gray
eyes betokeneth honeste/ & louynge peas. Bygge eyes betokeneth to
be enuyous/ unshamefast/ slowe & vnobedyent. | Eyes meane [f. H4ᵛ]
betwene blacke and yelowe is of good vnderstandyng/ curteys/
and trusty. Wyde retchynge eyes and a longe face betokeneth a 35

1 Physonomyas] Physononomyas   11] *All sections in Physonomy chapter
are run-on on same line as preceding words*   13 with] of a K   15 smyleth]
smighteth K   18 persone. Beware] *no punct. (at end of l.)*   21 whyte]
why *(at end of l.)*   23 of] if K: *see n.*   29 amerous] amorous K
to] vnto K   32 honeste] *(poss. for* honesté)*, honest K: *see n. and cf. 381/11,
383/4n. and 10n.*

is full of malice and yll disposicion. And he that hath yien like an asse, loking downward, he is a foole and of harde nature.

Whan the yien ben mevinge lightly, and his face is longe, suche a man loueth debate, falshede, and vntrouthe.

5 Whan the yien of a man ben rede, he is stronge and of grete corage. But the worst yien that ben, ben thoo that hauen spottes a-boute, white, rede or blake. And suche a man is of the worst disposicion that is.

HE that hath the browys thikke of here, he is euill tunged. And
10 he that hath thaim longe, nygh the earis, he is nat true.

And he that hath mykell here betwixt the browes, he is nat true. And he that hath th[aim faire] of here, and nat to longe, and that they ben of grete here, suche a man is of grete vndirstandinge.

And he that hath the nose slendyr, he will lightly be wroth. And
15 he that [hath] it longe downe to the mouthe, he is well-disposed and hardy. And he that hath it shorte and lowe, he is easely troubled. And he that hath grete holes in the nose, he is slaughfull, rude and soone meevid. And he that hath the nose large in the
19 myddys, going vpwarde, he is a grete talker and lyere. But the
[f. 67ᵛ] best nose of alle is that that is of meane lenght | and the holys
p. 133 nothir to grete ne to smale.

THe visage that is plat and playne, and is nat sharpe nor grete, it is ill. Suche a man is enuious, iniuriouse, and loueth plee. But he that hath the visage is a meene forme, and the cheekes nothir to
25 fatt nor to lene, he is a true man, lovinge, and of grete vndir-standinge, wyse, and full of good seruice.

HE that hath a large mouthe, he is manlye and loueth batailes. And he that hath grete lippes, he is a foole and malapert. And he that hath a slendre visage, he is wyse and of grete vndirstandinge.
30 And he that hath a litle face and of yelowe coloure, he is deceyu-able, drunkelewe and of yll condicion. And he that hath a longe face is vn-jantill. And he that hath the earis full and swollen, and the cheekes full, he is oft meeuid and angry. And he that hath the earis to litle, he is a foole, atheest and luxurious.

35 HE that hath the vois grete sownynge, he is a grete langager, and loueth batails. And he that spekith hastily, with a small vois, he is a lyer and of yll disposicion. And he that hath a grete vois, he is lightly wroth. And he that hath the voys swete and sownynge,

---

12 thaim faire] thynne: *see n.*   14 And . . . wroth] *repeated, each instance occupying entire line*   33 cheekes] s *ins. above*

man malycyous and yll. Eyes lyke an asse alway lokyng downe is
of harde nature and nought. Waueryng eyes with a lon[g] face
betokeneth gyle/ rennynge mynde and vntrusty. Reed eyes betokeneth to be stronge and of a grete courage. He that hath spekles
about his eyes/ whyte/ blacke/ or reed/ is the worst of all other 5
men. Thycke heered eye lyddes is an yll speker/ he that hath them
hangynge longe to his eyes/ is neyther true nor clene. He that
hath heere ynough betwene his two browes and be thynne and not
to longe/ is of a good and grete vnderstandyng.

℃ A sklendre nosed man is soone angry. A longe nose hawked 10
to the mouthe/ is a token of honeste and hardynesse. A snytted
nose is a token to be soone vexed. Wyde nosethrylles in a man is
slouth and boystousnesse and soone angered. A brode nose in the
myddes is a grete speker/ and a lyer. But þe best is he that is
meane neyther to wyde nor to close. The vysage that is ful & flat/ 15
and that is not swollen nor to bygge is a token of an yll persone/
enuyous/ iniuryous/ and a wrangeler. But he that hath a meane
vysage of fourme of chekes and eyes/ neyther to fat nor to leane/
he is trusty/ louynge/ and of grete vnderstandynge/ wyse and full
of seruyce and wytte. 20

℃ He that hath a wyde mouthe loueth batayle and is hardy. He
þat hath thycke lyppes is folysshe. And he that hath a wrynkled face
is a lyer/ and careth not of many debates. He that hath a sklender
face is of grete reason. He that hath a lytell vysage and yelowe of 24
colour is a deceyuer/ dronken/ and euyll. Full eyes & | smothe [f. J1]
chekes is soone angry.

℃ Small eeres betokeneth foly/ and lechery.

℃ He that hath a small voyce & speketh thycke loueth feyght-
ynge. He that hath a meane voyce/ neyther to bygge/ nor to lytell/
is folysshe and vnreasonable. And he that speketh to moche with 30
a sklender voyce/ is not ouer honest/ and of smal care. He that hath
a femynyne voyce is soone angry/ and of yl nature. A softe voyced

---

1 alway] alwayes K   2 nought] naught K (*regular substitution: not indi-*
cated hereafter)   long] lon (*at end of l.*) C long K   3 vntrusty. Reed] *no*
punct. (*at end of l.*)   5 or] and K   10 sklendre] slender K (*regular*
substitution: not indicated hereafter)   11 honeste] honest K   12 nose-
thrylles] nosthrels K   32 yl] euyll K

[he is of envious disposicion and vntrusty]. And he that hath a faire vois, he is a foole and of high corage.

He that meevith often, [and] in his spekinge meevith his handis, he is yll and deceyuable. And that spekith and mevith nat his
5 handys, he is of parfite vndirstandinge, wyse and good.

[And he that hath the nek longe, he is of harde vndirstandyng.] And he that hath it short, he is hote and deceyuable. And he that hath a grete bely, he is proude and luxurious. He that hath a large
9 brest, grete shulders, and grete bake, he is good, hardy, wyse, and
[f. 68] of good vndirstandinge. And he that hath a | slender bak, he will
p. 134 neuir agree to no man. And he that hath the brest in a meane and the bak playne, it is a signe of good disposicion. And he that hath high shulders he is sharpe and of yll feith.

HE that hath the armes longe, comynge downe to knees, he is
15 a man of grete manhode, good and large. And yf they ben shorte, it is a signe that he loueth discorde, and that he is a foole.

And he that hath the palmys and the fingers longe, he is apte to lerne many artes and sciences, and in espesiall hande craftes, and he shall be of good reule. And he that hath the fingers grete and shorte,
20 he is nyce and a foole and iniuriouse. And he that hath the feete grete and full of flessh, he is a foole and iniurious. And he that hath thaim litle he is light and of harde vndirstandyng.

HE that hath smale legges, he is meek and vnkunnynge. And he that hath thaim grete, he is harde and straunge. And the brede of
25 the heelys and of the legges betokne strenght of body. And he that hath miche flessh in the knees, he is soft and weyke. And whan a man goth a large paas and by layser, he shall doo well his besinesse. And he that goth fast with litle pace, he is to hasty and evill willed.

HE is of good complexion, that hath the flessh soft and moiste,
30 and in a meane betwixt euen and sharpe, and that he be nat to longe nor to shorte, and of coloure betwixt white and rede. And that he haue a swete looke, and the here of the hede swete and playne, and the yien in a meane grete and greye. And the hede
34 in a meane well made by mesure, and good nekke and of a suf-
[f. 68ᵛ] fisaunt lenght, and that the | shulders stoupe som-what, and that
p. 135 the legges and knees be nat to full of flessh, and the vois temperatly cliere, and the palme of a suffisaunt lenght, and the fingers longe

man is often angry and enuyous. He that hath a fayre voyce/ is
folysshe/ and of hyghe courage. He that speketh lyghtly/ lyeth
often/ and is a deceyuer. And he that speketh without moeuynge
his handes/ is of grete wysdome and honeste.

❧ He that hath a sklender necke/ is hote/ deceytfull/ and 5
folysshe. He þat hath a grete bely is proude/ lecherous/ and vnwyse.

❧ He that hath a large brest/ thycke sholdres/ and bygge fyngers/
is hardy/ wyse/ gentyll/ and of good wytte. He with a sklender backe
agreeth neuer with ony other. He þat hath his brest & backe egall/
is a token of honeste. Hye reysed sholdres/ is a token of lytell 10
fydelyte/ nought/ and sharpe. He that hath longe armes re-
chynge to the knee/ is of grete boldenesse/ sadnesse/ & lyberalyte.
Shorte armes betoken that he loueth socour/ and is folysshe.

❧ Longe palmed handes with longe fyngers/ is ordeyned to
lerne many scyences/ and artes/ and specyal handy craftes/ and 15
be of good gouernaunce. Fyngers short and thycke/ betoken
foly.

❧ Shorte thycke fete and flesshy/ betokeneth to be folysshe/ and
full of iniury. A lytell lyght fote/ is a man of smal vnderstandynge.
A sklender fote sheweth a man to be symple/ and of small know- 20
lege. He that hath a thycke fote is hardy and folysshe.

❧ The length of þe legges/ & the heles | betoken strength of the [f. J1ᵛ]
body. A thycke flesshy kne/ is soft and weyke.

❧ A man that gooth a grete pace/ is wyllynge in all thynges, and
to hasty. 25

❧ He is of a good nature and complexyon/ that hath softe flesshe
and moyst/ meanely smothe and rough/ and that is kyndly betwene
reed and whyte.

❧ He that hath a smothe contenaunce/ softe heere & playne/
with meane eyes of bygnesse/ with a well proporcyoned heed/ 30
a good necke and suffycyent in length/ with sholders somdele
lowe/ and his legges and knees metely flesshed/ his voyce competent clere/ þe palmes of his handes and fyngers longe/ and not

3 moeuynge] mouing of K   4 honeste] honestie K   10 honeste]
honestie K   12 knee] knees K   15 specyal] specially K: cf. 315/9
18 betokeneth] betoken K   30 heed/] heed ʃ   31 somdele] somewhat
K   32–3 competent] compotent K

and nat to grete. And that he laugh litle, and mokke no body, and that his face be laughinge and mery.

Notwithstandinge, deere sonne, thou maist nat juge a man alle-oonllye by oon signe, but considre alle his signes. And looke what
5 signes ben moost habundaunt in the man, and than holde the on the better parte and moost profitable.

Explicit &c.

3 Notwithstandinge] *illuminated initial* N *omitted, but space contains minuscule catch-letter* n *supplied by scribe for illuminator* 7 Explicit] *design in shape of scroll around extended tail of* p *contains* tous mon [*cuer*] aues, *the word* cuer *being represented by drawing of heart*

thycke/ and that he laughe but lytell/ and that is no mocker/ with
a smylyng chere and mery/ is of good complexyon. Howbeit dere
sone I commaunde the not to Juge al vpon one sygne/ but
consydre all the tokens of a man whiche moost habounde and
sheweth þe foly in hym/ and holde the to the best and moost 5
prouffytable party.

⟨ Deo gratias.

⟨ Thus endeth the abstract of the secrete of secretes of Arystotle
prynce of Phylosophres.

⟨ Here folowe certayne reasons of the grete phylosophre Sydrac 10
to the kynge Boctus/ whiche I haue translated out of the Pycardes
speche/ thynkynge it necessary in this sayd treatyse.

⟨ How one ought to vttre his speche. |

YF thou hast ony mater of grauyte or sadnesse of reason/ to
shewe and declare before noble and wyse audyence/ tell it breuely 15
and wysely/ with a good bolde courage and wyll/ and than they
wyll take it hertely/ and wyll gyue credence to thy wordes and
alowe thy saynge. For wyse men wyll gladly gyue eeres to wyse
and short informacyon. And therfore be not shamefast nor aferde
to tell the trouth. For many one haue loste theyr ryght by shame- 20
fastnesse and feare of theyr vtteraunce of wordes/ though theyr
causes were good.

⟨ The maner of angre.

THou oughtest not to be angry though thy brother or frende 25
shew the heuy chere somtyme/ for peraduenture he hath some
cause wherfore he can shew the/ nor other no fayre semblaunt.
And this thou mayst consydre in thy selfe. For yf thou were angry
thou coude shewe hym/ nor none other good chere or counte-
naunce/ and so it is with hym. And yf thou hast had ony wordes 30
with ony man/ and he shewe the yll countenaunce, therfore yet
thou ought not to be angry with hym. For perchaunce he is too
lewde or vnwytty of hymselfe that he can do no better/ and yet he
weneth that he doth wel/ for euer the lewdest sheweth moost anger.

---

18 eeres] eare K   19 aferde] afrayde K   27 semblaunt] semblance K
29 coude] couldst K   none] no K   32 too] so K

For whan a wyse man is angry/ he sheweth it not outwarde by his
reason. A man ought more to feare the anger of a wyse man than
of a foole/ for the wyse man can better reuenge his angre than a
[f. J2] foole | howbeit that a foles angre is often comberous.

5   ℭ To vttre secretes.

IN one maner onely thou ought to shew thy secretes/ that is to
wyte to almyghty god that knoweth al thyng/ that is to be vnder-
stande/ to his lyeftenaunt in erth/ and other wyse not. For yf thou
dyscouer it to thy frende/ and yf thy frende be but lewde/ & hath
10 another frende þat he loueth/ to whome he telleth thy secrete/ and
his frende hath another frende that telleth hym the same/ and
so frome one to another tyll a grete meyny do knowe it/ & so thy
secrete may come out to thy grete shame and rebuke. For whyles
thou kepest thy secrete within the/ it is sure. For thou mayst
15 shew thy secrete to suche one that whan he knoweth it wyl do the
some wronge/ and for feare that thou hast of hym þu dare not
gaynsay hym leest he bewrey the. And yf thou can none otherwyse
but that thou must vttre it by thy foly/ and that thy stomake wyl
swell for to tel it/ go out of company and tell it to thy selfe as yf
20 thou wolde tell it to another man/ and thy hert wyll coole and thy
stomake swage. And for ony nede that thou hast to dyscouer it/
take hede to whom/ but yf it be to suche one that for ony anger
that thou doost to hym wyl not rebuke the with it. And neuer lete
thy neyghboure knowe thy nede/ for therby thou mayst be the
25 lesse set by in places where thou dwellest.

                     ℭ How thou oughtest to sporte with thy frende. |
[f. J2ᵛ] LOke wysely how thou playest or bourdest with thy frende (or
other) with thy handes or with thy mouth/ for yf thou do hym
harme/ harme may come to the. With sportyng with handes cometh
30 angre and murdre/ whyther it be thy brother or frende. For yf
thou hurt hym or wryng his hande/ or cast hym downe/ or smyte
hym otherwyse/ it shall greue hym/ & shame hym in his mynde/
albeit that he be lytell and weyke/ for eche in hym selfe counteth
hym stronge/ bolde and fyers/ and yet he wyll prayse hym selfe

7 ought] oughtst K   8 lyeftenaunt] lifetenaunt K   10 frende/ and]
frende. And   12 meyny] many K

thoughe he be a cowarde and nought. And yf thou mocke hym/ thou shalt spyte hym to the hert/ for he wyll thynke that thou dyspysest hym/ & þat thou reputeth hym at nought. And yf thou mocke hym before people/ thou doost hym yet more spyte/ & he shall owe the yll wyll and hate the deedly. For of mockynge 5 cometh angre and grete hate/ though it be thy brother or other frende. But thou ought to pastyme with fayre wordes/ and to shewe goodly auctorytees and reasons to drawe theyr loue to the/ for by that pastaunce thou mayst come to þe goodnesse/ loue & curteysy of people. 10

⟨ The maner to doubt and trust thyn enemy.

WHyther thyn enemy be stronge or weyke/ thou ought not to doubt hym to moche/ nor trust to moche to hym/ For he þat is ouercome today/ may be vyctour tomorow. And he that is vyctour 15 today may be ouerthrowen to morow. And he that doubteth none/ none wyll haue doubt of hym. To moch doubt | maketh to moch trust/ and to moche trust maketh to moche domage. For he that [f. J3] bereth doubt alwaye with hym/ hath a grete burden & payne. 20 And he that hath trust in hym selfe/ bereth his owne domage/ and his dethe. For þu ought to doubt whan tyme is to doubt/ and to trust whan tyme is to trust.

⟨ Finis.

⟨ Lenuoy and excuse of Robert Coplande the translatour and 25
Imprynter of this boke

⟨ In humble maner/ and moost due reuerence
Tremblynge for drede afore thy souerayne
Yf thy chaunce be to come in presence
Where ony person shall the there retayne 30
Submytte thy selfe as one that wolde be fayne
His grace to please in all maner degre
And of thy rudenesse for to pardon the.

⟨ And where as thou art but as an abstract 35
As touchynge the auctours compylacyon
Yf I therfore be ony wyse detract
In defaut of thy abreuyacyon

12 WHyther] WHether K   ought] oughtest K   15 today] to day
24 Finis] omitted K   25 Lenuoy not included in K; Table of Contents, as on
pp. 231–51 above, follows here in K   34 the.] no punct.

Lay thou the blame in the frensshe translacyon
Whiche I haue folowed as nygh as I can
[f. J3ᵛ] Under correccyon of euery wyse man.

℃ Yf ony may dyspyse the language rude
5 Whiche barayne is/ of puryd eloquence
Desyre them that they do not delude
Thy fronysate mater full of sentence |
But in theyr hertes/ enprynt thy morall sence/
Which compyled is/ by wysdome naturall
10 Of prudent men/ the veray gouernall.

℃ Where many wedes be in a felde of corne
All though the weders thynke to wede it clene
Some shall remayne/ whan the fylde is shorne.
Drawke or cokle/ yet there wyll be seen
15 The fawtes therof/ is in the handes and eyen
Lykewyse where many/ wordes and lettres be
No mervayle is/ though I some ouerse.

℃ Yf by impressyon/ ony thynge be amys
In worde/ in sence/ or in ortography
20 I you requyre/ to mende where the faute is
In the best wyse/ it for to Justyfy
For though all be not to your fantasy
In formall maner/ do ye it dyscus
Saue onely god, nemo est perfectus.

25   ℃ Deo gratias.
                ℃ Dytee du translateur

                ℃ Tost ou tard/ pres ou loing
[f. J4]   A le fort du foible besoing. |

℃ Thus endeth the secrete of secretes of Arystotle with the
30 gouernayle of prynces and euery maner of estate with rules of
helthe for body and soule very prouffytable for euery man/ and
also veray good to teche chyldren to lerne to rede Englysshe. Newly
translated & enprynted by Robert Copland at London in the

---

10 gouernall.] *no punct.*   17 ouerse.] *no punct.*

Flete-strete at the sygne of the Rose garlande the yere of our lorde .M.CCCCC.xxviij. the .vij. day of August þe .xx. yere of the reygne of our moost dradde souerayne and naturall kynge Henry the .viij. defender of the fayth.

[Printer's device] 5

2 .xx.] *no final punct.; at end of l.*

IX

SIR WILLIAM FORREST
THE PLEASAUNT POESYE OF
PRINCELIE PRACTISE
1548

From British Library MS. Royal 17.D.iii

[f. 2] TO the **moste** worthie **and** famouse **prince**, Edwarde, **Duke of Somerset**, Earle **of** Herteforde, **Vicounte** Beaucham, **Lorde** Seymour, **vncle** vnto **owre** moste **dreade** soueraigne **lorde**, Kynge **Edwarde** the **Sexthe**, Protectour **also** ouer **his** moste royall person, **Realmes**, and **Dominions**, bee **honour**, healthe, and hyghe **prosperité**, withe, **after** this **lief**, æternall **foelicité**. So wisshethe **his** daylie **oratour**, Sir William Forreste, **preeiste**.

(1)
AS the olde feeldis bringeth forthe our nwe corne,
the ethymologie too all men is playne,
so dothe olde tutours children younge borne
produce and furdre too knowledge soueraine,
the olde for the younge too caste and ordayne   5
by education, as sittethe the case,
that after their tyme the younge maye take place.

(2)
Suche sorte sage **Cicero**, that famouse Romayne,
prouided for **Marke**, his dear beloued soon,
at **Athenis** withe **Gratippe**, a yeare or twayne,   10
too lerne and knowe thinges after too bee doon
when, in this lief, his dayes weare paste and roon,
too bee thapter the **trybune** seate too steade.
Oh, worthie parentes, that so their youthe can leade.

(3)

[f. 2ᵛ] The steye of the lifes exercitation   15
    takethe great force, as authours dothe endight,
    by yowthes firste breakinge and education,
    while they bee pliant too frame in ordre right;
    thoughe Nature workethe vertue too despight,
    yeat crooked ymps by handelinge are made streight,   20
    so yowthe muste bee woone on Reason too weight.

(4)

Suche liquour, they saye, as entrethe the vessell
    when firste the same is put in vsage,
    eauer after it will therof smell.
    Whiche maye bee applied too younge tendre age: 25
    breake yowthe tymelie from viciowse owterage,
    plantinge thearin vertuouse exercise,
    so shall it sweete sente too eache mannys deuise.

(5)

Vnto the purpose nowe present in hande.
    What shall I wright, comprise, or prolate   30
    of owre noble Edwarde, Kynge of Englande,
    althoughe hee bee yeat in his infantes date,
    of princelie nature withoute peere or mate?
    Neadis muste hee of highe worthynes sent,
    as proofe maye bee by reason consequent.   35

(6)

Firste, tochinge the giftes that Nature may geeue,
    he wantethe none: his features dothe shewe
    of graces superne that in hym dothe meeue;
    it shewithe hee hathe dronke of the heauenlye dewe,
    for, in the numbre of the fyneste fewe,   40
    too what thinge witt perspicuat maye reache,
    hee hathe whearewithe withe the beste too searche.

(7)

[f. 3]   The same (his witt) in woorthie wise tapplye,
of literate knowledge toptaine some substaunce,
hee hathe too **Gouernour** a Duke moste worthye,   45
Edwarde of **Somerset,** a man of puisaunce
whoe workethe highest meanis his honour taduaunce,
as dothe appeare in his procedinges all:
Scotelande theareof can make memoriall,

(8)

  wheare, the laste yeare, the firste of his reigne,   50
hee wrought suche feate and princelie entreprise
in the behaulfe of owre saide souereigne
as hathe not bene herde so passinge precise,
withe the losse of **fiuetie** or fewe moe certise,
XV thousande for too confownde.   55
Miraculowse it was: God was his grownde.

(9)

  Of more his endeuer too wright or saye,
althoughe the thinge I heere preposterate:
when his famowse father was rapte awaye
bie **Clothois** cuttinge the threade of his date,   60
howe, bie all meanys hee dyd accelerate
with suche highe honour as neauer in booke was fownde,
in **Westmynster** Churche too haue his Grace crownde.

(10)

  This is a **Protectour** to hym moste enteere,
this is an **vncle** moste faithfull too see,   65
this is a freende at hande eauer neere,
this is a father for his fidelitee!
This is not **Richarde,** rager of crueltee,
too whome the **fowrthe Edwarde** his children beetooke.
This is the true **Theseus,** and hee an hell whooke.   70

50] 1547 *added in margin, immediately next to the rhyming word.*

(11)

[f. 3ᵛ] **This** is the Duke **Epaminedon**
whiche in Athenis beere scepture and ball,
too whome **Amintas, Philippe** his son,
beeinge kinge of **Macedonye** all,
can commit for his fame royall: 75
the woorthynes that hee hym indude
heere to reherse, my phrase is too rude.

(12)

The same hee seemithe, I dare vndretake,
that in thaffairs of oure noble **Edwarde**
his helpinge hande at no tyme dothe slake,   80
bothe lief and goodis therin too ieobarde,
to whome I saye, this my warke too forwarde,
Ohe woorthie **Duke,** attende my pretence
whiche I in suete haue too your excellence.

(13)

This symple booke whiche yee in hande nowe haue,   85
I haue comprised in sorte as yee see,
firste deuised bye **Aristotele** graue
vnto Kinge **Alexandres** maiestee,
too thende it maye like your magnanimitee
as yee cause see, bye your discretion,   90
too bee preferred, or take direption.

(14)

As children that bee of highe progeniture
owght not too eate but as their nurice shall assyne,
the wief no lettre or tokne too recure
withoute her husbonde the same dothe diffyne,   95
so yee, bothe Nurice and Husbonde collateryne,
the neareste that eauer anye **Orphan** maye finde,
ought firste in this too declare your mynde.

80 no tyme] notyme

(15)

[f. 4] **Leste** his highe maiestie heereof might taiste,
yee not alowınge the same for hym meeite,   100
for lacke of foresight too make suche waiste
then had I growned all on a wronge greeite:
therfore too yow, as man moste discreeite,
ohe noble **Duke,** I itt firste heere present,
humblye besechinge too tendre myne entent.   105

(16)

As signe I geue it of myne allegeaunce;
for, vnto anye, what can bee higher prayes
that in enditinge hathe anye furtheraunce,
then to his soueraigne bye some humble wayes
hym too present withe sumwhat in his dayes,   110
too whome bee reigne that beste maye accorde
withe healthe and longe lief too yow, my good lorde?

The table **conteynynge** the **title** of **all** and **singulare** the **chapiters** in **this** present **booke.**

Page

Title of Caput 8: realmes] s *ins. above*

heading to Caput 16: as well] aswell

Caput 22

Caput 23

Caput 24

Caput 25

Caput 26

Caput 27

Caput 28

Howe a kinge shoulde endeuer (so muche as he may without to muche wronge offerde) too haue peace with all men, and in thexecutinge of warre not too shewe vttre vltion towardis the membres for the wronge demeanynge of their heade, consyderinge as thus: subiectes muste doo as their headis shall assigne.

Caput 29

Certayne documentes for conseruation of bodelie healthe, withe a description of the fowre elementes whereof man is made, and of their effectes.

Caput 30

What thinges by dyete prescribed for healthes preseruation are too bee obserued, and what meates and | drynkes are   [f. 7]
cheiflie too bee vsed for the same entent.

Caput 31

Of thexercise of tyme ymmediatlie beefore meate, withe a dwe maneire in feeadinge, not too the full contentation of thappetyte.

Caput 32

After what sorte a man, myndinge his health, shall behaue hym-selfe after his refections.

Caput 33

An admonition for dwe conseruation of natural heat, and what thinges too bodelie healthe are profitable, and what nociuouse.

Caput 34

Of certaynge thinges whiche dothe conforte the bodye, ympinguat, or macerat the same.

Caput 35

A meanys too knowe goode and howlesome wynes, and of the moderate maners in vsynge of them.

heading to Caput 28: So muche] somuche

Caput 36

At what season bedde reste is beste to be taken, in what howre for too arise, and howe a man shall vse hym-selfe after his reste-takynge.

Caput 37

Of theis fowre seasons in the yeare: ver, estas, autumnus, hyemps, and of their varieties and qualities, what ordre also is to be taken in them.

At thende of this worke shal ensue certaine narrations, exemplifijng sundry of the maters of the aforesaide tytles, to be fownde by the fygures at thende of the saide titles or their chapiters.

[f. 8] **Here ensuithe a notable warke called the** Pleasaunt Poesye of Princelie Practise, composed of late in **meatre royall: by the symple and vnlearned Sir William** Forrest, preeiste, muche parte collecte owte of a booke entiteled **The Gouer-naunce of Noblemen, which booke** the wise philosopher Aristotele wrote too his discyple **Alexandre, the great and mightie conqueroure.**

1548

To the moste mightie and puisaunte Prynce Edwarde the Sexthe, Kynge of Engelande, Fraunce **and Irelande, Defendour of the Faithe, and heere** in earthe (vndre Christe) the Supreme Heade of bothe **Churches, Englande and Irelande, bee regne in** state moste fortunate, with thuppre hande ouer his enemies **alweyes, thorowe His ayde by Whome all kynges** heere dothe governe.   William Forrest.

(17)

THe nobleste of nobles, **Alexandre** the greate,
when moste hee sought too florische in his reigne,
whoe in chyvalrie wrought manye a feate,   115
as monumentis olde of hym dothe conteine,
his throne too stablische in state souereigne,

Title to Caput 36: reste-takynge] restetakynge
Title to Caput 37] Foll. by f. 7ᵛ, taken up by the picture of Forrest presenting his book to the king.

Here ensuithe A notable warke / called the pleasaunt Poesye of Princelie Practise, composed of late in
meetre royall, by the symple and vnlearned, j Willia~
forrest preeiste, muche parte collecte owte of A booke
entituled, The gouernaunce of noble men, which booke
the wise philosopher Aristotele / wrote too his discyple
Alexandre / the great and migotie Conqueroure,
1548

O the moste mightie and puissante Prynce
Edwarde the Sexthe, kynge of Engelande / ffraunce /
and Irelande, Defendour of the faithe / And next
in earthe (vndre Christe) the supreme heade of bothe
Churches / Englande, and Irelande, beereigne in
state moste fortunate: W thumpie hande ouer his enemies
alweyes / thorowe his ayde / by whome all kynge
heere dothe governe.   William fforrest.

The nobleste of nobles / Alexandre the greate.
When moste hee sought / too florische in his reigne:
Whoe, in chyvalrie / wronght manye A feate:
as monumentis olde / of hym dothe conteine,
his throne too stablische / in state souereigne:
this caste hee caste / bye wisedome decorate,
too woorke by cownsell / of men approbate.

As artes
omnia agit
circonsilio.

this caste hee caste bye wisedome decorate:
too woorke by cownsell of men approbate.

(18)

[f. 8ᵛ] **Emonge** all men that in his fauour stoode,   120
Aristotele wan fauoure synguler,
whois fame appeared too his purpose goode,
thoughe from his presence his beeinge weare fer,
whoe in thois dayes shone like the daye ster:
in fresche philosophie so dyd hee admownte,   125
for souereigne wise men dyd hym then accownte.

(19)

Vnto this man, this Philosop[h]er sage,
Alexandre his lettres can deuise,
vnto his presence too dres his voyage,
in sundrie causes too haue his aduise.   130
When **Aristotele** herde thambassadise,
whoe ferr in age that tyme his dayes had spent,
not able too themperour hym-selfe too present,

(20)

whearfore in studye hee setteled his mynde
by answere too rescribe what weies hee might take,   135
consyderinge as thus: a man of suche kynde
no subiecte becummethe his pleasure too forsake,
thoughe feblenes hyndrede his iourney too take.
A while the case hee dyd delyberate,
concludinge this wise his mynde too satiate: 140

(21)

well dyd considre this auncyent man
what weightie affaires hym sundrie weies befel
too bee debated and weyed nowe and than,
bye office due all errour too expel,
in whiche was neade of politike counsel.   145
For whoe of powre hathe muche in hande too wilde,
sage aduysours maye not bee theare exilde.

119 *in margin, in red ink, in holograph*: *Astutus* omnia agit cum consilio

(22)

[f. 9]   **Vnto** that ende this booke that dothe ensue
Aristotele full wiselye can comprise,
withe all intent of obedyence due   150
for **Alexandre** kynge too exercise
bye a dwe meane of princelie iustice,
as too his persone an ordynarye rule,
withe sage respecte thearfrome not too recule.

(23)

Whiche booke ensuynge his fame made far too shine,   155
for in his doinges men dyd muche honour note,
so that thear-thorowe kynges of right highe lyne,
mooste of the worlde, vnto his powre hee gote.
So was his reigne in glorie set a-flote
bycause hee liste bye cownsell too proceade: 160
the whole worlde yeat recomptethe muche his deade.

(24)

Suchewise this prudent philosopher olde
satisfied themperours expectation:
from muche hawte outerage it dyd his harte colde
when furied hee was bye inclynation   165
rigour textende towardis anye person:
vnto this booke suche credyte gaue that kynge
that moste it ordrede hym in hole his lyuinge.

(25)

Not onlie this booke aduertisement gaue
in outewarde assayes what beste was tamplecte,   170
but also it taught meanys hym-selfe to saue
frome sundrye occasions his healthe tenfecte.
So that too all sortis of eache manere secte
it is a myrroure of perfection true,
heerein too contemplate their office due.   175

(26)

[f. 9ᵛ] **Vnto** my handis wheare late this booke dyd chaunce
and had seene what treasure it dyd conteyne,
anon it mooued in mye remembraunce
the same too turne in to owre Englische veyne,
for youre onlie sake, my cheif souereyne,   180
beseachinge youre myghtie Domynation
too graunte it youre woorthie acceptation.

(27)

Thoughe it bee thinge too youre Magnificence
not neadinge, or woorthie in presence tappeere,
bycause yee haue men of like equiualence,   185
or ferdre surmountinge, in knowledge cleere,
too prompte youre Grace in the regale speere,
thoffice, I meane, of princelie behauour,
then tenn tymes can doo this my present labour,

(28)

yeat as the **panther,** moste preaciouse in araye,   190
in his pasturinge dothe not his dyett dresse
vppon wone kynde of herbys too feeade alwaye,
but what hee fyndethe meete his hungre toppresse,
so, noble Kynge, thoughe grose bee his processe,
for dyuersité youre Grace maye it reade,   195
thoughe yee not so doo compelled of neade,

(29)

in whiche I haue gathered and knyt of intent
sundrye fresche sentencies too the purpose meeit,
like too a poesye of flowres redolent
that too the odour geuethe pleasaunt smell sweeite,   200
so namynge the same (if yee saye, so bee-it)
The Pleasaunte Poesye of Pryncelie Practise:
whiche I heere present in my humblest wise,

(30)

[f. 10] **acknowledginge** myselfe in this pretence
too passe my bondis, and that no small deale,   205
that I, so symple of intelligence,
in too your presence by this meanys shoulde steale.
Construe what men I liste, I wische your heale,
with reigne moste fortunat that eauer had kynge:
suche of my purpose is hole the meanynge.   210

**An argument concerninge what dreade and feare a man
stondithe in, that taketh in hande too write or cownseile
a kinge or heade potentate.**

Caput primum

(31)

RIght well I wote full ieoberdowse it is,
and also harde, a kynge too cownsell,
or too admonische, in that or this.
His mightie powre dothe so far excell,
althoughe wone meanythe neauer so well,   215
if hee it take too the contrarye,
for lief or deathe whoe dare with hym replye?

(32)

This is wheare will and powre togither
regnethe aboue the vertues cardynall.
But vntoe whome they bee sent for thither   220
eache thynge is take in the weye dextrall,
tavoyde all daungre that myght beefall.
Beefore **Aristotele** his warke beegone,
hee humblie beesought **Alexandres** perdone,

(33)

[f. 10ᵛ] **leste** thorowe his brute and pleynnes of stile   225
hee myght that touche whiche his harte myght offende,
thearbye frome his fauour hym-selfe texile:
then weare too late his pennynge too amende.

Too whois example I humblie myselfe bende,
if, by translation, addition or so, 230
I chaunce in this my-selfe too ouer go.

(34)

Dye had I rather then offende my leeche.
For trulie in this if it shoulde so chaunce,
(whiche God forbydde, I hartelye beeseeche)
it is then thorowe cause of ignoraunce, 235
lacke of learnynge and wittie remembraun[c]e.
Thearfore I make this protestation:
if owghtes heere myshappe, too graunte mee perdon.

(35)

For in this warke whiche **Aristotele** wrote
I doo not thorowlie his pathes ensue: 240
hee was an Ethnyke, I haue not forgote,
and was in tholde tyme, and I in the nwe;
they woorshipped ydollis, and wee the God true.
Theis thynges consyderyed, muche of his writinge
I muste then alter too a Christian kinge. 245

(36)

Hee manye thynges mooued nowe nowghtes sett bye,
whiche at that season serued in a sorte,
sowndinge too owre purpose nowe farr awrye,
of which in this I will make no reporte.
In studye hee dothe themperoure exhorte 250
in physonomye too applie his witt,
whiche in this warke I wholie omytt.

(37)

[f. 11] The pryncyple selfe ys false, I dare saye,
and mannys judgementes necligent and frayle.
Then false and frayle makethe a mad medlaye: 255
when the fundation it-selfe doithe fayle,
itt can no-mannys seakinge oughtes countreuayle
vnto purpose the truthe too verifie:
then is it not meete for a kynges studye.

257 no-mannys] nomannys

(38)

For the saide science makethe a pretendinge　　　260
by outewarde signes the thought too descrye.
As, if wone hathe in his face suche a thinge,
too bee freende or foe, too judge hym thearbye,
likewise bye wryncle thorowe **palmystrye.**
So maye a kynge caste aweye manye wone:　　　265
too knowe mannys thought it longethe too God alone.

(39)

But oother his lessons necessarye
I shall trauerse in sorte as I maye,
consyderinge as thus in my fantazye:
abowte a kynge too frequent alwaye　　　270
copie of counselours their myndys too saye,
but yeat too all men it is not full knowne
the cause of greefis beefore they bee growne.

(40)

In euerye case some kynge listethe nott
his Cownsell too counseile, for disquyetnes,　　　275
or shamefastenes that anye shoulde wott
thynwarde concepte of his pensifenes:
softenes of nature maye moove hym no les.
Yeat cownsell secreat that bookes can geeue
may frome his harte suche occasions dreeue.　　　280

(41)

[f. 11ᵛ] **Lyke** as bookes teachethe withoute maister
and hathe too learnynge furthrede manye wone,
so by bookis some gatherethe his plaister,
too heale his aiche, bothe of flesche and bone.
By bookis, deadys doone manye daye a-gone　　　285
are freschelie renued too oure remembraunce,
as histories olde geevithe vs resemblaunce.

278 no les] noles

(42)

And bookis agayne too owre posterytee
shall sundrye thinges too knowledge represent
after oure dayes bye longe antiquytee,   290
whiche wee haue seene in practise euydent.
Bookes of wisdome lefte for a preasydent
date too the hawghteste reherse his fawte playne,
wheare dyuerse, for feare or fauour, will fayne.

(43)

For ofte it happenethe in sundrye countreyes,   295
too what thinge cheeiflie a kynges harte is bent,
hee shall haue counsell too followe his owne weyes,
althoughe they woorke too no woorthie intent:
for feare, some dare geeue none admonyschement;
some, thorowe flaterye, too stande in fauoure,   300
and some, bicause they sent of like sauour.

(44)

Suche hathe beene seene, and suche shall ensue,
in sundrye royalmys, for the worlde is large.
Thoughe not in **England, Flaundries,** or **Gascue,**
yeat hathe it chaunced bothe in **Ilyon** and **Arge,**   305
when kinge **Priamus** wolde neadis take in charge
Helene too mayntayne, that **Paris** frome Grece fett,
his Cownsell inclynde as his harte was sett.

(45)

[f. 12] **Thoughe** woorthie **Hector** thereagainste heelde,
withe dyuerse that knwe the daungre of warre,   310
oother, inexperte, too the kynge dyd yeelde
his purpose prefixed not to differre,
whiche counsell theire wealthe dyd cleane set aiarre,
as vttre procuringe of their propre soyle,
the deuastation and moste spytefull spoyle.   315

(46)

For at that season **Priamus** was slayne
and sundrye his soonnys moste woorthie of renowne,
withe manye a kynge and noble capitayne
the royalme thorowe, and **Ilion** their towne
cleane depopulate and pessundate downe.   320
Yeat whoo cownsell gaue too auoyde suche,
for their soothe sayinge obteyned no thanke.

(47)

Iff kinge **Jamye** that gouerned **Scotelande**,
whoo was slayne at **Brankestowne** feelde,
had followed the counsaile laide in his hande   325
of sundrie right sage whois powles hee off peelde,
and wolde not vntoo their wise cownsell yeelde,
hee had not thorowe his headye woorkynge
beene brought too **Windesour**, nowe deade there loorkynge.

(48)

Howe manye hathe loste bothe goodis, londe and life,   330
that kinges in their causes hathe contraried,
bye highe wisedome of studye excessife,
when theye from the **publike weale** hathe varied?
It weare heere voyde the tyme too bee taried,
as, too this purpose, histories tenduce: 335
kinges indignations hathe none excuse.

(49)

[f. 12ᵛ] **In** this too make more sermocynation
I will cut off, for this concluyson:
eache godlie witt by inspiration
will leane too right and leaue abusion,   340
after the mynde of highe **Omousion**
whoe hathe leuyd what kinges owght too doo,
and what obeisaunce wee owe them vntoo.

---

323 *in margin*: 1513   336 Indignatio principis mors est *in red ink in*
holograph in margin

(50)

What more dothe remayne, I will heere now steye,
o puysaunte Prynce, and too yowe remytt   345
as yee in processe shall pondere and weye
when yee are come too perfection of witt,
the meane-tyme, with **Christe** emonge the wise too sitt,
heearinge and learnynge, that knowledge may come,
Whoo prospere your Grace withe age and wisedome.   350

**A notable description what a kynge is, and what significa-
tion in his regales, as firste** anoyntinge, **swoorde,** bawle,
crowne and throne, **dothe reste, with fowre notable ladies
to attende on the same throne.**

Caput 2

(51)

A kinge sorted vnto the regale **throne**
by election, succession or so,
enoynted, with **crouwne** his heade set vppon,
in highe estate before oother too go,
his liegis too hym obeysaunce too doe   355
so far as his domynyon dothe strache,
thearin too regne withoute peere or mache,

(52)

[f. 13] **firste** in a closett, deckte withe dwe araye,
his bodye made bare vnto the girdle steade,
withe **sacrede oyle** his right arme for the waye   360
bye thexecutour is theare anoyntede;
his reynes also, too signifie indeade
his lief too bee pure frome viciouse pretence,
and no-man on hym too woorke violence.

(53)

In the **anoyntinge** in forme aforeseide,   365
a certayne grace in hym infused is
frome the Higheste that althinges hathe weide
in the praescience of His aeterne blis,

inenerrable goode too all that bee His.
Whiche cerymonie offende maye no eare: 370
Dauid for that dyd **Saul** forbeare.

(54)

In his right hande a **swoorde** hee hathe to holde,
and in his lefte a **bawle** of golde all rownde,
of whiche the signification too vnfolde
it askethe meanys withe studye too compownde.   375
A meanynge was ment when it was first fownde:
whither I can vppon the true sense gesse,
too saye my mynde I will my deauer dresse.

(55)

The swoorde that wone too hym dothe commende
and in his hande all naked dothe beare,   380
it meanethe hee muste all right defende,
as thearewitheall offendres too feare.
The **crowne** whiche hee on his heade dothe weare,
glorie, honour, and powre dothe represent,
by that too bee knowne as kynge excellent.   385

(56)

[f. 13ᵛ] **The bawle** of golde, rightlye too discerne,
meanethe the precinctes of his empredome,
whiche in his hande hee hathe too gouerne,
by the rownde compacinge of hye wisedome.
Whiche **bawle** appropried is but too some,   390
too suche as regnethe by name **Imperiall** :
oother hathe **scepture** in steade of the **ball**.

(57)

Whiche scepture hathe too signification
the signe and steye of open veritee:
too the vnrightfull, is castigation,   395
and too the goode, the rule of pitee,
the prowde too disperse bie due equitee:
wheare so this **mace** or **scepture** shall come,
it threatenethe **justice** too all and some.

(58)

Then in his **throne** hee is inthronizate,   400
withe **crowne** on heade and **scepture** in his hande,
as place of God too hym theare delegate,
thearbie obliged well too vndrestande
justice and **lawe** too mayntayne in his lande;
his **regale robes** confirmethe the same   405
in woorthie honour too florische by fame.

(59)

Nowe is hee a **kynge** perfecte at all poyntis,
no iote wantinge vntoo that office dwe,
in sowle, bodye, veyne, synue and ioyntis,
so longe as his lief shall heere contynue,   410
his rewarde immortall after tensue,
as shall in truthe his gouernynge appeare
of Hym whois powre regnethe euerywheare.

(60)

[f. 14] Too stablische his **seate** in honour condigne,
this weies or that too slippe nor declyne,   415
in feare of fallinge too threat suche a kinge,
theis noble ladies that so far dothe shyne
as patronesses of prouidence dyuyne,
called the **fowre vertues cardynall**,
the fowre corners of his **throne** steye shall.   420

(61)

Dame Prudence the firste, the seconde **Justice,**
the thirde **Fortitude** or **Magnanymytee,**
the fowrthe **Temporaunce,** ladies of hie price:
too theis no woorthie comparison may bee,
for too attende a kynges maiestee;   425
whoo by theis ladies liste too bee ordrede,
his brute muste neadis too his honour bee sprede.

(62)

Firste at his elbowe on the right syde,
Ladye **Prudence** her standinge shall take,
in prudent wise his procedinges too gide,   430
no ferdre then shee signethe too medle or make;
whiche ladie is a celestiall flake
yssuynge frome the Gohoste moste Holie,
vnto the wise nothinge more iolie.

(63)

For this saide ladie wheare shee dothe manure   435
teachethe the cowrse of all hye woorthynes,
for whome eache potentate shoulde caste and cure
too doo hym steade in his moste busynes;
her nature vuede in vearie perfectnes,
whoo so by her his dooinges dothe dispose,   440
hee may bee sure he shall neauer lose.

(64)

[f. 14ᵛ] **Shee** is a maistres incomparable wise,
yea, rather a Queene for her woorthynes.
Of goode and badde shee trulie can decise
the iuste difference, nother more or les,   445
what is too allowe, what is too depres;
so iustelie shee can all that determyne,
for kingis too rule bye, shee is the streight lyne.

(65)

On the leafte syde, at his oother elbowe,
Justice right woorthelie maye theare take place.   450
As when bye **Prudence** hee dothe duelie knowe,
hee maye bye **Justice** then ordre the case,
whoe of no partie respectethe the face,
for kithe or kyn, frendeshippe or otherwise,
but as the beame weiethe by ballaunce of iustice,   455

---

455 ballaunce] ballunce *with contraction-sign usually used for* au *added above
the* n: *intended form possibly* ballaunnce

(66)

the beame whiche shewethe by his ostencer
when the scales thearuntoo dependinge
dothe eavenlie weye and in no poynte differ.
Suche is thoffice of **Justice** pretendinge,
by playne open truithe falsehode reuenginge,   460
in judgement attendinge bothe ende and induction,
by **Justice** too saue, or bringe too destruction.

(67)

Too scan of **Justice** the propretie true:
shee teachethe too loove and also too hate,
as shee cause seeithe in furtheringe vertue,   465
too chearische, chaisten or repudiate,
too God and man shee stentethe the rate,
as thus too doo or not too entreprise:
too comment on this belongethe too the wise.

(68)

[f. 15] **At** the back pummell on the right parte   470
Dame **Fortitude** shall take her stondinge,
in valyaunt wise too corage his harte,
too shrinke for none the truthe furtheringe,
too all woorthynes his harte inclyninge,
by suche hyghe force of **Magnanymytee**   475
that what **Right** willethe the same will [he].

(69)

If Fortune vnfortunate at him liste caste looke,
disdaynynge his wealthe and prosperowse estate,
all her false frowardnes hee easelie can brooke,
consyderinge his cause too **Justice** applicate.   480
At tyrauntes threateninges hee stondethe intrepidate.
Soaner shall they the bright light darkness prooue,
than from that right is his haste too remooue.

(70)

So strongelie shee stondethe too steye hym in this,
that arme, foote and hande at no tyme shall fayle.   485
Hee leanethe vnto her and ofte dothe her kys.
In her hee more trustethe then in his cote of mayle,
for, followinge her, hee can no tyme quayle.
Her sister **Prudence** ensencethe hym so,
that her hee louethe as behouethe hym too doe.   490

(71)

Jumpe evin withe her at the oother pummell,
Ladye **Temperaunce,** withe cheare full of grace,
shall, as becomethe her, contynuallie dwell.
Whearso shee restethe the better is the place.
Shee temperethe mannys meanis in conuenient case: 495
bothe woorde, deade and looke, whoo liste to aduerte,
shee doithe too all theis assigne their due parte.

(72)

[f. 15ᵛ] **In** meate, drinke and sleepe, traueile or pastime,
shee doithe determyne a temperature,
in theis and oother all owterage topprime.   500
In eauerye reasonable creature,
in seeakinge and reeakinge shee monischethe measure:
the mynde too moleste withe superabundaunce,
that doithe deteste this ladye **Temperaun[c]e.**

(73)

Shee wolde haue man hymselfe too dispose   505
Reasons gouernaunce eauermore tobeye,
superfluouse riches not too vpgrose:
in no manere wise shee can thearwithe aweye
exceadinglie too caste and purueye,
for treasure mundayne shee forefendithe cleane,   510
bycause eauer measure is the meriest meane.

485 no tyme] notyme

(74)

Theis ladies bestowed in sorte aforesaide,
what kinge can take fall that steyethe hym by them?
His fame muste florische, it cannot be denaide:
they are eache too hym moste preatious gem, 515
and cause shall too springe, as braunche oute of stem,
imps of renowne, incomparable sweete,
pleasinge too God, and heere too gouerne meete.

(75)

This little addition of my conceyte,
vnto this purpose as mee thought condinge, 520
this wise concluded, I will nowe aweyte
vppon thintent of my autours meanynge,
vnto his lectures from hensforthe leanynge,
excepte wheare cause shall ootherwise compell.
Thus of this lesson I byd nowe farewell. 525

An excusation of Aristotele **too** Alexandre, **of his let in commynge vnto hym thorowe debilitee of age, for that cause this present booke comprysinge, too bee as a balaunce too pondre and weye his warkis heerebie as thoughe he weare present alweies hymselfe too counsell hym.**

Caput 3

(76)

Wheare late in lettres your Maiestie did sende
that I my iourneye towards yow sholde addres,
thinke not I doo your pleasure vilipende
bycause I take not on mee that progres:
I am impedite bie ages feoblenes, 530
and not able your pleasure taccomplische
as wolde God I cowlde, I hartelie wische.

(77)

Well I considre my duetie noles
as at your sendinge my poure too prepare
too payne myselfe in your busynes: 535

suche of all subiectes their due dueties are.
But, nowe in case as withe mee it dothe fare,
wheare Impotencie your will dothe refuse,
your benynge Grace suche partie muste excuse.

(78)

Merueile I thinke your Maiestie will no-les,　　540
whie I frome your venerable presence
sholde absent myselfe for anye distres,
chalenginge mee thearfore, by this sentence,
in your affaires too neglecte my diligence,
not curinge, as too saye, howe your causes went.　　545
O Emperour, knowe yee, I meane no suche intent.

(79)

[f. 16ᵛ] **Trulie** in state as mee is nowe beefall,
consyderinge myne age and imbecillitee,
yee ought not mee an obstinate too call,
or ootherwise reprooue of equitee,　　550
but that mee enuoluethe suche debilitee
of age and bodie, makinge mee ponderowse,
not able too passe scante owte of my powre howse.

(80)

That yee shall yeat thinke I tendre your pleasure,
and that my true harte my duetie dothe attende:　　555
for theis twoe causes, withe all busie cure,
this booke haue I framed and brought too an ende,
and to your Highnes the same doo commende
too bee as a balaunce, so call it I maye,
your warkes by true justice euermore to weye,　　560

(81)

as howe vnto God yee shall your selfe behaue,
wheare too shewe mercie, wheare too bee rigorouse,
wheare, and in what wise, yee shall spende or saue,
wheare too bee streyte, and wheare too bee bownteouse:
this shall too yow an honeste meane discus,　　565
withe muche more matier decent too your degree.
O noble Kinge, receaue it heere of mee,

(82)

as full in it-selfe bye contentation,
for suche pretence of your necessaries,
as I weare present in propre person   570
too open all dowbtes before your owne iyes,
my place supplijnge in sufficient wies.
What then more neadethe, but your goode will,
as too endeuer the same too fulfill?

(83)

[f. 17] **Els** what shall it profitt the patient sore,   575
wounded and dryuen bie necessitee,
too seeke for saulue his hea[l]the too restore,
so too bee cured of his infirmytee,
if bie his leache hee will not ordrede bee?
As goode no medycine as not too bee vsed.   580
So farethe withe counsell wheare it is refused.

(84)

But, Alexandre, too yow shall I saye,
sithe yee in mee parte put your affiaunce,
reade auncient writinges, and beare them awaye,
that treatethe of wise and princelie gouernaunce,   585
whiche, beeinge placed in your remembraunce,
shall thearunto ofte mynistre effecte
what yee shall ensue, what yee shall reiecte.

(85)

For thinges sett in writinge more pithe dothe contayne
then I or any can sodaynlie preferr.   590
It is thinge gathered by propensed payne,
wheare sodayne tawlke is geuen oftetymes too err.
As men see too walke by the daye sterr
their weye too conueye from daungre of the darke,
so dothe wise writinges illumyne mannys warke.   595

(86)

In trifelinge trifles I will yee no tyme spende,
but wheare maye bee gathrede fruite delectable:
by readinge vayne thinges theare suethe no goode ende,
and too your Highnes muche discommendable.
Men as yee are, of state honorable,   600
that ought too delite too reade, heeare and see,
whiche teachethe right orderinge of a commontee,

(87)

[f. 17ᵛ] too whiche I haue heere sufficientlye,
as I suppose, sett my scribelinge pen.
If owghtes heere-after of matier weightye   605
in your aspecte shall happe nowe and then,
of dowbtes too bee doone, or still too let ren,
for the solution rightlie in that case
but sende, and I shall satisfie your Grace.

An answere of Aristotele too an Epistle of Alexandres, concernynge the Percians, whome hee mynded uttrelie too haue
slayne, bycause they weare men of nature politike and also
of highe corage, contrarious too his purpose, muche rather
geuin to gouern then obeye.

Caput 4

(88)

Amonge all matiers, o souereine Kinge,   610
whiche in your lettres yee liste to propone,
thearin too haue myne answere, answeringe
too that whiche moste myght magnyfie your throne,
specyallye yee mooued this alone,
concernynge the Percians, whome yee of late   615
vnto your powre haue made subiugate.

(89)

After this sorte your mynde mentionynge:
they too bee people of syngulare witt,
aboundinge withe reason and vndrestondinge,

too compace thinges too their publike profitt, 620
whois behauoure in your sight dothe not sitt,
bicause they delite, as your lettres tell,
ouer oother in honour too precell.

(90)

[f. 18] SO that I perceaue they hathe beene cumberous
for too convince, and too your purpose bringe. 625
Yeat, notwithestondinge their wit ingenious,
their politike woorkinge, and craftie cumpacinge,
yee haue them capiued for the tyme beeinge.
Howe longe they shall vntoo your pleasure lowte,
I partelie feele yee stonde muche parte in dowte. 630

(91)

Wheare yee doo mynde them clearlie too deleye,
as too destroye by powre of your great might,
and so foreauer deuastate that countreye:
leste heereafter enuyous appetight
their wronges too reuenge their hartes might excite, 635
reuokinge their neckis from your subiection,
so rather of them too make interfection.

(92)

Too whiche, yee shall thus myne answere receaue
(and note my meanynge, it shall your Honour sit):
if yee can firste that regions rightis beereaue, 640
as the ayre theare too altre bye your witt,
their se[ay]es too stoppe, that they nowey flitt,
their cities also of their disposition,
then let your pleasure take expedition.

(93)

But, noble Emperour, and soon moste entere, 645
(pleasinge your Maiestie, I maye yow so call,
bicause yee please too write mee your fathere,

642 seayes] seyaes

of looue sincere that towardis mee dothe fall
of your beneuolence abundantiall)
in that aforsaide too make transmutation,   650
too man is graunted no suche domynation.

(94)

[f. 18ᵛ] **The** ayre and water are elementis twoe,
too whiche are added the earthe and the fyre.
Too frustrate their effectes no man maye doe:
that dothe beelonge too Thimperiour empire.   655
What, by nature, Hee liste too enspire,
muste neadis take force, by inclynation,
excepte wheare Grace withstondethe constellation.

(95)

This wise excusinge the **Percians** pretence,
bicause they woorke but natures motionynge,   660
whiche liethe not in your Magnificence
as too depryue the occasion gevinge.
Whie vntoo yow then sholde they bee grevinge,
sithe your affectis, by that, they muche ensue,
for, of nature, yee appetite too subdue?   665

(96)

But, if by all your witt and polecye,
yee can suche propreties noweies depryue,
then withe benignitee dres your fancye
too reigne ouer them as wisedome shall contriue,
with gentle handelinge shewe tenderinge their liue,   670
with giftes also, their magistratis too wyn.
Too make them yealde, suche weis yee muste begin.

(97)

For nature grosse, sturdye and contrarious,
inflexible too bringe easelie too bende,
by witt muste bee woone, sobre and cautelous,   675
and not by meanys rasche thearbye too contende.
Politike wisedome bringethe too goode ende

muche soaner thinges sundrye in difficulte case
then dothe ofte mayne powre and headlinge manace.

(98)

[f. 19] **Woorkinge** this weies, yee shall yourselfe assure   680
that, bye the ayde of the powre supernall,
theis men shall yealde yow mynistrature
(in the avoydinge of daungre not small,
vntoo bothe parties muche preiudiciall)
after the wischinge of your full intent: 685
suche is of wise woorkinge the fruite consequent.

(99)

Wynnynge their fauours in forme aforesaide,
so shall yee quyetlye gouerne their hole trayne,
by fame tryumphant, woorthelie displaide,
too bee in this worlde moste noble capitayne,   690
theye thearof ioyinge, withe hartis glad and fayne,
for what can more a subiectes mynde content
then a loovinge lorde in deadis excellent?

(100)

Whiche wise answere by **Aristotele** sent,
as hym beste seamed, too **Alexandre** greate,   695
whearwithe hee was moste woorthelie content,
and steyde anymore the **Percians** too threate,
bye gentle meanys hee can their fauours geate
in so farforthe that, before oother all,
they did obeye his see imperiall.   700

**Howe the distinction of kinges consistithe in fowre pro-
preties or kyndis, descriued here by** Aristotele **too** Alexandre
in this present chapiter foloweinge.

Caput 5

(101)

[f. 19ᵛ] **OF** kinges I note fowre sundrie sortes too bee,
whiche vnto your Grace I shall heere streite discus.
The firste is la[r]ge, bountious and free
too hym and his, in exercise as thus:

not passinge at all of anye ouerplus,   705
but plentiouslie too bothe hee dothe dispose
that neadfull is, whither hee wynne or lose,

(102)

as too hymselfe; this largenes hee can vse.
Nowght is that neadethe to a princis estate
(so that of rapyne none shall hym accuse)   710
but hee it hathe, his mynde too satiate:
palecis pight, of pleasure prefulgeate,
forestes and lawndis, his freendis too solace,
his healthe too conserue in semblable case.

(103)

Hee pynchethe or wynchethe at none expense,   715
so it bee doone in honorable wise.
Plentie appearethe in his presence;
fresche Frugalitee freatethe eache office.
Whoo, of all his, can anye thinge deuise,
whearein hee may hym profite or prefer,   720
hee dothe shewe forthe his princelie endeuer.

(104)

The nexte frome the firste dothe far discent,
for too hymselfe hee is specyall neare,
and too his seruantis, by byll or patent,
no maner largesse hee will shall appeare.   725
By treasure hee thynkethe all too conqueare,
so that, rather then his hunche too mynische,
hee will from his table spare many a dische.

(105)

[f. 20] Catche what hee catche can, catchinge will hee bee:
howe eauer the worlde weare, waiste shall none of his.   730
So hee haue richesse, for nought els passithe hee:
onlie in vayne lucre fixed is his blis.
Manye hee lettithe looke for that they shall longe mys,
for their true labours contentation:
too departe withe-owtes is not his fashyon.   735

(106)

Althinges hee lookethe too come easelie bye,
muche readier too take then anyethinge too paye.
Whoe of his pleasure dothe hym owghtes denye
shalbee assured too haue a fowle daye:
suche thinkethe in althinges they may haue no naye.   740
So dothe false couetise his inwarde iye blynde
that from all goode deadis exiled is his mynde.

(107)

The thirde in ordre heere streyte forthe too bringe,
is hee that faschyonethe his propretee
like too the seconde in eauerye thinge   745
concernynge himselfe, as heere yee maye see.
Nowght hee dothe tendre his owne state and degree
the same too set forthe in all princelie porte,
but pleiethe Jack Snydge in a nygards sorte.

(108)

But vnto thois that longeth hym vnto,   750
whiche hathe free entré vntoo his presence
and can craftelie pleye Placebo,
of his to vpholde eauery sentence,
too suche no small appearethe his expense.
Thoughe streyte hee bee in furtheringe his fame,   755
as well myght hee keepe and saue still the same,

(109)

[f. 20ᵛ] **for** giftes geeuyn vnprouydentlie
vnto vayne tryfelers woorkinge wickednes,
cannot be called but open folie,
or, more proprelie, lascyuyousnes.   760
Abrode too sundry too bee too laues,
and pynche at whome, where plentie sholde appeare,
trulye it is no pryncelye maneare.

(110)

The fowrthe too recorde, hath too propretee
towardis hym-selfe too shewe plentiousnes,　　765
but too his subiectis moste nygarde is hee,
callinge and catchinge withe muche busynes.
Of all aforesaide my mynde too expres,
too bee abhorred of eache noble state,
this kinde of kynges I vituperate.　　770

(111)

Too launche at luste withoute aduisement,
no-whit too spare what neade eauer shall come,
and then your seruauntes too pynche and stent:
doo reacon that no poynte of wisedome.
Dyuyde youre state in-too this ordrede some:　　775
some saue, some take, some liberallie dispose;
so shall yee the honor of your name not lose.

(112)

Of theis foure sortis, O moste puysaunte kynge,
for your example let the firste bee,
whiche geeuethe yowe woorthye instructinge　　780
too vse pryncelye lyberalytee
bothe too your-selfe and your communtee.
A prince too bee pynchynge, sittethe as well
as a busserde too beare an hawkes bell.

[f. 21] **Howe a kynge ouwght too humble hymselfe towardis God, and too mayntayne Hys lawes, tauoyde pryde, and too consydre hymselfe a mortall man as oother men are.**

Caput 6

(113)

The sortis of kinges sithe heere wee haue discuste,　　785
vntoo whiche ordre yee are sorted frome a-hye,
too treate somedeale in this proces wee muste,
what towardis God consistithe youre duetye.

772 no-whit] nowhit　　　783 as well] aswell

Thoughe heere in earthe youre fame bee moste woorthye,
yeat heere your reigne is but dispensatyue, 790
as a mynystre, while yee are heere alyue.

(114)

Itt is not yowe, the woorthieste of renowne,
or whoo else anye of qualitee famouse,
in wisedome, strenght, that heere bearethe crowne,
but is so sorted in the superne howse 795
of **Prima Causa,** in powre affluowse,
in Whois affayres, by rightfull justice
bothe yow and all muste trulie exercise.

(115)

Of creatures heere the natures too compace,
thoughe muche wee haue of tyme thearin spent, 800
of soone, moone and sterris, eache in their place,
howe ouer Man they hathe the regiment,
contrariouse ofte, sometyme expedyent,
by excitation of course naturall,
whearbye Man is mooued too rise and fall, 805

(116)

[f. 21ᵛ] yeat of necessittee their force takethe effecte
no m[o]re but as man liste graunte his consent.
As when too anye owghtes is obiecte,
too take or forsake hathe choyce indifferent,
the planetes for man hathe their assignient, 810
and man not for them: God can so ordayne,
whome hee owght tacknowledge his cheif souerayne.

(117)

For heere of Hym hee dothe althinges receaue,
bothe witt, wisedome and vndrestondinge,
and too his vse this worldis monarche dothe leaue, 815
on His lieue-teanaunt too haue thorderinge,
Hee onlye causinge heere althinges too springe

807 no more] nomere

by procreation, as Hee liste tassigne,
against whois woorkynge owght none too maligne.

(118)

In His highe power Hee dothe all powres suspende: 820
no rayne maye rayne, no wynde may heere els blowe,
but thearuntoo Hee liste too condescende,
for highest of all Hee will man sholde Hym knowe.
No herbe, no plante, no grasse can man make growe,
doo what hee can, by all hee can inuent,   825
but cheiflie God graunte theartoo His consent.

(119)

Too wage battell with weapon, sheelde, and mayle,
against his enemye, whoe liste tentreprise
withoute His defense, hee cannot preuayle:
the victorie hangethe as Hee dothe decise,   830
in fewe or manye, all wone in His iyse.
So that yee owght, in all yee go abowte,
His fauour toptayne: then are yee owte of dowte.

(120)

[f. 22] Doo duelie your deuer His lawes too mayntayne,
doo streytelie punysche transgressours of the same,   835
doo woorke all meanys too bee moste glad and fayne
too keepe His faythe in right ordre and frame.
Wheare dwe honour is doone too His name,
theare all procedinges takethe fortunat succes,
in storms contrarious moste sureste fortres.   840

(121)

See that your lawes from His dothe not discent;
see, and foresee, that Hym yee not displease;
see that your owne cause dothe not His preuent,
so maye yee by vengeaunce His wrathe vprease.
In woorkinge His weies fynde ye shall moste ease,   845
for thoughe yee as judge doo reigne heere emonge men,
too bee judged yowr-selfe, the tyme shall come when.

(122)

Too wade for honour in this trobolowse seaye,
withe more then ynowghe too bee heere posseste,
enuolued withe daungres manyfolde waye,　　850
of fortunys fallacies the mynde too moleste,
ere yee too your purpose haue featherde your neste,
and then **Atropos** your date heere too fyne,
will not that sumwhat your harte make enclyne?

(123)

So too consydre this worldis brittlenes,　　855
and eache degre too ordre hymselfe so
when he shall walke, too bee in a redynes,
for neadis hee muste hense, whither hee will or no:
this sholde expell all pryde mannys harte fro.
His goodelie crispe skyn and eache oother parte　　860
is but woormys meate, if hee liste too aduerte.

(124)

[f. 22ᵛ] **This** write I heere, o Alexandre Kynge,
that yee not too muche in this worlde sholde delyte,
but heere so eauenlie too beare yow in althinge
that yee woorthelie this sayinge saye myght,　　865
'The worlde I haue ouercome in fyght,
and mee not the worlde,' meanynge thearbye,
by vayne worldelie thingis too sett not a flye.

(125)

Yeat muste yee neadis haue worldelie exercise,
not as his druge but as his gouernoure,　　870
and muste endeauer in all priuelie wise
for too contynue your regale honoure
in the monarche wheare yee are Emperoure.
So iustelie rule bothe towardis God and man,
that in your reigne no blott any spie can.　　875

(126)

Too lose that rightly your auncetours wan,
and hathe heere lefte too youre gouernaunce,
no honoure it weare for a noble man
that sittethe of office too youre attendaunce.
But yow and yours too put too encumbraunce   880
ouer realmys manye too reigne of hawte mynde:
defende well your owne and leaue that behynde.

Howe a kynge owght tattende his estate and too gouerne,
whome hee shall chuse too hys cownsellowrs, and after
what gentle and famyliar sorte hee shall vse and make of
them.

Caput 7

(127)

[f. 23] A kynge or prince sett in his maiestee
owght too consydre the state hee hathe in honde,
and theartoo accordinge too woorke in degree   885
that most woorthelye withe his honour maye stonde.
Suche state a publike persone is reaconde,
in whois wealthe, or hynderaunce lyke-so,
the publike weale is compted too and fro,

(128)

as if the prince dothe floorische and prospere,   890
the commons ioye in plentie then dothe flowe,
if hee perchaunce sholde chaunce in daungere,
then weare their wealthe by ebb layde a-lowe.
As his wealthe wriethe, theirs muste followe:
so that suche persone his state whoo dothe discerne,   895
bothe ought and muste searche howe heere too gouerne.

(129)

But sithe a kynge is but wone man alone,
and can no more doo then some oother can,
and hathe too gouerne so manye a wone,

898 no more] nomore

it muste of necessitee dreeue hym than,   900
his causes duelie too debate and scane,
some woorthie too chuse in counsell experte,
that headye woorkinge his wealthe not peruerte;

(130)

For that behaulfe, deere Lorde Alexandre,
let seeke and sende all your royalms abowte   905
for men wittie, wheare eauer they wandre,
and also learned, too discusse all dowte,
whois lyuynge knowen, bothe within and withowte,
by honeste prooif, so far as man may trye,
disceauerde cleane from cankerde myserye;   910

(131)

[f. 23ᵛ] men sobre, discreete and of conscience pure;
men that can meane what beste is too bee wrought;
men that beste can mennys hartis heere allure,
frome wronge too right agayne too bee brought;
too saye that right leadithe, whoo fearithe nought,   915
for dreade or meede, prysonment or so:
suche are that sholde in a publike weale go.

(132)

A prince also ought not, of hawte mynde,
in causes weightie his owne will tensue,
and thois too entreate with threatnynges vnkynde   920
that hym dothe admonische of the weye true
in sobre wise, as sittithe their office dwe,
but them too harken and keepe owte of dreade,
for sage counseile helpethe beste at neade.

(133)

Too cownseile a kynge in his causes greate   925
it longethe for no babis or younge younkinge bloode:
men graue thearin beste can speake and intreate.
Thoughe witt pregnaunte ofte yssuithe from childhood,
yeat hathe not youthe experyence so goode

as hathe sage age, sobre and dyscreete: 930
in weightie mattiers they are fownde moste meete.

(134)

Yeat meane I not yowght wittie and towarde,
withe learnynge indude and oother graces moe,
whiche in their dooinges liste not bee frowarde,
but of intent will harke wisedome vntoe: 935
suche maye commyxte withe oother wise also.
No youthe I repell but yowthe sauage,
for wisedome alweies goethe not by age.

(135)

[f. 24] Thus too counsell when yee haue men woorthye,
chearische all suche in conuenyent wise: 940
vse them as freendis famyliarlye;
in all your affayres they must bee precise,
preferr and set them in condigne office,
and as yee see their procedinges preeue,
from meane too higher so doo them remeeue.   945

(136)

If false reporte by enuyous hate
emonges your cowrte shoulde chaunce too arise,
anye your counselours for too abate,
beefore your judgement yee clearelye decise
haue due probation, and, in anyewise,   950
thoughe the mattier appeare euydent,
yeat doo neauer geeue haistie judgement.

(137)

Doo not condempne for any maner thynge
thee partie absent in prison kepte close:
againste conscience it weare vnsittynge,   955
so men his facte vnrightwiselye maye glose.
Nother his enemye facinge at his nose,
on hym too diffyne in his rage cruell:
for enuye, yee wote, dothe neauer woorke well.

(138)

For so it maye remediles befall   960
too caste aweye this daye for eauer
that whiche too-morowe forthinke yow shall,
and wolde muche fayne agayne rekeauer
then thousands of golde. A greate deale leauer
herken, steye, the case fullye consydre,   965
and then judge withe wisemen togidre.

(139)

[f. 24ᵛ] **The** wiseste of all a woorde maye escape
whiche sore his harte may aftrewardis repent.
Thoughe theare owght none withe his soueregn **to iape,**
or woorke any poynte withoute aduisement,   970
yeat, **Alexandre,** herke myne entent:
if hee shewe cheare repentynge his deade,
doo shewe mercye in suche extreame neade.

(140)

But if the case bee execrable,
no les toochinge then your owne person,   975
thearagainste too woorke meanys vengeable
of highe treason, withe full intention
your lief too depryue or els your region,
or ootherwise suche myserable deede:
bye justice then rewarde hym his meede.   980

(141)

Or in his cowntreye oppressethe the poore
bye false extortion vndre your pretence,
againste whois dooinges theare dare none stoore,
bycause hee is neare vntoo your presence,
thearbye fortressinge his heynous offense: 985
doo suche dissolue; the poore dothe them cursse;
wheare they dothe reigne the realme is the wursse.

975 no les] noles   978 or els] orels

[f. 25] **In what sorte a kynge owght taddres his studye for tat-
tayne knowledge in the dyuersyté of tunges and sciencis.
Howe also hee shall caste and prepare for the furtheraunce
of learnynge thorowe all his realmys and | domynyons.**

Caput octauum

(142)

Moste woorthelie a kinge it dothe become
his speache too polische in moste facownde wise
withe termys and sciencies of highe wisedome,   990
that of the wittie are had in moste price,
in present causes that beste maye suffise,
withoute stuttinge, staggeringe or suche:
in a kynges mowthe it shoulde offende muche.

(143)

Too haue in this suche promptytude and grace   995
as dothe bye office theartoo appertaynge,
fresche rhethorycians alweyes in place
it beste dothe a-gree withe hym too retayne,
of them too gathere the florischinge vayne,
bye consuetude too answere or exhorte,   1000
and thois too bee sought of the pickedeste sorte.

(144)

I meane not onlie of the Latyne tunge
too haue suche promptnes too answere all men,
but Greeke therwithe too bee mengled emunge,
too doo hym steade by mowthe or by pen,   1005
as shall occasions happ nowe and then;
if writinges come from forayne cowntraye,
then shall hee not neade too woorke by heerre-saye.

(145)

Other languages, Frenche, Duche or suche,
if hee can them speake and well vndrestande,   1010
vndoubtedlie it shall profite hym muche
if noble men from any suche lande

1008 *first* r *of* heerre *corr. from* i

sholde chaunce withe hym too haue dooinge in hande,
as ambassadours, excellent of fame:
the better hee maye for their answere frame.   1015

(146)

[f. 25ᵛ] For whiche hee maye in this wise prouyde
of eauerye suche cowntreye some too retayne
in whome honeste gracis maye bee espyde,
woorthie aboute a kynge too remayne,
withe whome ofte commonynge, hee shall attayne   1020
in thois saide tunges feelynge sufficient
that maye too his purpose ynoughe content.

(147)

The tunge, too tell truthe, is like an instrument,
althoughe it tattle in that speache or this
whiche, beeinge pleyde on withe an inscipient,   1025
no musycall armonye thearin herde is.
So tunge withoute knowledge walketh ofte a-mys,
wherfore too furnysche talkynge the better,
let tunge talke reason sought owte by letter.

(148)

Thorowe knowledge, Tholome of Egipte Kynge,   1030
as clarkys sundrye makethe memoryall,
all kynges of the worlde passed in gouernynge,
whoys fame in earthe shalbee immortall,
thearbye woorkynge or lettinge his case fall.
Thoughe God the fate of althinges hathe in holde,   1035
yeate may by science much thinges to come be tolde,

(149)

and vntoo God no derogation,
for Hee hathe set signes naturallie too woorke,
and hathe geeuyn man suche inspiration
by science too fynde that longe vnknown did loorke,   1040
aswell Thenglysch as Grecyan or Turke,
as cowrse naturall geeuythe inclynation,
thearbye too saye muche too constellation.

2550 C74   F f

(150)

[f. 26] **The** fowle, the fayre, the prosperous, the peruerse,
as the nyne speeris shewithe disposition,   1045
knowledge too man all theye dothe reherse,
if hee solertlye make inquysition.
Of God hathe man suche exhybition
by that, the more too rendre Hym thankes dwe,
all evyll tauoyde, and the goode too ensue.   1050

(151)

Whiche knowledge of man byndethe God no-whit,
the case too take force of necessitee,
but suche disposition threatenethe it
if cowrse naturall not impedite bee.
Whoe, knowinge the signes bent taduersitee,   1055
and will vncompelled thearagaynste try,
judge hym wise whoe liste: it shall not bee I.

(152)

Thoughe vndrestondinge bee geevin vntoo man
naturallye too judge and discerne,
yeat shall hee by scyence muche moe thinges scan   1060
then onlye by witt, bee it neauer so superne.
No wise man thearfore owght learnynge too sperne,
but the more hee is withe chargis onerate,
the more hee neadethe of knowledge literate.

(153)

Thearfore too yow, my soueraigne Lorde,   1065
I will geeue cownsell, withe all that I maye,
for many commodities thus taccorde
in places sundrye for learnynge too puruaye,
by vniuersities as I myght saye,
wheare assemblement myght bee had as thus,   1070
when neade shall requyre all dowbtes too discus.

1051 no-whit] nowhit

(154)

[f. 26ᵛ] Theare-too plante scoolis for them that begynnys,
Grammer, Sophistrie and Logike toptayne,
withe hawlis, collegis, hostels and innys
on higher learnynge toccupye their brayne.   1075
Thearuntoo added, studentis too mayntayne,
their myndis in studye too quyet the more,
honeste stypende conuenyent thearfore,

(155)

not too lau⌐is or passynge sumptuous,
but as maye serue sufficyentlye   1080
too bee dysburste by chargis of the house
for meate, drynke and clothe necessarye,
withe bookis, and althinge neadfull too studye,
so that freelie, withoute all maner lett,
they maye endeauer learnynge too gett.   1085

(156)

The sciencies seauen are called liberall,
free too the poore as well as too the riche;
not onlie thearfore wee doo them so call,
but freelie, withoute care of lesse or myche,
studentes thearunto their myndis sure too stiche,   1090
lackynge nothinge their studye too aduaunce:
in wittis setteled regnethe beste remembraunce.

(157)

When thus yee haue for studentes prouyded,
make statutis honest, godlie and discreete,
by whiche in ordre they maye bee guyded.   1095
Too range as vnbrydeled it weare vnmeete:
wheare obedience is trodde vndre feete,
too looke for vertue bye learnynge too sprede,
I cannot see howe it can bee constrede.

1087 as well] aswell

(158)

[f. 27]   **Too** gather learnynge in sciencis sundrye,   1100
and let vertue walke as an abiecte:
suche leawde learnynge let all men diffye.
It is vngodlie, withe fylthynes infecte.
If learnynge woorke not too vertues effecte,
it neadis must then bee detestable,   1105
muche more superfluous then profitable.

(159)

Ouer all places for **studies** assigned,
chuse honeste headys, prouydent and wise,
whois sage weyes their yowthe may make inclined
frome all owterage apperteynynge too vice.   1110
An honeste heade ys of muche highe price,
far more preaciowse then can bee well tolde,
whither hee bee younge, of mydde age, or olde.

(160)

So, when withe vertue and learnynge also
yee haue your realmes furnysched yn suche wise,   1115
if any withe yow sholde haue nowe too doe
in cawse dowbtfull too tempte your aduise,
yee are then able the case too decise,
which withoute learnynge cowlde not bee wrought.
Too furdre the same, then, trulie of right yee owght,   1120

(161)

and them too chearische, anymate and bolde,
for their necessaries too wante nothynge,
withe suche prerogatiue of yow too holde
that beste maye bee thought for their furtherynge,
by whiche yee shall geeue oother excitynge   1125
for too achieue literate knowledge,
when they freelye may entre without pledge.

(162)

[f. 27ᵛ] **Their** supplications when theye shall prefer,
    by verse or epistle, too your presence,
    benynglye your grace vntoo them confer,   1130
    geuynge them prayse vndre some sweete sentence,
    their paynes bownteouslye too recompense.
    Oh, what encoragement shall they thearbye take,
    of your hie woorthynes too bragge and make crake.

(163)

Suche soueraigne prudence seene in a kynge   1135
    passethe all other comparysons far.
    When they shall fynde a kynge so benynge,
    it shall oothers pryde cleare dysabar.
    Your woorthye woorkyngis and prowes in your war,
    or what noble featis shall happe yow nowe and then,   1140
    they shall take cawse too your hie prayse to pen.

(164)

By meanys of suche renowmed is your fame,
    your see imperiall made fresche and decorate.
    For too approoue by woorthy meanys the same:
    what dyd the reigne of the Greekis sublymate?   1145
    whoo dyd their featis thorowe the worlde publicate?
    Certaynlye that, too shewe in breeue sentence,
    was of the learned the probate dilygence.

(165)

In Greece the pithe of lyterate learnynge
    hathe hitherto florisched by estymation,   1150
    that damoysellis younge, withe their parentes beinge,
    hauynge theareof suche participation,
    the cowrse of sterrys, and their constellation,
    whye this tyme shorte, or that tyme lenger,
    in this, and muche more, cowlde true cause render.   1155

(166)

[f. 28] Saue tyme too detracte muche wolde I more write
concernynge learnynge, it is so preacyowse:
mannys duetie too God yt dothe recyte,
and also too kyngis in maner seryowse.
A goode thinge, theye saye, cannot bee too tedyowse; 1160
but in that sayinge, I will not nowe stande:
the surplusage I leaue as in your hande.

**Of the maner and solacynge most conuenyent for a kynge,
bothe at table, in the feeldis, and other places, at tymes
suche as hee shall thinke pleasinge too his mynde to recreat
his spyrytis.**
Caput 9

(167)

IN decent wise it sittethe eache noble kinge
certayne priuate famyliar freendis to haue,
withe whome hee maye vse his solacynge,   1165
not withe eache histrion, seruaunte or slaue;
it sholde hys maiestie muche parte depraue.
Hee is a persone frome oother exempte:
muche famyliarytee breedethe contempte.

(168)

The mynde of man dothe naturallye affecte   1170
in musicall myrthe too take his repose,
after tyme tedyous, the eare too reflecte,
the sensys settelynge in their office close,
solycitude of thinges too wordelye purpose
thearbye abiected by meanys attentife: 1175
moste salubryte sawce for lengthinge of life.

(169)

[f. 28ᵛ] More perfecte forme of solacynge tenduce,
as I can gesse bye wittis inuention:
if sikenes bee not your lefull excuse,

addicte your dyett withe inwarde intention,   1180
in the daye-springe, withoute exemption,
(the naturall, I meane, whiche holdethe twelue howres)
too owte in the feeldis emonge the sweete flowres.

(170)

Att season, take it, when vear doth vernate,
florischinge withe flowres of odour fragraunte,   1185
depeyntynge eache pasture with daysies delicate,
bothe coweslippe, prymerose and violet pleasaunte.
The medowes at suche tyme I wolde yowe too haunte,
and vpp the hyllis too payne your-selfe on foote,
theare to take ayer, that too healthe breedethe beste
    boote.   1190

(171)

Yowre howndis after this if yee shall so please,
maye run the hare or some oother wylde beaste,
your hors assumynge then, for your more ease,
and after too haisten till the game bee ceaste.
Thus for an howre or twoe at the leaste,   1195
yee maye your bodye put too exercise,
then after too eate as yee shall deuyse.

(172)

When dyner tyme commythe, this weyes yee may take:
your seruice serued, too your appetite dwe,
too voyde vanities yowe gladde for too make,   1200
some sowght for the nonys that can by cnackis nwe
fashyon hym selfe that myrthe maye ensue,
withe tawlke honeste moste decent too the same,
freelye too saye, appeyringe no mannys name.

(173)

[f. 29] And suche wone on yowe alweyes attendynge,   1205
        I thynke conuenyent, and so doo affyrme,
        his truste vndre yow too haue defendynge

<hr>

        1204 no mannys] nomannys

if any withe hym by hatrede sholde skyrme.
Suche merye fellowe maye cease manye chyrme.
When dyuerse the greate the small wolde deuoure,   1210
his meerye moouyngis maye wynne them socour,

(174)

as vndre cooloure of his iestinge sporte,
the truthe too infer of the poorys dammage,
wheare yee maye gather by suche his reporte
howe often the poore is browght in bondage,   1215
wheare yee maye signe meanys their greefes too suffrage,
redressynge wheare they are so ouer-throwne:
the poore mannys cawse yee muste take as your owne.

(175)

Suche wise weyes woorkinge makethe mery menye
that stoode in sorowe saylynge bye nyght and by daye, 1220
desperate of cheare, as hopynge for enye
that wolde for them withe their aduersary waye.
Emonge all your myrthes thinke on this playe,
and at meate bee mearye, endeuer euer so:
what myght that perturbe, let for the season go.   1225

(176)

When straungers greate youre presence hathe none,
take of youre nobles youe compenye too keepe.
Doo not your selfe sitt santeringe alone
as wone that weare in studye moste deepe:
at meale is no maner too sitt as a-sleepe.   1230
Haue communication as yee beste thynke:
suche solace as seemelie is as meate or drynke.

(177)

[f. 29ᵛ] Dynner onys ended, rise not vpp lightlye.
Haue then some noyse of musycall sownde,
as harpe, vyall, lute or some symphonye,   1235
virginallis, rybecke, withe taberlet rownde,
that too the eare moste sweete dothe rebownde,
sensyblye handeled in their monochorde.
No higher solace maye bee too a lorde.

(178)

In steade of whiche, as for dyuersytee,   1240
yee maye haue els the lyuelie musyke
set forthe in voyce of humayne facultee,
by men or chyldren after their best trike,
that, formallye handeled, hathe not the like,
for God Hym-selfe mannys organ ordayne can,   1245
and oother instrumentis deuysed by man.

(179)

All this set a-parte, yee maye ootherwise els
att tables, chesse or cardis, awhile your selfe repose,
or oother pastyme that pretendethe novels,
not passinge at all whither yee wynne or lose;   1250
but, playnelye my mynde too saye and not glose,
after your meale, but the weather dothe lowre,
in sittinge solacinge spende not paste wone howre.

(180)

If weatheringe bee not abrode for too walke,
the tyme then passe in some wisedome readinge,   1255
or withe your Cownsell too debate and tawlke
of mattiers weightie to a comone-wealthe leadinge,
before-hande castynge what after maye bee neadinge.
Then if fresche **Phebus** liste shewe his fayre face,
after this sorte yee maye yourselfe solace: 1260

(181)

[f. 30] all syttynge pastymes are seelden fownde goode,
excepte at nyght when walkynge cannot bee
(it is an hynderaunce too purifyed bloode:
in your dyatorye yee shall more playne see),
thearfore vse practise of hostylitee,   1265
as withe the longe bowe too pricke or too roue,
or chacynge the fox thorowe thickett or groue,

(182)

or oother vermyne withe begle or hownde.
Trulye suche moovinge of bodelye exercise
shall keepe yow in healthe moste perfectlye sownde;   1270
more bettre physike can no man deuise.
Or, leauynge all this, yee maye poynte in this wise:
too see your knyghtis in tornaynge or justes,
or oother warre featis too practise in their lustes,

(183)

and yee nowe and then, in armur armed sure   1275
withe some liste to trye suche as yee shall assigne,
in featis aforeseide too haue the more ure:
the nature of kyngis the same dothe dyffyne,
aduertinge as howe all daungre too declyne.
Thus for pastyme of eache noble man   1280
I haue the rule layde, the beste wise I can.

Howe a kynge owght tauoyde infamy, and, aboue althyngis,
nexte his duetie vnto God, tendeuer his honorable fame,
chosinge for that rather too reigne, then for thonlye glorye
of his pryncely estate.

Caput 10

(184)

[f. 30ᵛ] Knowe yow Alexandre, prepotent prynce,
for your instruction conservinge of fame,
I haue conceauyd inwardelye synce
an honeste lesson, concernynge the same.   1285
In thexercitation shyne shall your name
so far as Phebus his beamys shall displaye.
No treasure theartoo compare any maye,

(185)

bicause mankynde bye vndrestondinge,
whiche by reason takethe comprobation,   1290
frome the brutall hathe greate differinge,

1271 no man] noman

withe muche furtheraunce by education,
deadys sundrye too deeme by speculation,
theartoo accordinge too shewe exercise,
for knowledge takethe force cheeiflye by practise,   1295

(186)

for vndrestondynge of thingis in dwe place,
is too bee take of regyment cheeif grownde.
The perfecte healthe of the mynde in like case:
the conseruation withe vertues tabownde,
the meanys too espye eache viciowse wownde,   1300
as thearbye too knowe what yee sholde abiecte,
and what of dwe yee owght also telecte.

(187)

This kynde heere mente of vndrestondinge
ys the begynnynge of vertues all:
the roote also, withoute dissemblynge,   1305
of hole that wee cyvile maners heere call,
vntoo a kynge moste contubernyall,
as freende woorthieste of acceptation,
not too bee put in sequestration.

(188)

[f. 31] **The** firste instrument of intellection   1310
is the desyre of honorable fame.
Whoo thearon passethe shall haue reflection
bye **Ecchois** voyce, too make famous the same,
the worlde too bee ment the brute too proclame.
And whoo so of pride settithe thearbye no forse,   1315
his honour for nowghtis hee doothe awey scorse.

(189)

Therfore I saye that fame principallye
owght, in gouernynge, by it selfe too bee sought,
for seate of honour in her true partes too trye
is not for the same in thappetyte wrought,   1320

but florischinge fame too breede as it owght.
Thoughe grosenes the bodye hynderethe frome flight,
Fame hathe wyngis and tellethe talys far-of quyght.

(190)

So, after the mynde of this Ethnyke man,
the sole beginnynge of all sapience   1325
is tendeuer, bye all the meanys hee can,
of honeste fame too haue a preamynence,
for whiche, after his former sentence,
lordeshippe and domynion is take,
and not for the imperiall see sake.   1330

(191)

Thoughe this morall philosopher sage
the grounde of wisedome liste so too diffyne,
honeste fame too bee the true gage
too cause potentatis in glorye too shyne,
otherwise sayethe the sapient dyuyne   1335
Salomon, whois sayinge seamethe odde:
'The growne of all wisedome is the feare of Godde'.

(192)

[f. 31ᵛ] But too concorde their sentencies so,
either their meanyngis in ordynat place,
they currantlye togithers maye go,   1340
concernynge eache his naturall grace:
whoo passethe for goode fame in any case,
bee hee lorde, prince, kynge or emperowre,
it meanithe hee fearithe some higher powre.

(193)

Thus yee see serue in sorte conuenient   1345
bothe their sage sayinges too wone godlie ende:
too wyn fame woorthie, eache noble preasident
owght withe all dyligence for too attende,
not vnto purpose his state too commende,
but that his dooingis, bothe lowe, highe and meane, 1350
frome all owtrage shoulde see them seauerde cleane.

(194)

If for oother purpose highe romethe bee requyred
then is heere saide in sufficient wise,
then is suche fame vnseemelie tyred,
not sought in sorte of princelie deuise.   1355
Too woorke thorowe enuyous auarice
fame too achieue, oother too expell,
theirs too eclyps that hee maye bere the bell,

(195)

suche fame infamowse is too bee herde.
For Enuye suchewise storethe Mendation,   1360
whiche is the graffinge stock, muche too bee ferde,
of all myscheuous abhomynation.
Vntruithe, of enuious operation,
bredethe Detraction. And so proceedithe
odyous Hatrede, that nowheare needithe.   1365

(196)

[f. 32]   **Whiche** heynowse Hatrede in harte conceauyd,
speciallye wheare it maye ouercome,
woorkethe iniurye of right bereauyd:
then Pertynacye entrethe the bosome,
whearuppon growethe, for lack of wisedome,   1370
rygorowse Rancre, furyouse and fell,
withe hawte Repugnaunce togithers too dwell.

(197)

And whoe proternouslye lyste too repunge,
in thingis contrariowse too woorke againste right,
anon it fyerithe bothe lyuer and lunge   1375
by breache of looue on the brydle too bight.
Then dothe suche discorde Battell excight
thorowe whiche ensuethe, all men too teache,
of all goode ordre moste desolate breache.

(198)

For whoe of selfe-will in suche wise is bent,   1380
his fame full farr too his diffame shall spredde,
whiche too a kynge weare inconuenyent,
yeat this ensuethe wheare suche thingis are bredde.
Well maye it make a prince too bee dredde,
but looued, in sorte as might his fame set forthe,   1385
I wote it well, it helpethe lyttle worthe.

(199)

Compose your actis, thearfor, soueraigne Kinge,
after suche sorte as syttethe too your degree,
that thorowe the same euerywheare may springe
the famouse brute of highe nobylitee.   1390
For the true meanynge of right reason, perdee,
by famowse desyre, at conclusyon
furdrethe truthe, too falsehods confusyon.

(200)

[f. 32ᵛ] As of wone vice proceedithe another,
exampliﬁed in this present peece,   1395
so wone vertue too other is mother,
in pullulation frome greece to greece,
whearbye is conquestrede the golden fleece,
famowse renowne, that sobrethe a kingis seate
by due relation, as woorkethe his feate.   1400

(201)

Too call a kynge noble, and is ignomynyowse,
too fame hym royall, and vsethe weies beastlye,
shynynge withe vertue, and is moste viciowse:
suche adulation ought no man set bye.
Bee noble in deade, and flaterye diffye.   1405
Rather let lyinge abbreache your gode name
then thearbye too purches yow any vayne fame.

1380 selfe-will] selfe will   1385 set forthe] setforthe   1404 no man]
noman

(202)

For Truthe at lengethe will for her selfe speake,
and shewe as shee is, magre her foes all.
Vertue shall florische when Vice shall crye creake,   1410
and sit withe scepture vndre the riche pall.
Fauer then Trouthe: shee is no nuryce small,
she generatethe Justice, and shee, Confydence,
by whiche growethe vertues of passinge excellence.

(203)

The issue that dothe of Confidence sprynge   1415
as I doo note, is Liberalitee.
And her ensuethe, of her owne nurischinge,
the gentle damoysell Famyliaritee,
hauynge too offspringe frendelye Amytee,
whoo, too furdre all princelye affayres   1420
bryngethe Ayde and Counsell as her chief heyres.

(204)

[f. 33] **Wone** pryncipall thinge too a kinge dothe pertayne,
too thende that the prayse of his princelie name
myght bee dyuulgate in lawde souerayne,
as in speakinge his woordis wiselye too frame,   1425
his auditours too note no mysse in the same,
but placed in ordre withe his dwe grace,
so shall hee bee lauded in eauerye place.

(205)

So shall [h]ee bee honowred and feared also,
of his, and oother that foryners bee,   1430
when they aduerte, withe oother thingis mo,
his prudent speache and sage sobryetee
too answere or perswade: in hym they see
suche promptytude in all hee goithe abowte
that woorthye hee is too rule the whole rowte.   1435

1429 hee] ee *prec. by erasure*

(206)

Of wone that is of maners insolent,
dissolute in speache and his behauour,
it maye bee saide, by prooues euydent,
of princelie prudence hee sentithe no sauour,
for by the furtheshewe of his lyfes vapour   1440
it maye bee knowne whither of theis twayne,
wisedome or folye, in hym dothe moste rayne.

(207)

What kynge soeuer his reigne dothe subiecte
vntoo the lawes prescrybed of Godde,
woorthye hee is too rule in full effecte,   1445
withe dyademe, crowne and the scepture rodde
in peacible wise, els Godde forbodde:
and whoe contempnethe Goddis seruice and lawe,
hee shall of men bee had in small awe.

(208)

[f. 33ᵛ] Thus iustelye dealynge bothe towards God and man, 1450
geeuynge too eache their ordynarye parte,
towards your selfe woorke in dwe sorte than.
Yee maye not that in anyewise ouerstarte:
let leacherowse lustis not reigne in your harte,
content your selfe withe your weddid make.   1455
So of this lesson my leaue I heere take.

**Howe a kynge owght to lyue cleane, too auoyde carnal
voluptee and inordynat couetyse, for the manyfolde dys-
commodities ensuynge the same.**

Caput 11

(209)

Alexandre, nowe am I come vntoo
too geeue yow counseile suche as I can,
howe, for your owne wealthe yee chieflie must doo,
too voyde voluptee, that men beastlye scan,   1460

whiche manye vsinge at lengethe dothe sore ban.
Thearfore I saye as too hym I moste looue,
auoyde the same for youre owne behooue:

(210)

carnall appetite, inclynynge the mynde
too beastiall delytis inordinatlye sett,   1465
in whiche the bodye, so beeinge inclynde,
whoelye reioycethe withoute anye lett,
throughe whiche the conscience dothe wamble and frett
withein the sowle whiche hathe immortall lief,
well too bee called a spirituall strief.   1470

(211)

[f. 34] **As** for mannys carkes, whoo liste for too marke,
bee it of shape neauer so beawtiowse,
it is too bee likened too the treeis barke,
rugged, mossye and muche contrariowse:
so is mannys carkes moste far vngratiowse,   1475
thoughe it the Sowle clothe, I wote well so,
yeat ofte it cawsethe her naked too go.

(212)

Too clothe and vnclothe, as thus too bee ment,
whiche sensiblye too all men maye appeare:
the Flesche too the Sowle is as a garment,   1480
so longe as they togithers dwell heare.
The Sowle is immortall: that is knowne cleare;
the Bodye not so, but earthe, dowiste and claye:
wee thearof see tryall heere daye by daye.

(213)

They bothe are thingis twoe, and yeat but wone: 1485
the Sowle and Bodye makethe but wone Man.
And as they are twoe in wone persone,
so are their natures dyuerse too scan.
The Flesche of it selfe nowghtis appetite can
but lustis leacherous, beastlye and nowght.   1490
The Sowle no suche thinge wolde too bee wrought:

(214)

in Man, whiche I meane heere beeinge alyue,
there regnethe a Will as maister of the soyle,
thorowe whome althinge dothe prosper and thryue,
or els suynglye put too a foyle,   1495
Reason hathe Man too make hym recoyle.
But if Will and Sensualitee dothe meeite,
Reason anon is then caste vndre feeite.

(215)

[f. 34ᵛ] **Reason** laborethe the Sowle too preferr.
Sensualitee meanethe nothinge lesse.   1500
What the Flesche wolde too mayntayne herr
throughe thick and thyn, hee dothe his busynes.
So, commonlye, but God sende redresse
by His greate goodnes and grace specyall,
the Sowle gothe too wreake, and takethe a great fall.   1505

(216)

So that throughe Frayltie, another shrewde geste,
oftener Man fallithe then gettithe thupper honde.
Then is the Sowle, when the Flesche hathe her keste,
despoylde and made bare, it maye bee reaconde.
The staff of Cleanes whearbye she dyd stonde   1510
is her depryued throughe fowle Voluptee.
Thus beeinge clothed wee naked her see.

(217)

Naked is mannys Sowle when Vertue is reiecte.
As she is immortall, so muste her habite bee
Faithe and suche Warkis as longethe too her secte,   1515
Purenes of lief, with Longanimytee.
Wheare theis are secluded, and false Voluptee
entrede their place (the harte of man, I meane),
then is the Sowle bare and made naked cleane.

1495 or els] orels

(218)

Consydre thearfore, thow noble Emperoure,   1520
thy Sowle is a thinge thow neadis muste respecte
aboue all rychesse and wordelye honoure.
Geeue heede thearfore the same too protecte.
Let not fowle Voluptie thy mynde infecte,
leste when Atropos thye lief shall dissolue,   1525
the floodis infernall the same maye envolue.

(219)

[f. 35] Auarice entrede onys in-too mannys harte,
desyre of riches dothe daylye encrease.
What eauer hee seeithe contentithe hym no parte,
withoute hee maye vppon the hole sease.   1530
Shiftes makethe hee manye his longinge too please,
shiftinge, God wottithe, by shiftes that hee vsithe,
that manye for feare their owne right refusithe.

(220)

For, will they or nyll they, haue it hee will
by whooke or by crooke, as the prouerbe is.   1535
Hee hathe a nose and a vengaunce longe bill,
that what hee smellithe it shalbee sure his.
His byll will so pecke, hee make will no mys,
althoughe it distaunce seauyn myles of and more.
So are sheepe oft of a wronge sheaperde shore.   1540

(221)

No small are the thingis that maye hym content.
Whole vppon trasche is his solycitude:
hee choppethe, hee chaungethe, hee reysethe his rent,
and all too huche vpp, his mattiers too conclude,
withe vsurall wynnyngis his fyngres embrude,   1545
all hee hoordethe vpp in a bottomles coffer,
withe what thinge els that any will offer.

(222)

When withe riches hee is meetelie well spedde
(but too his full purpose that neauer maye bee),
hee is theare-throughe not belouyd, but dredde.   1550
So then hee lyuethe at his owne voluntee,
and dalliethe daylie withe his Voluptee,
that shamefastnes hee nowhit settethe bye:
thus Abundaunce breedethe shameles Folye.

(223)

[f. 35ᵛ] **And** thearuppon ensuethe Presumption.   1555
For whatsoeauer hee dothe entreprise,
hee reaconethe no man maye looke hym vppon,
so is hee blynded thorowe false Auarice,
as eauer the nowghtes the woorste dothe deuise,
and, no-tyme the better, wee daylie heere see,   1560
so breedethe Presumption Infidelitee.

(224)

Hee beeinge onys withe herr fealishipp frett,
by God or man hee settethe not a flye.
His will is his guyde, hee owethe God no dett.
Thus withoute shame hee liuethe moste beastlye,   1565
too mayntayne his luste with Voluptie too dallye,
hee dothe extorte and powle in playne preeif:
none so myscheuouse as the great theeif.

(225)

So is hee had in detestation:
God so prouidethe, too punysche his fawte,   1570
Whoe abhorrethe his abhomination,
bringeinge suche loweste that lookethe moste hawte,
and causethe hym as captyue to bee cawte,
whiche leadethe hym too the lawes torment.
Suche is for synners Goddis punyschment.   1575

1557 no man] noman

(226)

If hee in lief bee lotted heere too lyue,
yeat shall hee obloquye of bodye sustayne.
Common rumour his goode fame shall depryue,
so longe as his sowle in the bodye dothe reigne,
his faculties confiscated playne,   1580
losse of famyliars, for eauer and a daye,
thoughe nature grudge, theis muste hee neadis obaye.

(227)

[f. 36] **This** exempler too this intent I write,
not onlye yowe too admonysche heerebye
false Voluptie too abolische quyte,   1585
withe all her braunches and genealogye
(thoughe the reste toochethe yow in no partye)
but too thende wheare yee suche owterage see reigne,
the same textirpe too doo your busye payne.

**Of a kyngis endeckinge, and howe nothinge for hym maye
bee too deare or precyowse. Howe all woorthie featis doone
by any of his redoundethe too his honour speciallye. Howe
hee shall chuse chyualours and actyue men abowte hym.
Howe also hee shall chearische and mayntayne suche.**

Caput 12

(228)

Whoo too the honour of a kynge dothe attayne,   1590
what kinde of thinges behouethe suche estate
too haue dwe knowledge in suffisaunce playne,
it sittethe the office wee nowe mynystrate.
A kynge in nowise maye haue mynde elate,
althoughe his porte, in cheare and araye,   1595
in maner thearat dothe muche parte saye naye.

(229)

Nothynge for a kynge maye bee too deere
too glase his glorye in princelieste wise,
golde nor asure, or preacious stonys cleere,
tyssue, withe sylkes of inestimable price,   1600

none in his realme too walke in like deuise,
for, as his honour surmowntethe oother all,
so his endeckynge must bee princypall.

(230)

[f. 36ᵛ] **The** fresche furnyture, both in hall and towre,
wheare dothe manure his princelie presence,   1605
it muste transcende by cawse of his powre
all oother powres bye farr difference.
The maister is eauer of more excellence
then the seruaunte, it seruithe so of right:
a kynge is a kynge, and a lorde but his knight.   1610

(231)

Althoughe it maye his pleasure stonde withe so
in tyme of tryumphe, his fame to delate,
too cause whome he liste in glorye too go,
yeat from his sorte theirs owght too rebate,
and they thearbye too flasche nor efflate,   1615
of anye vayne prayse acquyringe the lawde:
so sholde they their lorde his honour defrawde.

(232)

Too see an hoste royall sett in araye,
so soueraignlye as may by witt bee thought,
the commendation men muste of right laye   1620
vntoe the prince at whois commaundement wrought
theye are so in-too assemblaunce brought.
So that what woorkethe anye chyualour,
it ought too redownde too his lordis honour.

(233)

For hee, men knowithe, his capitayne is,   1625
and brought hym vpp in suche exercise;
bothe horsse and armure, the whole is his.
Owght not hee then too haue the chief price?
Hee dothe thearin but his true seruice.
Whois teachinge causethe the scolar texcell,   1630
chief prayse too the maister maye bee geeuyn well.

(234)

[f. 37] **Yeate** hee princelye his paynes muste recompense
by office, rewarde, as hee dothe cawse see.
Men mynystringe too a kinges magnificence
owght not longe stande unrewardyd too bee.   1635
Paynes consydered in dwe degree
causethe free hartis no storme too refuse,
wheare els they wolde grudge and fayne some excuse.

(235)

Lyke as in araye a prince is peerelesse,
so in cowrte keepinge his plentie muste passe,   1640
his breade, his wyne, at eauerye messe,
and oother vytayle, bothe in plate or glasse,
that eache maye saye, in place wheare hee wasse,
the like in ordre nowheare maye bee fownde:
oh, howe shall that too a kynges lawde redownde!   1645

(236)

Hys powre, peereles, without peere must appeere,
too his bountiousnes oothers too geeue place.
As his scepture streachethe bothe farr and neere,
so muste hee woorke woorthelie, his fame too blase,
that his true lieges maye bragge of his grace,   1650
too bee not the like the whole worlde within,
so vsynge hym selfe their hartis for too wyn.

(237)

Oh, whoo is hee lyuynge, or eauer hathe beene,
by witt, learnynge or wisedome decorate,
althoughe hee hathe the seauyn sciencies seene,   1655
as their essentialles too enucleate,
that can for a kinge duelie inuestigate
what vnto hym in full some dothe beelonge?
Saye whoo so saye can, I saye hee saythe wronge.

(238)

[f. 37ᵛ] **Thoughe** heere I patche vpp suche wise as I can   1660
my symple conceyte concernynge this case
of the endeckynge so noble a man,
and oother thinges as seruithe in this place,
yeat wote I welle I leaue muche voyde space,
the surplusage for oother too supplye,   1665
that can conceaue more then as nowe can I.

(239)

Vnto whiche thinge theare restithe muche in this:
pleasure of princys, what els they will take,
vsage of cowntreys as custome theare is,
that wone vsethe another will forsake,   1670
whearfore longe tale neadethe not heere too make.
Wisedome and Prudence, lett theis ladies twayne
the dwe for eache prynce in this case ordayne.

(240)

Too doo hym mynysterye in feelde and howse,
or what place els his persone shall beecome,   1675
from all myshappes of sourges dawngerowse
that myght his harte bringe in anye thraldome,
too attende on hym, theare owght no small some
of famouse men in chyualrie tryde,
that, if neade bee, dare boldelye by hym byde.   1680

(241)

His lief and deathe is sorowe and blis
vntoo his true and loouynge liegis all,
as if hee shoulde perische or chaunce amys
it shoulde moste greatlye their hartis appall.
Hee dooinge well, steyethe many a sore fall,   1685
sythe in hym restethe the lief of many wone:
owght not the same then too bee tended vppone?

(242)

[f. 38] **This,** weyed and peyced in memoryall,
shall mooue yow, my renowmed soueraigne,
too sett by men of whome yee knowe tryall,   1690
as of necessité of suche too bee fayne.
The more your fame, the noblere your trayne:
whiche of a kynge, whoo so the truthe wiste,
dothe muche parte in suche his honour consiste.

(243)

Or if chalengers of realmys far or nye   1695
too juste or torneye shoulde chalenge pretende,
or what feate els in all kindes of maistrye,
in honour of hym whoo suche dothe too yow sende,
if yee haue not then able too diffende,
it shoulde redownde tyme, yearis, dayes, and howrs,   1700
too the great blankynge bothe of yow and yowrs.

(244)

Thearfore by men of actiuytee sett,
ordayne for them that necessarye is,
geeue them too keepe them from daungre and dett:
sithe yee in nowise may suche abowte yow mys,   1705
no small is the case yee owght caste in this:
for, bee yee sure, the more yee of them make,
the more will they payne them selfes for your sake.

**Howe a kynge owght too marrye, what wise and circum-
specte weyes hee shall vse yn chusinge his ladye and
soueraigne spowses, and howe hee shall, in moste amyable
wyse, chearische, looue, and make of her.**

Caput 13

(245)

[f. 38ᵛ] **Whoo** hathe too gouerne in this present orbe,
kingedome, prouynce or oother monarche,   1710
leste lacke of ysswe his name might absorbe,
whiche, peace too mayntayne, is moste sureste arche

if forayne enemyes towards his shoulde marche,
it muche conuenia[n]tethe too suche an estate
too haue some ladye too hym assocyate,   1715

(246)

suche wone as maye hym thorowlye content,
as for her looue all oother too forsake,
of amytee pure too graunte her suche stent,
that none the same shall cawse anywise slake,
of fresche beawtie his inwarde iye too make,   1720
wholie agreeinge her sole too amplecte.
Oh highe treasure, wheare suche wone is electe!

(247)

Yeat meane I not, but that suche ladye
whiche shoulde bee macht withe suche a potentate,
vntoo herr yowthe and soueraigne beawtye   1725
shoulde haue vertues the same too adornate.
But they togithers doo communycate,
thoughe herr fresche semblaunce shyne as the soone,
too ioyne withe suche wone weare bettre vndoone.

(248)

Thearfore before the firme knot bee upp knyt   1730
of earneste weddelocke and godlye spowsayle,
too voyde all daungre that myght ensue yt,
this is my mynde and prouydent cownsayle:
of her behauour, bye secreat trauayle,
prudentlie searche too haue perfecte reporte,   1735
for seelde prouethe goode that are of the light sorte.

(249)

[f. 39] **Sende** theare abowgtes suche as are circumspecte,
excellent wise and fyne in judgement,
seene in sciencis euyn too the full fecte,
that can in this frame your purpose too content,   1740
whither her nature geauethe preasident
of honeste likelyhede fruyte too forthe-brynge.
Suche foreseene sightes shall cause quyetnes sprynge.

(250)

A kynge Godde forbeade too bee nue fanglede,
his wief texchaunge for his lustis dalyaunce.   1745
Thearfore make searche if shee bee entanglede;
let her not reste then in your remembraunce.
A kingis wief in perfecte resemblaunce
too vue whoo shall so, his dooinges too stande,
hee hathe by office no small charge in hande.   1750

(251)

Too haue withe some ladye realms twoe or three,
or talentes of golde, as hathe beene well knowne,
and scace in her persone wone goode propretee,
but is withe vices sundrye ouergrowne:
what vaylethe too hym too haue his name blowne   1755
withe lordeships so manye too bee posseste,
and hathe too ioye hym no wone daye in reste?

(252)

Thoughe like vnto like is moste agreeynge,
noble bloode royall withe like for too matche,
by meanys suche, muche amytee breedynge,   1760
contackes and grudgis in peace so too patche,
I graunte it well, I will not thearat snatche,
but if shee serue not too his appetite,
then is suche woorkynge put in error quyte.

(253)

[f. 39ᵛ] Too matche for riches or realms domynyon,   1765
withe suche wone as looue listethe not too abyde:
more decent it weare in myne opynyon
too marrye for looue, and lett riches slyde.
The rakinge vpp riches is but vayne pryde.
Ynoughe is ynoughe: then holde I hym blynde   1770
that marriethe riches, too troble his mynde.

(254)

But wheare ill neighbours, adiacent or no,
that trobolowse are in poyntis manyfolde,
if cooplinge togithers maye breede meanys so,
thorowe their nobles, peace perfecte too make holde,   1775
by leage and looue lynked, moste surelye enrolde,
or otherwise the partyes too agree,
suche woorthye wedlocke neadis alowed muste bee,

(255)

and owght too bee sowght in dilygent wise,
and prosequuted of all that loouethe peace.   1780
Whoo theartoo can helpe and will not deuise,
pitee it weare their troobles shoulde cease.
But yeat I harpe on mye former lease:
for too auoyde eache breache and fowle blott,
I wolde haue looue too knyt upp the knott.   1785

(256)

Too ioyne in mariage babis in their cradle,
or infantis, ignoraunte of wedlockis yoke,
withe that sacrament suche-wise too fable
it is ynoughe their lyues too vpchoke.
Theare owght no man his childe so too prouoke,   1790
for landis or like, till they haue discretion,
then too matche at their free election.

(257)

[f. 40] **But** yeat, if this weye their parentis liste take,
suche as theye mynde too their children prefer
too haue in howseholde, and off them too make,   1795
withe his thoother too bee famylier
vntoo suche time pubertie dothe offer,
bye age too bee apte for father and moother,
then too adhere, if either like oother,

1790 no man] noman

(258)

theare cannot in wedlocke the wiseste of all   1800
too muche honeste meanys for quyetnes caste.
A younge damoysell her mynde too let fall,
for worldelie riches whiche fadethe aweye faste,
vppon an olde jaade, that is his luste paste,
or a fresche youngelinge vppon an olde wiche,   1805
too herkne thearunto it makethe my backe iche.

(259)

They cannot prospeire, vnlikelye it weare:
yowthe will by cowrse haue sum exercise.
Matche like too like, so beste frame shall this geare,
as godlye wisedome can heerein deuise.   1810
Bycawse this busynes wee entreprise
dothe chieflye compare for princies too treat,
wee will leaue the lowe and furthe withe the greate.

(260)

Wheare Kynge and Queene walkethe arme in arme,
in wone monochorde my meanynge is ment,   1815
theare can no wight their woorthye fame doo harme;
if they so doo of inwarde looue feruent,
eache withe oother at full too bee content,
withe contynuaunce suche as theare owght,
suche looue eauer too goode ende shalbee browght.   1820

(261)

[f. 40ᵛ] **Shee** loovethe hym withe ardent desyre,
and hee herr agayne most amorouslye:
so are their hartis by looue sett on fyre
that none maye well mysse oothers compenye
if neede shall so dreeue, their hartis ioynethe surelye.   1825
Man maye theare none her harte from hym wynne,
nor wooman his, from herr too doo synne.

(262)

This is all honeste, and thus it shoulde bee.
Looue dyuyded neauer in suche bredde goode.
Too use withe sundrye carnall voluptee,   1830
whiche neauer yeat withe highe honour stoode,
it mooue shall myschief and murmuringe moode,
withe many mysfortunys, evill too bee sowght,
but woorste of all when they are owte wrought.

(263)

Heere, Alexandre, my mynde yee haue herde,   1835
sittynge yowre honowre, and oothers also
that will bee cownseled beefore they ieoberde,
of nobles that shall abowte weddinge go.
The knott of cooplynge cummythe not too and fro,
of and on, as man his mynde dothe bende,   1840
but stondethe in effecte vnto the lyues ende.

(264)

While yee are yeat sole, looke well ere yee leape,
knowe ere yee knytt, bye the counseile of mee,
of manye mysspedde are knowe a greate heape:
let oothers entreatinge your exemple bee.   1845
An honeste wief is highe felycitee,
and ootherwise shee is an hell payne:
woourke as yee cause see; yee knowe the beste gayne.

(265)

[f. 41] **Joyne** not youre thighe, ham, or bare parte
by carnall commyxture withe commune harlote,   1850
in sorte of swyne by coitynge peruerte,
whois weies abhore and in anyewise vse not.
What glorye of reigne shalbee thearby gote,
if odyowse vsage of the vyle brutall,
man, hauynge reason, shoulde theare-untoo fall?   1855

1844 knowe] *curly horizontal-contraction sign over* o: *conceivably* knowen *or* knowne *is intended form*

(266)

Credite my cownseile, for vndoubtedlye
muche carnall coopelinge abbreuiatethe the life,
weakenethe the powres and strenght of the bodye,
corruptethe all vertues by meanys excessife,
destroyethe also the lawes prerogatife,   1860
and laste nowe of all too determynate,
it dothe mannys maners cleane effemynate.

(267)

Too knytt upp the whole whi[ch] is in hande nowe,
that after no-more wee shall neade heereof wright,
of muche medelinge, I admonysche yowe,   1865
withe wief or wooman, by daye or by nyght,
it shall greate hynderaunce woorke too your sight,
weaken your bodye, and shorten your dayes:
let **Reason** in all thynges ordre your wayes.

Howe a kinge shoulde make of ambassadoures, **bee they
freendis or ootherwise, of** merchauntes, **straungers or of his
owne cowntrey, also beehaue hym selfe too his** communtie,
**in difficulte cawses, too heeare their greefes, and withe sage
respecte, accordinge too right, too determyne the same.**

Caput 14

(268)

[f. 41ᵛ] **Yee** noble kinges that hathe the gouernaunce   1870
of realmys, prouyncis, domynyons also,
no small disquyet tossethe your remembraunce,
as sowrgis of seayes dothe shippe too and fro,
for of office it beelongethe yowe vnto,
too hym and hym, whatsoeauer they bee,   1875
too herke and answeare of necessitee.

(269)

Thoughe in some cawses yee substitute some
too answere some, suche some as yee signe shall,
yeat some sometyme vnto yow shall come,

          1863 which] whis   1864 no-more] nomore

that at their mowthes will not bee answerde at all: 1880
their busynes only vnto yow dothe fall.
Althoughe your Cownseile yee thearof preevye make,
yeat at your mowthe they will their answeare take.

(270)

Att leaste wise suche maye in your realme arryue,
that vnto none they will their cawse relate,   1885
so yee doo not their arryuaile depryue,
but onlye vnto yowre noble estate,
bee it too yowe hyghe pleasure or hate;
theye beeinge, yee knowe, but messengers sent,
the maisters malice may not the seruant shent.   1890

(271)

And woorthy hee is in suche beehaulfe too walke,
that shrynke will not his maisters mynde too saye,
so hee presume not passinge his bowndis too tawlke,
but in dwe wise as a messenger maye,
consyderinge, if yee like charge on yours shoulde laye,   1895
if they yowr pleasure wolde feare too set foorthe,
yee myght woorthelye accompte them small woorthe.

(272)

[f. 42] For whiche cawse and consyderation,
A kynge it beecommethe as I consydre,
too compase in his ymagination,   1900
when vnto hym suche men are sent thydre,
for peace or warre, their cawse shewinge whydre,
too arme hym-selfe for the purpose meete,
them to entretayne in weyes moste discreete.

(273)

If they bee freendis, whiche yee soone maye trye   1905
by the some of their ambassadise,
as freendis vse them moste amyablye,
in all woorthye weyes that yee can deuise.
Poynte for them pastymes of pleasaunte practise,
meete vntoo men of suche authorytee,   1910
the more their cheare, the more your lawde too bee.

(274)

Haue somewhile withe them communycation
vppon graue cawses of woondrefull weyte,
beaten before in yowre estimation,
whearin yee maye attempte their conceyte,   1915
leyde beefore them in maner as a beyte,
too prooue their wisedoms and sage iudgement,
for lightlye no babes in suche cawses are sent.

(275)

In wittie wise yee framynge the same,
no les solutynge if stickinge bee made,   1920
it shall muche highelye furdre your fame
a kynge in suche wise so wiselye too wade,
evyn as too freendis this doothe yow perswade,
too shewe pryncelye lyberalytee,
like so make of foes, thoughe no suche cawse bee.   1925

(276)

[f. 42ᵛ] They muste neadis leane as their maisters mynde liethe,
thearfore no blame vnto them maye bee layde.
After her husbands eache goode wifes harte wriethe,
and so eache true subiecte on his kinges cawse is stayde.
For their lordis sake they owght not bee abbrayde,   1930
so theye behaue them in sorte as theye shoulde,
too shewe them gentlenes noble bloode woulde.

(277)

Sayinge as thus, 'Freendis, welcome are yee,
howe eauer the mattier dothe in his case stande
bytweene the Prynce your maister and mee.   1935
Wee twoe shall reacon by proces at hande;
bothe hee and I the tytle of owre lande
bee sworne too defende by fyre, swoorde and myght,
as I mynde no les in that is my ryght.

1920 no les] noles   1939 no les] noles

(278)

But as for yowe, whiche but messengers are,   1940
I maye not chalenge for your princis cawse.
Hym I diffie, let hym mee not spare.
As I mynde hym, witheowte takinge longe pawse,
sithe hee by yowe so hawtelye dothe mee hawse,
his answeare shalbee, "Whoo dothe the oother wronge   1945
muste make thamendis." This is the shorte and longe.'

(279)

By this shalbee knowne a cowragiowse harte,
by this shall they gather yee feeade withoute feare,
by this shall they feele yee passe for your parte,
by this too bee dreade of your foes eauerywheare,   1950
by this they maye lerne too tell heere and theare
the nobleste of princis, too name and not feyne,
dothe at this season in suche a realme reigne.

(280)

[f. 43] **After,** when hense frome yow they shall departe,
withe placable cheare, bothe too frende and fo,   1955
that they maye bragge of your golden marte,
dispose youre rewardes largelie ere they go.
Too eache noble prince it appertaynethe so:
thoughe not too bothe like reason will so bynde,
yeat so may yee make of your foe your frynde.   1960

(281)

Withe merchauntis, too tell what too yow dothe belonge,
straungers, or oother of your owne cowntreye,
shewe them ofte fauour and thankes emonge,
for that they doo for yow and yours purueye.
Your woorthie woorkinge by them far dothe streye,   1965
vntoe the earys of manye a straunge kynge:
too make then of suche it is muche sittynge,

(282)

Let not your officers too sore them extorte
for custome, cartage, portage or suche like.
So maye yee dreeue them too some oother porte,   1970
and yow too flee froe, as frome pyrate or crike.
Greeuous exactours are woorse then a mastike
whiche them behalethe that commethe within his taye.
As yee doo vse them, so will they by yow saye.

(283)

Itt is thearfore for a kynge too auoyde   1975
all maner iniuries, offenses also,
whearbye anye suche myght bee annoyde,
of right occasion your realme too parte fro.
For theye, as is sayde, a-broade as theye go,
of youre princelye prayse the portatours are: 1980
too suffre them wronged, I cownseile yow beware.

(284)

[f. 43ᵛ] **By** suche your iestis are thorowe the worlde borne,
by suche your cities hathe fortification,
by suche are renued olde ornamentis owte-worne,
and too your reuenues great augmentation.   1985
So of youre fame is made locupletation,
so shall youre enemyes of yow stonde in awe,
so as yourselfe liste yee shall althinges too yow drawe.

(285)

Whoo of your subiectis, other hye or meane,
hauynge too your Grace some singulare sute,   1990
your earis beningelye doo thearuntoo leane,
if they so requyre doo make no depute:
of suche beningnitee rise shall a brute,
howe noblelye yee your subiectis dothe tendre,   1994
whiche shall them muche mooue true seruice too rendre.

1993 a brute] abrute

(286)

Itt is not heere ment eauerye suetour so
too troble a kynge in hearinge his cawse,
no sicke or vncleane owght neare hym too go,
but nowe and then, at conuenyent pawse,
wheare stickinge is in a difficulte clawse,   2000
thearbye too geeue knowledge in princelie wise
how hee tendrethe the furtheraunce of justice.

(287)

For trulie what thinge a kinge takethe payne yn
too quyet his commons in case perticulere
or vnyuersall, it shall bee spokyn   2005
of manye wone too his prayse singulere,
howe muche their wealthe hee duelie dothe pondere,
by whiche suche meanys their hartis are too hym knyt,
that what so they hathe hee maye commaunde it.

(288)

[f. 44] What is a royalme wheare diuision is,   2010
wheare headde and commons greeithe not in wone?
Goethe not theare manye thingis a-mys
attingent vntoo their owne destruction?
Hee hawte, they stooburne, this is induction
of vttre decaye bye warre intestyne,   2015
whiche chauncethe not wheare bothe drawethe by wone lyne.

(289)

Hee muste commawnde, they owght too obeye.
Hee muste foresee in studyowse wise
howe in goode ordre hee shall them conueye
in thobseruynge of legale justice,   2020
not burthenynge them no more then shall suffice,
in whiche consyderyd a temperature,
hee maye their looues assuredlye allure.

2016 chauncethe] *between* h *and* c, u *and* n *written in clearly differentiated manner; above the* u *the usual abbreviation sign for* au, *apparently intended for* a *alone: Cf. l. 455*   2021 no more] nomore

(290)

A kynge cheeiflye and aboue althinge
a commone-wealthe owght too respecte,   2025
and they towardis hym their duties ministringe,
withe all their powres his persone too protecte.
Thus headde and membres setteled in wone secte,
what forayne potentate withe batt, byll, or clubbe,
dare theare entreprise the peace too disturbbe?   2030

(291)

When so it shall happe, suche headde potentate
too passe his progresse his commons emonge,
whoe, preasinge too see his pryncelye estate,
or stondinge styll in companyes alonge,
it shall beecome hym, els dooinge them wronge,   2035
his pryncelye face, withe moste cheerfull harte,
towardes them all lowlye too conuerte.

(292)

[f. 44ᵛ] **Signifiinge,** 'Your prince I am and headde,
and yee my subiectis, moste faithefull on too truste;
yee, too see mee thynke youre selfe well speadde,   2040
as mee heere seeamythe by forecinge as yee thruste,
whiche hartie greetyngis I thanke and thanke muste,
for yow my treasure abooue oother all
I accompte alweyes, and eauer compte shall.

(293)

Yee gladde too see mee, youre naturall lorde,   2045
right so muste I yow, if I naturall bee.
If at your dooinge I shoulde oughtis remorde,
then of ingratytude yee myght chalenge mee.
I wische your wealthe withe all prosperitee,
as yee doo myne witheoute dissemblaunce.'   2050
Whiche thinge shall muche mooue in their remembraunce.

(294)

Althoughe they bee but symple plowe-draggis,
yeat muste eache gouernour neadis make of suche.
If byckeringe bee and rappynge on the raggis,
they sure bee theye then that susteynethe muche.　　2055
Heere withe the stone wee haue geeuyn a sure tuche
of right behauoure sittynge too a prynce:
grose thoughe it bee, I can it no better mynce.

**Howe a kynge hauynge ysswe ought by all diligent meanys
tendeuer their woorthye education, moste accordinge vnto
their noble byrthe, bee they manye or fewe, as Godde shall
please too sende.**

Caput 15

(295)

[f. 45] **Emonge** all mattiers oure mattier too supplye,
whiche heere in hande wee haue too exercise,　　2060
for so muche as it is necessarye,
wee owght and muste too the purpose deuise,
if vnto a kinge ysswe shoulde arise,
too shewe heere in dylygent fashion
what doth serue too suche education.　　2065

(296)

A kinge too bee barayne great pitie it weare,
so Godde dothe not the same so decree:
throughe malice of men that myght hym so steare,
for that theye will not his adherentis bee.
Hee, we knowe, cawsethe ofte sterilitee,　　2070
and also fertilenes, in all kynde of thyngis,
in Whois hande restethe the hartis of all kyngis.

(297)

Lett man deuyse all the meanys hee maye
for procreation too spreade or springe,
by herbys, potions in portion too weye,　　2075
or meatis too the purpose moste furtheringe,

withe dyett, complection in aptitude too bringe,
or what meanys els by witt maye bee sought,
but God saye 'Yee', it cannot too pas bee brought.

(298)

The seadman sowethe, the dewe geeuethe moysture,   2080
thearthe in her matrice enuoluethe the seade,
Apollo geauethe heate too nurische nature,
and dryethe aweye that buddinge dothe forbeade,
yeat fruyte for all this maye nowheare spreade,
tyll Nature naturaunce her helpe sendithe,   2085
then too perfection of fruyte it kendlithe.

(299)

[f. 45ᵛ] **In-too** this lief brought after humayne cowrse,
what kynge hathe ysswe, male or woomankynde,
too fostre the same hee bownde is no wourse
then all kynde of lawes as howe hathe diffynde.   2090
As in kyngis offspringis hangethe in the wynde
of no small fewe the disquyet or reste,
so owght their breakynge too bee of the beste.

(300)

As fruyte geeuithe taiste accordinge too the tree,
and tree too burgien by powre of the roote,   2095
if eyther corrupte or rotten bee,
the fruyte will shryuyll and fall vndre foote.
Graffe, proouynge a wyldinge, geevithe sent vnsoote,
not too bee eate off or hadde in regarde,
too serue honestlye nother goode roiste or parde.   2100

(301)

The roote is the perfection of nature,
grownded as longethe too male and femynyne,
whiche beeinge sowne defected or vnpure,
in feelde forayne or menstruatyne,
by roote and treeis suche fruyte adulteryne   2105
must neadys aryse, for roote and tree nowght
neauer naturallye goode fruyte foorthe browght.

(302)

More playnlye this case too elucydate,
what father by feedynge or frankynge vnclenlye
on meatys manye that crudenes dothe mynystrate,   2110
by surfeites sundrye that woorkethe semblablye,
or vppon drunkennes sowethe too multyplye,
trulye, I saye, note well this my sentence,
it muste neadys breede some inconuenyence.

(303)

[f. 46] Or bee the woman vncleane or vnchaiste,   2115
other of sorte as is 'of the man' sayde,
the childe of the moother shall muche parte taiste;
practice will shewe prooife, it shall not bee denayde.
Thearfore wiselye bee this mattier wayde
of eache potentate that ysswe desyrethe,   2120
for their framynge their childis affectes fierethe.

(304)

Thoughe wisedome, Grace and prudent demeanynge
maye natures motions mynysche or moderate,
I speake howe disposition is leanynge,
too the parentis propreties appropryate,   2125
too whiche fra[il]tie will man muche excitate,
that natures cowrse, in some, dothe oftener take place
then wisedome, reason or Goddis speciall Grace.

(305)

Too haue althinge well, so muche as man maye,
the beste weyes eauer is beste too bee taken;   2130
knowinge the beste and will trye another waye,
I saye it owght too bee rather forsaken.
Ferdre in this owre sense too bee waken,
for chyldren borne we shall forthwithe devise
too their education, as beste maye suffise.   2135

2126 frailtie] il *rubbed away*   2131 another waye] anotherwaye

(306)

Bycause greate ladies for cawses immynent
listethe not their ysswe too nurische at their breste
(althoughe Nature weare muche thearwithe content
yeat I conceaue it weare not for the beste:
the cawse too all men is ynowghe manyfeste),   2140
thearfore by all circumspection at onys
bee there forthesowght a nurice for the nonys.

(307)

[f. 46ᵛ] **In** choyce of whome this muste bee pondered well:
that shee bee woman of complexion pure,
of honeste trade, not drownken, hawte, or cruell,   2145
or geeven withe sundrye too haue commyxture.
Too fyne can shee not bee, I am well sure,
that shoulde vppon her suchewise take in hande
too haue in cure the treasure of a lande.

(308)

Thoughe suche wone be hadde meete for the purpose, 2150
yeat owght shee to haue wone her touer-see,
some duches or cowntes of maners not grose,
that as it owght eauerye thinge maye bee.
What longethe too the nurcerye-women passethe mee;
it is their office, and to them moste fytt,   2155
whearefore the resydue too them I commytt.

(309)

But after the tyme of ablactation,
and can commone in the vulgare speache,
knowledge tenduce, make preparation
for suche as shall hym his elementis teache,   2160
and as hee too more maturytee dothe reache
of age and witt, too mynystre hym more,
as his capacitee shall serue thearfore.

(310)

For easye weyes and quycke expedition,
hym too accempenye, matche twoe or three,   2165
withe whois tawlke and ofte inquisition
hee maye the soaner instructed bee.
Eauen nowe at the firste it shall well agree
too haue abowte hym, doo hee lerne or playe,
that can too hym tawlke in sundrye tungis alwaye.   2170

(311)

[f. 47] Yeate in this place we ought too admonysche
that honeste instructours bee ouer suche sett,
withe languagis moste pure his tunge too polische,
as daye bye daye somewhat thearin too gett.
When knowledge, wisedome, and judgement are mett 2175
in any prince withe dwe discretion,
theare althingis muste come to right perfection.

(312)

All whiche instructours ought too bee adornde
as well withe vertue as soueraigne doctryne.
If they thearwithe bee not sauerlye cornde,   2180
their dooingis myght seeme entrickeled withe vermyne,
of lustis lewide that too lightnes dothe enclyne,
for trulye whoe merkethe shall fynde this ofte true:
the scolar his teacher in sundrye poyntis tensue.

(313)

Suche sobre demeanour sought, as is meete,   2185
in breakynge too vertue and pluckynge frome vice,
maye cawse hym florische too furnysche the fleete
of noble champatours, too wynne hym the price,
when yearis, as too reigne, shall fullye suffice
too trayne them in trace of trade tryumphaunte,   2190
in highe honowre his estate too warraunte.

2179 as well] aswell

(314)

For onys a prince woorthelye brought vpp
in kyndis of learnynge and vertue also,
and is of wisedome made sauerlye too supp
by men prudent whiche hathe withe hym too do,   2195
his gouernynge neadys muste cleaue the tuche vnto,
as thus too meane: what sittethe a noble kynge,
hee knowethe in full some the perfecte orderinge.

(315)

[f. 47ᵛ] As learnynge furderithe in forme aforesaide
thearbye too gouerne by witt and science,   2200
so muste a prince, at some conuenient brayde,
in featis of maistries bestowe some diligence.
Too ryde, runne, leape, or caste by violence
stone, barre, plummett, or suche oother thinge,
it not refusethe anye prynce or kynge.   2205

(316)

In the longe bowe hymselfe too exercise,
by cleane handelynge in furtheringe his shote,
the iye on his marke, howe hee shall deuise,
and also orderinge bothe bodye and foote,
too sent the right weies it shall doo hym boote,   2210
by princelye cowrage his harte too attende,
oother nobles too chalenge or defende.

(317)

And, breeuelye too saye the some of my mynde,
I wolde no prynce too bee ignoraunte
of anye feate that is of honeste kynde.   2215
It shall hym rendre muche prompte and pleasaunte.
Movinge exercises are for a prince too haunte,
and not too muche on literate cure too care:
ynowghe is ynowghe, the reste hee maye spare.

(318)

Thoughe heere wee haue, as oure fancye dothe leade,   2220
saide too the purpose wee traueyle vppon,
yeat meane wee not but whoe so hathe in steade
a prince tenstructe, shoulde geeue hym in lesson
too honowre God for anye condition,
his noble parentis too reuerence and obeye: 2225
too prospere and reigne this is the redieste weye.

(319)

[f. 48] **For** thus I saye: yowthe vertuouslye vpp brought
shall eauer lightlye vertuouse trade ensue,
and contrarye, yowthe bredde vpp in weyes nought
seelde hathe beene seene too embrace vertue.   2230
And this I woulde men shoulde note too bee true:
whiche weyes of bothe a prynce dothe invre,
the more parte of his will vse the same sure.

(320)

More too entreat of this shall not heere neede,
for eache princelye parent withe this is enurde,   2235
that is descendyd of suche noble breede,
for lyneallye they are thearwithe assurde.
Owre processe ferdre may bee thearfore up-murde,
for Nature will of all maner kynde prouyde,
their little youngelingis too foster by their syde.   2240

(321)

And what shoulde mooue too woorke their hynderaunce,
they will endeauer maynlye too withestande.
The sealye byrdis shewithe suche resemblaunce;
muche more Man then is clampte in that bande,
too shifte and caste for the heyre of his lande,   2245
bee it hee or shee, all lawes dothe so dyffyne,
their education too sett in right lyne.

2232 invre] v *over a corr.*   2241 hynderaunce] hynder*auu*nce

Howe a kynge his judgis and chief offycers vndre hym, as
well spirituall as temporall, ought to admonysche and
entretayne, layinge to them the due administration of their
officies. And that for like fawte like punyshment tassigne,
withoute respecte of anye persone, except in some cases
in this chapiter followinge mentioned.

Caput 16

(322)

[f. 48ᵛ] **[A] lesson** at lengethe heere mynde wee to write,
    howe yee, my lorde and chief souerayne,
    owght in due sorte and withe all delyte,   2250
    your **judges** and **sage men** that takethe payne
    right religion in your realmes too mayntayne,
    too chearische and fauour in all freendelye sorte:
    they are youre treasure and speciall comforte.

(323)

For, doo yee sleepe, wake, walke, woorke or pleye,   2255
    if theye bee suche as indeade theye ought,
    theye caste althinges too keepe in goode steye,
    or in right ordre deuise too bee brought,
    disburdenynge yow of muche carefull thought,
    for whiche yee ought, they so endeueringe,   2260
    too shewe them fauoure and grace benynge.

(324)

Withe them too confer, debate, and consulte,
    your welthe too furdre, too steye and too guyde,
    all daungres tauoyde of the commone tumulte,
    too reigne in honour and not in vayne pryde,   2265
    withe their sage supportes upsteide on eache syde,
    fall can yee not in the diche of displeasure,
    so longe as men suche your cawse takethe in cure.

*Heading to Caput 16: as well] aswell   2248 A] From here to end illuminated
initial at head of each chapter missing, a blank space being left in every case*

(325)

The nobler they bee in wisedome and science,
semblablye seene sorted withe vertue,   2270
the higher withe yow take them in credence;
they shall yowre honour in althinges pursue.
Chaunge not the true triede for the vnknowne nwe,
for what kynge too hym hathe suche assistaunte
too sleepe the quyeter I dare hym waraunte.   2275

(326)

[f. 49] **Suche** too your purpose conuented and hadde,
them tadmonysche your duetie sittithe noles,
the goode too chearische, and chaisten the badde,
after the rule rated of rightyousnes,
their lyfes depured from vitious exces.   2280
So shall they oother from all enormytee
reduce vntoo a dwe conformytee.

(327)

A rightfull **judge** by this yee shall well knowe:
that whoelye endeuerthe vyce too suppres,
and too geeue justice fearithe highe nother lowe,   2285
althoughe the case partely toochethe your highnes.
If yee make lawes yee muste them fortres,
too suffre wronges reigne your lawes dothe forbydde:
then ought not in yow suche thinge too bee spydde.

(328)

Tenacte or make **statute** after this sorte,   2290
no-man to commense suche kynde of abuse,
the same too take force by generall reporte,
so that none of all hym-selfe shall excuse,
if yee shoulde offende, wolde not men then muse,
oother too bynde, and yee the same too breake?   2295
Yeas, bee yee certayne, they wolde therof speake.

(329)

All if a kynge bee ruler of his lawes,
and maye withe the same sundrye weies dispense,
yeat, **Alexandre,** respecte well this clawes:
punysche not the poore for dooynge offense, 2300
and too the greate too graunt your indulgence,
whois fawte is equall or dothe rather surmownte.
No justicer men will yow then accownte.

(330)

[f. 49ᵛ] **The** poore for an oxe, a sheepe, or a cowe,
a hors, or suche like too bee caste awaye, 2305
whoe dyd so for neade, as hathe beene ere nowe,
lackinge for howse roomethe, meate and drinke, too paye,
and a ruffeler, ryotous in araye,
robbinge and sleynge, whoe had goode and landys,
too let goe at large: this passethe lawes bandys. 2310

(331)

Thearfore I saye, sithe lawe is generall,
not made for wone pertycular person,
let justice serue the great as the small
if their offense in quantytee bee wone.
If meanys bee made too purches your perdone, 2315
consydre the likelyhoode after too come,
whiche is a poynte of syngular wisedome.

(332)

If thoffendre shewe sorowefulnes greate,
beweylinge his fawte, detestynge the same,
by signes so-muche as man maye knowledge gete, 2320
as in dyuerse maye bee had a great ame,
the meanys consyderyd of his feare and shame,
whiche wiselye weyed, maye [ye] soone gesse by lot
whither theare owght too bee perdon or not.

(333)

A deade deadlye, doone casuallye by chaunce,   2325
vnpropensed for anye greeif or grudge,
theare ought not bee shewed the lawes iuste peanaunce,
but hym for too feare, too geeue hym a pudge,
of some satisfaction weyed by his judge.
God forbeade, in eache offensed case,   2330
the lawes rigour shoulde euermore take place.

(334)

[f. 50] A publyke persone that yll maye bee spared
somewhile maye incurre the daungre of the lawe.
Of some suche the peanaunce maye bee pared,
excepte it too far in daungre dothe drawe,   2335
and that in no-wise without feare and awe,
and speciall signe of emendation:
of suche maye bee borne thaccumulation.

(335)

Thoughe lawe is leadde by justice and right,
yeat lawe muste sometymes mercye respecte,   2340
els weare lawe vengeaunce and horror quyght,
able all men withe dispeyre tenfecte.
I beeinge fawtie and therof defecte,
maye not my judge in his conscience feele
hym-selfe infecte withe lyke absurded zeele?   2345

(336)

Howe can hee then well his doome on mee caste,
beeinge in fawte as culpable as I?
but that Synderisis shall saye at the laste,
'Alas, on this wretche yeat shew some mercye!
Heere stondethe hee tremblinge in shame openlye,   2350
and thow sittynge, vnknowne, far woorse then hee.'
Sholde not this mooue a judgis harte too pytee?

2336 no-wise] nowise

(337)

Althoughe hee neadys muste execute judgement,
yeat maye hee use some tolleration,
the playntief thearwithe-all too bee content,   2355
vppon full truste of his emendation,
so too let cease his accusation.
This is not in all cases too bee take,
but wheare the partie maye honeste mendys make.

(338)

[f. 50ᵛ] **Heere** is a note too bee looked vppon,   2360
of what syncere lief a judge ought to bee.
Hee maye not bee the Dyuyllis dungeon,
a vessell implete withe iniquytee,
prowde, covetous, deuoyde of pytee,
affectionat too wone or oother,   2365
but too doo justice too his owne broother,

(339)

except, præexcept, for Mercies only sake,
for a **judge** mercyles ought not too reigne,
althinges at the woorste euermore too take:
suche seueritee is cruelnes pleyne.   2370
Mercye and **Justice**: let theis ladies tweyne
sit on eache syde of the trybunall seate,
vppon the gyltye his judgement too pleate.

(340)

As of highe judgis ouer the laye fee
wee haue heere treated the beste wise wee can,   2375
withe more streyte chardge, if possible maye bee,
is too bee saide too the spirituall man,
whoe in his office must bee as a phan,
the peoples lyuynge too purge from all ruste,
as corne is clensed from darnell and duste.   2380

(341)

Not by his woorde or highe authorytee,
correction or so, their lyfes too euerse,
but chief of all, by dwe conformytee
of holy exemple thearbye too coerce
their hardenyd hartis from synne too reuerce,   2385
vndre suche forme by wisedome owte sought
that theye maye vntoo goode ordre bee brought,

(342)

[f. 51] sometyme offendours reprouynge streytelye,
sometyme blamynge their wylfull wyckednes,
sometyme perswadynge, withe woordis moste gentelye, 2390
too emendation their weyes too addres.
Wheare nought appearithe but stoborne sturdynes,
and no maner signe of turnynge too grace,
theare ought correction of dwe too take place.

(343)

In this sufficient wee thinke too bee sayde.   2395
That more dothe wante youre maiestie may adde.
What kynge hathe suche faithefull men too ayde
hee hathe in his harte highe cawse too bee gladde.
Honour the woorthie, abolische the badde.
False dyssemblers, payntynge holynes,   2400
as dyvillis deceytefull detest them no les.

Howe prudentlye a kynge ought to searche the miseries
moste accustomed emonge his people, and for thextirpation
therof, and other vitious enormyteis, tenacte statutes and
ordynauncis, not too austere or streyte, but as hee maye
fynde in his harte partely to beare therwithe-all hymself.

[Caput 17]

(344)

[C]Onsyderinge and weyinge al-thinges well,
of all estatis in this waueringe lief,
howe muche doth they stande, obiurge and rebell
againste the quyet myndys prerogatief,   2405

too thinke thearuppon it makethe mee pensief:
for the whole discommodyties too wryte,
truly I am not able too recyte.

(345)

[f. 51ᵛ] **None** that in this worlde hathe habitation,
bee hee **kynge, duke, baron** or **capitayne,**   2410
knyght, squyre or **man** of domynation,
that hathe too conducte anye maner trayne,
yeae, the poore **ploweman,** is not free from payne,
but eache, for his parte, muste caste for that and this,
accordynge as his vocation ys.   2415

(346)

Whoe moste hathe too wylde, the more is his care,
for muche harueste manye handes requyrethe.
The gallye that is freatted withe muche riche ware,
of wittye rectours of neade desyrethe.
Recheles folke moste soneste their howse fyrethe.   2420
In all estatis, their charges well too frame,
let wise circumspection fore-see the same.

(347)

If all degreeis ought heereunto too harke,
howe muche chieflye too kynges it dothe pertayne.
For if they by ignoraunce bee made darke,   2425
as not too knowe for theirs howe too ordayne,
goode ordre muste neadys thearevppon complayne.
Therfore, o kynge of hyghe generation,
your iye conuerte to this exhortation.

(348)

Emonge althinges that in your mynde dothe mooue,   2430
caste and conueye your realme too keepe in awe,
in whiche appearethe a perfecte pryncely looue,
so it bee doone by due ordre of lawe.
Let not wone anothers throte owte gnawe,
for lacke of rules too rule them in rule right.   2435
Wheare ordre is none, all is in errour quyght.

(349)

[f. 52]   **Of** decreis and ordynauncis cyuyle
somewhat too saye for due obseruation
as mee semythe sittinge heere will I compyle,
for your peoples exercitation,   2440
the same too bee had in veneration.
What els helpethe too institute a lawe,
but it bee had in due reuerence and awe?

(350)

Wheare is no disordre, offense or trespace,
theare neadethe no lawe: all is in saufegarde.   2445
But sithe offendres regnethe in euerye place,
lawes must be made, their merytes tawarde.
Lawe in-no-wise ought too bee disabarde;
for thoutragious it is ordayned so,
els wolde the euyl the goode ouergo.   2450

(351)

Firste, tuchinge lawes of right religion,
due vnto God of man heere too bee kepte,
see them vpsteyde for any condition:
they bee of force without anye excepte.
If hynderaunce theretoo bee anywheare crepte,   2455
dyrecte theare-againste otherwise then well,
see meanys deuysed the same too expell.

(352)

As God is **Justice** and **Verité** endeles,
permanent in His promyses all,
so are His lawes of moste highe worthynes,   2460
too bee obserued tyme perpetuall.
The meryte great, the daungre not small
that shall ensue wheare breache shal-bee founde:
the more vsed, the greuouser the wounde.

2444 is] *ins. above*

(353)

[f. 52ᵛ] **Too** cawse all florische too Goddis complacence,   2465
    and Hym too o[bb]e[i]e, oother too feare,
    His lawes tobserue, applie your dyligence,
    throughe whiche, no doubte, muche quietnes shall appeare.
    If yee doo make lyght, and sett them areare,
    the more parte your exemple will cleaue too.   2470
    So maye yee profitt: so maye yee harme doo.

(354)

For suyngelye suche as gouernethe the cytee,
    bee they goode or bee they vitious,
    suche communlye the inhabytauntes bee.
    So farethe bye maister and seruauntes of his howse.   2475
    Thus wicked headys are repudyous.
    A hearde that wise is and circumspecte,
    auoydethe that whiche myght his grege infecte.

(355)

Toochinge as nowe of ordynauncies tentreat,
    for the mayntenaunce of a publike weale,   2480
    in whiche consistethe a wondrefull feate:
    howe too eache sorte yee muste their due partes deale
    so that no cawse maye bee had too appeale,
    as, this too bee kepte, this too bee forborne,
    vnto the same eache subiecte too bee sworne   2485

(356)

their soueraigne heade, as yee for the tyme,
    too honour, reuerence, and lowlye tobeye,
    and yee, by mayne powre, them not to oppryme,
    but by true lawe too holde in a right weye,
    robbers and reauers too chaisten deye by deye,   2490
    by suche due ordynaunce as yee shall sett,
    that oother toffende maye bee a maner lett.

    2466 obbeie] offende   2468 no doubte] nodoubte

(357)

[f. 53] **By** meanys as physike too the bodye sore
woorketh endeauer by maisters of that arte,
the patient syke too health too restore,   2495
that after, agayne, hee maye bee in goode quarte,
semblablye the lawe mynistreth her parte,
too the enormous in rule too reuoke,
or-els withe lawes rewarde their lyues tupchoke.

(358)

For whiche goode ordre eachewheare too bee kepte,   2500
offycers honeste, dyscreeite and trustie,
vyces that are emonge the people crepte
too see reformed dylygentlye,
muste bee owte sought withe circumspecte iye.
Schryues, baylifes, cunstables and suche,   2505
vyce too auoyde, their helpe shall doo muche,

(359)

whoe, in their walkes yowre powre muste present,
too punysche and pryson, none them too wistonde.
To ayde them, too haue at their commaundement
suche as they liste too requyre at honde,   2510
if anye contende, obiurginge lawes bonde,
your saide officers too streeke or too threate,
as too your persone let lawe hym entreate.

(360)

If vndre saufegarde, vnchekte or vnharmde,
your officers maye not passe peacyblye,   2515
thorowe malefactours togithers swarmde,
but too bee streeaken or fared withe fowlye,
they will geeue backe texecute their duetye.
So shall eache peasaunte rage at lybertee,
and honeste ordre dryuen textremytee.   2520

(361)

[f. 53ᵛ] **For** true it is, bothe in citye and towne,
if your officers bee not had in feare,
the quyet ordre fadethe and goithe downe.
Myschief and mysrule muste neadis reigne theare,
the rumour therof too roare at youre eare: 2525
as thus too meane, it shall youre earys glowe,
that men will not too goode ordre bowe.

(362)

The chief adoo is, and shalbee alweyes,
emonge slaues, vagabundes and suche lyke,
whoo are the moouers of myscheif and frayes,   2530
wheare the honeste too goode ordre dothe sticke.
Therfore lawe muste suche noughtypackes pricke.
If lawe bee weake, not able them too tame,
let ordayne streighter, too bringe them in frame.

(363)

Oother errours emonge the riche dothe rise,   2535
when of that sorte some wolde the poore oppres,
for too satisfie his fowle couetise,
by wronge the poore-mannys lyuynge too posses.
In suche case, use this kynde of righteousnes:
hee that hathe too muche and dothe the poore greue,   2540
let hym paye dooble that hee dothe bereue.

(364)

Dyscretion, Justice, Wysedome and **Truthe,**
theis muste bee autours and factours of lawe,
for too reclayme the vnbrydeled yuthe
and oother bye-walkers in right rule too drawe.   2545
Sharp, eagre bryne suckethe furthe the bloode rawe:
so lawes ordynaunce reformythe eache wronge,
when they bee dysperste the people emonge.

(365)

[f. 54] **As** to this disease, this medycyne dothe serue,
so too this trespace, this peanaunce assigne.   2550
Let lawe to transgressours digne punyschment kerue,
so shall goode ordre euerywheare shyne,
at whiche so dooinge no goode will repyne,
for wheare lawe lackethe not greinge too this,
theare goithe too ruyne all that euer ys.   2555

(366)

Whoe lawes shall deuyse, institute or make,
the natures of men hee muche muste respecte,
wheare-as hee the jurisdiction hathe take,
too what disposition inclynethe their secte,
thearto accordinge his lawes too dyrecte,   2560
this too bee doone withe counseile of the wise:
vppon this I can no bettre deuise

(367)

but that no man of authorité sholde
withe burthens too sore his people ouerlaye.
Vngodlye it weare, sure, if hee so wolde.   2565
Wisedome in that muste for the poore saye,
too whiche Discretion will not saye naye.
Thoughe Fortune the greate too gouerne hathe brought,
yeat oother touerpres their office streachethe nought.

**Howe a kynge speciallye ought tattende and prouyde for
a commone wealthe, and, too his powre, too abolische
vttrelye all kynde of meanys that workethe anye annoyaunce or hynderaunce vnto the same.**

Caput decimum octauum.

(368)

[f. 54ᵛ] **[I]f** men shoulde gather and perpende in mynde,   2570
why kinges and rulers firste ordeyned weare,
sithe wee are all come of wone stirpe or kynde,
this hathe heeretofore bene scanned manywheare.

2569 streachethe] *r ins. above*

As scarcitee of thinges causethe dearthe tappeare,
so, in fewe, at this worldis erection   2575
thinges weare not brought too their due perfection.

(369)

By proces as the same can springe and growe,
and men of experience gathered the fruyte,
wone then labored another touerthrowe,
thorowe highe preamynence too beare the bruyte.   2580
As suche prospered in their saide pursuyte
at laste it fell by wyse perswasyon
men too beare rule and haue domynation

(370)

whoe, by wisedome and magnanymytee
ordered their weyes so wondrefull too tell,   2585
vndre the forme of highe nobylytee,
vntoo the peoples contentation so well
that they them heelde as woorthieste of the bell,
in peace and warr afore them too take place,
and they tassiste them in all maner case.   2590

(371)

When thus too rule men had the state in hande,
and had woone people at their commaundement,
they caste all meanys in state suche still too stande,
as bettre too rule then bee obedyent,
aduoydinge althinges of daungres immynent,   2595
by suche behauyour of highe woorthynes,
that more and more their fauour dyd encres.

(372)

[f. 55] In all their studye and wise compasynge,
their priuate wealthe they dyd postponerate,
the commune commoditie firste preferrynge,   2600
of thoise that they had too them made subiugate,
vndre higheste weies of looue affectionate,

2588 woorthieste] r *represented by* ur-*contraction, as though* woourthieste

as, if thynges stoode in indifferencye,
their ayde inclyned too the more partye.

(373)

Of wone that thus can fashion his affeires,   2605
as fame the same in due kynde can dylate,
another tooke light too bee of his heires,
in suynge the steppes of suche men approbate,
too whome then was geven the brute of estate,
as woorshippe, honour and highe nobylitee: 2610
thus woorthye woorkinge sett men firste in degree.

(374)

As ferdre in reigne grue their contynuaunce,
theye caste and purueyed for the weale publyke,
by moste honeste meanys of lawes ordynaunce,
sought owte wondreslye by witt polytike,   2615
In Europe, Asya, and also Affryke.
The barbarouse behauyour beastelye and nought
too cyuyle maners at the firste was thus brought,

(375)

sythen contynuynge in wondrefull wise,
withe muche furtheraunce too many a region,   2620
wheare noble princes moste excellent precise
hathe on them weytinge many a legion,
as yee, of the highest accompted for wone,
whois wise endeuer attendethe no les
in semblable sorte too doo your busynes,   2625

(376)

[f. 55ᵛ] **not** as too saye of free liberalitee
too chuse in the same whither yee will or not,
but bownden by office of principalitee
(Nothinge should els more a princis honour blot)
what knyttethe too the contrarye, too loose the knot,   2630
and what goethe loose, in hynderinge the same
too see a restreynte: els are yee too blame.

(377)

Of meanys too speake concernynge the saide case,
firste is too bee had in consyderation,
by streyte punyschinge vice in euerye place   2635
that vertue maye bee hadde in digne estymation,
when synne so is hadde in detestation;
that whiche seemed by custome afore light
shal-bee seene odyouse in euerye mannys sight.

(378)

Vertue thus mayntenyd and vice depressed,   2640
then are the people like the gardeyne plot,
that is depured, leauelyd, and dressed,
too sowe or sett theare what thowner will allot,
as your wisedome and counseile dothe well wote,
for the commune-wealthes beste preseruation   2645
nowe maye yee put in exercitation.

(379)

See, and well pondre in all your dooinges,
whiche thearunto dothe any meane conclude,
that wone pryuate persone in vse of thinges
dothe not annoye or harme a multytude: 2650
wone, withe the lyuynges of fyue too bee endude,
of twentie or threscore, eache wise man maye saye,
the publike weale holdethe not theare the right waye.

(380)

[f. 56] **Or** if yee shall of affabylytee
vnto some wone suche libertie graunte   2655
temparke or enclose for his commoditee
that the hynderaunce of moe myght waraunte,
or any suche weyes taccustome or haunte,
by byinge or sellynge too others hynderaunce,
no suche thinge suffrethe a cyuyle ordynaunce.   2660

(381)

In tyme of plentie the riche too vpp mucker
corne, grayne, or chafre, hopinge vppon dearthe,
for his pryuate wealthe so daylye too hucker,
this criethe for vengeaunce too heauyn from the earthe.
Leste it shoulde happen it manye wone fearthe.   2665
For suche solayne snydges caste reformation
by forfeture too the poores sustentation.

(382)

The poore, for neade, is dreeuyn too make sale,
the riche reseruethe and muckerthe vpp more:
by whiche risethe this commune prouerbe tale,   2670
'Some muste bee sauers, store is no sore'.
So is it indeade if the riche therfore
wolde woorke after this neighbourlye deuyse,
too helpe the poore for a reasonable pryce.

(383)

A kyngis honour, disertlye too aduerte,   2675
is not vpsteyed, mayntened, and fortified
by wone, twoe, or thre, or the fewer parte,
but by the more some it hathe euer bene tried.
Then ought a kynge for his commons prouyed
that wone clubbed cobbe shoulde not so encroche   2680
an hundred mennys lyuynges: it weare greate reproche.

(384)

[f. 56ᵛ] Your realmys commodytee, in what it dothe consiste,
for twoe or thre too haue the specyall trade,
the publike weale is sore in that place myste,
and goethe too decaye, as flowres dothe fall and fade.   2685
In this eache potentate by witt muste wade,
bothe by hym selfe and his wise counseile,
that pryuate commoditee not so maye preueile.

(385)

If merchauntes that be too yow but straungers,
althoughe your custome by them bee copiouse,   2690
shoulde bee enriched and made great geyners,
your owne hynderyd, and made indigeouse:
this weare a mattier in maner litigiouse,
too make them murmure and their hartes withdrawe
from the due obseruation of the lawe.   2695

(386)

Chieflye your owne yee ought too respecte,
for yee of them in your neade may bee bolde,
wheare straungers passethe not your fauour to reiecte,
or in your right title will oughtes withe yow holde.
Custome vncumlye is too bee controlde,   2700
wheare priuate woorkinge shall shewe euydent,
too a commontie too doo detryment.

(387)

Heere too wryte all too this mattier meanynge
I cannot compase or caste thuttermuste,
but ferdre I shall yeat tuche this wone thinge,   2705
as shalbee pleasinge too your Grace, I truste.
Let not of yours wone another owte thruste
furthe of his lyuynge, his lease, or his holde:
Res publica thearat her harte wexithe colde.

(388)

[f. 57] **A** pooreman whiche hathe bothe children and wief,   2710
whoe withe his parentes vppon a poore cotte
hathe theare manured manye a mannys lief,
and trulye payed bothe rent, scotte, and lotte:
a couetous lorde whoe conscience hath notte,
by rent enhauncynge or for more large fyne,   2715
suche wone too caste owte, it goethe oute of lyne.

(389)

This too bee seene too, the publike weale criethe:
of reformation it sittethe your office.
Manye iniuryes too the poore pliethe,
done by the bygger without all justice. 2720
As the great fowle the small dothe supprise,
deuour and eate vpp all flesche too the bone:
so farethe the riche if they bee let alone.

(390)

That kynge, bee sure, can neauer bee poore,
wheare-as his commons lyuethe welthelye. 2725
If they bee not able to keepe open doore,
it muste withe hym then but small multyplye,
for kynges of their commons sumtyme muste ayde trye.
The more therfor the publike weale dothe afflowe,
the more is their wealthe: this reason prouethe nowe. 2730

(391)

And true it is, the highe Opificer
sendethe not His giftes too wone pertycularlye,
but that a multytude, wone withe other,
the same shoulde particypate mutuallye.
Sithe hee althinges heere dothe make too multyplye 2735
too thende aforesaide, o kynge of God electe,
see then the same stonde in her full effecte.

[f. 57ᵛ] Howe a kynge ought too deteste ydlenes, the moother of all
myschief, and too ordayne meanys too haue his subiectis
euermore occupied in honeste exercises, to the may-
tenaunce of theire own lyuynges, and furtheraunce of the
common weale, that the ydle shall not deuour that which
þe diligent doth truly get by the labour of their sweate.

Caput 19

(392)

[L]este kinges and gouernoures that heere dothe rule
myght this neglecte, whiche is expedyent,
wee shall make remembraunce in this schedule 2740
of Ydlenes, that hydeouse serpent,

whoe, loighteringe like a peasaunt pestilent,
lurkethe in corners vnoccupied,
too doo any goode lothe too bee espiede.

(393)

This beastelye bodye, this mawltische matrone, 2745
deuowres of the true laborers frute,
of nature desirethe too bee let alone,
as too contynue in her maners brute.
Too sleepe, eate, and drinke, suche is her sute,
and what els longeth too lustis dalyaunce, 2750
she is readye too shewe herr furtheraunce.

(394)

The daye in too the nyght shee can conuerte,
the nyght in to daye, for dalyaunce sake.
Too pleye is shee preste, woorke is a deserte,
too hiere therof tawlke herr harte will not wake. 2755
Whoe too herr compenye shee maye onys take,
for seauyn yearys after, I dare the truthe mooue,
the woorser husbonde hee shall surelye prooue.

(395)

[f. 58] **Or** bee it woman, in like maner wise,
no profite risethe wheare shee dothe frequent, 2760
but propagation of vice owte of vice:
the prooif shall shewe practice moste euydent.
Let loyterers lyue as they are content
and they shall plucke too their societee
feloshippe that neauer will after goode bee. 2765

(396)

Yowthe, brought vpp ydlelye in games and pastyme,
not taistinge the trade of honeste busynes,
as vice detestethe vnto vertue too clyme,
so farethe withe all that loouethe Ydlenes;
of all maner myschief shee is patrones 2770
againste whome the heauyns dothe openlie exclame,
by plage to punysche this Ydlenes by name.

(397)

What kynge is hee in this worlde so greate,
or potentate els, fewe or manye,
what clarke also in his studyous seate,   2775
or whoe that hathe too gouernaunce anye,
but moste their tyme liste not too dallye
withe Ydlenes heere mentioned,
then of their mattiers they myght bee euyl sped.

(398)

Kynges can noles but compace, searche and caste   2780
how too prouyde for the publike weale,
the same too contynue in state stedfaste,
as too eache partie true iustice too deale,
oother magistrates hauynge like zeale
vnto their offices dwe admynistration: 2785
shoulde loyterers lyue then in their ydle fashion?

(399)

[f. 58ᵛ] **For** reformation of suche nowghtyepackes,
bee it proclamed vnto their earys all
that whoe endeuorethe any suche knackes,
at ale howse too sitt at mack or at mall,   2790
tables or dyce, or that cardis men call,
or what oother game owte of season dwe,
let them bee punysched without all rescue,

(400)

owte of season in this sorte too bee take.
When dayes of labour are presently come,   2795
eache man too his arte his voyage too take
withe willinge harte, not too glomer or glome,
it is cyuyle iustice and no thraldome,
for as the byrde is heere ordeyned too flee,
so is man too woorke, olde writinges tellethe mee.   2800

(401)

Trulye, I wolde in all that [in] mee liethe
wright all I cowlde this vice tabolische,
for Ydlenes all vertue despisethe,
wheare honeste exercise the lief dothe polische.
Thearfor all kynges I doo admonysche   2805
heereunto too geeue goode aduertence,
for noughtes it breedithe but wretched indigence.

(402)

As in honeste artis wee wolde haue occupied
eaueryman after his vocation,
so wolde wee haue youthe too vertue applied,   2810
that are not readye for occupation
of hande crafte too use thadmynistration,
infantes I mean vndre eight yearis of age.
Their tyme I wolde thus too bee put in vsage:

(403)

[f. 59] at fowre yearis olde let suche too scoole bee sett,   2815
too gather and lerne some literature,
bye whiche they maye after knowe their due dett
too Hym that is Authour of eache creature,
bye readinge in bookes His will and pleasure.
For, whoe-so listethe to remembraunce call,   2820
too woorke in that age their powre is but small.

(404)

Leste some perhaps at this myght thus obiecte,
the pooreman his childe cannot so prefer,
bycawse hee hath not substaunce in effecte
for so longe season to fynde his scoler,   2825
as for his scoolinge too paye his maister,
to whiche I answere, it muste prouyded bee,
in eauerye towne the scoole too go free.

(405)

Suche townes whiche hathe a curate to bee ment,
dueties too persolue that bee spirituall, 2830
whome too bee ydle weare inconuenient
beyonde all oother, eauen the wurste of all:
thearfore, to teache it dothe their office fall,
and bringe vpp yowthe to saye, to singe, or write,
that God too serue they after maye delite. 2835

(406)

Suche honeste stipende towardis hym to remayne,
that for his paynes hee nothinge scholde expecte,
for so longe tyme as a-fore dothe contayne.
Mee thynkethe this sowndethe too goode effecte.
If vnto office they after bee electe 2840
when reade they can and their vulgare speache knowe,
their princis pleasure they maye bettre followe.

(407)

[f. 59ᵛ] **When** they hathe knowledge indifferentlye so,
too oother artis then maye theye bee preferde:
and not loyteringe ydlelye too go, 2845
thorowe whiche the publike weale is ofte merde.
Thearfore this lesson I wolde to bee herde,
in townes, goode ordre too shyne and florische,
this obseruation I wolde gladlye wische.

(408)

An ouerseeer, **Controwler** to bee calde, 2850
to see vnoccupied none to remayne,
vnles they bee withe sicknessies appalde,
or by debilitee of age ouerlayne;
if case theare bee, too punysche them by payne
of stockes or scowrginges, whiche suche maye compell 2855
to earne their fooade, els to haue no morsell.

(409)

And the saide officer to haue by fee,
owte of the towne coafer, thre or fowre pownde,
that for suche stipende the rather maye hee
to thexecution thearof bee bownde;   2860
if in thoffice hee negligent bee fownde,
to bee depryued withe reproache and shame,
and neauer againe too entre the same.

(410)

In thelection of suche ouerseeer,
this owght, and muste, firste consydrede bee: 2865
that hee bee knowne an honeste towne-beeer,
and hath a zeale too cyuile equytee,
too cawse hym earnestlie thearto too see.
But wone yeares space let hym thearin endure
excepte hee bee fownde moste fitte for the cure.   2870

(411)

[f. 60] **True** it is, no lyuynge man this daye
can presentlie for the publike weale frame
so syncerelie the vttremuste too saye,
that maye bee breache or staye too the same,
inviolablie too byde withoute blame.   2875
But, as tyme wearithe mannys maneirs vued,
so muste custome and lawe bee renued,

(412)

the soyle and people consydered also.
That will not serue heere that seruithe elsewheare.
Some hathe commoditeis, some lesse, some mo,   2880
which dothe the chargis of the publike weale beare,
bye merchaundise conueyde heere and theare,
as, heere in **Englande** wone speciall haue wee,
woole, for whiche manye great suetours hither bee.

2884 hither bee] *apparently added in fainter ink*

(413)

Of whiche to saye, as my fancye dothe leade   2885
(the judgementis of bettre not offendyd),
I wolde it weare duelie consyderede
howe **foryners** by **woolle** are assendyd
and owre weale publike little amendyd,
for by owre **woolle,** of Christians and Turke,   2890
thowsandis thowsandis hathe daylie handye wurke,

(414)

and wee the same of them agayne to bye,
sixefolde doble price moare then of them had wee.
Oh, some witt politike shewe reason whye
myght not the same heere so perfected bee,   2895
wee to profite by owre owne commoditee?
If honeste meanys myght bee thearto espied,
how sholde owre **commons** then bee occu[p]yed!

(415)

[f. 60ᵛ] **So** manye **beggers** sholde not reigne as reigne,
so manye **neadye** sholde not for conforte crye,   2900
so manye **rouers** sholde not vse the pleyne,
so many sholde not then lyue ydlelye,
a few to profyte to hynderaunce of manye,
as **thowsandis** to lacke and **twentie** to abownde,
oh, howe it geauethe a myserable sownde!   2905

(416)

Moste worthie it is a kynge to excell
in honowre, richesse and glorye decorate,
lordys in degre in woorthynes to dwell,
withe **gentyls** also as sittethe their estate,
and they to the meane to communycate,   2910
that theye maye lyue bothe childrene and wife,
and them not to streyne by meanys excessife.

(417)

The pooreman to toyle for twoe pense the daye,
some while thre haulfe pense, or-els a penye,
hauynge wief, childrene, and howse rent to paye,   2915
meate, clothe, and fewell withe the same to bye,
and muche oother thinges that bee necessarye,
withe manye a hungrye meale susteynynge.
Alas, makethe not this a doolefull compleynynge?

(418)

The worlde is chaunged from that it hathe beene,   2920
not to the bettre, but to the warsse farre:
more for a penye wee haue before seene
then nowe for fowre pense, whoe liste to compare.
This suethe the game called 'Makinge or marre':
vnto the riche it makethe a great deale,   2925
but muche it marrethe to the commune weale.

(419)

[f. 61] Too reyse his rent, alas, it neadethe not
of fyne texacte, for teanure of the same,
fowrefolde dooble; it is a shrewde blot,
to the greate hynderaunce of some mennys name.   2930
I knowe this to bee true, els weare I to blame
too mooue this mateir in this present booke
at whiche Respublica lookethe a-crooke.

(420)

A rent to reyse from twentie to fiftie,
(of powndis, I meane, or shealingis whither),   2935
fynynge for the same, vnreasonablye,
sixe tymes the rent, adde this togither:
muste not the same great dearthe bringe hither?
For, if the fermoure paye fowrefolde dooble rent,
he muste his ware neadys sell after that stent.   2940

(421)

So, for that **oxe** which hathe beene the like solde
for **fortie shealingis,** nowe takethe hee fyue pownde,
yea, **seauyn** is more, I haue herde it so tolde;
hee cannot els lyue, so deeare is his grownde.
Sheepe, thoughe they neauer so plentie abownde,   2945
such price they beare whiche shame is to here tell,
that scace the pooare man can bye a morsell.

(422)

Twoe pense **in beeif** hee cannot haue serued,
other in mutton, the price is so hye:
vndre a groate hee can haue none kerued.   2950
So goethe hee and his to bedde hungrelye,
and risethe agayne withe bellies emptie;
whiche turnethe to tawnye their white Englisch skyn,
like to the swarthie-coolored Flawndrekyn.

(423)

[f. 61ᵛ] **Wheare** they weare valiaunt, stronge, sturdy and stowte,
to shoote, to wrastle, to dooe anye mannys feate,   2956
to matche all natyons dwellinge heere abowte,
as hitherto manlye they holde the chief seate;
if they bee pinched and weyned from meate,
I wisse, o kynge, they, in penurye thus pende,   2960
shall not bee able thye royalme to defende.

(424)

Owre Englische nature cannot lyue by rooatis,
by water-herbys or suche beggerye baggage,
that maye well serue for vile owtelandische cooatis:
geeue Englische men meate after their olde vsage,   2965
beeif, mutton, veale, to cheare their courage
and then, I dare to this byll sett my hande,
they shall defende this owre noble Englande.

(425)

[T]he Tytle heere nowe whearon wee entreate,
bicawse it dothe suche weightynes contayne   2970
(a publike weale, whiche is a matter greate)
wee shall deuyde it into lessons twayne,
declaringe as seruethe my symple brayne,
howe, thorowe God and yowe His mynyster,
thinges owte of frame maye bee brought in order.   2975

(426)

[f. 62] If that I heere speake bee to no purpose,
perdon I haue askte for my symplenes:
if it maye serue withowte coment or glose,
moste happelie then seruithe this busynes.
Eache mannys writingis dothe not althinges redresse   2980
accordinge as his trauelinge dothe tell:
thoughe this like so, yeat wolde I althinges well.

(427)

Too saye howe ydlenesse maye bee expellyd,
and this owre royalme enriched by the same,
somewhat thearto all-readye is tellyd: 2985
for the reasydue wee shall nowe heere frame.
Woolle is the thinge wee will steye on, by name:
thoughe oother thinges moe geauithe assistence,
yeat woolle, for this tyme shall haue preamynence.

(428)

The woolle that staplelers dothe gather and packe,   2990
owte of this royalme to cowntreys forayne,
bee it reuoked and steyed abacke
that owre cloathiers the same maye retayne,
all kynde of woorkefolkes heere to ordayne,
vppon the same to exercise their feate,   2995
by tuckynge, cardinge, spynnynge, and to beate,

2969 *Nine-line space left before this stanza, as for seven-line stanza or for heading to chapter. Though numbering of chapters shows no missing title, first three lines of stanza are set back to right, leaving space for missing illuminated initial.*

(429)

weauynge, fullinge, withe dyinge if theye liste,
and what sorte els to cloathinge dothe belonge,
by suche true handelinge that nothinge bee myste,
whiche myght chalenge their woorkinge to bee wronge, 3000
that whearsoeuer they shall come emonge,
thorowe Christendome or heathenes grownde,
no fawte theare bee in the woorkemanshippe fownde.

(430)

[f. 62ᵛ] **Shrynked** befoare and perfected at full,
gaged and sealed iustelye as it is: 3005
if it bee fawtie in woorkinge or in wooll,
owre foalkes to weare them, I gree beste to this,
rather than straungers sholde fynde vs amysse,
for owre false dealinge owre cowntrey tappeache:
what the salys-man is, the ware ofte dothe teache.   3010

(431)

No towne in Englande, village, or burrowe,
but thus withe cloathinge to bee occupied:
thoughe not in eache place cloathinge cleane thorowe:
but as the towne is, their parte so applied;
heere **spynners,** heere **weyuers,** theare cloathes
     to be **died,**   3015
withe **fullers** and **shearers** as bee thought beste,
as the cloathier maye haue his cloathe dreste.

(432)

When they haue groaced vnto a some
of scoarys or hundredis as they appoynte shall,
owre Englische merchauntes by custome to come,   3020
and them receaue to go ouer withe all;
or, bee they fechte bye greement speciall,
by forayne merchauntes as they haue agreede,
moneye receaued, God geeue them goode speede!

(433)

Heere is not meaned the Kinges Maiestee 3025
his custome to loase or thearof wone joate
that heeretofore accustomed hathe bee,
but hee to haue still the vttremuste groate;
befoare they hense passe by shippinge a-floate,
the cloathes knowne what of a packe dothe come, 3030
and thearto accordinge to paye custome.

(434)

[f. 63] **Withe** all oother dueties in eauerye place,
both vnto his Grace and oother also,
as of conuenyence sittithe the case.
Wee will by no meanys theare-againste go, 3035
but heere this peece wee shall adde nowe vnto,
whiche withe conscience is muche agreable,
that **woolle** maye bee at a price reasonable.

(435)

The leaste price to bee, the **todde** accowntinge,
not vndre **ten shelinges,** beeinge no reffuse, 3040
the beste **fyuetene shealinges** not surmowntinge:
betwene theise pricis conuention to vse.
Theise pricis to lymyte let no-man muse:
it hathe beene so seene att within twentie yearis,
and so maye agayne withe helpe of owre hedde pearis. 3045

(436)

But heere liethe a mateir muche difficulte,
whiche greatlie I feare neauer to take force,
thoughe I with manye sholde thearin consulte,
and crye theare-vppon eauyn till wee weare horse:
pryuate comodye withe **commone** wealthe to
  scorse, 3050
as **rentis** to come downe from owterage so hye
too **price** indifferent to helpe manye bye.

3039 todde] T *in black ink; remainder of word in red*

(437)

Theis raginge **rentis** muste bee loked vppon,
and brought vnto **tholde accustomed rente,**
as they weare let att **fortie yearis** agone.   3055
Then shalbe **plentie,** and moste men content,
thoughe greate **possessioners** liste not tassent:
yeate bettre it weare their **rentis** to bringe vndre,
then **thowsandis thowsandis** to perische for **hungre.**

(438)

[f. 63ᵛ] **In** whiche youre Highnes this ordre maye take,   3060
discreit men of youre Cownsell too assigne,
that wilbee corrupted for no mannys sake,
and theye withe helpe their endeuer tenclyne,
ouer youre royalme wheare this is owte of lyne,
growndis and **fermys** to peruse and surueye: 3065
rentis to reforme that bee owte of the weye.

(439)

And as their wisedoms withe conscience shall see,
the soyle consydered, barrayne or fertyle,
the owners by them ordered too bee,
their **rentis** tabate, enhaunced so longe while,   3070
pryuate commodye to put to exile,
ratynge the same indifferentlie so:
the **fermers** to lyue and by them oother moe.

(440)

Not in thraldome and pynchinge penurye,
to bee as drudges vnto their landelordis;   3075
but as yeomen becomethe honestlye,
and of Goddys lawe conuenyatethe the conchordis.
At too muche bondage **Englische hartis** remordis.
for what kinge heere will lyue honorablye,
hee muste then make of **Englande yeomanrye.**   3080

3056 plentie] p *in black ink; remainder of word in red*   3060 In] I *in red*
nk; n *in black*   3078 Englische] E *in black ink; remainder of word in red*

(441)

For they, all men knowethe, are the maior parte
whiche by all lawes ought to bee seene vntoo
speciallye withe moste intentife harte,
sithe they for their princis their daylie labour doo,
the myndis of whome they can no bettre woo,   3085
to lyue and dye in furderinge their enquestis,
then to see mayntened their olde enterestis.

(442)

[f. 64] **Suche** poore lyuynges as their fathers dyd enioye,
meanlye to lyue, their lyues to contynue:
alas, a pooreman it greatlie dothe annoye,   3090
when hee for a lyuynge shall eauermore sue,
and withe non assuraunce hym-selfe can indue,
custome nor **copie** can keepe hym in, scace,
if **fawnynge fyne** attemptethe his lordis Grace.

(443)

Thoughe he bee dyuyllische that byddeth for it so,
more diuyllische is hee that thearto dothe graunte,
and for their dooinges shall too the Dyuyll go,
els false vnto vs is Goddis couenaunte;
for hee them cursethe and byddithe 'Auaunte!'
that so procurethe his neighbours lyvinge.   3100
To see heereunto sittethe thoffice of a kinge.

(444)

For what is it in **ferme** or **copye-holde,**
or oother semblable habitation,
owte of the same to bee bought and solde,
for lucre sake, to the lordis contentation?   3105
the sealye **pooreman** by suche euasion
withe wief and children so forced to go begge:
so they maye profite they passe not an egge.

3092 non] nō, *perh. for* no(e)

(445)

Anoother disordre of oppression,
aduerte this wone whiche is muche odyous: 3110
a lorde geauyn to pryuate affection,
lettinge the pooareman an olde rotten howse,
which hathe, to the same, profyttes commodious
as cloase and common, with lande in the feelde,
but noate well heere howe the pooareman is peelde.   3115

(446)

The howse shall hee haue and a gardeyne plott,
[f. 64ᵛ] but stonde hee muste to the reperation:
close, comon, or londe fallithe none to his lott,
that beste myght helpe to his sustentation.
The whoale rente payethe hee for his habitation,   3120
as thoughe hee dyd thappurtenauncis possesse.
Suche soare oppression neadethe speadye redresse.

(447)

Thoughe some will obiecte hee is the more asse
so to bargayne to bringe hym in thraldome,
hee can none otherwise bringe it to passe,   3125
els muste hee paye largelie for his income.
To settle hym-selfe, place muste hee haue some,
his wief and childrene in like maner wise,
whoe for pure penurye ofte waterethe their iyse.

(448)

Thus thorowe rentes-reysinge and pillinge the poore, 3130
Pouertie regnethe and is induced muche,
compelled to begge nowe from doore to doore,
as tyll owre tyme hathe not beene herde of suche.
Your Highnes, o Prince, this case dothe sore tuche,
for chieflie youre crowne to this intent yee weare, 3135
wronge to reforme that equité may rule beare.

(449)

No right it is the pooare to bee so vsed,
and some to the Dyuyll throughe richesse to flytt
(Christian charité of them refused)
which drowned **Dyues** in the deepe hell pytt.   3140
More occasion to treate on this as yeitt,
is wheare some wone the lyuynges dothe possesse
of twoe thowsandis well knowen to bee no-lesse.

(450)

[f. 65] **Firste** in goode rentes a thowsande powndis or more
in fermys and abbeys coequall to the same,   3145
reuenues by sheepe, thowsandis by tayle score,
oxon and neate, greate multytude to name,
personages of profites wondrefull in fame,
and yeat is as greadye more to procure
as hym to mayntayne: this weare but small sure.   3150

(451)

And what hee onys into his clampis catche maye,
the pooreman thearof no peece shall come bye,
cowe leayse, horse grasse, or one loade of **haye,**
thoughe hee before had theare-for his monye:
his chargis, hee saithe, are so passinge hye   3155
that for hym-selfe all is little ynowghe,
yeat on his whoale growndis hee keapeth not one plowghe.

(452)

To speake or repyne againste his fell factes,
alas, theare dare none their lippes to open;
the like togithers hathe dryuen suche compactes   3160
that truthe into an whoale is nowe cropen,
and for his tawlke his hedde all to-broken:
the more is the pité, conscience knowithe.
Goode kinge, thearfore searche wheare such darnell
      growithe,

(453)

and set an ordre of reformation   3165
that eache maye lyue to his gree accordinge;
dukes and lordis of highe domynation
ouer the people to haue thorderinge,
that the meane sorte abowte them borderinge
maye lyue by them and their neighbours become   3170
[f. 65ᵛ] by Christian loue, and not holde in thraldome.

(454)

For lordys and men of highe nobilitee,
or oother indude withe possessions greate,
to vse thoffice of thinferior degree
to choppe and chaunge, aduantagies to geate,   3175
as merket men dothe, it sittethe not their feate,
or fermys tencroche whiche oother myght releeue:
suche doinges, no dowbte, dothe many hartes greeue.

(455)

I will not saye all that neadethe to be saide,
to longe then sholde I heere tyme occupye,   3180
but by suche meanys common wealthe is decaide
and hathe heere of late cawsed great owte-crye
by muche disordre moste sclaunderouslye,
cheif to them-selfes to woorke so withoute witt,
and next to those that weare cawsers of itt.   3185

(456)

If great bee their charges, the wiseman ought
them to rebate, accordinge to his stent
to keepe a porte. In hatrede to bee brought
thorowe meanys whiche are inconuenient,
holde whoe thearewithe will, I will not assent: 3190
bettre is meane estate hauynge frindys manye
then highlie to ruffle, scace to fynde anye.

3169 borderinge] *medial* e *corr. from* r   3175-6 *written in inverse order:*
marked for reversal by letters a *and* b *in margin in red*

(457)

Moste merieste it is in eache cowntrey
when euery degre obseruethe his dwe
Dame **Justicis** lawe trulie to obeye:　　　　　3195
theare muste then neadys great quietnes ensue.
And wheare **diuision** by grudge dothe renue
it breadethe nowght els but desolation,
[f. 66] from all quyet wealthe to dissipation.

(458)

And all this makethe the goodis of the worlde:　　3200
for that will men toyle, for that will men scrache
for that olde frendeshippe shalbe all to-chorlde,
the wone brother readye thother to dispache,
the soone withe the father also to mache,
by vttre diffiaunce his deathe to exopte,　　　　3205
thoughe thousandis for the like hathe into hell dropte.

(459)

The highest of all that regnethe in estate
hathe in this worlde but meate, drinke and vesture:
then what dothe mennys myndis so intoxicate
inordynatlye to toyle for treasure,　　　　　　3210
purchacinge thearbye so muche displeasure
bothe of God and their neighbours heere neadinge,
whiche hungrethe ofte soare throughe their fatt feadinge?

(460)

Of this this tyme I will no-more entreate;
by wone woorde the wise perceaue can the whoale.　3215
I doo this mateir but roughlye heere beate:
the disposition, partelye and soale,
o noble kynge, belongethe to youre doale,
as to perceaue the comon-wealthes noyaunce
and for the same to deuise ordynaunce.　　　　　3220

3202 to] *followed by canc.* be

(461)

So that the pooare bee eauer seene vntoe,
the riche hym-selfe will sure saue harmelesse.
A little hynderaunce the poore dothe vndoe,
and can no remedye againste distresse,
but still susteynethe all busynesse.   3225
Thoughe drudges muste bee, yeat Christian loue wolde
that iuste rewarde redownde to them sholde.

(462)

[f. 66ᵛ] Too thresche all daye for peanye haulfe-peanye,
and delue in diches upp to the harde kneeis
for like valure, howe can hee lyue thearbye?   3230
God wote it risethe but to a small feeis:
with that he laiethe vpp hee maye well bye beeis,
and after go begge when age on hym dothe fall,
for noughtes can he saue to helpe hym then with all.

(463)

A laborer trulie doinge his duetye,   3235
as well the woman, I meane, as the man,
let them haue for their traueile worthelye,
so shall they delyte to doo what they can,
els will they loighter euer nowe and than,
comptinge as goode to bee ydle vnwrought   3240
as soare to traueile and profite right nowght.

(464)

So ordre that eache doinge their labour
iustelie and trulie withe most diligence,
may bee worthe them and theirs to succour,
fyndinge them-selfes on shorteste daies sex pense,   3245
and oother lengre, as the soone takethe ascense,
seauyn or eight pense. So shall they bee able
meanlye to lyue, and mayntayne their cradle,

3236 as well] aswell

(465)

and townes let downe to grase sheape vppon
withe dwellinge howses, as fermys and abbeyes,   3250
reduced agayne to habitation,
for lack of which muche lyuynges nowe decayes
and dothe great hynderaunce as this wone waies.
Thowsandis thear bee that right gladlie wolde wedde
if they had holdinges to coauer their hedde,   3255

(466)

[f. 67] **of** journeyemen and seruynge-men also,
withe oother dyuerse of oure owne nation
that nowe a-roauynge in oothers growndis go,
to this royalmys great depopulation,
at whiche the heauyns maketh exclamation,   3260
burdeynynge your Grace by othe that yee haue take
of this, as yee can, redresse withe speede to make.

**Howe a kinge sholde ordre his expensis, howe to retayne,
and wheare to bee free, that althinges bothe in takinge,
kepinge, and spendinge, maye bee done as they owght,
haistie rigour and all oother meanys resemblinge lightnes
and folye to be voyded and set aparte.**

Caput 20.

(467)

[T]hoffice and maner of expensis dwe,
whiche euerye prince ought to respecte,
by right description heere shall ensue,   3265
so well as oure witt can bringe to effecte.
Thoughe withe all plentie a kinge ought to bee decte,
yeat is it goode and requysite perdee,
that althinges sholde in a dwe ordre bee.

(468)

For that behaulfe and consyderation,   3270
to yowe, **Alexandre**, I fyrmelie saye
that what-euer kinge vsethe this fashion
superfluous expensis to flasche and furthe laye

ootherwise then his royalme easelye beare maye,
vndowbtedlye eauerye suche kynge   3275
vndoethe oother, and workethe his owne hynderinge.

(469)

[f. 67ᵛ] **Thoughe** plentie in a kinge ought to appeare,
yeat muste **Discretion** haue the ouersight.
And what plentie is, yee firste muste enqueare,
that thobseruation hathe his office right,   3280
whiche difficulte is, thoughe dyuerse makethe light.
But the mysusinge of largesse indeede
is easie to fynde if yee take not heede.

(470)

If thearfore yee please your selfe tendeuer
the vertue of **plentie** for to acquyre,   3285
consydre your coafers and reuenues eauer,
and what tyme of neade shall chaunce to requyre
the mearites of men that woorkethe your desyre,
in which is ment this prouydent meanynge:
in their fauour to bee sumwhat leanynge,   3290

(471)

meanynge suche as hathe, or heere-after shall,
in your affaires ieoberde goodes and lief,
whois seruice yee ought to remembraunce call,
and shewe your Grace bothe to children and wief
in deadys of pytie euer to bee rief,   3295
cawses aforesaide seene and looked too.
Trulye, suche-wise yee shall prudentlie doo.

(472)

Of princelie duetie yee ought doo no lesse,
suche thinges as yee maye conuenyentlie spare
but to bestowe them of your bountyousnes,   3300
firste, to the symple that indigent are,
and oother suche as your selfe can compare,
woorthie of rewarde their state to sustayne:
suche largesse sittethe a prince souerayne.

(473)

[f. 68] **What** kinge so eauer endeuorethe otherwise,   3305
hee dothe offende and the lawe transgresse
of liberalities leafull practise,
to the disgracinge of his worthynes.
The poore suffringe to departe penilesse,
and to thunworthye to shewe his almys deade: 3310
it is but vayne, it purchesse shall no meede.

(474)

And whoe-so the treasure that hee hathe reached
lanchethe heere furthe without aduisement,
his doinges are worthie to bee appeached,
for thearbye hee shall bee brought incontynent   3315
vnto the shoare of trobles indigent.
Thea[r]fore, I admonysche eache princelie hearde,
superfluouse expensis are to bee fearde.

(475)

For whatsoeuer kinge or emperoure
the goodes dothe deuaste inordynatlye   3320
of his kingedome, ouer whiche hee hathe poure,
or them bestowethe by meanys vnworthye,
suche wone a waister maye bee called aptelye,
a destroyer, a depopulator bothe,
vnworthye to rule: to lye I wolde bee lothe.   3325

(476)

By whiche demeanynge hee maye bee called well
a prodigall persone muche lascyuyous,
bicawse from his dwe hee far off dothe dwell,
the prouydent **Prudence** that makethe kinges famous:
discentinge from her, all goethe contrarious.   3330
To voyde the daungre of all suche owterage,
let **Prodigalité** bee **Reasons** page.

(477)

[f. 68ᵛ] **Thearfore** eftesones to Your Maiestie I saye,
as I haue ofte saide to remembre the more,
that, wryinge from **Prodigalité** awaye,   3335
yee use good **gouernaunce** to purge that sore,
as partelye wee haue mentioned before,
whiche of all kinges the glorye makethe cleere,
by longe contynuaunce of their reigne heere.

(478)

And that doethe ensue when euery suche kinge   3340
withe his propre rentes can holde hym content,
greuous exactions clearlye aduoydinge,
which his **commons** moleste myght or torment:
except great neade of stormys ymmynent,
his royalme to conserue from daungre of conqueste,   3345
then to take ayde wheare it spared maye bee beste;

(479)

other rebellyous to bringe in frame,
to owe obedyence to their souerayne,
or what great cawse els, to furdre the same,
helpe muste bee had, Discretion shewethe playne.   3350
But **howe, wheare, when,** and **of whome** certayne,
let **Wisedom** thearin your Grace aduertise:
so shall yee woorke in moste woorthieste wise.

(480)

If yee use weies your commons to keepe bare,
as vppon them to bee callinge ouersore,   3355
it shall their frayle hartes bringe in suche care,
that murmure maye rise when yee looke leaste thearfore.
If they bee wealthie, your parte is the more,
for what vnnaturall subiecte is hee
that grudgethe his prynce in his necessitee?   3360

(481)

[f. 69] **Greuous** exactions of subiectes taxed
hathe beene the cawse of muche subuersion
of dyuerse royalmys, when princis hathe axed
inordynatlye, to their destruction,
vndre pretence of false seduction,   3365
alledginge cawses for the publike weale,
when it hathe differde frome that a great deale.

(482)

And that hathe happened, wee maye gather so,
thorowe the meanys of superfluous expense,
when that the rentes of assise dothe ouer go,   3370
so, wantinge wealthe to mayntayne their pretence,
then dothe they extorte by powre and violence
their subiectes lyuynges, to season vppon,
whearbye arisethe muche sedition.

(483)

Then dothe the people, at Goddis excitation,   3375
againste suche tyraunys greuouslye arise,
their names in this worlde, to their detestation,
clearlye deleye and vttrelye recise.
And, wheare not Goddis mercye aboue His justice,
piteinge the people to bee so annoyed,   3380
their royalme for eauer weare cleane destroyed.

(484)

Consydre therfore, theis rychesse mundayne
cawsethe in manye the lief to persiste,
whoe, for the same, hathe taken great payne,
that for them and theirs it cannot bee myste: 3385
their rentes and oother charges it dothe assiste,
so that if thearof they bee depryued,
trulye then can they not bee longe lyued.

(485)

[f. 69ᵛ] **Thearfore** aduerte in all dyligent wise,
by all circumspection that maye bee sought,   3390
to spende so and saue that no rumour rise,
but that all suche thinges bee done as they ought.
Honour the woorthye, amende that is nought,
furyous tawlke, superfluous and inane,
repryme and exchue: it breadethe muche bane.   3395

(486)

Euerye iniurye doo not revenge,
vnles it bee heynous not to bee borne:
all small dyssymull, and make no chalenge,
vntill suche tyme your furye bee owte worne.
Flee flickeringe folye that men lawghe to scorne,   3400
then shall this lesson profite yowe so muche
as neauer erste I had moued any suche.

**Of the pité and prouydence of a kinge bothe in aduersité and
againste the same, in mynistringe of charité to the neadye
and penitent, in punishinge of malefactours to thexemple
of oother. And to beeware cawseles of humayne bloode
sheadynge, for the feare of Goddis vengeaunce.**

Ca[put] 21

(487)

[T]he pité and prouydence nowe texpresse
that dothe belonge to a kingis maiesté,
which shall muche garnysche his hie worthines,   3405
bothe towardis God and eauery degré:
firste by **prouydence** hee muste afore see,
by wise aspecte and polecye prudent,
daungers tauoyde of sourges immynent.

[f. 70]   ### (488)

Firste, to consydre what hee hathe in holde,   3410
a kindome of people in numbre not small.
In tyme of plentie hee maye well bee bolde
of theirs to take and liberallye to call.

But after, when **dearthe** maye fortune to fall,
and hathe not by muche, them-selfes to sustayne,   3415
howe shall hee then woorke his royalme to mayntaine?

(489)

Hee wil be fedd thoughe thowsandis perische,
yeat, pité and nature muste in hym meeue
againste suche daungre to caste and accomplische,
that his saide subiectes no suche thinge sholde greeue,   3420
as by wise meanys aforehande to preeue,
of straungers adiacent, or oother some,
to bee in suertie if suche chaunce dothe come.

(490)

And he, agayne, in sembleable neede,
of princelye **pité** them to consydre,   3425
suche foarehande driftes ought in his harte to breede,
daungers tauoyde that so myght chaunce hither,
or in tyme plentyous to gather to-gither
that in necessité myght steade or serue,
rather then for lack his people to sterue.   3430

(491)

If oother affliction bee hither soarted,
and that by mannys helpe ineuitable,
for syn, so sent, from whiche hee was exhoarted,
and wolde not ceasse to bee-come culpable,
let hym not grudge by meanys damnable,   3435
but withe meeke harte to tolerate the same:
to stryue againste God weare woorthy muche blame.

(492)

[f. 70ᵛ] **For** synne wee see muche plages to appeere,
as pestilence, pockes, with agues ardent,
some throughe mysdyet, bothe yondre and heere,   3440
and some by euyl ayre, corrupte and pestilent,
in which afflictions man muste bee content,
all if it doo vppon his owne headde light:
God dothe the great emonge the small ofte smyght.

(493)

Or, what oother els calamytee　　　　　　　　3445
maye chaunce or happe the mynde to moleste,
patience vincethe aduersytee,
as in all daungres the remedye beste:
enemyes moouynge withe mortall meanys preste,
or traytor vntrue, your royalme to bereaue,　　3450
yeat, for all this, still to patience cleaue.

(494)

Beinge assauted withe trobles so saide,
or oother what kinde so eauer they bee,
wrought by mannys meanys, they maye bee downe laide,
obseruynge patience as yee haue herde mee.　　3455
Wisedome moste helpethe in extremytee,
vnight withe patience, colde and discreeit:
so are all enemyes sonest brought vndre feeit.

(495)

So that, what myschefe so eauer dothe rise
againste a kinge or headde gouernour,　　　　3460
arme hym withe patience after this wise,
so shall he conuerte into sweete all sowre.
Euerye thinge is not woone by mayne powre,
nor euerye wronge reuenged at full,
but, vice to punysche, hee maye not bee dull.　3465

(496)

[f. 71] A kinge, indeade, it dothe conuenyate
to bee gentle, pitefull, and meeke,
the wrathe of oother to hym subiugate
for to appeace, some quyet meanys to seeke,
not in his furye to geeue them a gleeke,　　　3470
but to endeauer, withe gladde deuotion,
all meanys tauoyde that cawsethe commotion,

3462 sowre] r over a corr. (apparently an unfinished s)

(497)

and that before it commense anye acte,
for a **commontee** harde it is to staye
when theie togithers are onys compacte,   3475
except wise handelinge their malice delaye.
Thearfore a **prince** muste prudentlie waye
that hee, nor his, occasion sholde geeue
whiche thearunto his **commons** myght dreeue.

(498)

Yeat more againe to a kynge dothe belonge   3480
to knowe his errowre if hee bee fawtie,
and not to persiste in his doinge wronge
but of free harte, discreete and wiselye,
the same tacknowledge and reuoke lightlye,
for the higheste grace that a **kinge** maye haue   3485
is in right ordre his honour to saue.

(499)

When hee knowethe anye thinge to bee doone,
profitable, expedyent and goode,
let hym withe **discretion** complete it soone,
not raschelye in anye furyowse moode,   3490
noather to tractinge, as chowinge the coode,
but, tyme oportune, by **Prudencye** spidde,
to put in prooife so shee it not forbydde.

(500)

[f. 71ᵛ] **If** subiectes sholde their owne myndys ensue
vnyoaked by anye princelye restraynte,   3495
then myght goode ordre bydde farewell adwe,
and the **publike weale** become theare attaynte.
But, þat tauoyde, headde powres maye not wax faynte,
other to haistye or to remyssyue:
let **Reason** woorke their folye to depryue.   3500

(501)

As ouermuche **haistines** dothe confounde,
rather then bylde to perfection dwe,
so to muche **pité** peuyschnes dothe sownde:
the meane betwene bothe is beste to ensue.
Eache **prince** is bownde, his right to rescue,   3505
no **pité** or **patience** that to rebate:
bettre, saithe the wise, betyme then to late.

(502)

The **pité** that a **kingis** harte sholde contayne
is, not to punysche withe extremytee:
thoughe his **offenders** deserue deadlye payne,   3510
yeat **pité** mouethe to shewe **charyté,**
speciallye wheare hee **repentaunce** dothe see,
weyinge in ballaunce of misericorde,
sithe hee of the lawe is bothe **judge** and **lorde.**

(503)

Pyté bredethe **patience,** whiche quenchethe all **ire**   3515
that is accended by passyons colerike,
whiche, in anye, beinge onys set on fyre,
disposethe thinwardis to bee soare and sicke,
moultringe the lyuer like ouer-brent bricke,
withe more inconuenience then I can wright   3520
so soare at the harte it gnawethe and bight.

(504)

[f. 72] Patience, thearfore, is moste soueraigne salue,
rancre to heale that dothe so the **harte** frett,
cawsinge manye wone his lief to vpp caulue
before the date of his dwe dyinge dett.   3525
Let **Disposition** no suche maistrye gett,
but as **Reason,** for healthes preseruation,
shall in your eare geeue determynation.

(505)

Ferdre yeat more of pité to speake,
make searche to knowe wheare **pouertie** dothe reigne; 3530
of that is neadfull their myserye to wreake
do gladlye departe to qualyfie their payne.
Oh, it shall purchesse yowe tenne doble gayne!
All if they bee of forayne cowntreyes borne,
sithe they of man come, take at them no scorne.   3535

(506)

Doo some assigne that honest are and goode,
and can their language speake and vndrestande,
in your behalfe to mynistre them foode
withe oother neadys as geauyn of your owne hande,
of their pouertie subleuyinge the bande.   3540
Suche wise what **prince** dothe heere his seade sowe,
his meryte a-fore God shall greatlye growe.

(507)

Of pité also moste speciallye
bownden yee are the **poore** to respecte,
that in your **warrys** are maymed in bodye,   3545
or, thorowe the same, ootherwise infecte,
withe lyuynges likelye them to protecte.
Sithe they their lyfes for yow ieoberde can,
yee ought no-lesse but prouyde for them than.

(508)

[f. 72ᵛ] One thinge more, o Alexandre, I haue to saye,   3550
whiche to omyt I wolde for no worldys goode:
beware by all meanys yee possible maye
of wronge effusion of humayne bloode.
Doo not vppon yowe in your raginge moode
assume thoffice dwe vnto the highe Godde,   3555
so, beatinge oother, yee maye taiste the same rodde.

(509)

Tauoyde suche kynde of dealinge damnable,
thus writethe the famous **Hermogenes:**
when a creature that is reasonable,
anoother, formed to his owne likenes,   3560
liste by violence his lief to oppresse,
whoe uniustelye suche thinge dothe commense,
the Heauyns of vengeaunce criethe owte for sentence,

(510)

this wise to **God** makinge exclamation,
'O **Lorde**, beholde, a wretche inhumayne   3565
of pompous pryde and hawte elation
vppon hym takethe thy powre to disdayne,
to bee consilimate to Thee, his soueraigne,
in spillinge the bloode of his equall borne,
Thye powre vsurpinge as Thowe weare owte-worne.   3570

(511)

'**Hee** that so sleyethe', thus dothe the case crye,
'let hym like deathe, of Thye **justice,** sustayne,
Thowe that doiste saye, as the **Judge** moste hye,
"Let Mee take vengeaunce: I shall poynte hym his payne".'
So dothe the Heauyns on hym still complayne   3575
till suche offense bee punysched in hell.
This in remembraunce thearfore imprent well.

[f. 73] **Howe a kynge ought to be muche desyrowse too | knowe
thopynyon of his commons towardys hym, by thexploration
of some secreat wittie seruaunte whome he doithe beste
credyte, and thearto accordinge to reforme hym-selfe, that
hee and they may bee in looue togithers knytt as one head
and membres.**

Caput 22
(512)

[S]O sure in this lief hathe none his holdynge
to stande in estate deuoyde of greefes all,
but in some parte he may haue controwlinge   3580
to his exoptation partelye synystrall.

In manye headys manye masinges ofte doithe fall.
Althoughe to some no-deale it doithe belonge,
yeat vayne clatteringe ofte risethe men emonge.

(513)

And owte of doubte their tunges shall walke and chatt   3585
euyn as their heade doithe cheiflye exercise,
be it of vertue, of this vice or that.
Comone rumor thearin will entreprise,
mutteringe, as whoe saithe, in secreat wise,
muche more chalenginge his vicyous factes   3590
then oughtes commendinge his notable actes:

(514)

if hee bee geauyn to carnalytee
besydis his ladye twoe or three to keepe,
'Suche wone vnlawfullye oure kinge keepethe hee,'
dislaudinge hys name, doithe hee wake or sleepe.   3595
Or doithe couetise into his headde creepe,
eauermore callinge his coafers tencroache,
they wylbe tawlkynge to his great reproache.

(515)

[f. 73ᵛ] **Or** bee hee beastlye withe drounkenes oppreste
customablye, whiche odyous weare to heeare,   3600
emonges them-selfes they wolde thearof then ieste,
'Whye not wee drounke, as well as owre heade peeare?'
Or shoulde hee shewe forthe prowde disdainfull cheeare
to thois whiche to hym hath some certayne sute,
as his sorte shewethe so wyll they hym repute.   3605

(516)

Or after this maner: if hee shoulde pretende
a boacherlye beaste, rauenous and wylde,
that hathe delyte dyuyllischlye to contende,
by whome manye are of their right begylde,
dysquyeted sore and cruellye reuylde,   3610
to sett and mayntayne in authorytee,
to their lordys chardge they wolde laye it perdee.

(517)

For hee on his prynce bearethe hym so bolde,
that 'Wee', they will saye, 'dare speake nother stooare'.
Thorowe whiche risethe vpp this true prouerbe olde: 3615
the great thorowe force oppressethe the pooare.
Woorse is his dealinge then the strumpet whooare
for her may they stock and bannysche with shame,
but they are blanked at sownde of his name.

(518)

Sythe better is goode name then golde or treasure, 3620
whiche aboue althinges garnyschethe a kinges reigne,
and that so purelye lyuethe no creature
but some mysdemeanynge the same maye disteyne,
speciallye whois factes maye none restreyne
withoute wondrefull Grace doithe theare consiste, 3625
thearfore this deuyse ys not to bee myste:

(519)

[f. 74] some secreat seruaunte let hym owte espye
that hathe discretion and pregnaunte wytt
to walke abroade in sorte moste secreatlye,
in commone companyes to tawlke and sytt, 3630
and what hee heearethe for-to commende ytt,
other disprayse, to this ende and effecte
that hee maye so walke withoute all suspecte.

(520)

And surely hee shall, o noble kynge, I saye,
of that ys amysse thorowe youre occasion 3635
heeare suche reporte that muche profyt maye
when hee to youre eare shall make relation.
Yee, weetynge thinge worthye of reformation,
and sholde neglecte youre princelye endeauer,
then doe yee vniustelye from justice dysseauer. 3640

3636 muche profyt] profyt muche *marked for reversal by letters* b *and* a
added above in red

(521)

If ytt youre honour personallye ympeache
of this synne or that to your conscience knowne,
no better instruction can youre Grace teache
then to acknoledge suche fawte of youre owne.
All if it hathe in yowe longe season growne,   3645
no synne so sore in the wise taketh place
but hee can extirpe ytt as seruethe the case.

(522)

As in yowre royalme wheare your throne is erecte,
wee haue heere signyfied owre true entent,
so wolde wee haue yowe some wyttie electe   3650
in forayne cowntreyes slylye to bee sent,
to heeare and debate of kynges regyment,
by whiche hee shall gather, I dare bee bolde,
what opinion the worlde of yowe doithe holde.

(523)

[f. 74ᵛ] **For** trulye a prince, what soeauer hee bee,   3655
cannot caste meanys moe then shall suffice
for to vpholde his pryncelye maiestee,
suche instabilité ofte tymes doithe arise,
sometymes thorowe some accustomed vice.
Howe-eauer it bee, when hee the case knowethe,   3660
hee maye it remedye wheare the greeif growethe.

(524)

No-man so wise in this worlde can bee fownde,
but some inconuenience his fame maye blott.
Knowinge the same, muche more hee is then bownde
to stoppe or reforme, that it ferdre growe nott.   3665
As smoake is not seene withoute some fyre hott
so commone Rumor takethe occasyon
to treate and frame his communycation.

3662 No-man] Noman   3663 blott] l *corr. from* r.

(525)

A prince, bee hee neauer so noble of myght,
to herken his fawte it shall hym well become,　　3670
els myght hee bee geauyn into errour quyte,
and ren in hatred of no lyttle some.
Hee that endeauerthe the scoole of wisedome
can bee contented his fawte to heeare tolde
in sorte as it ought, withe termes not to bolde.　　3675

(526)

But, as wee haue heere geauen monytion
men to bee sent in sorte aforesayde,
and hathe thearin had expedition
of thinges neadfull in balawnce to bee wayde,
suche messengers ought not to bee abbrayde,　　3680
doithe his relatyon content or byte,
but his endeauer withe meede to requyte.

(527)

[f. 75] And as the case rehersed shall assigne,
of youre partie or oothers if it bee,
doe yowe by cownsell spedelye inclyne　　3685
to bringe althinge to goode conformyté
that yowe, youre nobles and whoale comontee
maye bee vnyte as membres and wone hedde:
then is that royalme moste happelye spedde.

Howe a kinge ought muche to haue in remembraunce the
highe worthynes of his creation; his sowle, bodye, and
senses, howe theye vnyte in wone globe or mateir, seruethe
eache in his propre office too the furnyture of a perfecte
reasonable creature: þe sowle, hedde maister; the bodye,
his castell; the fyue senses as baylyffes or offycers vnto
the same.

Ca[put] 23

(528)

[A]lexander, my moste redowbted kynge,　　3690
knowe yee, that when the Creatour of all
had to His purpose ordeyned althynge,

Hee formed Man, passinge ymperiall,
withe doatys sundrye, surmountynge the brutall,
bye whiche hee had a certaigne maiestee   3695
to subiecte them to his soueraigntee.

(529)

The same saide Lorde Mannys corps can ordayne
as it weare a cytee fensed all rownde,
in whiche **Vndrestondinge** as cheif soueraigne
had place to gouerne the saide soyle or grownde,   3700
the **fyue Senses** as bayliffes to bee bownde
to Vndrestandinge, withoute cauyllation
to doe their iuste admynistration.

(530)

Whiche is to meane, to the same presentynge
their officies moste necessarye,   3705
bothe of **Seeinge** and also of **Heearynge**,
[f. 75ᵛ] **Taistinge, Feelynge** appropyatlye,
Smellinge also, to sauer thearbye
the goode and hoalsome from the infectyfe,
as posterns to the Sowle Intellectyfe.   3710

(531)

Whiche Sowle hathe state of immortalyté
by consymylation vnto Ens-beeinge,
thorowe the respiratyon of theis thre,
Reason, Memorye and **Vndrestondinge**,
to weeit the weye what ys belongynge   3715
to **justycies** parte proporcyonatlye,
the wronge from the right to seauer and trye.

(532)

By Reason to knowe hee had hys begyn[i]nge
of Cawse cawsinge all procreatyon,
and hathe agayne a hense-returnynge   3720
to seeke elswheare hys habytation,
for **Atropos** shall geeue mynatyon

bye cowrse and custome of hys fate cruell
owre **Mycracosme** from this lief to expell.

(533)

By Memorye thinges in mynde to conceaue   3725
passed, as present in playne apparence,
to caste and conteyne as knowledge grauntethe leaue,
bye maneire impressynge, and sure permanence.
Althoughe eache hathe hys propre dyfference,
Reason, Memorye, and **Intellectyon,**   3730
one withoute all cawsethe ymperfectyon.

(534)

Vndrestondinge hathe this soueraigne grace:
to feele and perceyaue the substaunce of thynges.
Reason geauethe judgement in euerye case,
whither agaynste or withe **justice** it wrynges,   3735
[f. 76]   moste needefull of place in all noble kynges,
bycawse yt fallethe theyr mynysterye
in their **officies** to traueyle daylye.

(535)

For whoe-so hee bee that them abusethe,
hys fame dysgracethe of noble estate,   3740
and for that hee them suche-wise refusethe,
a beaste brutall men maye hym nuncupate.
Hys deadys then ragethe far illicytate:
nothinge more odyble can bee trulye
then man vnmanlye to become beastlye.   3745

(536)

Specyallye, the myghtyer thowe arte,
set in degree ouer oother to reigne,
the more greater of them ought to bee thy parte,
sythe theye include all polecye humayne.
Wheare wantethe **Reason,** feoble is the brayne.   3750
And lyke so, **Reason** withoute her dwe vse
is as treasure in a muckehyll tencluse.

(537)

As theare bee graces infused in man,
so bee theare graces acquysite, no naye,
some moe, some lesse, as prooif well prooue can,   3755
geauen by Nature, the fyrste, as wee saye,
thoother, by studyous industrye alwaye.
The more withe eyather whoe so doithe abownde,
the more to gouerne suerer is hys grownde.

(538)

Whoe theis gyftes hathe abundantlye so,   3760
and doithe confownde them by fowle abusyon,
not vsynge them as **Reason** wolde to doe,
hee hathe them, then, to hys owne confusyon.
For what can bee a more illusyon
to hym that ys withe **Reason** heere indude   3765
[f. 76ᵛ] and leauethe **Reason** as thearof destytude?

(539)

Concludinge thea[r]fore my meanynge in thys,
moste worthye **Emperour,** pondre youre parte,
what noble workynge by God in yowe wrought ys
freelye by His moste perfecte dyuyne arte,   3770
not bought or gote in anye mundayne marte
but, as wee haue sayde, from the Cowrte Superne.
Doe not thearfore theis graces prowdelye sperne.

(540)

Confownde not **Reason** by madde immanyté,
or weyes sensuall furyous and nought.   3775
Brydle the breathynges of **Sensualyté**
by **Reasons** rayne, sithe shee knowethe what beste ought.
Vndrestande also, and peyse in youre thought,
betweene goode and evyll thyndyfferencye,
and chuse the beste, to lyue honorablye.   3780

(541)

Marr not youre **Memorye** withe muche meatynge,
surfeites, or suche inordynate crapull.
Beastelye bancatynge, drynkeinge and eatynge,
that **needefull freende** dothe dampnyfie and dull,
whearuppon suethe the myndys sore trobull,   3785
forgettynge matiers expedyent to frame.
Knowinge the dawnger, whoe recketh not is to blame.

Howe a kynge ought to bee ware of all maner thynges that
myght in anywise maculate hys conscyence, for the mercyfull rewarde hee doith aspecte at the handys of God,
thorowe His benygne goodenesse, for hys juste admynys-
tration in his pryncelye offyce and gouernaunce heere.

Caput 24

(542)

[I] **Synge** of kynges this solempne idyome,
or idiograph, whyther yt bee sayde.
Although yt procede froe mee, moste rude mome,   3790
to traueyle it styll I holde me well apayde.
Emonge matiers manye heere shalbe layde
a matier muche compendyous and meete
to bee consydered of nobles dyscreete.

(543)

The some thearof this wise I shall vnfolde   3795
to yowe, moste nobleste of noble men all,
wearinge the dyademe and crowne of golde
thorowe thys royalme of reigne imperyall,
that yee wyll vouchesauf to remembraunce call
youre woorthye estate in full effecte moste stronge,   3800
what to the same in eache parte dothe belonge.

(544)

Fyrste, in honowre howe yee doe heere excell
the whoale orbe of your domynation,

Heading to Caput 24: His] H *with contraction-sign normally standing for* -es
3802 howe] e *indistinct*

and are a persone, as yee doe wote well,
pryuate and publyke in estymatyon.   3805
For pryuatlye yee haue coronation
withoute compare, the publike weale to see,
and yee protected of your commontee.

(545)

Sythe suche highe honour your Grace dothe ensue,
all men to yowe to kneele and to bowe,   3810
yee must adorne yowe withe godlye Vertue,
whoe cawsethe Honour to florische and flowe
as parte supreame, I am bolde to tell yowe.
For **Vertue,** wheare shee extendethe her grace,
before **Honour** eauer chalengethe place.   3815

(546)

Honour heere maye bee feared and obeyde
withe salutatyons dwe to the same,
but in the Hyghe Cowrte it is not so weyde:
[f. 77ᵛ] abbreachement maye bee, bye some kynde of blame.
Vertue cheiflye settethe furthe Honours fame,   3820
whoe vntoe her, successe of thinges foareseene,
subiectethe **Fortune** as her maistresse or queene.

(547)

In whome so **Vertue** dothe predomynate,
and hathe hymselfe knyt to her in alyaunce
fyrmelye foreauer, non to cancellate   3825
his saide godlye and faithfull affyaunce,
let hym neauer passe for mannys annoyaunce,
other the Dyuyllys, capytayne of all myscheif:
Vertue vtterlye expellethe all greif.

(548)

Thearfore, Alexandre, to yowe I wryte,   3830
withe all cyrcumspectyon keepe and defende
thy moste noble sowle and angelyke spiryte
to yowe deputed to the prescrybed ende,

as **Hermogenes** cownsell dothe pretende,
that by synnes vsage and fowle enormytee　　　　3835
it bee not brought to beastis difformytee.

(549)

But rather that shee by youre woorkinge sage
bee withe Vertue garnysched and endecte.
Whiche, if yee so endeauer your courage,
when yee this worlde shall clearlye reiecte　　　　3840
emonges the heauenlye yee shalbee electe,
in the Presence moste excellent to name,
to Whois symylytude hers shewethe the same.

(550)

If by youre neglygence and mysdemeanour
shee bee difformed ootherwise then soe,　　　　3845
shee shalbee downe throwne to payne and dolowre
[f. 78]　voyde of all p[l]easure, neauer to parte froe.
so **Vice** shall peryshe and **Vertue** shall goe
in estymatyon æternallye sure
withe the heauynlye in glorye to endure.　　　　3850

(551)

For, knowe yowe certaynlye, o noble kynge,
that Godde nothinge made vacuat or in vayne
in the creation of his dyuyne workeinge,
but althinges to an ende, perfecte and certayne,
of cawse probable, as Hee liste tordayne:　　　　3855
then, if yee sholde dyfface that Hee hathe wrought,
so maye your honour to dishonour bee brought.

[Manuscript breaks off without completing the page]

3847 voyde ... pleasure] voyde ... preasure (sine spe placendi Deo B132)

APPENDIX A

X

JENKYN GWYNNE

THE translating into the Englische tonge of the Epistle which Aristotiles wrote to the greate Emperor Alexander, intitlede, **De conseruatione sanitatis,** and owt of an Arabique booke called

Tyrocaesar

translatede into the Latyne by one Joannes Hispanus, a famous cleark.

1569

From *Wellcome Medical Historical Library MS. 71*, fols. 2–22

To the Right Honorable Syr Wa[lter] Myldmay, Knyht, [f. 2]
Chauncellour of the Maiesties Highe Courte of Escheaquer.

To the Right Honorable Syr Wa[lter] Myldmay, Knight, [f. 3]
Chauncellour of the Quenes Maiesties Highe Courte of Es-
cheaquer, and Threasurour of the same, one of Her Highnes 5
most Honorable Pryueye Counsaill, your humble orator,
Jenkin Gwynne, one of the particuler Surueyours of the same
Courte, and Seruante to the Right Honorable Earle of Penbrok,
Lorde Stewarde of the Queenes Highnes most noble householde,
wishith continuall healthe, longe lyeffe, with increase of honor. 10

Sundry occasions do move me to salute your honour withe this, the
argumente of my good will, of whose goodnes I haue tastede more then
20 yeares nowe paste; neyther did passe any one yeare syns, but such as
ministrede vnto me good cause to aknowlege hit with all obsequye and
seruice; yea, the leanger I do lyve, the more I remaine bounde to re- 15
taine the same in good remembraunce. And whear the protestation of an
inferior, whiche otherwise cannot yelde the recompens, may be taken
for mere fflatery, howe then may one of my sorte shewe himself a
gratfull rememberer of beneffytes, but by some outwarde signe or
token. Iff, therefore, I had your Honors ffurtherance, I cane declare hit 20
in perticularities, and a greter falte it were to fforegett then to aknowe-
ledge the same.

19 rememberer] remembrerer   21 a *inserted above line*

[f. 3ᵛ]　Your late sicknes, Right Honorable, offerede me the occasion | to aquite my sellf, bothe of debte and duetye. For vnto the sycke eache counfortable woorde ys a probable remedye. And, vppon this grounde, I ffell to examyn withe my self howe I might perfforme my long de-
5　syrede affecte towardes Your Honour. And loo, among certaine odde bookes I ffounde writtyn in an olde texte the transcrypte of the Epistile which Aristotiles wrate to the greate Emperor Alexander, in-titlede, **De conseruatione sanitatis,** and owt of an Arabique booke callede **Tyrocæsar** translatede into the Latyne by one **Joannes His-**
10　**panus,** a famous clearik. Hyt muche encoragede me to geve the ad-venture in the translating of the same into the Englishe tonge, vppon this ffull truste, that Your Honor, adornede with a mylde surname, wolde with myldenes and affabilitie dayne to accepte the good lore of Aristotiles, thoughe offerede by the symple and ignorant.
15　Therunto also ys addede some thing not ympertynent to the matter, as by the sequeale dothe appere. And, ffynding that nothing in earthe doth ensample man more lyvelye to the ymage of God then dothe the **præscience** and foreknowlege of thinges yet to come, and that man, taking pleasure therin, ys neuer satisfiede vntill he do acheve his owne
20　Centre, whiche ys God, as hit ys writtyn, **Sic enim homini manci-pantur terrestria, fauent Cælestia, quia Cælestium, et terres-trium, uinculum est et nodus,** I have therefore in the later ende
[f. 4]　hereof wryttyn | of the destruction of the Sea of Rome, of the defection and revoulte against the Empyre, spoken of by the holy Apostle [2]
25　**ad Thessalonii Caput 2,** of the commynge of Antichriste, off the libertie and conuersion of the Jewes, of some other mysteryes in magik naturall, and fynallye of the peryode of periodes, that ys, the laste ende of the woorlde, wherin Your Honor shall see sundry probable coniec-tures, and reasonable authoritie touching the sames: and the processe
30　of the matter dothe shewe that I am but a gatherer of other mens woorkes: the aucthoritye ys theirs, the credite and dyscredite ys theirs whose woordes and sentences I alledge, the order and ymperfection I do chalenge for my portion. And withall, my paynes were the more, in that my desire was greate, and my arte oversleander, to deale with so
35　wightye a cause, and withe so honorable a counsaillour as yow bee.
Thereffore the matter I do present vnto your woorthynes as a con-fusede chaos: Your Honor cane fframe the bodye and substaunce thereof vnto some proportionable quadrature: and hit ys true that ther ys not
39　writyn so yll a booke but hit ys woorthe the readinge to some ende or
[f. 4ᵛ]　other. And hit ys also expedient to geve sometymes eare to the | vn-

5–6 *in margin* Epistola Aristotilis ad Alexandrum magnum　　7 Epistile]
Epistitle　　21–2 *in margin* Homo vinculum omnium rerum et nodus
25 *ad Thessalonii,* Caput 2] *in margin, again,* 'Ad Thessalonii' 2 of Antichriste]
of *ins. above*　　29 sames] *form intended perh.* same

learnede; and hit were the parte of the writer not to write, rather then
the reader not to reade, specially whear a ffole differeth not from a wiseman whiles he vsithe scilence.

Vnto Your Honor, and to none other, I have writtyn: vnto Your
Honor I committe the correction of my writinge, and thexposition of my   5
syncere meaninge, which was to preserve your healthe by good diete and
the readinge of pleasaunte and woorthy coniectures, touching the
matters before remembrede. And of Your Honor I most humbly crave
pardon for my boldnes. **Et si aliquid in hoc opere imperfectum
inueniatur, humanæ imperfectioni deputetur, nec ideo quod**   10
in eo utile erit uituperetur.

Hec enim, propter unum male dictum, bona sunt uituperanda,
neque propter unum bene dictum sunt mala laudanda : quan-
doque enim uiĝilat Tharsites et dormitat Vlyxes.

Your Honors most humbly   15
at commaundemente
1569

Jenkyn Gwynne |

O Alexander, Monarche and Emperoure of the vnyuersall woorlde,   [f. 5]
consyder that as touchinge your bodye yow are corruptible as other men   20
bee. And by reason of whote and colde humors yow ar subiecte to meny
incomodytyes, ffor the advoydinge whereof I have determynede to
wryte vnto Your Grace certaine rules vearye proffitable and necessarye,
drawen ffrom the seacreate of Nature, and the bowelles of Phisycke,
and whiche maye contente Your Grace, syns hit ys not honorable for   25
so mightie a Prynce to make all his greffes and deceases knowen to any
phisicien. Yff therfore Your Magnyfycence doo observe this dyscypline
and example, Your Grace shall not nede the phisicien, excepte when
casuall woondes which require surgerye do happen, and therin also
may healpe.   30

I beseche Your Grace therefore that, ymediatly when yow do arise
from your sleape and naturall reast, that yow ffaill not to walke and
to kyme your heade, and withall to extende and streache your membres.
For the extention of membres dothe cause strength to the body, and the
kymmynge of the heade drawethe furthe the fumosytyes and vapors   35
which whiles yow sleypte ascendede from the stomake to the heade.

Then I do notyfye that hit is holsome to wasshe your handes in

---

1 and hit] and *ins. above*   25 not] *ins. above*   34 extention of mem-
bres] *in margin* Extensio membrorum   36 sleypte] *final five letters over*
erasure, and unclear. In outer margin, sleypte *repeated, with asterisks in text*
and margin as guides   37 is holsome] *ins. above*

sommer withe colde water, ffor colde water constraynethe the naturall
heate to remayne in his natyve place, restrayninge his commynge
ffurthe, whereby a more better appetyte to dayly meales ys sturrede
4 and excitede.

[f. 5ᵛ]   Then consequently, hit ys a pryncypall rule to be clothede | withe
ffyne and honnorable garmentes, ffor suche do gladde the mynde, and
the nutrytyve vertewe takethe pleasure in the bewtie and vse of robes.

I require also that yow doo rubbe your teathe and jawes withe whote,
plesaunte, and aromatick rootes, whose propertys are to drye vpp the
10 rawe and moist humors. For such rootes doue proffite muche, do
counfforte the teathe, cleanse the mouthe, raryfye the ffleugme, make
the tonge more diserte, the voice more shrill, and ffynally doo sturre
good stomake and appetyte.

Also to incence and fume into the mouthe and nosethrilles suffumiga-
15 tions answerable to the season of the yere, ys very necessarye for the
preseruation of healthe. For by suche meanes the closures and rystes
of the brayne are oponede, the armes maide more stronge, the neacke
more fatte, the fface more bewtiffull, the senses more quicke, and consequently whore and whit heares, which be accidentes of olde aege,
20 are staide and kepte backe.

And pursuante herevppon, the vse of swete oyntementes ys agreable
vnto Nature. For by good odours the mynde ys reffreasshede, and the
soule of man being therby counfortede, causethe the bloode to joye and
rynne in-to all the vaynes, to the counforte of the membres, wherunto
25 yow muste adde electuarye of rubarbe and aloys: therby fleugme ys en-
forcede from the mouthe of the stomake, the heate of the bodye ys excitede, wyndes ar expulsede, swete breathe and good taste ar inducede.

[f. 6]   Then | to sytte withe the noble and wise, and to treate of wisdome
and vertewe, answerable to the tyme and place, to vse the accustomede
30 houres at meales, withe a moderate exercise to the bodye, are commendable, and very naturall for the preseruation of healthe. For thereof
meny commodities do springe, to the helping of nature, as wynd-
breches, heate of the stomake, the closing of the ligatures in the body,
the dissolution of superfluous humors, and, ffynally, the digestion of the
35 meates, whiche do descende in-to a boilling and a whote stomake.

And for a pryncypall rule I warne Your Grace to have respecte and
good regarde to the differences of meates servede at your table: to
begynne therefore your meale withe one good disshe of light digestion,
ys allowable, but to make commyxtures of meny sortes of meates, grosse

---

1 *in margin* vsus aquae frigidae ad manus lauandae   6 *in margin*
pulchra indumenta prosunt   9–10 *in margin* fricatio dentium prodest
16–17 *in margin* suffimentum laudatur   31 ff. *in margin* Diaeta secundum
Ciceronem est ea pars medicae, quae uictu morbos curat: Ad At[t]i[cum] 56,
sed ego diaeta curari incipio.

and ffyne togethers, ys not to be allowede, specially the vse of grosse
meates after fyne meates, but rather the grosse meate ys to be receavede
ffurst in-to the bottome of the stomake, for the bottome of the stommake,
beinge so nere the lyver, ys of more heate and streangthe then the vpper
parte of the mouthe of the stomake, and therefore makethe an equallitie 5
in the digestion.

And forgett not in any wise to staye from eatinge whiles yet the
appitite dothe partly remayne, for superfluytye of meates doth | make [f. 6ᵛ]
narrowe the passage of the stomake, and the meate remayninge in the
bottome of the stomake ys not digestede. And in like maner beware 10
overmuche drynkinge and carrosinge, and drynke no waters vppon
meates, exceapte yow have vsede so to doo: for water after meates
coolethe the stomake, quenshith the naturall heate, confoundethe the
meate, and dothe ingender ympedymente in digestion, then the whiche
nothinge ys more pernicious to the healthe of man. But if the heate of 15
your stomake be suche that yow cannot refraine from the drynking of
water, in such extreamytye lett the water be colde, and drynke a small
quantitie thereof. And ffurthermore, after dyner to laye downe vppon
a conveniente softe couche, and therevppon temperatlie to reste, and to
take a swete nappe, ys not against the rule of phisick; but to sleape be- 20
fore dynner wasteth the bodye and makethe hit macylente and leane,
and dryethe vppe the bloode and naturall moisture: so, sleape after
meate reffreasshithe and doth noorisshe hit.

And amonge the nombre of which naturall preceaptes, marke that at
no tyme yow doo ingorge one meale vppon another, but rather refrayne 25
from eatinge vntill the stomake be purgede and well emptiede of the
formor meates receavede, which yow shall perfitly knowe by your
appetyte and by the subtillitie of the spettell | descendinge in-to the [f. 7]
mouthe: whiche dyete iff yow will negleacte, and ffall to your vittaill
contrary to this dyscyplyne, then your meate shall fynde the naturall 30
heate ffrosen; but contrarye wise, iff yow do vse your meate at neade and
withe appetite, then the meate which yow do take shall fynde the
naturall heate a kyndlede ffyre. Therefore as yow ought not to eate
witheout appetite, no more ought yow to refrayne from meate when
that yow have desire there-to. For by such abstynence the stomake 35
shulde be fylled with yvell humours which he drawethe from the
superfluetyes of the bodye, and therby the brayne ys troblede of a most
wickede vapor, and the stomake maide rawe, in sort that he cannot doo
his naturall offyce.

24 which] wᶜʰ: *conceivably error for* these   34 no more] nomore   *in mar-*
gin Abstinentia nocet   38 vapor] *written over an erasure of which the latter*
portion is still visible. In outer margin vapor *is repeated, with an asterisk over the*
word in the text, and another preceding the marginal repetition

And having by these ffewe preceaptes prescribede an order of dyete
vn-to Your Magnificence, ther ys yet vntouchede a due consideration to
be hade to the ffoure seasons of the yeare, **Vær, Æstas, Autumnus,
and Hyems.** Therefore like as **Vær,** whiche we call the springe, ys
5 whot and moist, and therby the ayre ys temperate and the blood sturred,
even so meates of that complexion, and agreable to that season, ar
conveniente to be eaten, as chikyns, quaylles, newelaid eagges, withe
the wilde leatise callede of the Latynes **Scariola,** and goates mylke,
[f. 7ᵛ] and no tyme more conveniente to leatt bloode. | **The motions of the
10 Bodye, withe the vse of Venus, purgations, bathinges, laxes,
spicede and artificiall drynkes,** do well accorde withe thys season,
the springtyme. And whatsoever errors do happen by meanes of formor
medicines, the spryngtyme, thrughe his humydytye, for the more parte,
dothe quallifye and resarciate.

15 Then **Aestas,** whiche wee call Sommer, ffoloweth, by nature whote
and drye. In this season reade **Colera** ys ingenderede. Beware, therefore, duringe that season, from all thinges that be of whote and drye
complexions, whiche are theese: muche heate, whote drynkes, but
speciallie surffeates, ffor thes before remembrede do queanshe the
20 heate naturall. Also duringe all the sommer, suche meates must be
vsede that are of colde and moist complexions, as veale, vinegre,
cowcumbres, feadde chickyns, and suche fruetes that ar sowre in taste,
as crabbes and pomegranates, withe the like. And during the sommer
season **Dame Venus** may be sparede, and licencede to beholde her
25 glasse, or myrror, by which priuilege she may pamper herself for the
winters seruice.

The sommer ones endede, **Autumnus** presentethe hymself in-to the
theatre, withe his colde and drye complexion, sturringe vppe blacke
Colera, an Impe of his owne generation. During all this season, eate
30 no coloricke meates. And, in especiall, **Venus, purgations, and
bathinges** are most inconueniente. |

[f. 8] For therby may yow the better receave winter withe his colde and
whorye blastes, whiche by nature ys colde and [moist], in whiche
season, touchinge your meates and drinkes, the diete ys to be alterede
35 alltogethers. For in wynter your meates ought to be of whote complexions, as pygyons, fleasshe of the male kynde callede of the Latynes
Carnes castratiuæ, pyping whote, and rather rostede then boyllede,
fygges, nuttes, good claret wyne, and whot electuaries. Purgations and

5–6 *in margin* vaer durat a medio Martii usque ad medium Junij.   8
Scariola] *repeated in margin*   15 *in margin* Aestas du[r]at a medio Junij
usque ad medium Septembris   27–8 *in margin* Autumnus durat a medio
Septembris usque ad medium Decembris.   28 colde] *partially rubbed out*
33 moist] *drye*   35–6 *in margin* Hyems durat a medio Decembris usque ad
medium Martij

laxes ar not conueniente, neither bloode leattinge, **but in cases of extremities. But Venus, for feare of her mallice, and doubte of her frowninge aspecte, may be well admitted and reclaymede.** And the more meate may be eaten withe the leasse dangier, because digestion ys stronge.　　　　　　　　　　　　　　　　　　　5

Adde thereunto joye, myrthe, and solace, ffor honor, and hope of glorye, joyned withe musycall harmony, the reading of good bookes, the vse of ffayre garmentes, and good company, doo make ffatte, counfforte and moiste the bodye. But to eate litle, to drinke muche, longe watche, sulphureous bathes, ofte leatting of bloode, overmuch **venerye,** 10 **feare, and heuynes,** do drye and make weke the bodye.

Beware, therefore, o **Alexander,** most victorious prynce, from thees forebooden thinges, and observe the formor preciouse rules and admonitions, and with all circumspection preserve the heate naturall. For as longe as temperate heate is within man, and that humiditie 15 excede not measure, | man ys in perffitt healthe. For by these twoo the [f. 8ᵛ] naturall heate ys reffreasshede, and vndoubtedelye the lyeff of eache lyvinge creature ys prolongede. Man, therefore, waxethe olde by twoo maner of meanes, the one naturallie, proceding of drynes, which destroithe and conquerethe nature, the other accydently, that ys, by in- 20 fyrmities, and dothe procede of most wickede causes.

I ffounde, Right Honorable, a pece of the said epistill Englisshed by some auncient learnede man, whose name I colde not fynde, whiche I thought good to place here for the more clere vnderstandinge of Aristotiles mynde. The copie was ffalsiffiede and corruptede by the 25 iniquitie of tyme, which at leangethe drawethe all thinges withe hit in-to the doongion of Obluuion. And the said verse, conteigning the said epistle, doth ensue in this maner:

Naturall philosophers assented all in one . . .

　　　[This is line 1240 of the rime royal version of the 'Secretum 30 *Secretorum' written by John Lydgate and Benedict Burgh, and published by Robert Steele, under the title 'Secrees of Olde Philisophres' as no. 66 of the Old English Text Society (1894). From here to f. 16 Gwynne gives his version of the section of this poem which deals with hygiene and corresponds to his prose translation of the Hispaniensis tract. This section* 35 *runs from l. 1240 to l. 2016: up to l. 1491, the work is Lydgate's, and thereafter, Burgh's. Gwynne omits the following lines: 1254–60, 1282–8, 1293, 1286–1449, 1492–1589, 1634–5, 1649, 1674–80, 1716–29, 1772–*

---

3 reclaymede] *unclear in body of text, first five letters over a corr.;* reclaimede
repeated in margin, with asterisks in text and margin as guides　　29] *preceded,
as last l. of text of f. 8ᵛ (not written in position of catch-phrase, by the words*
Naturall philosophers &c.)

1820, 1856–1904, and 1982–95. There are some dozen Latin marginalia, a few of which constitute glosses, while the remainder are indications of the subject discussed in the text: Gwynne then concludes with a Latin aphorism, as given below, and resumes his own contribution.]

[f. 16]   **Naturae assecla medicus.**

6   And nowe, Right Honorable, having endede the Epistill in prose, and also in verse, wherin the matter ys to be considerede more then the obseruation of the trowe nombre of sillables, hit may be said that those verses ar not rare, but comon, and therfor not woorthy to be presentede

10   vnto your honnour, **quia nihil praecl[a]rum est, quod idem non sit rarum.** To that I answere for my parte, I do fynde the said verses very auncient, and also rare, full of pithe and syncerytye, and therfore not to be reprovede, syns peradventure the Martilog also cannot shewe the like of his owne invention.

15   Also a ffurther question may growe, whither any man cane at all tymes observe the before-remembred and prescribede dyete, and, if

[f. 16ᵛ]   not, than wrate | **Aristotiles in vaine.** Therunto I say, that the obseruation of the said rules must nedes be very necessary and proffitable for mans healthe. Albeit I do graunt that hit were over-greate a taske

20   for eny man allwayes to be tiede to suche obseruations, wherin marke what **Roger Bachon the frere wrate in his book 'De admirabili potestate Artis et Naturae', thus:**

Est impossibile, ut sanitas regatur in omnibus sicut exigit regimen sanitatis, mediocritate, quia neque diues, neque

25   **pauper, neque sapiens, neque incipiens, nec ipsi medici quantumcumque perfecti, possunt hoc regimen in se nec in aliis perficere. Sapientes tamen uias excogitauerunt, non solum contra defectum regiminis, sed etiam contra corruptionem parentum, non ut reducatur homo ad uitam Adae, seu Artephij,**

30   **sed ad centenarium annorum, uel plus, in vita prolongetur, et passiones senectutis retardarentur, ultra estimationem humanam.**

Whiche tendethe to thus-muche in effecte, that wisemen have founde within the lymites of nature reasonable means to kepe an vnyformitye

35   in mans body. And that accordithe well withe the difinition of philosophy and phisick. Thus:

Philosophia est sapientiae studium diuinarum humanarumque notitia. Philosophia est eorum quae sunt et uidentur, et eorum quae sunt et non uidentur certa comprehentio. Et phisica

40   **est de natura causis et effectibus, et accidentibus corporis naturalis mobilis scientia.**

---

10 praeclarum] praeclurum   23–4 *in margin* Ro[gerus] Bachon[us]
24 mediocritate] mediocrietate   37–9 *in margin* Philosophia quid

Then by good consequence hit ffolloweth that philosophy and
phisick tende to a certaine knoweleage of naturall effectes, causes, and
accidentes of mans bodye. | But experience doth teache vs that ther [f. 17]
be certaine sycknes whiche our phisiciens do pronounce to be incurable,
as the leapre, the ffawling sycknes, the inveterate goute, and the like, 5
and therefore the formour difinition ys ffalse. But that may not be
grauntede, for the ymperfection ys not in the science, but in the ignorant
phisicien, whiche ffawlling to practise before he become an absolute
theoricien, omittethe to searche out and seeke the kyrnell, sappe, and
sparme, whiche ys hydde in the philosophers tree. Against whom 10
Arnaldus Nouauillanus dothe with open mouthe exclame in this
maner ffollowinge:

Reduxit me fortuna in medium, et in eo inueni tres doctrinas
principi dignas, quarum una docet aequum ab iniquo, iustum
ab iniusto, discernere, alia docet sanum in sanitate regere, et 15
egris reddere sanitatem. Et hec inuenitur in libris scientiae
medicine, licet imperfecte, et ideo sequentes eius operationem,
propter illius doctrinae defectum, et intellectum occultum,
errare sepissime consueuerunt.

Loo, Right Honorable, how Arnold (whom Chauser in the Chanons 20
Tale callethe the greate clerck) ys not affraid to accuse our phisiciens
of ignoraunce, affyrm[i]ng further that the certaintye of phisyck was
never sett furth by writing in sorte as may be vnderstandede by every
student, or by any one amonge a thowsande, wherunto agrethe Aristotiles thus: 25

Esset fractor sigilli caelestis, qui com[m]unicaret secreta
naturae et artis, et multa mala sequ[u]ntur eum qui reuelat
secreta, etiam rerum minuit maiestatem, qui diuulgat mis-
tica. 29

And agayne our | countreyman saithe that In pellibus caprarum et [f. 17ᵛ]
ouium non traduntur secreta naturae, ut a quolibet intelligan-
tur: Whereunto Raymunde doth agree as followith:

Pauci perueniunt ad notitiam rei talis quia medici et philo-
sophi nostri temporis nichil faciunt nisi pecuniae desiderio,
quare Deus nequaquam hoc uult illis conferre. 35

Many of the like testymonies might be vouchede out of auntient
and newe writters, were hit not a thing over-superfluous, to stande
vppon the proffe of that whiche daylye experience teachethe vs. The
philosophers doo therefore all conclude that ther ys lefte of God

10 philosophers] *prec. by* phisol *crossed through*   15 *f. in margin* Arnaldus
in sua epistola 'De accidentibus senectutis et senij'   22 affyrming] *only five
minims between* r *and* g   26 *f. in margin* Aristoteles in libro Secretorum.
30 our countreyman] *in margin* Ro[gerus] Bachon[us]   33 *f. in margin*
Raymundus, dist[inctio] prima libri sui de quinta essentia

amonge men one heavenly medycine, whiche prolongethe mans lyef,
and dothe preserve hit from all deceasses, and from the tokens and
messengiers of olde aege, vntill the tyme appointed of allmightye God,
whiche no man canne passe, as ys wryttyn, **Constituisti michi ter-**
5 **minos, quos preterire non possum. Breues dies hominum, et**
numerus eorum apud te est. Then hit were a ffantastycall thing to
seke perpetuation to mans bodye, whear as ther ys no healpe or meane
to reskue any from the ffynger of God, as the heathen theymself do
confesse:

10   **Mors etiam saxis marmoribusque venit.**

And nowe, again, to the better proffe of this necessary and most
vndoubtede medycyne. **Diascorides hathe thes woordes : Possibile**
est, ut sint medicinae aliquae, quae prohibent hominem a
[f. 18] **uelocitate senectutis, et frigore et siccitate membrorum, ut | per**
15 **illud elongatur uita hominis.** And also Haly Regalis, in Libro de
operationibus simplicium medicinarum, Canone 2 : Est una
medicina que ponit et diuidit omnem complexionem ad partem
quam meretur. The noble Englisshe philosopher **Joannes Gar-**
landius, whiche lyved Anno Domini [12]40 was not ignorant thereof
20 when he wrat in this maner:
Est quadam aqua uitae summe rectificata, quae conseruat
corpus, et contra omnes infirmitates est curatiua, et huic aquae
nichil est extraneum appositum, sed omnes eius amouentur
superfluitates, vincet omnem rem subtilem, et omnem rem
25 **solidam penetrabit.**
And of this mynde was **Hypocrates** in his aphorismes, wher thes
woordes ar:
Est etiam quoddam caeleste, quod ipsum medicum preuidere
oportet, cuius si tanta sit gratia prudentiaque, fit admira-
30 **bilis, nimiumque stupendum, rerum periculum prohibebit, et**
salutem competenti adminiculo administrato, tollerabilius
facit.
And **John Damascene, in his book of symple medicines, hath**
a lyke conclusion thus as followeth : Nulla querenda est causa,
35 **nisi a Caelo,** calling thys medicine **Caelum** by reason of the purenes
thereof. Wherunto **Raymunde** bearethe the like witnes:
Et haec medicina (saith he) futurum periculum a corporibus
euitari potest, quia omnem corruptibilitatem, ex qua infirmitas
prouenire solet, expellit, et humores inequatos equat, preterea

---

12 Diascorides] *margin repeats* Diascorides   15 *in margin* Haly Regalis
19 1240] 4040   21–2 *in margin* Garlandius Anglus   26 *margin repeats*
Hypocrates   33 *in margin* Joannes Damascenus   38 *in margin*
Raymundus

admirabilis est sapientia magistri hanc naturam cognoscentis,
quia, cum hac natura talia opera in medicina faciet, quae
miracula uideantur.

And Plynye dothe make | mention that Octauian the Emperour de- [f. 18ᵛ]
maundede of a certaine olde man, whiche was very aegede in yeares 5
and very yonge to the sight and apparraunce of men, howe he pre-
servede hymself, and his answere was, 'Posui oleum exterius, et
mulsum interius', by which woordes he ment the medicyne nowe
treatede of. And so the great clerck Arnolde expoundeth the said
woordes as followith: Hic sermo occultam habet interpreta- 10
tionem. And a lik recorde we do ffynde, that in the tyme of King
Ostus, king of Scicilia, a certayne laborer, dygging in the ffelde, founde
a golden vessell withe a certaine lyquor in hit, whereof he drank, and
thereby was restorede to his fformor strengthe, and woonderfully
alterede in mynde and bodye, and, being a heardeman, was appointed 15
one of the kinges offycers.

The noble Prynce Barnarde, Earle Frauerense, had the vse of
this dyvyne medycyne, as he hymself dothe reporte by thes woordes
ensuinge:

Hac medicina usus sum in caducis, hydropicis, hecticis, pti- 20
sicis, colicis, lientericis, melancholicis, et omni denique morbo,
quod longum esset recensere, et nunquam credidissem hanc
medicinam habere tantas uirtutes, nisi uidissem et probassem.

And Euonimus writethe that of late at Padua, not ffarre from
Venetia, ther was founde an earthen potte having vppon hit wryttyn 25
this hexasticon in maner and fforme ensuinge: |

Plutoni sacrum munus ne attingite, fures: [f. 19]
ignotum est uobis hoc quod in urna letet.
Nam elementa graui clausit digesta labore,
vase sub hoc modico, maximus Olibius: 30
adsit fecundo custos sibi copia cornu,
ne premium tanti depereat laticis.

And ys thus Englisshede by an Oxforde man:

This sacred, theues, ware that ye touche not:
Vnknowen hit ys unto you all, this that ys hydde in potte. 35
For the elementes hath upshut, digested with many payne,
In this small vessell, the great Olibius certayne.
Plentye with the frutefull horne, as a garde be thow present,
Least the pryce perryshe of this liquor most excellent.

1 magistri] ins. above   4-5 in margin Plinius   15 heardeman] man
ins. above   15-16 in margin Baiulus regis factus est ex bubulco   20-1 in
margin Barnardus Comes Frauerensis   27 in margin Euonimus   30 maxi-
mus] for Maximus: see n.

2550 C74   N n

And within that potte was a litle potte, withe the inscryption hereafter
ffollowinge:

    Abite hinc, pessimi fures:
    uos quid uultis cum vostris oculis emissitijs?
5   Abite hinc, uostro cum Mercurio petasato caduceatoque:
    Maximus maximo donum Plotoni hoc sacrum facit.

Thus Englisshede:

Away from hens, ye mightye theues, trudge elswher and goo bye:
What seke ye with your espeynge eyes? why doo ye pore and
10   prye?
Hens with your hatede Mercurye, and with his rode also:
Thys ys sacrede, by the greateste, vnto the greate Ploto.

    And hit were over-tedious, and also nedeles, here to sett furthe
what **Bartholomeus Amantius, Hemolaus, Democritus, Ap-**
15 **pianus, Trismagistus, Merlinus, Socrates, Plato, Thrytemius,**
[f. 19ᵛ] **Paracelsus, Agryppa, yea, and all the rowte** | of the philosophers
do wryte touching this matter, and againest whom ther do not want
some yonglinges whiche do ympugne, and infferre suche small knowe-
lege they have, and frame this argumente: **Quicquid aliud conuer-**
20 **tendo mutat, eundem mutari necesse est.** As, for example, wee
do norrishe our bodyes by eating and drinking: likewise, by eating and
drynking wee do destroye the same invisiblye and vnknowen vnto vs,
by the meanes of the vnequall natures of the sustynance we receave.
And againe this ys another of their maximes: **Continua resolutio re-**
25 **quirit continuam reperationem:** otherwise, saye they (whose
iugementes ar most ffallible) wee were ymortall. For healthe ys nothing
elles but a good disposition of the bodye, by the whiche the same bodye
dothe or suffrethe some **action or passion** naturall vnto hyt, without
any notable greffe. For dyvers men haue dyvers complexions, and hit ys
30 not possible to ffynde twoo men in all the woorlde of one equall complexion **secundum gradum totaliter.** Then hit ys consequente that
dyuerse men do want dyuerse regymentes, and this ys gathred out of
Galene, whose woordes ar these: **Cum enim regimen sanitatis fit**
34 **per similia, et si complexiones diuersorum hominum sunt dif-**
[f. 20] **ferentes, oportet quod per huiusmodi** | **differentiam conseruen-**
tur. Then howe cane hit be that one medycyne shulde be curatiue to
all men, to all aeges, and for all deceasses? This invyncible argumente
and **Gordians** knotte may be thus easelye answerede, and that **sine**
puluere as the proverbe goithe: **Vnum simile, additum sibi simili,**
40 **facit maius simile, et nulla res quae non habet inclinationem ad**

---

    11 his] *ins. above*   15 Thrytemius] *for* Trythemius   28 naturall]
over canc. notable   31–2 *in margin* Galenus 3 regni

consimilem rem, conseruari potest per consimilem rem. Then,
if any one substaunce or nature hathe contrarye operation, and dys-
posithe himself according to the matter that he ffyndithe, and ys diver-
siffyede according to the nature of the patient, the fformor argument ys
quite overthrowen. As, for example, the sonne, by his heate, mollifiethe 5
waxe, and makethe the claye harde, yet the proper acte of the sonne ys
but one, and woorkethe in the obiecte whereunto he ys infusede. I
persuade therfor that this medycyne I meane ys elevated into such
symplicitie and purenes, and hathe appetite to this or that complexion,
and ys to be maid of the 4 elementes, as did **Olibius,** and in him 10
actiuely the 4 elementes ar with all their actes settlede respectiuelye, as
in the **eye of the basilisk.** And as the heaven dothe powre vppon vs
sometymes colde, and sometymes heate, drynes, and humidytye, so
dothe this medycyne, by appleynge vnto hit certaine | hearbes, stounes, [f. 20ᵛ]
and mineralles whiche be the proper starres of this hevenlye medicine, 15
and which dothe augmente the vertue of every symple ioynede vnto hit
in **millecuplo,** a thousande-ffolde. Quia **qualitates primas, siue
elementa prima, quae a naturali sym[m]etriam deflectuntur, et
actiones labefactas, humoresque peccantes, et corruptionis
causas, siue internas, siue extrinsecus incidentes, ad naturam** 20
suam reducit. For **Aristotiles** saythe that the elymentes of naturall
thinges in their owne centres are most pure. Therefore, take from theym
their **heterogenall** partes, whiche they have **per accidens,** then the
most pure **homogenall** parte, that ys the **sperme, sperite, and soule**
of theym, will remayne. Then, to conclude, **the philosophers medi-** 25
cyne ys only a multiplication of naturall heate in a durable and permanent substaunce. And by this tyme I trust that the fformor grave
argumente of our comon scolemen ys more than answerede.

Then hit dothe rest to knowe how to come by this medycyne, and
whereof hit ys maid, elles hit may be said that all the fformor comenda- 30
tion may seme to be but a heape of ffrutles woordes, for **Principium
et medium** allway is **propter finem tantum, et spes premij
solatium est laboris.** Theunto this shalbe myne answere:

I was neuer no expert iueller, with suche matters to putt my-
self in prese : 35
With philosophers myne eyne were not clere, nether withe
Plato nor Socrates,
Excepte the prynce, Arystotiles, of philosophers, to Alexander [f. 21]
kinge
Wrate of thes secreates the greate maruaill and woorkinge. 40

5 sonne] *prec. by canc.* sinne   *In margin* qualitas solis   12 *in margin* oculus
basilisci.   And] *repeated*   21 *margin repeats* Aristotiles   25-6 *in margin*
Difinitio   32 allway is] *in italics, like preceding and succeeding Latin phrases*

Notwithstanding, touching my sinceritie, I will not be nyce to ymparte
vn-to Your Honnor what the aforenamede **Arnolde** dothe declare,
and that the matterialles are ffounde in the bowelles of the earthe,
adding further that all the secreates dothe consist in the preparation
5 thereof. And I swere that **Quicquid queritur, inueniri potest in
spermate Solis et Mercurij tantum.** Studye thereffore aboutes the
preparation, and be assured that hit is **donum Dei,** the whiche God of
His mercies graunte vnto yow, and then shall yowe be more then
Aristotoles **felix.** And this Your Honnor may take for the ffurst pryn-
10 cipall:

Vnusquisque nascentium, a progenitore suo trahit famula-
tum demonum, sicuti humanam naturam. Et hiis expulsis
virtute sancti ba[p]tismatis, per fidem Christianam, et stu-
diosam orationem, sanctum spiritum aduenire certissimum
15 est. Et quicumque hanc impetrauerit gratiam, futura preui-
det, et prescientem euadet, Deo propitio. Nam humanam
scientiam reddit crebra meditatio, et exercitatio meliorem
scientiam, eamque uero que gratia Dei conceditur, quia mens
quidem spirituali intellectu potita, perfecte purgatur. De
20 prouidentia et iuditio, apud temetipsum exerce sermones, et
studij materiam memoria retine, et tale quiddam Sanctus
Bernardus de so ipso testatur. Nullum denique tempus magis
[f. 21ᵛ] se perdere, | dixit, quam quando dormierit, et propter suam
magnam abstinentiam ad cibum accessit quasi ad tormen-
25 tum. Quicquid de sacris scripturis dedicerat, maxime in siluis
et in agris meditando et orando hauserat, nec alios se habuisse
magistros, quam quercus et fagos fatebatur. Et preterea consimilem habemus testimonium de illo Sancto Anthonio quem
Constantinus Imperator unice amabat, litteras uero neque
30 sciebat, neque mirabatur, sed potius mentem bonam litteris
antiquor[u]m, et laudabat et predicabat ueram namque
beatitudinem in Dei cultura. Dicebat, et itaque docebat,
oportere quemlibet animam purgare suam, quo posset in-
spicere, et futurorum notitiam possidere, Deo uero huius-
35 modi prescientiam declarante. Idem Anthonius Didymum
quondam Alexandrinum, eundem caecum, hijs magnificis
consolatus est uerbis : Nil te, in quid offendat, o Didyme, quod

3 and] *ins. above*   5–6 *in margin* The spearme of golde and quycksiluer
7 is] *ins. above*   11 *ff. in margin* Calodaemon bonus angelus: 'calon' est 'bonus';
'daemon', id ist 'sciens'   13 baptismatis] babtismatis   15 *ff. in margin*
Cacodaemon malus angelus, quia 'cacos' est 'malum'   18 conceditur] *prec.
by canc.* cons.   21–2 *margin repeats* Bernardus   28 *in margin* Anthonius
31 antiquorum] antiquiorem: *possibly for* antiquioribus   35–6 *in margin*
Modus peruveniendi ad omnes scientias.

carnalibus oculis uideris orbatus, desunt tibi oculi illi, quos
mures et muscae habent : sed letare, quia habes oculos quos
angeli habent, per quos uidetur Deus, per quos magnum tibi
scientiae lumen accenditur.

And ffynally, Right Honorable, make not comon the secreates of 5
nature, but note the woordes of God to **Esdras, libro 4, capit[e] 14,**
thus : **Scripti sunt autem per quadraginta dies libri quatuor et
ducenti, quibus quadraginta diebus peractis, locutus est
supremus hijs uerbis : Quae prima scripsisti, in propatulo
propone, et dignis et indignis legenda, sed ultimos septuaginta** 10
**seruabis, quos doctis popularium tuorum tradas, in hijs enim
ingenij uena, sapientiae lumen et scientiae fons inest.**

Proffane not therfor | the mysteryes of God, least yow make your- [f. 22]
self, by your owne negligence, **not capa[b]le of the grace that our
Sauiour Chryst most frely doth offer. Quia nec oculus uidit, nec** 15
**auris audiuit, nec in cor hominis ascendit, quae preparauit
Dominus diligentibus se, Cui sit laus, honor et dignitas per
omnem aeternitatem. Amen.**

Finis

---

3 magnum tibi] *prec. by canc.* tibi   6 *in margin* Esdra lib[ro] 4,
Cap[ite] 14   14 capable] capaple   17 dignitas] dignitatas *with some sign
of alteration through erasure, expuncting and writing-over.*

APPENDIX B

XI

THE 'WALWYN' VERSION:

ARISTOTLES'S SECRET OF SECRETS
CONTRACTED

Printed for H. Walwyn, 1702.

1520 = Achillini recension of *Secretum secretorum* as printed Paris, G. de Pré, 1520

[p. i] ARISTOTLES's / Secret of Secrets / Contracted; / Being the Sum of his Advice / TO / *Alexander* the Great, / About / The Preservation of Health / and Government. / Formerly Translated out of the / Original **Greek** into **Latin**, and di-/vers other Languages, and being /
5 very scarce, is now faithfully ren-/dred into *English,* / *For the Good of Mankind* / [line] / LONDON, / Printed for *H. Walwyn*, at the three Legs in / the *Poultry*, 1702.

[p. iii] **The Bookseller to the Reader.**

THE following Treatise in my Opinion hath justly merited a rescue
10 from Obscurity, on two the most considerable Accounts. First, the Credit of its Author *Aristotle*, a Person so famous for many Ages throughout the whole learned World; that to name him is to tell what he was, and forbids me the needless attempt to say any thing of him. Secondly, the Excellency of the matter contain'd therein, which singly
15 consider'd, is enough to recommend it (as divers Authors have done, particularly *Bacon* of Old Age) and what methinks should have given
[p. iv] this Discourse a | place in the Volumes of the rest of the Author's Writings, which, for what Cause I know not, is not to be found, either there or in its Original Greek Language; being for a long time since
20 (as far as I can find) to be found only in a somewhat barbarous Latin Translation, or in an *English* Abstract, but sorrily translated into now obsolete Language. Which Abstract coming to the Hands of a real Lover of Mankind, who now gives it a Resurrection from its obscurity, did discover so much Excellency under all its blemishes, and a Design
25 so well agreeing with his own, *the Good of Mankind*, that he could not

be satisfied till he had with some Trouble and Charge got as near the
Fountain as he could, viz. the *Latin* Edition of *Paris 1520*: the *English*
printed at *London 1572*, he found to be out of Print, and that the
Latin was not be bought or seen (as far as he could find) any where
but in the *Bodleian* Library at *Oxford*, and with one Gentleman 5
in *London*, who was pleased to give him the perusal of it; by which
he had not only the means to supply his Abstract, which | was not [p. v]
compleat, but to see with how little Judgment the old *English* Grapho-
chymist had attempted to separate the Quintessence of *Aristotle*'s
Instructions to Alexander, leaving out some things very material, 10
and putting in others not much to the purpose, and even missing
the true sense of the Author in divers places. Whereupon he soon
resolved with himself to make a new Translation and Abstract of
the most excellent Counsel of the greatest Philosopher to the greatest
King, which he knew would be of the greatest Advantage to what- 15
soever Prince and People in general, who shall observe it as to the
Government of the Body Politick, and to every Man in particular, who
shall follow these Rules as far as they are of general Concern, in preserving the Health of the Body Natural. I know it is not common for
Physicians to be very sedulous in teaching Mankind how they may 20
preserve their Health, and thereby prevent their advising for its Re-
covery; yet the Publisher from a generous Philanthropy, willing to
serve the World as well in the Preservative, as in the Curative part of |
Physick, gives this publick Specimen, of what he has been more [p. vi]
privately used to desire, and do for the Head and Body of his beloved 25
Country. And I will be bold to say, how little soever this his Gift may
seem, had it been received according to the intent of the first Author, or
shall it be us'd according to the desire of the present Restorer, *Alexander* might in all probability have died an aged and lamented Governour
of happy Subjects, and any other Prince may live the desire of a Healthy 30
and Blessed People. And wheresoever the Bodies Politick and Natural
shall be govern'd according to these Rules, the churlish and ungrateful
Remedies of Statesmen and Physicians shall have but little or no use,
because there will not be easily found a diseased State of either Bodies
to work upon. 35
　　That which *Alexander* seems to have desired of *Aristotle* was some
of the great Hermetick Secrets, if not the grand Aurifick Elixir which
that Philosopher was as likely to be Master of as any, but seems un-
willing to discover to his Pupil, | probably judging it might be abus'd [p. vii]
to serve his Ambition, and which perhaps might be a great cause of his 40
excusing his Absence. But thinking it not prudent positively to deny
the Request of so great a Prince, he tells him he hath said enough to
him Enigmatically, and under a Veil; which indeed seeming abundantly

more abstruse than many other things written on that Subject, it was
not thought fit to trouble the *English* Reader with it any more, than
with some other things not so directly relating to the better design of
Aristotle, and the Author of this Abstract. Yet this I must say for that
5 noble Philosopher, he hath given his Scholar a Lesson as much better
than the communication of the great Hermetick Secret, as moral Riches
are than natural, and Eternal than Transitory. And had he only given
the Rules of preserving the Health of the natural Body, so necessary to
all the due Purposes of this mortal Life; they are more precious and
10 eligible than all the Remedies even Chymists boast of for the recovering
[p. viii] the damages of indulg'd Debauches, the most | common Causes of
Diseases. But I will no longer withhold my *English* Reader from the
Legacy the antient *Greek* Philosopher hath left him by the hands of
a Modern *English* one, wishing him as much Profit in the use of the
15 Treasure, as I had pleasure in reading over the Will, I must call it,
of both of them. |

[p. 1]   **The Introduction.**

WHILST *Aristotle* lived, *Alexander* became Potent, by the Observation of his wholesom Counsel, and by keeping his wise Precepts. He
20 subdued Cities, and triumphing, got to himself Kingdoms, and held
alone the Monarchy of the World; and his Fame was heard in all
Parts, and Nations subjected themselves to his Command and Empire;
nor was there any People that durst resist him in Word or Deed. Now
when he had subdued the *Persians*, and made their Nobles Captives,
25 he directed a Letter to *Aristotle*, after this manner. |

[p. 2]   **Alexander to Aristotle.**

Excellent Master, and teacher of Justice; I signify to your Wisdom,
that I have found in the Land of *Persia*, certain Persons having great
Reason, and penetrating Understandings, studying to rule over others,
30 and to get the Kingdom; whence we have propos'd to put them all
to Death. Signify to us by Letter what you shall think right in this
matter.

                    Aristotle to Alexander.

'IF you are able to put them to death, in this the Power is in your
35 Hands, and then you cannot slay them for the Kingdom. If you can
change the Earth, the Air, the Water of the Land, and also the Disposition of the Cities, you shall fulfil your purpose. But will you rule over
them with Goodness, hear them with Benignity? Which if you do, I
[p. 3] trust, with the Help of God, they will be all sub-|ject to your Pleasure

35 and then . . . Kingdom] . . . in hoc propter regnum, tamen non poteris
occidere terram *1520: see n.*

and Command; and for the Love they will have for you, you shall rule
them with Triumph in Peace.'

Alexander therefore having received this Letter, followed his Counsel
diligently, and the *Persians* were more obedient to his Government than
all other Nations.   5

Aristotle to Alexander.

GLorious Son, and just Emperor, God confirm you in the way of
knowing the path of Truth and Vertue, and repress in you brutish
Lusts, and confirm your Government, and enlighten your Understanding to his Service and Honour. I have received your Epistle honour-   10
ably, as becomes me, and I understand that you have a Desire that I
should be with you personally, and wonder that I care but little for
your Business: For this cause I have determin'd to make a Rule for
your Clemency, which shall be | a Book to weigh all your Actions,   [p. 4]
supplying my Place, a certain Rule to all that you desire, and what I 15
should teach you, if I were present with you: Therefore you ought not to
blame me, when you know, or should know, that I refuse not to come to
see your spreading Glory, by reason of Contempt, but because the un-
weildiness, and weakness of my Body hath made me incapable of Travel.
The thing that you have asked, and desire to know, is such a Secret   20
which human Understanding can scarce bear. But as to that which
becometh you to enquire, and is lawful for me to discourse of, I am
bound to answer, as you are obliged by the Debt of Discretion not to
require me to teach you more of this Secret than I have deliver'd to you
in this Book; which if you shall read attentively, and understand, and
shall fully know what is contain'd in it, I undoubtedly believe that 25
there shall be no hindrance between you, and what you desire to know.
But this is the Cause wherefore I figuratively reveal the Secret to you,
discoursing with you in Examples, *Enigmas*, and Signs, because | I [p. 5]
fear, lest the Book should come into the hands of Infidels, and into the
power of the Proud, and so the Divine Secret should be disclosed to 30
them, whom the most High hath judged unworthy; so should I be
a Transgressor against the Divine Grace. Know therefore, that he that
reveals Secrets brings many Misfortunes upon his Neighbour, from
whence he cannot be safe: Therefore the Lord keep you and me from
the like, and from every dishonest Deed. After all I put you in mind 35
of that wholesom Document, which I have always been us'd to explain
to you, and to inform your Noble Soul; and this shall be your Comfort
and salutary Mirror.

It behoveth therefore every King of necessity to have two Helps
sustaining his Kingdom: the one of them is strength of Men, by which 40
his Government is defended and fortified, and this cannot be had, but

when the Ruler rules among his Subjects, and the Subjects likewise obey
their Ruler; as by the Disobedience of the Subjects the Power of the
[p. 6] King is weakned, and the Subjects rule. And I will tell you | the Cause
from which the Subjects are induced to obey their Ruler; and this
5 is twofold, Extrinsick and Intrinsick: I have lately told you the Extrinsick, viz. That he dispense his Riches to them wisely, and exercise
his Bounty, by rewarding all according to their Merits. And with all
this, it behoveth Kings to have another Caution, of which I will make
mention in what follows in the next Chapter, of Riches and Aids. The
10 other is to bring their Minds to Operations; and this precedes, and is
in the first Degree; but this second has two Causes, one Intrinsick, the
other Extrinsick: The Extrinsick is, that the King exercise Justice
about the Possessions, and Mony got by the Subjects, sparing and
having Mercy. But the Intrinsick Cause is the secret of the Philosophers,
15 and Rulers, whom the glorious God hath fore chosen and endowed
with Knowledg. And I give you this Secret, with some others which
you shall find in divers Titles of this Book; in which you shall find ex-
trinsically great Wisdom and Learning, but intrinsically the final
[p. 7] Cause | intended is contained; for there is your Principle, and final
20 Purpose. When therefore you shall perceive the significations of the
Sayings, and the Mysteries of the Examples, then you shall fully and
perfectly attain your Desire. The most Wise and Glorious God therefore enlighten your Reason, and give you Understanding to perceive
the Secret of that Science, that you may deserve therein to be my Heir,
25 and faithful Successor, by his Help who gives his Riches abundantly to
the Souls of the Wise, and to those that study the Grace of knowing; to
whom nothing is difficult, and without whom nothing can possibly
be had.

Of the manner of Kings about Liberality and Covetousness.

30   THERE are four sorts of Kings; a King liberal to his Subjects, and
liberal to himself; a King covetous to his Subjects, and covetous to
himself; a King covetous to himself, and liberal to his Subjects; a
[p. 8] King liberal to him-|self, and covetous to his Subjects. [The *Italians*
say that it is no Vice in a King if he be covetous to himself and liberal
35 to his Subjects.] The Indians say, a King covetous to himself is good:
The Persians affirming the contrary, and contradicting the *Indians*
and *Italians*, said, A King is good for nothing, who is not liberal to
himself, and his Subjects. But in my Opinion he is the worst of them,
and to be rejected, who is liberal to himself, and covetous to his Sub-
40 jects, by which the Kingdom will be soon destroyed. It behoveth us
therefore nicely to enquire of those Virtues and Vices, and to consider

9 next Chapter] *see n.*

what Liberality is, and what Covetousness, and where lies the Error
of Liberality, and what Evil follows the want thereof; for it is plain,
that these Qualities are to be disapproved, when they depart too much
from the Medium; and we know, that the Observation of Liberality
is hard, and the Neglect of it easy; and it is easy for any one to be 5
Prodigal and Covetous, but hard to be Liberal. If therefore you will
acquire the vertue of Liberality, consider your Ability, the Times, Neces-
sities, and Deserts of Men; you ought therefore to give your Gifts |
according to your Ability, with measure, to indigent and worthy Men: [p. 9]
He that gives otherwise sins, and goes beside the Rule of Liberality, 10
because he that gives to those that do not want, has no Praise; and he
that gives not in due time, is like one that sprinkles salt Water on the
Sea-shore. And whatsoever is given to the Unworthy is lost; and he that
gives his Wealth beyond measure will soon come to the bitter shores of
Poverty, and is like one who always gives himself a prey to his Enemies. 15
The King therefore that gives of his Goods in a time of Need to Men
in want, is liberal to himself and Subjects; his Kingdom shall prosper,
his Commands shall be obeyed; such a King the Antients praised; such
a one is said to be vertuous, liberal, and moderate. But he that wastes
the Goods of his Kingdom on the Unworthy, and those that do not 20
want, he is a destroyer of the Commonwealth, and a spoiler of the
Kingdom, and unfit for Government; whence he is called a Prodigal,
in as much as his Wisdom is alienated from the Kingdom. | But the [p. 10]
name of Covetousness does much dishonour a King, and is not be-
coming Kingly Majesty. If therefore any King hath either of those Vices, 25
Covetousness, or Prodigality, if he will consult his own Interest, he
ought with all Diligence to provide a faithful discreet Man, chosen out
of many, to whom he should commit the management of the Affairs
of the Commonwealth, and the keeping the Treasure of the Kingdom.
O *Alexander*, I tell you verily, what King soever shall superfluously 30
continue his Gifts beyond what his Kingdom can bear, such a King
without doubt will be ruined, and ruin his Kingdom. I tell you therefore
again, what I never omitted to tell your Clemency, that the avoiding
Prodigality and Covetousness, and the acquiring Liberality, is the
Glory of Kings, and the Continuation of Kingdoms; and this comes to 35
pass when a King abstains and withdraws his hand from the Goods
and Possessions of his Subjects. Whence I have found it written in the
Precepts of the great Master *Hermogenes*, That Charity is the | chief [p. 11]
and truest Virtue; and that abstinence from the Mony and Possessions
of the Subjects is the Understanding of the highest Law, and a sign of 40
Perfection in a King. This was the Cause of the Destruction of the
Kingdom of the *Calculi*, that the superfluity of the Expences exceeded
the Revenue of the Citys; and so the Revenues failing, the Kings seized

the Goods and Revenues of others; and the Subjects, because of the
Injury, cried unto the High and Glorious God, who sending a destruc-
tive Wind, afflicted them vehemently; and the People rose against them,
and utterly ras'd their Name from the Earth: and unless the Glorious
5 God had helped them, and had sent what he did, the Kingdom had
been utterly destroyed.

Know therefore, that Riches are the cause of the Duration of the
animal Soul, and are part of it; and it cannot continue such, if such a Life
be destroyed. Therefore it is necessary to beware of the superabundance,
10 and superfluity of Expences: And that Temperance and Liberality
[p. 12] may be acquir'd, foo-|lish and superfluous giving is to be avoided:
It is likewise of the substance of Liberality and Vertue to omit, and not
enquire of hidden Secrets, nor to call to mind the thing given: And it is
of the nature of the Good, and the substance of Vertue, to reward the
15 Deserving, and to forgive an Injury, to esteem the Honourable, to help
the Simple, and supply the Defects of the Innocent; to answer those
that salute you, to hold your Tongue, to dissemble an Injury for a time,
not to know how to feign foolishness. I have taught you what I always
used to teach you, and implant in your Mind. I would therefore be
20 confident that that teaching shall be in your Deeds, a Light always
shining, and a sufficient Knowledg to govern your self by all the days
of your Life; which ought to suffice in all your Works in this World,
and in that to come. |

[p. 13]   **Of the final Intention of Kings.**

25 KNOW therefore that Understanding is the head of Government, the
Health of the Soul, the Conservation of Vertues, an intuitive Mirror;
for in it is beheld the things to be avoided, by it we chuse the things
to [be] chosen; it is the origin of Vertues, the root of all good, laudable,
and honourable things. And the first instrument of Understanding is
30 the desire of a good Report; because he that desires a good Report will
be famous and glorious, and he that does not so will be confounded by
Infamy. Fame therefore is that which is principally, and by it self
desir'd in Government: for Government is not desir'd for its own sake,
but for a good Report. The beginning therefore of Wisdom and Under-
35 standing is the desire of a good Report, which is got and acquired by
Rule and Dominion. If Dominion or Rule is acquired or desir'd for
some other Reason, there will be no getting of Fame, but of Envy, and
[p. 14] so Envy be-|getteth a Lie, which is the Root of things to be disapproved,
and the matter of Vices. A Lie begetteth Detraction, Detraction be-
40 getteth Hatred, Hatred Injury, Injury begets Obstinacy, Obstinacy
Anger, Anger Resistance, Resistance Enmity, Enmity begets War, and

18] stulticiam stulti fugere [*v.r.* fingere] et ignorare: *B* 45/7f. *and n.* 2: *see n.*

War dissolves Laws, and destroys Cities; and this is contrary to Nature, and that which is contrary to Nature destroys all. Study therefore, and love the desire of a good Report; for Reason, by the desire of a good Report, brings forth Truth, and Truth is the Root of whatsoever is laudable, and the matter of all good things: for it is contrary to Fals- 5 hood, and begets the desire of Justice, and Justice begets Confidence, and Confidence Liberality, and Liberality Familiarity, and Familiarity Friendship, and Friendship begets Counsel and Help. And by this it was that the Earth was settled, and Laws made for Men; and on this account it agrees also to Nature. It appears therefore, that the desire of 10 Rule for a good Report is durable, good, and laudable. |

Of the Evils which follow carnal Desire. [p. 15]

O *Alexander*, avoid the desire of brutish Pleasures, for they are corruptible; for carnal Desires incline the mind to the corruptible Pleasures of the bestial Soul, without any Discretion; and there is a 15 rejoycing in the corruptible Body, and the incorruptible Understanding is grieved. Know therefore, that the desire of bestial Pleasure begets carnal Love, carnal Love Covetousness, Covetousness the desire of Riches, the desire of Riches Immodesty, Immodesty Presumption, Pre- sumption Infidelity, Infidelity Robbery, Robbery Reproach; from 20 whence comes Captivity, which leads to the detriment of the Law, and the destruction of Familiarity, and the Wretchedness of the whole Body; and this is contrary to Nature. |

Of the Wisdom and Religion of a King. [p. 16]

IT is first, and principally convenient for a King, in as much as 25 pertains to himself, that his Name should be famous for laudable Wis- dom, and that he reason wisely; because thence he shall be praised and honoured, and he shall be feared by Men when they see him eloquent in his Wisdom, and acting prudently in his Affairs. Moreover, it may be easily known whether Wisdom or Folly rules in a King; for what King 30 soever subjects his Kingdom to the divine Law, is worthy to reign, and to rule honourably: But he that makes the divine Law serve, subjecting it to his own Rule and Command, is a Transgressor of the Truth, and a Contemner of its Law. But he that contemns its Law shall be con- temned of Men; for he is condemn'd in Law. But I will say what the 35 wise Philosophers, speaking divinely, have said of the Reli-|gion of [p. 17] a King; That in the first place it becomes Kingly Majesty to obey legal Ordinances; not in feigned Appearance, but in evidence of Fact; that all may know that he fears the high God, and is subject to the Divine Power. Then Men are wont to reverence and fear the King, when they 40 see that he reverences and fears God. If therefore he shews himself to

be Religious only in appearance, and in his Deeds is an Evil-doer (and
it is hard to conceal his wicked Works, so as they shall not be known to
the People) he shall be reproved of God, and contemn'd of Men, and his
Deeds shall be infamous, and his Empire shall be diminished, and the
5 Diadem of his Glory shall be dishonourable. What shall I say more?
there is no Price, no Treasure that can redeem a good Report. Moreover,
it becometh a King to honour the Law-Makers, to reverence the Religious, to raise the Wise, and confer with them, to move doubtful
9 Questions, honestly to ask, and discreetly to answer; and to give more
[p. 18] honour to the more Wise and No-|ble, according to what becomes the
State of every one.

Of the Prudence of a King.

It also behoveth a King to think of things to come, and prudently to
provide for future Chances, that he may more easily bear adverse things.
15 It also becometh him to be Pious, to restrain Anger, and the commotion
of his Mind, lest an unwary Commotion proceeds into act without de-
liberation; and to acknowledg his Error reasonably, and wisely to recal
it; for it is the greatest Wisdom in a King to rule himself. And when a
King sees any good or profitable thing to be done, let him do it with
20 Discretion, not too slowly, nor too hastily, lest he seem negligent or
rash. |

[p. 19]   ## Of the Silence of a King.

O *Alexander*, how fair and honourable is it in a King to abstain
from much Speech, unless Necessity require it; for it is better that the
25 Ears of the people be always desirous, than weary of his words: for their
Ears being weary, their Minds will also be weary, nor will they much
care to see him. Also it becomes a King not much to frequent the Company of his Subjects, especially of mean Persons, because too much
Familiarity breeds contempt of his Honour; and for this the *Indians*
30 have a good Custom, in the disposition of their Kingdom, and Ordina-
tion of their King, who have ordain'd, That their King shall appear
publickly but once a Year in his Royal Robes, and with the armed Host,
sitting on his Chariot in very fine Armour, the People standing at a
distance, but the Nobles and Barons about him; and then he uses to
35 dispatch great Affairs, to avoid various and pressing Events, to shew
[p. 20] the Care and Pains he | hath faithfully taken about the Commonwealth.
He uses also on that day to give Gifts, and a Goal-Delivery of smaller
Criminals; to relieve great Oppressions, and to do many pious Works.
The Speech being ended, the King sits down, and then there arises one
40 of the Princes by him, who is reputed the most Wise and Eloquent, and
makes a Speech to his Honour and Commendation, giving thanks to

37 Goal] *see n.*

the glorious God, who hath so well ordered the Kingdom of the *Indians*, and hath honour'd his Country with so wise a King, and hath confirm'd the honest, unanimous, and obedient People of *India*. And after he hath praised and commended the King, he turns himself to the Praises of the People, in commemorating their good Manners, in receiving Benevo- 5 lence, inducing them by Examples and Reasons to Humility and Obedience, and to reverence and love the King; which being done, the whole People study to extol the King's Praises, to commend his good Works, to pray God for his Life, to declare his Deeds and Wisdom 9 thro | their Cities and Families; and for this cause they teach their [p. 21] Children from their infancy, and induce them to love, honour, obey, and fear their King; and by this means the Fame of the King is pub- lish'd, and increases in private and publick. They use also at such a time to punish the Malefactors, and wicked Persons, and to put some to death, that the more presumptuous may be hinder'd from hurting, and 15 the rest amended. They use also at that time to lighten the Taxes, to dispense with Merchants, to remit part of the Customs to them, to defend and preserve them with their Merchandizes; and this is the cause that *India* is very populous: For thither Merchants come freely from all Places, and are well received, and the rich and poor Citizens 20 and Courtiers get gain; and thence it is that the Royal Tributes and Revenues are increas'd. Therefore you ought to beware that you injure not, nor offend Merchants; for they are the spreaders of Praises, and publishers of mens Fame over all the World: to every one therefore 24 is to be given that which is his due; | for so the Cities will be strengthned, [p. 22] and Revenues multiplied, and the Kings Honour and Glory will in- crease; so will his Enemies tremble, and be restrain'd, and the King will live peaceably and safe, and so he will attain his Desires.

What a Man ought to desire.

O *Alexander*, covet not that which is corruptible and transitory, and 30 that which you must soon leave; seek incorruptible Riches, an un- changeable Life, an eternal Kingdom, and a glorious Continuance: Direct therefore your Thoughts to good, always render yourself venerable and glorious; shun the ways of Lions and brute Beasts in their Uncleanness; be not cruel and inflexible, but spare those whom you 35 have conquer'd: think of future things, and cases that may befal, be- cause you know not what the Day to come may bring forth. |

Of Chastity.   [p. 23]

Do not follow your desires in untimely Banqueting, Drinking, Whor- ing, and much Sleep. O gentle Emperor, do not incline to lust after 40

---

11 honour, obey] *no punct.* (*at end of line*)

Women; for Lust is a property of Swine. What Glory will it be to you, if you exercise the Vices of irrational Beasts, and the Acts of Brutes? Believe me without doubt, that Whoring is the destruction of the Body, a shortning of Life, the Corruption of Vertues, a transgression of the
5 Law, makes a Man effeminate; and lastly, it brings the Evil which we have foretold.

Of avoiding too much Laughter.

IT also becomes a King, amongst other things, to be discreet, and to abstain from too much Laughter, because frequent Laughter makes
10 a Man disesteem'd. Moreover you ought to know, that a King is more
[p. 24] oblig'd to | honour Men in his Court and Country than elsewhere; for then he is amongst his own. If any one does an Injury, he is to be punished according to the Quality of his Person, that others may fear and learn to abstain from Injuries: a noble and high Person is to be punished,
15 after one manner, a mean Person after another. It is good to be grave and sober, that there may be a distinction between the King and his Subjects. It is written in the Book of the *Esculapii*, That the King is to be praised and loved, who is like unto the Eagle that rules among the Birds; not he that is like unto one of the inferior Birds. If therefore
20 any in the Court, or Presence of the King's Majesty, presumes to do any Injury, or commit an Offence, it is to be consider'd in what manner he did it, whether in Sport, or in Contempt and Dishonour of your Dignity; if the first, he is to be corrected lightly, if the second, according
24 to his Offence. |

[p. 25]   ### In what the Obedience of a Ruler consists.

O *Alexander*, the Obedience to a Ruler comes from four things; his being Religious, Beloved, Courteous, and Reverend. O *Alexander*, get the love of your Subjects, take away all Injuries and Injustice from them, give no occasion for Men to speak evil of you; for what the
30 People can say of you, they can easily do. Keep your self so that nothing can be said against you, and by this you shall avoid what they can do: Know moreover, that Discretion is the Glory of Dignity, and the Reverence of a Master, and the Exaltation of a King; and it is your greatest Prudence rather to be honourable in the Minds of the People,
35 than only beloved. |

[p. 26]   ### Of the Mercy of a King.

O *Alexander*, enquire of the Want and Necessity of the miserable and weak Persons; help the Needy in their Distress, and out of your Clemency choose a Man understanding their Language, Eloquent, and
40 a lover of Justice, that may be in your stead, and rule them mercifully,

and love them; for in this is the keeping of the Law, the Joy of Honour,
and the good Pleasure of the Creator.

Of Prudence, and its Profit.

O *Alexander*, treasure up to your self Pulse, and other Grain for
Food, that may suffice your Land in time of Scarcity and Want, that 5
when Famine and Scarcity comes, as it sometimes happens, your Prudence may relieve your People. And in time of Necessity you must
relieve your Cities, opening your | Granaries, and proclaiming through- [p. 27]
out your Kingdom and Cities, your Corn and Grain that you have
provided. This is a matter of great Caution and Prudence; a defence of 10
the King, Health of the People, preservation of the Citys; then your
Precepts shall be obeyed, then your work shall prosper by your Providence; Health shall come to all, and then all shall know that your Eyes
see afar, and for this they will applaud your Clemency, and fear to
offend your Majesty.   15

Of the Evils that follow putting Men to death unjustly.

O *Alexander*, I have often admonish'd you, and still admonish, that
you keep my Doctrine, which if you keep, you shall get your Purpose,
and your Kingdom shall be lasting. See that you shed not Man's Blood,
because it belongs only to God, who knows the Secrets of Mens Hearts. 20
Take not there-|fore that which belongs to God; for it is not given to [p. 28]
you to know the Divine Secret. Beware therefore what you can of
shedding Man's Blood; for the famous Doctor *Hermogenes* saith, That
when a Creature slays a Creature like himself, all the Powers of Heaven
cry to the divine Majesty, saying, Lord, thy Servant would be like thee; 25
and if he hath unjustly kill'd him, the high Creator will answer, Suffer
him, for the Slayer shall be slain; leave Vengeance to me, and I will
repay: And the Powers of Heaven present the Death of him that is
slain, until Vengeance is taken of the Slayer, who shall be one of those
that continue in eternal Punishment. O *Alexander*, you have knowledg 30
in all Punishments, you have learnt many kinds of Evils by Experience;
call to mind the Acts of your Fathers, search their Annals, thence you
may draw many good Examples; for past Facts give sure Documents
of the Future. Contemn not those that are less than your self; for he 34
that is little and low, as it often happens, may soon ascend to Ho-|nours [p. 29]
and Riches, and then he will be stronger, and more able to hurt.

Of keeping Faith.

BEware lest you break your Faith and Leagues, when confirm'd. To
break Faith agrees with Infidels and Whores: Keep your faithful
Promise faithfully, for all Infidels come to an ill End; and if in breaking 40

Faith there happen any Good, yet it is a kind of Evil, and a wicked
Example. Know therefore, that by keeping Faith comes the congregat-
ing of Men, peopling of Cities, uniting of Men, and government of
Kings; by Faith Camps are holden, and Cities preserved. If you take
5 away Faith, all Men will become as Brutes, and be like wild Beasts.
Beware therefore, faithful King, lest you break your Faith given; keep
firmly your Oaths and Covenants, tho they are grievous. Know you not,
that, as *Hermogenes* witnesseth, there are two Spirits that keep you,
[p. 30] of | which one stands on the right, the other on the left Hand; keeping,
10 and knowing your Deeds, and reporting to your Creator whatsoever
you do. And in truth you, and every one ought to abstain from every
dishonest Deed. Who forces you to swear so often? It is not to be done,
but for some great Cause and Necessity. A King, tho much intreated,
and often required, ought not to swear; know you not that it does not
15 agree to your Dignity, and that you derogate from your Honour when
you swear? It is more fit for Servants and Subjects to swear. If you ask
the cause of the Destruction of the Kingdom of the *Heubaii* and
Syrians; I answer you, their Kings used to swear for Deceit, to deceive
Men and their neighbouring Cities, breaking the Leagues which were
20 made for the good and profit of Mankind. Those wicked Infidels abus'd
their Oaths to the subversion of their Neighbours; therefore the Equity
of Justice could not bear them any longer. |

[p. 31]   **Of the ordering of the Empire, and of your own Family.**

LEarned Son *Alexander*, I would have you know, that in the order-
25 ing of your Empire and Government, there are certain special Instructions, and very Moral, belonging to you, as to the Government of your
own Family, and all your People; but they have no place here; but I
will give them you in some part of this Book, and they will be wholesom
Instructions abbreviated, and very profitable to you, in the Observation
30 of which you shall prosper, by God's Permission. Repent not for the
thing that is past, for this is proper to weak Women; shew your self
Honest, be Courteous, exercise Goodness; this is the perfection of a
Kingdom, and the destruction of the Enemy. |

[p. 32]   **How a King ought to order Studys.**

35 PRepare Schools in the Cities of your Dominions, permit and command your Subjects to teach their Sons the knowledg of Letters, and
cause them to study in noble and liberal Sciences; and it ought to be
your care to assist them in things necessary. Let those that study well,
and profit, have some Prerogative, that by this you may give an Example
40 to other Scholars, and an occasion of Diligence. Hear their Petitions,
receive their Epistles, and attend to them: praise those that deserve to

be praised, and reward those that deserve to be rewarded; and by this
you shall excite the Learned to set forth your Praise, and to perpetuate
your Acts in their Writings. This is commendable and prudent, and in
this the whole Kingdom shall be honoured, the Court inlightned, and
the Annals and Acts of Kings the better remembred. What rais'd the 5
Kingdom of the *Greeks*? What makes their Acts perpetually fa-|mous [p. 33]
throughout the World? Certainly the diligence of their Students, and
the honesty of their wise Men, that they greatly love Sciences, and for
this have deserved so much. And even their Girls in their Fathers
Houses, knew by Study the course of the Year, the Feasts, and solemnity 10
of the Months, the course of the Planets, the Cause of the shortning of
the Day and Night; the Revolution of the *Pleiades* and *Bootes*, the
Circle of the Days, the Signs of the Stars, the Judgment of things to
come, and other things pertaining to Astronomy.

Of keeping your self from Women.   15

O *Alexander*, never confide in the Works and Services of Women,
commit not your self to them; but if need require, commit your self to
her that will be faithful and loving to you; for when you are in a
Womans hands, you are as a thing deposited and com-|mitted to her, [p. 34]
and your Life is in her Hands. Beware of deadly poison, for it is no new 20
thing for Men to be poison'd. It is known what a multitude of Kings
and Rulers have died before their time, by poisonous Potions.

Of Justice, and its Commendation.

JUSTICE is a laudable Condition, one of the Properties of the most
high, glorious, simple Being; whence the Kingdom ought to be his 25
whom God chuseth, and sets over his Servants, to whom the Business
and Government of the Subjects are to be committed; who ought to
watch over them, and defend the Possessions, Riches, and Lives of the
Subjects, and all their Works, as their God, and in this he is likened to
God; and therefore the King ought to be like, and imitate the most High 30
in all his Works. God is wise and knowing, and his glorious Praises, and
his Names are in himself, and the greatness of his Do-|minion is [p. 35]
greater than, and above all Commendation. Wisdom therefore is contrary to Injustice, and the opposite of Injustice is Justice: In Justice the
Heavens were made, and set over the Earth. In Justice were the holy 35
Prophets sent. Justice moreover is the form of the Understanding,
which the glorious God created, and brought his Creature to it; and by
Justice the Earth was made, and Kings are constituted, and the terrible
Subjects obey, are tamed, and come to that which is right, and their

33-4 Wisdom . . . is Justice] contrarium ejus injuria et ejus oppositum est
injusticia B 123/21, *intended reading of* Injustice[1] *perh.* Injury: *see n.*

Souls are saved, they are freed from all Vice, and from all Corruption
towards their Kings. For this Reason the *Indians* said, That Justice
in a Ruler is more profitable to the Subjects than a fruitful Season:
And again, that a just Ruler is better than the Evening Rain. And it was
5 found written on a Stone in the *Chaldean* Tongue, That a King, and
Understanding, are Brothers that stand in need of one another, and that
one cannot do without the other. And every thing in the World is
[p. 36] created of Justice, and it is the cause of Understanding which | brings
Essence and Operation into being, and is its Act, and it is a just Judg.
10 The Essence therefore of Justice, and its Root is Understanding, and it
is working and deducing it, and is its Power, and Operation, and Intention; and it is the speculation of Science, a working Judg receiving that
which comes from the Act in that which receives. It appears therefore
that Justice is twofold, Manifest and Occult. The manifest is that which
15 appears from the Act working on personal Actions; it is right Justice,
weighed, and measur'd by the Understanding, and Judgment, and
thence it has its name. The Occult is the Faith or Belief of the Judg
working his Works, and the Certitude and Confirmation of his Words. It
therefore appears, as is said, That a King by Justice is likened to the
20 Simple, Glorious, most High Being. And hence it is convenient that he
be firm in all his Works, proper and common. When he declines from
his proper or common Justice, the Justice of God, and the Will of the
[p. 37] most High is not in these | his doings. And let him wholly believe this;
for by this Faith he shall keep the Law, which is the Perfection of
25 Government; and as it shall appear in his Deeds, so has he the Heart
of his Subjects; that is as his Works appear, his Subjects will judg of
him. And Property and Community are in divers Degrees, and the
Transgressors of Justice differ in them. And Justice is a Relative Term
to something said, and a Correction of Injury, a just Ballance; and the
30 form of Measure is a collective Name, respecting Courtesy, the Mount
of Liberality, and the Operations of Liberality and Goodness. Now
Justice is divided into two parts; there is first Justice, which pertains to
the Judgment of Judges; and there is, secondly, Justice pertaining to
a Man in his own reasoning in the things between him and his Creator.
35 The World is an Orchard or Garden, its Matter or Species is Judgment;
Judgment is a Ruler fortified by Law. The Law is the Government by
which the King reigns. |

[p. 38]   **Of Counsellors.**

Wʜᴇɴ you call together your Counsellors to consult in your Presence,
40 mix not other Council with them, but hear them in what they agree. If
they speedily answer with one accord, then resist them, and shew them

29 Injury, a] *no punct.* (*at end of line*)   29–31 the form . . . Liberality]
see n.

the contrary, that their thoughts may be prolong'd and retarded to the last in Council. And when you perceive the Truth and right Counsel in their Words, or in the words of any one of them, let them cease, and shew them not in what you acquiesce, until you put it in Practice and Trial: and consider subtilely and diligently who leads most to right 5 Counsel; and according to the love he has to you, and desire of the Prosperity of your Government, take Counsel; and beware not to prefer one before another in Gifts and Degrees. What is a greater cause of the Destruction of a Kingdom, than to honour some Ministers above others? And it is not always inconvenient to follow the Counsel of a 10 young | Man, if it be wholesom: for Judgment imitates the Body; when [p. 39] the Body is weakned, the Judgment is weakned, unless there be Experience. Do not contemn a low State in Men; those that you see to love Science, and to abound in the way of Wisdom, and good Morals, and to decline and shun the path of Vices, such love and have about you, 15 and especially when you shall see one exercising his Mind in these Vertues, such a one uses to be of good Speech, pliant, courteous, and skill'd in Histories of preceding Nations: propose, or postpone nothing to be done without such a ones Counsel; love his Society, because such a one loves the Truth, and consults what becomes Kingly Majesty, 20 and removes the contrary; is firm in his Mind, constant in his Heart, faithful and just in his Actions, and good to the Subjects. Do nothing preposterously, those things which should be done first last, or those that should be done last first, nor act altogether without the Counsel of Physicians; for the Philosophers have said, that Counsel is the Eye of 25 future things. | And one of the old Philosophers said, That the Wisdom [p. 40] of a wise King shall be increased by the Counsel of his Ministers, as the Sea by the reception of the Rivers. And one of the *Medes* commanded his Son, Son it is necessary for thee to have Counsel, because thou art but one among Men. 30

Of a King's own Counsel.

ABound not in your own Sense, nor let the highness of your Condition hinder you, but that to your own Counsel you add that of others; for if it seems profitable it is to be embraced, and let your own always remain with you. But if another's Counsel differ from your Judgment, then 35 it is your part to consider; if it may be a help, and profitable to that which you have considered, embrace it; and if it be unprofitable, abstain from it. I earnestly admonish you, and give you good Counsel, never set a Minister to rule in your stead; for his | Counsel may destroy [p. 41] your Kingdom, Subjects and Nobles; he may intend his own Profit, and 40 consult your Fall.

The trial of Ministers of State.

ONE thing by which you may try a Minister, is, to shew him that you
want Mony; and if he induces you to spend what you have in your
Treasury, and shews it to be expedient, you may know he has no value
5 for you; and if he induces you to take the Mony of your Subjects, there
will be a Corruption of your Government, and they will hate you
beyond measure; but if he offers you what he has, he is to be commended, and praiseworthy. You may also try your Ministers with
Gifts and Rewards, and whomsoever you shall find to endeavour after,
10 and desire Gifts too much, hope for no good in him. That Minister
that is greedy to get Mony, and heap up Treasure, trust not in him;
[p. 42] for he serves for Gold, | he is a depth without a bottom, and there is no
bound nor end in him; for as much as his Mony increaseth, so much
will his desire of getting increase. And this is a Cause of Corruption
15 in many Cases; perhaps the love of Mony will induce him to be your
death. But he is the most profitable Minister of State, who loves Vertue
most, and he will most induce your Subjects to love you; and he that
has these Vertues and Manners, which I will reckon up. 1. Perfection of
Parts. 2. Goodness of Apprehension, and readiness of Understanding.
20 3. That he has a good Memory, not forgetful. 4. Is considerate, when
there comes any Difficulty. 5. That he be courteous, affable, well
spoken; but so that his Tongue and his Heart agree: That he be also
ready of Speech. 6. That he be of a penetrating Understanding in all
Science, and especially in Arithmetick, which is the most certain and
25 demonstrative Art. 7. That he be a lover of Truth, a hater of a Lie, of
[p. 43] good Manners, sweet, mild, tractable. 8. That he be no Glut-|ton or
Drunkard, or Whoremaster, but avoiding Plays and Sports. 9. That he
be magnanimous in his Purpose, and loving what is honourable. 10.
That he contemn Gold and Silver, and other accidental things of this
30 World, and that he covets no more than what is convenient for his
Dignity and Rule, that he love his Neighbour, and the Stranger. 11.
That he love and embrace the Just, and Justice, hating Injury and
Offence, giving every one his due, relieving the Oppressed, and those
that suffer Injury, removing wholly all Injustice, making no difference
35 at all in Persons and Degrees of Men, whom God hath created equal.
12. That he be firm and resolute in his Purpose, in those things which
he sees fit to be done, bold without Fear and Pusillanimity. 13. That he
know the going out of all Expences, that he be ignorant of nothing
that may be profitable to the Kingdom, that the Subjects complain
40 not of him. 14. That he be not verbose, or given much to laughter;
[p. 44] for Temperance is very pleasing to Men. 15. That he be none of | them
that are given to Wine, that his Court be open to comers; that he be
intent in trying and getting Intelligence of all, relieving the Subjects,

correcting their Deeds, comforting them in Adversities, bearing with
every one, and suffering their Simplicities.

O *Alexander*, compare your Subjects to an Orchard, in which are
divers kind of Fruit-Trees; let them not be as Fields that bear Wormwood and Thorns, and produce nothing fruitful, but as Trees having 5
many Branches and Boughs, bringing forth Seed and Fruit profitable to
multiply their kind. It behoves you that they be well governed, and
that you look to their Necessities, that you remove Injuries from them,
and that you be never weary to look to their Conditions, and to enquire
what they want, and let them have one only purpose appointed by you, 10
which is not to the destruction of the Trees, but their Preservation.
If it is not so, the Hearts of the Subjects will be rebellious, and their
Thoughts will be corrupted, which before were pure. |

That you ought not to trust in one Physician.   [p. 45]

O *Alexander*, trust not in one Physician, because one Physician is 15
able to hurt, he will easily attempt Wickedness and effect it. Therefore
if you can, have not less than ten, but let them all agree; and if you
are to take a Medicine, take it not, but by the Advice of the most. And
then the King ought to have among them one faithful Person knowing
the Kinds and Qualities of Drugs, who ought to collect all things that 20
are necessary in the Composition, and to make all up with due Weight
and Measure, according to the Direction of the Physicians.

Of preserving of Health.

Now I will give you the Doctrine of Medicine, and some other 24
Secrets, which will be enough for you in | preserving your Health, so [p. 46]
that you may not want a Physician. For the preservation of Health
is better and more precious than any Medicine, and very necessary to
you for the Government of this World. Know therefore, that there is no
way to get any Science but by Power, and there is no Power but by
Health, and there is no Health but by an Equality of Complexions, and 30
there is no Equality of Complexions but by a Temperature of Humours:
And the glorious God hath ordained a Method and Means to attemper
the Humours, and to preserve Health, which he hath revealed to
Philosophers, and holy Prophets, and others whom he hath chosen,
and enlightned with the Spirit of Divine Wisdom, and hath given them 35
Gifts of Knowledg; and from them those that followed had the Principles and Grounds of Philosophy. Now the wise Men, and natural
Philosophers agree, that Man is compounded of opposite Principles,
and four contrary Humours, which always need to be supplied with 39
Meats and Drinks, which if a Man want his Substance | is corrupted: [p. 47]
if he takes too much, or too little, he falls into Weakness and Infirmity,

and many other Inconveniences: But if he uses them temperately, he will find the Help of Life, Strength of Body, and the Health of his whole Substance. They have unanimously agreed, that he that transgresseth the due Measure, in Fulness and Emptiness, in Sleeping and Waking,
5 in Motion and Rest, in Loosness or Binding of the Belly, or in taking away Blood, he cannot avoid the Fury of Sickness, and the Troubles of Infirmities, of all which I am about to give you in short, certain Instructions. All agree, that he who avoids Superfluity and Want, keeping an Equality and Temperance, he shall have Health and length of Days. I
10 have not found any of the Philosophers differing from this Opinion, That all delectable things of this World's Delights, Riches, Honours, Pleasures, are all what they are from their durableness. He therefore that desires to live and abide, let him study to get that which is convenient for
[p. 48] durability, and to preserve | Life; and let him renounce the desire of
15 his Pleasure, and not add eating upon eating. I have heard it said of *Hippocrates*, that he used a very slender Diet; to whom his Scholar said, Excellent Master, if you will but eat well, you shall not have such a weakness of Body; but *Hippocrates* said unto him, Son, I eat that I may live, I do not live that I may eat. And indeed I have known many
20 who have kept a spare Diet, living temperately, who by this means had a sound Body, long Life, good Appetite, quick Motion, and were better for Business; and this is manifest in the *Arabs*, and those that often travel the Desarts, and go long Journeys. This is therefore a great Argument, that to abstain from too much eating, and to purge Super-
25 fluity, is most conducive to Health. O *Alexander*, there are in Medicine most certain and true Documents; for the Conservation of Health consists principally in two things: the first is, that a Man use Food agreeable to his Age, to the time in which he is, and to the Custom of his
[p. 49] Nature, *viz.* that he use Meats | and Drinks, with which he hath been
30 used to be nourished, and in so doing he will strengthen his Substance. The second is, That he purge himself of all Superfluity, and from corrupt Humors. Know therefore, that the Bodies of Men, which are the receptacles of Meat and Drink, are diminish'd and dissolved, as well the Bodies themselves receiving, as the Food it self received. They are
35 dissolved therefore in the first place by Natural Heat, which dries up the moisture of the Body, and is nourished and fed by the Moisture. Secondly they are dissolved by the heat of the Sun, and by Winds which dry up the Humidity of all Bodies, and are fed by the moisture of Bodies, as well as of Rivers. When therefore the Body is hot, and enclining to
40 Sweat, gross meats are good; because that which is dissolved, and emitted from such a Body, will be much and gross, by reason of the great Heat, and perspiration of the Body. But when the Body is low and dry, light and moist Food is good; whenas that which is dissolved of

such a Body is of small | Quantity, by reason of its strait Passages. It is [p. 50]
therefore a certain Rule to preserve Health, that a Man use Food convenient to his Complexion in Health, *viz*. If one is of a hot Nature,
Meats temperately warm are convenient: If of a cold Complexion,
temperately cool; and the like of a moist and dry Body: but if the Heat 5
is increased and inflamed too much by hot and strong Meats, or by
predominant external Heat, then the opposite and contrary help, *viz*.
cold Meats, *&c*. When the Stomach is hot, strong and good, strong and
gross Meats are better for such a Stomach, because such a Stomach is
as a strong Fire, able to burn much hard Wood: but when the Stomach 10
is cold and weak, for such a Stomach subtile and light Food is better;
such a Stomach is compared to a Fire burning Reeds, and small Wood. |

Of the signs of a good, and bad Stomach.   [p. 51]

THE signs of a good Stomach are lightness of the Body, clearness of
the Understanding, readiness to Motion. But the signs of a bad Stomach, 15
and of a weak Digestion, are heaviness of the Body, softness, dulness,
bloated Face, often yawning, heaviness of the Eyes, filthy and unsavory
Belchings, *viz*. when one belches acid, insipid, or bitter, aqueous or
stinking; and by this wind is generated, and inflammation of the Belly,
and loss of Appetite. And when things grow worse, then there are 20
spittings, with reaching, extensions of the extreme Parts, reflections of
the Members, trembling of the Heart, Yawnings, and other evils which
are always contrary to Health, destroying the Body, and corrupting
Nature. You ought therefore, most merciful King, diligently to keep
your self from the abovesaid Inconveniences. | 25

Of the government of Health.   [p. 52]

WHENAS the Body is corruptible, and is corrupted from the opposition
of Complexions and Humours which are in it; it seems good to me to
write unto you in this present Work, some profitable things of the
Secrets of the Art of Medicine, which are very necessary, and with 30
which you shall be contented, because it is not honourable that all the
Infirmities of a King should be discovered to the Physician. And if you
will follow this example, and keep your self according to this excellent
Order, you shall not want a Physician, except in Cases that may fall out
in War, and others, which cannot be avoided.   35

What is to be done after Sleep.

WHEN you arise from Sleep, O *Alexander*, you ought to walk a little,
and equally to extend your | Limbs, and also to comb your Head; for the [p. 53]
extension of the Limbs strengthens the Body, and combing the Head
brings forth the Vapours arising from the Stomach in time of Sleep. 40

In Summer wash with cold Water, because it straitens the Pores, and retains the Heat of the Head, and will be a cause of an Appetite to eat. Then dress your self with fine Clothes, and adorn your self with fair Ornaments, because your Mind will be naturally delighted in be-
5 holding such things. Then rub your Teeth and Gums with the Rind of some hot and dry Tree of a bitter Taste. This much helps the Teeth, for it cleans them, taketh away the stink of the Mouth, and clears the Voice, and moreover excites an Appetite to Meat. Then perfume your-self with convenient Perfumes; for this is very profitable, for it openeth
10 the clausures of the Brain, makes the Neck thick, and the Arms fat, clears the Countenance, and keeps off grey Hairs and strengthens the Senses. After this you should use pretious and sweet Ointments, agree-
[p. 54] able to the time; for the Spirits are | refresh'd with Odours, which are their sweetest Food; and when the Spirits are refreshed, fortified, and
15 delighted, the Body will be strengthened, the Heart will rejoice, and the Blood will run briskly in the Veins from the Joy of the Heart. After-wards take Wood of Aloes, and then of Rubarb a fourpenny Weight; this is very profitable, and draws Flegm from the Mouth of the Stomach, stirs up the heat of the Body, expels Wind, and gives a good Taste.
20 Then sit with your Nobles, and discourse with your wise Men, and do what becomes you to do according to Custom. And when you have a Stomach to eat, near your usual Hour, use some moderate Exercise of Body, as riding, walking, or the like; for this much helps the Body, expels Wind, makes the Body apt and strong, and nimble, stirs up the
25 heat of the Stomach, strengthens the Joints, dissolves superfluous Humours and Phlegm, and makes the too hot and dry Food descend from the Stomach. If you have many Dishes of Meat before you, eat of
[p. 55] them that you like best, | with Bread well levened; and eat those things first which ought to be eat first, viz. if a Man eat thin Pottage, loosening
30 the Belly, and something binding follow, if the thin Food go before, the Digestion is lighter; but if one eat hard and binding Food first, and afterwards thin and loosening, both digest ill. Likewise if a Man take much thin Pottage, which is of easy digestion, there ought to be some-thing first harder in the bottom of the Stomach, because the bottom
35 of the Stomach is hotter and stronger to digest, the parts thereabout being more fleshy; and it is near to the Liver, by whose heat the Food is concocted. And in eating you ought to hold your hand, that is, leave off whilst you have yet an Appetite: For the Stomach is distressed by superfluity of Meat, the Body oppress'd, the Mind hurt, and the Food
40 remains in the bottom of the Stomach, heavy and hurtful. Likewise abstain from drinking Water with your Meat, until you are used to it; because by drinking cold Water upon the Meat, the Stomach is chil'd,
[p. 56] and it extinguishes the | heat of Digestion, and confounds the Food,

and breeds an impediment, if much is drank, than which nothing is
worse for the Heart. But if there is a Necessity of drinking Water, from
the heat of the Weather, the heat of the Stomach, or the heat of your
Food, take but a small Quantity, and let it be very cool; and when you
are refreshed lie down on a soft Bed, and sleep temperately, and rest   5
one Hour on the right Side, and then turn on the Left, and so sleep
out your Sleep; for the left Side is cold, and so wanteth heating: And
if you find a Heaviness in your Stomach, and gripings in your Belly, then
the Remedy is to put upon your Belly a hot thick Cloth: But if you find
sour Belchings, it is a sign of the coldness of the Stomach: The Remedy 10
for this is, *to drink warm Water with Syrup of Sorrel, and to vomit;*
for the retaining of the corrupt Food in the Stomach is the destruction
of the heat of the Body. And Motion before Dinner stirs up the heat
of the Stomach, but after Dinner it is naught, because then the Food   14
descends unconcocted | to the bottom of the Stomach, and causes   [p. 57]
Obstructions, and other Evils.

Of the Efficacy of divers manners of Sleeping.

SLeeping before Dinner makes the Body lean, and drys up its moisture, but after eating strengthens and nourisheth; for while a Man
sleeps, the Body resteth, and then the natural Heat which was diffus'd   20
over all the Body, is drawn to the inward parts of the Stomach, and then
the Stomach is strengthned for the concoction of the Food; then the
natural Power seeks its Rest: and for this Reason some Philosophers
said, That it is more profitable to eat in the Evening than at Noon, because Noon has the heat of the Day, and then the Senses are at work,   25
and the Mind is troubled by those things which a Man hears and thinks,
and many Inconveniencies which attend the Body from Heat and
Motion; whence at Noon the natural | Heat is diffus'd through the out-   [p. 58]
ward Parts, and so the Stomach is much weakned, and is not so able to
concoct the Food; but at Evening it is quite contrary, for then the Body   30
has rest from Labour, then the Senses and Mind are at quiet, and the
coldness of the Night brings the natural Heat to the inward parts of the
Stomach. Also you ought not to be ignorant, that he that is used to eat
twice a day, and shall eat but once, will find himself certainly hurt,
as it happens to him who is used to eat but once, and begins to eat   35
twice; for the Stomach cannot digest the Food, but it remains an in-
digested Nutriment: and he that uses to eat at a certain Hour, and
changes his Eating to another Hour, will soon perceive that he does his
Nature no good, but much hurt; for Custom is a second Nature. If
therefore any Necessity, which has no Law, compels to that which   40
Custom is against, it ought to be done discreetly and wisely, *viz.* that
the change of Custom be by little and little, and so by the help of God

[p. 59] all will be well. And beware | that you eat not till you find your Stomach empty, and discharg'd of the former Meat, and this you shall know by your Appetite; that is, when your Stomach begins to crave Food, and by the subtileness of your Spittle coming into your Mouth. For if any
5 one eats when the Body has no need, that is, when he hath no Appetite to Meat, he will find the natural Heat very weak: but if he eats when he hath an Appetite, then he will find the Heat as a Fire blown up: and when you begin to have an Appetite, you ought presently to eat, because if you do not eat presently, the Stomach will be fill'd with ill Humours,
10 which it draws to it self, of the superfluities of the Body, which will trouble the Brain with an ill Vapour; and when you eat afterwards, the Food will be lukewarm, and will not profit the Body. |

[p. 60] ### Of the four Seasons of the Year.

IT is now our Intention to treat briefly of the four Seasons of the
15 Year; of the Quality, Property, and Variation of each of them. The Spring begins when the Sun enters the sign *Aries*, and continues ninety two Days, an Hour and a half; from the tenth day of *March*, to the tenth day of *June*. In this Season the Day and Nights are equal, the Weather grows pleasant, the Air mild, the Winds blow, the Snow melts,
20 Torrents run, and Fountains flow between the Hills; the Sap rises to the tops of the Trees, and the ends of the Branches; Seeds spring up, and Corn grows; the Medows are green, the Flowers bud forth and blow; Trees are adorn'd with new Blossoms, the Earth with Grass; Animals generate, Pasture grows, all things resume their Strength;
25 Birds sing, the Nightingal warbles, the Earth receives all its Ornaments and Beauty, and becomes as a fair Bride, adorn'd with divers Colours,
[p. 61] that she may appear on | her wedding Day. The Spring is warm and moist, and temperate, like the Air; the Blood is moved, and diffus'd through all parts of the Body, and makes in it an equal Complexion;
30 that is, a temperate: and in this Season are eaten Chickens, and Eggs not too many, *viz.* unto 5; and Lettice, [and] Goats-Milk, for no time is better for Diminution: and now the Use and Motion of the Body is profitable, purging the Belly, Bathings, and Sweatings, and Pouders, and Digestive Potions. If purging Medicins are to be taken, whatsoever Diminution
35 happens by purging, this time restores by its moisture.

Of the Summer.

THE Summer begins when the Sun enters the first Point of the Sign *Cancer*, and contains 92 Days, an Hour and a half; that is, from the
39 10*th* Day of *June*, to the tenth of *September*; in this Season the Days
[p. 62] are lengthened, | and the Nights are shortned, Heats increase, the Winds are hot, the Sea calm, the Air serene, the Corn grows hard,

Serpents are bred, Poisons are poured forth, the Virtues of Bodies are
strengthned, and the World becomes like fair Bodies perfect in Age,
enflamed with Heat. The Summer Season is hot and dry, in which red
Choler is stir'd up; and there is need to beware of it, because it will
be of a very hot and dry Nature and Complexion. We must also abstain 5
in Summer time from too much eating and drinking, lest the natural
Heat be extinguish'd. You may eat in this Season whatsoever is of a
cold and moist Nature, as Veal with Vinegar, Gourds, fed Chickens,
Barley-broth, Fruits of sharp taste, as Pomgranates and sour Apples:
abstain from Women, and all Evacuations, unless on Necessity; use 10
Motion of the Body, and Baths sparingly. |

Of Autumn.   [p. 63]

Autumn begins when the Sun enters into the first Degree of *Libra*,
and contains 91 Days, and an Hour and a half; that is, from the tenth
of *September*, unto the tenth of *December*. In this Season the Days 15
and Nights become equal, and then Nights lengthen, and the Days
grow short, the Air grows cold, the North-Winds blow, the Weather
changes, the Rivers decrease, and the Fountains are diminished, the
Gardens wither, the Fruits fall, the face of the Earth loseth its Beauty,
Birds go to hot Countries, Animals desire their Caves, creeping things 20
their Holes, where they gather their Food for Winter; and the World is
compar'd to a Woman of full Age, wanting her Garments, her Youth
departing, and old Age coming on. Autumn is a Season cold and dry,
in which Melancholy ariseth: Hot and moist things are to be used in
this Season, as Pullets, Lambs, old Wine, sweet Grapes; abstain from 25
things that b[r]eed Melancho-|ly. The motion of the Body, and the [p. 64]
use of Women hurts more than in Summer; purging, if there be a Necessity, may be in this Season. If a Man wants a Vomit, let it be taken at
Noon, and in the hottest time of the Day, because in such Hours Superfluities are bred in Man. Purgation ought to be at this Season by things 30
which purge Melancholy, and repress Humours.

Of Winter.

Winter begins when the Sun enters *Capricorn*, and contains ninety
Days, an Hour and a half, from the tenth of *December* to the tenth of
March. In this Season the Days are shortned, and the Nights lengthened, 35
Cold increases, Winds are rough, Leaves fall from Trees, and green
Herbs for the most part die, and are hardned like a Stone; Animals hide
in the Bowels of the Earth, and Caverns of the Mountains; and by too
much coldness and moistness the Air is obscure and dark; Cattel quake, 39
the | Virtues of Bodies are weakned; and the World is like an old [p. 65]
Woman, languid, decrepid by Age, naked, and ready to die. The Winter

is cold and wet, in which there ought to be a change, to hot Medicines
and Meats, as Pullets, Hens, and Mutton, and roasted Meats, all hot
Confections, Figs, and Nuts, the best new red Wine; and take hot
Electuaries. Abstain also from purging, and blood-letting; use not
5 abundance of Food, lest the Digestion be weakned; anoint your Body
with hot Ointments, and use Baths; much Drink and Women hurt not
so much this Season, nor much eating, because by reason of the great
cold the natural Heat is collected into the inward parts of the Body;
therefore the Digestion is better in Winter: but in the Spring and
10 Summer the Stomach is cold, because in those Seasons the Pores are
open'd by heat, and the natural Heat is diffus'd through all parts of the
Body, and by reason of the little heat of the Stomach Digestion is
hinder'd, and Humours are moved. Therefore know these things, and
[p. 66] the Lord be with you. | Farewel, *Alexander*; keep this precious Rule
15 of Diet I have given you, in preserving your natural Heat; for as long as
the natural Heat remains temperate in a Man, Health will be kept. For
a Man grows old, and decays two ways: One is natural, which comes
by the Debt of Nature, *viz.* old Age, which overcomes and destroys
the Body. The other is accidental, *viz.* from Infirmities, and other ill
20 Causes.

Of those things which make the Body fat.

THESE things fatten and moisten the Body, Rest and eating well,
pleasant and divers kinds of Meats, drinking of Milk, and sweet Wines,
sleep after eating on a soft Bed perfum'd with things convenient for
25 the times, bathing in fresh Water a little while, for bathing long weakens
the Body; Odours, and good smells in their Seasons: drink Wine
[p. 67] seldom, but what's temper'd with Wa-|ter; in Winter *Alchitimum*,
which is a kind of Flower of a hot Nature, Roses and Violets, and whatsoever is cold in Summer; if moreover, with the use of these things,
30 you are so happy as to have Joy and Gladness, Respect and Honour, &c.
*And use your self to vomit once a Month, especially in the Summer; for
vomiting washeth the Body, and cleanseth the Stomach from evil and
putrid Humours; and if there are but few Humours in the Stomach, the
Heat will be strengthened for Digestion, the Body will be filled with
35 humidity and fatness, and many other Advantages will come from hence.*
For a Confirmation of the profitable use of Vomiting, the Translator
thinks fit to add the following Observations.

The late Dr. *Short* in a Manuscript relates, that the Lord *Cambden*,
every Morning gargl'd a quart of warm small Beer, and with his Finger
40 forced by vomiting much Flegm, and other ill Humours out of his
Stomach, whereby he preserved himself from Diseases; and that his

eldest Son has done the same these thirty Years, and seldom or never
was sick. |

Also the late famous Dr. Rugely seldom fail'd once in two or three   [p. 68]
Months, to take a Vomit of Small-beer Posset-drink, and recommended
it as one of the best Remedies, for preventing all, and curing most 5
Diseases from Indigestion; and by this use he lived to be near 85 years
of Age, and enjoy'd a very healthful Life; which Practice was taught
him by his Father, an eminent Physician, who had us'd it all his Life
time, and lived to a great Age.

The Emperor *Aurelian* died in the sixty sixth Year of his Age, in 10
all which time he never purg'd, blooded, or physick'd any otherwise,
than by bathing once a Year, vomiting once a Month, fasting one day
in a Week, and walking one Hour in a Day. Much more might be said
from his long Experience, and many Instances given of the happy Effects
of this rinsing or washing the Stomach, which for brevity sake is omitted; 15
as also what *Hippocrates*, and many other great Men have said of it.

And to conclude, we find Vomiting recommended, *Ecclesiasticus*,
Chap. 31. | Ver. 21. *If thou hast been forced to eat, arise, go forth, vomit,* [p. 69]
and thou shalt have rest.

Of things which make the Body lean.   20

ON the contrary, these things make Lean, and weaken the Body, and
dry it; to eat and drink but little, to labour much, to go often in the Sun,
to walk above measure, to sleep before Dinner on a hard Bed, to be in
Care and Sorrow, to go into sulphureous Baths, to eat salt Meats, to
drink much old Wine, and to [ve]nt much, and to take away Blood, 25
and that beyond measure, to have evil and sad Thoughts. And it
is a Rule of *Hippocrates*, If one bathes with a full Stomach, he shall
have pain in his Bowels: and if one lie with a Woman with a full Belly,
he shall have the Palsy. Neither let any one run or ride too much. Those
that often eat Milk and Fish, get the Leprosy; Wine and Milk do the 30
like. |

Of the Division of the Body.   [p. 70]

THE Body is divided into four parts: The first is the Head. When
therefore superfluities are gathered in it, you may know it by these
Signs, dimness of the Eyes, heaviness of the Eye-brows, drawing in of 35
the Temples, trembling of the Ears, drawing in of the Nostrils. If
one perceives this, let him take Wormwood and boil it in sweet Wine,
and with the Roots of Organy, till half be boiled away, and hold it
in his Mouth every Morning until he finds it do him good; and let him
use with his Meat Mustard seed, of which you shall boil a Dram, and 40

---

25 vent] want *Walwyn* egere *1520*, f. 23ᵛ, i.e. sig. c7ᵛ; purgacio ventris
B 95/28: *see n.*

take going to Bed. If you omit this, you may fear dangerous Infirmities, *viz.* weakness of Sight, Headach, and many other sicknesses; from which the Lord keep you always. As for the Eyes, he that labours to keep his Eyes sound, ought to keep them from Dust and Smoke, from the
5 Intemperance of the Air in heat and cold, and from ill Winds; let him
[p. 71] not use to look sted-|fastly on one thing, nor look much on things in Motion; let him avoid weeping, and too much of Venery, and too much Meat and Drink, and especially Drinks and Meats that send up a gross Vapour to the Head, as Leeks, Pot-herbs, Ale, Beans, and the
10 like; neither let him sleep, when full. But the things which are good for the Eyes are, Vipers Buglos, Water or Juice of Fennel, of Vervain, Roses, Selandine, and Rue; submersion of the Eyes in clear Water, and opening them in it, and looking on it.

Of the Breast.

15   THE Breast is the second part of the Body; if therefore there are Superfluities gathered in it, these signs follow, the Tongue is heavy, the Mouth Salt, and there is perceived sour Food in the Orifice of the Stomach, and a painful Cough; you must in this case eat but little,
[p. 72] and *Vomit, and after vo-|miting take Ginger, with Roses, and Wood of*
20 *Aloes*; and after eating take the quantity of a Nut, of the Electuary *Dianisum.* He that shall not do this, may soon get the pain of the Side, or Reins, or many other Sicknesses. The drinking the Decoction of Hysop is wonderful, taken fasting.

Of the lower Ventricle.

25   THE third part of the Body is the Belly, and if it abound with ill Humours it is known by these signs, it will swell with pain, and there will be stiffness in the Knees; for preventing whereof use a spare Diet, with Meats of easy Digestion, and vomit, as before mention'd. If you do not thus, you'l be troubled with Disorders in the Spleen, Pains in
30 the Hips, Back, and other Joints, and heat of the Liver, with Indiges-tion. |

[p. 73]   ## Of the Testicles.

THE Testicles are the fourth part of the Body: When therefore there is a Superfluity and ill Humours in them, these signs follow; The
35 Appetite will abate, redness will appear upon them, and upon the Prepuce. He that perceives this, let him take the Seed of Smallage, and Fennel, and the Root of Mugwort, or of another Herb which is call'd *Achem* or *Arianes*, and of their Roots; let him steep these in good White-wine, and take of it every Morning tempered a little with Water

and Honey, and abstain from much eating. If he omits this Remedy, he may fear the Pain of the Testicles and Lungs, and danger of the Stone.

It is written in the Histories of the Antients, that a potent King call'd together the best Physicians of the *Indians*, *Greeks*, and *Medes*, 5 and commanded that each of them should study to make such a Medicine, which if a Man used it would do him good, and he should | want [p. 74] no other Remedy. *Sanages* a Greek said, That to take two Mouthfulls of Water, will keep a Man in Health, and he shall need no other Medicine. A *Mede* affirm'd, that it's very profitable to take of the Seeds of 10 Millet. But, I say, he that eats every Morning seven Drams of sweet Raisins, need not fear the Diseases of Phlegm, his Memory shall be strengthned, and his Understanding cleared; and he that uses it in a Season agreeable to his Complexion shall be secure, and need not fear Quarten Agues; and he that eats Figs with Nuts, and a few Leaves of 15 Rue, no Poison shall hurt him that day.

Of the Preservation of natural Heat.

O Mighty King, study how to preserve and keep your natural Heat; for Health consists in two things, the temperature of the Heat, and of the natural *Moisture* of a Man. Also you must | know here, that the [p. 75] Destruction and Corruption of the Body comes from two Causes; one 21 Natural, and the other against Nature. The natural comes from the Repugnance and Contrariety of contrary Qualities, as when, for Instance, Dryness bears rule in the Body: but the Corruption against Nature comes from some accidental Cause, as a Weapon, a hurt by 25 Stones, or other Casualties, from Infirmity, or evil Advice.

Of the Qualities of Meats.

MEATS are some subtile, some gross: the Subtile generate subtile Blood, clear and good; such are Wheat, Chickens well fed, and Eggs: Gross Meats are good for those that abound with hot Humours, those 30 that labour, and in fasting, and those that sleep after Dinner. But Meats of a middle nature do not breed Inflammation, or Superfluity, as the Flesh of Lambs, and things gelded, and all sorts of Flesh of a | hot and [p. 76] moist Nature; but it fails in those things that are roasted, because they are made hard, hot, and dry, by roasting. If such sorts of Flesh are 35 roasted, let them be eaten presently, and then they are good, when they are eaten with sweet Spices. Some Meats breed Melancholy, as Buffles, and Cows-Flesh, and all that are gross, dry, and rough. But others that have subtile Flesh, which are fed and nourished in watry and moist places, are better and more wholesom. 40

Of Fishes.

THE like is to be said of Fishes: Know therefore, that Fish of small Substance, and thin Skin, easy to be chewed, bred in running Waters that are Salt, are better and lighter than those that are bred in the Sea, 5 or fresh Water. But Fish bred in the Sea is wholesomer than that which is bred in fresh Water. You ought to beware therefore of Fish of large substance, and hard Skins, for such use to be venomous. |

[p. 77]   ## Of Waters.

YOU must know, that subtile Waters are profitable to every living 10 thing, as well Animals as Vegetables: and remember what I have taught you, and shewed you, that all Waters, as well sweet as bitter, take their rise from the Sea, and of this I have given you a Demonstration. Now take it, that the lighter and more wholesom Waters are those that are running near Cities, where the Earth is pure from Rocks, not abound- 15 ing with Fumes; but Water that comes out of stony Earth abounding with Fumes is heavy, and unwholesom; and Waters wherein are Frogs, Snakes, and other venomous Animals, as Lakes, are naught. The signs of good Waters are lightness, clearness, good colour, when they are easily heated, and soon cold; in such Nature delights. But Salt-Waters, and 20 of the Sea, are said to be fumous, and loosen the Belly; Sea-Water is hot and heavy, because it stands, and does not run, and because the [p. 78] Sun | is long upon it; therefore it breedeth Choler, and makes a great Spleen and Lungs. The drinking cold Water on an empty Stomach, hurts the Body, for it quenches the Heat of the Stomach; but the drink- 25 ing it after Dinner breeds Phlegm; and if much be drank, it corrupts the Meat in the Stomach. You ought to drink cold Water in the Summer, and warm in the Winter; and not the contrary, for drinking warm Water in the Summer mollifies and weakens the Stomach, and destroys the Appetite: so the drinking of cold Water in the Winter extinguishes the 30 Heat, and hurts the instruments of the Breast, and the Lungs, and breeds many Mischiefs.

Of Wine.

As to the knowledg of Wine, you must know that Wine that cometh 34 from Mountains, expos'd to the Sun, is of a more drying Nature than [p. 79] that which comes from the Plains, and moist and | shady Places. Wine is good for old Men, and those that abound with Moisture and Phlegm, but hurts young Men, and those of a hot Constitution. First, it heats and frees from cold and gross Superfluities. How much the redder and thicker Wine is, so much the more Blood it breedeth. But when it is 40 strong, and of a great bitterness, then it is call'd the first Blood, and first Nourishment, and has the nature of Drink and Medicine, and being

long took hurts much; and when this sort of Wine is sweet, it hurts
the Stomach, and breeds Wind. But the best Wine, and most agreeable
to all Complexions, is that which comes from Ground extended between
the Mountains and Valleys, in a subtile Air, whose Grapes are sweet,
fully ripe, which are not gathered until they have the strength of their 5
Substance, from a Vine of a moist Bark, thick Branches, the colour of
the Seeds of the Grapes being golden, or between yellow and red, the
Wine of an acute and pleasant taste; the Lees settled, the Wine subtile
and clear. And when you can get such Wine, drink | moderately of it, [p. 80]
according to your Age, and the quality of the time; for it comforts the 10
Stomach, strengthens the natural Heat, and helps Digestion, preserves
from Corruption, concocts the Food, and carries it purified to all the
Members, and concocts it in the Members till it is changed into sub-
stantial Blood, and goes to the Neck with temperate Heat, and makes
the Head secure from unfortunate Chances, chearing the Heart, makes 15
the Tongue fluent, frees from Cares, and makes a Man bold, stirs up an
Appetite, and has many other good Effects.

Of the Evils which follow too much Drinking.

BUT Wine, when it is took in too great a quantity, causeth the following Evils; it darkens the Understanding, dulls the Sense, troubles the 20
Brain, weakens the natural and animal Powers, causes forgetfulness,
hurts all | the five Senses, by which the whole operation of the Body is [p. 81]
rul'd and carried forth, spoils the Appetite, weakens the Ligaments and
Joints, begets tremblings of the Members, blear Eyes, enkindles
Choler, destroys the Liver, by making its Blood more gross, blackens 25
the Blood of the Heart; and thence come Horror, Fear, Trembling,
talking in Sleep, fantastical Visions, destruction of Heat, weakness of
the Genitals, destruction of the Seed, Loathings, a distemper'd Complexion; it makes the Body gross, and what is worse, brings the Leprosy,
and then it is of the nature of Poison. Therefore beware that you go not 30
beyond the measure, because Wine changes Nature, and the Complexion.
Rubarb, which is said to be the Life of the Liver, and hath many Virtues, yet sometimes it is equivalent to a deadly Poison to those who
take it beyond measure. Wine is compar'd to the nature of Serpents,
out of whom an Antidote is made, and great Mischiefs are driven forth 35
by their Medicine, yet it is known to all, that they have a d[e]adly
Poison, and death in them. |

O *Alexander*, never think much to take a sharp Syrup in the Morn- [p. 82]
ing fasting, and not fasting when Humidities abound, and Phlegm
predominates; for it is very sanative. *Aristos*, a certain wise Man, hath 40
commended good Wine, saying, it is a wonder how a Man can be weak,
or die, who eateth Bread of the best Wheat, good Meat, and drinketh

good Wine, and useth them temperately, abstaining from too much
Eating, Drinking, Venery, and Labour. He that does otherwise shall
have some Sickness; and it behoveth him who is drunk with too much
Wine, to wash himself with warm Water, and that he sit over Rivers of
5 running Water, and have Willows and Myrtle, and anoint his Body with
a Confection of Sanders, and to fumigate with cold and odoriferous
things burnt; this is a good Remedy for Drunkenness. But if any one
has a mind to leave off wholly the drinking of Wine, he ought not wholly
9 to forbear it at once, but to go by degrees from drinking Wine to a drink
[p. 83] of Raisins, and thence to mix Water by little and | little day after day,
until he comes to pure Water; for by such an Order the Body shall be
kept from great Sicknesses.

Moreover you must know, that some of these things strengthen and
fatten, some make lean and moisten, and some dry; some things give
15 Vigour and Beauty, some make dull and cool. Those things which
strengthen the Body are pleasant and light Meats, agreeing with the
Constitution, taken in due time, and when one wants them, as I have
said. Those things that fatten and moisten the Body are, rest of the
Body, Joy of the Mind, pleasant Company, hot and moist Meats,
20 drinking sweet Wine, the taking of good Hony; and nothing does so
much as sleeping after Dinner on a sweet Bed in a cool place, and to
bath in hot Baths, and stay but a little while therein, lest the moisture
of the Body be too much spent; and to use Odours refreshing the
Spirits, and agreeable to the time: *To vomit two or three times in a*
25 *Month, especially in the Summer, because Vomits wash the Stomach,*
and purge it from ill Humours and moistures of the Body. And | corupt
[p. 84] matters are *expell'd from the Stomach, the natural Heat increased and*
strengthened to digest the Food.

Govern your Body well therefore, if you would have it thrive, and
30 observe my Counsel. And moreover, if herewith you have Comfort and
Riches, and are fear'd by your Enemies, live in Pleasure, hear Musick,
behold, and be delighted with beautiful things, read pleasant Books, hear
joyous Songs with beloved Friends, wear fine Cloths, confer with wise
Men of things past and to come, strengthen the rational Powers with
35 Ointments agreeing with the Season; with these things Men are made
fat. And the things which on the contrary make lean, are eating and
drinking too little, much Exercise and Labour in the Heat, long Watch-
ing, sleeping before Dinner on a hard Bed, because the Heat is hinder'd
by too much moisture in the Body; to bathe in sulphureous and salt
40 Waters, cold, or very hot; Hunger and drinking old Wine, often purging
the Belly, and Bleeding, too much Venery, Poverty, Cares, and Fears,
[p. 85] evil Thoughts, | anxiety, Pains often happening, and ill Chances.

40 cold, . . . hot;] *comma and semi-colon transposed*

Of a Bath.

A Bath is one of the Wonders of the World, for it is built according to the four Seasons of the Year. Cold is ascrib'd to the Winter, moist to the Spring, hot to the Summer, dry to Autumn. In short, it is good to make in Baths four Mansions, so order'd, that the first is cold, the 5 second warm, the third dry, the fourth hot: and when any one will go in, he ought to stay a little in the first, and then go into the next and stay a little there, and then in third and there make a little stay; and lastly, in the fourth, and there you must wash you; and when you will go out you ought to keep the same Order, staying a little in each 10 Chamber, and not go out from too much Heat to too much Cold. And let a Bath be built in a high and airy place, and have large flaming Furnaces, and sweet Water; and in it | must be us'd Odours convenient [p. 86] to the time, as in Spring and Summer must be us'd Ointment a triple and quadruple Quantity, in Autumn and Winter double: then sit on a Seat 15 moistened with Rose-water, then you must be rub'd with a clean flaxen Cloth; when this is done, and you are well wash'd, go out to other Mansions, and use the following Rules and Ointments. If you are overcome with Heat, be comb'd, and use, in the Spring, Ointment of Sanders, and *Emleg*. In Autumn and Winter Ointment of *Myrrh*, and of the 20 juice of the Herb *Blites*; cast upon your Head artificial Waters, and temperate; then let your Body be wash'd and rub'd well till it is clean, then anoint you with convenient Ointments, and go out gradually; then wipe your self well; and if you thirst drink Syrup of Roses, and take an Electuary with Musk, then stretch your Arms a little; then after 25 about an Hour take Meat with quiet, and drink good Wine temperately, with a little Water, as you are used; then fume your self with Incense convenient to the | time, and rest in a soft Bed, and take a good Nap [p. 87] which helps much; then continue the rest of the day in Joy and Quiet. He that is old, or has too much moisture and coldness, must not stay 30 long in the Bath, but just till his Body receives the moisture of the Bath; and let him cast warm Water on him as soon as he will. The Phlegmatick ought not to go in but with an empty Stomach, and must be anointed with hot Ointments. He that is of a hot Nature, let him keep the former Doctrine. 35

O *Alexander*, when you shall know, and keep the Documents I have given you, you shall not want a Physician all your Life, by the Help of God.

FINIS

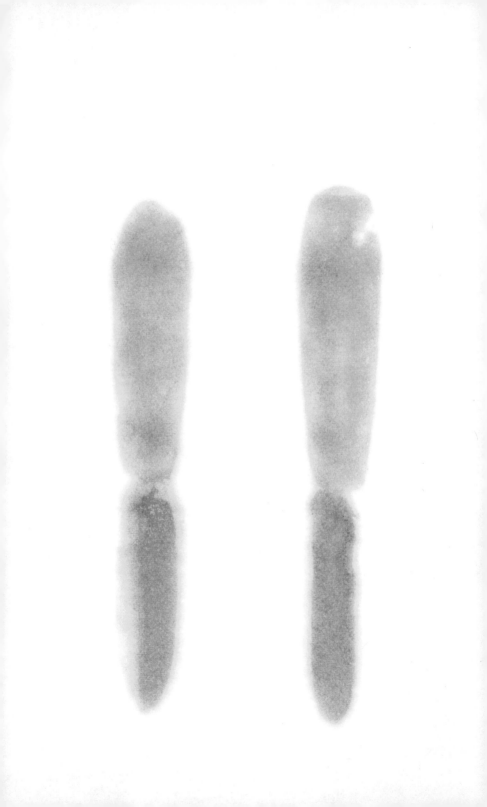